World War II

A CHRONOLOGY OF WAR

World War II

A CHRONOLOGY OF WAR

Edited by Colonel Raymond K. Bluhm Jr., USA (Ret.)

THE ARMY HISTORICAL FOUNDATION

NAVAL HISTORICAL FOUNDATION

MARINE CORPS ASSOCIATION

THE AIR FORCE HISTORICAL FOUNDATION

UNIVERSE

The content of this book is based on the text originally written for four separate service chronologies: *U.S. Army: A Complete History* by Colonel Raymond K. Bluhm Jr., USA (Ret.), with Major General Bruce Jacobs, AUS (Ret.); *U.S. Navy: A Complete History* by M. Hill Goodspeed; *USMC: A Complete History* by Colonel Jon T. Hoffman, USMCR (Ret.); and *U.S. Air Force: A Complete History* by Lieutenant Colonel Dik A. Daso, USAF (Ret.), with the Smithsonian Institution, National Air and Space Museum. Special thanks to these contributors for their tremendous work on the World War II sections of the original chronologies.

THE ARMY HISTORICAL FOUNDATION

The Army Historical Foundation, a nonprofit charitable organization, was founded in 1983 by Generals Lyman Lemnitzer, Bruce Palmer, and Orwin Talbott, with the support of Secretary of the Army John Marsh and Army Chief of Staff General Edward Meyer. The foundation's goal is to promote greater appreciation for the contributions that America's Army—Active, Reserve, and National Guard—has made to the nation in more than 230 years of service. The motto of the Army Historical Foundation—"Preserve the Heritage, Educate the Future"—summarizes its mission. The Foundation's top priority is building The National Museum of the U.S. Army, due to open in 2013, for America's oldest military service and the only branch of the American armed forces currently without its own national museum. The Foundation also supports Army history by presenting annual Distinguished Writing Awards for outstanding books and articles on Army history; awarding small grants to museums within the Army museum system to assist them with exhibits and programs; providing funds for acquisition and preservation of artifacts, books, and documents for the Army's collections; and sponsoring public historical education and research assistance programs.

Individuals may learn more about The Army Historical Foundation and become a member at www.armyhistory.org.

The Army Historical Foundation
2425 Wilson Boulevard
Arlington, Virginia 22201
tel: (703) 522-7901; fax: (703) 522-7929
www.armyhistory.org

NAVAL HISTORICAL FOUNDATION

In 1926, Commodore Dudley Knox wrote in the U.S. Naval Institute *Proceedings* about the "glaring deficiencies" in collecting and preserving the Navy's written records. Knox's article on "Our Vanishing History and Traditions" gave birth to the Naval Historical Foundation in 1926 under the sponsorship of the Secretary of the Navy. From its initial focus on safeguarding the material culture of the Navy, the Foundation has developed into a nonprofit organization dedicated to preserving and promoting the full range of U.S. naval history.

Today, in addition to providing much-needed support to the Navy's historical programs and its flagship National Museum of the United States Navy in Washington, D.C., the Foundation collects oral histories of Navy veterans from World War II through the Cold War, and publishes articles and sponsors symposia on important naval history topics. To provide increased access by the public to the Navy's historical collections of art, artifacts, documents, and photographs, the Foundation provides historical research and both document and image reproduction through its Historical Services Division.

The Foundation provides high quality gifts at the Navy Museum Store to satisfy both young tourists looking for memorabilia of their Washington visit and Navy commands seeking special presentation gifts such as the Foundation's signature Truxtun Bowl replica. To enhance the accessibility of the Navy Museum, the Foundation has an exclusive license with the Navy to rent the museum for evening and weekend events, providing a unique venue for corporate, Navy, and personal dinners or receptions.

Individuals may learn more about the Naval Historical Foundation and become a member at www.navyhistory.org.

Naval Historical Foundation
1306 Dahlgren Avenue, SE
Washington Navy Yard
Washington, DC 20374-5055
tel: (202) 678-4333; fax: (202) 889-3565
e-mail: nhfwny@navyhistory.org
www.navyhistory.org

MARINE CORPS ASSOCIATION

At Guantanamo Bay, Cuba, on 25 April 1913, Marines of the Second Provisional Brigade formed the Marine Corps Association. John A. Lejeune, then a lieutenant colonel, headed its first executive committee. The purpose of the MCA was defined then and continues to drive the Association into the 21st century: "to disseminate knowledge of military art and science to its members; to provide for professional advancement; to foster the spirit and preserve the traditions of the United States Marine Corps."

For all who have earned and worn the Eagle, Globe, and Anchor, the Marine Corps Association is the professional organization for active duty, Reserve, retired, and Marine veterans. The MCA understands and identifies with the sacrifices made and the services rendered as a Marine to this great country. Once a Marine, always a Marine!

A member of the Marine Corps Association is part of a brotherhood rich with history, traditions, and accomplishments. Membership is the lifeblood of the MCA. Regardless of status—active duty, Reserve, retired, or veteran—we urge eligible individuals to become members of the professional association of the Marines.

Individuals may learn more about the Marine Corps Association and become a member at www.mca-marines.org.

Marine Corps Association
715 Broadway Street
Quantico, Virginia 22134
tel: (703) 640-6161; fax: (703) 640-0823
e-mail: mca@mca-marines.org
www.mca-marines.org

THE AIR FORCE HISTORICAL FOUNDATION

Founded in 1953, The Air Force Historical Foundation is a 501(c)(3) independent, nonprofit, tax-exempt organization dedicated to promoting the preservation and appreciation of the history and heritage of the United States Air Force and its predecessors. The Foundation seeks to inform and inspire the men and women who are, or have been, affiliated with the Air Force and depends on membership dues, private contributions, and institutional subscriptions to operate and foster America's rich air power history and heritage. The Foundation serves members representing all components of the United States Air Force, including the active force, the Reserve, the Air National Guard, the civilian force, retirees, veterans, and families of those members. The Foundation is proud of its role in presenting an authoritative history of many aspects of the Air Force and strives to make available to the general public, and to government planners and decision-makers, historical information on policies and actions related to air and space power. By doing so, the Foundation believes that the nation profits from past experiences as it helps the U.S. Air Force remain the world's most respected air and space force.

Past presidents of the Foundation read like a Who's Who of air power pioneers and leaders, including General Carl A. Spaatz, General Hoyt S. Vandenberg, Major General Benjamin D. Foulois, General Curtis E. LeMay, and General Bernard A. Schriever. The logo of the Foundation, a Wright aircraft designated Signal Corps No. 1, was the first aircraft accepted by the United States Army in 1909.

The Foundation provides active support of its membership through sponsorship of biennial symposia on diverse aspects of aerospace power, sponsorship of eleven annual awards, publication of books on aerospace power and leaders, and publication of the quarterly journal *Air Power History*.

Individuals may learn more about the Air Force Historical Foundation and become a member at www.afhistoricalfoundation.org.

Air Force Historical Foundation
P.O. Box 790
Clinton, Maryland 20735-0790
tel: (301) 736-1959
e-mail: execdir@afhistoricalfoundation.org
www.afhistoricalfoundation.org

Published by UNIVERSE Publishing
A Division of Rizzoli International Publications, Inc.
300 Park Avenue South
New York, NY 10010
www.rizzoliusa.com

Project Editor: Melissa C. Payne
Series Editor: James O. Muschett
Copy Editor: Wendy Leland
Production Coordinator: Candice Fehrman
Designers: Veronica Naranjo and Charles J. Ziga,
Ziga Design, LLC

2008 2009 2010 2011 / 10 9 8 7 6 5 4 3 2 1

Printed in China

ISBN-13: 978-0-7893-9983-0

Library of Congress Catalog Control Number:
2008922676

Front Matter Credits
Page 2: (Corbis); Page 6: (National Archives)
Page 8, Top: (U.S. Air Force); Page 8, Bottom: (U.S. Navy)

CONTENTS

WORLD WAR II:
A CHRONOLOGY OF WAR

FOREWORD BY
PRESIDENT GEORGE H. W. BUSH

As a combat veteran of World War II, this wonderful, unique book strikes a particularly strong personal note, especially the chapter on the war in the Pacific.

Like most young men in high school in the late 1930s, I was more interested in sports and social activities than world politics. We paid little attention to the looming storm of global war, but the attack on Pearl Harbor, December 7, 1941, changed all that. And like most of the young men my age, we signed up as soon as we could. In my case, I enlisted six months later, on my 18th birthday, and became a naval aviator.

This book is more than a history of the war; it is a chronological record in words and pictures of American courage in one of the most dangerous periods of our history. By this simple approach, the vast scope of the war, the complexity of the operations and the deadly ferocity of the fighting are easily followed for all our military services.

In the more than sixty years since the war ended, I have met and worked with many other veterans of the conflict, men and women, representing all the military services and all the theaters of fighting—Pacific, Mediterranean, North Africa, France, Germany, Burma and the Aleutian Islands, and all the seas of the globe. None of those veterans considered themselves to be something special. They were ordinary Americans caught up in extraordinary circumstances and called upon to do exceptional things.

We veterans of World War II are now passing from the scene in daily increasing numbers, but when the last Soldier, Sailor, Marine, Aviator, and Coast Guardsman have gone, they will leave behind a legacy of service, determination, and bravery. Their story is told in this book that is unique in both its clarity and comprehensive detail. I am honored to even be mentioned, given that I was one of millions of my fellow Americans with whom I served in those trying days.

G Bush

EDITOR'S NOTE

This book is a chronological compilation of the events and activities of the United States military forces in the critical years of World War II. In this book, a simple, straightforward approach is taken that enables a reader, no matter what level of military historical expertise, to quickly find a specific date or event, or get an overview of a long-term operation for each service branch of the military.

For clarity and consistency, several editorial decisions were made that I hope add to the reader's experience. First, this book focuses on the American military forces. Second, the entry headings identify the military service(s) involved with each entry in alphabetical order, not by seniority, as is the standard protocol. There are many entries titled "Air Force" even though today's Air Force did not exist as a separate service until July 1947. This heading covers events and activities of the Army Air Corps, and later the Army Air Forces, and is used for the benefit of modern readers who may not realize that today's Army and Air Force share a common aviation history.

Likewise for clarification, the full name of an individual is used rather than a nickname (e.g., Ike, Tooey, Hap, etc.), and full official unit designations are used (e.g., regiment, squadron, division, etc.) rather than the usual military shorthand number system. Aircraft are identified as fighters, bombers, etc., along with the service name (Lightning, Wildcat, Invader, etc.) and service identifier (PBY, SB2C, P-39, etc.). In addition, U.S. Navy ships are referred to only by their names, not by hull numbers.

I feel strongly that this is an accurate presentation of the most important events of World War II. I tried to convey a feeling for the scope of the immense complex activity, both organizational and operational, that each service experienced during the war, and to give a balanced snapshot of how each service responded to the demands of the war. But as with any historical chronology, there was not enough space to include it all.

Most regrettably, it was not possible to include more than a sample of the Medal of Honor recipients. This in no way diminishes their awesome heroism, nor the debt of this nation to them.

A collective, multi-service team of editors and historians reviewed this text in its entirety, but I assume full responsibility for the choices that were made. There is no doubt that some may disagree with entries in this book. I apologize for any errors, historical or otherwise, that may have crept in despite the valiant efforts of this dedicated team.

COLONEL RAYMOND K. BLUHM JR., USA (Ret.)

PRELUDE TO WAR
1938–1941

Tom Freeman
© 1993

PRELUDE TO WAR
1938–1941

"Once we had plenty of time but no money; now the Army has all the money it needs, but no time."

—General George C. Marshall, Army Chief of Staff

THE ISOLATION YEARS

It was a time of troubled peace for the United States. For most Americans, the years between the world wars were a focus on home. These were the years of the Great Depression filled with hardscrabble days to simply survive. The nation's focus was on day-to-day struggles to hold a job, find sufficient food, and have a place to live. Foreign events taking place thousands of miles away were of little interest as a strong isolationist sentiment swept the country after the World War I demobilization. After all, it was the "war to end all wars"—right? And America had its own problems.

By 1938, the last year of official "peace," the storm flags of world war were plainly flying in both Europe and Asia. The growth of Japanese militarism in the 1920s culminated in the takeover of Manchuria by the Japanese army in 1932. This was followed the next year by the rise to power of the Nazi party in Germany and the appointment of Adolph Hitler as German chancellor. Within months, both Japan and Germany left the League of Nations. Japan then abrogated the 1922 Washington Naval Treaty in 1934, and Germany abandoned the Versailles Peace Treaty in January 1937. In July of that same year, a staged "incident" at the Marco Polo Bridge near Peking, China, was used by the Japanese to justify assaults against Chinese forces in north China. The Japanese army captured Shanghai, China, and in December 1937, rampaged through Nanking, China, "accidentally" attacking and

Pages 10–11: *The U.S. Navy gunboat* Tutuila *is shown at anchor near Chungking, China, circa 1939. She is one of several lightly armed gunboats assigned to the Navy's Yangtze River Patrol. A sister gunboat,* Panay, *is sunk near Nanking, China, by the Japanese in an "accidental" attack on 12 December 1937. ("Far Yangtze Station," Tom Freeman)*

Left: *As the Army transforms into a mechanized force, it retains horses and mules. An Army warrant officer explains the mysteries of properly harnessing a team of field artillery horses to perplexed Soldiers, circa 1930s. ("The Quiet Professional," Don Stivers)*

Left: *Machine gun crews from the 4th Marine Regiment practice their street combat drills in Shanghai, China, in 1937. Along with a small detachment of sailors from the heavy cruiser* Augusta, *the Marines have the mission of helping secure the city's International Settlement as the undeclared war between Japan and China spreads. The regiment is withdrawn to the Philippines in 1938. (National Archives)*

sinking the U.S. Navy gunboat *Panay* in the process.

All these foreboding events fell on the mostly deaf ears of an America absorbed with its own problems. Successive administrations and Congress severely reduced military budgets and imposed skeleton force structures on the U.S. Army and Navy. Army strength fell to 132,000 men in 1923 and remained at that level until the mid-1930s. When President Franklin D. Roosevelt took office in 1933 with a New Deal to salvage the American economy, he proposed cutting the Army's budget by another 51 percent and reducing officer strength by 10,000. Only an emotional protest by Army Chief of Staff Douglas MacArthur prevented the catastrophe. Even as late as 1939, there were only 175,000 or so Army Regulars. The National Guard and Army Reserve languished as well.

The Marine Corps, seen by isolationists as the tool of American foreign intervention, was the target of political pressure to greatly reduce its ranks, or even be eliminated completely. The 1919 congressional authorization for a Marine Corps of 27,400 was threatened several times during the 1920s and 1930s with proposals to reduce it to only 13,000. Low budgets and recruiting problems even during the Depression years kept actual Marine Corps strength hovering around 18,000 officers and men, well below the authorized total.

The Navy fared little better. Bound by the 1922 Washington Naval Treaty and the 1930 London Naval Treaty, which were intended to prevent an international naval arms race, the Navy was limited in both tonnages and types of warship. Year after year the Navy was prevented from even building up to its authorized treaty strength. A remarkable feat was the Navy's commissioning in 1927, within treaty restrictions, of the large aircraft carriers *Lexington* and *Saratoga*, converted from battle-cruiser hulls. These later became heroic fighters in the approaching war. With careful planning, the Navy was also able to modernize a number of older World War I–era ships, and eventually build some new cruisers, destroyers, and battleships.

THE ALARM SOUNDS

The German invasion of Poland in September 1939 was a rude awakening to world reality for many Americans. In mid-1940, the Germans turned west and attacked Belgium and France. Paris fell in June, and an alarmed Congress began to open its purse. But despite a growing sense of impending war, the small gains in military readiness were not without a bitter political fight from antiadministration, antiwar, and isolationist elements.

During the early 1930s, all the military services continued efforts, within their modest budgets, to develop and test new technology, especially in the fields of aviation and electronics. As money was gradually made available during the period 1938–1941, they were able to do more. A Naval Expansion Act, passed in May 1938, permitted a 20 percent increase in active ships and additional aircraft. Later that year a prototype radar was installed on the battleship *New York*. After extensive testing by the Marine Corps, the Navy adopted a new landing craft, the Higgins boat, in 1940.

America's air strength also grew. The Army Air Corps, established in 1926, continued to refine its

flying skills and shifted its interest from lighter-than-air craft and bi-planes to monoplanes. America's first heavy long-range bomber, the Boeing B-17 *Flying Fortress*, delivered in March 1937, was given an intercontinental trial when six Army Air Corps crews flew their planes to Argentina. Other new Army aircraft, like the experimental P-39 Airacobra, P-40 Warhawk, and P-38 Lightning fighters, were also tested in 1939, and the B-25 Mitchell bomber was flown for the first time. The Navy contracted for the SB2C-1 Helldiver dive-bomber, which became critical during the war.

Meanwhile, the ground branches of the Army also started modernizing. Quantities of new items were small, however, as American industry was still in its Depression shock. A new eight-round, semiautomatic rifle, the M1 Garand, was adopted in 1939 to replace the venerable bolt-action 1903 Springfield, while advocates of mechanized warfare fought for changes in tactical doctrine and money to develop new tanks. A unique little utility vehicle that became known as the "jeep" soon made an appearance, and was adopted by all services.

President Roosevelt's declaration of a "limited national emergency" on 8 September 1939 and directive to strengthen national defense brought funding for full manning of the services. In 1940, Congress provided major military budget increases that put new energy into the military services' reorganization initiatives. Finally, in September 1940, the president signed the first peacetime Selective Training and Service Act, and a month later the first draft numbers were drawn. Draft service, however, was only for one year and a bitter political fight was waged

a year later when Congress proposed extending the tours of duty by another year. The law passed by only one vote. Roosevelt also authorized mobilization of the National Guard. Manpower and money now began to pour into the military.

New commands were activated as all the military services reshaped themselves from a reduced peacetime force. The Army activated new divisions and organized them into a "triangular" configuration with three infantry regiments and artillery. Fully mechanized armored divisions were created for the first time, and the Army's horse cavalry began its transition to tracks and wheels. The first parachute unit was formed and tested, combining air mobility with ground power, and an Army General Headquarters was activated to train the growing number of Soldiers. By mid-1941 the Army had 15

divisions in various stages of readiness, and a newly renamed Army Air Forces of almost 100,000 officers, cadets, and enlisted men.

The Marine Corps activated its reserves, added additional regiments, and opened new facilities. New Defense Battalions organized to defend U.S. naval bases were soon deploying to Pacific bases. The 1st Marine Brigade (Provisional) was sent in June 1941 to protect strategically important Iceland until the Army's "Indigo Force" arrived in September.

A series of naval expansion acts in 1940, passed over antiwar opposition, increased the size of the fleet, and authorized the officers and men needed to man the new ships, planes, and facilities. A year later *North Carolina*, the first new battleship since 1923, joined the fleet. New submarines were commissioned, and naval aviation grew dramatically as new carriers were launched and planes delivered.

While joint service exercises occurred in the early 1930s, they were relatively small. Now the pace and size of these Navy-Army-Marine Corps exercises picked up, and plans included at least one joint Army-Marine Corps division-size unit, forming the basis for later interservice cooperation. Each service also conducted its own training exercises; the largest were a series of Army maneuvers in Louisiana and the Carolinas utilizing aircraft, tanks, and thousands of Soldiers.

TOO LITTLE, TOO LATE

The fall of France in June 1940, Great Britain's struggle to survive the German blitz, and the Japanese advance into Southeast Asia brought the American mobilization efforts to a frenzied pace by mid-1941. In response to British pleas for help, an alarmed Congress had passed the Lend-Lease Act in March, trading U.S. destroyers for access to British territory for bases. An undeclared war at sea began when U.S. Navy destroyers were given responsibility for escorting North Atlantic convoys of equipment and ammunition to England and the USSR. To help protect the Atlantic convoy routes, a Marine Corps brigade was sent in July to reinforce British troops defending the Iceland bases. The inevitable clash with German submarines came in October 1941 with the damaging of the destroyer *Kearny* and the sinking of the destroyer *Reuben James*.

Air and ground reinforcements were also sent to the Pacific island outposts and the Philippine Islands, but many never arrived. Both the Navy and Army sent out a series of war-warning messages to all commands in November, but the attacks against Pearl Harbor, Hawaii, and the Philippines on 7–8 December 1941 were still a surprise. The losses in ships and planes devastated American strength in the Pacific. The United States declared war against Japan on 8 December, and the same day the first Japanese troops landed in the Philippines. War declarations by Germany and Italy were answered in kind by Congress, making the war truly global. Active service tours for all military members were extended for the duration of the war plus six months. With grim determination, a shocked America prepared for a long, desperate struggle back to peace.

1938
THE STORM APPROACHES

7 JANUARY
ARMY
The use of spiral khaki wrap-around leggings is discontinued, and the Army adopts more practical canvas leggings, long a prerogative of the cavalry, as a standard item for the field uniform.

13 JANUARY
MARINE CORPS
Marines participate in Fleet Landing Exercise 4 at Culebra, Puerto Rico. The exercise continues through 15 March.

2 FEBRUARY
NAVY
Participating in naval exercises, two PBY Catalina flying boats collide in the darkness. On board one

of the planes, Lieutenant Carlton B. Hutchins remains in the pilot's seat, maintaining control of the aircraft so that four members of his crew can parachute to safety. He is awarded the Medal of Honor posthumously.

17 FEBRUARY
AIR FORCE
A flight of six B-17 Flying Fortress bombers under the command of Lieutenant Colonel Robert D. Olds takes off from Miami, Florida, en route to Buenos Aires, Argentina, to participate in the inauguration of President Roberto Ortiz.

18 FEBRUARY
MARINE CORPS
The 2d Brigade headquarters and 6th Marine Regiment depart Shanghai, China, after the Japanese force the Chinese army from the city, and the threat to the International Settlement is reduced.

28 FEBRUARY
ARMY

The United States withdraws the 15th Infantry Regiment after 26 years in and around Tientsin, China. Thus ends the mission of the command known as U.S. Army Troops in China and a presence dating back to the 1900 Boxer Rebellion. The 15th Infantry heads for Fort Lewis, Washington, and soon is assigned to the 5th Brigade, 3d Division.

MARINE CORPS

Following the withdrawal of the Army's 15th Infantry Regiment from Tientsin, China, a detachment of about 200 Marines is sent from the Legation Guard at Peiping to establish a post at the former Army barracks.

15 MARCH
MARINE CORPS

Marine Corps units participate in Fleet Problem XIX in Hawaii, practicing the occupation of an advance base.

6 APRIL
AIR FORCE

The Bell XP-39 Airacobra flies for the first time at Wright Field, Ohio. Bell test pilot James Taylor makes the flight. P-39s will be produced in large numbers as part of the Lend-Lease program between the U.S. and the Soviet Union, which will utilize some 4,800 P-39s in the ground attack role on the Eastern Front.

12 MAY
AIR FORCE/NAVY

Attempting to validate the Army Air Corps' mission of coastal defense, three B-17 Flying Fortress bombers intercept an ocean liner, *Rex*, at a range of 700 miles from U.S. shores. The U.S. Navy reacts by demanding that a 100-mile limit be enacted on Army coastal defense responsibility to limit Army bombers.

NAVY

The aircraft carrier *Enterprise*, destined to become one of the most decorated ships of World War II, is commissioned.

17 MAY
NAVY

Congress passes the Naval Expansion Act, which provides for a 20 percent increase in active naval vessels and not less than 3,000 aircraft.

Above: *The "Old China Hands" of the Army's 15th Infantry Regiment, illustrated here in their summer field and garrison uniforms, are stationed in Tientsin, China, 1912–1938. China service is represented by the dragon on the regimental insignia. As young officers, George C. Marshall and Joseph W. Stilwell serve with the 15th Regiment in China. ("15th Infantry, American Barracks, Tientsin, China, 1927," Frederic E. Ray Jr., Company of Military Historians)*

Opposite: *Six Army Air Corps YB-17 bombers pass over New York City as the planes begin their flight to Argentina in February 1938. The "Y" indicates the planes are prototypes. (U.S. Air Force)*

23 JUNE
MARINE CORPS

President Franklin D. Roosevelt signs legislation providing that the active-duty strength of the Marine Corps be 20 percent of the active-duty enlisted strength of the Navy. That act adds 97 billets to the 27,400 already authorized for the Marine Corps. Congress does not provide sufficient funding for that number, however.

25 JUNE
MARINE CORPS
The Naval Reserve Act reorganizes the Marine Reserve into three groups: Fleet Marine Corps Reserve (active-duty retirees still subject to recall), the Organized Marine Corps Reserve (units), and the Volunteer Marine Corps Reserve (individuals).

NAVY
Congress passes a naval appropriation act providing for the construction of two battleships, one aircraft carrier, two light cruisers, and a sizeable number of auxiliary vessels.

30 JUNE
MARINE CORPS
The strength of the Marine Corps on active duty is 1,359 officers and 16,997 enlisted.

21 SEPTEMBER
AIR FORCE
Major General Oscar Westover, Chief of the Army Air Corps, is killed when the Cessna AT-17 aircraft he is flying crashes in Burbank, California. The accident board reveals that the crash was caused by gusty and unpredictable wind conditions coupled with rising heat currents near the ground. Westover's mechanic, Staff Sergeant Hymes, is also killed in the crash.

Right: *The A-20 Havoc is used as a light bomber and night fighter (P-70). It is one of the most produced aircraft of the war and sees service in both the European and Pacific theaters. The A-20 receives many modifications and is provided to several U.S. allies during the war. The British name it the "Boston." (NASM)*

29 SEPTEMBER
AIR FORCE

Major General Henry H. Arnold, pilot certificate No. 29, circa 1911, is confirmed as the Chief of the Army Air Corps. Arnold had been immediately named chief and promoted to major general the day after Major General Oscar Westover's untimely death.

14 OCTOBER
AIR FORCE

The Curtiss XP-40, the prototype for the P-40 Warhawk fighter, flies for the first time near Buffalo, New York. Test pilot Edward Elliot conducts the test. Almost 14,000 P-40s will be built before the end of the construction run in 1944.

26 OCTOBER
AIR FORCE

The Douglas Model 7B, later the A-20 Havoc, flies for the first time near El Segundo, California. The A-20 Havoc will become the most produced Army surface attack aircraft and will see service in all combat theaters.

14 NOVEMBER
AIR FORCE

During a top-level White House conference, President Franklin D. Roosevelt suggests that the size and scope of the Army Air Corps be increased. Major General Henry H. Arnold calls the meeting the "Magna Carta" of American airpower.

9 DECEMBER
NAVY

A prototype shipboard radar, designed by the Naval Research Laboratory, is installed on board the

battleship *New York* for trials. During World War II shipboard radar proves a tremendous advantage in combat between U.S. and Japanese warships.

16 DECEMBER
NAVY

The K-2 non-rigid airship, the prototype for a successful class of blimps that prove valuable in antisubmarine operations during World War II, arrives at Naval Air Station Lakehurst, New Jersey, for evaluation.

Left: *The K-ships are a class of non-rigid blimps used by the U.S. Navy for antisubmarine warfare and convoy protection in both the Atlantic and Pacific ocean areas. First purchased in 1938, K-ships had crews of 10 and were equipped with radar, sonobuoys, four depth charges, and a .50 caliber machine gun. (Naval Historical Center)*

1939
AN AWAKENING NATION

JANUARY
MARINE CORPS

The General Board of the Navy approves a formal mission statement for Marine Corps aviation: "To be equipped, organized, and trained primarily for the support of the Fleet Marine Force in landing operations and in support of troop activities in the field; secondarily as replacements for carrier-based naval aircraft."

3 JANUARY
MARINE CORPS/NAVY

The report of the Hepburn Board (a Navy fact-finding group led by Admiral Arthur Hepburn established to examine the Navy's requirements for overseas bases) recognizes the need for expanding naval aviation's infrastructure. The board recommends the enlargement of 11 existing air stations and construction of 16 others, half of which will be built on Pacific islands, including Wake Atoll, Midway Atoll, and Guam Island. This work will eventually be facilitated by the 1st, 3d, and 6th Marine Defense Battalions.

9 JANUARY
ARMY/MARINE CORPS

The Army adopts the .30 caliber M1 semi-automatic Garand (named for inventor John Garand) as its standard rifle. The Marine Corps follows suit after more testing. This will be the principal weapon for the individual infantryman in the U.S. military and the armies of many allies in and after World War II, and it will remain in production until the 1950s.

27 JANUARY
AIR FORCE

Experienced test pilot 1st Lieutenant Benjamin Kelsey flies the XP-38, later the P-38 Lightning fighter, at March Field, California, on its maiden flight. In February, Kelsey attempts to break the transcontinental speed record in the XP-38, but crashes just before landing. Nonetheless, the performance until that point convinces the Air Corps to purchase the plane in large numbers.

Left: *A flight of Grumman F3F-3 fighters is shown in the bright pre-war color scheme common in the 1930s. Designed for aircraft carrier service, the single seap plane is armed with one .30 caliber and one .50 caliber machine gun, both in the nose. The F3F-3 is the last biplane ordered by the Navy, but is flown well into the war years by both Navy and Marine Corps pilots. (Naval Historical Center)*

Opposite: *Army gunners of the 13th Coast Artillery Regiment go through their practice drill at a 12-inch mortar battery of Fort Taylor, Key West, Florida. Reduced budgets and insufficient men in the 1920s and early 1930s left the coastal defenses of the U.S. outdated and in poor shape. Open batteries like this are very vulnerable to air attack. In 1940 a desperate catch-up effort is made to rearm and modernize coastal defenses. (National Archives)*

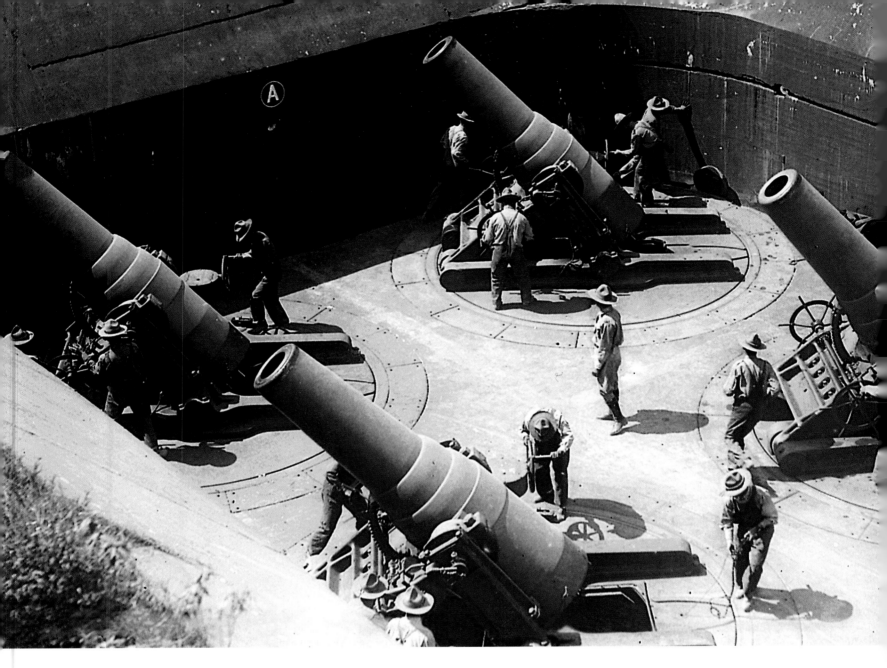

10 FEBRUARY
AIR FORCE
The North American NA-40, later the B-25 Mitchell bomber, flies for the first time, piloted by test pilot Paul Balfour. The B-25 will become famous when 16 Mitchell bombers are launched from the aircraft carrier *Hornet* in a daring raid on Japan in April 1942.

15 MARCH
MARINE CORPS
Following tests of Andrew Higgins' Eureka boat during Fleet Landing Exercise 5 in the Carribean, Marines enthusiastically endorse it as the best landing craft available. The Higgins boat is finally adopted by the Navy in 1940. Later improved with a bow ramp, it becomes the standard U.S. landing craft of World War II. Higgins soon develops larger models to carry tanks.

1 APRIL
ARMY
Major General Joseph A. Green is named the chief of Coast Artillery. He will be the last officer to serve in this assignment as the position is destined to be eliminated soon after the attack on Pearl Harbor, Hawaii, in 1941. The Coast Artillery will merge with the Field Artillery in 1950.

3 APRIL
AIR FORCE
President Franklin D. Roosevelt signs the National Defense Act that will direct military spending for the following year. Army Air Corps strength is expanded to 48,000 personnel, 6,000 aircraft are authorized, and the budget explodes to $300 million for 1940. The act also authorizes training for African American pilots and crew.

18 APRIL
AIR FORCE
Major General Henry H. Arnold recalls Colonel Charles A. Lindbergh, USAR, to active duty and assigns him the task of evaluating the weaknesses in military airpower expansion underway at that time.

21 APRIL
MARINE CORPS

The Division of Operations and Training of Headquarters Marine Corps is renamed the Division of Plans and Policies.

1 MAY
MARINE CORPS

Aircraft One (Quantico, Virginia) and Aircraft Two (San Diego, California) are renamed the 1st and 2d Marine Aircraft Groups, respectively.

15 MAY
NAVY

The Navy issues a contract for the procurement of the XSB2C-1 Helldiver, prototype of the unpopular aircraft that nevertheless forms the backbone of U.S. Navy dive-bombing squadrons in the latter part of World War II.

17 MAY–18 OCTOBER
NAVY

A landing party from the gunboats *Asheville* and *Tulsa* and the destroyer *Whipple* protects the U.S. Consulate and a hospital at Kulangsu, China, following the landing of Japanese forces in the area.

23 MAY
NAVY

The submarine *Squalus* sinks while executing a practice dive off Portsmouth, New Hampshire. Employing the new McCann Rescue Chamber, rescuers are able to bring 33 of 59 crew members to the surface. The boat is subsequently raised, repaired, and renamed *Sailfish*.

1 JUNE
AIR FORCE

Civilian flying schools around the country are tasked to train Army Air Corps flying cadets in an effort to rapidly produce a large trained flying force. This is

Above: *The "propeller" shoulder insignia is adopted by the General Headquarters, Air Force in 1937. This unit controls all Army Air Corps combat units until creation of the Army Air Forces under Major General Henry H. Arnold in 1941. (American Society of Military Insignia Collectors)*

Right: *The U.S. Navy submarine* Squalus *surfaces during salvage operations. The new sub had sunk with a 59-man crew in 250 feet of water during a test emergency dive on 23 May 1939. Thirty-three survivors are brought up in a rescue chamber. (Naval Historical Center)*

Left: *Denied tanks by a 1919 Army decree that gave them to the Infantry branch, the Cavalry branch continues to experiment with mechanized mobility and armored vehicles, such as this M1 armored combat car. (Hunnicutt Collection, Patton Museum)*

Below*: Troopers of the 13th Cavalry (Mechanized) show off their "modern" combat cars, as cavalry tanks were called, at the 1939 World's Fair. (Patton Museum)*

part of Major General Henry H. Arnold's balanced air plan that he had put into effect after becoming Chief of the Army Air Corps.

11–13 JUNE
NAVY

The aircraft carrier *Saratoga* and the oiler *Kanawha* participate in underway replenishment trials off the West Coast. The first underway replenishment operations occurred in 1917 when the oiler *Maumee* refueled destroyers steaming across the Atlantic to European waters. Her executive officer at that time was Lieutenant Chester W. Nimitz, whose work on at-sea refueling during World War I led to the perfection of a logistical operation essential to the ships under his command winning the far-flung naval war in the Pacific during World War II.

30 JUNE
MARINE CORPS

The strength of the Marine Corps on active duty is 1,380 officers and 18,052 enlisted.

1 AUGUST
NAVY

Admiral Harold R. Stark becomes the eighth Chief of Naval Operations.

8 AUGUST
ARMY

The 7th Cavalry Brigade (Mechanized) arrives at Plattsburg, New York, following a journey from Fort Knox, Kentucky. The unique, experimental unit under Brigadier General Adna R. Chaffee participates successfully in First Army maneuvers. The brigade participates in the New York World's Fair, Flushing Meadows, New York, on 30 August.

1 SEPTEMBER
ALL SERVICES

Germany invades Poland after aerial bombardment of the Polish lines by Junkers Ju-87 Stuka dive bombers. France and Great Britain declare war on Germany two days later. World War II in Europe begins.

ARMY

General George Catlett Marshall becomes Army Chief of Staff. An alumnus of the Virginia Military Institute, Marshall is the first Chief of Staff to be commissioned from a civilian college training program.

2 SEPTEMBER
AIR FORCE

At the annual Cleveland Air Races, songwriter Robert Crawford sings "Nothing Will Stop the Air Corps Now," designated the official Army Air Corps song. A group of Air Corps wives had selected the song from over 700 entries.

5 SEPTEMBER
NAVY

President Franklin D. Roosevelt declares American neutrality in the European war, and orders the Navy to inaugurate the so-called Neutrality Patrol off the eastern seaboard to monitor all foreign vessels entering a zone extending 300 miles from the East Coast of the United States. The first ships put to sea to establish the patrol on 6 September.

8 SEPTEMBER
ALL SERVICES

President Franklin D. Roosevelt calls for "strengthening of the national defense within the

Above: *During the 1930s the Marine Corps refines its amphibious warfare doctrine and techniques, testing several designs of landing craft. The draft of boat shown here does not permit it to approach near the beach and forces the Marines to exit awkwardly over the bow. (National Archives)*

Left: *One of the few surviving examples of the original Bantam ¼-ton Reconnaissance Car that became known worldwide as the Army "jeep." This tough vehicle is credited by some as a major factor in winning the war. (Patton Museum)*

limits of peace-time authorizations." The Army and the Navy are put on notice that training and increased "preparedness" are now the order of the day in a time of "a limited national emergency." This results in an order to increase the strength of the Marine Corps to 25,000 enlisted men; increase Navy enlisted strength from 110,813 to 145,000; and to recall retired officers, enlisted men, and nurses.

16 SEPTEMBER
ARMY

Following field testing by the provisional 2d Division under the command of Major General Walter Krueger, the Army decides upon the "triangular" structure for its new divisions. The new divisions are built around three combat infantry regiments with appropriate field artillery as well as service and support elements. The 2d Division is the first to convert to the new structure, quickly followed by the 1st and 3d Divisions.

23 SEPTEMBER
ARMY

After an emergency call to U.S. industry, the American Bantam Car Company delivers a prototype vehicle to Camp Holabird, Maryland, for testing. Officially to be known as the "truck, one-quarter ton" and soon to be mass produced by the Willys-Overland Company and Ford, this is the Army's, and the world's, introduction to the "jeep." There will be approximately 650,000 produced in the next five years.

1 OCTOBER
ARMY

Fort Humphreys, District of Columbia, takes on a new name—the Army War College. After World War II the name will change to Fort Lesley J. McNair.

2 OCTOBER
ARMY

The 5th Division, formed at Fort McClellan, Alabama, returns to the active rolls. Next to be formed is the 6th Division, on 12 October at Fort Lewis, Washington. The new divisions will feature a strength of approximately 15,000 in contrast to the 28,105 required to man the old four-regiment "square" divisions.

5 OCTOBER
NAVY

The Hawaiian Detachment, U.S. Fleet—consisting of the aircraft carrier *Enterprise*, two heavy cruiser divisions, a light cruiser, two destroyer squadrons, and auxiliary ships—sails for Pearl Harbor, Hawaii. This measure establishes a sizeable naval presence at this Pacific base, deemed important given Japan's continuing aggression against China.

10 OCTOBER
MARINE CORPS

The 3d Defense Battalion is established at Parris Island, South Carolina. The mission of this new type of unit is to provide fixed defenses for expeditionary bases against air and surface attacks. The primary armament is antiaircraft artillery, machine guns, and coast defense guns, though some later units also include infantry and tank elements. All told, 18 of these units serve in World War II.

Right: *The submarine* Swordfish *is launched from the Mare Island, California, shipyard on 3 April 1939. In December 1941 and the early months of 1942,* Swordfish *successfully evacuates American and Philippine officials from the Philippine Islands including President Manuel L. Quezon. She departs on her 13th combat patrol in December 1944 to an area near the Ryukyu Islands. After a last radio communication on 3 January 1945,* Swordfish *is never heard from again. (National Archives)*

Left: *After the draft begins in October 1940, early morning formation and drills at Fort Lewis, Washington, become a familiar ritual for millions of young Americans. (Jeffery Ethell Collection)*

Below: *More than 18,000 B-24 Liberator bombers are built during the war. The aircraft serves in every theater, but vulnerability to fuel tank fires makes it less reliable than the B-17 Flying Fortress. (NASM)*

Opposite: *("Fleet Maneuvers," James Dietz)*

1 NOVEMBER
ARMY

The infamous "corned willy" canned beef is to be a thing of the past as newly designed "C-rations" are adopted as standard for the Army in the field.

4 NOVEMBER
ALL SERVICES

President Franklin D. Roosevelt signs the Neutrality Act into law. The measure repeals the arms embargo, prohibits U.S. vessels from entering combat zones, and establishes the National Munitions Control Board. Roosevelt immediately declares the waters around the British Isles a combat zone.

1 DECEMBER
NAVY

Submarine Division 14, consisting of *Perch*, *Permit*, *Pickerel*, *Pike*, *Porpoise*, and *Tarpon*, arrives on the Asiatic Station to provide the Asiatic Fleet with some degree of offensive firepower in the event of a Pacific war.

14–19 DECEMBER
NAVY

U.S. Navy warships trail the German passenger liner *Columbus*, as British destroyers pursue it from Mexican waters to a position some 450 miles east of Cape May, New Jersey. On 19 December, the crew of *Columbus* scuttles the ship to prevent her capture by the British. The heavy cruiser *Tuscaloosa* rescues 573 passengers and crew and transports them to New York City.

20 DECEMBER
MARINE CORPS/NAVY

Chief of Naval Operations Admiral Harold Stark directs the establishment of a Marine detachment on Midway Atoll.

29 DECEMBER
AIR FORCE

The Consolidated XB-24 Liberator bomber makes its maiden flight, piloted by company test pilot Bill Wheatley. More than 18,000 B-24s will be built, a total exceeding any other U.S. military aircraft in history.

1940
A CALL TO ARMS

2 JANUARY
NAVY
Charles Edison, son of the famous inventor Thomas Edison, takes office as the 46th Secretary of the Navy.

11 JANUARY
MARINE CORPS/NAVY
Fleet Landing Exercise 6 begins at Culebra, Puerto Rico. The exercise force includes the 1st Marine Brigade; the 1st Marine Aircraft Group; and one transport, the four-stack destroyer *Manley*, recently converted to an amphibious transport and later redesignated APD 1. *Manley* serves throughout World War II, landing her first troops in combat at Guadalcanal in 1942 and her last in the Philippine Islands in 1945.

15–22 JANUARY
ARMY/NAVY
In a training exercise that foreshadows joint operations in the Mediterranean and European theaters during World War II, Army and Navy forces practice amphibious landings at Monterey, California. A major focus of the training is familiarizing Army troops in embarking and disembarking landing craft.

23 JANUARY
AIR FORCE
The Army tests the feasibility of movement of ground units by air. A battalion of the 65th Coast Artillery is loaded into 38 bombers at Hamilton Field, California, and flown 500 miles to a test destination.

15 FEBRUARY
NAVY
President Franklin D. Roosevelt departs Pensacola, Florida, in the heavy cruiser *Tuscaloosa* to inspect the Panama Canal and discuss defense of this vital asset.

26 FEBRUARY
ARMY
The Army establishes the Air Defense Command to plan and supervise the U.S. air defenses.

25 MARCH
AIR FORCE
Under the liberalized release policy, Army Air Corps aircraft contractors are authorized to sell modern Army aircraft to anti-Axis nations. This establishes a production base for future Army Air Corps expansion.

1 APRIL
MARINE CORPS
The 8th Marine Regiment is reactivated at San Diego, California, and assigned to the 2d Marine Brigade.

7–13 APRIL
NAVY
The destroyer *J. Fred Talbott* makes rendezvous with the Japanese merchantman *Arimasa Maru* off the Panama Canal Zone and provides urgent medical treatment to a member of the steamship's crew.

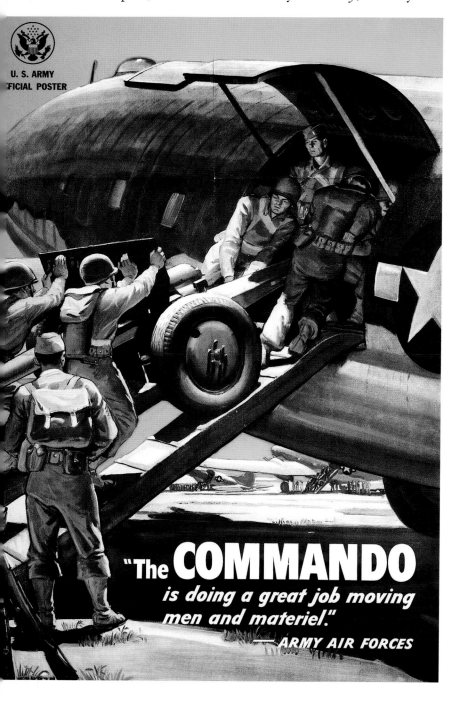

U.S. ARMY OFFICIAL POSTER

"The **COMMANDO** is doing a great job moving men and materiel." — ARMY AIR FORCES

Opposite: To answer the Army's need for a larger transport aircraft, the 1937 Curtiss-Wright CW-20 commercial aircraft is adopted and becomes the C-46 Commando. (NASM Poster Collection)

Right: The carrier Wasp *on sea trials in the Atlantic before being commissioned on 25 April 1940.* Wasp *is considered an experimental design and no others like her are built. In October 1940, she becomes the first carrier used for flying Army aircraft. After antisubmarine service and two risky ferry missions to deliver British planes to Malta,* Wasp *sails to the Pacific, arriving in time to support the Guadalcanal invasion. (Naval Historical Center)*

15 APRIL
AIR FORCE
The War Department issues Field Manual 1-5 concerning the employment of air power and advocating centralized control of aerial assets. A more detailed regulation, FM 100-20, will not be published until 1943.

21 APRIL
AIR FORCE
Captain Robert M. Losey, an Army Air Corps military attaché in Norway, is killed in a German air raid in Oslo, Norway. He is the first American military officer to die in World War II.

25 APRIL
NAVY
The aircraft carrier *Wasp* is commissioned.

7 MAY
NAVY
President Franklin D. Roosevelt orders ships of the U.S. Fleet to remain in Hawaiian waters indefinitely as a gesture of American strength aimed at Japan. Admiral James O. Richardson, the fleet's commander, protests that Pearl Harbor's facilities are inadequate to support the fleet and are poorly protected against attack. The manner in which he expresses his opinions to the president results in his removal from command on 1 February 1941.

9 MAY
MARINE CORPS
British troops occupy Iceland due to its key location along sea lanes in the Atlantic. In the coming months, U.S. Marines will also garrison the island.

14 MAY
MARINE CORPS
Impressed by German success with airborne operations, Marine Corps Commandant Major General Thomas Holcomb orders his staff to "prepare plans for the employment of parachute troops."

16 MAY
ALL SERVICES
President Franklin D. Roosevelt asks Congress for $1.18 billion to strengthen the nation's defense. The funds requested include $250 million for the Navy and Marine Corps, along with $186 million to contract for equipment and other services.

AIR FORCE
After weighing advice given him by Chief of the Army Air Corps, Major General Henry H. Arnold, President Franklin D. Roosevelt calls for increased aircraft production—up to 50,000 planes per year.

28 MAY
AIR FORCE
Dr. Robert H. Goddard meets with Major General Henry H. Arnold to discuss rockets and their

Above: *Professor Theodore von Kármán (center) discusses the number of rockets needed to allow an Ercoupe test plane to take off without its propeller. The head of the Caltech Aeronautics Laboratory, Kármán is key to the Army Air Corps' development of jet-assisted takeoff technology. (U.S. Air Force)*

potential for military uses. Despite showing limited interest in Goddard's work, Arnold had already directed Caltech professor Theodore von Kármán to begin work on rocket-propelled takeoff devices to increase flight range of heavy bomber-type aircraft.

JUNE
MARINE CORPS/NAVY
Congress authorizes the Navy Department to begin a program to build 10,000 new planes, of which 1,167 will go to the Marine Corps. The Marine planes will form four aircraft groups of 11 squadrons each.

3 JUNE
ARMY
The 4th Division is activated at Fort Benning, Georgia. Three other divisions are activated soon thereafter—the 8th Division (1 July at Fort Jackson, South Carolina), the 7th Division (7 July at Fort Ord, California), and the 9th Division (1 August at Fort Bragg, North Carolina).

14 JUNE
NAVY
The Naval Expansion Act of 1940, authorizing an 11 percent increase in the fleet, is signed into law. The measure also increases naval aircraft strength to 4,500

planes, which is elevated to 10,000 the next day by order of President Franklin D. Roosevelt. The expansion act is approved on the same day that German troops enter Paris; France asks for an armistice three days later.

17 JUNE
NAVY

Chief of Naval Operations Admiral Harold R. Stark asks Congress for $4 billion to increase the authorized strength of the Navy by 70 percent. The Two-Ocean Navy Act quickly passes the House and Senate and is signed into law on 19 July.

20 JUNE
NAVY

The Bureau of Construction and Repair is merged with the Bureau of Engineering to form the Bureau of Ships. In addition, the office of Undersecretary of the Navy is established.

The heavy cruiser *Quincy* arrives in Montevideo, Uruguay, to assist in countering German propaganda in the Central American nation. She is later joined by the heavy cruiser *Wichita*, and the two ships embark on a tour of South America as a demonstration of U.S. strength.

24 JUNE
NAVY

Charles Edison leaves the post of Secretary of the Navy.

25 JUNE
NAVY

Congress abolishes the Naval Construction Corps and gives its officers "engineering duty only" line status.

30 JUNE
MARINE CORPS

The strength of the Marine Corps on active duty is 1,732 officers and 26,545 enlisted.

6 JULY
AIR FORCE

Major General John F. Williams, Chief of the National Guard Bureau, reports that the Guard, comprising 235,000 men, is ready for active service. He notes that Guard divisions and air observation squadrons will participate in August maneuvers on a record scale.

8 JULY
MARINE CORPS

The Joint War Planning Committee earmarks the 1st Marine Brigade for a projected mid-July occupation of Martinique, the most important of the French colonies in the Caribbean. The operation is never executed.

10 JULY
AIR FORCE

President Franklin D. Roosevelt announces that the administration is seeking equipment for a land force of 1,200,000. He also calls for procurement of 15,000 airplanes for the Army.

Opposite, below: *Soldiers in Oahu, Hawaii, stand by for a full equipment inspection during a field training exercise, January 1941. With war on the horizon, having all clothing and equipment in serviceable condition is paramount. (National Archives)*

Right: *During the large Army maneuvers in Louisiana during 1940 and 1941, efforts to create integrated horse-mechanized units are unsuccessful. By 1943, horses are removed from cavalry units. (Patton Museum)*

Left: *The Grumman F4F-4 Wildcat fighter, like those in this formation, is first delivered to the U.S. Navy in 1941. Flown by both Navy and Marine Corps pilots, it has six .50 caliber machine guns and can carry two 100-pound bombs. Its speed is 320 mph with a range of 770 miles. (Marine Corps Historical Center)*

Opposite: *World War I-era destroyers like these are exchanged with the British for the right to use British bases in the Caribbean and Newfoundland, Canada. These bases are used for anti-German submarine patrols and to protect the Atlantic entrances to the Panama Canal. (Naval Historical Center)*

ARMY

Former Ambassador and Secretary of State Henry L. Stimson becomes the 55th Secretary of War. Stimson is a veteran of World War I. He was Governor General of the Philippine Islands and a brigadier general in the Organized Reserve Corps.

No longer required by law to keep its tanks under the Infantry branch, the Army forms the Armored Force and announces that it is to be led by Brigadier General Adna R. Chaffee.

11 JULY
NAVY

Frank Knox, a Chicago newspaper publisher and one of Theodore Roosevelt's famed "Rough Riders," takes office as the 47th Secretary of the Navy.

15 JULY
ARMY

The Army forms its first two armored divisions. With the 7th Cavalry Brigade (Mechanized) as its core element, the 1st Armored Division (eventually to earn fame as "Old Ironsides") is activated at Fort Knox, Kentucky. On the same date the 2d Armored Division is activated at Fort Benning, Georgia.

18 JULY
ARMY

With 48 enlisted volunteers from the 29th Infantry Regiment, the parachute test platoon is established at Fort Benning, Georgia. It is headed by Lieutenants William T. Ryder and James A. Bassett, with Warrant Officer Harry M. Wilson as the jump technique instructor.

20 JULY
MARINE CORPS/NAVY

The Two-Ocean Navy Act authorizes a vast expansion in the size of the fleet and naval aviation. Under this plan, Marine Corps aviation will increase to 1,500 aircraft.

25 JULY
ARMY

For the first time in 20 years the Army opens a General Headquarters much like the one that directed World War I field operations. The new command, under Brigadier General Lesley J. McNair, is concerned only with enhancement of training. McNair reports directly to General George C. Marshall, Army Chief of Staff.

10 AUGUST
MARINE CORPS

Great Britain announces the withdrawal of all its forces from Shanghai and North China, leaving the U.S. Marines as the only non-Axis western force in those areas.

16 AUGUST
ARMY

The Army Parachute Test Platoon makes its first parachute jump at Fort Benning, Georgia, led by 26-year-old Lieutenant William T. Ryder. Later in the month, the test platoon is moved to a special training field near Hightstown, New Jersey, where two 125-foot parachute jump towers have been constructed.

19 AUGUST
AIR FORCE

Test pilot Vance Breese makes the first flight of the North American B-25 Mitchell bomber. The original design, the NA-40, was significantly modified and renamed the NA-62. Larger engines and redesigned wings and tail were part of the modifications that became the famous B-25.

22 AUGUST
NAVY

James V. Forrestal, a World War I naval aviator, becomes the first to hold the post of Undersecretary of the Navy.

2 SEPTEMBER
MARINE CORPS/NAVY

The U.S. agrees to give Britain 50 World War I–era destroyers in exchange for leases on British bases in the Caribbean, including the Bahamas, Jamaica, Antigua, Saint Lucia, Trinidad, and British Guiana. Marine detachments later occupy these bases. The British also give the United States bases in Bermuda and Newfoundland, Canada. The transfer of ships begins four days later.

16 SEPTEMBER
ALL SERVICES

President Franklin D. Roosevelt signs the first peacetime Selective Service and Training Law. It requires all military services to enlist African Americans.

ARMY

In addition to draftees, the Army gets authority to mobilize National Guard units and to call up members of the Officers Reserve Corps. Four divisions—the 30th (Tennessee, Georgia, North Carolina), 41st (Washington, Oregon), 44th (New

Jersey, New York), and 45th (Oklahoma, Arizona, Colorado, New Mexico)—are in the first increment of National Guard units called for "one year of training."

27 SEPTEMBER
AIR FORCE/ARMY

President Franklin D. Roosevelt creates 84 new brigadier generals and promotes 29 to major general. The list of new brigadier generals includes many who will become key figures in World War II, such as Colonels George S. Patton Jr., Robert L. Eichelberger, William H. Simpson, Leonard T. Gerow, Lewis H. Brereton, John C. H. Lee, and Carl Spaatz. Among the new major generals are Brigadier Generals Jacob L. Devers, Jonathan M. Wainwright, Joseph W. Stilwell, and Lesley J. McNair.

ARMY

Brigadier General George S. Patton Jr. is named acting commander of the 2d Armored Division ("Hell on Wheels") at Fort Benning, Georgia, and in December the assignment is made permanent. He leads the division to acclaim in the 1941 Tennessee Maneuvers.

The War Department announces that Citizens Military Training Camps will be suspended until the summer of 1941 in favor of development of an officer candidate school program.

29 SEPTEMBER
MARINE CORPS

The Midway Detachment arrives on Midway Atoll and begins establishing defenses. It consists of nine officers and 168 enlisted men, with one-third of the equipment of the 3d Defense Battalion.

OCTOBER
MARINE CORPS

The Marine Corps receives its first prototype of Donald Roebling's Alligator, a tracked aluminum

CADETS for Naval Aviation take *that something extra* .... have you got it? *Apply nearest U.S. Navy Recruiting Station*

vehicle capable of swimming in the water and crawling onto land.

1 OCTOBER
MARINE CORPS
Marine Corps units of the East Coast Fleet Marine Force participate in Landing Operation 2 in the Caribbean, which lasts until 9 December. Following the exercise, the 1st Marine Brigade goes into camp at Guantanamo Bay, Cuba.

2 OCTOBER
ARMY
With Major William M. Miley in command, the 501st Parachute Battalion is formed at Fort Benning, Georgia. Early training is conducted with specially rigged T-4 Air Corps parachutes from B-18 bombers and C-33 transports, the latter being the military version of a DC-1 airliner.

5 OCTOBER
MARINE CORPS/NAVY
Secretary of the Navy Frank Knox orders the Organized Marine Corps Reserve to active duty by 9 November. These units add 236 officers and 5,009 enlisted men to the strength of the active Marine Corps.

MARINE CORPS
An airstrip is opened at Parris Island, South Carolina, to serve as an outlying field for aviation units based at Quantico, Virginia. On 1 February 1942, Parris Island is designated a Marine Corps Air Station.

12 OCTOBER
AIR FORCE/NAVY
Army Air Corps P-40 Warhawk fighters and O-47 observation planes launch from the aircraft carrier *Wasp* during an evaluation of takeoff runs of military and naval aircraft. This marks the first operation of Army aircraft from a carrier.

16 OCTOBER
ARMY
The second increment of mobilized National Guardsmen includes the 27th Division (New York), 37th Division (Ohio), and 32d Division (Michigan and Wisconsin). Nearly 100,000 National Guardsmen and thousands of Reserve officers are now on active duty.

Right: *Soldiers of the 501st Parachute Battalion line up for an equipment check before boarding an aircraft at Fort Benning, Georgia. The earlier success of the Parachute Test Platoon convinces the Army to create its first parachute infantry unit, and the 501st is activated 1 October 1940. Wartime expansion brings more battalions, then regiments, and finally five divisions of parachute and glider troops. (National Archives)*

25 October
NAVY

During a Japanese bombing raid against Shanghai, China, bombs fall 300 yards from the U.S. Embassy and the U.S. river gunboat *Tutuila*. Japan attributes the act to equipment malfunction.

26 OCTOBER
AIR FORCE

The North American NA-73, later the P-51 Mustang fighter, makes its first flight near Inglewood,

California. Company test pilot Vance Breese makes the flight. Once the original Allison V-1710 V-12 liquid-cooled engine is replaced with a Packard-built Rolls Royce Merlin V-1650 engine and additional fuel tanks added, the Mustang becomes the premier escort fighter of the war.

MARINE CORPS

Volunteers already serving in the Corps report to Lakehurst, New Jersey, to form the first class of trainees for eventual Marine Corps parachute units.

29 OCTOBER
ALL SERVICES

The military service "lottery" begins as the sequence for induction is established by numbers drawn from a fishbowl in Washington, D.C. Secretary of War Henry Stimson draws the first—No. 158.

25 NOVEMBER
ARMY

The 31st Division (Alabama, Mississippi) and the 36th Division (Texas) report for active duty as does the 192d Tank Battalion (Wisconsin, Illinois, Ohio, and Kentucky tank companies).

1 DECEMBER
MARINE CORPS

Major General Thomas Holcomb is appointed to a second term as Marine Corps Commandant.

Right: *On 29 October 1940, with war still 14 months away, President Franklin D. Roosevelt (left) initiates the first national peacetime draft in U.S. history. Secretary of War Henry Stimson, standing behind the container of numbers, is blindfolded and reaches into the container, drawing out number 158. (National Archives)*

Below: *In addition to the draft, Reserve and National Guard units are called to active duty. On 6 October 1941 the 127th Observation Squadron, Kansas National Guard, stands in formation near its planes at Wichita Municipal Airport to listen to the mobilization order. (National Guard Bureau)*

23 DECEMBER
AIR FORCE

The 35th Division (Missouri, Kansas, Nebraska) reports for duty and is quickly headed to Camp Robinson, Arkansas. By this date 13 National Guard observation squadrons are on active duty with the Army Air Corps.

27 DECEMBER
MARINE CORPS

The 10th Marine Regiment is reactivated as an artillery regiment at San Diego, California, to serve with the 2d Marine Brigade.

31 DECEMBER
ARMY

As the year ends, the Army's overall strength includes 104,000 members of the Officers Reserve Corps. Also in the ranks are 8,000 mobilized enlisted Reserve members. National Guardsmen called to the colors total 147,700 officers and men.

1941

TO THE COLORS

JANUARY
ARMY
Mobilization is now bringing more than 140,000 men per month into the active Army. However, draftees and Guardsmen have only a one-year tour. Army General Headquarters is expanding the training while the General Staff plans for the organization of the forces. In various stages are 15 infantry, 6 armored, and 2 cavalry divisions, plus support units sufficient for 11 corps. The Army Air Corps has expanded to 6,180 officers, 7,000 flying cadets, and 88,000 enlisted men.

MARINE CORPS
The 2d Marine Aircraft Group deploys from San Diego, California, to Hawaii.

1 JANUARY
MARINE CORPS
The 7th Marine Regiment is reactivated at Guantanamo Bay, Cuba, to serve as the second infantry regiment in the 1st Marine Brigade.

NAVY
During this year Navy personnel strength reaches 383,150.

6 JANUARY
NAVY
The heavy cruiser *Louisville*, after taking aboard over $148 million in British gold, departs Simonstown, South Africa, bound for New York City. She arrives on 22 January, and the gold is deposited in American banks.

9 JANUARY
NAVY
The first group of contractors arrives on Wake Island to begin construction of an air station there.

11 JANUARY
AIR FORCE
The Army Air Corps successfully tests robot planes that are controlled by radio signals sent either from ground stations or from another airplane. Further development of guided glide bombs and torpedoes is initiated in February.

27 JANUARY
MARINE CORPS
The Chief of Naval Operations orders the remainder of the 3d Defense Battalion to Midway Atoll, the advance echelons of the 1st Defense Battalion to Johnston and Palmyra islands, and the 6th Defense Battalion to Pearl Harbor, Hawaii.

Left: *An Army Air Forces bombardier guides by radio an unmanned B-17 Flying Fortress "robot flying bomb" whose crew has bailed out. The experimental Project Aphrodite was stopped after a number of crews were killed arming the bomb. ("Controlling a Drone Plane in Flight," Milton Marx, USAF Art Collection)*

Right: *A squadron of Marine F4F Wildcat fighters are lined up on the flight line at Marine Corps Air Station, Ewa Field, Hawaii. Ewa Field is a major staging point for Marine Corps pilots and aircraft during the war. (National Archives)*

29 JANUARY
ARMY

Major General Stanley D. Embick heads the U.S. delegation to the British-American staff talks (the "ABC meetings"). Under discussion is a strategy for possible future coalition warfare.

FEBRUARY
AIR FORCE

The Army Air Corps experiments with and adopts a special flash technique for taking night reconnaissance photographs. Major George W. Goddard works with technicians at Eastman Kodak to develop heavy cylindrical flares that are dropped from a plane and explode in mid-air to create a burst of light of several million candle power, activating a camera in the photo aircraft. Up to 20 square miles may be photographed using this technique.

1 FEBRUARY
MARINE CORPS

The 1st Marine Brigade is redesignated the 1st Marine Division as it sails from Guantanamo Bay, Cuba, to Culebra, Puerto Rico, for exercises. Simultaneously, the 2d Marine Brigade in southern California is redesignated the 2d Marine Division. The 2d Marine Regiment is reactivated at San Diego, California, to serve as the third infantry regiment of the 2d Marine Division. The 4th Defense Battalion arrives at Guantanamo Bay to garrison that base.

NAVY

In a reorganization of fleet structure, the Atlantic and Pacific Fleets are reestablished. The following day Admiral Husband E. Kimmel is appointed to command the Pacific Fleet and, also, the U.S. Fleet when the ships of the two fleets operate together. Admiral Ernest J. King receives command of the Atlantic Fleet, and Admiral Thomas C. Hart commands the Asiatic Fleet.

3 FEBRUARY
MARINE CORPS

An airfield for Marine Corps use is established at Oahu's Ewa Mooring Mast Field (originally constructed for dirigibles in the 1930s) when the 2d Marine Aircraft Group deploys there from Ford Island, in Pearl Harbor, Hawaii. Ewa becomes a Marine Corps Air Station in September 1942.

4 FEBRUARY
ARMY

The Alaska Defense Command is established at Fort Richardson, Alaska, under the Western Defense Command. Brigadier General Simon Bolivar Buckner Jr. is designated commander.

7 FEBRUARY
ARMY

Walter C. Short is promoted to lieutenant general and appointed the commanding general of the Hawaiian

Left: *Wearing their blue denim work uniforms, Soldiers of the 186th and 162d Infantry Regiments sit outside their barracks at Fort Lewis, Washington, to practice the lessons they have received on the M1903 Springfield rifle. As part of the 41st Infantry Division, both regiments are among the first Army units sent to the Pacific. (National Archives)*

Department, with headquarters at Fort Shafter, Hawaii.

NAVY
The U.S. Naval Academy Class of 1941 graduates four months early because of the national emergency. Forty-one members of the class will be killed in action during World War II.

14 FEBRUARY
MARINE CORPS
The remaining elements of the 3d Defense Battalion reach Midway Atoll.

Right: *A new Marine receives personal instruction in the proper stance for firing an M1 carbine. (National Archives)*

Opposite: *Oregon National Guardsmen of the 186th Infantry attempt to dry their bedding after a wet night during a field exercise in mid-1941. (National Archives)*

15 FEBRUARY
MARINE CORPS
Congress approves the purchase and construction of a new Marine Corps base at New River, North Carolina. Formally established on 1 May, it is eventually named Camp Lejeune.

1 MARCH
MARINE CORPS
The 1st Marine Regiment and 11th Marine Regiment (artillery) are reactivated at Guantanamo Bay, Cuba, to serve with the 1st Marine Division. The 6th Defense Battalion is formed at San Diego, California.

3 MARCH
MARINE CORPS
The advance echelon of the 1st Defense Battalion lands at Johnston Island.

5 March
ARMY
With the call-up of the Illinois' 33d Division, the Army completes the mobilization of the National Guard's 18 combat divisions, although many non-divisional units are still to be called as training sites become available. The 33d is among the nine Guard divisions destined to see combat in the Pacific.

11 MARCH
ALL SERVICES
President Franklin D. Roosevelt signs the Lend-Lease Act into law. The act authorizes industry to lend war materiel to several Allied nations. The majority of goods go to Great Britain and the Soviet Union. More than 43,000 aircraft are eventually shipped to these nations to fight the war against Nazi Germany.

15 MARCH
MARINE CORPS
The Fleet Marine Force is administratively divided, with the 1st Marine Division reporting to the Atlantic Fleet and the 2d Marine Division reporting to the Pacific Fleet.

17 MARCH
ARMY
The headquarters for Western Defense Command is co-located with Headquarters, Fourth Army, at San Francisco, California. Lieutenant General John L. DeWitt commands both organizations. Western Defense Command includes Alaska.

18 MARCH
MARINE CORPS
The 7th Defense Battalion reaches American Samoa and secures naval and air facilities on the island of Tutuila.

22 MARCH
AIR FORCE
Captain Harold R. Maddux takes command of the 99th Pursuit Squadron at Chanute Field, Illinois. The 99th is the Army's first African American flying squadron and is one of three squadrons in the 332d Fighter Group.

MARINE CORPS
The 2d Parachute Company is formed as part of the 2d Marine Division. It is the first Marine Corps parachute unit and becomes the nucleus for the 2d Parachute Battalion.

Above: *The battleship* North Carolina *with her six forward 16-inch guns is pictured on her maiden voyage in April 1941. She is the first battleship built by the U.S. since 1923. (Naval Historical Center)*

26 MARCH
AIR FORCE
The Air Corps Technical Training Command is established.

27 MARCH
ALL SERVICES
Authorities for the United States and Great Britain sign a base-lease agreement which stipulates that the U.S. may use eight air and naval bases located in the British Atlantic and Caribbean possessions in exchange for a number of U.S. naval destroyers. The agreement is implemented in September.

Representatives of the United States, Britain, and Canada sign the ABC-1 Staff Agreement in Washington, D.C., outlining a framework for strategic cooperation in the event that the United States enters World War II. The agreement establishes a Combined Chiefs of Staff and stipulates that the U.S. Atlantic Fleet will, as soon as possible, assist the Royal Navy in convoying ships to Britain.

28 MARCH
AIR FORCE
The first of three American Eagle Squadrons, made up of American volunteers under British command, becomes fully operational. In 18 months, the squadron will be integrated into the American 4th Fighter Group in England.

1 APRIL
ALL SERVICES
The U.S. and Mexico sign an agreement allowing reciprocal transit of military aircraft through each other's territory.

9 APRIL
ALL SERVICES
A United States–Danish agreement gives the U.S. the right to build and use airfields in Greenland.

NAVY
North Carolina, the first battleship to join the fleet since 1923, is commissioned.

11 APRIL
AIR FORCE
Anticipating the eventuality of world war, and fearing that Europe might fall under complete Nazi control, the Army Air Corps requests both Consolidated and

Boeing Aircraft companies to submit concept designs for a very long-range bomber. These early conceptualizations are later realized in the Convair B-36 Peacemaker.

NAVY

The destroyer *Niblack*, while rescuing survivors from a torpedoed Dutch freighter, drops depth charges on a sound contact believed to be a German submarine. It turns out to be a false contact, but the action illuminates the growing involvement of the U.S. Navy in the Battle of the Atlantic.

14 APRIL
MARINE CORPS

Elements of the 1st Defense Battalion arrive on Palmyra Island.

15 APRIL
ALL SERVICES

President Franklin D. Roosevelt authorizes Reservists who are on active duty to resign from the Air Corps and other services and sign up for duty with a new P-40 Warhawk volunteer group under the command of former Army Air Corps officer Claire L. Chennault. The American Volunteer Group, also known as the Flying Tigers, created by a secret and unpublished executive order, is tasked to help China fight the Japanese in the air.

You GIVE HIM WINGS!

U.S. ARMY

The Army needs LUMBER for Training Planes

18 APRIL
AIR FORCE

Construction on the new $50 million Consolidated Aircraft plant begins near Fort Worth, Texas. The factory will become a major builder of B-24 Liberator and B-32 Dominator bombers during World War II.

Above: *Posters like this encouraged Americans to economize on critical war materials and support the war effort. (NASM Poster Collection)*

Left: *This experimental LVT-1 coming ashore on the beach of the Caribbean island of Culebra in 1941 is the result of years of Marine Corps testing and evaluation. The successful LVT-1 design, with modifications, becomes the famous "Alligator" used to assault many Pacific beaches. (USMC)*

Left: *The Republic P-47 Thunderbolt—affectionately called the "jug" because of its large body and stub nose—is a workhorse of the Army Air Forces after its introduction in 1942. The rugged fighter-bomber excels at ground attack and is heavily armed with eight .50 caliber machine guns. It can carry 1,000 pounds of bombs or 10 rockets. The P-47s depicted belong to the 56th Fighter Group (Wolfpack) led by Colonel Herbert Zemke. The plane on the far right belongs to Major Francis Gabreski, the highest scoring ace in Europe. ("A Wolfpack Salute," Roy Grinnell)*

MARINE CORPS/NAVY

Admiral Husband E. Kimmel, U.S. Pacific Fleet commander, asks for a Marine Corps defense battalion for Wake Island.

3 MAY
ARMY

With the assignment of Lieutenant General Walter Krueger to command the Third Army, all four of the U.S.-based field armies are commanded by non-West Point graduates. The others are Lieutenant Generals Hugh A. Drum (First Army), Ben Lear (Second Army) and John L. DeWitt (Fourth Army).

6 MAY
AIR FORCE

Republic test pilot Lowery Brabham flies the XP-47B Thunderbolt fighter for the first time. This durable aircraft flies in every combat theater during the war as both an escort fighter and ground attack aircraft.

13–14 MAY
AIR FORCE

In the first mass flight of bombers across the Pacific, the U.S.-based 19th Bombardment Group delivers 21 B-17D Flying Fortresses to the Hawaiian Air Force (later Seventh Air Force) without a single mechanical failure. All 21 aircraft land within 30 minutes of each other.

19 MAY
ARMY

Major General James E. Chaney is designated the Special Army Observer, London, England, reporting directly to the Army Chief of Staff.

Opposite, bottom: *Soldiers of an infantry division descend a cargo net during amphibious training in Monterey Bay, California, in November 1941. Behind them a 37mm anti-tank gun is lowered to a waiting landing craft. (National Archives)*

Right: *Marines practice landing from a Landing Craft, Vehicle and Personnel (LCVP) during an exercise in Puerto Rico. Its shallow draft and bow ramp permit the vessel to run onto the beach and quickly discharge its troops and cargo. (USMC)*

21 MAY
AIR FORCE

The Army Corps Ferrying Command is created. By the end of the war in Europe, the command (later renamed the Air Transport Command) possesses nearly 2,500 transport aircraft, one-fourth of which are four-engine heavy lifters.

ARMY/MARINE CORPS/NAVY

Based on tests in Louisiana, a bow-ramp version of the Higgins boat is determined to be fully functional and preferable to the non-ramp boats previously being built for the Navy. This design goes into production and becomes the forerunner of the Landing Craft Vehicle, Personnel (LCVP).

NAVY

En route to Africa, the U.S. freighter *Robin Moor*, with American flags painted prominently on her sides, is torpedoed by the German submarine *U-69* and later sunk by fire from the sub's deck gun. This marks the first sinking of an American merchantman during World War II.

26 MAY
NAVY

A British Royal Air Force PBY Catalina flying boat searching for the German battleship *Bismarck* finds her quarry in the Atlantic some 300 miles west of France. The pilot of the Catalina is a U.S. Navy observer, Ensign Leonard B. Smith. British Royal Navy surface and air forces sink the battleship the following day.

27 MAY
ALL SERVICES

President Franklin D. Roosevelt proclaims an unlimited state of national emergency.

28 MAY
MARINE CORPS

The 1st Parachute Battalion is established at Quantico, Virginia.

29 MAY
ARMY/MARINE CORPS

The Joint Board approves a plan for a landing force of 28,000 troops (half Marine Corps and half Army) under the command of Major General Holland M. Smith to occupy the Portuguese Azores Islands. Although the plan is never executed, it becomes the basis for the first Marine Corps-Army joint command of the war.

1 JUNE
MARINE CORPS

The 2d Marine Division begins moving to Camp Elliott, California, located on Kearney Mesa in the vicinity of what is now Marine Corps Air Station Miramar. The government purchases and uses a total of 32,000 acres here before the end of World War II.

Left: *Army Air Corps cadets march in formation to a training class at Randolph Field, Texas. Known as "West Point of the Air," the air base is the home of the School of Aviation Medicine and the Air Corps Flying School. (National Archives)*

2 JUNE
NAVY

The aircraft escort vessel *Long Island* is commissioned at Newport News, Virginia. A converted merchantman, she is the first of what are later called escort carriers, small "flattops" that serve in the Atlantic campaigns against U-boats, and provide close air support for amphibious assaults in North Africa, Europe, and the Pacific.

4 JUNE
AIR FORCE

The grade of aviation cadet replaces the flying cadet designation. Once a cadet earns his wings, he is commissioned as an Army officer.

9 JUNE
ARMY

Plans are underway to introduce a new-style combat helmet to replace the World War I–era British-style "tin hat" helmet. The new helmet is a steel shell with a fiber (soon to be plastic) helmet liner adjusted to the individual soldier's head size.

Right: *A rite of passage for every new Soldier and Marine is his first GI haircut, a visible sign of the transition from civilian to military life. (National Archives)*

Opposite: *World War I hero Army Colonel William J. Donovan is selected by President Franklin D. Roosevelt to establish and head the secret Office of Strategic Services, forerunner of the Central Intelligence Agency. (U.S. Army)*

13 JUNE
ARMY/MARINE CORPS

Major General Holland M. Smith relinquishes command of the 1st Marine Division to become commander of the newly created I Corps (Provisional), composed of his old division and the Army's 1st Infantry Division. This force changes its name several times and ultimately is renamed Amphibious Force Atlantic Fleet, which focuses on training for amphibious assaults.

15 JUNE
NAVY

Echoing an amazingly similar incident on 25 October 1940, during an attack against Chungking, China, Japanese planes drop bombs near the river gunboat *Tutuila*, the office of the U.S. military attaché, and a U.S. Navy canteen. The Japanese military terms the attack "wholly unintentional," though the U.S. representatives on the scene doubt the truthfulness of this assessment.

16 JUNE
AIR FORCE

The Consolidated B-24 Liberator bomber begins Army service.

MARINE CORPS

Following a 5 June decision by President Franklin D. Roosevelt to commit American forces to the defense of Iceland, the 1st Marine Brigade (Provisional) is established at Charleston, South Carolina. It is formed around the reinforced 6th Marine Regiment, newly arrived by sea from California and originally destined to reinforce the 1st Marine Division for the Azores Islands operation. The other major elements of the brigade are the 5th Defense Battalion and the 2d Battalion, 10th Marine Regiment. The brigade sails on 22 June. Marines receive the mission because U.S. law prevents draftees and National Guardsmen from serving overseas.

20 JUNE
AIR FORCE

The Secretary of War directs a consolidation of the Army's Air Corps division with the Air Force Combat Command into a single command called the Army Air Forces. Major General Henry H. Arnold is appointed as Commanding General, Army Air Forces, reporting directly to the Army Chief of Staff.

NAVY

The submarine *O-9* (SS 70), while engaged in submergence trials off Portsmouth, New Hampshire, sinks during a test dive with the loss of all 33 members of her crew.

24 JUNE
MARINE CORPS

Marine Fighting Squadron 121 is organized at Quantico, Virginia. It finishes World War II as the highest scoring Marine fighting squadron with 205 enemy aircraft shot down.

28 JUNE
ALL SERVICES

President Franklin D. Roosevelt creates the Office of Scientific Research and Development when he signs Executive Order 8807.

30 JUNE
AIR FORCE/NAVY

A joint Army-Navy contract is awarded to Northrop Aircraft to design an aircraft gas turbine engine rated at 2,500 horsepower and weighing less than 3,215 pounds. Named the Turbodyne, it is the first turboprop power plant to operate in North America.

MARINE CORPS

The strength of the Marine Corps on active duty is 3,339 officers and 51,020 enlisted.

1 JULY
AIR FORCE

Lieutenant Colonel C. V. Haynes flies a B-24 Liberator bomber from Bolling Field, D.C., to Scotland. His route takes him and his crew through Montreal and Newfoundland, Canada. This is the first Army Air Forces overseas transport service flight, made even before direct U.S. involvement in the global conflict.

ARMY

Four of 10 new Officer Candidate Schools open. The initial goal is to commission 10,000 new second lieutenants each year. The Army now has 1,400,000 in uniform organized into four armies, with 9 corps and 29 infantry divisions, 4 armored divisions, and an Army Air Forces of 54 combat groups.

NAVY

Admiral Ernest J. King, Commander in Chief, U.S. Atlantic Fleet, organizes 10 task forces to support the defense of Iceland and escort convoys between the United States and Iceland. The effort is in response to an agreement between the two countries for U.S. troops to occupy and defend the island nation.

3 JULY
ARMY

General George C. Marshall, Army Chief of Staff, approves a plan to create the American Military Mission to China to monitor lend-lease distribution. The Army selects Major General John Magruder as the Chief of the Military Advisory Group, China.

7 JULY
AIR FORCE/ARMY/NAVY

A force of 469 officers and men under Colonel Benjamin F. Giles arrives to begin work on "Bluie West," the first major Army and Navy base in the subpolar region.

ARMY/MARINE CORPS

The 1st Marine Brigade (Provisional) arrives in Iceland. The Army is alerted to ready a divisional force to take over this mission and ensure an adequate defense.

MARINE CORPS

The 1st Marine Aircraft Wing (MAW) is established at Quantico, Virginia, by the addition of a headquarters squadron to the 1st Marine Aircraft Group. It is the first of five MAWs that will eventually serve in World War II.

8 JULY
AIR FORCE

A force of 20 B-17C Flying Fortress bombers given to the Royal Air Force is used to attack the German city of Wilhelmshaven. Largely ineffective because of the RAF's bombing doctrine, it is the first operational use of the B-17 in combat. The British name for the B-17 is Fortress I.

15 JULY
MARINE CORPS

A Marine Corps detachment is established to guard the U.S. Embassy in London, England.

16 JULY
AIR FORCE

At Langley Field, Virginia, full-scale wind tunnel tests of the A-1 weapon—a power-driven controllable bomb—are conducted.

19 JULY
AIR FORCE

Claire Chennault, a retired Army Air Corps pilot, assumes duties as chief instructor of Marshall Chiang Kai-shek's Chinese Air Force. Chennault is called back to active duty in 1942.

26 JULY
ARMY

Douglas MacArthur is recalled to active duty as a major general to command the U.S. Armed Forces Far East. Since his retirement in 1937 he had been serving in an advisory capacity as field marshal of the Philippine National Army. On 29 July he is promoted to lieutenant general.

30 JULY
NAVY

During a Japanese air raid against Chunking, China, a bomb splashes eight yards astern of the river gunboat *Tutuila*. Like the two previous close calls, the Japanese term this incident an accident.

4 AUGUST
AIR FORCE

The Air War Plans Division (AWPD) begins to formulate the Army Air Forces' strategic bombardment campaign plan that will eventually be executed in Europe and then Japan. Designated

Left: *The U.S. heavy cruiser* Augusta *is the scene of a critical prewar meeting between British Prime Minister Winston Churchill and President Franklin D. Roosevelt. Pictured aboard the cruiser anchored in Placentia Bay, Newfoundland, on 1 August 1941 are, left to right, Ensign Franklin D. Roosevelt Jr., USN; Undersecretary of State Sumner Wells (obscured); Prime Minister Winston Churchill; President Franklin D. Roosevelt; and Major Elliot Roosevelt, USA. During the meeting, the two leaders create the Atlantic Charter, a statement of principles should the U.S. enter the war. (Naval Historical Center)*

AWPD-1, the plan is completed on 12 August after around-the-clock War Department sessions.

5 AUGUST
AIR FORCE
The Panama Canal Air Force is designated the Caribbean Air Force. It becomes the Sixth Air Force on 5 February 1942. Its initial primary task is the defense of the Panama Canal.

NAVY
President Franklin D. Roosevelt secretly boards the heavy cruiser *Augusta* in Vineyard Sound, Massachusetts. With the heavy cruiser *Tuscaloosa* and five destroyers, *Augusta* sets course for Argentia, Newfoundland, where the President meets with British Prime Minister Winston S. Churchill.

6 AUGUST
AIR FORCE/NAVY
The 33d Pursuit Squadron (Interceptor) flies its 30 P-40 Warhawk fighters off the deck of the carrier *Wasp*, to set up its new base in Reykjavik, Iceland. A 1,100-man U.S. task force also includes two infantry companies, an aviation engineer regiment, aircraft warning elements, and quartermaster port troops.

9–12 AUGUST
ALL SERVICES

In a historic meeting, President Franklin D. Roosevelt and British Prime Minister Winston S. Churchill formulate the Atlantic Charter during discussions on board the heavy cruiser *Augusta* and the British battleship *Prince of Wales*. Though not a formal treaty, the charter serves as a declaration of American intent should the United States be drawn into World War II.

10–15 AUGUST
ARMY

The Fourth Army under Lieutenant General John L. DeWitt initiates a major field exercise in Washington state, pitting the 3d and 41st Divisions (IX Corps) and the 7th and 40th Divisions (III Corps) against a mythical invading "oriental" army.

12 AUGUST
AIR FORCE

Captain Homer Boushey makes the first takeoff in an Army Ercoupe aircraft specially modified with three small solid-propellant rockets fastened beneath each wing. Dubbed jet assisted takeoff, the system is designed to save fuel on takeoff and thus extend range and increase payload capability of heavy combat aircraft.

16 AUGUST
MARINE CORPS

The first man is enlisted in the 1st Samoan Battalion, Marine Corps Reserve. Its purpose is to provide an infantry element to reinforce the 7th Defense Battalion on Tutuila Island.

18 AUGUST
ARMY

Major General Charles H. Bonesteel is informed that he is to command the "Indigo Force," destined to become the main Army component in Iceland.

MARINE CORPS

The command that will become Marine Corps Air Station, Cherry Point, North Carolina, is established. The first air operations commence in March 1942. Cherry Point becomes one of the primary Marine airfields on the East Coast.

19 AUGUST
MARINE CORPS

The advance echelon of the 1st Defense Battalion arrives at Wake Island.

23 AUGUST
AIR FORCE

In a follow-on rocket-assisted takeoff test, the propeller is removed from an Army Air Forces

Right: A Marine Corps pilot walks over to check on the ground crew servicing his plane in fall 1941. (National Archives)

Above: *Major General George S. Patton Jr., a career cavalryman and early proponent for tanks, assumes command and develops the new 2d Armored Division at Fort Benning, Georgia. His aggressive leadership of that unit made him a standout in the precedent-setting 1941 Louisiana Maneuvers. (Patton Museum)*

Below: *This overhead photo taken from an aircraft on 22 October 1941 shows the first stages of what will become one of the largest and most well-known office buildings in the world—the Pentagon. It is completed in less than 18 months, an amazing feat of engineering and construction. (U.S. Army)*

Ercoupe aircraft and six rocket motors are mounted under each wing. Pilot Captain Homer Boushey holds a rope tied to a pickup truck, which tows the aircraft until it reaches about 30 miles per hour. Boushey releases the rope, hits the switch that ignites the rockets, and accomplishes the first rocket-powered flight, briefly attaining an altitude of 10 feet.

26 AUGUST
ARMY
The Hawaiian Division, which dates back to 25 February 1921, trades its name for a number and is reorganized as the 24th Infantry Division.

27 AUGUST
AIR FORCE
Pilot Officer William R. "Wild Bill" Dunn, flying a Hawker Hurricane fighter as a volunteer with 71 Squadron of the Royal Air Force, is the first U.S. citizen to become an aerial ace during World War II when he shoots down his fifth and sixth enemy aircraft over Belgium. Three RAF Eagle Squadrons are composed primarily of American volunteers under RAF command.

28 AUGUST
AIR FORCE
The 19th Heavy Bombardment Group under Lieutenant Colonel Eugene L. Eubank begins deploying its 35 B-17 Flying Fortress bombers to Clark Field in the Philippine Islands. The long trans-Pacific route is via Hawaii, Midway, and Wake islands to a staging point in Australia or New Guinea before the final leg north to the Philippines. By the first week in November all 35 B-17s have completed the long journey from the U.S. West Coast.

31 AUGUST
ARMY
President Franklin D. Roosevelt issues a proclamation mobilizing the 10 reserve divisions of the Philippine National Army and authorizes Lieutenant General Douglas MacArthur to equip them from U.S. resources.

SEPTEMBER
AIR FORCE/NAVY
During this month, Dr. Robert H. Goddard begins work on development of liquid propellant jet assisted takeoff engines for the Army Air Forces and the U.S. Navy. He delivers useable units one year later.

Right: One of the miracles of American industry during the war is the creation of the mass produced Liberty ship. Time is saved by welding rather than riveting, and making the ship in sections to be joined together. Eighteen shipyards launched 2,751 of these cheap cargo ships between 1941 and 1945, the first of which is Patrick Henry. *They are designed to last five years, but many of the ships are still around for years after the war ended. (Naval Historical Center)*

1 SEPTEMBER
NAVY
The U.S. Navy assumes responsibility for convoying transatlantic merchant convoys from a point off Argentia, Newfoundland, to a mid-ocean meeting point south of Iceland. The first such escort voyage, in company with Canadian escort ships, begins on 16 September.

4 SEPTEMBER
NAVY
The destroyer *Greer*, operating 175 miles southwest of Iceland, maintains sonar contact with the German submarine *U-652* for several hours. A British patrol plane drops depth bombs and leaves the area. The German submarine fires a torpedo; *Greer* drops depth charges; and *U-652* fires another torpedo, which misses. The destroyer cannot regain contact, and resumes its voyage. In response, President Franklin D. Roosevelt issues an order to U.S. ships to fire upon any vessel threatening American shipping or ships under American escort, and declares that German and Italian warships enter U.S.-controlled waters "at their own risk."

6 SEPTEMBER
AIR FORCE
The Boeing B-17E bomber makes its first flight. The B-17E, larger and more heavily armed than previous Flying Fortress models, includes a stabilizing fin that extends forward of the tail to provide high-altitude stability.

11 SEPTEMBER
ALL SERVICES
Ground is broken on a new headquarters building to house the War Department in Arlington, Virginia. The five-sided design soon leads to its being known as "the Pentagon." Under the direction of Brigadier General Brehon B. Somervell, the job is completed in just 16 months at a cost of $83 million and the lives of eight construction workers.

MARINE CORPS
The 6th Defense Battalion relieves the 3d Defense Battalion on Midway Atoll.

15–16 SEPTEMBER
ARMY
Major General Charles H. Bonesteel's task group ("Indigo Force") arrives in Reykjavik, Iceland, to form the future Iceland Defense Command. The force includes the 10th Infantry Regiment, 5th Engineers, 46th Field Artillery Battalion, and support elements.

Left: *Young volunteers and draftees find they are quickly challenged by the rigors of military life, among them daily physical training and obstacle courses run under the watchful eye of their platoon drill sergeant. (National Archives)*

Left: *Lieutenant General Walter C. Short reviews the reorganized Hawaiian Division in September 1941. The division is renamed the 24th Infantry Division on 1 October 1941. Many of its officers and non-commissioned officers are used to form the 25th Infantry Division. (National Archives)*

Below: *With a hole in its hull from a German torpedo, the damaged destroyer Kearny lies alongside another destroyer at Reykjavik, Iceland. (Naval Historical Center)*

15–30 SEPTEMBER
AIR FORCE

The Second (Red) Army under Lieutenant General Ben Lear is pitted against the Third (Blue) Army under Lieutenant General Walter Krueger in the largest maneuver ever held during peacetime in the United States. More than 350,000 troops in 22 divisions (including two armored) and four Army Air Forces wings take part in the two-phase Louisiana Maneuvers in a 30,000-square-mile area.

MID-SEPTEMBER
MARINE CORPS

Marine Scout Bombing Squadron 131 participates in the Army's Louisiana Maneuvers.

17 SEPTEMBER
AIR FORCE

Paratroopers are dropped in a tactical combat exercise for the first time when 13 DC-3 aircraft drop a parachute company during the Louisiana Maneuvers.

20 SEPTEMBER
AIR FORCE

Philippine Department Air Force—the parent to the Far East Air Force and, later, the Fifth Air Force—is established at Nichols Field, Luzon Island. Since 4 August the fledgling Philippine Air Force, a token force of 210 obsolete aircraft, has been under U.S. command.

24 SEPTEMBER
ARMY/MARINE CORPS

The 1st Provisional Marine Brigade is detached from the Department of the Navy for service with the Army.

26 SEPTEMBER
ARMY

A Corps of Military Police is established for the first time since 1918. All officers and men performing police duties as a principal function become members of the military police.

The transport ship *President Coolidge* arrives in Manila, Philippine Islands, with long-awaited reinforcements. Arrivals include the 200th Coast Artillery (Antiaircraft) Regiment (New Mexico National Guard). Also, the 194th Tank Battalion, a light-tank battalion of National Guard tank companies (Minnesota, California), arrives with accompanying 17th Ordnance Company (Armored). The 194th has 54 new M3 light tanks and 23 late-model half-tracks.

27 SEPTEMBER
ARMY
Brigadier General Omar N. Bradley, commandant of the Infantry School, Fort Benning, Georgia, presides over the first graduating class of infantry officer candidates.

NAVY
Patrick Henry, the first of over 2,700 "Liberty"-type cargo ships that become famous during World War II for their mass production and widespread use, is launched at Baltimore, Maryland.

1 OCTOBER
ARMY
The Army searches for ships to transport 500,000 tons of supplies and 20,000 reinforcements for the Philippine Islands. Eleven transports sail over the next three months.

MARINE CORPS
The 1st and 2d Barrage Balloon Squadrons are organized at Parris Island, South Carolina.

9 OCTOBER
AIR FORCE
A week-long test of the U.S. air defense network begins. More than 40,000 civilian aircraft spotters of the Aircraft Warning Service search the skies for "enemy" bombers using searchlights and antiaircraft artillery sighting mechanisms. The communications network is evaluated when more than 1,800 observation stations are tested.

10 OCTOBER
ARMY
Built around two infantry regiments and a cadre from the 24th Infantry Division, the 25th Infantry Division is formed at Schofield Barracks, Hawaii. In addition to the 27th and 35th Infantry Regiments it will later add the 161st Infantry Regiment from the Washington National Guard. The new division is destined to earn fame as the "Tropic Lightning" division.

Major General John Magruder, after a stopover in Manila, Philippine Islands, to confer with Lieutenant General Douglas MacArthur, assumes his post as chief of the American Military Mission to China in Chungking. Magruder soon sends Washington a gloomy report on the status of China's armed forces.

16–17 OCTOBER
NAVY
U.S. Navy warships participate in the defense of convoy SC 48 during a mass U-boat attack, marking the first time an American-escorted convoy engages German U-boats on the high seas. On 16 October, the destroyer *Livermore* depth charges *U-553*, while the destroyer *Kearny* drops depth charges astern of the

Right: *U.S. Navy Captain Arthur W. Radford, senior American representative, stands to the left of a British officer at the commissioning of the U.S. Naval Air Station Trinidad in October 1941. American use of the British facility is part of the Lend-Lease agreement. The air station is used as the base for antisubmarine patrols in the Caribbean. (Naval Historical Center)*

convoy in an effort to discourage attacks. On 17 October *U-568* puts a torpedo into *Kearny*'s starboard side, killing 11 of her crew and wounding 22 others. The destroyer regains power in about 10 minutes and reaches Iceland under her own steam.

23 OCTOBER
ARMY
The Philippine Department in Manila, Philippine Islands (a U.S. Army command since 1913), becomes a service command under U.S. Army Force Far East, and its commander, Major General George Grunert, returns to the U.S. for reassignment.

30 OCTOBER
NAVY
In the Atlantic Ocean some 700 miles off the coast of Newfoundland, Canada, the German submarine *U-106* torpedoes the oiler *Salinas* as she steams as part of convoy ON 28. Throughout the remainder of the day, escorting U.S. destroyers carry out 10 depth

charge attacks, and the destroyer *Bernadou* fires on a U-boat, forcing it to submerge.

31 OCTOBER
NAVY
While escorting convoy HX 156 west of Iceland, the destroyer *Reuben James* is torpedoed by the German submarine *U-552*. The torpedo detonates in the destroyer's magazine, and she sinks quickly with the loss of 115 men. *Reuben James* is the first U.S. warship lost to hostile action during World War II.

1 NOVEMBER
ARMY/MARINE CORPS
The 2d Joint Training Force is established at Camp Elliott, California, under command of Marine Major General Clayton B. Vogel. A West Coast counterpart of the Amphibious Force Atlantic Fleet, it is composed of the 2d Marine Division, 2d Marine Aircraft Wing, and the Army's 3d Infantry Division.

NAVY
President Franklin D. Roosevelt issues an executive order placing the Coast Guard under the operational control of the Navy for the duration of the national emergency.

2 NOVEMBER
MARINE CORPS
Additional elements of the 1st Defense Battalion reach Wake Island, bringing the Marine Corps force to 15 officers and 373 enlisted men.

3 NOVEMBER
AIR FORCE
Major General Lewis H. Brereton arrives at Nielsen Field, Philippine Islands, to assume command of the

newly formed Far East Air Force (FEAF). The Philippines garrison now boasts the largest concentration of U.S. Army aircraft outside of the continental U.S., including 107 P-40 Warhawk fighters and 35 B-17 Flying Fortress bombers. The FEAF, composed of the V Bomber Command and V Interceptor Command, is officially activated on 16 November.

7 NOVEMBER
AIR FORCE
The Army Air Forces launches its first guided glide bomb, the GB-1.

10 NOVEMBER
MARINE CORPS
The U.S. Asiatic Fleet receives permission to withdraw gunboats and Marines from China.

10–28 NOVEMBER
ARMY
During two-phased manuevers in the Carolinas, the First Army (under Lieutenant General Hugh Drum) is pitted against a force composed of the IV Corps (under Major General Oscar W. Griswold), reinforced by the I Armored Corps. Drum and Griswold employ 13 divisions including the 1st and 2d Armored Divisions fresh from the Louisiana Maneuvers.

12 NOVEMBER
AIR FORCE
The Army Air Forces launches its first radio-controlled glide bomb—the GB-8. The GB series of weapons are part of Project Aphrodite, a program centered on developing standoff weapon capability and more precise guidance for bombs.

15 NOVEMBER
ARMY
The Army activates its first unit designed specifically to fight in mountain terrain, the 1st Battalion, 87th Mountain Infantry, at Fort Lewis, Washington.

20 NOVEMBER
ARMY
The 192d Tank Battalion (Kentucky, Illinois, Ohio) and a company from Wisconsin, which goes to the understrength 194th Battalion, arrives in the Philippine Islands. The two tank battalions form the new 1st Provisional Tank Group with 108 light tanks. The Philippine garrison now numbers 31,095, marking a 40 percent increase in 120 days.

27 NOVEMBER
ARMY
The Tank Destroyer and Firing Center is activated at Fort Meade, Maryland. It is under direct War Department control. Orders are issued for the activation of 53 tank destroyer battalions. Division antitank battalions are redesignated tank destroyer battalions and placed under the General Headquarters.

NAVY
Chief of Naval Operations Admiral Harold R. Stark

Right: *Soldiers and Marines headed overseas in troopships found their staterooms more than a little crowded. Men, their personal gear, and equipment are jammed into every nook of the ship for the long and dangerous voyage. Enemy submarines, hostile aircraft, and rough weather may lie ahead for their ship. (National Archives)*

sends "War Warning" messages to the Pacific and Asiatic fleets. This measure comes a day after a Japanese carrier task force secretly departs the Kurile Islands and sets course for Hawaii to attack the U.S. fleet base at Pearl Harbor in the event negotiations between the United States and Japan break down.

27–28 NOVEMBER
MARINE CORPS

The 4th Marine Regiment embarks and sails from Shanghai, China, for the Philippine Islands. The regiment arrives at Olongapo on the 30th.

28 NOVEMBER
NAVY

The aircraft carrier *Enterprise* departs Hawaii for Wake Island to deliver F4F Wildcat fighters of Marine Fighting Squadron 211. Based upon a war warning issued the previous day, Vice Admiral William F. Halsey Jr. issues his famous War Order No. 1 stating that *Enterprise* is operating "under war conditions."

30 NOVEMBER
AIR FORCE

The Army's oldest pilot, Brigadier General Frank P. Lahm, retires. Lahm was the Army's first military aviator.

MARINE CORPS

Total strength of the active Marine Corps reaches 65,881 officers and enlisted.

LATE NOVEMBER
MARINE CORPS

Marine Corps officers begin training as glider pilots in civilian schools to form the cadre of a Marine glider program for carrying troops into combat. The program ends on 29 May 1943 with no gliders having gone into combat with the Marines.

1 DECEMBER
AIR FORCE

An executive order establishes the Civil Air Patrol, with the primary mission of coastal patrol and detection of enemy submarines.

ARMY

With most of 10 undermanned and poorly equipped Philippine Army divisions now incorporated with U.S. forces, Lieutenant General Douglas MacArthur reorganizes for the possibility of ground combat in defense of the Philippine Islands. The Northern Luzon Force is under Major General Jonathan M. Wainwright; the Southern Luzon Force is under Brigadier General George M. Parker Jr.; the Visayan-Mindanao Force is commanded by Brigadier General William F. Sharp; Major General George F. Moore commands the Harbor Defense forces; and the command's Reserve is directly under MacArthur.

MARINE CORPS
The 2d and 4th Defense Battalions arrive at Pearl Harbor, Hawaii, destined for eventual deployment to Wake Island.

2 DECEMBER
NAVY
The first U.S. Naval Armed Guard detachment, a gun crew trained to serve in merchant vessels, boards the freighter *Dunboyne*. All told, some 145,000 men serve in the Armed Guard during World War II, manning 6,236 merchantmen. A total of 1,810 men lose their lives, and five receive the Navy Cross for extraordinary heroism.

4 DECEMBER
MARINE CORPS
Twelve F4F Wildcat fighters of Marine Fighting Squadron 211 fly from the carrier *Enterprise* to Wake Island. They begin aerial patrols the next day.

5 DECEMBER
AIR FORCE
Despite incomplete facilities, Major General Lewis H. Brereton moves two B-17 Flying Fortress squadrons comprising 16 aircraft to Del Monte Field, Mindanao, Philippine Islands, to initiate a dispersion plan. The 14th and 93d Squadrons from the 19th Bomb Group,

Below: *A stunned Sailor looks at the destruction around him during the Japanese attack on the Ford Island Naval Air Station, Hawaii. Of the Navy's 148 combat aircraft, 36 survived. (National Archives)*

Overleaf: *Japanese dive-bombers attack Pearl Harbor's Battleship Row on 7 December 1941. The surprise attack on military installations in the Hawaiian Islands decimates U.S. forces there. All of the eight battleships anchored at Pearl Harbor are either sunk or damaged; numerous other ships are damaged or destroyed. Attacks on airfields throughout the islands destroy the majority of U.S. combat planes based there. ("Battleship Row," Robert T. McCall, NASM Art Collection)*

commanded by Majors Emmett O'Donnell Jr. and Cecil Combs, find no natural cover to camouflage airplanes and use a single spray gun to convert the shining silver finish of the aircraft to olive drab.

NAVY

The aircraft carrier *Lexington* sails from Pearl Harbor, Hawaii, for Midway Atoll to deliver SB2U Vindicators of Marine Scout Bombing Squadron 231.

7 DECEMBER
ALL SERVICES

Early in the morning, the destroyer *Ward,* operating in the entrance channel to Pearl Harbor, Hawaii, attacks and sinks a Japanese midget submarine with the help of a PBY Catalina flying boat from Patrol Squadron 14. Despite this, no general warnings are issued.

At 7:55 a.m. Hawaiian time, two waves of 353 Japanese naval aircraft strike U.S. facilities on Oahu, Hawaii. The Japanese aircraft hit the naval base at Pearl Harbor, Hickam and Wheeler Army Air Fields, Schofield Barracks, and other installations. Great devastation occurs on Battleship Row where *Oklahoma* capsizes, and *West Virginia* and *California* are sunk. The battleship *Arizona* is destroyed by a catastrophic explosion when a bomb detonates her forward magazine. Despite damage from bombs and torpedoes, the battleship *Nevada* manages to get underway, but is eventually beached. The battleships *Tennessee, Maryland,* and *Pennsylvania* as well as the heavy cruiser *New Orleans* and the light cruisers *Honolulu, Raleigh,* and *Helena* suffer damage. Three

destroyers and other support ships are also hard hit; in all, 19 ships are lost. The Sailors and Marines on ships and ashore suffer 2,008 dead including Rear Admiral Isaac Kidd, the first Navy flag officer killed in the war.

Soldiers and Marines ashore scramble to defense positions and use rifles and machine guns to engage the enemy. At the airfields, Japanese planes destroy or damage almost 200 parked aircraft. A flight of unsuspecting and unarmed B-17D Flying Fortress bombers of the 38th and 88th Reconnaissance Squadrons arrive in the midst of the attack. At least one bomber breaks in half on landing, but none are shot down. In contrast, some other arriving planes,

including SBD Dauntless dive-bombers from the aircraft carrier *Enterprise*, are not so lucky and are shot down. The Army sustains the loss of 96 aircraft, 233 soldiers killed and 364 wounded. The Marine Corps suffers 33 aircraft destroyed and 12 damaged.

During the attack, Army Second Lieutenants Kenneth Taylor and George Welch of the 47th Pursuit Squadron at Haleiwa Airfield get their P-40 Warhawk fighters into the air and pursue the Japanese. Together they earn credit for shooting down six enemy aircraft.

MARINE CORPS
Over 1,100 miles west of Hawaii, two Japanese destroyers appear off the island of Midway and bombard it, inflicting 14 Marine Corps casualties.

8 DECEMBER
ALL SERVICES
Calling 7 December 1941 a "date that will live in infamy," President Franklin D. Roosevelt asks Congress for a declaration of war against Japan. A joint resolution passes the same day. Subsequent action is taken to declare war on Germany and Italy. Immediate action is taken to halt the discharges of draftees, and National Guard units due to be returned to state status are retained under federal control.

Japanese forces attack U.S. military installations in the Philippine Islands. More than 100 aircraft, including 18 B-17 Flying Fortress bombers, 56 P-40 Warhawk and P-35 fighters, and 26 other types, are destroyed on the ground at Clark and Iba airfields. About 80 American servicemen are killed in these attacks. Five Army Air Forces pilots shoot down seven Japanese aircraft during the attack. Lieutenant Randall B. Keator is credited with shooting down the first Japanese aircraft over the Philippines in his P-40.

AIR FORCE
Bell test pilot Robert Stanley makes the first flight of the XP-63 Kingcobra fighter near Buffalo, New York.

MARINE CORPS
Japanese aircraft attack Wake Island, destroying seven of Marine Fighting Squadron 211's aircraft. Enemy planes strike Wake daily until it falls on 23 December. Elsewhere, Japanese aircraft execute raids against Guam Island, Mariana Islands, and the Philippine Islands.

Marine Corps detachments in Peiping, Tientsin, and elsewhere in China surrender to superior Japanese forces.

NAVY
After unsuccessful efforts to scuttle their ship, the crew of the river gunboat *Wake* surrenders the ship to a Japanese boarding party off Shanghai, China. This is the only time a U.S. Navy vessel strikes her colors in World War II.

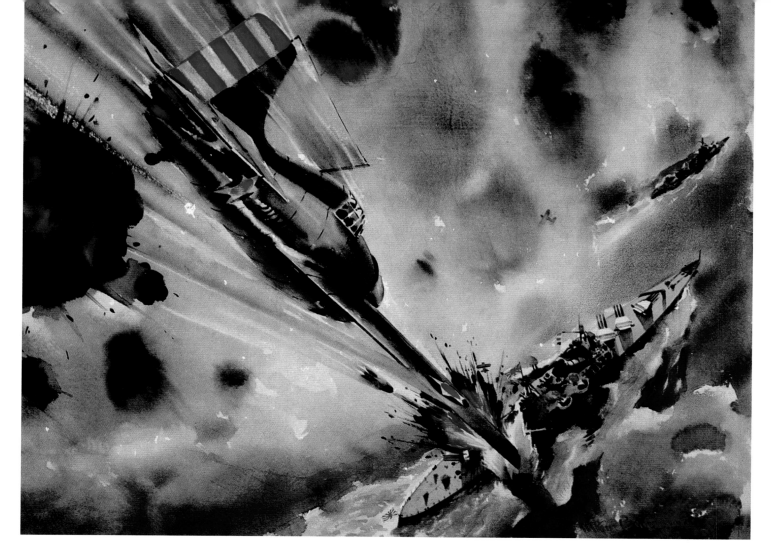

9 DECEMBER
NAVY

The submarine *Swordfish* executes the first U.S. Navy submarine attack of the war, claiming the sinking of a Japanese ship 150 miles west of Manila, Philippine Islands. The sinking is not confirmed in postwar records, which indicate that *Swordfish* sinks her initial victim of the war on 16 December, hitting the cargo ship *Atsutasan Maru* with three torpedoes.

10 DECEMBER
AIR FORCE

In the first U.S. offensive operations against Japan, five B-17 Flying Fortress bombers attack Japanese targets off Aparri, near Luzon, Philippine Islands. These 93d Bomb Squadron planes are the first U.S. aircraft to sink an enemy vessel by aerial bombardment. In one such attack, the aircraft flown by Captain Colin P. Kelly Jr., is hit by enemy fire. Kelly orders the crew to bail out of the bomber, but is killed when he fails to escape the crippled plane himself. He is posthumously awarded the Distinguished Service Cross for his attack upon the heavy cruiser *Ashigara*.

ARMY

Defense forces are unable to mount resistance to the first Japanese landings in northern Luzon, Philippine Islands, at Aparri and Vigan.

Above: *The men of Marine Fighting Squadron 211 defending Wake Island fly their F4F Wildcats against air and naval surface attackers, exacting a high price for the final surrender of the island. They sink a Japanese destroyer with a bomb and help defend against two landings. ("Wake Island," Arthur Beaumont, Art Collection, National Museum of the Marine Corps)*

MARINE CORPS/NAVY

A Japanese force of nearly 6,000 men lands at three points on Guam Island, Mariana Islands. The 153 Marines of the garrison and the 80 Chamorros of the Insular Guard, armed with rifles and four machine guns, fight back for a time, but Captain George J. McMillin, USN, the governor of Guam, surrenders the island to the Japanese to avoid needless casualties. Marine Corps losses are 4 killed and 12 wounded.

NAVY

Japanese aircraft bomb the Cavite Navy Yard in the Philippine Islands, destroying shore facilities and, sinking one vessel and damaging six more. During the attack Chief Boatswain Earl D. Payne, a gunner in a PBY Catalina of Patrol Squadron 101, downs a Japanese Zero fighter, the Navy's first air-to-air kill of the war.

An SBD Dauntless dive-bomber from the carrier *Enterprise* sinks the Japanese submarine *I-70* off the Hawaiian Islands, the first sinking of a Japanese vessel by U.S. Navy carrier aircraft during World War II.

Right: *The tiny P-26 Peashooter is the first all metal pursuit fighter purchased by the Army. Armed with two .30 caliber machine guns, it is the top Army fighter in 1938. (John H. Batchelor)*

11 DECEMBER
ALL SERVICES
Germany and Italy declare a state of war with the United States.

AIR FORCE
Pilot Officer John Gillespie Magee Jr. is killed during a midair collision over Great Britain. An American serving with the Royal Canadian Air Force, and only 19 years old at the time of his death, Magee had authored the poem "High Flight" during the previous summer and had mailed a copy to his parents. The poem, which captures the ethereal experience of flight, has since been widely distributed and reproduced.

ARMY
The Western Defense Command, headquartered in San Francisco, California, and responsible for the protection of the west half of the country, is redesignated from an administrative status to being a theater of active military operations. Nine additional antiaircraft regiments are rushed from various parts of the U.S. to vulnerable western cities.

MARINE CORPS
The Wake Island defense force defeats an attempted Japanese amphibious assault. Four F4F Wildcat fighters sink two enemy destroyers, while Marine Corps shore batteries damage three cruisers, two destroyers, a destroyer-transport, and a transport. Marine Corps losses are a handful of wounded.

12 DECEMBER
AIR FORCE
Captain Jesus Villamor, Philippine Army Air Corps, shoots down a Japanese bomber over the Philippine Islands. Villamor is flying the Army's first monoplane fighter, the obsolete P-26 Peashooter. This aerial victory is one of the few credited to a Peashooter.

ARMY
Southeast of Manila, Philippine Islands, in the sector defended by the Southern Luzon Force under Major General George M. Parker Jr., the Japanese land at Legaspi unopposed and move north on the coastal road.

Left: *The Japanese attacks on Wake Island are met with fierce resistance by the mixed garrison of Marines, Sailors, Soldiers and civilians. ("Wake Island," E. Franklin Wittmark, Art Collection, National Museum of the Marine Corps, Triangle, Virginia)*

Left: *The Japanese attacks on Pearl Harbor, Hawaii, and the Philippine Islands in December 1941 create an outpouring of patriotic fever among young Americans. These hopeful recruits are lined up outside the Navy recruiting office in Quincy, Massachusetts. Before the attack the Navy counts less than 400,000 men; in 1942 the Navy grows to more than three times that number. (Naval Historical Center)*

NAVY
The Naval Air Transport Service is established.

14 DECEMBER
ARMY
The Army hurriedly moves a corps of two infantry divisions (27th and 35th) with other corps troops to block the latest Japanese landing on Luzon, Philippine Islands.

General George C. Marshall approves a plan for a 2-million-man Army with 100 divisions over the next two years. This soon gives way to a blueprint for a strength of 3.6 million and 69 new divisions within one year. Three years later the Army numbers 8 million men and women and 89 combat divisions.

15 DECEMBER
MARINE CORPS
Two Japanese ships bombard Johnston Island. The defending Marines suffer no casualties.

NAVY
The seaplane tender *Tangier*, the oiler *Neches*, and four destroyers sail from Pearl Harbor, Hawaii, as part of a force gathered in an effort to relieve the beleaguered garrison on Wake Island.

16 DECEMBER
AIR FORCE
Lieutenant Boyd D. Wagner, commander of the 17th Pursuit Squadron, becomes the first American ace of World War II. Flying a P-40 Warhawk fighter, he shoots down his fifth enemy aircraft in air-to-air fighting near the Japanese landing site at Vigan, Philippine Islands.

NAVY
Task Force 14—the aircraft carrier *Saratoga*, three heavy cruisers, and nine destroyers—departs Pearl Harbor, Hawaii. Under the command of Rear Admiral Frank Jack Fletcher, the force's objective is the relief of Wake Island.

17 DECEMBER
MARINE CORPS/NAVY
Led by a Navy patrol bomber, 17 SB2U Vindicator dive-bombers of Marine Scout Bombing Squadron 231 make what is then the longest mass overwater single-engined flight recorded, covering the 1,137 miles from Oahu, Hawaii, to Midway Atoll in 9 hours and 45 minutes. They represent the first combat aircraft on the island.

NAVY
Vice Admiral William S. Pye becomes Acting Commander in Chief, U.S. Pacific Fleet, relieving Admiral Husband E. Kimmel.

19–20 DECEMBER
ARMY
The Japanese begin landing operations in the northern sector of Davao, Mindanao, in the southern Philippine

Islands. They overwhelm a Philippine Army battalion commanded by U.S. Army Lieutenant Colonel Roger B. Hilsman. The Japanese soon use Davao as a launching point for attack, which results in the capture of Jolo on Christmas Eve. The enemy now has forces in position for an attack against Borneo.

19 DECEMBER
NAVY
The United States Naval Academy Class of 1942 is graduated six months early due to the national emergency. Forty-eight members of the class are killed during World War II service.

20 DECEMBER
ALL SERVICES
The China-based American Volunteer Group flies its first missions against the Japanese. Led by the dynamic Claire Chennault, the Flying Tigers fly the P-40 Warhawk painted with distinctive shark teeth on the engine intake.

MARINE CORPS
The commander of the Asiatic Fleet places the 4th Marine Regiment under command of Lieutenant General Douglas MacArthur. Japanese troops invade Mindanao, Philippine Islands.

21 DECEMBER
MARINE CORPS
Japanese carrier planes destroy the last remaining aircraft of Marine Fighting Squadron 211 on Wake Island.

22–24 DECEMBER
ALL SERVICES
President Franklin D. Roosevelt and British Prime Minister Winston S. Churchill open the Arcadia Conference in Washington, D.C., which results in the commitment to a "Germany-first" strategy,

Above: *Recruiting posters like this are designed to appeal to different motives that may attract a young man into the Marine Corps. This poster offers the recruit a life of adventure and action. (USMC)*

Right: *The American Volunteer Group (AVG), nicknamed "Flying Tigers," is formed in 1941. It becomes the scourge of the Japanese in the air over Burma and China, destroying more than 400 Japanese planes with a loss of only 12 P-40 Warhawk fighters. The AVG is disbanded in July 1942. ("The Flying Tigers," Robert Taylor, © The Military Gallery, Ojai, CA)*

Left: *With only four F4F Wildcats, Marine Fighter Squadron 211 sinks a Japanese destroyer and downs several planes while defending Wake Island in 1941. ("Cat and Mouse Over Wake Island," Marc Stewart, Stewart Studios)*

Below: *To delay the Japanese advance on Bataan, Philippine Islands, the horse-mounted 26th Cavalry (Philippine Scouts) makes the last mounted charge in Army history. (Blandford Press)*

creation of a Combined Chiefs of Staff to direct the war effort, and an agreement that a supreme commander should be appointed for both the Pacific and Atlantic theaters.

ARMY/NAVY
Douglas MacArthur is promoted to full general as he deploys his battered forces in the Philippine Islands to continue the fight in the face of overwhelming odds. The main assault of the Japanese 14th Army is underway as 76 Army transports and 9 Navy transports, with 43,110 troops, enter Lingayen Gulf, Luzon, with a strong naval escort. Major General Johnathan M. Wainwright maneuvers elements of the North Luzon Force to meet the enemy. But by 24 December one enemy column is in Baguio; the main thrust south toward Manila reaches Binalonan and is driving toward the Agno River.

23 DECEMBER
ARMY
Hoping to stave off civilian casualties, General Douglas MacArthur declares Manila an open city. He evacuates troops from the city and orders American and Filipino units to fight a delaying action as he withdraws the Army into the Bataan Peninsula, where it is hoped that defensive positions will deter the enemy attack. Commander, I Philippine Corps Major General Albert M. Jones orders the withdrawal of troops from the Bicol Peninsula as another Japanese invasion task force (the Lamon Bay Force) appears off Atimonan on the east coast.

MARINE CORPS/NAVY
Following a dawn landing by a Japanese Special Naval Landing Force and 12 hours of fighting, the battered

garrison of Wake Island, under the command of Commander Winfield Scott Cunningham, surrenders. Total Marine Corps casualties are 56 killed and 44 wounded. A U.S. Navy relief expedition carrying Marine Fighting Squadron 221 and the 4th Defense Battalion turns back to Pearl Harbor, Hawaii.

24 DECEMBER
AIR FORCE
Major General Lewis H. Brereton closes down his headquarters at Fort McKinley, Luzon, Philippine Islands, and leaves to join his bombers near Port Darwin, Australia. Surviving B-17s Flying Fortresses have been moved to Australian or Netherlands East Indies bases.

ARMY
Two Army transports carrying critically needed supplies reach Australia, but no way can be found to

transport the troops or cargo north to the Philippine Islands. General Douglas MacArthur has not received a single piece of equipment or any additional soldiers to reinforce his beleaguered army.
.
The prewar plan WPO-3 anticipating the possibility of a withdrawal of U.S. and Philippine forces into the Bataan Peninsula is activated. The Bataan Defense Force is created, with Major General George M. Parker Jr. in command of II Philippine Corps. In the retrograde action toward Bataan, Colonel Clinton S. Pierce's 26th Cavalry, Philippine Scouts, makes a mounted charge at Binalonan in an effort to stem the Japanese tide.

The Japanese Lamon Bay Force encounters little resistance as it lands at three points on the east coast of Luzon, Philippine Islands, and opens a drive northwestward toward Manila.

MARINE CORPS

Elements of Batteries A and C of the 4th Defense Battalion reinforce the garrison on Midway Atoll.

25–31 DECEMBER
ARMY

In the Philippine Islands, the Northern Luzon Force (NLF) withdraws below the Agno River and starts a phased retrograde action to the final and most southerly position, D-5, stretching from Mt. Arayat to Sibul Springs. D-5 is organized for a protracted defense to enable the South Luzon Force to slip past San Fernando and into Bataan before the NLF closes the road.

25 DECEMBER
MARINE CORPS

The 14 F2A Buffalo fighter planes of Marine Fighting Squadron (VMF) 221 fly off the carrier *Saratoga* and land on Midway Atoll. The next day, Battery B of the 4th Defense Battalion and the ground elements of VMF-221 arrive at Midway. The 4th Marine Regiment begins moving to its assigned defensive positions on the fortress island of Corregidor, Philippine Islands, guarding the entrance to Manila Bay. The deployment is completed two days later. Two antiaircraft batteries of 3d Battalion, 4th Marines (recently created from units of the former Marine Barracks, Cavite Navy Yard) remain on Bataan.

29 DECEMBER
ARMY/MARINE CORPS

Japanese aircraft begin daily attacks on Corregidor, Philippine Islands, and slowly destroy its fixed fortifications.

30 DECEMBER
AIR FORCE/ARMY

The Army Air Forces formally requests that the National Defense Research Committee begin development of "controlled trajectory bombs." Eventually, programs like Azon and Razon guided weapons result from this request.

MARINE CORPS

The 1st Barrage Balloon Squadron arrives in the Panama Canal Zone to assist in the canal's defense.

Right: *At the start of World War II, American outposts in the Pacific stretch from Alaska to the Philippine Islands. These and other bases were the sites of many of the key battles in the Pacific war. (Map by Edgeworx)*

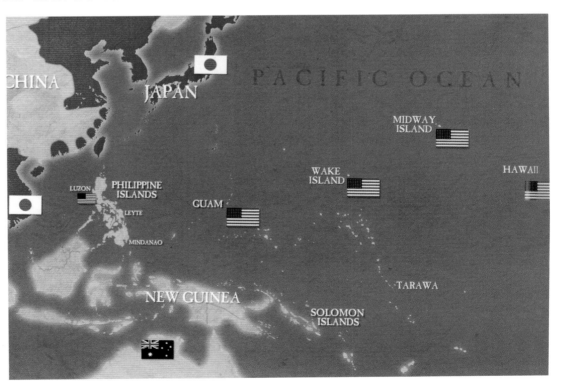

Left: *A Japanese roadblock intended to stop American withdrawal into the Bataan defenses in Luzon Island, Philippine Islands, is smashed on 26 December 1941 by an M3 Stuart light tank of Company C, 194th Tank Battalion. The battalion, considered one of the best in the Army, is composed of three National Guard companies. The small number of tanks and other armored vehicles greatly hinders the American efforts to throw back the Japanese invasion of the Philippine Islands. ("At A Roadblock on the Road to Bataan," D. Millsap, Army Art Collection, U.S. Center of Military History)*

NAVY

Admiral Ernest J. King assumes duties as Commander in Chief, United States Fleet. One of his first actions is to change the acronym of his new command from CINCUS, which he thinks sounds like "sink us," to COMINCH.

31 DECEMBER
ARMY/NAVY

As a result of the increased Japanese naval presence, a new trans-Pacific route has to be developed. Army task forces are organized to move rapidly to secure Christmas and Canton islands and to establish U.S. facilities in the Society Islands (Bora Bora), Fiji, and New Caledonia.

ARMY

The withdrawal of troops to Bataan, Philippine Islands, is covered by the Provisional Tank Group of light tanks. In the extrication of the Southern Luzon Force, the 192d Tank Battalion and six of Lieutenant Colonel David S. Babcock's self-propelled 75mm guns battle Japanese forces in Baliuag. Eight Japanese tanks are destroyed with negligible damage to the U.S. force.

NAVY

Admiral Chester W. Nimitz, a submariner and most recently Chief of the Bureau of Navigation, takes command of the Pacific Fleet on the deck of the submarine *Grayling* at Pearl Harbor, Hawaii.

Right: *In a ceremony befitting his career as a submarine officer, Admiral Chester W. Nimitz assumes command of the U.S. Pacific Fleet on the submarine* Grayling *on 31 December 1941. (Naval Historical Center)*

Opposite: *Each service generated posters to appeal to potential recruits. (Clockwise from top left: National Archives; Naval Historical Center; NASM Poster Collection; "Fly with the Marines," Howard Chandler Christy, Art Collection, National Museum of the Marine Corps)*

THE WAR AGAINST JAPAN

1942-1945

THE WAR AGAINST JAPAN
1942–1945

"I fear all we have done is awaken a sleeping giant and fill him with a terrible resolve."
—Admiral Isoroku Yamamoto, Japanese Imperial Navy, 8 December 1941

*"Sixteen hours ago an American airplane dropped one bomb on Hiroshima . . .
The force from which the sun draws its power has been loosed
against those who brought war to the Far East."*
—President Harry S. Truman, 6 August 1945

DESPERATE TIMES, DESPERATE MEASURES
Following the official declarations of war with Japan, Germany, and Italy in December 1941, U.S. planners faced the challenge of fighting a two-ocean, multicontinent war. Such a war would require close cooperation with allied forces. To this end, the U.S. and Britain created the Combined Chiefs of Staff to oversee the Anglo-American war effort. The U.S. Joint Chiefs of Staff (JCS) was then established to replace the long-standing joint Army-Navy Board. The JCS was given the responsibility of directing the Pacific war. A two-pronged offensive strategy was eventually hammered out. The key was to recapture the Philippine Islands and use them as a base for final attacks on, and a possible blockade of, Japan.

When the Japanese cut the sea routes to the Philippines, American forces already en route were

diverted to Australia. This became the new Pacific base for American forces. Some Marine Corps units managed to reach the remaining Pacific outposts like Midway Island, Bora Bora, and Samoa. By mid-January 1942, U.S. and Japanese naval forces were already trading blows as American aircraft carriers and other ships that had escaped the December 1941 attacks intercepted Japanese invasion fleets. The hard-won prewar investment in carriers as well as Navy and Marine Corps aircraft, was paying dividends.

The Americans and Filipinos, pushed into the last defensive lines on the Bataan Peninsula on Luzon Island, in the Philippines, soon realized that help was not coming. In March 1942, senior commander General Douglas MacArthur was ordered to Australia to regroup American forces. He promised, "I shall return." Starving and battered by Japanese air and ground attacks, the American–Filipino defenders were finally overwhelmed in May and forced to surrender. This was the largest surrender in American history—12,000 U.S. and 63,000 Filipino officers and enlisted personnel, including many female Army and Navy nurses. The prisoners were then forced on a 60-mile death march that killed thousands. At the end of the death march, prisoners underwent hellish mistreatment for three years in Japanese prison camps. Some prisoners were deported as slave laborers to Japan and Korea, but many thousands more did not survive. A few men escaped to form guerrilla bands in the Philippine hills.

Only days after the Philippine surrender in April 1942, the Army Air Forces struck back at the Japanese home islands. In a daring raid, the aircraft carrier *Hornet* approached within one-way flying distance of Japan and launched a flight of 16 Army Air Forces B-25 Mitchell bombers. The planes, led by Lieutenant Colonel James Doolittle, hit Tokyo and three other

Previous spread: The bold, low-level surprise attack by Army Air Forces B-25 Mitchell bombers on the Japanese homeland in April 1942 is only a hint of retribution to come. ("Doolittle Raiders Bomb Osaka," George Guzzi, USAF Art Collection)

Opposite: A Soldier of the 2d Service Command shines his shoes in the spartan barracks built in the early days of the war. ("Barrack Scene," M.W. Slaughter, Army Art Collection, U.S. Army Center of Military History)

Right: By early 1942, the Japanese have reached the greatest extent of their advances. (Map by Edgeworx)

cities. The attack shocked the Japanese, boosted American morale, and foreshadowed the destruction that would ultimately rain down on Japan.

American political and military leaders, driven by resource limitations, the pleas of Britain and Russia, and the dire prospect of a total Nazi Europe, developed a "Europe first" offensive strategy. However, at the same time, men, ships, and planes were dispatched to slow the Japanese in the Pacific and Asia, where they had occupied two Alaskan islands, invaded New Guinea Island, and routed Allied forces in Burma. The Allies struck back at every opportunity. Submarines waged a constant underwater war, while on the surface aircraft carriers replaced battleships as the key warship. For the first time in history, U.S. fleets dueled against an enemy who was miles away, using far-ranging aircraft rather than naval guns. At the same time, the mobilized military turned out trained Sailors, Soldiers, and Marines, and the industrial base provided new equipment, and more ships, and ground and air units were built up and sent to the front.

TIPPING THE BALANCE

In accordance with the two-prong Pacific strategy, American forces were divided into two theaters of operations—the Southwest Pacific Area, under General Douglas MacArthur, and the Central Pacific Area, under Admiral Chester Nimitz. Each commander had his own strategic vision for defeating Japan. MacArthur favored a push north out of Australia to New Guinea Island, through the island groups to the Philippine Islands, and then up the Ryukyu Islands to Japan. Nimitz wanted a western approach using the Solomon, Caroline, Mariana, and Bonin Island groups to reach Japan. Both strategies recognized the necessity of progressively seizing islands for use as naval and air bases to support advanced operations.

Two events occurred in the summer of 1942 that shifted the strategic initiative in the Pacific from the Japanese to the Allies. On 3 June, the U.S. Navy sprang a carefully laid trap on the Japanese fleet. Using translated intercepts of the secret Japanese code, the Navy pounced upon a Japanese invasion fleet approaching Midway Island in the central Pacific. While suffering heavy losses itself, the Navy dealt a crippling blow to the Japanese fleet by sinking its four aircraft carriers, and sent the Japanese reeling back.

Less than 90 days later, Vice Admiral William F. Halsey Jr. landed the 1st Marine Division on Guadalcanal Island in the Solomon Islands. The bitter jungle battle marked the first American offensive ground action in the Pacific. The purpose was to eliminate the island's airfield as a Japanese base. The Army's American and 25th Infantry Divisions joined the struggle for the island, which lasted almost six months. A series of tough fights contested landings

by Soldiers and Marines on other Solomon Islands, culminating with an assault on Bougainville Island in November 1943.

With the destruction of the major Japanese base on Rabaul Island as his target, MacArthur launched an offensive in July 1942 with the Army's 32d Infantry Division and Australian troops to clear the Japanese from New Guinea Island. It took two years and several more Army divisions before the mission was done, but it opened a southern path back to the Philippine Islands. MacArthur then seized the Admiralty Islands, and in October 1944, he stepped ashore with his troops on Leyte Island, Philippine Islands. As promised, he had returned, but the bloody contest to free the islands lasted five more months, including a three-month fight to liberate Manila, which had some of the worst city fighting the Army had seen.

As MacArthur's troops struggled through New Guinea toward the Philippine Islands, Nimitz waged a series of island campaigns in the Central Pacific. In November 1943, two major landings took place in the Gilbert Islands. The Marines took Tarawa Atoll with heavy casualties, while the Army seized Makin Island in four days of fighting. The Marshall Islands were next in February 1944, followed by more invasions that included Saipan and Guam Islands in the Mariana Islands. By October, Nimitz had pushed the Japanese defensive perimeter back more than 4,000 miles, and Army Air Forces B-29 Superfortress bombers were using the captured bases to strike at the Japanese home islands.

Far to the west in Burma, the ragged provisional force known first as Merrill's Marauders, and later as the Mars Task Force, spearheaded the return of the Allies into Burma. As they moved through the jungle toward the Burma–China border, they were followed by engineers who built the almost impassable mountain trail known as the Ledo Road. The road served as a logistics link between the supply bases in India and the forward-based airfields in China that were used by the Army Air Forces to attack Japan. The Japanese were forced out of the way and the last segment of the road opened in February 1945. The road served as a main route for supplies to the Chinese troops fighting the large Japanese forces that occupied China and Manchuria.

THE END GAME

At the start of 1945, it appeared that an invasion of the Japanese home islands was going to be necessary. Previous experience with fanatical Japanese defenders indicated that such an invasion would result in horrific casualties on both sides. As preparation, penetration of the inner ring of Japanese defenses continued. In February, a Marine Corps landing on Iwo Jima brought American forces within 700 miles of Tokyo. It took three weeks of desperate fighting to secure the tiny island. Less than a month later, units of the Tenth U.S. Army stormed Okinawa, Japan, an island held by 100,000 Japanese defenders. Ground fighting continued on the island through June as the Navy fought off hundreds of suicide planes. Even as the battle raged, men and equipment were shifted from liberated Europe to the Pacific and the waiting units steeled themselves for the expected invasion of Japan proper.

Unknown to all but a few, a unique weapon had been developed that offered an alternative to the dreaded invasion—the atomic bomb. The Army's super-secret Manhattan Project, underway since early in the war, brought the bomb to successful testing in July 1945, when one of the three existing bombs was exploded in the New Mexico desert. The two remaining bombs were moved to the Pacific island of

Above: *The battleship* New Mexico *fires her main guns in support of landings on Saipan Island, Mariana Islands, in June 1944. (Naval Historical Center)*

Tinian, and preparations were made to employ them against Japan. On 6 August 1945, an Army Air Forces B-29 bomber named "Enola Gay" dropped the second bomb, code-named "Little Boy," devastating the city of Hiroshima. Three days later, on 9 August, another B-29, "Bockscar," dropped the last bomb on Nagasaki with equal results. Four days later, Emperor Hirohito announced the unconditional surrender of Japan. The formal document of surrender was signed on 2 September 1945 in Tokyo Bay on the deck of the battleship *Missouri*. The war in the Pacific was over.

Opposite: *American Volunteer Group (Flying Tigers) P-40 Warhawk fighters cause the Japanese heavy losses in the air over China and Burma. ("Flying Tigers," James Dietz)*

Right: *Men from the 6th Marine Regiment train with M1903 Springfield rifles on a snowy rifle range in Iceland. (Dept. of Defense)*

1942
DOWN, BUT NOT OUT

1 JANUARY
AIR FORCE
Lieutenant General George H. Brett, a veteran airman, arrives at Port Darwin, Australia, from Chungking, China, to take command of U.S. Army Forces in Australia.

ARMY
In the Philippine Islands, the last of the U.S. tanks crosses the Calumpit bridge into Bataan at about 2:30 a.m. By 5:00 a.m. all units are safely across. Final preparations are made for demolition of the bridge. General Douglas MacArthur's army is in Bataan.

2 JANUARY
ARMY
The 26th Cavalry Regiment (Philippine Scouts) covers the left flank of the new Philippine defensive line anchored at the town of San Jose. Japanese aircraft start daily attacks on Corregidor Island.

5 JANUARY
ARMY
In the face of heavy enemy pressure, a new defensive line, manned by battered Philippine Army divisions, is established along the base of the Bataan Peninsula, Luzon Island.

NAVY
Operating just eight miles from Tokyo Bay, Japan,

the submarine *Pollack* torpedoes the Japanese cargo ship *Heijo Maru*. *Pollack* attacks two more ships off the coast of the Japanese home islands on 7 and 9 January.

6 JANUARY
NAVY
Eleven Navy nurses are among the military personnel captured at Manila, Luzon Island, Philippine Islands, when it falls to the Japanese. They eventually spend 37 months as prisoners of war.

7 JANUARY
AIR FORCE/ARMY
U.S. and Philippine forces are reorganized. The Northern Luzon Force becomes I Philippine Corps. The Bataan Defense Force is renamed II Philippine Corps. The combined force has 47,500 troops. I Corps is responsible for the western sector, II Corps for the Eastern sector. A provisional infantry unit composed of Army Air Corps personnel is formed near Marivales.

9 JANUARY
ARMY
Three Japanese regimental combat teams, with artillery support, attack defenses at Bataan, Luzon Island, Philippine Islands. The I Corps uses demolitions in an effort to slow the enemy on its Mauban line.

10 JANUARY
ARMY
The Japanese make their first surrender demand with a message dropped by aircraft in Bataan, Luzon Island, Philippine Islands. General Douglas MacArthur ignores it.

Left: *The B-17 Flying Fortress bombers of the 19oth Bomb Group arrive as reinforcement to the Philippine Islands in November 1941. ("They Fought With What They Had," John D. Shaw, Liberty Studios)*

Opposite: *Lieutenant Alexander R. Nininger Jr., 57th Infantry Regiment (Philippine Scouts) is awarded the Army's first Medal of Honor for his heroism at Bataan on Luzon Island. (National Archives)*

11 JANUARY
ARMY

While enroute to the Philippine Islands, with six artillery battalions, the 2d Battalion, 131st Field Artillery (Texas National Guard) is diverted to Surabaya, Java, Dutch East Indies, where it is assigned to join a mixed defense force of Dutch, British, and Australian troops.

NAVY

The Japanese submarine *I-6* torpedoes the aircraft carrier *Saratoga* as she returns to Hawaii after delivering aircraft to Midway Atoll. *Saratoga* is forced to head to the West Coast for repairs, reducing U.S. carrier strength in the Pacific to three.

12 JANUARY
ARMY

Wounded three times in hand-to-hand fighting near Abucay, Bataan, Philippine Islands, 2d Lieutenant Alexander R. Nininger, 57th Infantry Regiment, Philippine Scouts, finally succumbs. He is posthumously awarded the Medal of Honor.

15 JANUARY
AIR FORCE

The Alaskan Air Forces is activated at Elmendorf Field, near Anchorage, Alaska. In February it will be redesignated as the Eleventh Air Force.

MARINE CORPS

Brigadier General Henry L. Larsen, commanding general of the 2d Marine Brigade, is appointed the first military governor of American Samoa.

NAVY

The American–British–Dutch–Australian Command (ABDA) is established on the island of Java, Dutch East Indies, with British General Sir Archibald Wavell named as supreme commander of forces in the Southwest Pacific. Admiral Thomas C. Hart is named commander of ABDA's naval forces.

16 JANUARY
ARMY

The U.S. 31st Infantry Regiment enters the fight as the enemy launches an encirclement at Moron, Luzon Island, Philippine Islands. The I Corps engages the enemy for the first time as Japanese forces cross the Batalan River. Cavalrymen of the 26th Cavalry, Philippine Scouts, led by Lieutenant Edwin P. Ramsey, attack on horseback in an effort to secure Moron. The cavalrymen withdraw after taking heavy losses, and remaining horses are soon destroyed. This marks what

is possibly the last horse cavalry charge in the U.S. Army.

NAVY

Operating under strict radio silence, a TBD-1 Devastator torpedo-bomber flown by Chief Aviation Machinist's Mate Harold F. Dixon and his two-man crew is forced to ditch at sea when it runs out of fuel during a search mission from the aircraft carrier *Enterprise*. The three men spend the next 34 days drifting at sea in a life raft, their sole nourishment consisting of rain water, two birds, and whatever fish they manage to spear with a knife. When they reach Danger Island, Cook Islands, on 19 February, it is estimated that the trio has traveled about 1,200 miles.

22 JANUARY
ARMY

General Douglas MacArthur orders withdrawal southward to a final defense position on Bataan, Luzon Island, Philippine Islands, as the enemy starts an attack. In the I Corps' area, infantry elements supported by cavalry scouts and tanks are unsuccessful in their efforts to reduce an enemy roadblock.

MARINE CORPS

The 2d Marine Brigade (reactivated on Christmas Eve 1941) reaches American Samoa and joins with the 7th Defense Battalion in protecting that territory. It is the first American Expeditionary Force of the war.

Left: *Fighting in the jungles of Bataan Peninsula, Luzon Island, Philippine Islands, is desperate and close as the Japanese push American forces back. (Army Art Collection, U.S. Army Center of Military History)*

Below: *Philippine Scouts unhook and move their M3 37mm antitank gun into position during training. (U.S. Army)*

NAVY

With Japanese forces landing on the Bataan Peninsula, Luzon Island, Philippine Islands, the naval battalion under Commander Francis J. Bridget joins in the initial defense, helping drive the invaders back on 24 January.

In the first surface engagement by U.S. Navy forces in the Pacific, Destroyer Division 59 under Commander Paul H. Talbot attacks a Japanese invasion force bound for Borneo, Dutch East Indies, in what becomes known as the Battle of Makassar Strait. The flush-deck destroyers *John D. Ford*, *Parrott*, *Paul Jones*, and *Pope* sink three transports and a cargo ship before retiring.

27 JANUARY
ARMY/NAVY

Task Force Bobcat—sets sail from Charleston, South Carolina, in a six-ship convoy to construct a U.S. base at Bora Bora, Society Islands. The task force includes the 102d Infantry Regiment and the 198th Coast Artillery Regiment (Antiaircraft) (Semi-mobile).

27–28 JANUARY
MARINE CORPS

Dozens of Marines from two 3d Battalion, 4th Marine Regiment batteries assist a provisional naval battalion and Philippine units in containing a Japanese amphibious landing against the Bataan coast near Mariveles.

29 JANUARY
AIR FORCE

The 70th Pursuit Squadron sets up its base on Suva, Fiji, to help provide a link between New Caledonia and Samoa. Redesignated the 70th Fighter Squadron on 15 May 1942, it will later operate from Guadalcanal Island, Solomon Islands.

31 JANUARY
AIR FORCE/ARMY

Infantrymen, coast artillerymen, air corps elements, and supply troops man Army task forces destined for Christmas Island (Task Force Birch) in the Indian Ocean and Canton Island (Task Force Holly) in the central Pacific. Two thousand troops sail from San Francisco, California, on board the transport *President Taylor*.

1 FEBRUARY
NAVY

The U.S. Navy strikes at the Japanese with attacks against Kwajalein and Wotje Islands in the Marshall Islands and Jaluit, Makin, and Mili Islands in the Gilbert Islands. At Kwajalein, aircraft from the carrier *Enterprise* sink a transport and damage nine other vessels while the heavy cruisers *Northampton* and *Salt Lake City* sink a gunboat; the destroyer *Dunlap* sinks an auxiliary submarine chaser at Wotje. In the Gilbert Islands, aircraft from the carrier *Yorktown* strafe a gunboat and cargo ship. The raids provide a much-needed morale boost to U.S. Navy forces in the Pacific.

3 FEBRUARY
NAVY

The submarine *Trout* serves as an undersea transport, delivering ammunition to forces defending Corregidor Island in Manila Bay, Philippine Islands, and departing with a cargo that includes 20 tons of gold and silver from Philippine banks.

4 FEBRUARY
NAVY

Japanese naval land attack planes bomb an Allied naval force under the command of Rear Admiral Karel

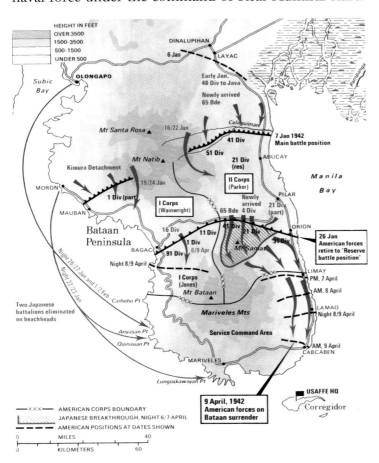

W. F. M. Doorman, Royal Netherlands Navy, in the Java Sea. Two Dutch light cruisers are damaged by near misses. The heavy cruiser *Houston*'s rear gun turret is put out of action and the light cruiser *Marblehead* is damaged to such an extent that she is forced to return to Java and thence to the United States for repairs.

5 FEBRUARY
AIR FORCE

The Far East, Caribbean, Hawaiian, and Alaskan Air Forces are redesignated the Fifth, Sixth, Seventh, and Eleventh Air Forces, respectively.

10 FEBRUARY
ARMY

Task Force Birch lands and sets up base camp on Christmas Island in the Indian Ocean.

MARINE CORPS

Marine Fighting Squadron 221 aircraft drive off a Japanese submarine after it fires two rounds from its deck gun against Midway Atoll.

11 FEBRUARY
NAVY

The Japanese destroyer *Yamakaze* sinks the submarine *Shark* with all hands east of Celebes Island, Dutch East Indies.

12 FEBRUARY
AIR FORCE

The Tenth Air Force is activated at Patterson Field, Ohio. During the war the unit will fight the Japanese in the China–Burma–India Theater, launching attacks from bases in southern Asia.

Above: *Antiaircraft gunners on the carrier* Enterprise *engage attacking Japanese planes off the Marshall Islands in February 1942. (Naval Historical Center)*

Below: *The light cruiser* Marblehead *receives repairs to her stern after being damaged by Japanese bombs in the Java Sea on 4 February 1942. (Naval Historical Center)*

MARINE CORPS

The 9th Marine Regiment is reactivated at Camp Elliott, California. The regiment is initially assigned to the 2d Marine Division to replace the absent 6th and 8th Marine Regiments.

13 FEBRUARY
ARMY

Entering the lagoon of Canton Island, in the central Pacific, the transport *President Taylor* goes aground short of the pier. Task Force Holly troops land without any loss of life, set up camp, and start a survey of the area to begin construction of an airstrip.

14 FEBRUARY
NAVY

Admiral Thomas C. Hart is relieved as Commander in Chief, Allied Naval Forces in the Southwest Pacific by Vice Admiral C. E. L. Helfrich, Royal Netherlands Navy.

16 FEBRUARY
MARINE CORPS

The 1st Separate Battalion (formerly 1st Battalion, 5th Marines) is redesignated the 1st Raider Battalion at Quantico, Virginia. On 19 February the 2d Separate Battalion (created at Camp Elliott, California, two weeks earlier) is similarly redesignated the 2d Raider Battalion.

17 FEBRUARY
ARMY

Task Force Bobcat arrives at Bora Bora, Society Islands, to develop a base on the vital supply line between the U.S. West Coast and Australia.

NAVY

The 1st Naval Construction Battalion, lead unit of the famed Seabees, arrives at Bora Bora, Society Islands.

17–18 FEBRUARY
MARINE CORPS/NAVY

Sailors without specific shipboard duties are assigned to augment the ranks of the 4th Marine Regiment on Corregidor Island, Philippine Islands. Survivors of other units eventually swell the Marine Corps regiment to almost 4,000 men (four times its pre-war size). The 4th Marines is responsible for the beach defenses of the island.

19 FEBRUARY
NAVY

An Allied naval force under the command of Rear Admiral Karel W. F. M. Doorman, Royal Netherlands Navy, engages Japanese ships retiring from support of the invasion of Bali, Dutch East Indies. In the resulting Battle of Badoeng Strait the Dutch destroyer *Piet Hein* is sunk; the U.S. destroyer *Stewart*, the Dutch light cruisers *Java* and *Tromp*, and two Japanese destroyers are damaged. *Stewart's* battle damage includes a hit aft below her water line, which floods the steering engine room. However, the

steering engine continues to operate under two feet of water, enabling the destroyer to return to Surabaya, Java, the following morning.

ARMY/NAVY

An attack against Darwin, Australia, by Japanese carrier aircraft results in the sinking of the destroyer *Peary*, which is hit by five bombs and loses 80 men killed; the U.S. Army transport *Meigs*; and the U.S. freighter *Mauna Loa*. The small seaplane tender (destroyer) *William B. Preston* is damaged along with two freighters. Japanese fighters attack a Darwin-based PBY Catalina flying boat of Patrol Squadron 22,

Above: *The "fighting bee" insignia of the famed Naval Construction Battalions (Seabees) was drawn by a civilian clerk working for the Navy. (Seabee Museum)*

Left: *Medical facilities like this field hospital become increasingly crude and supplies run low as the Japanese continue their attack on the defenses on the Bataan Peninsula in the Philippine Islands. (U.S. Army)*

wounding the pilot, who manages to put his damaged aircraft down on the water. A merchantman rescues the eight-man crew, but is subsequently sunk by Japanese aircraft. One of the PBY's crewmen is killed in the attack, but the remaining seven are eventually rescued for a second time. The pilot of the PBY is Lieutenant Thomas H. Moorer, who later becomes Chief of Naval Operations and Chairman of the Joint Chiefs of Staff.

20 FEBRUARY
NAVY

As the aircraft carrier *Lexington* approaches Rabaul, New Britain Island, for planned attacks against the Pacific stronghold, she is spotted by a Japanese flying boat. Subsequently a squadron of Japanese planes attacks the carrier. With the guns of his wingman's F4F Wildcat malfunctioning, forcing his return to the carrier, Lieutenant Edward H. "Butch" O'Hare of Fighter Squadron 3 is left to defend the ship against the attackers. In a heroic feat of airmanship, the fighter pilot is credited with destroying five Japanese bombers and damaging another in defense of the carrier (postwar records indicate he actually shot down four and damaged two). Antiaircraft gunners and other defending aircraft thwart the other enemy bombers. For his actions, O'Hare receives the Medal of Honor.

The submarine *Swordfish* embarks Philippine President Manuel Quezon, Vice President Sergio Osmeña, and their families, along with other government officials, to prevent their capture by the Japanese. They are brought from Mariveles to San Jose on the Philippine island of Panay.

22 FEBRUARY
NAVY

The damaged destroyer *Stewart* falls off the keel blocks in a Philippine drydock, necessitating her destruction in the face of invading Japanese forces. Subsequently salvaged and operated as a patrol boat in the Imperial Japanese Navy, she is eventually captured by U.S. forces at Kure, Japan. Recommissioned in the U.S. Navy on 29 October 1945, she is decommissioned the following May, ending a most unusual career.

23 FEBRUARY
AIR FORCE

The Japanese submarine *I-17* fires its deck gun at an oil refinery near Santa Barbara, California. Aircraft are sent to intercept and destroy the sub, but it escapes.

Six B-17 Flying Fortress bombers, survivors of the Philippine Islands campaign, make their first strike against Japanese installations at Rabaul, New Britain Island, as part of the Fifth Air Force.

24 FEBRUARY
NAVY

The ships of Task Force 16 (under Vice Admiral William F. Halsey Jr.), centered around the carrier *Enterprise*, attack Wake Island. While aircraft bomb and strafe the atoll, the guns of the heavy cruisers *Northampton* and *Salt Lake City* and destroyers *Balch*

and *Maury* bombard it from the sea. In addition to damage inflicted on shore installations, the attack sinks two enemy guardboats.

The submarine *Swordfish* continues its evacuation mission in the Philippine Islands, embarking the U.S. High Commissioner to the Philippine Islands, Francis B. Sayre, and his official party for transport from Manila Bay to Java.

27 FEBRUARY
AIR FORCE/NAVY

Allied air and naval units—including all available Army Air Forces B-17 Flying Fortresses, A-24 Banshees, P-40 Warhawks, and LB-30 Liberators—try to intercept a Japanese convoy of approximately 80 ships approaching Java.

NAVY

Japanese land attack planes conduct a series of bombing raids against the seaplane tender *Langley* (formerly the U.S. Navy's first aircraft carrier) in the waters south of Tjilatjap, Java. The ship, carrying Army Air Forces P-40 Warhawk fighters for service in Java, suffers such extensive damage that she must be abandoned. Her crew is picked up by the destroyers *Edsall* and *Whipple*. *Whipple* delivers the coup de grace to *Langley*, sinking the stricken ship.

Right: *Still painted in their prewar insignia, SBD-3 Dauntless dive-bombers from Bombing Squadron 6 prepare to take off from the carrier* Enterprise *for a raid against Wake Island. The striped tail and red ball in the center of the star are soon changed to prevent mistaken identity with the Japanese. (Naval Historical Center)*

27–28 FEBRUARY
NAVY

In the Battle of the Java Sea, an American–British–Dutch–Australian force consisting of 5 cruisers and 11 destroyers under the command of Rear Admiral Karel W. F. M. Doorman, Royal Netherlands Navy, engages a Japanese force covering an invasion convoy bound for Java. In the first day of action, Japanese guns and torpedoes sink two Allied destroyers; another sinks when she hits a mine. The following day a Japanese heavy cruiser sinks the Dutch light cruisers *De Ruyter* (Doorman's flagship) and *Java*. Admiral Doorman is killed in action, and the remaining Allied ships retire in an effort to reach Australia. The U.S. Navy submarines *S-37* and *S-38* rescue some survivors.

28 FEBRUARY–1 MARCH
NAVY

The heavy cruiser *Houston* and Australian light cruiser *Perth* engage three Japanese cruisers and nine destroyers in the Battle of Sunda Strait in the waters off Java. Torpedoes and gunfire from two Japanese heavy cruisers ravage the two Allied vessels, sinking *Perth* in one hour. *Houston* fights valiantly, damaging three Japanese destroyers. Eventually, she is stopped by torpedo hits and gunfire, and a shell burst kills her commanding officer, Captain Albert H. Rooks, who is posthumously awarded the Medal of Honor. *Houston*

sinks in the early morning hours of 1 March. Only 368 members of her crew of over 1,000 men survive the action, and they are captured by the Japanese.

1 MARCH
NAVY

With the impending fall of Java, the American–British–Dutch–Australian Command is dissolved.

The destroyer *Pope*, operating as part of a three-ship Allied force, comes under attack by four Japanese heavy cruisers in the waters off Java. *Pope* manages to avoid being hit by gunfire from the enemy ships; however, a near miss from a Japanese seaplane damages the destroyer and then enemy aircraft bomb her. *Pope* is eventually sunk by the Japanese heavy cruisers, and her surviving crew members are taken prisoner. One of them, Pope's executive officer Lieutenant Richard N. Antrim, later receives the Medal of Honor for heroic conduct while in captivity.

Just hours after the destroyer *Edsall* finishes transferring survivors from the seaplane tender *Langley* to the oiler *Pecos*, *Pecos* is sunk by planes from Japanese carriers in the waters south of Christmas Island. *Edsall* comes under fire from two Japanese battleships and two heavy cruisers, which together expend 1,141 shells in their effort to sink the resilient

destroyer. Carrier planes also participate in the attack, which kills all but five of *Edsall*'s crewmen, who are captured and eventually executed.

2 MARCH
NAVY
The destroyer *Pillsbury* is sunk by gunfire from Japanese heavy cruisers as she attempts to escape Java.

3 MARCH
NAVY
The submarine *Perch* is scuttled by her crew in the Java Sea after enduring three days of attacks by Japanese surface ships. The first depth charging, which occurs on the evening of 1 March, drives the boat to a depth of 135 feet and causes engine damage and flooding. Her attempt to surface and make repairs draws another depth charge attack that again forces the boat to submerge, damaging her ballast tanks.

Finally, able to make repairs, *Perch* makes a test dive in the early morning of 3 March, from which she is barely able to make it to the surface. She is then straddled by fire from two enemy cruisers and three destroyers, prompting the decision to scuttle her. All of her 59-man crew are taken prisoner. Six die in captivity.

The gunboat *Asheville* is sunk by Japanese destroyers south of Java with the loss of all but one crewman, who is captured and eventually dies in captivity.

4 MARCH
ARMY
After consultations in India, Lieutenant General Joseph W. Stilwell arrives to establish headquarters of the China–Burma–India theater of operations at Chungking, China.

NAVY
In another hit-and-run raid conducted by U.S. Navy forces, the carrier *Enterprise* launches SBD Dauntless dive-bombers against Japanese-held Marcus Island.

5 MARCH
AIR FORCE
Major General Lewis H. Brereton becomes the leader of U.S. Army Air Forces in India and Burma as he takes command of the newly activated Tenth Air Force. Its immediate duties are to defend the ferry route over the Himalaya Mountains. Initially it is also responsible for the Kunming-based China Air Task Force under Major General Claire L. Chennault.

Opposite, top: *"Battle of the Sunda Strait," John Hamilton, Navy Art Collection.*

Above: *Representative of the Army's transition to mechanized units, horsemen of the 26th Cavalry Regiment (Philippine Scouts) pass an M3 Stuart light tank as they move forward on Bataan, Luzon Island. The cavalrymen act as a screening force to delay the Japanese advance. (U.S. Army)*

Left: *One of the Provisional Tank Group's 80 M3 Stuart light tanks moves into position on Luzon Island, Philippine Islands. (Courtesy of Albert L. Allen Jr.)*

Left: *Soldiers arriving in Honolulu, Hawaii, from the U.S. in early 1942 carry M1903 Springfield rifles and wear World War I-style equipment. Hawaii is a training and refitting center for units headed for the frontline. (National Archives)*

Below: *Marines teach a group of Filipino soldiers the basics of a .30 caliber water-cooled Browning machine gun in a jungle clearing on Bataan Peninsula, Luzon Island. (National Archives)*

9 MARCH
AIR FORCE/ARMY

After fighting under Dutch command, the 2d Battalion, 131st Field Artillery is swept up in the Japanese conquest of Java. The ill-fated "lost battalion" of Texas artillerymen is among the prisoners forced to labor on the bridge over the Kwai River in Thailand, and remains imprisoned until 29 August 1945. Elements of the battered 19th Bombardment Group manage to evacuate to Broome, Australia.

10 MARCH
ARMY

The 27th (New York) Infantry Division is the first full division deployed from stateside to a Pacific area. The only unit to go overseas in the configuration of a "square" division of four infantry regiments, it is to be reconfigured to the newer three-regiment organization after it arrives in the Hawaiian Islands.

MARINE CORPS

The U.S. government purchases the 132,000-acre Santa Margarita Ranch on the Pacific coast between Los Angeles and San Diego, California, for use as a new Marine Corps base. It is soon named Camp Pendleton.

NAVY

Task Force 11 and Task Force 17, centered around the aircraft carriers *Lexington* and *Yorktown*, respectively, launch an air strike against Japanese shipping assembled at Lae and Salamaua, New Guinea Island. The raid, the first of the war to involve more than one American carrier, results in the sinking of an armed merchant cruiser, auxiliary minelayer, and transport, as well as damage to 10 other vessels. The most successful strike to date by U.S. Navy carriers, the raid prompts the Japanese to send aircraft carriers to the region to support offensive operations.

Right: *The Japanese attack on Hawaii in December 1941 causes the 2d Battalion, 131st Field Artillery, to be diverted from the Philippine Islands to Java Island. When Java falls in March 1942, 532 Soldiers of the battalion, along with 371 survivors of the heavy cruiser* Houston, *are prisoners. Of these, 668 are sent to Burma and Thailand as slave laborers to build a railroad through the jungle. Many die in captivity. ("Bridge on the River Kwai," James Dietz)*

11 MARCH
ALL SERVICES

With the imminent fall of the Philippine Islands to the Japanese, President Franklin D. Roosevelt orders General Douglas MacArthur to leave for Australia. After dark, MacArthur and Rear Admiral Francis Rockwell, along with family and a small number of staff members, depart Corregidor Island on four PT boats for a 560-mile trip to Mindanao Island, where they will board B-17 Flying Fortresses at a small civilian airstrip for the final leg. The dangerous PT boat trip takes three days; after delivering the MacArthur party on 14 March, the boats return to Luzon Island. The commander of the tiny flotilla, Lieutenant John D. Bulkeley, receives the Medal of Honor.

12 MARCH
ARMY

Army Task Force 6814, comprising 17,500 troops under Major General Alexander M. Patch, reaches the island of Nouméa, New Caledonia, where it will provide the core for the future Americal Division. Construction begins on an air base at Tontouta.

15 MARCH
ARMY

As Japanese forces push farther down the Bataan Peninsula, Philippine Islands, they are able to bring more artillery to bear on the U.S.-held islands in Manila Bay. The bombardment of Fort Drum and defensive gun positions on Corregidor Island is particularly heavy.

MARINE CORPS

Elements of Marine Aircraft Group 24 depart Ewa Field, Hawaii, for Efate, New Hebrides, to assist in establishing an airfield. Efate serves as a vital staging point supporting the subsequent Solomon Islands campaign.

17 MARCH
ARMY

General Douglas MacArthur lands at Darwin, Australia, and sets up his new headquarters. Regarding his departure from the Philippine Islands, he promises, "I shall return."

Left: *Motor Torpedo Boats, called PT boats, serve as water-borne scouts and patrol craft with a dangerous sting in their four torpedoes. Boats like these help evacuate senior American and Philippine officers and their families from the Philippine Islands. (Naval Historical Center)*

Opposite, top: *General Douglas MacArthur (right) and Major General Jonathan M. Wainwright, the two senior commanders in the Philippine Islands, confer during field maneuvers. Wainwright becomes a Japanese prisoner in May. (MacArthur Memorial and Archive, Norfolk, VA)*

Opposite, bottom: *Soldiers of the U.S. 31st Infantry Regiment prepare a camouflaged position on Bataan Peninsula, Luzon Island. (National Archives)*

MARINE CORPS
Engineers complete the airfield on Tutuila Island, American Samoa.

18 MARCH
ARMY
A small force of the 182d Infantry and engineers from the Americal Division arrive at Efate, New Hebrides, to build an airstrip.

19 MARCH
NAVY
Lieutenant John D. Bulkeley's *PT-41*, the same one used to evacuate General Douglas MacArthur, transports Philippine President Manuel Quezon and 13 others from Negros to Mindanao, Philippine Islands.

20 MARCH
MARINE CORPS
The United States assumes responsibility for defending Western (or British) Samoa. The 7th Defense Battalion moves from American Samoa to the island of Upolu, Western Samoa.

1 APRIL
ARMY
General Douglas MacArthur receives the Medal of Honor for his actions in the Philippine Islands.

MARINE CORPS
The 8th Defense Battalion is organized on American Samoa.

2 APRIL
AIR FORCE
The Tenth Air Force launches its first combat mission. Three heavy bombers, led by Major General Lewis H. Brereton, strike shipping targets near Port Blair, India.

MARINE CORPS
The first flight echelon of Marine Aircraft Group 13 flies into Tutuila Island and assumes responsibility for the air defense of American Samoa.

3 APRIL
ARMY/NAVY
Commander in Chief, U.S. Pacific Fleet Admiral Chester W. Nimitz assumes additional duties as

Commander in Chief Pacific Ocean Areas, directing operations in the North, Central, and South Pacific. General Douglas MacArthur is named Allied Supreme Commander, Southwest Pacific Area.

6 APRIL
AIR FORCE

In preparation for the arrival of 16 B-25 Mitchell bombers for the planned aerial raid on Tokyo, Japan, 10 Pan American Airways DC-3s begin to transfer 30,000 gallons of fuel and 500 gallons of oil from Calcutta to Asansol, India. The fuel is subsequently moved to China. This airlift is the first resupply mission over the Himalaya Mountains. The B-25s that are expected to land at these Chinese airfields never make it. After their daring raid against Tokyo, the aircraft are unable to locate the fields because the aircraft carrying the radio homing beacon crashes in poor weather.

NAVY

The river gunboats *Mindanao* and *Oahu* claim the destruction of four Japanese landing barges in a night attack in Manila Bay, Luzon Island, Philippine Islands.

8 APRIL
NAVY

The submarine *Seadragon* delivers food to forces on Corregidor Island and takes aboard naval radio and communications intelligence personnel, thus

completing the evacuation of the last group of these vital specialists from the Philippine Islands.

9 APRIL
ARMY/MARINE CORPS/NAVY

Badly outnumbered American and Filipino forces are overwhelmed and Bataan, Luzon Island, Philippine Islands, falls. With food and ammunition gone, Major General Edward P. King Jr. surrenders the surviving "Battling Bastards of Bataan," 75,000 American and Filipino soldiers. The surviving but surrounded American forces continue to fight from the island

fortresses of Corregidor Island and Fort Drum in Manila Bay, Luzon Island.

MARINE CORPS
Battery C of the 4th Marine Regiment escapes from Bataan to Corregidor Island, Philippine Islands, which Japanese heavy artillery continues bombarding.

NAVY
The surrender of forces on the Bataan Peninsula, Luzon Island, Philippine Islands, prompts the destruction of naval facilities at Mariveles to prevent their use by the Japanese, and the scuttling of the submarine tender *Canopus*, minesweeper *Bittern*, tug *Napa*, and drydock *Dewey*. Small craft, including ferries and motor launches, help transport retreating troops from Bataan to Corregidor.

The motor torpedo boats *PT-34* and *PT-41* engage a Japanese light cruiser and torpedo boat off Cape Tanon on the island of Cebu, Philippine Islands. A torpedo hits the cruiser but fails to explode. *PT-34* is later bombed and strafed by floatplanes and is beached at Cauiut Island. She is destroyed by a second air attack. Of her six-man crew, two are killed and three wounded.

9–11 APRIL
ARMY
The advance elements of the 41st Infantry Division arrive in Australia. The division assembles at a training base 65 miles from Melbourne.

10 APRIL
ALL SERVICES
The six-day Bataan Death March begins, with 76,000 Allied prisoners of war, including 12,000 Americans, making the 60-mile forced march from the Bataan Peninsula, Luzon Island, Philippine Islands. Approximately 10,000 die or are killed by their captors during the march in the sweltering heat. Those who

survive are kept in prisons near Manila, where an additional 1,600 Americans and nearly 16,000 others die from a variety of causes.

NAVY
In a reorganization of the U.S. Pacific Fleet, the following type commands are established:

Aircraft Carriers: Vice Admiral William F. Halsey Jr.
Amphibious Force: Vice Admiral Wilson Brown Jr.
Battleships: Rear Admiral Walter S. Anderson
Cruisers: Rear Admiral Frank Jack Fletcher
Destroyers: Rear Admiral Robert A. Theobald
Patrol Wings: Rear Admiral John S. McCain
Service Force: Vice Admiral William L. Calhoun
Submarine Force: Rear Admiral Thomas Withers

Opposite, top: *Faced with a hopeless situation, Major General Edward P. King, commander of American and Philippine forces on Bataan Peninsula, Luzon Island, surrenders his forces in April 1942. Corregidor Island holds for another month. (U.S. Army)*

Opposite, bottom: *An antiaircraft gun crew of the 200th Coast Artillery poses with an M2 3-inch gun. The unit is one of six coast artillery regiments in the Philippine Islands. (National Archives)*

Right: *A Japanese photographer took this staged photo of Americans and Filipinos surrendering on Bataan Peninsula, Luzon Island. (Hulton-Getty Archives)*

12 APRIL
MARINE CORPS/NAVY

Sailors in the Philippine Islands are formed into a unit designated the 4th Battalion, 4th Marine Regiment.

18 APRIL
AIR FORCE/NAVY

Sixteen B-25 Mitchell bombers under Lieutenant Colonel James H. Doolittle take off from the carrier *Hornet* to bomb targets in Tokyo, and three other cities in the Japanese homeland. When a Japanese guard boat spots the ships of Naval Task Force 16, the planes are launched early with insufficient fuel to reach airfields in China. After hitting their targets, the planes continue on. Fifteen planes crash or ditch in the sea near the China coast and two crews are captured. One plane makes it to Vladivostok, USSR,

where the plane and crew are interned. The crew escapes in 1943. Damage to Japan is minimal, but the raid is a great boost to American morale.

MARINE CORPS

Fighting Squadron 211 flies onto Palmyra Atoll from the carrier *Lexington*.

NAVY

The submarine *Searaven* completes the evacuation of Royal Australian Air Force personnel from Japanese-occupied Timor in the Dutch East Indies.

20 APRIL
MARINE CORPS

The Fleet Marine Force Training Center is established at Camp Elliott, California. Although initially used in

training battalions, it becomes the primary location for training men in individual skills prior to their assignment to a combat unit.

24 APRIL
MARINE CORPS
Glider Group 71 and Marine Glider Squadron 711, the only numbered units devoted to glider operations in the Marine Corps during the war, are formed from the Glider Detachment at Parris Island, South Carolina.

28 APRIL
MARINE CORPS
Major General Charles F. B. Price and his staff arrive in Samoa and establish the Headquarters Samoan Area Defense Force. The 1st Raider Battalion and 2d Barrage Balloon Squadron also reinforce the Samoan garrison.

1 MAY
MARINE CORPS
The 8th Defense Battalion arrives at Wallis Island to garrison this outpost west of the Samoas. Marine Fighting Squadron 223 under Major John L. Smith and Marine Fighting Squadron 224 under Major Robert Galer are organized at Ewa, Hawaii. Smith and Galer are destined to receive Medals of Honor for actions on Guadalcanal Island, Solomon Islands.

2 MAY
ARMY
With 26 Americans, 13 British, 16 Chinese, and a number of Chinese nurses from the Seagrave military hospital, Lieutenant General Joseph W. Stilwell starts

the long walk toward Allied territory in the wake of the collapse of Allied forces in northern Burma.

3 MAY
NAVY
In the last submarine evacuation of personnel from the island fortress of Corregidor Island in Manila Bay, Philippine Islands, the submarine *Spearfish* departs carrying nurses and other personnel.

4 MAY
NAVY
Aircraft from the carrier *Yorktown* strike Japanese shipping supporting the landing of ground forces on Tulagi in the Solomon Islands. Four vessels are sunk and four are damaged. The action foreshadows the Battle of the Coral Sea.

6 MAY
ALL SERVICES
Following days of almost constant air and artillery bombardment of Corregidor Island, Philippine Islands, a Japanese regiment comes ashore in the morning at several places on the island's north end. Men of the 4th Marine Regiment and several provisional groups of Army, Navy, and Air Corps personnel mount a defense and inflict heavy losses, but are unable to repulse the landings. By mid-day, the Japanese have fought their way up the island, almost to Malinta Tunnel, where the American headquarters and hundreds of wounded are sheltered. At mid-day Lieutenant General Jonathan M. Wainwright, acting commander of American forces, recognizes the inevitable and, wishing to avoid further casualties,

Opposite: *Hundreds of American and Philippine servicemen die on the brutal 60-mile "death march" from Bataan, Luzon Island, to a Japanese prison camp. ("Bataan Death March," James Dietz)*

Right: *B-25 Mitchell bombers of Lieutenant Colonel James Doolittle's Tokyo raiding force sit on the stern of the carrier* Hornet *as the secret task force sails for Japan. (U.S. Air Force)*

sends Marine Corps Captain Gollard L. Clark with a white flag bearer, a translator, and a musician blowing a trumpet to the Japanese lines to request negotiations. He also orders all documents and weapons larger than a pistol destroyed and the garrison's flag burned. Colonel Samuel L. Howard, commander of the 4th Marine Regiment, orders the regiment's colors burned. The surrender of all American and Filipino forces, including 19 generals, is signed at midnight. Avoiding capture, the crew of the minesweeper *Quail* scuttles their ship and sets out for

Australia in a motor launch. The 18 sailors, including their commander, Lieutenant Commander John H. Morrill, reach Darwin, Australia, on 6 June.

7 MAY
AIR FORCE/NAVY
The two-day Battle of the Coral Sea opens when surface ships under the command of Rear Admiral John G. Crace, British Royal Navy, attempt to intercept a Japanese invasion force bound for Port Moresby, New Guinea Island. The ships are bombed

Left: *National Guardsmen of the 102d Observation Squadron pose in front of a C-45A transport. The unit also flew O-47 observation planes in antisubmarine patrols along the U.S. West Coast. (National Guard Educational Foundation)*

first by land-based Japanese bombers and are later mistakenly attacked by Army Air Forces aircraft. Meanwhile, on board the aircraft carriers *Lexington* and *Yorktown*, aircraft launch for an attack against the Japanese ships escorting the Port Moresby invasion force. These planes send the Japanese light carrier *Shoho* to the bottom, which prompts Lieutenant Commander Robert Dixon, skipper of Scouting Squadron 2, to radio the electrifying message, "Scratch one flattop!" Meanwhile, Japanese aviators damage the oiler *Neosho* and sink the destroyer *Sims*. On board the oiler, Chief Watertender Oscar V. Peterson overcomes his wounds to close bulkhead stop valves, helping save the lives of shipmates. Severely burned, he soon dies,

and later is awarded a posthumous Medal of Honor for his actions. The fatally damaged ship he fought so hard to save is scuttled on 11 May.

8 MAY
NAVY
In the battle of the Coral Sea, aircraft of the two opposing carrier forces spot one another, triggering a launching of strike groups. Naval aviators from *Lexington* and *Yorktown* strike first, heavily damaging the Japanese carrier *Shokaku*. One pilot, Lieutenant John J. Powers, dives to within 200 feet of the enemy carrier's deck before releasing his bomb and is last seen attempting to recover from his dive. He receives a

Above: *Two SBD-3 Dauntless dive-bombers from Scouting Squadron 3 are depicted on a dawn mission in 1942. ("Dauntless Against a Rising Sun," William S. Phillips)*

Left: *The stricken carrier* Lexington *burns in the Coral Sea on 8 May 1942. The ship begins to recover after being hit by Japanese torpedoes and bombs, but gasoline vapors explode inside the ship. (Naval Historical Center)*

posthumous Medal of Honor for his actions. Japanese pilots score hits on *Lexington* and *Yorktown*, despite the heroic defense of pilots like Lieutenant William H. Hall who, while flying an SBD Dauntless dive-bomber in anti-torpedo defense, is credited with shooting down three aircraft. Hall receives the Medal of Honor for his actions. On board *Lexington*, the damage is made worse when gasoline vapors ignite, resulting in explosions that signal the carrier's end. The destroyer *Phelps* scuttles the stricken carrier. *Yorktown* suffers severe bomb damage, but the efforts of men like Lieutenant Milton E. Ricketts, who receives a posthumous Medal of Honor for fighting fires despite being mortally

wounded, save the ship. The Battle of the Coral Sea marks the first time a naval battle is fought without the opposing surface forces coming within sight of each other. The costly battle achieves the strategic goal of blunting Japanese aims on Port Moresby.

MARINE CORPS
The 3d Marine Brigade arrives at Tutuila, American Samoa, and begins building an airfield and defenses. It takes control of the 7th Defense Battalion.

13 MAY
ARMY
The last of the 41st Infantry Division arrives in Australia with advance elements of the 32d Infantry Division. The 32d and 41st Divisions are charter members of the U.S. I Corps under Major General Robert L. Eichelberger. The 32d is moved to Camp Cable near Brisbane in July.

18 MAY
AIR FORCE
The Seventh Air Force is placed on alert anticipating an attack at Midway Island. Immediately, older B-18 Bolo bombers, although still used, are rapidly replaced with newer B-17 Flying Fortresses.

20 MAY
ARMY
Lieutenant General Joseph W. Stilwell reaches Imphal, India, at the end of his march from Burma through mountains and jungle. The undiplomatic Stilwell

Left: *Lieutenant General Joseph Stilwell leads his men over jungled mountains on a 140-mile retreat out of Burma to India. ("Vinegar Joe Stilwell," by Mort Künstler, © 1960 Mort Künstler, Inc.)*

Opposite: *Soldiers en route to New Caledonia Island in the southwest Pacific practice firing their M3 37mm antitank gun at a floating target. New Caledonia is a major staging and supply point for American forces. (National Archives)*

declares, "We got a helluva beating." Stilwell learns that the Japanese have launched a major invasion of China.

NAVY

Rear Admiral John S. McCain assumes duties as Commander Air Force, South Pacific, a new command which plays a central role in the upcoming campaign on Guadalcanal Island, Solomon Islands.

21 MAY
NAVY

The North Pacific Force is established under Rear Admiral Robert A. Theobald to cover operations in Alaskan waters.

25 MAY
MARINE CORPS

Companies C and D of the 2d Raider Battalion and elements of the 3d Defense Battalion arrive on Midway Atoll to reinforce the garrison.

26 MAY
MARINE CORPS

16 SBD Dauntless dive-bombers and seven F4F Wildcat fighters of Marine Aircraft Group 22 arrive to reinforce Midway Atoll.

27 MAY
ARMY

The Americal Division under Major General Alexander M. Patch is formed on New Caledonia Atoll from the elements of Army Task Force 6814. It is the only U.S. division in World War II with a name instead of a number. In postwar years it becomes the 23d Infantry Division.

28 MAY
ARMY/MARINE CORPS

Soldiers and Marines occupy Espiritu Santo, New Hebrides Islands, to accelerate airfield development.

3 JUNE
AIR FORCE/ARMY

Nine B-17 Flying Fortress bombers from the Seventh Air Force attack the Japanese fleet consisting of 45 ships, nearly 600 miles southwest of Midway Atoll. The next day, other B-17s from Kauai, Hawaii, attack a different force only 150 miles north of Midway.

AIR FORCE/NAVY

The pivotal Battle of Midway opens when a PBY Catalina patrol plane flown by Ensign Jack Reid spots the Japanese occupation force carrying troops for the invasion of Midway Atoll. Aircraft from Midway attack the enemy ships. On the morning of 4 June, a PBY flown by Lieutenant Howard P. Ady radios a message indicating the sighting of Japanese carriers. Midway-based aircraft immediately launch strikes as do aircraft from the carriers *Yorktown*, *Enterprise*, and *Hornet* operating northeast of Midway. They seek out the enemy while aircraft from four Japanese carriers attack Midway. The initial attacks against the Japanese carriers meet determined antiaircraft fire and an umbrella of Zero fighters, which cut through the U.S. aircraft. The U.S. torpedo squadrons are hard hit, with only 4 of 41 aircraft managing to land back aboard their carrier. However, attacks against the lumbering TBD Devastator torpedo-bombers bring the Japanese fighters down to low altitude just as SBD Dauntless dive-bombers arrive on the scene. Within minutes, three of the four Japanese carriers are raging infernos and eventually sink. Later in the day, the SBDs knock the surviving carrier out of action, but not before she is able to launch two strikes that severely damage *Yorktown*. On 6 June, the Japanese submarine *I-168* torpedoes the damaged *Yorktown* and the destroyer *Hamman*, sinking the destroyer. A Japanese heavy cruiser is also sunk by air attack. *Yorktown* sinks on 7 June, the last casualty of the Battle of Midway. Some Army Air Forces bombers also participate in the battle. The American victory at Midway turns the tide of the Pacific War.

MARINE CORPS

In the initial aerial attacks of the Battle of Midway, 108 Japanese planes strike the atoll. Marine Fighting Squadron 221 loses most of its aircraft, though they combine with antiaircraft gunners on Midway Atoll to destroy 11 attackers and damage 14 others. Marine Scout Bombing Squadron 241 also suffers heavy losses among its dive-bombers, but fails to achieve hits on the enemy fleet. Captain Richard E. Fleming's aircraft crashes into the Japanese cruiser *Mikuma*, and he subsequently receives the Medal of Honor.

6 JUNE
AIR FORCE

Seventh Air Force commander Major General Clarence L. Tinker is lost while leading a flight of LB-30 bombers from Midway Atoll on a predawn bombing raid on Wake Island. Tinker is the first Army Air Forces general officer to be killed in action during the war. Major General Willis H. Hale takes command on 20 June.

6–7 JUNE
ARMY

The Japanese invade the western Aleutian Islands, landing 1,800 men on Attu and Kiska Islands.

9 JUNE
AIR FORCE

President Franklin D. Roosevelt awards newly promoted Brigadier General James "Jimmy" Doolittle, then assigned to the First Special Aviation Project, the Medal of Honor for his role in planning and leading the 18 April raid on Tokyo.

AIR FORCE/NAVY

Lieutenant Commander Lyndon B. Johnson, future thirty-sixth President of the United States, inspects facilities in the Pacific while on leave from his seat in the House of Representatives. He climbs aboard an Army Air Forces B-26 Marauder bomber for a raid against Lae, New Guinea Island, only to have his plane turn back short of the target because of engine trouble. The future Commander in Chief receives the Silver Star from the Army for the mission.

11 JUNE
AIR FORCE

Reconnaissance confirms Japanese garrisons have been established on both Attu and Kiska Islands in the Aleutian Islands. The Eleventh Air Force strikes Kiska for the first time. Five B-24 Liberator and five B-17 Flying Fortress bombers attack recently occupied Kiska Harbor installations and attack Japanese ships. For the next year, whenever the Eleventh Air Force has spare airpower, it bombs the island of Kiska.

Above: *The Japanese carrier* Shoho *burns after attacks by planes from the carriers* Lexington *and* Yorktown *during the Battle of the Coral Sea, on 7 May 1942. (Naval Historical Center)*

Left: *Two TBD-1 Devastator torpedo-bombers begin their attack on distant Japanese ships in the Battle of the Coral Sea. (Robert L. Rasmussen)*

14 JUNE
MARINE CORPS

The advance echelon of the 1st Marine Division arrives in New Zealand; the movement of all personnel is completed on 11 July.

19 JUNE
NAVY

The South Pacific Area and South Pacific Force is established and placed under the command of Vice Admiral Robert L. Ghormley.

The submarine *S-27* runs aground off St. Makarius Point on Amchitka in the Aleutian Islands. The crew employs rubber boats to get ashore and all are rescued by PBY Catalina aircraft on 24–25 June.

22 JUNE
ARMY

All units under Lieutenant General Joseph W. Stilwell are assigned to American Army Forces in India, China, and Burma.

25 JUNE
ARMY

With the Allies facing a critical situation in the Middle East, Major General Lewis H. Brereton is

Above: *The Japanese carrier* Akagi *is repeatedly hit by bombs from SBD Dauntless dive-bombers and set aflame during the Battle of Midway in early June 1942. Four Japanese carriers are sunk in the epic battle. ("The Famous Four Minutes," R.G. Smith)*

Below: *TBD-1 Devastator torpedo-bombers of Torpedo Squadron 6 prepare to launch from the carrier* Enterprise *at the start of the Battle of Midway. Only four of the planes return. (Naval Historical Center)*

ordered from New Delhi, India, to Egypt "with all available heavy bombers."

26 JUNE
MARINE CORPS
The 1st Marine Division receives the warning order for an amphibious assault against the Guadalcanal–Tulagi area in the southern Solomon Islands, after discovery of Japanese construction of an airfield on Guadalcanal.

30 JUNE
MARINE CORPS
The strength of the Marine Corps on active duty is 7,138 officers and 135,475 enlisted.

1 JULY
NAVY
The submarine *Sturgeon* torpedoes and sinks the Japanese transport *Montevideo Maru* off Luzon Island, Philippine Islands. Among those killed are 1,050 Allied prisoners of war being transported to Hainan Island, China.

2 JULY
ARMY/NAVY
A directive from the Joint Chiefs of Staff prescribes that the offensive on the islands of New Britain, New Ireland, and New Guinea be conducted in three phases, with 1 August as the target date. Boundaries between the South Pacific (Navy) and Southwest Pacific (Army) commands, as altered, place the lower Solomon Islands within the South Pacific zone.

4 JULY
AIR FORCE
The American Volunteer Group (AVG) "Flying Tigers" is replaced when the Chinese Air Task Force is activated. Major General Claire L. Chennault is named commander of the unit, which is incorporated into the Army Air Forces as the 23d Pursuit Group. The AVG had destroyed 300 Japanese aircraft

both in the air and on the ground, losing 50 aircraft of its own and only nine pilots. Only five pilots join the AAF after the merger; the rest of the volunteers return home.

10 JULY
MARINE CORPS
Marine Corps Air Station, El Centro, California, is established.

NAVY
A PBY Catalina of Patrol Squadron 41 spots the wreckage of a Japanese Zero fighter that crashed in a bog during strikes against the Aleutian Islands on 3 June. The aircraft is subsequently salvaged and restored to flying condition, proving beneficial in refining fighter designs and tactics.

13 JULY
AIR FORCE/NAVY
The German submarine *U-153*, after being damaged by the submarine chaser *PC-458* and an Army Air Forces aircraft, is sunk off Panama by the destroyer *Lansdowne*.

14 JULY
MARINE CORPS
The Marine Corps Glider Base, Edenton, North Carolina, is established. It is redesignated Marine Corps Air Station Edenton on 13 July 1943, following termination of the Marine Corps' glider program.

15 JULY
MARINE CORPS
Elements of the 4th Defense Battalion arrive at Espiritu Santo, New Hebrides, to help protect an air base there.

18 JULY
NAVY
The Amphibious Force, South Pacific is established under the command of Rear Admiral Richmond Kelly Turner.

21 JULY
MARINE CORPS
The 1st Base Depot establishes an advance echelon in New Zealand to provide logistics support to units in the area.

Above: *Ground crews prepare two 19th Bomb Group B-17 Flying Fortresses at Del Monte airfield on Mindanao Island for what may be the last mission before evacuating to Australia. ("Bottom of the First," James Dietz)*

Left: *Marines of the 1st Marine Division approach the shore of Guadalcanal Island, Solomon Islands, in landing craft on 7 August 1942. (Naval Historical Center)*

Right: *Japanese reinforcements land at night on Guadalcanal Island, Solomon Islands, to resist the U.S. invasion. ("Landing of Japanese Troops on Guadalcanal," John Hamilton, Navy Art Collection)*

Below: *Soldiers of the 32d Infantry Division wait with their equipment on board a ship sailing for New Guinea Island. They wear makeshift helmet covers and carry both M1 Garand and M1903 Springfield rifles. (National Archives)*

25 JULY
ARMY

Equipped with B-17 Flying Fortresses, four squadrons of the 11th Bombardment Group under Colonel LaVerne G. Saunders complete deployment from Hawaii. Two squadrons are based on New Caledonia Island; one is on Efate Island, New Hebrides Islands, and one on Fiji.

26 JULY
ARMY

In New Zealand, Major General Millard F. Harmon takes command of the newly created U.S. Army Forces in the South Pacific Area. Harmon plans to transfer his command post to Noumea, New Caledonia Island, as planning for offensive operations in the Solomon Islands gets into high gear.

2 AUGUST
MARINE CORPS

The first F4F-3P Wildcat photographic planes of Marine Observation Squadron 251 land on the recently completed airfield at Espiritu Santo, New Hebrides Islands.

4 AUGUST
NAVY

The destroyer *Tucker*, her crew unaware of the presence of a minefield in the waters off Segond Channel, Espiritu Santo, New Hebrides Islands, hits a mine and sinks with the loss of six of her crew.

6–7 AUGUST
AIR FORCE

Although he is not scheduled to fly, Captain Harl Pease Jr. leads a strike by the 93d Squadron, 19th Bomb Group, comprised of survivors of the Philippine Islands campaign. Flying a B-17 Flying Fortress bomber deemed "unserviceable for combat" and with only three hours' rest, Pease leads a foray that is

intercepted by 30 enemy fighters. He is lost on the mission. Earlier in the year Pease had flown the B-17 that carried General Douglas MacArthur from Mindanao Island, Philippine Islands, to Australia.

7 AUGUST
MARINE CORPS/NAVY

Operation WATCHTOWER begins as the Amphibious Force, South Pacific, under the command of Rear Admiral Richmond Kelly Turner, lands the 1st Marine Division on Florida, Tulagi, Gavutu, Tanambogo, and Guadalcanal Islands in the Solomon Islands, marking the first American offensive of the war. The 1st Marine Division (less the 7th Marine Regiment) and reinforcing elements (2d Marine Regiment, 1st Raider Battalion, 1st Parachute Battalion, and 3d Defense Batalion) are supported by air and surface forces under the command of Vice Admiral Frank Jack Fletcher. The Marines quickly advance inland and on 8 August capture an airstrip under construction on Guadalcanal, which they christen Henderson Field after Major Lofton Henderson, a Marine Corps aviator killed at the Battle of Midway. During the first two days of operations, Japanese air attacks damage the destroyers *Mugford* and *Jarvis* and transports *Barnett* and *George F. Elliott*, the latter to such an extent that she is scuttled.

9 AUGUST
MARINE CORPS/NAVY

A Japanese surface force consisting of four heavy cruisers, three light cruisers, and a destroyer under the command of Vice Admiral Gunichi Mikawa engage in a night action against U.S. and Australian ships protecting transports unloading off Guadalcanal Island, Solomon Islands. In the Battle of Savo Island, the Japanese score a stunning victory, sinking the heavy cruisers *Astoria*, *Quincy*, and *Vincennes*. The Australian cruiser *Canberra* is so badly damaged that she is scuttled, and the heavy cruiser *Chicago* and destroyers *Patterson* and *Ralph Talbot* suffer damage. Though no Japanese surface ships are sunk, American gunners score hits on four enemy ships, including Mikawa's flagship. Despite their victory, the Japanese ships fail to descend upon the defenseless transports. Nevertheless, the tenacity of Japanese air assaults since 7 August prompts the withdrawal of carrier air support and the transports without completing the unloading of supplies and forces. The Marines ashore are short of critical items, including food, and begin subsisting on two meals a day.

NAVY

The destroyer *Jarvis*, an enemy torpedo having already put a 50-foot gash in her side on 8 August, faces a determined attack by Japanese land-based aircraft as she steams towards Australia for repairs. Her gunners shoot down two of the attackers and damage a third to such an extent that it is forced to ditch. However, the destroyer, which first fired her guns at Japanese aircraft at Pearl Harbor, Hawaii, on the morning of 7 December 1941, is sunk with loss of all hands.

12 AUGUST
MARINE CORPS/NAVY

Lieutenant Colonel Frank Goettge, 1st Marine Division intelligence officer, leads a 25-man patrol to the Matanikau River area of Guadalcanal Island to

Right: *Terrain and vegetation on Guadalcanal Island, Solomon Islands, vary. Near the coast are palm groves, mangrove swamps, and jungle, while the interior of the island has many ridges and open tall grass areas. (Dept. of Defense)*

Below: *Lieutenant Colonel Evans F. Carlson (left), commander of the 2d Marine Raider Battalion, and his executive officer, Major James Roosevelt, hold a Japanese flag captured by their raiders on Makin Atoll during the August 1942 raid. (unknown)*

check out reports of Japanese willing to surrender. The patrol is attacked, and only three Marines escape alive. CUB-1, a Navy aviation ground support unit, arrives on Guadalcanal to provide the initial maintenance echelon for Marine Corps aircraft.

17 AUGUST
MARINE CORPS/NAVY
Companies A and B, 2d Marine Raider Battalion land from the submarines *Nautilus* and *Argonaut* on Makin Atoll in the Gilbert Islands to destroy enemy installations and conduct a diversionary raid in support of the offensive on Guadalcanal Island, Solomon Islands. The Marines, supported by fire from the deck gun of *Nautilus*, defeat the garrison, but heavy surf

disrupts their withdrawal and delays it until the next night. Marine Corps casualties during the raid are 18 dead, 16 wounded, and 12 missing. Of the latter, nine are captured soon after and beheaded on Kwajalein Atoll, Marshall Islands, by the Japanese. Major James Roosevelt, son of the President, participates in the raid as executive officer of the 2d Raiders.

19 AUGUST
MARINE CORPS
Three companies of the 5th Marine Regiment conduct attacks against Japanese forces around Matanikau and Kokumbona villages on Guadalcanal Island, Solomon Islands.

20 AUGUST
MARINE CORPS/NAVY
The escort carrier *Long Island* transports the first Marine Corps aircraft to Guadalcanal Island, Solomon Islands. The first echelons of Marine Aircraft Group 23 and the 1st Marine Aircraft Wing (19 F4F Wildcat fighters of Marine Fighting Squadron 223 and 12 SBD Dauntless dive-bombers of Marine Scout Bombing Squadron 232) land on Henderson Field.

21 AUGUST
MARINE CORPS
The roughly 900 Japanese soldiers of the Ichiki Force attack the 1st Marine Regiment along what was thought to be the Tenaru River (actually the Ilu River)

on Guadalcanal Island, Solomon Islands. After repulsing the assault, Marines cross the river and envelop the remaining enemy, almost completely wiping out the attackers. Major John L. Smith of Marine Fighting Squadron 223 scores the first aerial kill for a Guadalcanal-based fighter, shooting down a Japanese Zero fighter. This is the first of 19 aircraft Smith will down during the war. For his actions, he receives the Medal of Honor.

22 AUGUST
NAVY

Having completed the landing of Japanese troops on Guadalcanal Island, Solomon Islands, the Japanese destroyer *Kawakaze* encounters the destroyers *Blue* and *Henley*. *Blue* is torpedoed, killing 9 and wounding 21 members of her crew. The damaged *Blue* is towed to the Solomon Islands and scuttled off Florida Island the following day.

24 AUGUST
MARINE CORPS/NAVY

F4F Wildcats of Marine Fighting Squadron 223 fight their first big aerial battle with the Japanese at Guadalcanal Island, Solomon Islands, downing 16 enemy at a cost of 4 of their own aircraft. Captain Marion E. Carl becomes the first Marine Corps ace of the war after he destroys three enemy planes that, combined with two kills at Midway, brings his total to five. Air battles become an almost-daily occurrence hereafter. Eleven Navy SBD dive-bombers from *Enterprise* land at Henderson Field to temporarily reinforce what is now referred to as the "Cactus Air Force," after Guadalcanal's code name Cactus. Marine Aircraft Group 25 begins arriving in Hawaii.

Above: *A tired Marine Corps weapons squad moves forward on Guadalcanal Island, Solomon Islands. ("Weary Trail," Kerr Eby, Navy Art Collection)*

Left: *A camera catches the moment a Japanese bomb explodes on the carrier* Enterprise *during the Battle of the Eastern Solomons in August 1942. This bomb inflicts only minor damage, but other heavier battle damage requires the ship to withdraw to Hawaii for repairs. (Naval Historical Center)*

Right: *Heavy jungle and coastal swamps limit visibility and movement, making patrolling Guadalcanal Island especially difficult and dangerous. ("U.S. Marines in Dense Jungle on Guadalcanal," John Hamilton, Navy Art Collection)*

MARINE CORPS/NAVY

In the Battle of the Eastern Solomons, the carriers *Saratoga* and *Enterprise* engage Japanese carriers supporting a major effort to reinforce Japanese troops on Guadalcanal. SBD Dauntless dive-bombers and TBF Avenger torpedo bombers score hits on the Japanese carrier *Ryujo*, but fail to hit the large-deck carriers *Shokaku* and *Zuikaku*, whose planes attack *Enterprise*. The "Big E" is heavily damaged and retires to Pearl Harbor, Hawaii, for repairs. The following day the dive-bombers of Marine Scout Bombing Squadron 232 assist in sinking a Japanese destroyer and a transport, which turns back an enemy effort to land troops on Guadalcanal.

27–28 AUGUST
MARINE CORPS

Landing craft place the 1st Battalion, 5th Marine Regiment ashore near Kokumbona, leading to two days of inconclusive fighting with Japanese forces near the Matanikau River on Guadalcanal Island, Solomon Islands.

28 AUGUST
MARINE CORPS/NAVY

Marine Corps and Navy SBD dive-bombers operating from Henderson Field successfully turn back Japanese

destroyers attempting to land reinforcements on Guadalcanal Island, Solomon Islands, sinking one ship and damaging two others.

NAVY

The light minelayer *Gamble* employs repeated depth charge attacks to sink the Japanese submarine *I-123* off Florida Island in the Solomon Islands.

30 AUGUST
MARINE CORPS

Captain John L. Smith, commanding officer of Marine Fighting Squadron (VMF) 223, shoots down four Japanese Zero fighters at Guadalcanal Island, Solomon Islands, giving him nine total kills and temporarily making him the leading Marine Corps ace. Marine Fighting Squadron 224 and Marine Scout Bombing Squadron 231 arrive on Henderson Field, and a new Japanese brigade begins landing on the island. The commander of VMF-224, Major Robert E. Galer, will receive the Medal of Honor for his actions during the Guadalcanal campaign, including shooting down 11 enemy aircraft.

NAVY

Japanese land-based bombers attack the high-speed transport *Colhoun* off Kukum Point, Guadalcanal

Island, Solomon Islands, and the transport sinks with 51 members of her crew.

31 AUGUST
NAVY

The aircraft carrier *Saratoga* takes a torpedo from the Japanese submarine *I-26* while operating 260 miles southeast of Guadalcanal Island, Solomon Islands. The carrier is forced to retire from the combat zone for repairs.

PBY Catalinas of Patrol Squadrons 42 and 43 join the destroyer *Reid* in sinking the Japanese submarine *RO-61* off Atka Island, Aleutian Islands.

1 SEPTEMBER
AIR FORCE/ARMY/NAVY

Some 4,500 troops move ashore rapidly to secure Adak Island, Aleutian Islands. The advanced air base will be used to attack Kiska Island, some 250 miles distant. Army plans are to have 10,000 or more troops on Adak by mid-October. On 11 September a runway is completed.

MARINE CORPS

The 12th Marine Regiment is reactivated as an artillery regiment at San Diego, California.

NAVY

Vice Admiral Aubrey W. Fitch becomes the first Commander Air Force, Pacific Fleet.

The Sixth Naval Construction Battalion lands at Lunga Point on Guadalcanal Island, Solomon Islands, becoming the first Seabees to serve in a combat zone.

3 SEPTEMBER
AIR FORCE

Lieutenant General George C. Kenney takes command of the Fifth Air Force in Brisbane, Australia. Kenney replaces Lieutenant General George Brett, who had been recalled to the U.S. one month before.

In the first U.S. raid over the city of Hanoi, Vietnam, a B-25 Mitchell medium bomber drops both bombs and pamphlets on the city and an airfield, where munitions and nine aircraft are destroyed or damaged.

MARINE CORPS

Brigadier General Roy S. Geiger and the command echelon of the 1st Marine Aircraft Wing reach Guadalcanal Island, Solomon Islands, via a Marine Aircraft Group (MAG) 25 R4D Skytrain transport plane and assume control of all air elements on the island. MAG-25 begins shifting from Hawaii to New Caledonia Island. MAG-25 will become the nucleus of South Pacific Combat Air Transport Command (SCAT), which will remain in existence until February 1945. Highly productive in carrying men and material, in one six-month period SCAT aircraft carry 18 million pounds of freight and 130,000 passengers.

4 SEPTEMBER
MARINE CORPS

Two companies of the 1st Raider Battalion sweep Savo Island, Solomon Islands, for reported enemy, but find nothing.

5 SEPTEMBER
NAVY

A Japanese destroyer, assisted by a flare mistakenly dropped from a PBY Catalina patrolling the area, sinks the high-speed transports *Gregory* and *Little* operating off Lunga Point, Guadalcanal Island, Solomon Islands.

8 SEPTEMBER
MARINE CORPS

The 1st Raider Battalion and attached 1st Parachute Battalion conduct an amphibious raid at Tasimboko, Guadalcanal Island, Solomon Islands, and defeat the rear echelon of the Japanese Kawaguchi Brigade. Elements of the 3d Barrage Balloon Squadron arrive on Tulagi.

9 SEPTEMBER
CIVIL DEFENSE

A Japanese E14Y-1 floatplane is launched from a submarine near the U.S. West Coast. The aircraft makes two flights near the northern California border, drops four bombs, and starts a forest fire. This is the only direct attack upon the continental United States by enemy aircraft during the war.

11 SEPTEMBER
NAVY

In a first for Navy medicine, Pharmacist's Mate First Class Wheeler B. Lipes performs an appendectomy on Seaman First Class Darrell D. Rector on a mess table on board the submarine *Seadragon* while the boat is submerged on patrol in the South China Sea.

12–14 SEPTEMBER
MARINE CORPS

The 1st Raider Battalion and 1st Parachute Battalion defend a low coral ridge south of Henderson Field on Guadalcanal Island, Solomon Islands, during two nights of assaults by the Kawaguchi Brigade. Toward the end of the second night, 2d Battalion, 5th Marine Regiment is brought up to reinforce the raiders and parachutists. The Japanese are turned back after suffering heavy casualties in what becomes known as the Battle of Edson's Ridge, after the Raider's commanding officer, Lieutenant Colonel Merritt Edson. He receives the Medal of Honor for his leadership in the battle.

Right: *Dense brush and jungle brings fighting on Guadalcanal Island, Solomon Islands, down to the lowest infantry unit level, with ambushes and aggressive patrolling employed by both sides. ("Guadalcanal Ambush," James Dietz)*

14 SEPTEMBER
ARMY

Japanese forces on Kiska Island, Aleutian Islands, are attacked for the first time by B-24 Liberator bombers accompanied by fighters (42d and 54th Fighter Squadrons) from Adak Island. Despite heavy antiaircraft fire, bombers drop more than 100 tons of bombs in September and 200 tons in October.

MARINE CORPS

The 3d Marine Regiment arrives at Tutuila Island, Samoa.

15 SEPTEMBER
AIR FORCE/ARMY

General Douglas MacArthur orders the 32d (Red Arrow) Infantry Division under Major General Edwin F. Harding to reinforce hard-pressed Australian forces near Port Moresby, New Guinea Island. As part of MacArthur's offensive plan, the division makes an air and sea movement to Port Moresby. Elements of the 126th Infantry Regiment, the first U.S. infantry troops in New Guinea, are flown in by Fifth Air Force transports. They are followed by the 128th Infantry Regiment. On 17 September, patrols begin probing for advance air field sites and trails to bypass Japanese

units. Using this pioneering air movement, the entire division, less some rear elements, arrives in New Guinea by 29 September.

NAVY

The Japanese submarine *I-19* fires a spread of torpedoes at the ships of Task Force 18 covering a convoy bound for Guadalcanal Island, Solomon Islands. The battleship *North Carolina*, the destroyer *O'Brien*, and the aircraft carrier *Wasp* are hit. Feeding on aviation gasoline, fires on the carrier also trigger ammunition explosions and force Captain Forrest P. Sherman, a future Chief of Naval Operations, to give the order to abandon ship. The destroyer *Lansdowne* scuttles the carrier.

18 SEPTEMBER
MARINE CORPS

The 7th Marine Regiment lands and returns to the 1st Marine Division on Guadalcanal Island, Solomon Islands. The same ships depart with the depleted 1st Parachute Battalion.

19 SEPTEMBER
MARINE CORPS

Marine Corps Air Station Eagle Mountain Lake is established at Fort Worth, Texas, to serve as a glider training base. With the end of the Marine Corps glider program, the base is transferred to the Navy in 1943 only to be returned to Marine Corps service in 1944.

20 SEPTEMBER
MARINE CORPS

The 3d Raider Battalion is organized in Samoa.

22 SEPTEMBER
MARINE CORPS

The 5th Barrage Balloon Squadron arrives on New Caledonia Island.

23–27 SEPTEMBER
MARINE CORPS

In the second Battle of the Matanikau on Guadalcanal Island, Solomon Islands, the 1st Battalion, 7th Marine Regiment is briefly trapped behind enemy lines

following an amphibious landing, while strong enemy defenses prevent the 1st Raider Battalion and 2d Battalion, 5th Marine Regiment from crossing the river. Lieutenant Colonel Lewis B. "Chesty" Puller oversees the battalions fighting amphibious withdrawal.

24 SEPTEMBER
ARMY
The I Corps opens its first Pacific command post at Rockhampton, Australia, under Major General Robert L. Eichelberger. The 32d Infantry Division and the 41st Infantry Division are under I Corps.

Above: *The battleship* South Dakota *sets up a curtain of antiaircraft fire during the Battle of the Santa Cruz Islands in October 1942. ("Air Defense: Battle of Santa Cruz," Lt. Dwight C. Shepler, Navy Art Collection)*

Right: *A patrol receives its last instructions before starting a dangerous night mission on Guadalcanal Island. ("Final Instructions," Col. Donald L. Dickson, USMCR, Art Collection, National Museum of the Marine Corps, Triangle, Virginia)*

MARINE CORPS

Marine Corps Air Station Mojave, California, is established.

25 SEPTEMBER
AIR FORCE

In a rare day of acceptable flying weather, Eleventh Air Force aircraft team up with Canadian P-40 Kittyhawk fighters in attacks against Kiska and Little Kiska Islands, Aleutian Islands. This operation is the first combined mission of the Eleventh and the Canadians.

1 OCTOBER
AIR FORCE/ARMY

General Douglas MacArthur's Southwest Pacific General Headquarters issues its plan to force Japan out of New Guinea Island by recapturing the small ports on the north coast, starting with the encirclement and seizure of Buna. Allied advances will be made from three directions over the mountains and along the coast. The 2d Battalion, 126th Infantry Regiment with a field hospital begins its move over the mountains on 7 October. The trail and terrain are so bad that most supplies must be air dropped by the Fifth Air Force.

MARINE CORPS

Major General Holland M. Smith's Amphibious Training Staff, Fleet Marine Force is disbanded and takes over the duties of the headquarters element of the Amphibious Corps, Pacific Fleet at San Diego, California. The I Marine Amphibious Corps forms at San Diego under Major General Clayton B. Vogel.

4 OCTOBER
MARINE CORPS

Headquarters, Marine Aircraft Wing, Pacific arrives at Ewa, Hawaii, from San Diego, California.

5 OCTOBER
NAVY

The aircraft carrier *Hornet*, in an attempt to hinder resupply of Guadalcanal Island, Solomon Islands, by the famed "Tokyo Express," launches an air strike against Japanese staging areas in the area of Buin-Tonolei and Faisi on Bougainville Island, Solomon Islands. The raid results in damage to two Japanese destroyers and near misses on two seaplane carriers.

Above: *Marine Corps Captain Joseph J. Foss and his F4F-4 Wildcat (later an F4D Corsair) are a deadly combination in the Pacific sky. He ends the war with 26 kills. ("Joe Foss Downs a Zero," Robert T. Horvath, National Museum of the Marine Corps)*

Below: *The last moments of a Japanese destroyer are photographed through the periscope of the U.S. submarine that had torpedoed the ship. (National Archives)*

A PBY Catalina, the personal aircraft of Commander Aircraft South Pacific, sinks the Japanese submarine *I-22* near Indispensable Strait in the Solomon Islands.

7 OCTOBER
ARMY
Captain Alfred Medendorp sets out with a small force ahead of the 2d Battalion, 126th Infantry Regiment on a difficult march over the Kapa Kapa Trail across the Owen Stanley Mountain Range of New Guinea Island. On 10 October the main body of the 2d Battalion follows. The rugged march takes until 24 October.

7–9 OCTOBER
MARINE CORPS
In the third Battle of the Matanikau on Guadalcanal Island, Solomon Islands, the 3d Battalion, 2d Marine Regiment with the 1st and 2d Battalions, 7th Marine Regiment cross the upper Matanikau River and attack toward the coast, destroying a Japanese battalion, while the 2d and 3d Battalions, 5th Marine Regiment and the 1st Raider Battalion defeat a Japanese company holding the mouth of the river.

9 OCTOBER
MARINE CORPS
Aircraft of Marine Fighting Squadron 121 arrive on Henderson Field, Guadalcanal Island, Solomon Islands, to bolster the Cactus Air Force.

11 OCTOBER
NAVY

A powerful Japanese surface force aiming to reinforce the garrison defending Guadalcanal and bombard Henderson Field enters the "Slot"—the body of water running the length of the Solomon Islands chain from Bougainville to Guadalcanal Island. In response, a task group under the command of Rear Admiral Norman Scott maneuvers into a blocking position. In the resulting Battle of Cape Esperance, which begins late in the evening, gunners on board the heavy cruiser *Salt Lake City* and light cruiser *Boise* score numerous hits on the Japanese heavy cruiser *Furutaka*, which sinks the following day. The American task force also sinks the destroyer *Fubuki* and damages the destroyer *Hatsuyuki* and heavy cruiser *Aoba*. The Japanese force's commander, Rear Admiral Aritomo Goto, is killed in the engagement. The Japanese damage both *Salt Lake City* and *Boise*, and also score hits on the destroyers *Duncan* and *Farenholt*. *Duncan* sinks the following day.

12 OCTOBER
MARINE CORPS/NAVY

During action in the waters off Guadalcanal Island, Solomon Islands, Navy aircraft based temporarily at Henderson Field join their Marine Corps counterparts in sinking the Japanese destroyer *Natsugumo* and damaging the destroyer *Murakumo* to such an extent that she is scuttled.

13 OCTOBER
ARMY

The 2,852 soldiers of the 164th Infantry Regiment, Americal Division, under Colonel Bryant E. Moore, join the Marines on Guadalcanal Island, Solomon Islands. They quickly go into action near Henderson Field.

MARINE CORPS

The depleted 1st Raider Battalion leaves Guadalcanal Island, Solomon Islands, for recuperation on New Caledonia Island. That night, two Japanese battleships bombard Henderson Field, destroying half of the Cactus Air Force and large quantities of aviation gasoline.

14 OCTOBER
ARMY/MARINE CORPS

On Guadalcanal Island, Solomon Islands, Japanese planes and artillery bomb and shell Henderson Field by day, then two cruisers bombard the airstrip that night.

15 OCTOBER
MARINE CORPS/NAVY

American and Japanese naval aircraft trade attacks against forces attempting to reinforce Guadalcanal Island, Solomon Islands. While Navy and Marine Corps aircraft from Henderson Field attack a convoy heading up the Slot, carrier planes from the Japanese carrier *Zuikaku* stage attacks against vessels of Task Units 62.4.5 and 62.4.6. Three Japanese cargo ships and the U.S. destroyer *Meredith* are sunk. Seven officers and 56 enlisted men from the destroyer's crew survive the sinking and subsequent three days drifting in shark-infested waters.

16 OCTOBER
MARINE CORPS

Lieutenant Colonel Harold Bauer and his Marine Fighting Squadron 212 arrive at Guadalcanal Island, Solomon Islands, after a flight from Efate, New Hebrides Islands, just as a Japanese air attack is ending. Despite being nearly out of fuel, Bauer engages the enemy and shoots down four dive-bombers.

Right: *In October, Soldiers of the 164th Infantry Regiment, Americal Division, arrive on Guadalcanal to help the Marines secure the island. The troops off-load supplies and equipment on the beach, including four M3 37mm antitank guns, which are effective against bunkers and other dug-in positions. (National Archives)*

Right: *On Guadalcanal Island, Marines line up for hot chow, a welcome luxury even though it is rationed and uses captured rice and fish. (USMC)*

Below: *The carrier* Hornet *defends herself against attacking Japanese planes during the Battle of the Santa Cruz Islands in October 1942. The ship suffers fatal damage. ("The Fighting Hornet," Tom Lea, Army Art Collection, U.S. Army Center of Military History)*

For this feat he eventually receives the Medal of Honor, though the award is posthumous after Bauer is lost in combat in November 1942. Marine Aircraft Group 14 relieves MAG-23 as the aviation administrative and logistics element on Guadalcanal.

NAVY

The submarine *Thresher* plants mines in the approaches to the harbor at Bangkok, Thailand, the first such operation performed by a U.S. Navy submarine during World War II.

17–18 OCTOBER
AIR FORCE/ARMY

The Fifth Air Force air lifts the 128th Infantry Regiment and Australian troops to Wanigela, New Guinea Island, as the start point for their advance along the coast toward Buna. Heavy rain hinders the movement, but patrols are sent on 21 October.

18 OCTOBER
NAVY

Vice Admiral William F. Halsey Jr. relieves Vice Admiral Robert L. Ghormley as Commander South Pacific Area and South Pacific Force at the direction of Admiral Chester W. Nimitz, who decides that "a more aggressive commander" is needed.

19 OCTOBER
ARMY

The 25th Infantry Division under Major General J. Lawton Collins is ordered to prepare for deployment from Schofield Barracks, Hawaii, to the South Pacific. The plan is to stage through New Caledonia Island en route to Guadalcanal Island, Solomon Islands.

20 OCTOBER
NAVY

The Japanese submarine *I-176* torpedoes the heavy cruiser *Chester* southeast of San Cristobal, in the Solomon Islands. Hitting the ship amidships on the starboard side, the torpedo causes a blast that kills 11 sailors and wounds 12 others. The cruiser retires to Espiritu Santo, New Hebrides Islands, for repairs.

21 OCTOBER
AIR FORCE

Tenth Air Force B-24 Liberator bombers of the Indian Air Task Force attack the Lin-his coal mines near Kuyeh, China. The attack marks the first use of heavy bombers in China and the Allied Air Forces' first attacks north of the Yangtze and Yellow rivers.

23 OCTOBER
MARINE CORPS

Antitank guns and artillery crush a diversionary Japanese tank and infantry assault across the Matanikau River on Guadalcanal Island, Solomon Islands. The 4th Raider Battalion is organized in southern California.

24–26 OCTOBER
ARMY/MARINE CORPS

On Guadalcanal Island, Solomon Islands, the Japanese Sendai Division attacks the 1st Battalion, 7th Marine Regiment south of Henderson Field. Elements of the 164th Infantry Regiment reinforce the Marines' lines during the night and assume responsibility for the threatened zone the second night. The Japanese are repulsed with heavy losses. Another diversionary attack across the Matanikau River is defeated by the 2d Battalion, 7th Marine Regiment. In the air on the 25th, Captain Joe Foss shoots down five enemy planes during two sorties, bringing his total kills to 16, which he accumulates in a 12-day period.

25 OCTOBER
AIR FORCE/MARINE CORPS/NAVY

Navy, Marine Corps, and Army Air Forces aircraft from Henderson Field, Guadalcanal Island, Solomon Islands, damage one Japanese destroyer and bomb the light cruiser *Yura* to such an extent that she is abandoned. The Japanese sink the tug *Seminole* and district patrol vessel *YP 284*, and damage the high-speed minesweeper *Zane*.

26–27 OCTOBER
NAVY

In the battle of the Santa Cruz Islands, the carriers *Enterprise* and *Hornet*, under the command of Rear Admiral Thomas C. Kinkaid, engage four Japanese carriers under the command of Vice Admiral Chuichi

Right: *The destroyer* Smith *is struck near her forward 5-inch gun by a Japanese aircraft during the Battle of the Santa Cruz Islands in October 1942. One of two U.S. carriers also damaged in the fighting can be seen in the distance. ("The Smith Still Fights," Lt. Dwight C. Shepler, Navy Art Collection)*

Nagumo. American aviators hit the carriers *Zuiho* and *Shokaku* and damage the heavy cruiser *Chikuma* and destroyer *Terutsuki*. However, Japanese pilots find both *Enterprise* and *Hornet*, damaging the latter to such an extent that she is abandoned. Attempts to scuttle *Hornet* fail and she is sunk by Japanese destroyers on 27 October. Enemy fliers also score hits on the battleship *South Dakota* and light cruiser *San Juan*, and a damaged aircraft plunges into the destroyer *Smith*. In addition, the destroyer *Hughes* collides with *Hornet* while fighting fires on board the carrier and taking off survivors, and the destroyer *Porter* is damaged by a torpedo that accidentally fires when a battle-damaged TBF Avenger torpedo bomber ditches in her vicinity. She is later scuttled. The action ends in a tactical victory for the Japanese.

Above: *An SBD-3 Dauntless flown by Tech Sergeant John Fogerty takes off from Henderson Field, Guadalcanal Island, for a bombing mission on 22 October 1942. He does not return. ("Fogerty's Fate," Col. Albert M. Leahy, Art Collection, National Museum of the Marine Corps, Triangle, Virginia)*

Left: *Marines jump down from an amphibious tractor during one of several landings made on the Guadalcanal coast to bypass Japanese defenses. (National Archives)*

Right: *A long line of Marines wades through one of the many rivers that flow to the coast of Guadalcanal Island, often ending in malaria-infested swamps or tidal mud flats. (Marine Corps Research Center)*

28 OCTOBER
MARINE CORPS
The I Marine Amphibious Corps arrives at Noumea, New Caledonia Island. It is initially purely an administrative command to control Marine Corps units in rear areas of the South Pacific command.

29 OCTOBER
NAVY
A PBY Catalina of Patrol Squadron 11 sinks the Japanese submarine *I-172* off San Cristobal, Solomon Islands.

31 OCTOBER–1 NOVEMBER
MARINE CORPS
Marine Fighting Squadron 211 and Marine Scout Bombing Squadron 132 reach Henderson Field, Guadalcanal.

NOVEMBER
MARINE CORPS
Marine Aircraft Group 11 moves to Espiritu Santo, New Hebrides Islands.

1–3 NOVEMBER
ARMY/MARINE CORPS
With support from the division scout-snipers and the 3d Battalion, 7th Marine Regiment screening the flank, the 5th Marine Regiment attacks west across the Matanikau River to destroy a pocket of Japanese around Point Cruz, Guadalcanal Island, Solomon Islands. The 2d Marine Regiment and 1st Battalion, 164th Infantry Regiment move past Point Cruz to establish a new defensive line to the west.

2 NOVEMBER
AIR FORCE/ARMY
Using small coastal boats, units of the 128th Infantry Regiment move by night from Wanigela, New Guinea Island, to new positions near Mendarou on the coast. The Fifth Air Force completes transporting the last elements of the regiment from Wanigela on 4 November. Together with attached Australian troops, the 128th Infantry Regiment is designated Task Force Warren.

ARMY/MARINE CORPS
A battery each of Marine Corps and Army 155mm guns arrive on Guadalcanal Island, Solomon Islands.

3–9 NOVEMBER
ARMY/MARINE CORPS
The Battle of Koli Point, Guadalcanal Island, Solomon Islands, opens with the 2d Battalion, 7th Marine Regiment skirmishing with Japanese reinforcements arriving by sea to the east of the Marines' perimeter. The 164th Infantry Regiment and 1st Battalion, 7th Marine Regiment move up to assist and help destroy part of the enemy, with the rest escaping inland.

4 NOVEMBER
ARMY

The 147th Infantry Regiment under Colonel W. B. Tuttle heads to Guadalcanal Island, Solomon Islands. With support from a provisional artillery battery out of the Americal Division, the regiment makes an amphibious landing near Lunga Point.

ARMY/MARINE CORPS/NAVY

The 8th Marine Regiment and 1st Battalion, 10th Marine Regiment arrive at Lunga Point on Guadalcanal Island, Solomon Islands. Two companies of the 2d Raider Battalion secure a new beachhead at Aola Bay and are joined by the 1st Battalion, 147th Infantry Regiment, a battery of Army artillery, and a Navy Seabee unit. Brigadier General Edmund B. Sebree is given command of the section west of the Lunga River.

6 NOVEMBER
AIR FORCE/ARMY

The Fifth Air Force completes airlift of the 1st Battalion, 126th Infantry Regiment from Port Moresby, New Guinea Island, to rough airstrips inland. The 3d Battalion is brought by air on 12 November. The two battalions assemble at Natunga and prepare for the advance on Buna.

ARMY

General Douglas MacArthur's advance General Headquarters moves to Port Moresby, New Guinea Island. MacArthur arrives to direct operations.

MARINE CORPS

The 2d Raider Battalion companies set out from Aola Bay, Guadalcanal Island, Solomon Islands, to track

Above: *Keeping supplies flowing from ships to the shore units on Guadalcanal Island is a major undertaking, requiring many types of vehicles and good organization. ("Discharging Stores at Lunga Point," John Hamilton, Navy Art Collection)*

Left: *Brigadier General Nathan F. Twining (left), Major General Millard F. Harmon (center), and another officer examine a map in preparation for Operation CARTWHEEL. Harmon is commander of Army Forces, South Pacific Area. (National Archives)*

down enemy elements escaping the encirclement at Koli Point.

10 NOVEMBER
MARINE CORPS
Three more companies of the 2d Raider Battalion land at Tasimboko, Guadalcanal Island, Solomon Islands, and move to join the rest of the battalion.

11 NOVEMBER
ARMY/MARINE CORPS
Elements of the 2d and 8th Marine Regiments and the 164th Infantry Regiment pull back from Point Cruz to the eastern side of the Matanikau River in preparation for an anticipated Japanese assault on the main American perimeter on Guadalcanal Island, Solomon Islands. The 2d Raider Battalion engages Japanese forces at Asamama.

12 NOVEMBER
AIR FORCE
P-38 Lightning fighters of the 339th Fighter Squadron move to Henderson Field, Guadalcanal Island, Solomon Islands. One of the P-38s is destroyed the next night by Japanese naval artillery fire.

ARMY
The 182d Infantry Regiment under Colonel Daniel W. Hogan is the second major element of the Americal Division to land in Guadalcanal Island. During December, remaining elements of the Americal (16,196 troops) join the division in the frontlines.

MARINE CORPS
Captain Joe Foss shoots down three Japanese planes at Guadalcanal Island, Solomon Islands, making him the first American pilot to achieve 20 kills in the war. Marine Scout Bombing Squadrons 131 and 142 arrive on Guadalcanal.

NAVY
Rear Admiral Richmond Kelly Turner's Task Force 67 begins unloading reinforcements at Guadalcanal Island, Solomon Islands. Meanwhile 11 Japanese transports bearing 11,000 soldiers—escorted by 2 battleships, 1 cruiser, and 11 destroyers—enter the Slot and set course for the embattled island. Over the course of the next three days, the U.S. and Japanese navies wage two pivotal sea battles in the waters around Guadalcanal.

13 NOVEMBER
AIR FORCE/NAVY
After being forced to ditch in the Pacific Ocean some 600 miles north of Samoa, the crew of a B-17D Flying Fortress bomber—World War I ace Eddie Rickenbacker, Colonel Hans C. Adamson, and Private John F. Bartek—is rescued by a Navy OS2U Kingfisher seaplane. The trio had been afloat on a raft for 21 days.

ALL SERVICES
The Battle of Guadalcanal begins in the darkness just after midnight when two heavy cruisers, three light cruisers, and eight destroyers under the command of Rear Admiral Daniel J. Callaghan engage Japanese

Right: *Marine Corps Lieutenant A. C. Emerson flies his battered F4F Wildcat fighter in the Battle of the Santa Cruz Islands in October 1942. He adds two more enemy planes to his tally at the end of the battle. (Tom Lea, Army Art Collection, U.S. Army Center of Military History)*

Above: *"Battle of Guadalcanal," John Hamilton, U.S. Navy Memorial Foundation.*

Below: *A B-17 Flying Fortress banks away after a low level bombing attack on Japanese facilities on Gizo Island, Solomon Islands, in October 1942. (U.S. Navy)*

warships under the command of Vice Admiral Hiroaki Abe. The U.S. Navy ships turn back the enemy vessels, which intended to fire their guns on Henderson Field. Four destroyers and the light cruiser *Atlanta* are sunk or scuttled, one of the hits on the cruiser coming inadvertently from the heavy cruiser *San Francisco*, taking the life of Rear Admiral Norman Scott. On board *San Francisco*, enemy fire kills Rear Admiral Callaghan. Also among those killed on the ship are Boatswain's Mate First Class Reinhardt Keppler, who courageously battles fires and aids his wounded shipmates despite his own wounds. He receives a posthumous Medal of Honor. The light cruiser *Juneau* is damaged by enemy fire and later torpedoed by the Japanese submarine *I-26*. She sinks in 20 seconds. All but 10 members of her crew perish, including the five Sullivan brothers. Japanese losses include the battleship *Hiei*, damaged by gunfire and sunk by aircraft from the carrier *Enterprise* and Henderson Field. Two destroyers are also sunk and six ships suffer damage.

At daybreak, aircraft from the carrier *Enterprise* join planes from Henderson Field in attacking enemy ships in the Slot. During the three-day battle, Army airplanes from the 11th Bomb Group, 69th, 70th, and 72d Bomb Squadrons and the 39th and the 339th Fighter Squadrons participate. In the first strike a heavy cruiser is sunk and five other ships are damaged.

Later in the day airmen send seven transports and freighters to the bottom. Shortly before midnight on 14 November the battleships *Washington* and *South Dakota* along with four destroyers under the command of Rear Admiral Willis A. Lee Jr. engage in a night action with the battleship *Kirishima*, four cruisers, and nine destroyers. Japanese gunfire and torpedoes sink the destroyers *Preston* and *Walke*, with the loss of 204 sailors. The following morning, the main batteries of *Washington* sink *Kirishima* and the destroyer *Ayanami*, while the U.S. destroyer *Benham* is so damaged that she is scuttled. On the afternoon of 15 November, planes and artillery hammer ships carrying Japanese reinforcements, sinking four transports. This marks the end of the Battle of Guadalcanal, the last time major Japanese naval forces enter the waters around the island. It is the beginning of the end for Japanese forces on the island, and on 31 December the Japanese command decides to evacuate Guadalcanal. Organized resistance on the island ends on 9 February 1943.

16 NOVEMBER
AIR FORCE/ARMY
On New Guinea Island, the 126th Infantry Regiment (the 2d battalion) and Task Force (TF) Warren under Brigadier General Hanford MacNider initiate the attack toward Buna in concert with an advance by Australian infantry. The 126th Infantry marches overland, following its 2d Battalion sent ahead in October. TF Warren advances along the coast in two parallel battalion columns, with the 1st Battalion nearest the water and 3d Battalion on its left. A fleet of small barges with sorely needed supplies for TF

Warren is attacked and destroyed by 18 enemy aircraft; the 32d Infantry Division commander, Major General Edwin F. Harding, and surviving staff members must swim ashore. The Fifth Air Force begins emergency resupply by air.

19 NOVEMBER
ARMY
Task Force Warren continues its attack on New Guinea Island against stiff Japanese resistance. The two battalions of the 126th Infantry Regiment are diverted from their direction of march to assist the Australian 7th Division. Major General Edwin F. Harding receives a message from General Douglas MacArthur to press the attack "regardless of cost."

20–22 NOVEMBER
ARMY
On New Guinea Island, heavy enemy fire halts the 3d Battalion, 128th Infantry Regiment (Task Force Warren) with heavy losses. Completing its long, mountainous trek, the 2d Battalion, 126th Infantry Regiment arrives in the division area. After dark on 22 November, it crosses the Gira River on rafts to assist the task force.

23–29 NOVEMBER
ARMY
On New Guinea Island, Task Force (TF) Urbana is formed by combining the 2d Battalion, 126th Infantry Regiment, and 2d Battalion, 128th Infantry Regiment under the commander of the 128th Infantry Regiment. TF Urbana suffers more losses at a fortified trail crossing area known as the "Triangle," and makes little

Right: *P-40 Warhawk fighters like this one hidden in a jungle clearing are the main American strength in China. In July 1942, there are only 40 American aircraft there compared to more than 200 Japanese planes. (National Archives)*

Left: *M3 Stuart light tanks of the Australian 6th Armored Regiment join with U.S. and Australian infantry in December 1942 to reinforce the Allied effort to push the Japanese out of Buna, New Guinea Island. (U.S. Army Center of Military History)*

Below: *On 7 December 1942, the anniversary of the attack on Hawaii, the new battleship* New Jersey *is launched at the Philadelphia Navy Yard. (AP Images)*

headway. TF Warren commander Brigadier General Hanford MacNider is wounded and replaced. On 24 November, another assault by TF Urbana on the Triangle fails. TF Warren resumes its attack to secure an airstrip on 26 November with little success. Back at Port Moresby, the 32d Division's 127th Infantry Regiment

arrives. Both task forces repeat their attacks on the Buna Village complex and the Triangle with no gains.

30 NOVEMBER
MARINE CORPS
The 2d Raider Battalion surprises and routs a Japanese force on the slopes of Mount Austen on Guadalcanal Island, Solomon Islands.

NAVY
In the Battle of Tassafaronga, four heavy cruisers, one light cruiser, and six destroyers attack Japanese destroyers attempting to resupply troops on Guadalcanal Island, Solomon Islands. The Japanese quickly fire a spread of torpedoes that damage the heavy cruisers *Pensacola, Northampton, New Orleans,* and *Minneapolis. Northampton* sinks the following day, as does a Japanese destroyer.

DECEMBER
ARMY
Brigadier General Raymond K. Wheeler, commander of Services of Supply for the China–Burma–India Theater, is given responsibility to build a road from China through the mountains and jungle of Burma to Ledo, India, in order to supply U.S. and Chinese forces in China. This engineering marvel becomes known as the "Ledo Road."

1 DECEMBER
ARMY

The I Corps' headquarters remains in Australia as Lieutenant General Robert L. Eichelberger, accompanied by his chief of staff, reports to General Douglas MacArthur in Port Moresby, New Guinea Island. He is told to relieve the 32d Division commander and to "take Buna or not come back alive."

4 DECEMBER
ARMY

After inspecting the Task Force Urbana front near Buna Village, New Guinea Island, Lieutenant General Robert L. Eichelberger replaces the 32d Infantry Division commander, Major General Edwin F. Harding, with Brigadier General Albert W. Waldron.

5 DECEMBER
ARMY

Following a heavy air and artillery preparation, Task Forces Urbana and Warren again assault Japanese fortifications around Buna Village, New Guinea Island. TF Urbana makes some gains, but Brigadier General Albert W. Waldron is wounded during the attack and Brigadier General Clovis E. Byers takes division command. TF Warren's attack fails with heavy casualties.

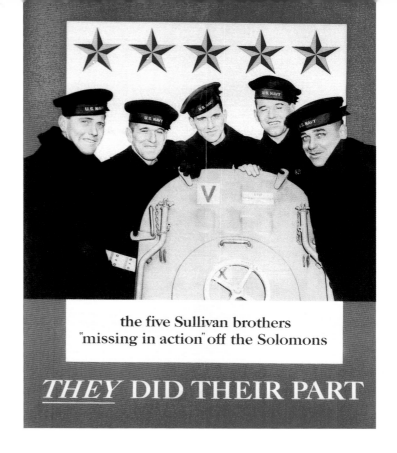

the five Sullivan brothers "missing in action" off the Solomons

THEY DID THEIR PART

Above: *This poster memorializes the sacrifice of the Sullivan brothers, who are killed when the light cruiser* Juneau *is sunk in November 1942. (Naval Historical Center)*

Below: *It takes four months of fighting to clear Japanese forces from Buna, New Guinea Island. ("Red Arrow at War: 32d Infantry Division at Buna," Michael Gnatek Jr., National Guard Bureau)*

Above: To make the most efficient use of the limited cargo space, large vehicles like trucks are shipped in pieces, then reassembled at the landing point. Twenty-five men can assemble six trucks a day. (National Archives)

Below: Army Air Forces Lieutenant Richard I. Bong uses his P-38 Lightning fighter to become the top American ace of the war. (U.S. Air Force)

8 DECEMBER
NAVY
Eight motor torpedo boats turn back eight Japanese destroyers attempting to land reinforcements on Guadalcanal Island, Solomon Islands. The following night *PT-59* sinks the Japanese submarine *I-3* in the waters surrounding the island.

9 DECEMBER
ARMY/MARINE CORPS
Major General Alexander A. Vandegrift turns command of Guadalcanal Island, Solomon Islands, over to Major General Alexander M. Patch of the Army's Americal Division. The 1st Marine Division begins its movement to Australia, with the 5th Marine Regiment departing, followed soon after by the 1st Marine Regiment. Hereafter, the 1st Marine Division's insignia features the name "Guadalcanal" over the "1."

12 DECEMBER
NAVY
Five motor torpedo boats continue their actions against Japanese ships. The Japanese destroyer *Terutsuki* and *PT-44* are sunk near Guadalcanal Island, Solomon Islands.

14–18 DECEMBER
ARMY
On New Guinea Island, the assaults by Task Forces Urbana and Warren on Japanese positions around Buna Village continue. TF Urbana finally clears an enemy strong point called the "Coconut Grove" on

16 December and enters Buna Village the next day, but attacks on the Triangle are repulsed with heavy losses. Lieutenant General Robert L. Eichelberger takes command of the 32d Infantry Division after Brigadier General Clovis E. Byers is wounded. Australian Brigadier George Wootten is placed in command of TF Warren with orders to seize nearby Musita Island in preparation for taking the next objective, Buna Mission. TF Warren's 18 December attack on the island fails, but TF Urbana has success, using tanks to destroy concrete bunkers as the troops take the airstrip and push to the shore.

15 DECEMBER
ARMY

Despite the lack of troops, the Army undertakes a limited offensive in the Mount Austen area of Guadalcanal Island, Solomon Islands. The mission is given to the 132d Infantry Regiment, last of the Americal Division's regiments to reach the battlefront. After a bitter fight lasting 22 days, the 132d Infantry Regiment succeeds in controlling part of Mount Austen.

MARINE CORPS

The 2d Raider Battalion departs Guadalcanal Island, Solomon Islands, for Espiritu Santo, New Hebrides Islands.

15 DECEMBER
NAVY

Patrol Squadron 12 officially becomes known as a "Black Cat" squadron in reference to its employment of PBY Catalinas painted black in night attack missions in the Solomon Islands. Other squadrons also serve as "Black Cats," conducting highly effective strikes in the South Pacific campaigns.

17 DECEMBER
ARMY

Hard pressed for troops, Major General Millard F. Harmon (Commander, U.S. Army Forces in the South Pacific Area) orders the Hawaii-based 25th Infantry Division under Major General J. Lawton Collins directly to Guadalcanal Island, Solomon Islands. The 35th Regimental Combat Team is first to land and is quickly pressed into perimeter defense.

17–19 DECEMBER
ARMY

A reconnaissance party lands on the island of Amchitka Island, Aleutian Islands, and reports to Western Defense Command that a fighter strip could be constructed in two to three weeks and a main airfield in three to four months.

Right: *The 41st Infantry Division arrives on New Guinea Island in December 1942 to begin almost 18 months of jungle fighting alongside Australian troops to fully secure the island. ("Jungleers," James Dietz)*

22 DECEMBER
MARINE CORPS

The 1st and 6th Barrage Balloon Squadrons arrive on New Caledonia Island.

22–23 DECEMBER
AIR FORCE

Twenty-six 307th Bombardment Group B-24 Liberator bombers from the Seventh Air Force carry out the first full-scale attack upon enemy airfields when they bomb Wake Island after staging through Midway Island.

23 DECEMBER
ARMY

The 7th Infantry Division under Major General Albert E. Brown at Fort Ord, California, is alerted to begin special mission training. Major General Charles H. Corlett is advised he is to command the task force. The 184th Infantry Regiment becomes the 7th Division's third regiment.

24 DECEMBER
AIR FORCE

South Pacific Allied Air Forces P-39 Airacobra fighters working with Marine Corps F4F Wildcat fighters and SBD Dauntless dive-bombers attack Munda, New Georgia Island, Solomon Islands, with

Above: *On all of the Pacific islands, it is critical to Allied victory for Army Engineers and Navy Seabees to build roads and bridges to carry supplies forward and move the wounded to the rear. (National Archives)*

Below: *An unidentified Soldier grabs a nap while waiting for air transportation to New Guinea Island. The handle of a cut-off Australian saber, issued in lieu of a machete, shows on the right side of his pack. (National Archives)*

devastating results. Twenty-four enemy aircraft are destroyed in the air and on the ground, with no friendly losses.

ARMY

Driving through enemy lines on New Guinea Island to reach a critical objective, the lead platoon of Company L, 127th Infantry Regiment, 32d Infantry Division encounters heavy fire from two enemy pillboxes. Sergeant Kenneth E. Gruennert advances alone and puts the enemy position out of action, but he is shot by snipers as his platoon attains the objective. He is awarded the Medal of Honor.

27 DECEMBER
AIR FORCE

2nd Lieutenant Richard I. Bong shoots down two Japanese aircraft while flying a P-38 Lightning fighter. Bong will go on to score 40 victories, all while flying P-38s, and ends the war as America's leading ace.

Above: *A ground crew member makes last minute preparations on a P-38 Lightning for an early morning patrol in the Pacific. The fast, heavily armed, and rugged fighter is well respected, even feared, by the Japanese pilots. (Jeffery Ethell Collection)*

29 DECEMBER
MARINE CORPS

Marine Aircraft Group 12 begins moving to Efate, New Hebrides Islands. The entire group completes the movement by 28 January 1943.

31 DECEMBER
ARMY

On New Guinea Island, the 32d Infantry Division's Task Force Urbana attacks eastward from Buna Village and Musita Island to encircle Buna Mission. Meanwhile, advance elements of the arriving 41st Infantry Division are flown to inland airfields from Port Moresby to continue the campaign to clear New Guinea Island.

1943
THE LONG ROAD BACK

2 JANUARY
ARMY

A coordinated attack by Task Force (TF) Urbana and TF Warren is launched to recapture Buna Mission, New Guinea Island. TF Warren, spearheaded by tanks, and TF Urbana overrun Buna Mission. By nightfall the coastline is in U.S. hands. Organized resistance ceases on 3 January, although mopping-up operations take another three weeks. Allied casualties in securing Buna are more than 2,800 men.

ARMY/MARINE CORPS

Lieutenant General Ernest N. Harmon activates the XIV Corps on Guadalcanal Island, Solomon Islands, under Major General Alexander M. Patch. Brigadier General Edmund B. Sebree takes the helm of the Americal Division. The XIV Corps consists of the Americal and 25th Infantry Divisions, the 147th Infantry Regiment, the 2d Marine Division, and other Marine Corps ground troops.

4 JANUARY
ARMY

Following arrival of the 27th Regimental Combat Team (RCT) on Guadalcanal Island, Solomon Islands, on 1 January, the 161st RCT lands to complete the 25th Infantry Division (under Major General J. Lawton Collins). The division is ordered by XIV Corps to relieve the 132d Infantry Regiment to complete the seizure of Mount Austen. Collins gives this mission to the 35th RCT.

MARINE CORPS

The command echelon of the 2d Marine Division and the 6th Marine Regiment arrive on Guadacanal Island, Solomon Islands.

5 JANUARY
AIR FORCE

Brigadier General Kenneth N. Walker, commander, V Bomber Command, Fifth Air Force, leads a bombing attack on a shipping harbor in Rabaul, New Britain Island, Solomon Islands, with direct hits on nine enemy vessels, for which he receives the Medal of Honor. During the mission, Walker is killed when his B-17 Flying Fortress bomber is brought down by enemy fighters.

ARMY

The 32d Infantry Division pushes against the Japanese units in delaying positions covering their withdrawal along the New Guinea Island coast. The recently arrived 163d Infantry Regiment joins the offensive.

THE PACIFIC AREAS
as of 1 August 1942

Left: *In 1942, the Joint Chiefs of Staff divide the Pacific region into two parts: the Pacific Ocean Areas (with North, Central, and South Pacific sub-commands) and the Southwest Pacific Area. (R. Johnston, U.S. Army)*

Opposite: *The 32d Infantry Division and Australian tanks fight on New Guinea Island. ("River Crossing," James Dietz)*

NAVY

Together with air raids against the island that commenced in December 1942, Navy surface ships of Task Force 67 under the command of Rear Admiral Walden L. Ainsworth bombard Munda, New Georgia, in the Solomon Islands. During a Japanese air attack against the task force, the light cruiser *Helena* becomes the first ship to employ projectiles equipped with proximity fuses in combat, downing a Japanese dive-bomber.

10 JANUARY
ARMY/MARINE CORPS

The 25th Infantry Division (reinforced) begins its largest campaign to eliminate Japanese forces on Guadalcanal Island, Solomon Islands. The division fires a 30-minute artillery preparation, the first divisional time-on-target concentration of the campaign. The 27th Infantry Regiment seizes most of its objective, as does the 35th Infantry Regiment. The offensive continues on 11 January against strong Japanese opposition.

NAVY

The transport submarine *Argonaut* attacks a Japanese convoy off New Britain Island. The escorting Japanese navy destroyers depth charge the submarine, forcing her bow to break the surface. The destroyers then pump shells into *Argonaut*, sinking her with the loss of all 105 crewmen on board.

11 JANUARY
AIR FORCE/ARMY

A small Army security detachment lands on Amchitka Island, Aleutian Islands, followed the next day by a combat team of 2,000 troops under Brigadier General Lloyd E. Jones. The landing meets with no opposition. By 16 February a fighter strip is ready. Eight P-40 Warhawk fighters arrive and are soon running patrols over Kiska Island.

MARINE CORPS

The 2d Parachute Battalion arrives on New Caledonia Island.

NAVY

Eleven motor torpedo boats attack a Japanese force of eight destroyers off Cape Esperance, Guadalcanal Island, Solomon Islands, damaging one of the enemy vessels. *PT-112* is sunk and *PT-43* is damaged.

13 JANUARY
AIR FORCE

The Thirteenth Air Force is activated in the New Hebrides Islands and New Caledonia Island. From there, fighters and bombers will operate throughout the Southwest Pacific under overall command of Major General Nathan F. Twining. They fly combat missions near Munda, New Georgia Island, Solomon Islands.

Left: *A Marine Corps ground crew works on Guadalcanal Island to prepare an SBD Dauntless for its next flight. ("The Ground Crews," Lt. Dwight C. Shepler, U.S. Navy Art Collection)*

Below: *A Marine Corps antiaircraft crew uses a range finder to direct their guns in defending Guadalcanal Island. (Marine Corps Research Center)*

ARMY/MARINE CORPS

The 2d Marine Division begins a coordinated attack with the Army's 25th Division to destroy remaining Japanese forces west of the American perimeter on Guadalcanal Island, Solomon Islands. The advance continues through 17 January. Captain Joe Foss shoots down three enemy planes, giving him 26 kills and tying Army Captain Eddie Rickenbacker's World War I American record. The 2d Marine Regiment departs Guadalcanal for New Zealand.

16 JANUARY
ARMY/MARINE CORPS

The Composite Army–Marine (CAM) Division is formed on Guadalcanal Island, Solomon Islands, under the XIV Corps. It consists of the 6th Marine Regiment, 182d and 147th Infantry Regiments, and artillery units from the Americal and 2d Marine divisions. CAM Division is tasked with making a coordinated attack with the 25th Infantry Division to envelop the left flank of the Japanese defenses.

ARMY

On New Guinea Island the advance is slowed by strong Japanese defenses around Sanananda. Efforts by the battalions of the 163d and 127th Infantry Regiments meet limited success.

18–19 JANUARY
ARMY/MARINE CORPS

The Composite Army–Marine Division advances on Guadalcanal Island, Solomon Islands, on the XIV Corps' north flank, while the 25th Infantry Division surrounds and attacks the village of Gifu.

ARMY

On New Guinea Island the Japanese defenders fight last-ditch battles against the 163d and 127th Infantry Regiments along the Sananada–Soputa Road. Mop-up of bypassed pockets of Japanese resistance continues.

23 JANUARY
ALL SERVICES

Japanese resistance on Guadalcanal crumbles as the Composite Army–Marine (CAM) Division and the 25th Infantry Division press their attacks. The two divisions link up on 24 January. On 26 January the CAM Division passes through the 25th Division and undertakes pursuit of the withdrawing enemy. The 25th Division is pulled from the line and sent to secure the airfields, which still are vulnerable to attack by groups of bypassed Japanese.

24 JANUARY
NAVY

In the Solomon Islands, ships of Task Force 67 bombard Japanese fuel and ammunition dumps on Kolombangara. Aircraft from Henderson Field, Guadalcanal Island, bombard the targets later in the day.

Three survivors from the torpedoed Dutch motorship *Zaandam*, one of whom is Seaman First Class Basil D. Izzi, USNR, are rescued from the Indian Ocean by the submarine chaser *PC-576*. The men have spent 83 days in a raft, subsisting on a diet of raw fish, birds, and rain water.

25 JANUARY
ARMY

The U.S. Sixth Army is activated at Fort Sam Houston, Texas, to become the major field command in the Southwest Pacific. Lieutenant General Walter Krueger takes command on 13 February.

27 JANUARY
AIR FORCE/NAVY

Thirteenth Air Force commander Major General Nathan F. Twining and his crew of 14 are reported down at sea. All 15 men are rescued by a Navy PBY-5 Catalina flying boat near Guadalcanal Island, Solomon Islands, on 1 February. The rescue raft was not equipped with a radio for signaling, thereby complicating the search. After this rescue, dinghy radio sets become standard equipment on rescue rafts.

Right: *The cruiser* Chicago, *recently returned to action after repairs to damage suffered during the 1942 Battle of Savo Island, suffers another hit by Japanese torpedoes off of Guadalcanal Island in January 1943. While under tow to port for repair,* Chicago *is again attacked by enemy planes, whose torpedoes finally sink her. ("Double Jeopardy," by Mort Künstler, © 1963 Mort Künstler, Inc.)*

Above: *The grim reality of war does not dampen the humor of American servicemen. By mid-1943 Walt Disney and other artists have created hundreds of squadron, ship, and unit cartoon insignia. Mostly used on signs and flight jackets, some are painted on planes as nose art. (Walt Disney Enterprises, Inc.)*

Below: *Although he is mortally wounded on deck, Commander Howard Gilmore orders his sub,* Growler, *to submerge, saving the rest of the crew. (Fred Freeman)*

29 JANUARY
NAVY

In the Battle of Rennell Island, Japanese land-attack planes strike U.S. Navy warships covering the movement of transports to Guadalcanal Island, Solomon Islands. The heavy cruiser *Chicago* is torpedoed on the night of 29 January. Taken under tow, she is attacked again the following day, sustaining four additional torpedo hits that sink her 30 miles east of Rennell Island.

31 JANUARY
MARINE CORPS

1st Lieutenant Jefferson J. DeBlanc of Marine Fighting Squadron 112 shoots down five enemy Zero fighters in a single mission over the central Solomon Islands, giving him a total of eight kills. For his exploits in the air, he receives the Medal of Honor.

1 FEBRUARY
NAVY

Japanese aircraft sink the destroyer *DeHaven* as she covers the landing of Army troops in the Japanese rear on Guadalcanal Island, Solomon Islands. The first of three bomb hits causes the ship to go dead in the water, and the second scores a direct hit on the bridge, killing the commanding officer. Meanwhile, the light minelayers *Montgomery*, *Preble*, and *Tracy* lay a minefield between Savo Island and Cape Esperance, which fatally damages a Japanese destroyer the following day.

7 FEBRUARY
NAVY

In the early morning hours, Commander Howard Gilmore maneuvers his submarine *Growler* for a night surface attack against the Japanese stores ship *Hayasaki* off Rabaul, New Britain Island. During the approach his quarry maneuvers to ram the submarine, prompting Gilmore to change course and ram *Hayasaki*. *Growler* hits the ship at a speed of 17 knots, and her bridge is soon raked by machine-gun fire. Gilmore remains on deck while his crew goes below, but before he can reach the hatch he is mortally wounded. Knowing he cannot make it, he gives the order to "Take her down," thus saving his boat and her crew. Gilmore is posthumously awarded the Medal of Honor.

9 FEBRUARY
ARMY/MARINE CORPS

Troops of the Americal Division and the 25th Infantry Division link up at Tenaru Village, Guadalcanal Island, Solomon Islands, marking the end of organized fighting on the island. There are more than 11,000 American casualties killed, wounded, or missing from all services during the campaign.

11 FEBRUARY
NAVY

The destroyer *Fletcher*, operating in concert with an SOC Seagull floatplane of Scouting Squadron 9 off the light cruiser *Helena*, sinks the Japanese submarine *I-18* in the Coral Sea.

12 FEBRUARY
NAVY

The submarine *Grampus* sails from Brisbane, Australia, to begin her sixth war patrol. She is never heard from again and is declared lost at sea.

14 FEBRUARY
NAVY

The submarine *Amberjack* sends her last radio transmission, reporting the capture of an enemy aviator and attacks by two enemy destroyers in the Solomon Sea. She is never heard from again and is presumed lost at sea.

15 FEBRUARY
MARINE CORPS

All land-based aircraft in the southern Solomon Islands are placed under a single new command, Aircraft Solomons. This is a joint (multiservice) and combined (multinational) force.

21 FEBRUARY
ARMY/MARINE CORPS

The 3d Raider Battalion makes an unopposed landing on Pavuvu Island, Russell Islands, in the central Solomon Islands. The 11th Defense Battalion follows the 43d Infantry Division ashore in unopposed landings on nearby Banika Island.

Above: *A squadron of Marine Corps F4F Wildcats awaits the pilots on Henderson Field, Guadalcanal Island, in April 1943. Allied operations push the Japanese farther away, greatly reducing the danger of attack on the field. (National Archives)*

Left: *Marines from the 3d Raider Battalion land on Pavuvu Island, Russell Islands, to conduct reconnaissance prior to an invasion of the island. The Marine in the bow holds a Browning automatic rifle. No enemies are found and the island is occupied without resistance. (National Archives)*

Left: *Two PT boats of Motor Torpedo Squadron 3 make a night attack against a Japanese destroyer group near Cebu Island. PT-41 is the same boat that had evacuated the MacArthur family and other senior officials from the Philippine Islands in 1942. ("Expendable," James Dietz)*

Opposite, top: *A photo of an early model of the twin-engine B-25 Mitchell bomber clearly shows the dorsal gun turret, cockpit, and bombardier's position in the nose. (NASM)*

MARINE CORPS
Marine Corps Air Station, Kearney Mesa is established adjacent to Camp Elliott, California.

NAVY
Ships of Task Unit 62.7.2 under the command of Captain Ingolf N. Kiland and carrier planes from *Saratoga* temporarily operating from Henderson Field, Guadalcanal Island, support successful landings in the Russell Islands, opening the campaign in the Central Solomon Islands.

28 FEBRUARY
ARMY
Army engineers push construction of the Ledo Road over the India–Burma border. Two Army engineer outfits are soon joined by 6,000 troops sent from the United States. Brigadier General Lewis A. Pick is to command the enormous undertaking.

2 MARCH
AIR FORCE/NAVY
Fifth Air Force B-17 Flying Fortresses and B-24 Liberators attack a convoy of 16 Japanese ships just north of New Britain Island, beginning the Battle of the Bismarck Sea. Attacking in coordination with the Royal Australian Air Forces, the bombers sink four of the transport ships on the first day. On the second day of the battle, B-25 Mitchell bombers, fighters, and PT boats from the U.S. Seventh Fleet engage the enemy convoy, sinking all but four escort destroyers. By the third day, the combined American force has finished off the rest of the Japanese ships, ending the battle. More than 40,000 tons of Japanese shipping are sunk, more than 50 enemy aircraft are destroyed, and approximately 75 percent of the Japanese troops bound for Lae, New Guinea Island, are killed at sea.

10 MARCH
AIR FORCE/ARMY
The Army Air Forces activates the Fourteenth Air Force at Kunming, China. Commanded by Major

General Claire Chennault, former Flying Tigers leader, the Fourteenth includes a flying wing composed of both American and Chinese pilots. Flying P-40 Warhawk fighters, these pilots conduct armed reconnaissance missions into Burma from Kunming.

11 MARCH
NAVY
The submarine *Triton* reports sinking a Japanese army cargo ship on 6 March in the northern Bismarck Sea. This is the last transmission received from the sub, which is never heard from again.

12 MARCH
MARINE CORPS
The first Marine Corps Vought F4U Corsair fighter planes enter combat when Marine Fighting Squadron 124 arrives at Henderson Field, Guadalcanal Island, Solomon Islands.

14 MARCH
MARINE CORPS
Marine Aircraft Group 21 begins deploying to Banika Island, Solomon Islands.

15 MARCH
MARINE CORPS
The 1st Raider Regiment is established to command all four raider battalions. The 3d and 4th Raider Battalions had arrived in Espiritu Santo, New Hebrides Islands, in February.

17 MARCH
MARINE CORPS
Marine Corps Air Station El Toro is established in southern California.

20 MARCH
MARINE CORPS
Marine Scout Bombing Squadron 143 conducts the first aerial minelaying mission in the South Pacific, near Bougainville, Solomon Islands.

21 MARCH
MARINE CORPS
A small group of Marine Raider scouts land at Segi Plantation on New Georgia Island, Solomon Islands, to reconnoiter landing beaches for a planned invasion.

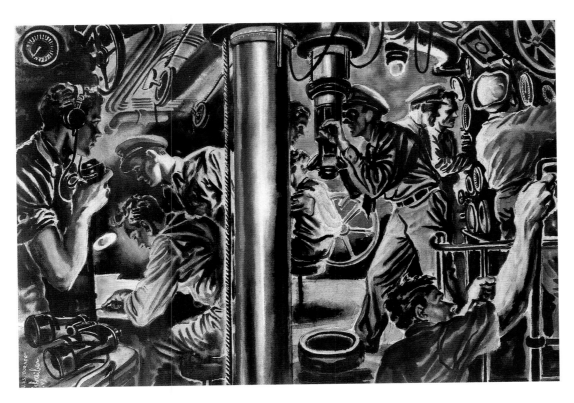

Left: *For a submarine crew, bringing the periscope up for a look around adds even more tension. It is a moment of vulnerability and potential discovery by searching enemy eyes. ("Up Periscope," Georges Schreiber, Navy Art Collection)*

Below: *Even aboard transports, living conditions are cramped and crowded. ("Transport Quarters Aboard Ship," William F. Draper, Navy Art Collection)*

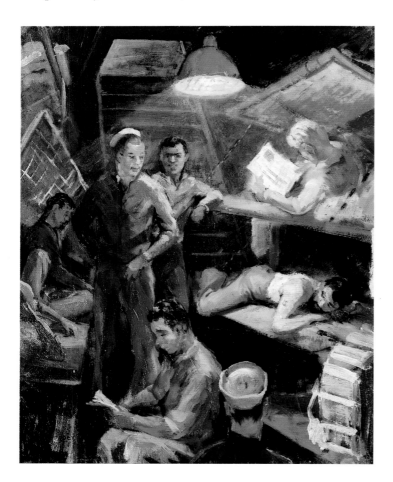

23 MARCH
NAVY

While operating near Formosa Island, the submarine *Kingfish* undergoes an intense depth charge attack that damages the boat. Her crew destroys secret codes in preparation for abandoning ship. Damage to the sub's main piping causes an air bubble to rise to the surface, which leads her attackers to believe they have sunk her. *Kingfish* cuts short her patrol, is repaired, and conducts 12 war patrols during World War II.

25 MARCH
NAVY

The submarine *Wahoo* sinks three Japanese cargo ships in the Yellow Sea. Under the command of the legendary Lieutenant Commander Dudley W. Morton, the sub attacks on the surface. On one occasion her crew throws homemade "Molotov cocktails" at one of the cargo ships as the submarine pulls alongside.

26 MARCH
ARMY

Second Lieutenant Elsie S. Ott, an Army nurse, receives the first Air Medal awarded to a woman in the military for gallantry in escorting five patients more than 10,000 miles from India to the U.S.

NAVY

In the Battle of the Komandorski Islands, Task Group 16.6 (under Rear Admiral Charles H. McMorris) prevents a Japanese surface force from reinforcing their garrison on Kiska Island, Aleutian Islands. The heavy cruiser *Salt Lake City* damages a Japanese heavy cruiser in the engagement despite suffering damage that briefly renders her dead in the water. The destroyers *Bailey* and *Coghlan* are also damaged by Japanese gunfire.

28 MARCH
ARMY

On New Guinea Island, Task Force MacKechnie (under Colonel Archibald R. MacKechnie) is formed around the 1st Battalion, 162d Infantry Regiment, 41st Infantry Division. Its mission is to land at and secure Morobe Harbor. The task force lands at the harbor and sets up defensive positions on 3 April.

1 APRIL
ARMY

Although it has been training for months for desert mechanized warfare, the 7th Infantry Division (under Major General Albert E. Brown) is selected to make the amphibious landing to retake Attu in the Aleutian Islands, planned for 7 May. Unit leaders begin a crash training program to prepare the division for seaborne warfare. Fortunately, the division is based at Fort Ord, California, right on Monterey Bay.

4 APRIL
MARINE CORPS

Marine Aircraft Group 12 moves to Guadalcanal Island, Solomon Islands, in place of MAG-14, which shifts to New Zealand.

5 APRIL
NAVY

The destroyer *O'Bannon* sinks the Japanese submarine *RO-34* operating on the surface near Russell Island in the Solomon Islands.

7 April
MARINE CORPS/NAVY

A raid carried out against shipping off Guadalcanal Island, Solomon Islands, by about 170 Japanese dive-bombers and fighters damages numerous U.S. Navy vessels. The destroyer *Aaron Ward* is hit by bombs and sinks with the loss of 27 men. Bombs also start fires on board the oiler *Kanawha*, which is eventually beached, and sinks the following day. On his first combat mission, 1st Lieutenant James E. Swett of Marine Fighting Squadron 221 shoots down seven dive-bombers before crash landing his damaged plane in the water. For this action he receives the Medal of Honor.

9 APRIL
MARINE CORPS

The 3d Barrage Balloon Squadron arrives at New Caledonia Island.

Right: *Soldiers of the 32d Infantry Division cross a Japanese built footbridge as they advance against enemy positions on Papua, New Guinea, in January. The long, but successful, campaign is over by the end of the month, reducing the danger of Japanese attacks against Australia. (Dept. of Defense)*

Above: *Flashes from the ship's guns illuminate Sailors aboard the destroyer* Nicholas *as she fires at the enemy near the Solomon Islands in May 1943. (National Archives)*

Below: *Initially based in Australia, the 431st Fighter Squadron, nicknamed "Hades," begins its combat operations in July 1943. ("Major Tom McGuire Flying in Pudgy V with the 431st FS," Francis McGinley, USAF Art Collection)*

14 APRIL
AIR FORCE/MARINE CORPS/NAVY

The Fleet Radio Unit, Pacific Fleet, intercepts and decodes a "hot" Japanese naval communiqué that Admiral Isoroku Yamamoto is planning an inspection visit to three bases of operations near Bougainville Island, Solomon Islands. A fairly precise itinerary, escort aircraft force, and the date for the inspection are deciphered. The decoded message is immediately transmitted to Admiral Chester W. Nimitz, Commander in Chief Pacific Fleet, who assigns the planning of the attack to Admiral William F. Halsey Jr. Marine Corps aviators participate in planning the operation. Army Air Forces P-38 Lightning fighters stationed on Guadalcanal Island are selected for the intercept mission.

15 APRIL
NAVY

The Navy begins playing a role in unconventional warfare in China with the establishment of the Sino-American Cooperative Organization (SACO). The deputy to the organization's Chinese leader is Commander Milton E. Miles. SACO is involved in training Chinese guerrillas, gathering intelligence, reporting the weather, and establishing a medical organization manned in part by U.S. Navy personnel.

17 APRIL
MARINE CORPS
Part of Marine Observation Squadron 155 goes on board the escort carrier *Nassau* to participate in the reconquest of Attu, Aleutian Islands, which begins on 11 May and ends on 3 June.

18 APRIL
AIR FORCE
Major John W. Mitchell leads a flight of 16 P-38 Lightning fighters on a daring surprise attack to intercept and shoot down Admiral Isoroku Yamamoto near Bougainville Island, Solomon Islands. The P-38s fly at very low altitude in a circuitous route to a predetermined location 35 miles from Kahili. At about 9:35 a.m., the fighters identify two Betty bombers and six Zero fighters. The Betty carrying Yamamoto takes evasive action, but Captain Thomas G. Lanphier Jr. and 1st Lieutenant Rex T. Barber rake the bomber with machine-gun fire, and it crashes into the jungle. The following day, Yamamoto's body is recovered from the wreckage.

6 MAY
ARMY
General Douglas MacArthur's General Headquarters issues warning instructions for units under his command for Operation CARTWHEEL—the offensive to destroy the major Japanese base at Rabaul, New Britain Island.

11 MAY
ARMY/NAVY
Task Force 16 and Task Force 51 support the landing of the U.S. Army's 7th Infantry Division on Attu in the Aleutian Islands The 7th Infantry Division finds initial resistance light, but mud immobilizes its tracked vehicles. As troops progress inland, the division encounters heavy fighting. Surface ships, including the battleships *Pennsylvania* and *Idaho*, provide gunfire support for the assault troops, and aircraft from the auxiliary carrier *Nassau* fly close air support missions, marking the first use of this type of direct support of an amphibious assault in the Pacific. Japanese submarines attempt to interfere with the landings, unsuccessfully attacking *Pennsylvania* and the light cruiser *Santa Fe*. Subsequently, the destroyers *Edwards* and *Farragut* sink the Japanese submarine *I-31*.

ARMY
Army engineers under Brigadier General Lewis A. Pick have pushed the Ledo Road construction through the mountains and jungle at the Burma–India border to within 47 miles of Ledo, India. Arrival of the monsoon season forces a temporary halt to the work.

13 MAY
MARINE CORPS
1st Lieutenant Kenneth A. Walsh of Marine Fighting Squadron 124, a former enlisted pilot, shoots down three Zero fighters in the Solomon Islands, giving him a total of six and making him the first F4U Corsair ace.

13–15 MAY
ARMY
Efforts by two battalions of the 32d and 17th Infantry Regiments, 7th Infantry Division, to break through Japanese defenses at Massacre Bay, Attu, Aleutian

Right: *A puff of dark smoke in the air marks the explosion of a Japanese artillery shell as men run to seek cover on the landing beach of Attu Island, Aleutian Islands, in May. Landings occur at both Holtz Bay and Massacre Bay. (Dept. of Defense)*

Islands, are repulsed with heavy losses. At Holtz Bay, the 3d Battalion, 32d Infantry also fails in its attempt to break out of the beachhead. Dense fog and rain hinder air support, though naval gunfire is provided.

14 MAY
NAVY

The motor torpedo boats *PT-150* and *PT-152* sink the Japanese submarine *RO-182* in Vitiaz Strait, New Guinea Island.

16 MAY
ARMY/NAVY

On Attu in the Aleutian Islands, Major General Eugene M. Landrum replaces Major General Albert E. Brown as the assault force commander. The 3d Battalion, 32d Infantry Regiment seizes high ground overlooking Holtz Bay, forcing the Japanese to retreat. Before dawn on 17 May, patrols from Holtz Bay and Massacre Bay link up and find the enemy has pulled back. At the north landing area, the 2d Battalion, 32d Infantry breaks through Clevesy Pass after heavy fighting, but Japanese troops continue to hold high peaks.

19 MAY
MARINE CORPS

Marine Scout Bombing Squadron 143 conducts another aerial minelaying mission in the waters around Bougainville Island, Solomon Islands, losing two TBF Avenger torpedo bombers to heavy antiaircraft fire. Repeat attacks on 20 and 23 May complete the mission without further loss.

Above: *Japanese troops use the mountainous terrain on Attu Island to their advantage in resisting the 7th Infantry Division. After 18 days of fighting, the island is secured. ("Death in the Snow," Edward R. Laning, Army Art Collection, U.S. Army Center of Military History)*

Right: *Japanese-American Soldiers assist in questioning the few enemy troops captured during the Aleutian Islands campaign. ("Interrogation," Edward R. Laning, Army Art Collection, U.S. Army Center of Military History)*

23 MAY
ARMY

Units of the 7th Infantry Division continue to fight to clear the high ridges, peaks, and valleys of Attu in the Aleutian Islands. The 2d battalion, 17th Infantry Regiment penetrates an extensive tunnel system after hard fighting. To the north, the 3d Battalion, 32d Infantry Regiment reaches a fortified trench line below a key peak and begins clearing it of enemy. By 28 May Japanese forces have been pressed into a small area near Chichafo Harbor. A desperate predawn counterattack on 29 May by the Japanese is repulsed, and the defeated enemy disperses into small groups to hide in caves that must be cleared one by one.

26 MAY
NAVY

The submarine *Trout* lands a party on Basilan Island, Philippine Islands, to establish a coastwatcher network, conduct surveys, and assist in supplying Filipino guerrillas.

27 MAY
NAVY

The submarine *Runner* departs Midway Atoll on her third war patrol. She is never heard from again and is presumed lost.

30 MAY
ARMY

In the Aleutian Islands, organized Japanese resistance ends at Attu and the 7th Infantry Division rounds up the remaining survivors. U.S. Soldiers also occupy Shemya Island without a fight.

7 JUNE
MARINE CORPS

The Japanese make an unusually large aerial attack against Guadalcanal Island, Solomon Islands, in an effort to erode growing U.S. power on the island. Allied fighter planes turn back the attack and inflict heavy enemy losses. Similar large Japanese air attacks on 12 and 16 June meet the same fate.

10 JUNE
NAVY

While escorting two vessels near Shemya Island, Aleutian Islands, lookouts on board the submarine chaser *PC-487* spot two periscopes, prompting the chaser to increase speed and make a depth charge attack. The blasts force the Japanese submarine *I-24* to the surface. With guns blazing, *PC-487* rams the I-boat twice, causing her to eventually sink.

Left: *Operation CARTWHEEL begins with the 172d Infantry, 43d Infantry Division landing on Rendova Island in June. (National Archives)*

Below: *A combat artist sketch depicts a tattered Soldier guarding Japanese prisoners. (Howard Brodie, Army Art Collection, U.S. Army Center of Military History)*

Opposite: *The objective of Operation CARTWHEEL is to destroy the large Japanese base at Rabaul, New Britain Island. (U.S. Army)*

13 JUNE
ARMY/MARINE CORPS/NAVY

Reconnaissance patrols go ashore on New Georgia Island to survey possible landing sites for the planned invasion of the central Solomon Islands.

13 JUNE
NAVY

While operating near Kiska Island in the Aleutian Islands, the destroyer *Frazier* spots a periscope and attacks. Gunfire hits the Japanese submarine *I-9* as she submerges, and subsequent depth charge attacks sink her.

16 JUNE
AIR FORCE

Captain Jay Zeamer Jr., Fifth Air Force, pilots a B-17 Flying Fortress bomber on a photographic mission on Buka Island, Solomon Islands. During the mission, Zeamer's bomber is attacked, and he receives wounds in both arms and legs. Zeamer continues to pilot the plane and destroys at least five enemy aircraft. 2nd Lieutenant Joseph R. Sarnoski volunteers as bombardier of the B-17 crew and fights off 20 enemy fighters. Even after he is knocked under the catwalk by a 20mm shell, he crawls back and keeps post until he collapses dead on his guns.

21 JUNE
ARMY/MARINE CORPS

The 4th Raider Battalion (less two companies) and two Army infantry companies from the 103d Infantry Regiment (43d and 37th Infantry Divisions) land at Segi Point, New Georgia Island, Solomon Islands, to stave off a Japanese advance against a coastwatcher. This opens the campaign to seize New Georgia earlier than planned.

22 JUNE
NAVY

The destroyer *Monaghan* attacks and damages the Japanese submarine *I-7*, which later runs aground near Kiska Island, Aleutian Islands. This marks *Monaghan*'s third brush with an enemy submarine, the first having come when she sank a midget submarine at Pearl Harbor, Hawaii, on the fateful morning of 7 December 1941.

23 JUNE
NAVY

The Japanese submarine *RO-103* sinks the cargo ship *Aludra* and damages the cargo ship *Deimos* to such an extent that she is scuttled. Both transports are en route to Guadalcanal Island, Solomon Islands, when attacked.

26 JUNE
ARMY/MARINE CORPS

The Army agrees to assume responsibility for all barrage balloon missions in the Pacific. The six Marine Corps balloon squadrons gradually begin to transition to operating 90mm antiaircraft guns.

27 JUNE
MARINE CORPS

On New Georgia in the Solomon Islands, the 4th Raider Battalion (less two companies) moves by boat and overland from Segi Point to support a planned amphibious landing at Viru Harbor. The Raiders have several skirmishes along the way.

30 JUNE
ALL SERVICES

Operation CARTWHEEL—the offensive to seize the port of Rabaul, New Britain Island—begins with Operation TOENAILS, the capture of New Georgia Island, Solomon Islands. Navy Task Force 31 (Rear Admiral Richard Kelly Turner), supported by aircraft from the Thirteenth Air Force, lands the New Georgia Occupation Force (under Major General John H. Hester) composed of the 43d Infantry Division reinforced with Marine Corps units, before dawn on New Georgia and nearby islands. The 4th Marine Raider Battalion also begins a day-long slogging overland trek from Segi Point to capture Viru Harbor, where they encounter Japanese defenders. Heavy rain, high winds, and rough seas cause major problems with the landings on New Georgia at Wickham Anchorage, but the assault force, a battalion of the 103d Infantry Regiment and two companies of 4th Marine Raiders, makes it ashore and begins clearing the Japanese defenders. Two companies of the 169th Infantry Regiment land unopposed on two small islands guarding the harbor approach, and by 7:00 a.m. the 172d Infantry Regiment is ashore on Rendova Island followed by the 9th Marine Defense Battalion. The 2d Battalion (reinforced), 103d Infantry Regiment, and two companies of the 4th Marine

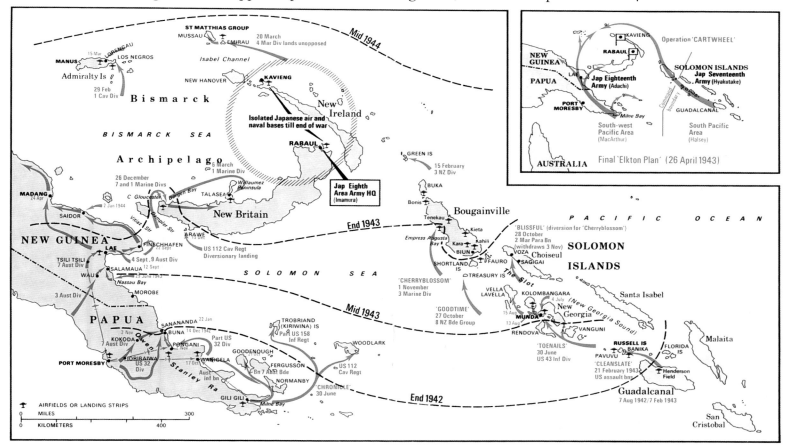

Raiders land on the nearby island of Vangunu, meeting light resistance. At mid-day the surprised Japanese respond with some 60 aircraft to attack the task force. They are engaged by planes of the Thirteenth Air Force and Marine Aircraft Solomons, which share claim for 101 enemy aircraft downed. The Japanese succeed in torpedoing Rear Admiral Turner's flagship, the attack transport *McCawley*, and damaging the destroyer *Gwin* with shore artillery.

ARMY/NAVY

In its first amphibious operation by Lieutenant General Walter Krueger's Sixth Army (later Alamo Force), Navy Task Force 76 (under Rear Admiral Daniel E. Barbey) lands troops on the tiny islands of Woodlark and Kiriwina, just north of New Guinea Island, Solomon Islands, to secure them and construct airfields. The landings are unopposed. The 112th Cavalry Regiment reinforced with artillery and the 12th Marine Defense Battalion, Seabees, and other support units lands on Woodlark Island, while the 158th Infantry Regiment with artillery, construction, and support units is on Kiriwina Island. On the north coast of New Guinea Island, Task Force MacKechnie makes an unopposed night landing at Nassau Bay. As the task force advances toward the Tabali River, it runs into Japanese resistance.

1 JULY
MARINE CORPS

The 4th Raider Battalion defeats the Japanese defenders of Viru Harbor on New Georgia Island, Solomon Islands. Major General Alexander A. Vandegrift takes command of the I Marine Amphibious Corps in place of Major General Clayton B. Vogel.

2 JULY
MARINE CORPS

Marine Fighting Squadron 123 is the last of the eight Marine Corps fighter squadrons in the South Pacific to convert from the F4F Wildcat to the F4U Corsair.

3 JULY
ARMY/NAVY

On New Georgia Island, Solomon Islands, the 43d Infantry Division (Major General John H. Hester) begins its operation to capture Munda Airfield with the landing of the 1st Battalion, 172d Infantry Regiment on Zanana beach, about five miles east of Munda. The 9th Marine Defense Battalion provides supporting artillery fire from Rendova Island. The landing is unopposed and the rest of the 172d and the 169th Infantry Regiments are ashore by 6 July. On 7 July, division advance along the narrow Munda Trail is stopped by determined Japanese resistance.

4 JULY
MARINE CORPS

Antiaircraft units from the 9th Defense Battalion move forward to New Georgia Island, Solomon Islands, to support the 43d Infantry Division.

Above: A Navy PBY-5 Catalina makes a bold attack on a Japanese naval base in the Pacific. Although designed for long range patrolling and rescue missions, Navy aviators also use them to attack enemy ships and for occasional dive-bombing. ("PBY Torpedo Attack," by Mort Künstler, © 1963 Mort Künstler, Inc.)

Below: Members of a Marine Corps defense battalion man their 40mm antiaircraft gun on a Pacific island. In mid-1943, elements of the 9th, 10th, and 11th Defense Battalions are deployed to defend bases in the Solomon Islands. (National Archives)

Marine guns on Rendova Island turn back a sizable Japanese air raid.

5 JULY
ARMY/MARINE CORPS

The 1st Raider Regiment headquarters and the 1st Raider Battalion spearhead the landing at Rice Anchorage on New Georgia Island, Solomon Islands. The 3d Battalions, 148th and 145th Infantry Regiments, 37th Infantry Division, join them ashore. There is no enemy opposition on the beach. The force under Colonel Harry B. Liversedge immediately moves overland toward their objective, a large base at Enogai Inlet.

5–6 JULY
NAVY

After bombarding positions on Kolombangara and New Georgia in the Solomon Islands, the ships of Task Group 36.1 (under Rear Admiral Walden L. Ainsworth) engage Japanese destroyers in a night action. The Battle of Kula Gulf results in the sinking of a Japanese destroyer and inflicts such damage upon another destroyer that she is beached and abandoned. Three other destroyers are damaged. The U.S. Navy suffers the loss of the light cruiser *Helena* and the destroyer *Strong*. Some of the cruiser's 900-man crew reaches the island of Vella Lavella, where they are aided by a coastwatcher and friendly natives. Taking to the jungle, the men are eventually rescued by U.S. Navy destroyers on 16 July. The engagement prevents four of the enemy destroyers from landing their cargoes of troops and supplies on Kolombangara.

6 JULY
NAVY

A PB4Y-1 Liberator of Bombing Squadron 102 piloted by Lieutenant Commander Bruce A. Van Voorhis makes a daring single-plane low-level attack on Japanese installations on Greenwich Island, Solomon Islands. The patrol bomber is shot down by Japanese seaplanes. Van Voorhis receives a posthumous Medal of Honor for his actions.

7–9 JULY
ARMY/MARINE CORPS

The 1st Raider Battalion, with two companies of the 145th Infantry Regiment, launches its attack on Japanese defenders at Enogai on New Georgia Island.

9 JULY
ARMY/MARINE CORPS

After eliminating a strongpoint the day prior, the 43d Infantry Division attacks the main Japanese defensive line around Munda, New Georgia Island, Solomon Islands. The 169th and 172d Infantry Regiments move abreast; the 172d Infantry gains about 1,100 yards, but the 169th is stopped. The 1st Raider Battalion's attack on Enogai also fails.

10 JULY
MARINE CORPS

Marine Corps Air Station El Centro, California, is established.

11 JULY
ARMY/MARINE CORPS

On New Georgia Island, Solomon Islands, Colonel Harry B. Liversedge's force of Marine Raiders and Army troops completes capture of Enogai. Supply problems are acute for the 43d Infantry Division as it struggles to break through the Japanese defense line to the Munda Airfield. The 172d Infantry Regiment is out of water and food, and the heavy jungle prevents air resupply.

12 JULY
MARINE CORPS

The 4th Raider Battalion elements at Viru Harbor and Vangunu on New Georgia Island return to Guadalcanal Island, Solomon Islands.

NAVY

The destroyer *Taylor* sinks the Japanese submarine *RO-107* off Kolombangara, Solomon Islands.

13 JULY
ARMY/MARINE CORPS

In the Solomon Islands, Lieutenant General Ernest N. Harmon arrives and replaces Major General John H. Hester as New Georgia operational commander, letting Hester focus on the 43d Infantry Division's difficulties. The 169th Infantry Regiment makes gains east of Munda, and the 172d Infantry Regiment fights its way to the beach at Laiana where it can be resupplied. On 14 July, Major General Oscar W. Griswold, XIV Corps commander, is ordered to New Georgia with some of his staff. Both the 25th and 37th Infantry Divisions (under Major General Robert S. Beightler) are alerted to send units. The 3d Battalion, 103d Infantry Regiment and the 9th Marine Defense Battalion with a light tank platoon come ashore at Laiana beach. On 15 July, Rear Admiral Richard Kelly Turner is replaced by Rear Admiral Theodore S. Wilkinson, and Griswold assumes command of the New Georgia Occupation Force ground forces. The first units of the 37th Division arrive at Zanana.

NAVY

In the Battle of Kolombangara, 3 light cruisers and 10 destroyers under Rear Admiral Walden L. Ainsworth engage 1 light Japanese cruiser and 5 destroyers. The pitched battle results in the sinking of the Japanese flagship with the loss of Rear Admiral Shunji Izaki, and damage to a Japanese destroyer. Torpedoes launched from Japanese destroyers damage all three light cruisers in Ainsworth's task group, and damage the destroyer *Gwin* to such an extent that she is scuttled. Two other destroyers are damaged in a collision while maneuvering during the battle.

16–18 JULY
ARMY/MARINE CORPS

With the support of Marine Corps tanks, the 172d Infantry Regiment expands the Laiana beachhead toward Munda Airfield on New Georgia Island, Solomon Islands. Beginning on 17 July, the Japanese launch a series of day and night attacks against the Army and Marine Corps troops closing on Munda. All the attacks are repulsed with heavy Japanese losses.

17 JULY
ARMY/MARINE CORPS/NAVY

U.S. and New Zealand aircraft strike shipping concentrated at the southern end of Bougainville Island, Solomon Islands. Marine Corps fighters claim 41 of the 52 enemy planes shot down, while dive-bombers assist in hitting four destroyers.

Right: *Soldiers wearing camouflage uniforms depart on a patrol into the jungle. The single piece camouflage uniforms, called "frog suits," are unpopular because they are hot and awkward to use, especially for Soldiers suffering from one of the many intestinal diseases found on the islands. The uniforms are soon replaced with a two piece olive-green uniform. ("Marching Through New Georgia," Aaron Bohrod, Army Art Collection, U.S. Army Center of Military History)*

Left: *Marine Raiders cross a jungle river on New Georgia Island. Two Marines carry long-barreled Boys .55-caliber antitank rifles. These weapons date to the early 1930s, but are still effective against the lightly armored Japanese tanks. (Marine Corps Historical Center)*

Opposite: *M3 Stuart light tanks of the Marine 9th Defense Battalion move forward to support regiments of the 37th Infantry Division in capturing Bilbilo Hill on New Guinea Island. (Dept. of Defense)*

17–18 JULY
AIR FORCE/MARINE CORPS/NAVY

In two days of air strikes, U.S. Navy aircraft join those of the Marine Corps, Army Air Forces, and Royal New Zealand Air Force in striking targets on Bougainville Island, Solomon Islands, sinking one destroyer and damaging three others.

18 JULY
MARINE CORPS

In the Solomon Islands, the 4th Raider Battalion arrives at Enogai, New Georgia Island, from Guadalcanal Island to reinforce the 1st Raider Regiment for the drive on Bairoko Harbor.

20 JULY
MARINE CORPS

Marine Corps land-based aircraft sink a Japanese destroyer and damage a cruiser south of Choiseul Island in the northern Solomon Islands.

20–21 JULY
ARMY/MARINE CORPS

The 1st Raider Regiment, supported by the Army's 3d Battalion, 148th Infantry Regiment, attacks enemy forces holding Bairoko Harbor on New Georgia Island, Solomon Islands. After fierce fighting against strong Japanese defenses, the Americans pull back with heavy losses. The withdrawal is covered by 250 Aircraft Solomons sorties, one of the largest air operations of the Central Solomons campaign.

Right: *The sturdy F4F Wildcat is the main fighter plane for the U.S. Marine Corps and Navy in the Pacific until the arrival of the F6F Hellcat in 1943. It was initially designed in the 1930s to be a biplane, which accounts for the Wildcat's thick, stubby body. Although outclassed in some respects by the Japanese Zero, the Wildcat is an effective fighter in the hands of a capable pilot. (Marine Corps Historical Center)*

22 JULY
ARMY/MARINE CORPS/NAVY
A six-man patrol of officers lands near Barakoma, Vella Lavella Island, Solomon Islands, to scout the area for a proposed amphibious operation.

MARINE CORPS
Torpedo bombers sink a Japanese seaplane carrier with a load of tanks off Bougainville Island, Solomon Islands.

25 JULY
ARMY
The XIV Corps opens the final offensive on New Georgia Island, Solomon Islands, to take the Munda Airfield. There is slow progress, as the newly arrived 37th and 41st Infantry Divisions get support from tanks and flame throwers.

26 JULY
AIR FORCE
Eight Seventh Air Force B-24 Liberator bombers fly the last mission against Wake Island from Midway Atoll. The formation is intercepted by enemy fighters, and the bombers claim that 11 of those are shot down during the engagement.

26–28 JULY
ARMY/MARINE CORPS/NAVY
The 43d and 37th Infantry Divisions, assisted by the light tanks of the 9th and 10th Marine Defense Battalions, assault the Japanese defenses around Munda, New Georgia Island, Solomon Islands. Strong Japanese bunkers limit the 37th Division's advance, but the 103d Infantry Regiment, 43d Division makes better progress and reaches the coast. Heavy fighting to clear bunkers continues with slow progress. Marine Corps and Navy aircraft attack Bibilo Hill overlooking the airfield.

29 JULY
ARMY
Major General John R. Hodge replaces an exhausted Major General John H. Hester as commander of the 43d Infantry Division. As the 172d Infantry Regiment is trying to break through Japanese defenses on New Georgia, 1st Lieutenant Robert S. Scott single-handedly stops an enemy counterattack despite serious wounds. Two days later, Private First Class Frank J. Petrarca is killed going through enemy fire to the aid of a wounded soldier. Both receive the Medal of Honor.

31 JULY
ARMY
Wounded as his platoon is forced to withdraw on New Georgia Island, Solomon Islands, Private Rodger Young, 148th Infantry Regiment, 37th Infantry Division battles back at the enemy with hand grenades until he is cut down. His action earns the Medal of Honor.

Left: *High tide forces Soldiers of the 165th Infantry Regiment, 27th Infantry Division, to wade 250 yards to shore on Butaritari Island, Makin Atoll, in November 1943. Fortunately, initial Japanese resistance is light. (Dept. of Defense)*

Below: *Lieutenant John F. Kennedy, future President of the U.S., poses with his crew on the deck of* PT-109 *in mid-summer. The boat sinks during a night action in August 1943. (Naval Historical Center)*

AUGUST
ARMY

Japanese resistance on New Georgia Island, Solomon Islands, crumbles as troops of the 43d Infantry Division reach the Munda Airfield runway; the advancing 37th Infantry Division finds enemy positions on Horseshoe Hill abandoned.

1 AUGUST
MARINE CORPS

Planes of Aircraft Solomons participate in a major strike against Japanese positions holding up the advance on Munda Airfield on New Georgia Island.

2 AUGUST
NAVY

The motor torpedo boat *PT-109*, while engaged in a night patrol off Kolombangara in the Solomon Islands, is rammed and sunk by the Japanese destroyer *Amagiri*. Two sailors are killed and the survivors, including the boat's skipper Lieutenant (junior grade) John F. Kennedy, swim to a nearby island. The 11 survivors are rescued on 6 August. Kennedy later becomes the 35th President of the United States.

5 AUGUST
ARMY/MARINE CORPS

After 12 days of heavy jungle fighting by Soldiers and Marines on New Georgia Island, Solomon Islands, Munda Airfield is taken. Units of the 25th Infantry Division continue on to clear the last pockets of Japanese defenders and to make contact with Colonel Harry B. Liversedge's force of Marine Raiders and the 148th Infantry Regiment. This is accomplished on 9 August.

6 AUGUST
MARINE CORPS

The major elements of the 9th Defense Battalion begin moving from Rendova Island to the Munda Airfield area to protect the newly captured landing strip on the island of New Georgia Island, Solomon Islands.

Build for your NAVY!

ENLIST!
CARPENTERS, MACHINISTS, ELECTRICIANS ETC.
FOR INFORMATION APPLY TO YOUR NEAREST RECRUITING STATION
U.S. NAVY - BUREAU OF YARDS & DOCKS

NAVY
The Battle of Vella Gulf, a night action between American and Japanese destroyers off Kolombangara in the Solomon Islands, results in the sinking of three Japanese vessels. The Japanese ships are engaged in an attempt to deliver troops and supplies to the island.

12 AUGUST
ARMY/MARINE CORPS
Operations to seize islands surrounding New Georgia Island, Solomon Islands, begin with landings on Baanga. The 169th Infantry Regiment, 43d Infantry Division's beachhead on Baanga meets heavy resistance. The 9th Marine Defense Battalion provides artillery with 155mm guns. On 16 August, the 172d Infantry Regiment is brought into the fight, and the island is secured on 20 August.

14 AUGUST
MARINE CORPS
Marine Fighting Squadrons 123 and 124 begin operating from Munda Airfield on New Georgia Island, Solomon Islands. They are followed in the coming weeks by Marine Scout Bombing Squadrons 144, 234, and 244, and Marine Torpedo Bombing Squadrons 143 and 232. The headquarters of the 2d Marine Aircraft Wing and Marine Aircraft Group 14 also shift to Munda.

15 AUGUST
ARMY/NAVY
A 34,000-man force under Major General Charles H. Corlett lands on Kiska Island, Aleutian Islands, only to find the Japanese have fled. Major troop elements include the U.S. 7th Infantry Division and the 1st Special Service Force.

Above: *Despite recruiting appeals like this poster, manpower demands for both the frontlines and the wartime supporting industries exceeded the suitable male population. Women enter the workforce and "Rosie the Riveter" replaces the Sailor on the poster. (Library of Congress)*

Right: *Soldiers of the 7th Infantry Division's task force landing on the Aleutian island of Kiska find it deserted. The Japanese are gone, leaving a dog as the sole inhabitant. ("Kiska Raid," Edward R. Laning, Army Art Collection, U.S. Army Center of Military History)*

ARMY/MARINE CORPS/NAVY

In the Solomon Islands, Task Force 31 (under Rear Admiral Theodore S. Wilkinson) lands the 35th Regimental Combat Team, 25th Infantry Division, on Vella Lavella Island. A beachhead is quickly secured and the 4th Marine Defense Battalion and Seabees of the 58th Construction Battalion follow ashore. Marine Corps fighters from Munda Airfield on New Georgia Island provide cover for the landings and down 17 enemy planes. The island will become an important air base.

16 AUGUST
AIR FORCE

Fifth Air Force aircraft attack oil tanks and transport vessels at various locations. P-38 Lightning and P-47 Thunderbolt fighters intercept a force of 25 enemy planes preparing to attack the Allied bomber force, and shoot down 12 Japanese fighters. This marks the first use of the P-47 in the Southwest Pacific Theater.

Above: *Soldiers and Airmen line up for hot food at their snowy tent encampment on one of the cold and foggy Aleutian Islands. ("Chow Line," Ogden Pleissner, Army Art Collection, U.S. Army Center of Military History)*

Left: *Two low flying B-25 Mitchell bombers blast Japanese positions at Dagua Airfield near Wewak during a five-day offensive against the enemy on the north coast of New Guinea Island. (NASM)*

17–18 AUGUST
AIR FORCE

More than 200 fighters and bombers make a surprise attack on the enemy airfields near Lae-Salamaua, New Guinea Island, destroying nearly all of the Japanese aircraft located on those fields.

18 AUGUST
AIR FORCE

During a mid-morning attack at locations around Wewak, New Guinea Island, Solomon Islands, more than 70 heavy and medium bombers covered by 100 fighters cause heavy damage to Japanese aircraft on the ground in those locations. Additionally, more than 30 enemy fighters are claimed to have been shot down.

Major Ralph Cheli, Fifth Air Force, dies near Wewak, New Guinea Island, while leading his squadron in an attack on the Dagua Airdrome. Cheli's B-25 Mitchell bomber is severely damaged by the enemy, but he chooses to complete the attack. Upon ending the mission, Cheli cannot gain the necessary altitude to parachute and he crashes his plane into the sea. He is captured by the Japanese, held prisoner, and dies in captivity. He is awarded a Medal of Honor for the mission.

19 AUGUST
NAVY

An OS2N Kingfisher of Scouting Squadron 57 and the New Zealand corvette *Tui* sink the Japanese submarine *I-17* off Australia.

20 AUGUST
AIR FORCE

At New Delhi, India, the Allied Air Forces, India–Burma Sector, China–Burma–India Theater, is activated with Major General George E. Stratemeyer in command.

21 AUGUST
AIR FORCE

Eleventh Air Force records show that since 3 June 1942, 69 enemy aircraft have been destroyed, 21 ships sunk, 29 ships damaged, and 29 of its own aircraft have been lost during the Aleutian Islands campaign. Preparations are made to redeploy Eleventh Air Force combat units to the U.S.

MARINE CORPS

The 2d Barrage Balloon Squadron is disestablished and its personnel join the 2d Defense Battalion on Samoa.

Right: *An Army Air Forces ground crewman and pilot prepare a P-38 Lightning fighter for a mission at one of the rough airfields in the Aleutian Islands. By mid-1943 at least two islands, Adak and Amchitka, are home to squadrons of P-40 Warhawk and P-38 Lightning fighters as well as B-24 Liberator bombers. ("The Itsy Bitsy," Ogden Pleissner, Army Art Collection, U.S. Army Center of Military History)*

Left: *Navy landing craft move Soldiers of the 43d Infantry Division to a beach on New Georgia Island, Solomon Islands. The battle to control key locations on New Georgia and smaller islands nearby lasts from June to August, requiring several landings by joint task forces of units from the 37th and 43d Infantry Divisions, 1st Marine Raider Regiment, and 9th Marine Defense Battalion. (Naval Historical Center)*

25 AUGUST
ARMY

Bairoko Harbor, the last main Japanese position on New Georgia Island, Solomon Islands, is secured by the 27th and 161st Infantry Regiments, ending the battle for the island. Army casualties are 1,094 dead and 3,873 wounded.

MARINE CORPS

Major General Holland M. Smith's Amphibious Corps, Pacific Fleet, Camp Elliott, California, is redesignated V Amphibious Corps in preparation for its employment as a tactical headquarters. Its training mission is passed to the newly established Troop Training Unit, Pacific Fleet.

NAVY

The destroyer *Patterson* sinks the Japanese submarine *RO-35* southeast of San Cristobal Island in the Solomon Islands.

27 AUGUST
AIR FORCE

Equipped with special radar equipment, 10 Thirteenth Air Force SB-24 "Snooper" bombers begin all-weather bombing operations from Carney Field, Guadalcanal Island, Solomon Islands.

MARINE CORPS/NAVY

The 2d Marine Airdrome Battalion and Navy Seabee units occupy Nukufetau Atoll in the Ellice Islands for the purpose of building an airfield to support future operations in the Gilbert Islands.

28 AUGUST
MARINE CORPS

The 1st Raider Regiment is withdrawn from New Georgia Island, Solomon Islands, and sails to Guadalcanal Island. Total Marine Corps casualties during the New Georgia campaign are 221 killed and 415 wounded. Losses among Navy personnel serving with Marine Corps units are 3 killed and 11 wounded. The 7th Defense Battalion occupies Nanomea Island, where Seabees will construct an airfield to support subsequent operations in the Gilbert Islands.

30 AUGUST
MARINE CORPS

1st Lieutenant Kenneth A. Walsh shoots down four Zero fighters while escorting bombers over Rabaul, New Britain Island, bringing his total kills to 20. Although forced to crash land his plane in the water due to damage, he survives and becomes the first F4U Corsair pilot to receive the Medal of Honor.

31 AUGUST
NAVY

The carriers of Task Force 15, under the command of Rear Admiral Charles A. Pownall, strike Marcus Island, hitting installations ashore and sinking three Japanese small craft. The raid marks the combat debut of the *Essex*-class and *Independence*-class carriers, as well as the first combat action of the Navy's newest carrier fighter, the F6F Hellcat.

Right: *A Navy squadron commander briefs his pilots alongside one of their F6F Hellcat fighters on board the carrier* Lexington *off the Gilbert Islands. (National Archives)*

Below: *In September 1943, paratroopers of the 503d Parachute Infantry are dropped by C-47 Skytrain transport aircraft to seize the airfield at Nadzab, New Guinea Island. Smoke screens from artillery and bombs help obscure the landing from enemy observers. (U.S. Air Force)*

1 SEPTEMBER
AIR FORCE

More than 70 Fifth Air Force B-24 Liberator and B-25 Mitchell bombers strike Alexishafen-Madang, New Guinea Island, with 201 tons of bombs. This is the heaviest single mission total dropped by the Fifth in one day.

NAVY

During landings on Baker Island in the Central Pacific, *Ashland* becomes the first dock landing ship employed in an actual operation.

2 SEPTEMBER
ARMY

In the Solomon Islands, the 172d Infantry Regiment lands on Arundel Island without opposition and begins searching the island for Japanese forces.

3 SEPTEMBER
NAVY

The destroyer *Ellet* sinks the Japanese submarine *I-25* in the waters near Espiritu Santo, New Hebrides Islands.

4 SEPTEMBER
ARMY

Patrols of the 172d Infantry Regiment find enemy forces in fortified positions along the Bomboe Peninsula, New Georgia Island, Solomon Islands. An assault on 5 September against the Japanese line is unsuccessful and small units attempt to slip around it. A battalion of the 169th Infantry Regiment arrives to reinforce the 172d Infantry on 8 September, but no progress is made. The units fall back and wait as a heavy artillery bombardment is used. On 9 September the 37th Infantry Division departs New Georgia to retrain for the invasion of Bougainville Island.

Above: *Dozens of landings, large and small, have to be made by Soldiers and Marines to clear the Japanese from the many islands clustered in the South Pacific. ("Amphibious Operations," Aaron Bohrod, Army Art Collection, U.S. Army Center of Military History)*

Below: *A destroyer defends itself against attacking Japanese aircraft during operations off the coast of Vella Lavella Island, Solomon Islands, in August 1943. (Naval Historical Center)*

NAVY

The ships of Task Force 76, under the command of Rear Admiral Daniel E. Barbey, land Australian troops on the Huon Peninsula near Lae, New Guinea Island. The offensive action prompts the Japanese to strike the invasion force by air, damaging the destroyer *Conyngham* and two tank landing ships. One of them is *LST-473*, which is hit by a bomb in the pilot house just as orders are given to turn the ship to avoid a torpedo. Despite his wounds, Seaman First Class Johnnie D. Hutchins grabs the wheel and turns his ship away from the oncoming torpedo, thus saving her. He receives the Medal of Honor posthumously for his heroic act.

5 SEPTEMBER
AIR FORCE/ARMY

On New Guinea Island, paratroopers of the 503d Parachute Infantry are dropped near Nadzab Airfield in the first such operation in the southwest Pacific. The Fifth Air Force uses 82 C-47 Skytrain transports to insert the forces after 52 medium bombers bomb the drop zone. Nadzab Airfield is quickly restored to operational status and becomes a major operating location for the Allies.

9 SEPTEMBER
NAVY

The submarine *Grayling* is lost in the South China Sea after being rammed by a Japanese transport.

11 SEPTEMBER
ARMY

Two battalions of the 27th Infantry Regiment, 25th Infantry Division land on Arundel Island, Solomon Islands, and the 27th Regiment commander is placed in charge of the operation to clear the island. Strong Japanese resistance prevents link-up with the 172d Infantry Regiment force.

MARINE CORPS

Marine Night Fighting Squadron 531 arrives in Banika in the Russell Islands and begins flying night intercept missions.

15 SEPTEMBER
MARINE CORPS

Major General Charles D. Barrett assumes command of the I Marine Amphibious Corps in place of Major General Alexander A. Vandegrift.

NAVY

The destroyer *Saufley* and a PBY Catalina of Patrol Squadron 23 sink the Japanese submarine *RO-101* east of San Cristobal in the Solomon Islands.

16 SEPTEMBER
ARMY/MARINE CORPS

The rest of the 27th Infantry Regiment is sent as additional reinforcements to Arundel Island, Solomon Islands, as well as the light tank platoons from the 9th, 10th, and 11th Marine Defense Battalions. With the tank support, the infantry pushes ahead to make contact with the 172d Infantry Regiment. On 21 September, the 27th's patrols find the Japanese have evacuated the island.

MARINE CORPS

Major Gregory Boyington, commander of the famed "Blacksheep" of Marine Fighting Squadron 214, shoots down five Zero fighters near southern Bougainville Island, Solomon Islands.

18 SEPTEMBER
AIR FORCE/NAVY

Carrier aircraft from Task Force 15, under the command of Rear Admiral Charles A. Pownall, join Army Air Forces B-24 Liberator bombers in striking the Gilbert Islands.

20 SEPTEMBER
AIR FORCE

1st Lieutenant Henry Meigs II, flying a 6th Night Fighter Squadron P-38 Lightning against Japanese night attackers over Bougainville Island, Solomon Islands, shoots down two aircraft within one minute.

22 SEPTEMBER
MARINE CORPS/NAVY

Two patrols comprised of Marine Corps and Navy officers and New Zealanders scout Choiseul Island and the vicinity in the northern Solomon Islands. The patrols complete their work on 30 September.

Right: U.S. Navy LSTs offload Australian army troops and equipment at Lae, New Guinea Island, in September 1943. Joint U.S.-Australian operations to secure New Guinea and the surrounding islands are common in the southwest Pacific area. (Naval Historical Center)

22 SEPTEMBER
NAVY

Task Force 76 (under Rear Admiral Daniel E. Barbey) puts Australian troops ashore at Finschhafen, New Guinea Island.

23 SEPTEMBER
MARINE CORPS/NAVY

A Navy-Marine Corps patrol lands from the submarine *Gato* on the northeast coast of Bougainville Island, Solomon Islands. After four days of scouting, they determine the area is unfavorable for an

Left: *A flight of B-25 Mitchell bombers completes a raid in September 1943 that leaves Japanese facilities on Bougainville Island, Solomon Islands, on fire. (U.S. Army)*

amphibious landing. A similar reconnaissance element goes ashore at Empress Augusta Bay on the west coast from the submarine *Guardfish*. It finds the area lightly defended and suitable for construction of an airfield.

24 SEPTEMBER
MARINE CORPS

Marines from the 1st Marine Division are part of a patrol that lands on western New Britain Island to scout the Cape Gloucester area. They remain ashore until 6 October.

25 SEPTEMBER
MARINE CORPS

Elements of the I Marine Amphibious Corps establish a forward staging area on Vella Lavella Island, Solomon Islands.

27 SEPTEMBER
MARINE CORPS

Marine Corps aircraft land at Barakoma Airfield on Vella Lavella Island, Solomon Islands, and begin operating from that base.

28 SEPTEMBER
NAVY

The submarine *Cisco* sinks in the Sulu Sea off Panay Island, probably the result of damage inflicted by a Japanese observation plane and gunboat.

3 OCTOBER
NAVY

The Japanese submarine *RO-108* sinks the destroyer *Henley* off eastern New Guinea Island.

5–6 OCTOBER
NAVY

Aircraft from six carriers of Task Force 14 (under Rear Admiral Alfred E. Montgomery) strike Wake Island.

6 OCTOBER
MARINE CORPS

Marine Aircraft Group 31 begins operations in Samoa after its move from the United States.

NAVY

In the Battle of Vella Lavella in the Solomon Islands, the destroyers *O'Bannon*, *Chevalier*, and *Selfridge* are damaged after engaging a superior Japanese force escorting troop-carrying barges. *Chevalier* and *Selfridge* both take torpedoes, but manage to torpedo and sink a Japanese destroyer. *Chevalier* is later scuttled.

7 OCTOBER
NAVY

A Japanese escort destroyer sinks the submarine *S-44* in the northern Pacific east of the Kamchatka Peninsula, USSR.

8 OCTOBER
MARINE CORPS

Major General Alexander A. Vandegrift reassumes command of the I Marine Amphibious Corps following the accidental death of Major General Charles D. Barrett.

11 OCTOBER
AIR FORCE

Colonel Neel E. Kearby, Fifth Air Force, leads a flight of four P-47 Thunderbolt fighter bombers to reconnoiter the enemy base in Wewak, New Guinea Island. Kearby single-handedly shoots down six enemy aircraft after observing enemy installations at four

airfields and securing important tactical information. Colonel Kearby is awarded the Medal of Honor for his accomplishment.

NAVY

While operating in the La Pérouse Strait between Japan and Russia, the submarine *Wahoo* is sunk by Japanese aircraft and surface ships. In July 2006, a Russian dive team discovers the wreck of the submarine.

12 OCTOBER
AIR FORCE

Allied Air Forces, including aircraft of the Fifth Air Force, assault Rabaul, New Britain Island. Approximately 350 B-24 Liberator and B-25 Mitchell bombers and P-38 Lightning fighters, along with Royal Australian Air Force aircraft, attack the town, harbor, and local airfields. Three enemy ships and 50 enemy aircraft are destroyed.

20 OCTOBER
MARINE CORPS

The 1st Joint Assault Signal Company is activated at Camp Pendleton, California. Its mission is to coordinate the fire of supporting arms, including air, during amphibious operations.

The commander of Aircraft Solomons displaces his headquarters from Guadalcanal Island to Munda, New Georgia Island. The headquarters of the 2d Marine Aircraft Wing moves to Efate in the New Hebrides Islands and begins serving primarily as a training command.

21 OCTOBER
ARMY

Alamo Force headquarters (under Lieutenant General Walter Krueger, XIV Corps) moves from New Guinea Island to Goodenough Island to the east in preparation for Operation DEXTERITY, the planned December seizure of Cape Gloucester on New Britain Island. The airfields there will support the attack on Rabaul.

25 OCTOBER
AIR FORCE

More than 60 Fifth Air Force B-24 Liberator bombers hit airfields near Rabaul, New Britain Island, destroying some 20 enemy aircraft on the ground and claiming 30 aerial kills. These attacks continue through the Allied landings on Bougainville Island, Solomon Islands, on 1 November.

Above: *Army engineers use a bulldozer to remove trees and clear undergrowth for a jungle base on a Pacific island. ("Jungle Clearance," Maltby Sykes, Army Art Collection, U.S. Army Center of Military History)*

Right: *Navy Lieutenant Walter Chewing, a catapult officer on the carrier* Enterprise, *climbs up the side of an F6F Hellcat to help the pilot, Ensign Byron Johnson, escape from the burning plane. Johnson has crashed on returning from a raid on Makin Island in November 1943. (National Archives)*

28 OCTOBER
MARINE CORPS/NAVY

In the Solomon Islands, the 2d Parachute Battalion makes an unopposed night landing from destroyer transports on the northwest coast of Choiseul Island to divert enemy attention from the pending assault on Bougainville Island. On 30 October, the Marines attack and destroy a Japanese barge staging point on the island.

31 October
MARINE CORPS

The 22d Marine Regiment is detached from the Defense Force, Samoan Group, and assigned to the V Amphibious Corps.

1 NOVEMBER
MARINE CORPS/NAVY

Following naval and air bombardment including

attacks by Marine Corps aircraft based on Munda, New Britain Island, Navy Task Force 31 (under Rear Admiral Theodore S. Wilkinson) lands the reinforced 3d Marine Division in an amphibious assault at Cape Torokina in Empress Augusta Bay, Bougainville Island, Solomon Islands. The 3d and 9th Marine Regiments and 2d Raider Battalion make the main landing and the 3d Defense Battalion comes ashore as well. Minimal resistance is met and a beachhead perimeter is set up. The 3d Raider Battalion makes a supporting landing on Puruata Island. Elsewhere in the Solomon Islands, light cruisers and destroyers of Task Force 39 (under Rear Admiral Aaron S. Merrill) shell Shortland Island and the Buka–Bonis area of Bougainville Island, where aircraft from the carrier *Saratoga* and the light carrier *Princeton* join in the bombardment.

2 NOVEMBER
AIR FORCE

In support of Allied operations at Bougainville Island, Solomon Islands, Fifth Air Force B-25 Mitchell bombers and P-38 Lightning fighters attack Rabaul Airfield and harbor on New Britain Island. During the intense air battle, 11 ships are sunk and dozens of enemy aircraft are destroyed in the air and on the ground. Antiaircraft fire and enemy fighters take a deadly toll, and by the end of the day, 21 U.S. aircraft are lost.

Major Raymond H. Wilkins, Fifth Air Force, leads the Eighth Bomb squadron in an attack over Simpson Harbor near Rabaul, New Britain Island. On his 87th combat mission, Wilkins' B-25 Mitchell bomber is hit by intense antiaircraft fire. Nevertheless, he strafes a group of harbor vessels and makes a low-level attack of an enemy destroyer. Wilkins destroys two enemy vessels, but his aircraft is uncontrollable and crashes into the sea. He is awarded the Medal of Honor for his heroism.

MARINE CORPS/NAVY

Elements of the 2d Parachute Battalion make a mortar attack on Japanese installations on Guppy Island off the coast of Choiseul Island, Solomon Islands. Two Navy torpedo boats, one commanded by Lieutenant (junior grade) John F. Kennedy, assist in returning the Marines to their main perimeter.

NAVY

A powerful Japanese surface force, intent on disrupting the American landings at Bougainville Island, Solomon Islands, runs into four light cruisers and eight destroyers of Task Force 39. In the resulting Battle of Empress Augusta Bay, U.S. destroyers sink a Japanese destroyer, while gunfire sends a light cruiser to the bottom. Four other Japanese vessels are damaged. Task Force 39 loses no ships, but four suffer damage. Raids against the Buka–Bonis area of Bougainville Island launched from the carrier *Saratoga* and the light carrier *Princeton* prevent the enemy from mounting serious air opposition.

Right: *Navy Seabees work on the surface of the airfield at Torokina on Bougainville Island, Solomon Islands, in December 1943. The use of interlocking panels of pierced steel planking greatly speeds the construction of all-weather landing strips and parking areas for planes. The rapid construction of such island fields permits Allied planes to extend their range as the Japanese are pushed back. (National Archives)*

The submarines *Seahorse*, *Halibut*, and *Trigger* attack the same Japanese convoy south of Honshu Island, Japan, with devastating results, sinking five transports and cargo ships.

4 NOVEMBER
MARINE CORPS

Before first light, the 2d Parachute Battalion conducts an unopposed amphibious withdrawal from Choiseul Island, Solomon Islands.

5 NOVEMBER
NAVY

Task Force 38 (under Rear Admiral Frederick C. Sherman) and including the carrier *Saratoga* and the light carrier *Princeton*, strikes the Japanese bastion at Rabaul, New Britain Island. The aircraft score hits on nine warships in Simpson Harbor. Six days later U.S. carrier aircraft hit Rabaul for a second time, with Task Force 38 aircraft joining those launched from Task Group 50.3 (under Rear Admiral Alfred E. Montgomery). The strike, which includes SB2C Helldiver dive-bombers on their first combat mission,

Left: *A Marine Corps pilot in an F4U-1D Corsair shoots down a Japanese Betty bomber. The D-model, introduced in April 1944, is fitted for a centerline drop tank and two 1,000-pound bombs. (Marc Stewart, Stewart Studios)*

Opposite: *Two Army M3 Grant medium tanks roll past a medical team on a road in Butaritari in the Gilbert Islands. The M3 has a side-mounted 75mm gun and a 37mm gun in the turret. (Dept. of Defense)*

sinks a destroyer and damages four other warships. Air strikes, primarily conducted by aircaft based at Solomon Islands airfields, continue to pound Rabaul, eventually making an invasion unnecessary.

6 NOVEMBER
AIR FORCE

Tenth Air Force B-24 Liberator bombers begin a series of night mining missions when they drop mines into the Rangoon River, Burma. Similar missions continue through November.

MARINE CORPS

The second echelon of the 3d Marine Division, including a battalion of the 21st Marine Regiment, arrives by sea at Cape Torokina on Bougainville Island, Solomon Islands.

7 NOVEMBER
MARINE CORPS

A Japanese battalion lands from destroyers just west of the Marine Corps perimeter on Bougainville Island, Solomon Islands, and attacks. Artillery and the Marines of the 3d Battalion, 9th Marine Regiment and 1st Battalion, 3d Marine Regiment turn back the enemy at the Koromokina River.

7–10 NOVEMBER
MARINE CORPS

The 2d and 3d Raider Battalions and elements of the 9th Marine Regiment battle Japanese defenders for control of the Piva Trail, the only route into or out of the jungle-choked eastern end of the perimeter on Bougainville Island, Solomon Islands. Marine Corps dive-bombers support the final attack on Piva Village on 10 November.

8 NOVEMBER
ARMY/MARINE CORPS

The 148th Regimental Combat Team, 37th Infantry Division lands at Cape Torokina on Bougainville Island, Solomon Islands, and takes over responsibility for the left flank of the beach position from the Marine Corps. The 1st Battalion, 21st Marine Regiment eliminates the last elements of a Japanese counterattack on the beachhead.

9 NOVEMBER
MARINE CORPS

Major General Roy S. Geiger assumes command of the I Marine Amphibious Corps and the Bougainville Island campaign in the Solomon Islands from Lieutenant General Alexander A. Vandegrift.

11 NOVEMBER
AIR FORCE/NAVY

In a joint attack, the Fifth and Thirteenth Air Forces along with U.S. Navy carrier aircraft attack targets on Rabaul, New Britain Island. This is the first time that the Thirteenth Air Force has attacked Rabaul.

Above: *Marines of the 2d Marine Division struggle ashore on Betio Island, Tarawa Atoll. ("The Seawall at Tarawa," Col. Charles Waterhouse, USMCR, Ret., Art Collection, National Museum of the Marine Corps, Triangle, Virginia)*

13 NOVEMBER
AIR FORCE

In one of the heaviest Allied raids on New Guinea Island, 57 B-24 Liberator and 62 B-25 Mitchell bombers of the Fifth Air Force attack Alexishafen and Madang airfields while P-40 fighters strafe targets in the same area. A second flight of B-24s attack targets at Gasmata, Kaukenau, and Timoeka. A B-25 Mitchell bomber and Royal Australian Air Forces Beaufighter fighters sink a small freighter.

The XX Bomber Command is activated at Smokey Hill Army Air Field, Salina, Kansas. Major General Kenneth B. Wolfe assumes command one week later.

Wolfe had assisted in the development of the B-29 Superfortress, which is assigned to the XX Bomber Command.

13–14 NOVEMBER
MARINE CORPS

In the Battle of the Coconut Grove, the 2d Battalion, 21st Marine Regiment defeats a Japanese force and gains control of an important trail junction on the eastern side of the perimeter on Bougainville Island, Solomon Islands. Marine Night Fighting Squadron 531 makes its first successful night intercept and shoots down a Japanese Betty bomber near the island.

16 NOVEMBER
NAVY

The Japanese submarine *I-176* sinks the submarine *Corvina* off Truk in the Caroline Islands.

17 NOVEMBER
MARINE CORPS/NAVY

Japanese aircraft attack a convoy carrying reinforcements to Bougainville Island, Solomon Islands, sinking the high-speed transport *McKean* in a torpedo attack that causes the loss of personnel from the 21st Marine Regiment.

19–20 NOVEMBER
MARINE CORPS

In the first phase of the Battle of Piva Forks on Bougainville Island, Solomon Islands, the 2d and 3d Battalions, 3d Marine Regiment expand the perimeter to the east and seize a key ridge in the face of strong Japanese opposition.

19 NOVEMBER
NAVY

The submarine *Sculpin* is heavily damaged by a

Japanese destroyer north of Truk in the Caroline Islands. Though he has time to escape *Sculpin* before she sinks, Captain John P. Cromwell, the submarine squadron commander, chooses to go down with the sub rather than face interrogation that might force him to reveal his knowledge of plans to seize the Gilbert Islands. For his sacrifice, he receives a posthumous Medal of Honor.

20 NOVEMBER
ARMY/MARINE CORPS/NAVY

Operation GALVANIC begins as U.S. forces invade Tarawa and Makin Atolls in the Gilbert Islands. Under overall command of Vice Admiral Raymond A. Spruance (Central Pacific Command), Task Force 54 (under Rear Admiral Richmond Kelly Turner) lands the 2d Marine Division on Betio Island in the Tarawa Atoll. The 2d and 8th Marine Regiments lead the assault into murderous Japanese fire. Only the use of

amphibian tractors allows the leading waves of Marines to get through the shallow water covering the coral shelf around the island. A beachhead is finally established after heavy losses and commitment of reserves. Navy losses include torpedo damage to the carrier *Independence* and damage to the destroyer *Ringgold* by fire from shore batteries. On Butaritari Island, Makin Atoll, the 165th Infantry Regiment, reinforced by the 3d Battalion, 105th Infantry Regiment and tanks, all from the 27th Infantry Division (under Major General Ralph C. Smith), makes a supporting landing. It is the Army's first amphibious operation in the Central Pacific Command.

MARINE CORPS
Major General Ralph J. Mitchell assumes command of Aircraft Solomons.

21 NOVEMBER
MARINE CORPS
The 2d and 8th Marine Regiments continue the attack on Betio Island in the Tarawa Atoll, Gilbert Islands, and reach the opposite shore, cutting the Japanese force in two. The 1st Battalion, 6th Marine Regiment gets ashore relatively unscathed that evening to reinforce the assault. The 2d Battalion, 6th Marine Regiment lands on nearby Bairiki Island to clear it for the use of artillery. The V Amphibious Corps Reconnaissance Company seizes an island on Apamama Atoll in the Gilbert Islands against light resistance.

21–25 NOVEMBER
MARINE CORPS
During the final phase of the Battle of Piva Forks on Bougainville Island, Solomon Islands, the 3d Marine Regiment, 2d Raider Battalion, and 1st Battalion, 9th Marine Regiment further expand the perimeter and establish firm control over the dominating high ground.

22 NOVEMBER
ARMY
Butaritari Island, Makin Atoll, is declared secured, though the 165th Infantry Regiment has mopping up to do.

MARINE CORPS
Reinforced by the landing of the 3d Battalion, 6th Marine Regiment, the 2d Marine Division seizes all of Betio Island, Tarawa Atoll, Gilbert Islands, except for

Right: *To overcome a lack of small boats, Marines use rafts to evacuate some of their wounded from Betio Island during the heavy fighting in the early stages of the battle to secure the Tarawa Atoll. (USMC)*

Below: *Soldiers of the 27th Infantry Division take cover on the beach as they land to seize Butaritari Island, Makin Atoll, on 20 November. A light tank of the 193d Tank Battalion is visible in the distance. (Dept. of Defense)*

small pockets near the original landing beaches and the long narrow tail of the island. That night the 1st Battalion, 6th Marine Regiment repels enemy counterattacks coming out of Betio.

NAVY
The destroyer *Frazier*, with the destroyer *Meade*, depth charges the Japanese submarine *I-35* near the Gilbert Islands, forcing her to the surface. *Frazier* then rams the submarine, sinking her.

22–26 NOVEMBER
AIR FORCE
During talks at the Cairo Conference, President Franklin D. Roosevelt, Prime Minister Winston S. Churchill, and Chinese leader Chiang Kai-Shek

discuss the use of the B-29 Superfortress bomber against Japan in what would be called Operation TWILIGHT. It is agreed that the long-range bomber will initially be based in the China–Burma–India Theater.

23 NOVEMBER
MARINE CORPS

In the Gilbert Islands, the 2d Marine Division completes the seizure of Betio Island, Tarawa Atoll. In the Solomon Islands, the 1st Parachute Battalion arrives at Cape Torokina, Bougainville Island, from Vella Lavella Island.

24 NOVEMBER
MARINE CORPS

The 2d and 8th Marine Regiments depart Tarawa Atoll, Gilbert Islands, for a new base camp in Hawaii. The 2d Defense Battalion arrives on Tarawa from Samoa.

NAVY

The Japanese submarine *I-175* penetrates the protective screen around the escort carrier *Liscome Bay* and sinks her off the Gilbert Islands. A total of 702 crewmen are lost, including Rear Admiral Henry M. Mullinix. *Liscome Bay* is the first of six escort carriers lost in action during World War II.

Above: *Planes from the carriers* Saratoga *and* Princeton *strike enemy ships at Rabaul, New Britain Island. (Naval Historical Center)*

Right: *Members of the Office of Strategic Services Detachment 101 sign up recruits of Kachin tribesmen in northern Burma to fight the Japanese. Loyal, determined fighters who gather intelligence, the Kachim suffer the most casualties in the mountain fighting. (U.S. Army)*

Right: *Unexpected heavy Japanese resistance forces Marines of the 1st Parachute Battalion and 3d Raider Battalion to fall back to the beach after a landing behind Japanese lines on Bougainville Island, Solomon Islands. (USMC)*

24–27 NOVEMBER
MARINE CORPS

The 2d Marine Division Scouts and 2d Battalion, 6th Marine Regiment complete the conquest of Tarawa Atoll, Gilbert Islands. Total Marine Corps casualties for the battle are 1,085 dead or missing and 2,233 wounded. Losses among Navy personnel serving with Marine Corps units are 30 killed and 59 wounded.

25 NOVEMBER
MARINE CORPS

The V Amphibious Corps Reconnaissance Company completes its conquest of Apamama Atoll in the Gilbert Islands.

NAVY

In the early morning hours Destroyer Squadron 23 (under Captain Arleigh A. Burke) engages five Japanese destroyers off Cape St. George, New Ireland Island. Burke's squadron, known as the "Little Beavers," sinks three enemy vessels and damages a fourth without suffering any damage. The destroyer *Radford* sinks the Japanese submarine *I-19* north of the Gilbert Islands.

28–29 NOVEMBER
NAVY

The submarines *Pargo* and *Snook* attack a Japanese convoy northwest of the Mariana Islands, sinking three ships.

29 NOVEMBER
MARINE CORPS/NAVY

The 1st Parachute Battalion, reinforced by Company M, 3d Raider Battalion, makes an amphibious raid at Koiari, about 10 miles east of the perimeter on Bougainville Island, Solomon Islands. They encounter a large Japanese force. The destroyers *Fullam*, *Lardner*, and *Lansdowne* rush to the scene. Along with land-based aircraft, the three ships silence shore batteries and permit the extraction of the Marines.

30 NOVEMBER
MARINE CORPS

The 2d Marine Tank Battalion's scout company searches for enemy on Abaiang and Makakei Atolls, north of Tarawa Atoll, Gilbert Islands, and finds only five Japanese. The first Marine Corps aircraft (six SBD Dauntless dive-bombers of Marine Scout Bombing Squadron 331) arrive on the airstrip on Betio Island in the Tarawa Atoll. The airstrip is named after 1st Lieutenant William D. Hawkins, posthumous recipient of the Medal of Honor for his actions in the battle.

DECEMBER
ARMY

Lieutenant General Joseph Stilwell, commander of the China–Burma–India Theater, directs the Office of Strategic Services Detachment 101, operating in Burma, to expand its recruiting of native tribesmen to build a force of 3,000 guerrillas for operations behind Japanese lines. Stilwell is planning a spring offensive into Burma.

1 DECEMBER
MARINE CORPS

The scouts of the 2d Marine Tank Battalion land at Maiana Atoll in the Gilbert Islands and determine it is not occupied by enemy forces.

Above: *P-38 Lightning fighters on patrol. The plane is one of the fastest Allied fighters and carries four .50 caliber machine guns and a 20mm cannon in the nose. (U.S. Army)*

Below: *A Soldier of the 27th Infantry Division helps his wounded buddy to the rear during fighting on New Georgia Island. (U.S. Army)*

Opposite, top: *A Soldier armed with an M1A1 2.36-inch rocket launcher takes cover on one of the Gilbert Islands. This early model "bazooka" is tried against Japanese bunkers with little success. (Dept. of Defense)*

3 DECEMBER
MARINE CORPS

The 1st Marine Parachute Regiment headquarters, weapons company and 3d Battalion arrive at Cape Torokina on Bougainville Island, Solomon Islands.

4 DECEMBER
NAVY

The carriers of Task Force 50 (under Rear Admiral Charles A. Pownall) launch air strikes against Japanese installations on Kwajalein and Wotje islands in the Marshall Islands. In addition to damage inflicted on land targets, the strikes result in the sinking of four enemy vessels and damage to seven other ships, including two light cruisers. During the Japanese counterattack an aircraft puts a torpedo into the carrier *Lexington*.

The submarine *Sailfish* sinks a Japanese escort carrier off Honshu Island, Japan. The submarine's crew is unaware that their quarry carries survivors of their sister ship, *Sculpin*, sunk the previous month.

9 DECEMBER
MARINE CORPS

The 3d Battalion, 1st Parachute Regiment begins an attack to seize Hellzapoppin Ridge, a heavily defended spur east of the perimeter on Bougainville Island, Solomon Islands. The parachutists are relieved by the 1st Battalion, 9th Marine Regiment and 1st Battalion, 21st Marine Regiment on the night of 10 December.

10 DECEMBER
MARINE CORPS

The Cape Torokina airfield on Bougainville Island, Solomon Islands, is declared operational. F4U Corsairs of Marine Fighting Squadron 216 arrive to make it their home, but for the near future, aircraft based on New Georgia Island will simply stage through this intermediate base for refueling.

15 DECEMBER
ARMY/MARINE CORPS/NAVY

Operation DEXTERITY—the campaign to capture New Britain Island—opens with Task Force 76 landing the Alamo's (XIV Corps) Task Force Director, Brigadier General Julian W. Cunningham, on the Arawe peninsula. The task force is composed of the reinforced 112th Cavalry Regiment. Coral reefs prevent use of landing craft, so amphibian tractors from the 1st Marine Division land the troops. Only scattered opposition is met.

ARMY/MARINE CORPS

The XIV Corps (under Major General Oscar W. Griswold) replaces the I Marine Amphibious Corps (Major General Roy S. Geiger) at command headquarters for the Bougainville Island campaign.

17 DECEMBER
MARINE CORPS/NAVY

Major Gregory Boyington of Marine Fighting Squadron 214 leads the first fighter sweep against Rabaul, New Britain Island. Results are disappointing since few Japanese planes challenge the 76 U.S. Marine Corps, Navy, and New Zealand aircraft.

18 DECEMBER
MARINE CORPS

The 21st Marine Regiment take Hellzapoppin Ridge

on Bougainville Island, Solomon Islands, after eight days of fighting, with the help of close air support by Marine Corps planes.

20–23 DECEMBER
AIR FORCE

Army bombers and aircraft of the Fifth Air Force move from New Caledonia Island to begin operations from Russell and Stirling Islands. On 23 December, bombers begin using Munda Airfield on New Georgia Island.

Right: *Initially, the Navy does not consider the F4U-1 Corsair as suitable for aircraft carriers. The first Corsairs in the Pacific area are given to land-based Marine Corps fighter squadrons that operate from airfields on newly captured islands. ("Marine Corsair," James Dietz)*

Left: Marine reinforcements, possibly members of the 1st Marine Parachute Regiment in camouflage uniforms, come ashore on Bougainville Island from Higgins boats in November. (National Archives)

21–22 DECEMBER
MARINE CORPS

Two patrols scout beaches on western New Britain Island near Tauali in preparation for the assault.

22–23 DECEMBER
MARINE CORPS

Elements of the 21st Marine Regiment seize Hill 600A overlooking the Torokina River. This is the last significant action by the 3d Marine Division on Bougainville Island, Solomon Islands.

23 DECEMBER
MARINE CORPS

Major Gregory Boyington of Marine Fighting Squadron 214 leads another fighter sweep of 48 planes against Rabaul, New Britain Island. This time claimed kills total 30, at a cost of 3 American planes. Boyington gets 4, to bring his tally to 24.

Five Marine Scout Bombing Squadron 331 SBD Dauntless dive-bombers from Tarawa Atoll, Gilbert Islands, participate in an attack against enemy shipping at Jaluit Atoll, Marshall Islands.

24 DECEMBER
AIR FORCE

The Fifth Air Force's bombardment of Cape Gloucester, New Britain Island, reaches its peak as 190 B-24 Liberator, B-25 Mitchell, and A-20 Havoc medium bombers pound the area during extensive daylight attacks.

Right: Two men of the 2d Marine Raider Battalion kneel in their flooded foxhole to man a machine gun along the Piva Trail on Bougainville Island. (National Archives)

Opposite: A PT boat makes a fast getaway after a successful torpedo attack on a Japanese destroyer. ("PT Score," James Dietz)

pre-invasion bombardment operations at Cape Gloucester, New Britain Island. Enemy targets are completely destroyed. As the 1st Marine Division lands at Cape Gloucester, B-25 Mitchell and B-24 Liberator bombers continue bombing enemy positions. P-40 Warhawk, P-38 Lightning, and P-47 Thunderbolt fighters provide air defense and claim 60 victories in the enemy-filled skies. The term "Gloucesterizing" is coined to describe such missions of total destruction flown by the Fifth Air Force.

ARMY

The Sixth Army's command post departs Australia and opens a new location at Cape Cretin, New Guinea Island. It is joined by the Alamo Force to train selected soldiers in reconnaissance and raider work. Graduates become known as Alamo Scouts.

MARINE CORPS/NAVY

Task Force 76 (under Rear Admiral Daniel E. Barbey) lands elements of the 1st Marine Division at Cape Gloucester, New Britain Island, with gunfire support from Task Force 74 (under Rear Admiral Victor A. C. Crutchley). The 7th Marine Regiment and 1st Marine Regiment (less the 2d Battalion) go ashore near the Japanese airfields at the cape. The 2d Battalion lands on the western coast to block trails. The heaviest

25 DECEMBER
ARMY/MARINE CORPS

The Army's Americal Division begins relieving the 3d Marine Division on Bougainville Island, Solomon Islands. In the Gilbert Islands, the 4th Marine Base Defense Aircraft Wing headquarters arrives on Tarawa Atoll, Gilbert Islands. The changeover is completed 28 December.

26 DECEMBER
AIR FORCE/MARINE CORPS

The Fifth Air Force accomplishes highly successful

Above: *A Marine Corps gun crew prepares to fire their 105mm howitzer in support of troops on Bougainville Island, Solomon Islands. (National Archives)*

Left: *A Marine and a Navy Seabee shake hands to celebrate the completion of a road on Bougainville Island. (Dept. of Defense)*

Opposite: *Three Soldiers provide cover for a fourth man armed with a flamethrower as he engages a Japanese defensive position near Munda Airfield on New Georgia Island. (Dept. of Defense)*

ground fighting comes when a Japanese battalion counterattacks the lines of the 7th Marines that night. F4U Corsairs from five Marine Corps fighting squadrons provide cover for the operation. The Japanese air attacks claim the destroyer *Brownson*, which sinks in 17 minutes, and damage five other ships.

27 DECEMBER
ARMY/MARINE CORPS
The Army's 164th Infantry Regiment replaces the 9th Marine Regiment at Bougainville Island, Solomon Islands. The Marine Corps regiment and the 3d Parachute Battalion sail for Guadalcanal Island the next day.

MARINE CORPS
Aircraft Solomons fighters conduct sweeps over Rabaul, New Britain Island, through 28 December.

28 DECEMBER
MARINE CORPS
The 3d Battalion, 1st Marine Regiment destroys Japanese forces fighting from a bunker complex, dubbed Hell's Point, astride the path to the Cape Gloucester airfields on New Britain Island.

29 DECEMBER
MARINE CORPS
The 5th Marine Regiment comes ashore to reinforce the drive on the Cape Gloucester airfields on New Britain Island. That night, the 2d Battalion, 1st Marine Regiment defeats a counterattack on its lines at Tauali by elements of a Japanese battalion.

NAVY
Operating off Palau, Caroline Islands, the submarine *Silversides* sinks a Japanese transport and two cargo ships, and damages another cargo ship.

30 DECEMBER
MARINE CORPS
The 1st and 5th Marine Regiments overrun the final enemy defenses and seize the airfields at Cape Gloucester, New Britain Island.

31 DECEMBER
MARINE CORPS
Commandant Lieutenant General Thomas Holcomb retires and is promoted to the rank of general. Lieutenant General Alexander A. Vandegrift becomes the 18th Commandant of the Marine Corps.

1944
CONTEST OF STRENGTH

1 JANUARY
AIR FORCE
In Burma, Tenth Air Force B-25 Mitchell bombers and P-38 Lightning fighters attack a bridge over the Mu River. Bombing from extremely low altitude, Major Robert A. Erdlin drops his bombs while pulling up to avoid a ground obstacle. The low-angle loft successfully drops two spans of the bridge. The "Burma Bridge Busters" are born.

Medium bombers strike troop concentrations and supply targets in preparation for the Allied invasion of New Guinea Island. The Fifth Air Force launches more than 120 B-24 Liberator, B-25 Mitchell, and A-20 Havoc bombers in attacks against targets in the Saidor area.

1–2 JANUARY
ARMY/MARINE CORPS
The 182d Infantry Regiment, Americal Division relieves the 21st Marine Regiment from positions on the perimeter on Bougainville Island, Solomon Islands.

2 JANUARY
AIR FORCE
Tenth Air Force medium and heavy bombers attack targets at Yenangyaung, Burma, setting fire to oil storage facilities and damaging a power plant.

ARMY/NAVY
Task Force 76 (under Rear Admiral Daniel E. Barbey) lands the Sixth Army's Task Force Michaelmas (126th Regimental Combat Team [reinforced], 32d Infantry Division) at Saidor, New Guinea Island. The surprise landing under cover of smoke enables the capture of an important port and airfield.

MARINE CORPS
On New Britain Island, the 7th Marine Regiment and 3d Battalion, 5th Marine Regiment attacks across Suicide Creek to enlarge the beachhead perimeter at Cape Gloucester and also stave off an enemy night attack against Target Hill.

In the Solomon Islands, the 2d Parachute Battalion sails from Vella Lavella Island to Guadalcanal Island to rejoin the 1st Parachute Regiment.

3 JANUARY
MARINE CORPS
Major Gregory Boyington shoots down three enemy planes during a fighter sweep over Rabaul, New Britain Island, only to be shot down himself soon after. His claimed kills give him 28 (including those scored during earlier service with the American Volunteer Group), two more than Captain Joe Foss' record. Boyington spends the rest of the war as a prisoner of war, receiving the Medal of Honor. Aircraft Solomons maintains a daily schedule of heavy attacks on Rabaul throughout the month.

Left: *A Zero is brought down by a Marine Corps F4U Corsair. ("What a Helluva Thing," Paul J. Clinkenbroomer, Art Collection, National Museum of the Marine Corps, Triangle, VA)*

NAVY

The submarine *Scorpion* departs Midway Atoll on her final war patrol. After she conducts a rendezvous with the submarine *Herring* on 5 January, *Scorpion* is never heard from again.

6 JANUARY
ARMY

In Burma, Brigadier General Frank D. Merrill assumes command of the 3,000-man 5307th Composite Unit (Provisional), code-named Galahad Force. It will soon win renown as "Merrill's Marauders." Since October, the unit has been training in India under the British in long-range penetration tactics.

6–11 JANUARY
MARINE CORPS

The 7th Marine Regiment and 3d Battalion, 5th Marine Regiment seize Aogiri Ridge to expand the Cape Gloucester perimeter on New Britain Island.

7 JANUARY
AIR FORCE

Lieutenant General Hubert R. Harmon assumes command of the Thirteenth Air Force. In June, he will

Above: F6F-3 Hellcats prepare to launch from the light carrier Cowpens for a January 1944 raid on the Marshall Islands. (Naval Historical Center)

Below: A Soldier of the 37th Infantry Division prepares to hurl a hand grenade at an enemy position on Bougainville Island. (National Archives)

Above: *A weary Marine Corps pilot stands alongside the wing of his F4U Corsair. ("Marine Airman," Kerr Eby, Navy Art Collection)*

Below: *A Marine slowly moves his M3 Stuart light tank down the ramp of a tank lighter. The Marine Corps uses the small M3 early in the war until larger landing craft become available. (National Archives)*

assume command of the Sixth Air Force (later the Caribbean Air Command). Harmon will be recalled from retirement in 1953 to be appointed as the first superintendent of the newly established U.S. Air Force Academy, effective 14 August 1954.

MARINE CORPS/NAVY
Dive-bombers and torpedo-bombers from New Georgia Island and fighters from Bougainville Island, Solomon Islands, stage a large raid against the Japanese base of Rabaul on New Britain Island. A similar attack is made two days later.

10 JANUARY
AIR FORCE
More than 100 Fifth Air Force medium and heavy bombers hit targets on New Britain Island near Madang, Alexishafen, and Bogadjim while P-39 Airacobra fighters strafe villages and barges.

AIR FORCE/NAVY
Lieutenant General Hubert R. Harmon's Thirteenth Air Force begins a night bombardment campaign against New Britain Island. B-24 Liberator bombers strike airfields at Lakunai and Vunakanau, as well as supply depots near Buka. Thirteenth Air Force and U.S. Navy fighters provide air cover while Navy dive-bombers hit targets at Cape Saint George. Similar missions are flown the next day.

10–11 JANUARY
NAVY
In a two-day attack against a Japanese convoy in the waters north of Okinawa, Japan, the submarine *Seawolf* sinks three cargo ships.

11 JANUARY
ARMY/MARINE CORPS
A company of the Marine 1st Tank Battalion is deployed to Arawe, New Britain Island, to reinforce the Army's Task Force Director (112th Cavalry reinforced) which is holding the peninsula. The next day elements of the 158th Infantry Regiment and a company of light tanks from the 1st Marine Division land to strengthen the Task Force Director's beachhead at Arawe.

13 JANUARY
AIR FORCE
Lieutenant General Kenneth B. Wolfe, XX Bomber Command, arrives at New Delhi, India, with his advance staff. His arrival marks the beginning of deployment for Operation MATTERHORN—the B-29 Superfortress bomber offensive against Japan.

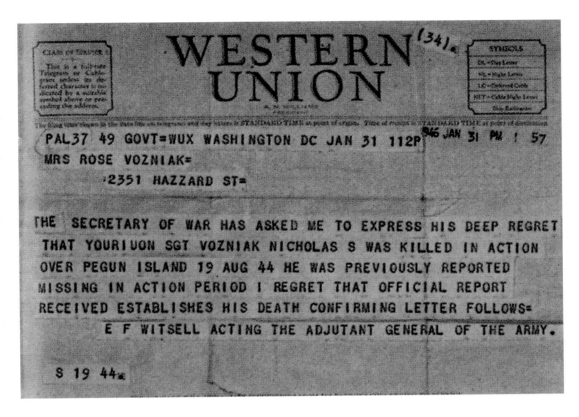

ARINE CORPS

The 9th Defense Battalion begins to move from New Georgia Island, Solomon Islands, to the Russell Islands.

13–14 JANUARY
AIR FORCE/NAVY

During a midnight raid, two dozen Thirteenth Air Force B-24 Liberators bomb the airfields at Vunakanau and Malaguna, New Britain Island.

At dawn, a dozen B-25 Mitchell bombers strike targets near Buna, New Guinea Island. P-39 Airacobra fighters join Navy SBD Dauntless dive-bombers in attacking Wakuni. During the day, a large joint operation is carried out when 70 Allied fighters support 50 Navy dive-bombers in an attack against shipping in Simpson Harbor.

MARINE CORPS

On New Britain Island, the 7th Marine Regiment seizes Hill 660, the last piece of terrain needed to complete the Cape Gloucester perimeter.

15 JANUARY
NAVY

Service Squadron 10 is established at Pearl Harbor, Hawaii. Under the command of Captain Worrall R. Carter, the squadron's ships will provide vital mobile logistic support to the Central Pacific campaign.

16 JANUARY
AIR FORCE/ARMY/MARINE CORPS

Following a preparatory bombardment on New Britain Island by attack and medium bombers, two companies of the 158th Infantry Regiment and a troop of the 112th Cavalry Regiment led by the Marine Corps light tanks gain over 1,500 yards, breaking the Japanese line. The next day, remaining pockets of Japanese troops are eliminated. Task Force Director casualties are 474 killed, wounded, and missing.

MARINE CORPS

The last elements of the 3d Marine Division return to Guadalcanal Island, Solomon Islands. Marine Corps casualties during the Bougainville Island campaign total 732 dead and 1,249 wounded. Losses among Navy personnel serving with Marine Corps units are 12 killed and 30 wounded.

18 JANUARY
AIR FORCE

In a very active day for the Fifth Air Force over New Guinea Island, 40 B-24 Liberators bomb Hansa Bay while another group of B-24s attacks Laha. More than 70 B-25 Mitchell bombers attack Madang and Bogadjim, New Britain Island, and other positions near Shaggy Ridge. More than 50 Allied Air Forces fighters engage 50 Japanese fighters over Wewak. Three P-38 Lightning fighters are lost. Similar attacks continue for the next three days.

Left: *Soldiers of the 7th Infantry Division set up communications in a shell crater on one of the three islands of Kwajalein Atoll, Marshall Islands. One Soldier carries an air marking panel on his pack to signal aircraft overhead if necessary, as ground and aircraft radios are not able to communicate. ("Radio Communications," Edward A. Sallenback, Army Art Collection, U.S. Army Center of Military History)*

19 JANUARY
ARMY

The Saidor beachhead on New Guinea Island is reinforced with the arrival of the 128th Regimental Combat Team, 32d Infantry Division. They are joined by the 863d Aviation Engineer Battalion on 29 January to begin airfield repair and construction.

22 JANUARY
AIR FORCE

Thirteenth Air Force medium and heavy bombers, flying under cover of 90 fighter planes, seriously damage the runway at Lakunai, New Britain Island. The bombers continue attacking the airfield until the end of the month.

MARINE CORPS

The 1st Marine Division begins aggressive patrolling of the interior of western New Britain Island.

NAVY

The Japanese submarine *RO-37* torpedoes the oiler *Cache* southeast of San Cristobal Island, Solomon Islands, and is then sunk by the destroyer *Buchanan*.

24 JANUARY
MARINE CORPS

F4U Corsair fighters of Marine Fighting Squadron 422 depart Hawkins Field on Betio Island, Tarawa Atoll, Gilbert Islands, bound for Funafuti, Ellice Islands, 700 miles distant. Due to bad weather, 22 of 23 planes ditch in the water and six pilots die.

28 JANUARY
MARINE CORPS

The 16th Marine Regiment (engineer) is activated at Camp Lejeune, North Carolina, for eventual duty with the 5th Marine Division.

29 JANUARY
AIR FORCE

Seventh Air Force B-24 Liberator bombers open a 'round-the-clock offensive against enemy bases in the Gilbert Islands as the Allied invasion forces approach. Single-plane night attacks and formation day strikes keep the Japanese on the defensive. Formations of P-39 Airacobra fighters flying in flights of four patrol the airfield at Mille, denying its use to the enemy. B-24 Liberators bomb Kwajalein Island, Marshall Islands, during the next 48 hours to soften the landing zone for the invasion forces.

NAVY

Task Force 58, the Pacific Fleet's carrier striking force under Rear Admiral Marc A. Mitscher, begins launching air strikes against the Marshall Islands in preparation for U.S. landings. Commanded by the pioneer naval aviator throughout the entire war, Task Force 58 spearheads the Central Pacific offensive toward the Japanese home islands.

30 JANUARY
MARINE CORPS

1st Lieutenant Robert Hanson shoots down four Japanese planes, giving him a total of 25 kills, 20 of them in the course of six missions over the previous

13 days. His tally is the highest of any Marine F4U Corsair fighter pilot during the war. He dies during a mission on 3 February, but eventually receives the Medal of Honor. Total aircraft Solomons sorties over Rabaul, New Britain Island, for the month are 873 by light bombers and 1,850 by fighters. They claim 503 enemy aircraft destroyed, at a cost of 65 planes lost.

The "Gilnit Group" is formed under the command of Lieutenant Colonel Lewis B. Puller. A battalion-size patrol composed of elements of all three regiments of the 1st Marine Division, it is tasked with clearing all enemy forces in the interior of western New Britain Island. The group continues operations until 18 February.

31 JANUARY
ALL SERVICES
Following an intense bombardment the previous day and supported by carrier aircraft, Marines and Army troops go ashore on Kwajalein and Majuro Atolls in the Marshall Islands from ships under the command of Vice Admiral Raymond A. Spruance.

ARMY
Provisional groups from the 7th Infantry Division (under Major General Charles H. Corlett) secure a number of small islands controlling the inlets into the Kwajalein Atoll, Marshall Islands. Battalion landing teams from the 17th Regimental Combat Team secure two larger islands. All the islands are only lightly defended.

Above: *Soldiers of the 148th Infantry, 37th Infantry Division, navigate narrow, muddy jungle trails to carry water and hot food to the front line units fighting to secure the Munda Airfield on New Georgia Island, Solomon Islands. (U.S. Army)*

Below: *The battleship* Idaho *uses her 14-inch main guns to provide support during an invasion in the Marshall Islands. The bitter experience of Tarawa Atoll taught planners that there is never too much pre-invasion bombardment. (USMC)*

Above: *Two Marine M4 Sherman tanks with 75mm main guns make their way through the jungle following the landing of the 1st Marine Division at Cape Gloucester on New Britain Island, Solomon Islands. ("Tank-Infantry Team, Cape Gloucester," Master Tech.Sgt. Victor P. Donahue, Art Collection, National Museum of the Marine Corps, Triangle, Virginia)*

Below: *Soldier or Marine, the infantryman's best friend is his rifle, and maintaining it is a full-time job. ("Marine's Best Friend," Col. Donald L. Dickson, USMCR, Art Collection, National Museum of the Marine Corps, Triangle, Virginia)*

MARINE CORPS

In the Marshall Islands, the 25th Marine Regiment seizes the islands of Mellu, Ennuebing, Ennumennet, Ennubir, and Ennugarret in the northern end of Kwajalein Atoll, against light resistance. The 14th Marine Regiment places artillery there to support the 4th Marine Division's landings scheduled for the next day on Roi-Namur Island. Meanwhile, the V Amphibious Corps Reconnaissance Company occupies Majuro Atoll.

1 FEBRUARY
AIR FORCE/ARMY/NAVY

Seventh Air Force fighter aircraft rapidly advance to occupy newly established bases in the Gilbert Islands. Operation CATCHPOLE begins with the goal of taking Eniwetok Atoll, Marshall Islands, from the Japanese and then using its airfields to strike important airfields in the Mariana Islands. Battalion landing teams from the 184th and 32d Infantry Regiments secure beachheads on the west end of main Kwajalein Island, Marshall Islands. Initial resistance is minimal. At mid-day, the 2d Battalion, 32d Infantry takes up the attack, and by the end of the day the 7th Infantry Division holds a third of the island.

ARMY

The Northern Area Combat Command is created in the China–Burma–India Theater with Brigadier General Haydon L. Boatner in command. All Allied forces entering North Burma are attached to it. Army engineers are working on improving the roads to support Lieutenant General Joseph Stilwell's Chinese divisions.

MARINE CORPS

In the Marshall Islands, the 23d Marine Regiment assaults Roi-Namur Island, Kwajalein Atoll, and overruns the entire island by late afternoon. The 24th Marine Regiment attacks Namur and captures about two-thirds of the island by nightfall. The 1st Raider Regiment, recently returned to Guadalcanal Island, Solomon Islands, is redesignated as the 4th Marine Regiment, resurrecting the regiment that had disappeared when the Japanese captured Corregidor Island, Philippine Islands, in 1942.

NAVY

Amphibious Forces, Pacific Fleet is established with headquarters at Pearl Harbor, Hawaii, and placed under the command of Vice Admiral Richmond Kelly Turner.

Right: *Two P-51A Mustang fighters of the 1st Air Commando Group fly over the mountains of Burma. The group marks its fighters and B-24 Liberator bombers with a distinctive candy-cane stripe paint scheme for easy identification. Only five of the group's 30 P-51s are lost during 1,500 combat missions. (U.S. Air Force)*

2 FEBRUARY
MARINE CORPS

The 24th Marine Regiment completes the seizure of Namur Island. When mopping-up actions are finished a few days later, the 4th Marine Division's casualties in the campaign for Kwajalein and Majuro Atolls in the Marshall Islands total 387 killed and 631 wounded.

NAVY

The destroyer *Walker* sinks the Japanese submarine *RO-39* east of Wotje Atoll, Marshall Islands.

3 FEBRUARY
AIR FORCE

Colonel Philip Cochran leads five P-51 Mustang fighters on the first air-commando combat mission, flying against Japanese targets in the China–Burma–India Theater.

Fifth Air Force fighters and bombers attack Wewak, New Guinea Island, destroying approximately 80 enemy aircraft on the ground. P-39 Airacobra fighters and B-25 Mitchell bombers continue to strike shipping targets in the Bismarck Sea.

5 FEBRUARY
ARMY

The 7th Infantry Division continues to work its way up the Kwajalein Atoll, Marshall Islands, toward the Marines, cleaning out pockets of Japanese resistance. Units of the 17th Infantry Regiment land and clear three other small islands of the atoll. On Bennett

Island, the 184th Infantry Regiment with two tanks assists the 7th Reconnaissance Troop in eliminating a group of defenders.

MARINE CORPS

The 5th Marine Regiment begins an advance eastward along the north coast of New Britain Island using landing craft for shore-to-shore movements.

NAVY

The destroyer *Charrette* and destroyer escort *Fair* sink the Japanese submarine *I-21* north of Jaluit Atoll, Marshall Islands.

7 FEBRUARY
MARINE CORPS

Ground elements of the 4th Marine Base Defense Air Wing arrive at Roi-Namur Island, Marshall Islands. The first aircraft of Marine Aircraft Group 31 arrive on 15 February.

8 FEBRUARY
MARINE CORPS

The 4th Marine Division departs Kwajalein Atoll, Marshall Islands. The 25th Marine Regiment is detached to remain behind as the garrison force.

10 FEBRUARY
ARMY

The Sixth Army declares a successful end to Operation DEXTERITY with the securing of New Britain Island and Saidor, New Guinea Island.

12 FEBRUARY
MARINE CORPS

A Japanese air raid strikes an ammunition dump on Roi-Namur Island in the Marshall Islands. The resulting explosions kill 26, wound 130, and destroy large quantities of supplies.

13 FEBRUARY
ARMY

As the next step in Operation CARTWHEEL, the elimination of the Japanese at Rabaul, New Britain

Island, General Douglas MacArthur directs the Sixth Army to seize Manus and Kavieng Islands in the Admiralty Islands (Operation BREWER). The small island of Los Negros offers the entry point. The 1st Cavalry Division (under Major General Innis P. Swift) with reinforcements, code named Brewer Force, will test the Japanese defenses on Los Negros and, if possible, secure the island.

15 FEBRUARY
AIR FORCE/NAVY

Lieutenant (junior grade) Nathan G. Gordon of Patrol Squadron 34 makes four water landings with his PBY Catalina patrol-bomber under intense enemy fire off Kavieng, New Ireland Island, to rescue crews of three downed Army bombers. Gordon flies 15 men to safety, and receives the Medal of Honor for his heroism.

16 FEBRUARY
AIR FORCE

The Allied air attack on Truk Islands, Caroline Islands, begins and will continue for one full month.

NAVY

The destroyer *Phelps* and minesweeper *Sage* sink the Japanese submarine *RO-40* northwest of Kwajalein Atoll, Marshall Islands.

17 FEBRUARY
ARMY/MARINE CORPS

The V Amphibious Corps Reconnaissance Company and the scout company of the Marine 4th Tank Battalion occupy three small islands in Eniwetok Atoll, Marshall Islands. Marine Corps and Army artillery batteries follow and set up to support the main landings the next day.

NAVY

Task Force 58 strikes the Japanese naval base in the Truk Islands, Caroline Islands, causing heavy damage to shore installations and sinking 33 ships in the harbor and surrounding waters. The aircraft carrier *Intrepid* takes a torpedo during a Japanese counterattack. (*Intrepid*'s propensity for suffering battle damage during World War II leads to her being dubbed "Evil I.") The attacks against Truk continue into the following day.

The destroyer *Nicholas* sinks the Japanese submarine *I-11* northwest of the Marshall Islands.

18–19 FEBRUARY
ARMY/MARINE CORPS/NAVY

Task Group 51.11 supports the landing of the 22d Marine Regiment on Engebi Island, Eniwetok Atoll, Marshall Islands, against limited resistance. Army artillery provides support. The next day, the 106th Regimental Combat Team, 27th Infantry Division, lands two battalions on Eniwetok Island. A strong enemy counterattack requires reinforcement by a battalion of the 22d Marine Regiment.

19 FEBRUARY
AIR FORCE

More than 60 Tenth Air Force A-36 Apache dive-bombers, P-51 Mustang fighters, and B-25 Mitchell bombers strike a variety of targets in Burma. Fuel supply depots, rail cars, and river traffic are attacked over a wide area. The Fourteenth Air Force continues flying "sea sweeps" in search of targets of opportunity from the Formosa Straight to Indochina. B-24 Liberator and B-25 bombers, and P-40 Warhawk fighters claim three ships sunk and bridges, trains, and depots also attacked. The same day, Seventh Air Force bombers pound targets near Ponape Island, Caroline Islands, and Wotje Island, Marshall Islands.

Opposite, top: *Thick jungle and brush on the Pacific islands limits visibility and hampers movement. The Japanese take advantage of this at every opportunity in making their defensive positions. (National Archives)*

Opposite, bottom: *Specially waterproofed M4A1 Sherman tanks land on Kwajalein Island, Marshall Islands, in January 1944 to reinforce the assault force. The high metal vent pipes on the rear of the tanks permit them to wade through deep water to come ashore. (U.S. Army)*

Right: *Crewman on the carrier* Saratoga *help a wounded turret-gunner out of his TBF Avenger torpedo-bomber after a raid on Rabaul, New Britain Island. Though injured, the gunner continued to fight off enemy planes on the return flight. (National Archives)*

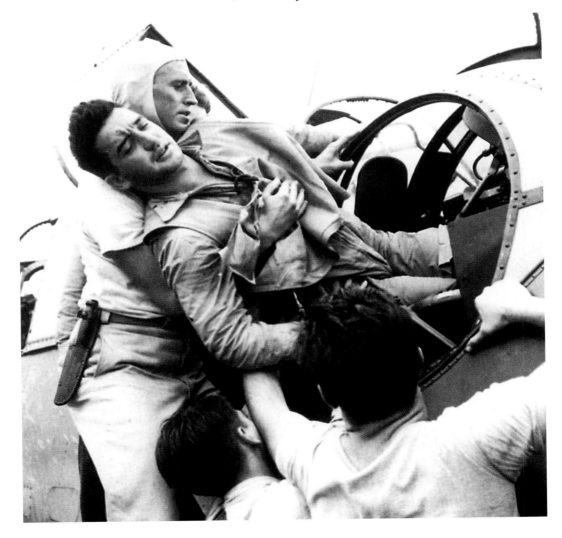

MARINE CORPS

In the last significant aerial battle over Rabaul, New Britain Island, an Aircraft Solomons 139-plane strike tangles with 30 enemy fighters and claims 23 kills. The Japanese withdraw their remaining planes from Rabaul. Air attacks continue for the remainder of the war against ground targets at the sprawling Japanese base complex.

NAVY

During operations in the South China Sea, the submarine *Jack* attacks a convoy of six enemy tankers

escorted by a lone destroyer, sending four of the tankers to the bottom.

20 FEBRUARY
ARMY/MARINE CORPS

The 3d Battalion, 22d Marine Regiment and the 1st Battalion, 106th Regimental Combat Team (RCT) complete clearing the southern end of Eniwetok Island, Marshall Islands. The 3d Battalion, 106th RCT continues the attack to capture the northeastern end.

21 FEBRUARY
ARMY/MARINE CORPS

Soldiers and Marines units complete the seizure of Eniwetok Island, Marshall Islands. Marine Scout Bombing Squadron 231 flies onto the airfield at Majuro Atoll. Aircraft Solomons bombers sink two Japanese merchant ships attempting to evacuate ground crews on Rabaul, New Britain Island.

22 FEBRUARY
AIR FORCE/MARINE CORPS

The Fifth Air Force sends B-24 Liberator and B-25 Mitchell bombers to attack Iboki Plantation as Marines advance on New Britain Island. One Seventh Air Force P-40 Thunderbolt fighter launches rockets against an airfield target. This is the first rocket attack made by any Seventh Air Force plane.

MARINE CORPS

The 22d Marine Regiment, reinforced by a 500-man provisional infantry battalion formed from elements of

the 10th Defense Battalion, overruns Japanese defenders on Parry Island, completing the seizure of Eniwetok Atoll, Marshall Islands. Marine Corps casualties during the Eniwetok campaign total 254 killed and 555 wounded. Losses among Navy personnel serving with Marine Corps units at Kwajalein, Majuro, and Eniwetok Atolls are 6 killed and 36 wounded.

NAVY
In the first carrier strikes launched against the Mariana Islands, the carriers of Task Force 58 send their air groups against the islands of Saipan, Tinian, Rota, and Guam. During two days of strikes, naval aviators sink three vessels and damage a fourth.

24 FEBRUARY
ARMY
The 5307th Provisional Unit (Marauders) marches toward the Hukawng Valley of Burma to harass Japanese forces and with the ultimate mission of capturing the two airfields at Myitkyina.

MARINE CORPS
Elements of the 5th Marine Regiment seize the Iboki Plantation on the north-central coast of New Britain Island.

25 FEBRUARY
MARINE CORPS
The 10th Defense Battalion assumes garrison duties for Eniwetok Island, Marshall Islands.

26 FEBRUARY
MARINE CORPS
In the Marshall Islands, Marine Scout Bombing Squadron 331 arrives on Majuro Atoll, and the 22d Marine Regiment arrives on Kwajalein Atoll to relieve the 25th Marine Regiment from garrison duty.

27 FEBRUARY
ARMY
Delivered off shore at night by a PBY Catalina patrol-bomber, a six-man patrol of Sixth Army Alamo Scouts paddles rubber boats ashore on Los Negros Island off the tip of larger Manus Island in the Admiralty Islands. Contrary to intelligence reports, the scouts find a large Japanese force.

MARINE CORPS
The 51st Defense Battalion relieves the 7th Defense Battalion in the Ellice Islands.

28 FEBRUARY
AIR FORCE
On New Guinea Island, Fifth Air Force B-24 Liberator bombers continue to attack landing areas for advancing Allied troops. Airfields in Nubia and Awar as well as targets in Hansa Bay area are also struck in anticipation of the landings.

The Thirteenth Air Force launches a multi-wave attack upon Rabaul, New Britain Island. First, 22 B-25 Mitchell bombers with fighter escorts bomb targets;

Right: *Marines of the 51st Defense Battalion pose around their 3-inch antiaircraft gun in a sandbagged position on Eniwetok Island, Marshall Islands. They name their gun Lena Horne in honor of a popular singer. (USMC)*

next, P-38 Lightning fighters drop glide bombs on the same targets; then, just minutes later, 11 B-24 Liberator bombers pound the same targets again. P-39 Airacobra fighters and Navy dive-bombers hit other targets as well.

29 FEBRUARY
AIR FORCE
Fifth Air Force bombers destroy two Japanese air bases at Alexishafen, New Guinea Island. These strikes are in support of Allied landings in the Admiralty Islands and complete the isolation of Rabaul, New Britain Island.

29 FEBRUARY–1 MARCH
AIR FORCE/ARMY/NAVY
With air and naval gunfire support, Task Group 76.1 (under Rear Admiral William M. Fechteler) lands the 1st Brigade (minus), 1st Cavalry Division on Los Negros Island, Admiralty Islands, as General Douglas MacArthur watches from the cruiser *Phoenix*. The assault waves, 2d Squadron, 5th Cavalry Regiment, meet light enemy fire. The airfield is secured and defenses set up. Throughout the night the cavalrymen battle enemy infiltrators; 67 Japanese are killed within the perimeter. Patrols the next day encounter stronger resistance, and enemy attacks resume in the evening. The Sixth Army orders Major General Innis P. Swift to bring the rest of his force to capture Manus Island and the rest of the Admiralty Islands.

1 MARCH
AIR FORCE
Supporting invasion forces, the Fifth Air Force strikes targets on Los Negros Island and near Lorengau on Manus Island, Admiralty Islands. More than 100 bombers and fighters attack targets near Wewak, New Guinea Island, including enemy positions at Madang and Saiba. These attacks continue until the landings on 22 April at Hollandia, New Guinea. Direct support continues as U.S. troops begin the process of taking the island.

The XI Strategic Air Force is activated at Shemya Island, Aleutian Islands. It is composed of the forces of the XI Bomber and XI Fighter Command and becomes a tactical operating agency along the Aleutian Islands.

1–2 MARCH
MARINE CORPS
Marine Aircraft Group 22 aircraft begin to arrive on Engebi Island, Eniwetok Atoll, Marshall Islands. The 5th Defense Battalion departs the Ellice Islands for Hawaii.

2 MARCH
ARMY/NAVY
Two squadrons of the 5th Cavalry Regiment attack and expand the beachhead to encompass the airfield on Los Negros Island, Admiralty Islands. The defenses are strengthened with the arrival of artillery,

engineers, and Navy Seabees. During the night of 3–4 March, a major Japanese attack hits the 2d Squadron, 5th Cavalry, but is repulsed. Sergeant Troy A. McGill defends a position until all eight of his men are dead or wounded. Ordering the wounded to the rear, he holds back the Japanese with a clubbed rifle until he is killed. He is awarded the Medal of Honor. Sixty-one soldiers and Seabees are killed or wounded, but the Japanese are thwarted and withdraw.

3 MARCH
AIR FORCE

Operation FORAGER begins to capture the Mariana Islands. Airfields there will allow B-29 Superfortress bombers to strike the Japanese mainland with efficiency. The Seventh Air Force is tasked to neutralize enemy air activity in the Caroline Islands and continue to bomb Wake Island while bypassing the Marshall Islands during the operation.

4 MARCH
ARMY

The 2d Battalion, 5307th Provisional Unit sets up a blocking position near Kumnyan, Burma, along the main route of Japanese withdrawal. Repeated Japanese efforts to break through are unsuccessful. An attack against a second block at Walawbum held by the 3d Battalion also fails with heavy losses. On 5 March, the 2d Battalion moves to join the 3d Battalion. They are joined by the joint Chinese–American 1st Provisional Tank Group.

MARINE CORPS

The 4th Marine Base Defense Air Wing, recently arrived in Kwajalein Atoll, begins its campaign against Wotje, Jaluit, and other atolls in the eastern Marshall Islands with attacks by Marine Scout Bombing Squadron 331. The aerial neutralization campaign continues until the surrender of Japan in August 1945.

Above: *The 6th Army Alamo Scouts are a group of specially trained Soldiers used for reconnaissance, small raids, and scouting. The volunteer Scouts, created by Lieutenant General Walter Krueger, locate enemy forces prior to landings. (Company of Military Historians)*

Right: *Soldiers of the 5th Cavalry Regiment, 1st Cavalry Division make a surprise landing at Los Negros Island, Admiralty Islands, in February 1944. The Japanese soon recover and launch a fierce night counterattack that nearly overruns the cavalrymen's lines. (U.S. Army)*

5 MARCH
AIR FORCE/ARMY

Under cover of darkness, Army gliders insert British Special Forces troops (under Brigadier General Orde C. Wingate) 50 miles northeast of Indaw, Burma. The gliders are flown by Colonel Philip G. Cochran's 1st Air Commando Group (not officially formed until later in the month). Almost half of the gliders land successfully, but some troops cannot deploy because the Japanese have cut trees across the second landing zone. U.S. Army engineers parachute in to assist. In total, 539 men, three mules, and more than 30 tons of equipment are delivered for the mission, which successfully halts the Japanese invasion of India.

6 MARCH
ARMY

The 12th Cavalry Regiment, 1st Cavalry Division lands with tanks, artillery, and more support units on Los Negros Island, Admiralty Islands.

MARINE CORPS

The 5th Marine Regiment, with the 1st Battalion in the lead, conducts an amphibious assault against the Willaumez Peninsula, New Britain Island. In three days of fighting, the regiment clears the area of Japanese forces.

7 MARCH
ARMY

A Japanese counteroffensive on Bougainville Island, Solomon Islands, aims to recapture Hill 700 from the 148th Infantry Regiment, 37th Infantry Division with artillery fire and a night attack. Attacks continue on 8 March with penetrations into the 148th Infantry lines. The 145th Infantry Regiment loses part of Hill 260 on 9 March and is unable to retake it. The next day the 182d Infantry Regiment, Americal Division is forced off the hill, and a counterattack by the 145th has limited success. Heavy fighting continues on 11 March in both the Americal and 37th Division sectors as the main Japanese attack hits the 127th Infantry, 37th Division.

11 MARCH
AIR FORCE

Seventh Air Force B-24 Liberator bombers operate from runways on Kwajalein Island, Marshall Islands, for the first time. Their first attack against Wake Island from bases in the Marshall Islands is supported by P-40 Warhawk fighters and B-25 Mitchell bombers operating from the Gilbert Islands.

ARMY

In the Admiralty Islands, patrols scout landing sites on Manus Island and nearby islands for Japanese artillery that could harm the Manus landing. The patrol landing on Hauwei Island is ambushed and

barely escapes with rescue by a PT boat. The 2d Squadron, 7th Cavalry Regiment returns to Hauwei the next day and hits strong resistance. Using tanks, the island is secured on 13 March.

On Bougainville Island, Solomon Islands, combined infantry-tank counterattacks by regiments of the 37th and Americal Divisions restores most of the lost positions on Hills 700 and 260 after intense fighting.

12 MARCH
MARINE CORPS
The Joint Chiefs of Staff direct the return of the 1st Marine Division from General Douglas MacArthur's Southwest Pacific Area to control of Commander in Chief Pacific Area Command, Admiral Chester W. Nimitz.

13 MARCH
NAVY
The submarine *Sand Lance* sinks a Japanese light cruiser and a cargo ship in the waters off Japan, but pays a penalty for her success by spending more than 18 hours submerged as Japanese escort vessels batter her with 105 depth charges.

15 MARCH
AIR FORCE

Seventh Air Force B-24 Liberator bombers, operating from Kwajalein Atoll, Marshall Islands, make the first land-based air attack on the Truk Islands, Caroline Islands. B-25 bombers from Tarawa Atoll, Gilbert Islands, strike Maloelap Atoll, Marshall Islands.

AIR FORCE/MARINE CORPS

Major General Ralph J. Mitchell ends his tour as commander of Aircraft Solomons. Lieutenant General Hubert R. Harmon takes command, and his forces continue to provide support throughout the region.

MARINE CORPS

Admiral William F. Halsey Jr., commander of the South Pacific area, orders the 4th Marine Regiment to seize Emirau Island, Admiralty Islands, on 20 March. Located 230 miles northwest of Rabaul, New Britain Island, it would complete the mission of surrounding the Japanese bastion. The 4th Marine Regiment receives the assignment, draws up plans, and embarks within two days.

15–18 MARCH
ARMY/NAVY

The 2d Brigade, 1st Cavalry Division (under Brigadier General Verne S. Mudge) lands on Manus Island, Admiralty Islands, at two beaches against light opposition. The 1st and 2d Squadrons, 8th Cavalry Regiment move on converging trails toward the Lorengau village and airfield, breaking through Japanese roadblocks and bunkers. Navy destroyers provide gunfire support. The airfield is secured on

18 March, but fighting on Los Negros, Manus, and other Admiralty Islands continues until mid-May. The Manus–Los Negros harbor becomes one of the largest Navy facilities in the Pacific.

20 MARCH
AIR FORCE/MARINE CORPS/NAVY

Task Group 31.2 (under Commodore Lawrence F. Reifsnider) lands the 4th Marine Division on Emirau Island, Admiralty Islands. Construction of air bases begins immediately. The Thirteenth Air Force provides support by attacking surrounding airfields. Radar-equipped SB-24 Snooper bombers cover the Marines' approach to the island. Meanwhile, four battleships, two escort carriers, and destroyers of Task

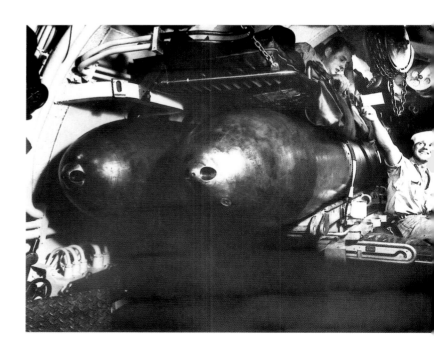

Right: *A PBJ bomber of Marine Bombing Squadron (VMB) 611 flies over a native village on Emirau Island, Admiralty Islands. VMB-611 is the first Marine Corps bombing squadron in the Pacific. During the war, VMB squadrons lose 45 aircraft and 173 crewmen. ("Marine Bombers Over Emirau," Robert T. Horvath, Art Collection, National Museum of the Marine Corps, Triangle, Virginia)*

Force 37 (under Rear Admiral Robert M. Griffin) bombard Kavieng, New Ireland Island.

MARINE CORPS

Plans for the invasion of the Mariana Islands assign the V Amphibious Corps (with the 2d and 4th Marine Divisions) the mission of seizing the islands of Saipan and Tinian, while the I Marine Amphibious Corps (3d Marine Division and 1st Provisional Marine Brigade) tackles Guam. Lieutenant General Holland M. Smith doubles as overall commander of both corps as well as the V Amphibious Corps.

21 MARCH
MARINE CORPS

The 3d Battalion, 22d Marine Regiment seizes Ailinglapalap Atoll in the southern Marshall Islands after a brief fight.

22 MARCH
MARINE CORPS

The 1st Provisional Marine Brigade headquarters is activated at Pearl Harbor, Hawaii. The primary components of the brigade will be the 4th Marine Regiment (on Emirau Island, Admiralty Islands) and the 22d Marine Regiment (on Kwajalein Atoll, Marshall Islands).

23 MARCH
ARMY

A general Japanese assault against the 129th Infantry Regiment, 37th Division, on Bougainville Island, Solomon Islands, is repulsed with heavy enemy losses. A renewed Japanese attack the next day is defeated, ending the main Japanese effort to defend the Solomon Islands.

In Burma, the 5307th Provisional Unit (Task Force Galahad) bypasses Japanese positions and tries to set up a road block along the Kamaing Road. Strong Japanese units in the area force Task Force Galahad to move to a new location.

MARINE CORPS

Elements of the 3d Battalion, 22d Marine Regiment attack Ebon Atoll in the Marshall Islands and clear it of the enemy.

25 MARCH
NAVY

Operating south of Wotje Island, Marshall Islands, the destroyer escort *Manlove* and submarine chaser *PC-1135* sink the Japanese submarine *I-32*.

26 MARCH
NAVY

A torpedo fired from the submarine *Tullibee* malfunctions, making a circular run and sinking the submarine north of the Palau Islands.

Left: *A squadron of Army Air Forces B-24 Liberator bombers sits on one of the Pacific islands. As islands are captured, Army engineers and Seabees quickly refurbish and expand the existing airstrips or build new ones to support the Allied advance. (U.S. Air Force)*

Below: *Taking advantage of a lull in action, a Marine Corps machine gunner eats a can of rations while keeping a wary eye on the jungle to his front. ("Mess on Machine Gun Watch," A. Draut)*

28 MARCH
MARINE CORPS

A reinforced company of the 2d Battalion, 22d Marine Regiment lands on Bikini Atoll, Marshall Islands, and raises the U.S. flag.

28–31 MARCH
ARMY

In Burma, the 2d Battalion, 5307th Provisional Unit establishes a roadblock on the Kamaing Road and defensive positions near Nhpum Ga. Japanese forces make repeated efforts to eliminate the block, but are defeated, trapping them between the American and advancing Chinese units. Japanese units finally succeed in surrounding the battalion.

29 MARCH
AIR FORCE

The 1st Air Commando Group is activated in India.

Thirteenth Air Force bombers—commanded by Lieutenant Colonel Philip G. Cochran and Lieutenant Colonel John R. Alison—carry out the first daylight raids on the Truk Islands, Caroline Islands. Many Japanese aircraft are destroyed, but two B-24 Liberator bombers are also lost.

MARINE CORPS

Admiral Ernest J. King, Commander in Chief, U.S. Fleet/Chief of Naval Operations, authorizes Lieutenant General Holland M. Smith to exercise administrative and logistical control over all Fleet Marine Force units in the Central Pacific.

30 MARCH
AIR FORCE

The Fifth Air Force carries out its first major daylight raid against Hollandia, New Guinea Island. Targets include airfields, fuel dumps, and troop concentrations along the north coast from Wewak to Madang. A mix of A-20 Havoc and B-25 Mitchell bombers, and P-39 Airacobra, P-40 Warhawk, and P-47 Thunderbolt fighters strike at will in these areas.

ARMY

Units of the untried 93d Infantry Division, composed of African American troops, land on Bougainville Island, Solomon Islands, to gain combat experience.

30 MARCH–1 APRIL
NAVY

Task Force 58 aircraft bombard Japanese airfields, repair facilities, and other installations in the Caroline Islands, sinking 41 vessels of various sizes and classes. TBF Avenger torpedo-bombers from the carriers *Bunker Hill*, *Hornet*, and *Lexington* mine the approaches to the Palau Islands, the first time carrier aircraft participate in sowing a minefield during World War II.

1–8 APRIL
ARMY

The 1st and 3d Battalions, 5307th Provisional Unit make repeated, but unsuccessful, attacks to reach the surrounded 2d Battalion near Nhpum Ga, Burma.

2 APRIL
AIR FORCE

Colonel Leonard F. Harman lands the first operational XX Bomber Command B-29 Superfortress bomber at Chakulia, India.

4 APRIL
AIR FORCE

The Twentieth Air Force is activated in Washington, D.C., under General Henry H. Arnold, who assumes direct command two days later. This command is established to ensure that the B-29 Superfortress bombers attacking Japan from India and China, then later from the Mariana Islands, come under direct supervision of the Joint Chiefs of Staff.

6 APRIL
MARINE CORPS

The V Amphibious Corps orders establishment of a Marine Administrative Command, composed of a headquarters and the Marine Supply Service, to perform administrative and logistical services for both the V and III Amphibious Corps. This marks the birth of the command that will later be called Fleet Marine Force Pacific.

7 APRIL
NAVY

The destroyer *Saufley* employs 18 depth charges to sink the Japanese submarine *I-2* in the South Pacific.

Right: *Navy LSTs unload troops, supplies, and equipment on Red Beach 2 at New Hollandia on the north coast of New Guinea Island in April. The well-planned invasion, codenamed Operation RECKLESS, employs both the 24th and 41st Infantry Divisions to seize the large airfields and facilities in the area. (U.S. Navy)*

Above: B-25 Mitchells attack enemy ships at Wewak, New Guinea Island. The planes drop their bombs at low altitudes so they skip off the water and impact the ships at the waterline. ("B-25s Skip Bombing Wewak," Tony Fachet)

Below: Student pilots prepare to go up in their PT-19 Cornell trainer aircraft. Easy to fly and to maintain, the two-seat plane is well suited for its role as an observation aircraft in Burma. (NASM)

9 APRIL
ARMY

In Burma, the 1st and 3d Battalions, 5307th Provisional Unit break through to relieve the 2d Battalion, which has been holding out against Japanese attacks for 10 days. In addition to 59 killed and 314 wounded, 379 Soldiers are lost to illness.

The XXIV Corps enters the rolls of the Army under the command of Major General John R. Hodge. The XI Corps is formed in the Southwest Pacific under Major General Charles P. Hall.

11 APRIL
MARINE CORPS

The 147th Infantry Regiment arrives to relieve the 4th Marine Regiment on Emirau Island, Admiralty Islands. The 4th Marine Regiment begins its movement back to Guadalcanal Island, Solomon Islands.

14 APRIL
MARINE CORPS

Marine Night Fighting Squadron 532 flies its first successful night intercept in its F4U Corsair fighters near the Marshall Islands.

15 APRIL
MARINE CORPS

The I Marine Amphibious Corps is redesignated III Amphibious Corps.

16 APRIL
AIR FORCE
More than 170 Fifth Air Force planes are sent to attack targets near Hollandia, New Guinea Island. Severe weather interferes with their return to landing fields. Unable to find suitable runways, 37 A-20 Havoc and B-25 Mitchell bombers are lost.

18 APRIL
NAVY
The submarine *Gudgeon* is sunk southwest of Iwo Jima Island, Japan, probably by Japanese naval aircraft.

19 APRIL
NAVY
The aircraft carrier *Saratoga* and three escorting destroyers join ships of the British Eastern Fleet in conducting air attacks against Japanese installations and shipping at Sabang, Dutch East Indies, the first joint offensive operations by the two nations in the Indian Ocean. Aircraft from *Saratoga* and the British Royal Navy carrier sink three enemy vessels.

20 APRIL
NAVY
The submarine *Seahorse* sinks the Japanese submarine *RO-45* off the Mariana Islands.

21 APRIL
NAVY
The submarine *Stingray* strikes an underwater pinnacle west of the Mariana Islands and sinks.

22 APRIL
ALL SERVICES
After six weeks of constant bombardment on Hollandia and Aitape, New Guinea Island, by Fifth Air Force and Navy aircraft, Navy Task Force 77 (under Rear Admiral Daniel E. Barbey) lands the 24th Infantry Division at Tanahmerah Bay, and the 41st Infantry Division at Humboldt Bay and Aitape. All the landings are unopposed and the infantry units begin expanding the beachheads despite swamps and thick jungle. Base development by engineers begins

Above: *Dozens of aircraft, including TBF Avenger torpedo-bombers and F6F Hellcats, warm up prior to taking off from the deck of the carrier* Yorktown *during the battles to capture the Gilbert and Marshall Island groups. (National Archives)*

Left: *A rifleman provides cover for a flamethrower operator to get close enough to use his weapon in the thick undergrowth on Bougainville Island, Solomon Islands . The dug-in Japanese positions on the Pacific islands often require the use of a flamethrower to neutralize them. (National Archives)*

Right: *Japanese ships and shore facilities at Rabaul Harbor on the northern tip of New Britain Island during an attack by U.S. aircraft. By February, the constant attacks force the Japanese to stop bringing surface ships to the port. That same month they also stop sending planes to intercept the U.S. attackers, signaling that the once important base is no longer a threat to Allied advances. (Dept. of Defense)*

immediately. A company of tanks from the 1st Marine Division supports the 24th Division. The Fifth Air Force provides close support and continues to attack Wewak and Hansa Bay.

23 APRIL
ARMY/MARINE CORPS

The Army's 40th Infantry Division begins to arrive at Cape Gloucester, New Britain Island, to replace the 1st Marine Division. The Marines turn over responsibility for western New Britain Island on 28 April.

24 APRIL
AIR FORCE

The first two Twentieth Air Force B-29 Superfortress bombers to fly across the Himalaya Mountains to

Chinese soil land at Kwanghan. The XX Bomber Command commander, Lieutenant General Kenneth B. Wolfe, pilots one of the Superfortresses.

ARMY

Task Force Myitkyina—composed of the 1st and 3d Battalions, 5307th Provisional Unit, two Chinese regiments, and some Kachin guerrillas—begins an operation to capture the town and airfield of Myitkyina, Burma. It requires a 65-mile march over the 6,000-foot Kumno Mountains. Supplies are carried on mules.

On New Guinea Island, the 31st Infantry Division arrives, while regiments of the 24th and 41st Infantry Divisions continue to push out from the beaches. Light resistance is encountered as Japanese units continue to withdraw.

25 APRIL
AIR FORCE/ARMY

Flying a YR-4 helicopter, Lieutenant Carter Harman, 1st Air Commando Group, rescues four men from the Burmese jungle. It is the first time that a helicopter has been used in a combat rescue operation.

26 APRIL
NAVY

Picking up a surface contact on radar off the Aleutian Islands, the destroyer escort *Gilmore* pursues what turns out to be the Japanese submarine *I-180*, which submerges. *Gilmore* launches a determined attack that eventually sinks the sub.

28 APRIL
AIR FORCE/NAVY

Seventh Air Force B-24 Liberator bombers flying from Eniwetok Atoll, Marshall Islands, attack enemy targets on Guam Island, Mariana Islands. This is the first time land-based bombers have attacked the island. The bombers are accompanied by a Navy PBY reconnaissance aircraft.

29 APRIL–1 MAY
NAVY

Task Force 58 (under Vice Admiral Marc A. Mitscher) returns to the Caroline Islands, launching two days of strikes against the Truk Islands, which unfortunately are devoid of many shipping targets. However, a TBF Avenger torpedo-bomber from the light carrier *Monterey* joins the destroyers *MacDonough* and *Stephen Potter* in sinking the Japanese submarine *I-174* with depth charges. In addition, battleships, cruisers, and destroyers (under Rear Admiral Jesse B. Oldendorf and Vice Admiral Willis A. Lee Jr.) bombard Satawan Island and Ponape Island in the Caroline Islands.

1 MAY
AIR FORCE

The first four very heavy bomber bases open in Chengtu, China. B-29 Superfortress bombers are arriving daily.

2 MAY
MARINE CORPS

Marine Fighting Squadron 115 is the first flight

element of Marine Aircraft Group 12 to arrive on Emirau Island, Admiralty Islands.

4 MAY
MARINE CORPS/NAVY

The last elements of the 1st Marine Division depart New Britain Island for Pavuvu Island, Solomon Islands. Marine Corps casualties for the New Britain campaign total 275 dead and 948 wounded. Losses among Navy personnel serving with Marine Corps units are 12 killed and 30 wounded. The 12th Defense Battalion remains on New Britain Island.

NAVY

In a coordinated attack against a Japanese convoy in the Luzon Strait, Philippine Islands, the submarines *Bang*, *Parche*, and *Tinosa* sink five freighters.

5 MAY
ARMY

Two groups from the 5307th Provisional Unit task force cut trails through the Burmese jungle to surprise and encircle the Japanese-held village of Ritpong. Attacks by Chinese troops finally drive the Japanese out on 9 May and the task force continues its march.

8 MAY
MARINE CORPS

The 3d Marine Aircraft Wing arrives in Hawaii and assumes control of all Marine Corps aviation units there.

Opposite, bottom: *The Bell P-39 Airacobra is one of the principal U.S. fighter planes at the start of the war. It plays a significant role in the southwest Pacific, giving effective ground support with a variety of cannon and machine guns. (U.S. Air Force)*

Right: *The first combat use of a helicopter takes place in Burma, where the still experimental YR-4 helicopter supports jungle operations. The YR-4 seen here comes to the aid of one of the 1st Air Commando Group's B-25 Mitchell bombers that has crash-landed in the tall grass. (U.S. Air Force)*

10 MAY
AIR FORCE/ARMY

After five months of intense labor by more than 400,000 Chinese laborers, five B-29 Superfortress bomber bases and six fighter bases are completed as part of Project Chengtu—the establishment of B-29 operations against Japan from locations near the city of Chengtu, China.

16 MAY
NAVY

The destroyers *Franks*, *Haggard*, and *Johnston* sink the Japanese submarine *I-176* north of the Solomon Islands.

17 MAY
NAVY

The carrier *Saratoga* and the British carrier *Illustrious* attack the harbor at Surabaya, Java, Dutch East Indies, in an operation that coincides with the landing of Army troops on New Guinea Island.

17 MAY
AIR FORCE/ARMY/NAVY

Air and naval bombardment by Task Force 77 (under Rear Admiral William M. Fechteler) precedes the unopposed landing of the 163d Infantry Regiment, 41st Division at Arare, New Guinea Island. The next day, the main objective of Insoemoar Island, with its strategically located airfield, is assaulted by two companies of the 163d Infantry. Despite moderate opposition from fortified defenders, the airfield and most of the island are secured by dark. Night attacks by the Japanese fail to dislodge the beachhead. Army losses are 40 killed and 107 wounded. On 19 May,

companies of the 163d Infantry search two adjacent islands and find them unoccupied, permitting radar from the Fifth Air Force to be set up.

ARMY

In Burma, Task Force Galahad makes a surprise attack on Myitkyina, capturing the south part of the airfield against light opposition, However, efforts to move into the town are repulsed by the larger-than-expected Japanese force. Before weather closes in, a company from the 679th Engineer Aviation Battalion lands by glider. Other support troops arrive the next day, but no infantry. Attacks by Chinese troops to take the town fail. Brigadier General Frank D. Merrill suffers a heart attack and is evacuated; Colonel John E. McCammon takes command.

19 MAY
NAVY

Assisted by radio intelligence that pinpoints the operating area for Japanese submarines in the waters around New Ireland Island, the destroyer escort *England* sinks *I-16*. The ship sinks five more subs in quick succession—*RO-106* on 22 May, *RO-104* on 23 May, *RO-116* on 24 May, *RO-108* on 26 May, and, with the assistance of other ships, *RO-105* on 30 May.

21 MAY
MARINE CORPS/NAVY

Following amphibious exercises, a tank landing ship (LST) carrying ammunition explodes in Pearl Harbor, Hawaii, and destroys five adjacent LSTs. Just over 200 men in the 2d and 4th Marine Divisions are killed or wounded.

23 MAY
MARINE CORPS/NAVY

Marine Corps and Navy torpedo bombers from Cape Torokina mine the waters off the Japanese-held southern end of Bougainville Island, Solomon Islands.

23 MAY
ARMY

On New Guinea Island, the 158th Regimental Combat Team (Task Force Tornado) relieves the 163d Infantry Regiment. The task force pushes west toward the village of Sarmi against increasing Japanese resistance. A two-company task force (the 32d Recon Troop and A Company, 127th Infantry) is forced back near the Aitape beach by Japanese attacks. Task Force Tornado uses tanks and flamethrowers to assault Japanese defenses the following day.

25 MAY
ARMY

The 209th Engineer Combat Battalion lands at Myitkyina, Burma, followed on 30 May by the 236th Engineer Combat Battalion. Both units are sent into the battle line as infantry. On 30 May, Colonel John E. McCammon is evacuated and replaced by Brigadier General Haydon L. Boatner. In Bombay, India, provisional unit GH 770 arrives. The unit's 2,600 men receive some training and are flown to join the 5307th Composite Unit. The surviving 300 men of Merrill's Marauders, reformed into one battalion, are combined with the two battalions of GH 770 and renamed the New Galahad Force.

27 MAY
AIR FORCE

Twenty-four rocket-firing Fourteenth Air Force P-40 Warhawk fighters strike military installations and enemy troops at Nanchang, China.

Above: *Navy ordnancemen load snow-covered bombs on the wing racks of a PBY Catalina on a base at Cold Bay, Aleutian Islands. By 1944, most of the action is in the South Pacific, but patrols are still flown to ensure the security of the northern approaches to U.S. territory. (Naval Historical Center)*

Right: *Moving cautiously through the jungle, Soldiers of the African American 93d Infantry Division search for the last pockets of Japanese resistance along the Numa-Numa Trail on Bougainville Island, Solomon Islands, in May 1944. (National Archives)*

202650-S

Previous Spread: *Soldiers of the 41st Infantry Division charge ashore on Wakde Island on 16 May 1944. Strong Japanese resistance lasts until August. (U.S. Army)*

Above: *The view from the cockpit of an Army Air Forces CG-4A Waco glider as it and others are towed toward their landing zone. (U.S. Army)*

AIR FORCE /ARMY/NAVY
Fifth Air Force B-24 Liberator and B-25 Mitchell bombers attack Babo Airfield and Biak Island, Schouten Islands, as Task Force 77 lands the reinforced 41st Infantry Division (Task Force Hurricane, under Major General Horace H. Fuller) on Biak against light resistance.

ARMY
On New Guinea Island, the 158th Infantry Regiment continues its unsuccessful efforts to take Lone Tree Hill. During the night, the Japanese make a series of attacks on the beachhead. On 28 May, the 41st Division units hit strong Japanese resistance near the airfield. The division sets up a defensive perimeter for the night and requests reinforcements.

29 MAY
ARMY
The first tank battle of any consequence in the southwestern Pacific occurs as Japanese light tanks clash with American medium tanks in support of the 162d Infantry Regiment on Biak Island, Schouten Islands. Eight enemy tanks are destroyed. As the battle grows more intense, the 34th Infantry Regiment enters the fight.

31 MAY
NAVY
The submarines *Barb* and *Herring* cooperate to sink all five ships of a Japanese convoy in the Kurile Islands, Japan. The next day, after *Herring* sinks a Japanese freighter, shore batteries sink the American submarine.

1–2 JUNE
ARMY
On Biak Island, Schouten Islands, Task Force Hurricane expands the beachhead against Japanese resistance as the 186th Infantry Regiment uses tanks to move north to make contact with the 162d Infantry Regiment.

5 JUNE
AIR FORCE

More than 75 B-29 Superfortress bombers assigned to the XX Bomber Command, Twentieth Air Force, strike rail targets in Japanese-occupied Bangkok, Thailand. This is the first B-29 bomber raid of the war.

ARMY

On New Guinea Island, initial elements of the 6th Infantry Division (under Major General Franklin S. Sibert) arrive and relieve the 158th Infantry Regiment. The division headquarters, 20th Infantry Regiment, and other division units land at Toem on 11 June. On Biak Island, Schouten Islands, Task Force Hurricane makes a major effort to complete seizure of the Mokmer Airfield with partial success.

MARINE CORPS

Admiral Ernest J. King designates Lieutenant General Holland M. Smith as commander of all Marine Corps ground forces in the Pacific theater and authorizes establishment of a headquarters Fleet Marine Force Pacific.

8 JUNE
NAVY

Task Forces 74 and 75, which include the U.S. light cruisers *Boise* and *Phoenix* along with an Australian cruiser and 14 Allied destroyers, finish the work begun by Army Air Forces medium bombers and turn back a Japanese convoy carrying reinforcements bound for Biak Island, Schouten Islands.

9 JUNE
NAVY

The submarine *Harder* completes four days of operations in the vicinity of the Japanese fleet anchorage at Tawi Tawi Island, Philippine Islands. She sinks three enemy destroyers, survives a determined depth charge attack, and evacuates coastwatchers from the nearby island of Borneo. The boat's skipper, Commander Samuel D. Dealey, will receive a posthumous Medal of Honor for his actions.

10 JUNE
NAVY

The destroyer *Taylor* sinks the Japanese submarine *RO-111* north-northeast of New Ireland Island. The destroyer escort *Bangust* sinks the Japanese submarine *RO-42* northeast of Kwajalein Atoll, Marshall Islands.

11 JUNE
NAVY

F6F Hellcat fighters from Task Force 58 open four days of strikes preparatory to landings in the Mariana Islands, conducting a massive fighter sweep of enemy airfields that decimates Japanese air power.

Right: *Brigadier General Frank D. Merrill (far left), commander of the 5307th Composite Unit (Provisional), known as the "Galahad Force" or "Merrill's Marauders," watches some of his troops cross into Burma on the Ledo Road. To move supplies on the almost non-existent mountain roads and trails, the Marauders turn to an old Army friend, the mule, for help. (U.S. Army)*

Subsequent missions strike installations ashore and attack two convoys near the islands, sinking 19 ships.

13 JUNE
NAVY
In the Mariana Islands, the destroyer *Melvin* sinks the Japanese submarine *RO-36* east of Saipan Island.

14 JUNE
NAVY
Battleships, cruisers, and destroyers of Task Group 58.7 (under Vice Admiral Willis A Lee Jr.) begin bombarding Saipan and Tinian Islands preparatory to landings in the Mariana Islands. Task Groups 52.17 (under Rear Admiral Jesse B. Oldendorf) and 52.18 (under Rear Admiral Walden L. Ainsworth) continue fire support during and after the landings the following day.

The submarine *Golet* sinks off Honshu Island, Japan, probably succumbing to attacks by Japanese ships and aircraft.

Above: *A Soldier of the 7th Infantry Division employs a flamethrower to destroy a Japanese block house while riflemen wait to engage any enemy soldiers who might emerge. Action was during the U.S. assault on Kwajalein in the Marshall Islands. (U.S. Army)*

15 JUNE
AIR FORCE
The Far East Air Force is created with command authority over the Fifth and Thirteenth Air Forces. General George C. Kenney assumes command with his headquarters at Brisbane, Australia. The Fifth Air Force strikes north in the Truk Islands, Caroline Islands, while the Thirteenth Air Force strikes south at airfields at Bougainville Island, Solomon Islands, and continues the mission of neutralizing Rabaul, New Britain Island, and attacking Bougainville.

In the first raid on the Japanese home islands since the carrier-launched strike on targets in and around Tokyo on 18 April 1942, 68 B-29 Superfortress of the XX Bomber Command bomb the steel works at

Above: *Soldiers with M4A1 Sherman tanks prepare for an assault on Pancake Hill near Hollandia, New Guinea Island. (Dept. of Defense)*

Below: *B-25 Mitchell bombers make a low-level attack on a Japanese airfield at Wewak on the north coast of New Guinea Island. (Dept. of Defense)*

Yawata, Japan. The target is more than 1,500 miles away from the bombers' forward area bases in China.

ARMY
Lieutenant General Robert L. Eichelberger arrives on Biak Island, Schouten Islands, and replaces Major General Horace H. Fuller as commander of Task Force Hurricane. Fuller retains command of the 41st Infantry Division, which continues its efforts to clear the island of Japanese defenders.

ARMY/MARINE CORPS/NAVY
The invasion of the Mariana Islands begins with the 2d and 4th Marine Divisions, V Amphibious Corps (Lieutenant General Holland M. Smith) landing on the west coast of Saipan Island. Task Force 52 (Vice Admiral Richmond Kelly Turner) provides naval gunfire and air bombardment support. Losing more than 2,000 dead and wounded as they fight their way ashore, the Marines hold a firm beachhead by nightfall and fight off enemy counterattacks. Carrier aircraft also strike the Bonin Islands and Iwo Jima Island, Japan, to stop Japanese aircraft from attacking the invasion force. The Army's 27th Infantry Division waits in reserve. On 16 June, the advance party of Army XXIV Corps Artillery and the first units of the 27th Infantry Division come ashore to support the Marines. On 17 June, some of the Task Force 52 ships withdraw to engage a Japanese fleet. That night, the Japanese launch a major attack using 44 medium tanks and 500 infantrymen against the 2d Marine Division. The enemy is repulsed with the loss of 31 tanks and 300 men.

MARINE CORPS
Aircraft Solomons is redesignated as Aircraft, Northern Solomons. Its new commander is Major

General Ralph J. Mitchell. Of its 40 flying squadrons, 23 are Marine Corps.

16 JUNE
NAVY

In the Marshall Islands the destroyers *Melvin* and *Wadleigh* sink the Japanese submarine *RO-114*, while the destroyer escort *Burden R. Hastings* sinks the Japanese submarine *RO-44*.

17 JUNE
ARMY/MARINE CORPS

American forces on Saipan Island, Mariana Islands, resume their attack, with the Army's 165th Infantry Regiment taking over the right flank of the 4th Marine Division zone. Progress remains slow, averaging a thousand yards across the extended front.

NAVY

A PB4Y-1 Liberator bomber of Bombing Squadron 109 sinks the Japanese submarine *RO-117* in the Caroline Islands.

18 JUNE
ARMY/MARINE CORPS

On Saipan Island, Mariana Islands, the 105th Infantry Regiment, 27th Infantry Division enters the fight on the right flank of the 165th Infantry Regiment, placing eight U.S. Army and Marine Corps infantry regiments in the front lines. The 4th Marine Division reaches the east coast at Magicienne Bay, thus cutting the Japanese garrison in two, while the 27th Infantry Division captures Aslito Airfield. On 19 June the 27th Infantry Division is given the task of clearing Nafutan Point and the south coast as Marines clear the north.

19 JUNE
NAVY

A TBM Avenger torpedo-bomber of Torpedo Squadron 60 off the escort carrier *Suwanee* sinks the Japanese submarine *I-184* off Guam Island, Mariana Islands.

The Battle of the Philippine Sea begins. In an effort to disrupt the landings at Saipan Island, Mariana Islands, a Japanese carrier force consisting of nine

aircraft carriers supported by five battleships and numerous cruisers and destroyers enters the Philippine Sea. The Japanese launch a mass air strike against the ships of the Fifth Fleet, hoping the aircraft can land at airfields in the Mariana Islands, where they can be refueled and rearmed for repeated attacks. The Japanese attackers, largely inexperienced pilots, run into a determined combat air patrol over the Fifth Fleet. In an engagement later called the Great Marianas Turkey Shoot, F6F Hellcat fighters decimate the Japanese strike group, shooting down nearly 300 aircraft. Many pilots achieve multiple kills, with Commander David McCampbell, Commander, Air Group 15 on board the carrier *Essex*, splashing nine enemy aircraft. Meanwhile, the submarines *Albacore* and *Cavalla* sink two Japanese carriers. Fearing an attempt by Japanese surface forces to go around his ships and descend on the invasion force,

Left: *Marines of the V Amphibious Corps pause for a moment on one of the beachheads on Saipan Island, Mariana Islands, before joining the battle inland. Two Marine Corps divisions and an Army division land against fierce Japanese resistance. (U.S. Army)*

Left: *Army surgeons work by flashlight to save the life of a seriously wounded Soldier. Jungle conditions, crude facilities, and the threat of enemy artillery and bombs challenge even the most skilled doctors. (Robert Benney, Army Art Collection, U.S. Army Center of Military History)*

Opposite: *Antiaircraft fire from a Navy carrier brings down a Japanese dive-bomber during the Battle of the Philippine Sea in June 1944. (U.S. Navy)*

Fifth Fleet commander Vice Admiral Raymond A. Spruance chooses to keep the carriers of Task Force 58 in the vicinity of Saipan on the evening of 19 June rather than allow them to pursue the Japanese fleet to the west. When Vice Admiral Marc A. Mitscher's Task Force 58 carriers are released the following day, aerial scouts do not spot the enemy carriers until late in the afternoon, necessitating a strike launched at extreme range with pilots having to return after nightfall. In the ensuing mission, carrier aircraft sink a Japanese carrier, damage two oilers that are scuttled, and damage three carriers, a battleship, and four other ships. The strike aircraft are assisted in finding their way back to their carriers by Vice Admiral Mitscher's order to turn on the lights of Task Force 58's ships as a guide.

Right: *A Soldier armed with an M1911 .45 caliber pistol peers into the door of a Japanese bunker on New Georgia Island, Solomon Islands, to ensure that it is clear of enemy troops. (U.S. Army)*

20 JUNE
ARMY/MARINE CORPS

The 4th Marine Division reorients its lines to drive north on Saipan Island, Mariana Islands, in conjunction with the 2d Marine Division. The 27th Infantry Division's 106th Infantry Regiment comes ashore and the division continues its attack to the southeast against enemy troops bottled up in Nafutan Point. An Army artillery battery on Saipan opens the bombardment against Tinian Island. By the time Marine Corps forces launch the Tinian assault, 13 battalions of artillery are executing preparation fires on that objective.

ARMY

In Burma, the New Galahad Force continues the long siege of Myitkyina. The situation remains serious as they suffer from lack of supplies, and jungle disease thins the ranks—75 to 100 men a day are lost to malaria, dysentery, and scrub typhus.

21 JUNE
ARMY

Lieutenant General Simon Bolivar Buckner Jr. arrives at Schofield Barracks, Hawaii, to organize the new U.S. Tenth Army. It is tentatively planned that Buckner will head the force to seize Formosa Island.

NAVY

The destroyer *Newcomb* and high-speed minesweeper *Chandler* sink the Japanese submarine *I-185* in the Mariana Islands.

22 JUNE
ARMY/MARINE CORPS

Following a day of consolidation, the 2d and 4th Marine Divisions gain ground in their drive north on Saipan Island, Mariana Islands, and confront the enemy's new defensive line. The 6th Marine Regiment seizes Mount Tipo Pale. The 105th Infantry Regiment holds its position around Nafutan Point, while the remainder of the 27th Infantry Division becomes the corps reserve. The following day, the 27th Infantry Division assumes responsibility for the center of the Marine Corps zone on Saipan.

23 JUNE
ARMY/MARINE CORPS

The 27th Infantry Division's mission is broadened on Saipan Island, Mariana Islands, to include clearing critical Purple Heart Ridge and Death Valley—which Lieutenant General Holland M. Smith mistakenly regards as minor "mopping-up" operations. The 27th Division's inability to advance results in a gap between Army troops and the 4th Marine Division.

Left: *A Marine Corps machine gun crew wades through a jungle stream in the Mariana Islands. On his shoulder one gunner carries an air-cooled M1919A4 .30 caliber Browning light machine gun, which can fire 400–600 rounds per minute. Other members of the crew carry the tripod and ammunition. (National Archives)*

ARMY

On New Guinea Island, the 20th Infantry Regiment, 6th Division throws back Japanese assaults at Lone Tree Hill in heavy fighting during the day, followed by night attacks. Two companies of the 1st Infantry Regiment make a landing to attack the west side of the hill. A small beachhead is secured, but movement inland is blocked by Japanese defenders.

24 JUNE
AIR FORCE
Seventh Air Force P-47 Thunderbolt fighters flying from newly captured airfields on Saipan Island, Mariana Islands, provide close support to Allied ground forces by strafing remaining enemy positions on Saipan and Tinian Islands.

ARMY/MARINE CORPS
The 4th Marine Division wheels east to clean out Kagman Peninsula on Saipan Island, Mariana Island. Disappointed by the slow advance of the 27th Infantry Division, Lieutenant General Holland M. Smith relieves its commander, Army Major General Ralph C. Smith. Major General Sanderford Jarman is designated temporary commander. On 27 July, Major General George W. Griner Jr. arrives to take command of the 27th Division, which he leads until the end of the war.

NAVY
The submarine *Tang*, attacking a Japanese convoy leaving the Koshiki Straits, Japan, sinks three cargo ships and a tanker.

25 JUNE
AIR FORCE
Continuing the campaign of reconnaissance and harassment in the Aleutian Islands, two Eleventh Air Force B-24 Liberator bombers bomb the suspected enemy airfield at Kurabu Cape. The Eleventh Air Force continues to fly bombing and reconnaissance missions against the Japanese forces in these islands for the remainder of the war. This was the only campaign in World War II fought on and over North American soil.

MARINE CORPS
The 2d Marine Division captures Mount Tapotchau, the key point for observers controlling Japanese artillery fire on Saipan Island, Mariana Islands. The 4th Marine Division completes its mission of destroying enemy forces in the Kagman Peninsula.

26 JUNE
AIR FORCE
The P-61 Black Widow night fighter begins flying night patrols over Saipan Island, Mariana Islands. Along with P-47 fighter sweeps during the day, these missions continue well into July.

Right: *Flying an F6F Hellcat, Lieutenant (junior grade) Ray Hawkins duels with a Japanese Zero on the first day of the Battle of the Philippine Sea in June 1944. ("Great Marianas Turkey Shoot," Robert L. Rasmussen)*

Below: *In a partnership of old and new means of transportation, ox carts carry ammunition and supplies from C-47 Skytrain transports to U.S. and Chinese troops in the front lines around Myitkyina, Burma. (U.S. Army)*

ARMY

In Burma, Brigadier General Haydon L. Boatner is evacuated with malaria; Brigadier General Theodore F. Wesels replaces him as commander of the New Galahad Force. Operations continue as Chinese units moving north link up with the isolated task force.

On Saipan Island, Mariana Islands, the 27th Infantry Division continues its attack with elements of the 106th Infantry Regiment battling to clear a Japanese strongpoint called "Hell's Pocket" in Death Valley,

and the 165th Infantry Regiment fighting on Purple Heart Ridge.

ARMY/MARINE CORPS

During the night, 500 Japanese troops infiltrate the lines at Nafutan Point on Saipan Island, Mariana Islands, and conduct attacks against Aslito Airfield, artillery positions, and a Marine Corps regiment in reserve. The enemy force is destroyed by dawn the next day.

27 JUNE
ARMY

On Saipan Island, Mariana Islands, the 105th Infantry Regiment clears Nafutan Point, counting over 500 dead Japanese. The 27th Infantry Division makes progress on Purple Heart Ridge and Hell's Pocket.

On Biak Island, Schouten Islands, the 34th Infantry Regiment continues its final clearing operations in the East Caves area and prepares to withdraw to participate in the planned invasion of Noemfoor Island, Schouten Islands. Task Force Tornado mops up remaining resistance around Lone Tree Hill on New Guinea Island.

MARINE CORPS

The 4th Marine Division resumes its position on the right flank of the front on Saipan Island, Mariana Islands.

Above: *A seaplane tender anchored off one of the Pacific islands provides a home base to PBY Catalinas and other sea-based aircraft. ("Safe Harbor," James Dietz)*

Below: *A jeep towing an M3A1 37mm antitank gun passes Soldiers of the 27th Infantry Division as they move inland on Saipan Island, Mariana Islands. (U.S. Army)*

In the New Hebrides Islands, the 2d Marine Aircraft Wing headquarters moves from Efate to Espiritu Santo.

2 JULY
ARMY/NAVY
Navy Task Force 77 (under Rear Admiral Fechteler) lands the 158th Regimental Combat Team on Noemfoor Island, Schouten Islands, after an intensive air and naval bombardment. Japanese resistance is light and a beachhead including the Kamiri Airfield is quickly secured. The 1st Battalion, 503d Parachute Infantry Regiment is dropped on the airfield the next day, and occupies a portion of the perimeter.

3 JULY
ARMY/MARINE CORPS
Following the enemy's withdrawal the previous day from its main defenses on Saipan Island, Mariana Islands, the V Amphibious Corps forces make significant progress on the island. The town of Garapan falls to the 2d Marine Division, which then is pinched out of the front by the 27th Infantry Division. The 27th Infantry Division and the 4th Marine Division push on to secure Tanapag Harbor.

4 JULY
ARMY

The 3d Battalion, 503d Parachute Infantry Regiment is dropped on Kamiri Airfield, Noemfoor Island, Schouten Islands, and replaces the 158th Infantry Regiment on the front line. The remainder of the 503d is air landed when the runways are repaired.

ARMY/MARINE CORPS

On Saipan Island, Mariana Islands, the 27th Infantry and 4th Marine Divisions advance together against sporadic resistance.

NAVY

Attacks by carrier-based aircraft against the Volcano and Bonin Islands result in damage to Japanese installations and the sinking of 10 vessels.

The destroyer *David W. Taylor* and the destroyer escort *Riddle* sink the Japanese submarine *I-10* in the Mariana Islands.

The submarine *S-28* is lost with all hands during a training exercise off Oahu, Hawaii.

6 JULY
AIR FORCE

A P-61 Black Widow night fighter piloted by 1st

Lieutenant Francis Eaton intercepts and shoots down a Japanese G4M3 Betty bomber over the Solomon Islands. This is the first victory scored by the P-61 during the war.

In China, Fourteenth Air Force B-25 Mitchell bombers and P-40 Warhawk and P-51 Mustang fighters support Chinese ground forces by striking Japanese targets along the Yangtze River. B-25s drop supplies to fielded armies and attack the Tien Ho airfield at Canton overnight. The aircraft conduct air superiority, close support, and supply missions over

Above: *Paratroopers of the 503d Parachute Infantry Regiment land on the Kamiri Airfield on Noemfoor Island as reinforcements in the battle against stubborn Japanese defenders. (U.S. Air Force)*

Right: *Three Navajo Marine Corps communicators take a break on Saipan Island, Mariana Islands. Both Marine Corps and Army units use American Indian servicemen as radio "code talkers" for tactical communications. Speaking in their native languages, which are mostly unwritten and unknown to the Japanese, these men are able to send messages to each other without fear of interception. (National Archives)*

the Himalaya Mountains for ground forces from Tsinan in the north to Indochina in the south; and from Chengtu in the west to Formosa Island in the east. At war's end, the Fourteenth Air Force will officially be credited with destruction of more than 2,300 enemy aircraft, 350 bridges, 1,200 locomotives, and 700 railroad cars.

ARMY/MARINE CORPS
Lieutenant General Holland M. Smith attaches the

77th Infantry Division to the III Amphibious Corps in preparation for landings on Guam Island, Mariana Islands.

7 JULY
ARMY/MARINE CORPS
On Saipan Island, Mariana Islands, about 3,000 Japanese launch a pre-dawn banzai attack that falls primarily on the 105th Infantry Regiment. After overrunning Army positions, enemy troops strike

batteries of the 10th Marine Regiment. Marines and Soldiers defeat the attackers, but American casualties exceed 1,000. The 2d Marine Division, with the 165th Infantry Regiment attached, attacks through the 27th Infantry Division to clear the remaining enemy. The struggle continues through 8 July.

9 JULY
ARMY/MARINE CORPS

As the 2d Marine Division and the 165th Infantry Regiment continue to mop up on Saipan Island, Mariana Islands, the 4th Marine Division reaches Marpi Point on the northern end of the island. Organized Japanese resistance ends. Among the Japanese dead is Admiral Chuichi Nagumo, leader of the raid on Pearl Harbor, Hawaii. Of the 14,000 casualties on Saipan, 3,674 are Soldiers and Marines.

10 JULY
ARMY/MARINE CORPS

The Army's 305th Regimental Combat Team on Eniwetok Atoll, Marshall Islands, is assigned to the 1st Provisional Marine Brigade.

ARMY

On Biak Island, Schouten Islands, the 163d Infantry Regiment makes good progress, while in the Aitape area of New Guinea Island, Task Force Persecution (1st Battalion, 128th Infantry Regiment and 2d Squadron, 112th Cavalry Regiment) crosses the Driniumor River without opposition. The 128th Infantry Regiment moves along the coast while the cavalry patrols into the jungle. During the night, a large Japanese attack penetrates the task force lines and causes heavy casualties; the next day the task force withdraws a short distance. On 13 July, the reorganized task force successfully attacks to recover its former positions along the river.

MARINE CORPS/NAVY

Elements of the V Amphibious Corps' Amphibious Reconnaissance Battalion and Navy Underwater Demolitions Teams 5 and 7 begin scouting the landing beaches on Tinian Island, Mariana Islands.

11 JULY
AIR FORCE

Seventh Air Force P-47 Thunderbolt fighters relentlessly attack Tinian and Pagan Islands in the Mariana Islands to soften up the beaches for the landings scheduled for less than two weeks from this date. In the coming days, B-24 bombers stage out of Eniwetok Atoll, Marshall Islands, and strike Tinian twice a day until the landings begin.

12 JULY
MARINE CORPS

Lieutenant General Holland M. Smith relinquishes command of the V Amphibious Corps to Major General Harry Schmidt, and becomes the first commander of Fleet Marine Force Pacific.

12–17 JULY
NAVY

Submarines of Task Group 17.16 (under Captain William V. O'Regan) attack Japanese shipping off Luzon Island, Philippine Islands, sinking nine ships.

13 JULY
MARINE CORPS

The 3d Battalion, 6th Marine Regiment seizes Maniagassa Island off the coast of Saipan Island, Mariana Islands. Marine Corps casualties on Saipan total 3,152 dead and 8,575 wounded. Losses among Navy personnel serving with Marine Corps units are 77 killed and 337 wounded. The 2d and 4th Marine Divisions begin recuperating and preparing for the assault on Tinian Island, Mariana Islands.

14 JULY
ARMY

The 31st Infantry Division (under Major General John C. Parsons) unloads onto New Guinea Island at Maffin Bay and begins replacing the units of the 6th Infantry Division to become Task Force Tornado. Task force command is passed on 18 July and the 6th Division prepares to conduct another landing near Vogelkop Peninsula. Near Aitape, New Guinea, Task Force Persecution units maneuver along the Driniumor River to close a gap between them, trapping a Japanese force.

NAVY

The destroyer escort *William C. Miller* joins the high-speed transport *Gimer* in sinking the Japanese submarine *I-6* in the Mariana Islands.

17 JULY
NAVY

Underwater demolition teams, supported by destroyers and LCIs (landing craft infantry-gunboats) successfully remove some 940 beach obstacles in four days, in preparation for landings on Guam Island, Mariana Islands.

Above: *A depth charge explodes at the location of a suspected Japanese submarine on 30 July 1944 off the coast of western New Guinea Island, where amphibious landings take place. (U.S. Army)*

Right: *Sailors of the crew of a U.S. Navy submarine gather for a meal in the cramped eating space that also serves as the library. Due to limited space, multipurpose areas are common in submarines. (U.S. Naval Institute)*

Right: *An LVT-2 amphibious tractor lands Marines on a beach during the assault on Guam Island, Mariana Islands, in July 1944. Although it is armored, the vehicle does not have a ramp, forcing troops to climb over the side. (National Archives)*

19 JULY
AIR FORCE
In the Caroline Islands, Far East Air Force B-24 Liberator bombers attack the airfield on Yap Island. They attack in two waves, while others bomb Ngulu and Sorol Islands.

Fighter-bombers lend close support to ground forces on the Sarmi-Sawar sector on the north coast of New Guinea Island.

19 JULY
NAVY
The destroyer escort *Wyman* sinks the Japanese submarine *RO-48* in the Mariana Islands.

20 JULY
AIR FORCE
American forces turn their attention toward Guam, the largest of the Mariana Islands. Seventh Air Force aircraft support the operation by attacking Japanese forces in the Truk Islands, Caroline Islands, and Tinian Island, Mariana Islands.

ARMY
The 43d Infantry Division arrives in the Aitape area of New Guinea Island, reinforcing the front for further offensive action along the Driniumor River lines.

21 JULY
ARMY/MARINE CORPS/NAVY
Task Force 53 (under Rear Admiral Richard L. Conolly), supported by naval gunfire and carrier aircraft, lands Marine Corps and Army troops on Guam Island, Mariana Islands. The III Amphibious Corps (also designated the Southern Troops and Landing Force) assaults the west coast of Guam. The 3d Marine Division goes ashore north of the Orote Peninsula with all three regiments abreast, while the 1st Provisional Marine Brigade lands to the south of the peninsula with the 4th and 22d Marine Regiments in the lead and along with the 305th Regimental Combat Team, 77th Infantry Division. The rest of the 77th Infantry Division (under Major General Andrew D. Bruce) is initially held in reserve with the III Amphibious Corps. By the end of the day, the corps has two separate beachheads on either side of Orote Peninsula. The 305th Regimental Combat Team lands to help hold the beachhead. The brigade fights off a strong Japanese counterattack that night. On 22 July elements of the 9th Defense Battalion land on Guam to provide assistance.

23 JULY
ARMY/MARINE CORPS
Elements of the 3d Marine Division complete the seizure of Cabras Island off the coast of Guam Island, Mariana Islands. The 14th Defense Battalion assumes control of the island. The Army's 77th Infantry

Left: *Private First Class Mary Jane Ford, Signal Corps, receives the Soldier's Medal for her efforts to save a drowning Soldier. (National Archives)*

Below: *Marines take cover in a shell-blasted palm grove on Guam Island. (U.S. Navy)*

Opposite: *Two servicemen raise the Stars and Stripes on a beach on Guam Island. (MacArthur Memorial Library & Archives)*

Division begins going ashore and replacing elements of the Marine Corps brigade in the southern perimeter.

24 JULY
AIR FORCE/MARINE CORPS/NAVY

Task Force 52 (under Rear Admiral Harry W. Hill) puts the 4th Marine Division ashore in an amphibious landing on the northwest coast of Tinian Island in the Mariana Islands. Naval gunfire and carrier air support, along with tactical air support from Seventh Air Force

bombers and fighters, aid in the landings. P-47 Thunderbolt fighters drop napalm to clear heavy jungle hiding enemy positions. A beachhead is secured against light opposition. The 2d Marine Division makes an amphibious feint in the south, then returns to the main landing site. That evening the Japanese fail in an attack against the beachhead.

ARMY/MARINE CORPS

The 77th Infantry Division completes the relief of the 1st Provisional Marine Brigade in the south on Guam Island, Mariana Islands, with the 305th and 306th Infantry Regiments.

25 JULY
ARMY/MARINE CORPS

On Guam Island, Mariana Islands, the 1st Provisional Marine Brigade seals off the base of Orote Peninsula and positions itself with both Marine Corps regiments abreast to assault the peninsula the next day. The 77th Infantry Division assumes complete responsibility for the southern beachhead facing toward the remainder of Guam. That night, the Japanese launch a strong counterattack, mainly against the northern beachhead, but it is repulsed.

MARINE CORPS

The 2d Marine Division comes ashore on Tinian Island, Mariana Islands, and assumes responsibility for the eastern half of the corps zone. The 8th Marine Regiment captures Ushi Point Airfield.

NAVY

The carriers of Task Force 58 launch three days of air strikes against the Caroline Islands, hitting Yap, Ulithi, Fais, Ngulu, Sorol, and Palau Islands.

26 JULY
ARMY

In Burma, the 5332d Brigade (Provisional) is activated to replace the worn-out 5307th Composite Unit (Provisional) "New Galahad Force" and to continue missions against the Japanese. Brigadier General Thomas S. Arms is named commander, but other than the survivors of the New Galahad Force who will be absorbed into the new 475th Infantry Regiment, no

combat units are yet available. The 124th Cavalry Regiment (dismounted), a mobilized Texas National Guard outfit, is en route from the U.S. to join the 5332d. The 5332d Brigade (Provisional), together with American support units and Chinese troops, will be designated "Mars Task Force."

ARMY/NAVY

Arriving at Pearl Harbor, Hawaii, on board the heavy cruiser *Baltimore*, President Franklin D. Roosevelt begins a four-day conference with senior military advisor Admiral William D. Leahy and Admiral Chester W. Nimitz and General Douglas MacArthur, the principal American commanders in the Pacific.

Above: *After a flight from their base in India, B-25 Mitchell bombers of the 12th Bomb Group release their bombs on Japanese defenders holding out in Myitkyina, Burma. (Jeffery Ethell Collection)*

Left: *Soldiers fire an M1A1 75mm pack howitzer in support of the Galahad Force during the two-month siege of Myitkyina, Burma. The small artillery piece is designed to be taken apart and carried by mules or horses. (U.S. Army)*

The conference results in the decision to liberate the Philippine Islands, a move opposed by many as detracting from the offensive toward the Japanese home islands.

MARINE CORPS

In the Mariana Islands the 1st Provisional Marine Brigade launches its assault on Orote Peninsula on Guam Island. The 2d and 4th Marine Divisions drive south on Tinian Island, with the latter organization seizing Mount Lasso, the highest terrain on the island.

27 JULY
ARMY

At Myitkyina, Burma, the weary infantrymen of the New Galahad Force capture the northern airstrip and turn it over to the 209th and 236th Engineer Battalions to defend.

28 JULY
ARMY/MARINE CORPS

On Guam Island, Mariana Islands, the 22d Marine Regiment captures the old Marine Barracks on Orote Peninsula. The 3d Marine Division and the 77th Infantry Division expand their beachheads and link them in one solid perimeter.

NAVY

The destroyer escorts *Wyman* and *Reynolds* sink the Japanese submarine *I-55* east of Tinian Island, Mariana Islands.

29 JULY
AIR FORCE

B-29 Superfortress bombers based in Chengtu, China, attack the Showa Steel Works at Anshan, China. The first combat loss of a B-29 occurs when a crippled bomber proceeds to attack a secondary target and is intercepted by five enemy fighters. A B-29 damaged by antiaircraft fire is forced to make an emergency landing on a small Soviet field at Tarrichanka, USSR. The crew is interned, and the aircraft, along with two other B-29s which fall into Soviet hands in August

Left: *Wary Marines try to convince Japanese soldiers to come out of their bunker and surrender on Tinian Island, Mariana Islands. The Marine Corps assault force from the 2d and 4th Marine Divisions lands at two small beaches away from the main Japanese defenses, taking the enemy by surprise. (MacArthur Memorial)*

Below: *Marines wounded in the fighting on Guam Island, Mariana Islands, are loaded on board an amphibious tractor for transport to waiting hospital ships. ("First Toll at Guam," William F. Draper, Navy Art Collection)*

and November, are given to the Tupolev Design Bureau to be copied. The resulting Tu-4 looks remarkably like an American B-29. The Tu-4, the Soviets' first strategic bomber, does not become operational until 1947.

MARINE CORPS

The 1st Provisional Marine Brigade defeats the last organized Japanese resistance on Orote Peninsula on Guam Island, Mariana Islands.

30 JULY
AIR FORCE/ARMY/NAVY

In a surprise landing without bombardment, Task Force 77 puts Task Force Tyhoon (6th Infantry Division) ashore on the Vogelkop Peninsula, New Guinea Island. A beachhead is quickly secured. Army Air Forces aircraft keep the Japanese occupied by bombing targets near Wewak and Aitape. Unopposed landings are also made on nearby New Amsterdam and Middleburg Islands. On 31 July, the 3d Battalion, 1st Infantry Regiment lands unopposed on Cape Sansadore, while near Aitape, the 124th Infantry Regiment reinforced by a battalion of the 169th Infantry Regiment attacks across the Driniumor River.

MARINE CORPS

In the Mariana Islands, the 4th Marine Division captures Tinian Town, Tinian Island. The airfield on Orote Peninsula on Guam Island goes into operation when aircraft from Marine Observation Squadron 1 land on it.

31 JULY
ARMY/MARINE CORPS

The 3d Marine Division captures Agana, the capital of Guam Island, Mariana Islands, while the 77th Infantry Division reaches the eastern coast of the island, cutting it in two. Most Japanese forces withdraw to the north.

MARINE CORPS

The 2d and 4th Marine Divisions meet stiff resistance along an escarpment in southern Tinian Island, Mariana Islands. By the end of the day, the 8th Marine Regiment has a toehold on the high ground.

Right: *Signalmen of "Merrill's Marauders" load their equipment on mules and horses as they prepare to continue their march behind Japanese lines in the Burma mountains. (U.S. Army)*

NAVY

A submarine group under Commander Lewis S. Parks attacks Japanese convoy MI 11 south of Formosa Island, sinking four ships and damaging three others. During the operation the submarine *Parche* engages in a daring predawn surface attack against the convoy, torpedoing four ships. Despite the flames from the burning convoy ships illuminating *Parche* and drawing fire from the convoy's escorts, the sub's captain, Commander Lawson P. Ramage, presses home the attacks and skillfully avoids an enemy ship about to ram him. Ramage receives the Medal of Honor for his actions.

1 AUGUST
AIR FORCE

Lieutenant General Millard F. Harmon assumes command of the Army Air Forces, Pacific Ocean Areas. The new command consolidates logistic and administrative functions as well as all tactical operations throughout the Pacific Theater, and assumes control of the Seventh Air Force. Harmon also assumes the position of Deputy Commander, Twentieth Air Force and is responsible for strategic operations.

In the Mariana Islands, as organized resistance on Tinian Island ends, P-47 Thunderbolt fighters and P-61 Black Widow night fighters from Saipan Island continue day and night combat patrols over Guam, Rota, and Pagan Islands.

ARMY

Newly named U.S. Army Forces, Pacific Ocean Areas (Lieutenant General Robert C. Richardson Jr.) supersedes U.S. Army in Central Pacific Area and now includes command of all Army elements of the South Pacific area as well.

ARMY/MARINE CORPS

The 1st Provisional Marine Brigade assumes responsibility for clearing the southern sector of Guam Island, Mariana Islands, while the 3d Marine Division and the Army 77th Infantry Division advance abreast to the north.

MARINE CORPS

The 2d and 4th Marine Divisions reach the southern coast of Tinian Island, Mariana Islands, and all organized Japanese resistance is finished. Marine Corps casualties on Tinian total 368 dead and 1,921 wounded. Losses among Navy personnel attached to the V Amphibious Corps are 26 killed and 40 wounded.

3 AUGUST
ARMY

In Burma, a final assault by Chinese and American troops takes the town of Myitkyina. The long battle has cost 272 American dead, 955 wounded, and 980 sick and evacuated.

Left: *On Bougainville Island, Solomon Islands, a Soldier checks out an enemy bunker that he burned out with his flamethrower. (U.S. Army)*

Opposite, top: *A Marine Corps crew sets up its Browning M1917A1 .30 caliber water-cooled heavy machine gun in the ruins of a destroyed house on Guam Island, Mariana Islands. Though heavy to carry, its rate of fire of 500-600 rounds per minute makes it good for defensive position. (MacArthur Memorial)*

Opposite, bottom: *Two Army M4 Sherman tanks burn after being hit by Japanese antitank guns near the town of Yigo, Guam Island. (USMC)*

4 AUGUST
MARINE CORPS
Marine Night Fighting Squadron 534 is the first squadron of Marine Aircraft Group 21 to arrive on Guam Island, Mariana Islands, followed soon after by Marine Fighting Squadrons 216, 217, and 225.

NAVY
Task Group 58.1 (under Rear Admiral Joseph J. Clark) attacks Japanese convoy 4804 off the Bonin Islands. Naval gunfire and carrier aircraft sink eight Japanese vessels. The force attacks the Bonin Islands again the following day along with Task Group 58.3 (under Rear Admiral Alfred E. Montgomery).

5 AUGUST
ARMY
The 475th Infantry Regiment is formed at Myitkyina, Burma, and assigned to the 5332d Brigade (Provisional). Replacements arrive and training soon begins. One of the brigade's units is the 612th Field Artillery (Pack), which uses 280 mules for transportation. On 16 September the 5307th Composite Group (Provisional), informally known as "Merrill's Marauders," is officially disbanded.

MARINE CORPS
The 3d Marine Division smashes through the Japanese defensive line around the town of Finegayan on Guam Island, Mariana Islands.

6 AUGUST
ARMY
Twelve days after the death of Lieutenant General Lesley J. McNair in Normandy, France, his son, Colonel Douglas C. McNair, 77th Infantry Division, is killed on Guam Island, Mariana Islands.

MARINE CORPS
The 2d and 4th Marine Divisions begin departing Tinian Island, Mariana Islands, with the 2d headed for Saipan Island and the 4th for Hawaii. The 8th Marine Regiment assumes responsibility for mopping up Tinian Island.

7 AUGUST
ARMY/MARINE CORPS
On Guam Island, Mariana Islands, the 1st Provisional Marine Brigade reenters the front on the left flank on the island's west coast. With the 3d Marine Division in the center and the 77th Infantry Division on the right, the III Amphibious Corps launches its final attack to seize northern Guam. Meanwhile, Marine

Fighting Squadron 225 launches the first combat air patrol and close air support missions from Orote Airfield on the island.

8 AUGUST
AIR FORCE
In China, Fourteenth Air Force aircraft hit targets in Hengshan, where they destroy several trucks, and at Hamoy and Swatow, where they destroy radio stations and munitions storage facilities.

10 AUGUST
AIR FORCE
From bases constructed on Guam, Tinian, and Saipan Islands in the Mariana Islands, American B-29 Superfortress bombers begin an aerial campaign against Japan that will last until mid-August 1945. In one of two missions flown during this period, 24 Twentieth Air Force B-29s flying out of Chengtu, China, bomb targets in Nagasaki, Japan. In the second mission, staged through China Bay, Sri Lanka (Ceylon), more than 30 B-29s bomb the oil refinery at Palembang, Sumatra, Indonesia, while eight others mine the nearby Moesi River. The mission from Ceylon to Sumatra—some 3,900 miles—is the longest single-staged combat flight made by a B-29 during the war.

The Seventh Air Force begins the air campaign to neutralize enemy defenses on Iwo Jima Island, Japan. B-24 bombers flying from Saipan Island, Mariana Islands, pound Japanese forces there. For the next six months, the Seventh Air Force will attack the islands

of Iwo Jima, south of Japan, as well as Chichi Jima, and other enemy locations in the Caroline and Mariana Islands in preparation for the amphibious landings on Iwo Jima.

MARINE CORPS
The 3d Marine Division destroys and captures the last handful of Japanese tanks on Guam Island, Mariana

Islands, and reaches the northern coast. The III Amphibious Corps declares the island secure, although mopping-up operations will continue until the end of the war. Marine Corps casualties during the assault phase on Guam total 1,568 dead and 6,933 wounded. Losses among Navy personnel serving with the III Amphibious Corps are 51 killed and 206 wounded.

12 AUGUST
ARMY/MARINE CORPS

Major General Roy Geiger departs Guam Island, Mariana Islands, for Guadalcanal Island, Solomon Islands. His III Amphibious Corps headquarters begins to follow the next day. Geiger and his staff assume responsibility for planning the Palau Islands campaign, slated to begin on 15 September. The Army's 81st Infantry Division is rehearsing for the operation.

13 AUGUST
NAVY

The submarine *Flier* strikes a mine north of Borneo, Dutch East Indies, and sinks.

14 AUGUST
AIR FORCE

The Seventh Air Force is reorganized into a new "mobile tactical airforce" which retains only functional combat units. In a typical day of combat missions, B-24 bombers based on Saipan Island, Mariana Islands, bomb Iwo Jima Island, Japan; B-25 bombers strike Pagan Island and P-47 fighters strike Rota Island in the Mariana Islands; B-25s flying from the Marshall Islands hit Ponape Island, Caroline Islands; B-24s attack the Wotje Atoll, Marshall Islands.

15 AUGUST
MARINE CORPS

Major General Henry L. Larsen and his Island Command headquarters takes complete control of Guam Island, Mariana Islands.

18 AUGUST
NAVY

In an attack on the Japanese convoy HI 71 in the waters off Luzon Island, Philippine Islands, the submarine *Rasher* sinks four ships and damages a fifth, and the submarine *Redfish* damages one vessel.

20 AUGUST
AIR FORCE

Seventh Air Force B-24 Liberator bombers based on Saipan Island, Mariana Islands, strike targets on Yap Island, Caroline Islands, for the first time. Marshall Island–based B-24 Liberators continue to bomb the Truk Islands.

Right: A Marine on Tinian Island, Mariana Islands, makes a new friend at a refugee camp. (Marine Corps Research Center)

Below: Marines offer Japanese defenders on Guam Island, Mariana Islands, the opportunity to surrender before sealing off the entrance to their cave with explosives. Small groups of Japanese hold out on the island for months after the main fighting ends. (U.S. Navy)

ARMY

Lieutenant General Walter Krueger, Sixth U.S. Army commander, declares the campaign on Biak Island, Schouten Islands, completed, though the 41st Infantry Division (Task Force Typhoon) continues mopping up for several months. American losses are 400 killed, 2,150 wounded/injured plus evacuated sick.

21–24 AUGUST
NAVY

U.S. submarines attack Japanese convoys off the Philippine Islands, sinking eight ships. One of the attacking boats is *Harder*, under the command of Commander Samuel D. Dealey, the most decorated submarine officer of World War II. On 24 August *Harder* is sunk by an enemy coast defense vessel off Luzon Island.

22 AUGUST
MARINE CORPS

The 3d Marine Division is assigned to the Guam Island Command to continue mopping-up operations. Numerous Japanese holdouts resist until December 1945. Not until 1960 does the last one emerge from hiding.

Left: *Long-range B-29 Superfortress bombers of the 468th Bomb Group drop their bombs on targets around Rangoon, Burma. (NASM)*

Below: *Marines on Guam Island, Mariana Islands, search for Japanese soldiers and civilians who are hiding out in the many caves and crevices of the island. (U.S. Navy)*

Opposite: *A horse loaded with supplies for British troops in Burma resists boarding a C-47 Skytrain transport of the 1st Air Commando Group. The "?" tail insignia symbolizes the secret nature of the unit. (U.S. Air Force)*

23 AUGUST
AIR FORCE

Thirty-two Tenth Air Force P-47 Thunderbolt fighters provide close support to British ground forces advancing from India to Burma by attacking troop concentrations, gun batteries, and headquarters buildings.

24 AUGUST
AIR FORCE

Brigadier General Emmett O'Donnell Jr. lands his 73d Bomb Wing Headquarters advanced echelon in the Mariana Islands. This is the first Twentieth Air Force contingent to arrive at these island bases.

25 AUGUST
ARMY

The Aitape operation on New Guinea Island is declared completed after eliminating two and a half Japanese divisions. Allied losses have been 440 killed, 2,550 wounded, and 10 missing plus evacuated sick and injured. On 31 August, the operations on Noemfoor Island, Schouten Islands (Task Force Cyclone) and Vogelkop Peninsula, New Guinea Island (Task Force Typhoon) are ended, with a total of 77 killed and 387 wounded.

28 AUGUST
AIR FORCE

Brigadier General Haywood Hansell assumes command of the XXI Bomber Command, and Brigadier General Laurence Norstad becomes Chief of Staff for the Twentieth Air Force.

29 AUGUST
AIR FORCE

Major General Curtis E. LeMay assumes command of the XX Bomber Command.

31 AUGUST
MARINE CORPS

The Commandant directs that Fleet Marine Force Pacific will consist of Headquarters Troops, III Amphibious Corps, V Amphibious Corps, Fleet Marine Force Supply Service, and other supporting elements. The future chain of command of Marine Corps aviation units in the Pacific Theater remains unresolved. The 20th Marine Regiment is disbanded as the 4th Marine Division shifts to the new tables of organization.

NAVY

Aircraft from carriers of Task Group 38.4 (under Rear Admiral Davison) attack the islands of Iwo Jima and Chichi Jima, Japan.

2 SEPTEMBER
NAVY

A TBM Avenger torpedo-bomber of Torpedo Squadron 51 from the light carrier *San Jacinto* is shot down over Chichi Jima Island, Japan. Two of the plane's crew are killed but the pilot, Lieutenant (junior grade) George H. W. Bush, successfully parachutes from his aircraft and is subsequently rescued by the submarine *Finback*. Bush eventually becomes the 41st President of the United States.

4 SEPTEMBER
AIR FORCE

Tenth Air Force B-24 Liberator bombers begin to haul thousands of gallons of fuel to staging areas in Kunming, China, for use by advancing forces. By this time, Brigadier General William H. Tunner has taken charge of the Air Transport Command and is responsible for the operations in the Himalaya Mountains.

6 SEPTEMBER
NAVY

Task Force 38 (under Vice Admiral Marc A. Mitscher) launches three days of air strikes against the western Caroline Islands, with surface ships supplementing the aerial attacks with shore bombardment. The action includes *Independence*, the first aircraft carrier in the U.S. Navy specially equipped to carry out night operations.

7 SEPTEMBER
ARMY

The U.S. Eighth Army is established at Hollandia, New Guinea Island, and Lieutenant General Robert L. Eichelberger is named to command. Army units are training for the invasion of Morotai Island, Dutch East Indies.

MARINE CORPS

The 1st Provisional Marine Brigade headquarters is deactivated on Guadalcanal Island, Solomon Islands, and its units (primarily the 4th and 22d Marine Regiments) are absorbed by the 6th Marine Division, organized the same day. The other main elements of

Right: *A camouflaged Marine peers over the side of his landing craft at the bombardment of Peleliu Island, Palau Islands, as the assault craft prepare to go onto the beach. (Tom Lea, Army Art Collection, U.S. Army Center of Military History)*

the division are the 29th Marine Regiment (infantry) and 15th Marine Regiment (artillery).

8 SEPTEMBER
AIR FORCE

Nearly 100 B-29 Superfortress bombers from Chengtu, China, bomb the Showa Steel Works in Anshan, China. During the night, Japanese bombers attack one of the Chengtu bases, damaging a B-29 and a C-46 Commando transport, and wounding two Soldiers.

MARINE CORPS

The 10th Defense Battalion relieves the 51st Defense Battalion in the Ellice Islands, and moves forward to Eniwetok Atoll, Marshall Islands.

9 SEPTEMBER
MARINE CORPS

Marine Base Defense Air Group 45 departs California for Ulithi Atoll, Caroline Islands, where it will provide air protection to the fleet anchorage that becomes the forward base for the Pacific Fleet. It arrives on 8 October.

NAVY

Carrier planes of Task Force 38 strike port facilities and airfields on Mindanao Island, Philippine Islands, and also sink 17 vessels. The attacks continue the following day.

10 SEPTEMBER
AIR FORCE

Troop carrier missions and cargo-hauling continue

Left: *A Vought OS2U-3 Kingfisher observation seaplane circles over the landing craft carrying the first assault waves of the 81st Infantry Division onto the beach at Angaur Island, Palau Islands, in September 1944. (U.S. Navy)*

Opposite: *Assaulting Marines scramble from their amphibious tractors on Peleliu Island, Palau Islands. (Tom Lea, Army Art Collection, U.S. Army Center of Military History)*

throughout the China–Burma–India Theater. B-24 Liberator bombers haul fuel over the Himalaya Mountains from India to China. Similar missions continue throughout September. During November and December, transport aircraft fly over the mountains an average of 300 times each day to resupply forces operating in China.

11–16 SEPTEMBER
ALL SERVICES
President Franklin D. Roosevelt and British Prime Minister Winston S. Churchill, along with the Combined Chiefs of Staff, meet at the Second Quebec Conference, with the discussions centering mainly on the British Royal Navy's role in the campaign against Japan. The conference approves Admiral William F. Halsey Jr.'s suggestion to push the invasion of Leyte Island, Philippine Islands, ahead, which is based in part on intelligence gathered from Filipino rescuers by a fighter pilot shot down off Leyte.

12 SEPTEMBER
NAVY
Aircraft launched from the carriers of Task Force 38 attack the Visayan Islands, Philippine Islands, causing heavy damage to airfields and sinking 38 enemy vessels in surrounding waters. Over the following two days carriers attack Cebu, Negros, and Legaspi in the Philippine Islands.

13 SEPTEMBER
NAVY
The high-speed minesweeper *Perry* strikes a mine and sinks off Angaur Island, Palau Islands.

15 SEPTEMBER
AIR FORCE/MARINE CORPS/NAVY
The Palau Islands campaign begins with an invasion of Peleliu Island. Ships of the Third Amphibious Force (Vice Admiral Theodore S. Wilkinson) land the 1st Marine Division (reinforced) (III Amphibious Corps) on the southwest coast of the island. Despite heavy air and naval bombardment, the division's three infantry regiments (1st, 5th, and 7th Marines) sustain heavy casualties as they fight their way ashore over the jagged coral. A beachhead is secured and withstands a Japanese tank-led counterattack late in the afternoon. The lead echelon of Marine Aircraft Group 11 goes ashore to work on the airfield.

ARMY/NAVY
Task Force 77 (Rear Admiral Daniel E. Barbey) shells Morotai Island, Dutch East Indies, for two hours, then lands three regiments of Task Force Tradewind (31st Infantry Division, under Major General John C. Persons) on two beaches—155th and 167th Infantry Regiments at Gila Peninsula and 124th Infantry Regiment to their south. The landings are unopposed.

Left: *As fighting continues to rage on Peleliu Island, Palau Islands, Navy Chaplain Rufus W. Oakley holds a religious service for Marines and Sailors just behind the battle line. (National Archives)*

Opposite, top: *Marines on watch at a forward post keep alert as a flare bursts overhead, while others try to get some sleep. (Tom Lea, Army Art Collection, U.S. Army Center of Military History)*

16 SEPTEMBER
ARMY
On Morotai Island, Dutch East Indies, the 31st Infantry Division expands the beachhead and the 125th Regimental Combat Team, 32d Infantry Division lands.

MARINE CORPS
On Peleliu Island, Palau Islands, the 7th Marine Regiment completes its turning movement to the right and isolates the southern promontory. The 5th Marine Regiment in the center drives straight across the island, seizing the airfield and reaching the opposite shore. The 1st Marine Regiment wheels left into a widening zone and begins the assault toward the rugged coral ridges that constitute the heart of the Japanese defenses.

NAVY
Lieutenant Arthur M. Preston leads the motor torpedo boats *PT-489* and *PT-363* through 60 miles of heavily mined waters and, despite being repeatedly fired on by Japanese shore batteries, presses forward through an 11-mile channel into Wasile Bay, Halmahera Island, Dutch East Indies. While within 150 yards of enemy guns on shore, Preston's PTs pull a downed fighter pilot from the water. During their high-speed retirement the PTs sink a small cargo vessel. For heroism above and beyond the call of duty, Preston receives the Medal of Honor.

In an attack against a Japanese convoy southeast of Hong Kong, the submarine *Barb* sinks a 20,000-ton

carrier and a tanker. The next day, the submarine *Sea Devil* sinks the Japanese submarine *I-364* off Yokosuka, Japan.

17 SEPTEMBER
ARMY/NAVY
Task Group 32.1 (under Rear Admiral William H. P. Blandy) lands the 81st Infantry Division (under Major General Paul J. Mueller) on Angaur Island, Palau Islands, where an airfield is established to support offensive operations in the Philippine Islands. In the Southwest Pacific area, 32d Infantry Division elements are winding up the campaign on Morotai Island, Dutch East Indies.

MARINE CORPS
On Peleliu Island, Palau Islands, the 7th Marine Regiment continues its assault on the southern promontory, while the 1st Marine Regiment and 2d Battalion, 7th Marine Regiment batter their way into the nightmare terrain in the north.

18 SEPTEMBER
ARMY
Against moderate Japanese resistance on Angaur Island, Palau Islands, the 81st Infantry Division pushes toward the center of the island and along the coastal trails.

MARINE CORPS
The 7th Marine Regiment completes the seizure of the southern promontory of Peleliu Island, Palau Islands.

19 SEPTEMBER
ARMY

The 81st Infantry Division commits the 321st Infantry Regiment and a battalion of the 322d Infantry Regiment into the line as the main effort to clear Angaur Island, Palau Islands. Other than one stubborn pocket, organized resistance ends the next day.

MARINE CORPS

The 5th Marine Regiment nearly completes the conquest of the eastern flatlands on Peleliu Island, Palau Islands, while the 1st Marine Regiment presses deeper into the coral ridges. Two light planes of Marine Observation Squadron 3 are the first to land on Peleliu's airfield.

21 SEPTEMBER
MARINE CORPS

The 7th Marine Regiment assumes responsibility for the center of the 1st Marine Division zone and takes up the assault on the coral ridges of Peleliu Island, Palau Islands. The 1st Marine Regiment focuses its remaining combat power on the narrow plain on the west coast of Peleliu while elements of the 5th Marine Regiment occupy two small islands off the northeast coast.

The 52d Defense Battalion departs San Diego, California, for the Marshall Islands, where detachments will guard Roi-Namur Island in the Kwajalein Atoll as well as the Majuro Atoll.

Left: *Soldiers of the 81st Infantry Division ignore a dead enemy and watch as a column of M4A4 Sherman tanks move past during fighting on Angaur Island, Palau Islands. (U.S. Army)*

Above: *A Marine Corps dog handler reads a message his war dog has just delivered. Radios are unreliable in the humid tropics and the dogs are dual-trained to scout and deliver messages when radio communication fails. (Marine Corps Research Center)*

Below: *A Marine stops to check the condition of a casualty slumped against a trench on Peleliu Island, Palau Islands. (National Archives)*

NAVY

Carrier planes from Task Force 38 strike enemy airfields and shipping in the vicinity of the Philippine Islands' capital of Manila and at Subic Bay. All told, 28 enemy vessels are sunk in the protected waters there, as well as during an attack against a convoy off Luzon Island.

22 SEPTEMBER
NAVY

Carrier aircraft from Task Force 38 sink nine enemy ships off Cebu and San Fernando, Luzon Island, Philippine Islands.

23 SEPTEMBER
AIR FORCE

The Thirteenth Air Force moves its base of operations from Hollandia, New Guinea Island, to Noemfoor Island, Schouten Islands.

Seventh Air Force B-24 Liberators continue to attack the islands of Chichi Jimi, Haha Jima, and Ani Jima, Japan.

23 SEPTEMBER
ARMY/MARINE CORPS

The 321st Regimental Combat Team, temporarily detached from the Army's 81st Infantry Division, arrives on Peleliu Island, Palau Islands, from Angaur Island and begins replacing the 1st Marines in the lines.

ARMY/NAVY

Task Group 33.19 lands the 323d Regimental Combat Team, 81st Infantry Division on Ulithi Atoll in the Caroline Islands. Ulithi becomes the forward base for the Pacific Fleet during the final campaigns of the war.

NAVY

The battleship *West Virginia* rejoins the Pacific Fleet at Pearl Harbor, Hawaii. She is the last veteran of the 7 December 1941 attack to return to active service.

24 SEPTEMBER
AIR FORCE

Eleventh Air Force B-24 Liberator bombers hitting the airfield at Kurabu Cape, Aleutian Islands, are attacked by a dozen Japanese fighters. One damaged B-24 is forced to land in the Soviet Union.

ARMY/MARINE CORPS

On Peleliu Island, Palau Islands, the 321st Regimental Combat Team begins a drive up the west coast to surround the coral ridges. The 7th Marine Regiment continues the assault against the ridges from the south and west. The first aircraft of Marine Night Fighting Squadron 541 arrive on Peleliu, joined by the headquarters of 2d Marine Aircraft Wing.

NAVY

Carrier planes of Task Force 38 continue their aerial onslaught against Japanese shipping off the Philippine Islands, sinking 15 vessels.

25 SEPTEMBER
ARMY/MARINE CORPS

The 5th Marine Regiment is committed to exploit the lack of significant enemy resistance on the west coast of Peleliu Island, Palau Islands. While the 321st Regimental Combat Team drives across the island north of the coral ridges to isolate the Japanese strongpoint, the 5th Marines continues north with the objective of seizing the less rugged ground at that end of the island.

27 SEPTEMBER
NAVY

On Bougainville Island, Solomon Islands, Special Air Task Force 1 carries out its first operational missions employing TDR-1 drones controlled from specially modified TBM Avenger aircraft. Four of the primitive guided missiles are launched and two strike their

Right: *A machine gun crew waits and watches in their jungle position while keeping their Browning M1919A1 light machine gun ready. ("Machine Gun Position," David Fredenthal, U.S. Army Art Collection, U.S. Army Center of Military History)*

target, a beached Japanese freighter that contains an enemy antiaircraft emplacement.

28 SEPTEMBER
AIR FORCE

More than 100 Fourteenth Air Force fighters perform armed reconnaissance missions throughout southeastern China, and to a lesser degree, in southwestern China and Indochina.

MARINE CORPS

The 3d Battalion, 5th Marines conducts a shore-to-shore amphibious assault off the coast of northern Peleliu Island, Palau Islands, to seize Ngesebus Island.

29 SEPTEMBER
MARINE CORPS

While the 3d Battalion, 5th Marine Regiment completes the conquest of Ngesebus Island, off Peleliu Island, Palau Islands, the rest of the 5th Marines and the 321st Regimental Combat Team wipe out the last significant Japanese positions in northern Peleliu. All enemy resistance is now bottled up in the central ridges, an area roughly one-half mile long by one-quarter mile wide known as the Umurbrogol Pocket. The 7th Marine Regiment assumes responsibility for squeezing out this position.

30 SEPTEMBER
ARMY

Rear Admiral George H. Fort, commander of the U.S. Western Attack Force, declares the islands of Peleliu, Angaur, Ngesebus, and Kongarur in the Palau Islands successfully occupied. The 81st Infantry Division and attached units count more than 3,275 casualties, including 542 killed in action.

2 OCTOBER
AIR FORCE

Tenth Air Force troop carrier flights continue, more than 250 each day, to locations throughout the China–Burma–India Theater. These missions continue to provide the lifeblood of supplies and troops during the month of October. By the 16th, more than 300 airlift flights will be flown during one day.

2 OCTOBER
MARINE CORPS

The remnants of the 1st Marine Regiment depart Peleliu Island, Palau Islands, for Pavuvu Island, Solomon Islands.

3 OCTOBER
ARMY/MARINE CORPS

On Peleliu Island, Palau Islands, the 7th Marine Regiment seizes Walt's Ridge and Boyd Ridge, further compressing the Umurbrogol Pocket on Peleliu. The 321st Regimental Combat Team finishes clearing Amiangal Mountain.

NAVY

While operating off Morotai Island, Dutch East Indies, the destroyer escort *Shelton* is sunk by the Japanese submarine *RO-41*. The destroyer escort *Richard M. Rowell* pursues the submarine, but, unaware that U.S. submarines are operating in the vicinity, sinks *Seawolf* with the loss of all hands.

The destroyer escort *Samuel S. Miles* sinks the Japanese submarine *I-177* off Angaur, Palau Islands.

4 OCTOBER
ARMY

Lieutenant General Walter Krueger ends the operations on Morotai Island, Dutch East Indies, though small clearing operations continue. Allied casualties are 30 killed, 85 wounded.

5 OCTOBER
MARINE CORPS

The 5th Marine Regiment relieves the 7th Marine Regiment around the Umurbrogol Pocket on Peleliu

Above: *No matter how bad or how old it might be, a movie is always a hit with the troops on the tiny Pacific islands. It is a rare pleasure seldom enjoyed by the front line units. (Paul Sample, Army Art Collection, U.S. Army Center of Military History)*

Below: *Senior leaders (left to right) Colonel John Walker, Lieutenant General Holland M. Smith, Major General Roy S. Geiger, and Admiral Raymond A. Spruance hold a conference on Guam Island, Mariana Islands. (MacArthur Memorial)*

Island, Palau Islands. On 7 October, an attack on the pocket by 5th Marines is repulsed. Elements of the 5th Marines seize Old Baldy, a key terrain feature in the Umurbrogol Pocket, on 10 October.

10 OCTOBER
NAVY
Shifting its operations to the west, Task Force 38 launches air strikes against Okinawa, Japan, destroying Japanese military installations and sinking 30 vessels in the surrounding waters.

11 OCTOBER
MARINE CORPS
Command relationships are formalized for Fleet Marine Force Pacific (FMFPAC). Lieutenant General Holland M. Smith is given the status of commander for all operational Marine forces reporting to Commander in Chief, U.S. Fleet/Chief of Naval Operations Admiral Ernest J. King. Aircraft FMFPAC is put under operational control of the commander of Air Force, Pacific Fleet, a Navy vice admiral.

12 OCTOBER
AIR FORCE
The first Twentieth Air Force B-29 Superfortress bomber, "Joltin' Josie, The Pacific Pioneer," lands on Saipan Island, Mariana Islands, to establish temporary headquarters. Brigadier General Haywood Hansell, commanding general of the XXI Bomber Command, pilots the aircraft. Elements of the 73d Bomb Wing also arrive.

12 OCTOBER
ARMY/MARINE CORPS

The assault phase of the Peleliu Island operation in the Palau Islands is declared over, but the III Amphibious Corps continues to battle to reduce the Umurbrogol Pocket. The 321st Regimental Combat Team takes responsibility for the eastern part of the island. Marine Corps Brigadier General Harold D. Campbell and his Island Command assume responsibility for the remainder of Peleliu. Among his forces is the 12th Antiaircraft Artillery Battalion.

NAVY

Task Force 38 begins attacking the heavily defended island of Formosa. Naval aviators also sink 17 Japanese vessels around Formosa. Despite the heavy damage, the Japanese launch determined aerial counterattacks. On 13 October, they damage the carrier *Franklin* and put a torpedo into the side of the heavy cruiser *Canberra*. On 14 October, enemy aircraft damage the carrier *Hancock*, light cruisers *Houston* and *Reno*, and destroyer *Cassin Young*. In an effort to draw the Japanese fleet into action in hopes of finishing off its damaged ships, 3d Fleet commander Admiral William F. Halsey Jr. directs two carrier task groups to withdraw to the east from where they can launch air strikes against any attackers. Enemy surface units do not sortie, but torpedo planes again damage *Houston* on 15 October.

14 OCTOBER
AIR FORCE

For the first time, more than 100 Twentieth Air Force B-29 Superfortress bombers from Chengtu, China, mass to attack targets. This raid against the aircraft plant at Okayama is the first in a series of attacks against Formosa Island, flown in conjunction with U.S. landings at Leyte Island, Philippine Islands.

Above: *In a pose evoking past Army leaders, Lieutenant General Daniel Sultan, new commander of the China–Burma–India Theater, uses a mule to move up and inspect his troops in Burma. (U.S. Army)*

Left: *Colonel Aubrey Newman, commander of the 34th Infantry Regiment, leads his men off of the beach on Leyte Island, Philippine Islands. ("Follow Me," H. Charles McBarron, Army Art Collection, U.S. Army Center of Military History)*

15 OCTOBER
ARMY/MARINE CORPS
On Peleliu Island, Palau Islands, the 321st Regimental Combat Team begins replacing the 5th Marines in the lines around the Umurbrogol Pocket, a Japanese zone that is now no larger than 400 yards by 500 yards. The 5th Marine Regiment goes into reserve.

17 OCTOBER
ARMY/MARINE CORPS
The 6th Ranger Battalion seizes two small Philippine islands in Leyte Gulf in preparation for the Leyte Island campaign. Four Marine Corps aviation officers, including Major General Ralph J. Mitchell, accompany the force as observers. Both landings are unopposed.

18 OCTOBER
NAVY
Task Force 38 launches two days of air strikes against targets in the Philippine Islands, hitting airfields around Manila, sinking eight ships in Manila Bay, and sending 12 enemy vessels to the bottom off Luzon Island. Seventh Fleet aircraft also attack Japanese shipping, sinking twelve ships off Cebu.

19 OCTOBER
ARMY
Culminating a tumultuous relationship with Chinese leader Chiang Kai-shek, Lieutenant General Joseph W. Stilwell is "recalled" from Chungking, China. The China–Burma–India Theater is split, with Major General Albert C. Wedemeyer to command U.S. troops in China; Lieutenant General Daniel Sultan is named to temporary command in India. After 32 months of frustrating duty, Stilwell leaves China on 26 October.

20 OCTOBER
AIR FORCE

Two Seventh Air Force B-24 Liberator bombers fly the first combat missions from Guam Island, Mariana Islands, attacking Yap Island, Caroline Islands.

ARMY/MARINE CORPS

In the Palau Islands, the 322d Infantry Regiment wipes out the last pocket of Japanese resistance on Angaur Island. The 81st Infantry Division assumes responsibility for ground operations on Peleliu Island in place of the III Amphibious Corps and the 1st Marine Division. The 5th Marine Regiment remains ashore attached to the 81st Division.

ARMY/NAVY

General Douglas MacArthur's return to the Philippine Islands begins with preliminary landings by the 21st Infantry Regiment, 24th Division to secure Panaon Strait. The 6th Ranger Battalion strikes inland targets prior to the invasion landing. At H-Hour, the 7th Fleet (Vice Admiral Thomas C. Kinkaid) lands two Sixth Army corps on Leyte Island beaches in Ormac Bay. X Corps units (1st Cavalry Division and 24th Infantry Division) receive heavy enemy fire, but advance quickly and secure Tacloban airfield. The XXIV Corps (7th and 96th Infantry Divisions) units find light resistance and establish a beachhead. Japanese counterattacks during the night are repelled. A fleet of more than 700 ships puts 160,000 troops ashore, with battleships and escort carriers of the Third Fleet lending support. Close-in fire support is provided by two groups of "mortar boats," each consisting of four infantry landing craft armed with 4.2-inch heavy mortars manned by troops of the 96th Infantry Division. Japanese air attacks against the landing fleet are fierce, with enemy bombers damaging the escort carrier *Sangamon*, light cruiser *Honolulu*, and a salvage vessel. Shore batteries damage a destroyer and tank landing ship.

21 OCTOBER
ARMY

On Leyte Island, Philippine Islands, advances are made against Japanese resistance. 1st Cavalry Division takes Tacloban, Utap, and Caibaan. The 34th Infantry Regiment, 24th Infantry Division stops an enemy counterattack and has units advancing west to Palo. The 96th Infantry Division runs into swamps and enemy pillboxes that slow it, but the 7th Infantry Division breaks through enemy defenses to seize the Dulag airstrip. The next day, with the assistance of

Opposite, top: *"Battle for Leyte Gulf," James Dietz.*

Opposite, bottom: *After wading ashore on Leyte Island, Philippine Islands, from a landing craft, General Douglas MacArthur discusses the status of the invasion with his senior staff. (Jeffery Ethell Collection)*

Right: *One of many explosions rocks the light carrier* Princeton *after being hit by a Japanese bomb on 24 October 1944. The ship sinks after eight hours of fires and explosions. (Naval Historical Center)*

Left: *An F4U Corsair loaded with bombs prepares to take off during the Battle of Leyte Gulf in October 1944. ("Corsair on Carrier," by Mort Künstler, © 1960 Mort Künstler, Inc.)*

Below: *Japanese naval shells with colored dye straddle the escort carrier* Gambier Bay *as she tries in vain to avoid being hit during the Battle of Leyte Gulf. Enemy gunners finally sink her. ("USS Gambier Bay," U.S. Naval Institute)*

naval air and artillery, advances continue to expand the beachheads despite difficult terrain and enemy resistance.

MARINE CORPS

V Amphibious Corps Artillery consisting of a headquarters element and a battalion each of 155mm guns and howitzers goes ashore on Leyte Island, Philippine Islands, to support the U.S. Sixth Army.

Marine Carrier Groups headquarters is established at Marine Corps Air Station Santa Barbara, California, as a subordinate echelon of Aircraft Fleet Marine Force Pacific. This marks the beginning of the process of deploying a significant number of Marine Corps squadrons in Navy carriers in World War II.

23 OCTOBER
ARMY

General Douglas MacArthur restores the Philippine civil government to President Sergio Osmeña. The 34th and 19th Infantry Regiments assault fortified positions blocking entry into the Leyte Valley. Supply shortages halt the 96th Infantry Division, while tanks of the 767th Tank Battalion spearhead the advance of the 7th Infantry Division to take San Pablo airfield.

NAVY

In the first stage of the Battle of Leyte Gulf, the largest naval battle in history, the submarine *Darter* detects a sizeable Japanese surface force heading toward Leyte Island, Philippine Islands. *Darter* joins with the submarine *Dace* in sinking the heavy cruiser *Atago* (the flagship of Vice Admiral Takeo Kurita), and the heavy cruiser *Maya*. *Darter* also torpedoes the heavy cruiser *Takao*, which withdraws under the escort of two destroyers.

24 OCTOBER
NAVY

Carrier planes of Task Force 38 strike ships of a Japanese surface force under the command of Vice Admiral Takeo Kurita as they enter the Sibuyan Sea, Philippine Islands. Japanese land-based aircraft from the Philippines hit the light carrier *Princeton*. As surface ships assist the stricken carrier, fires reach her ammunition storage magazines, triggering a massive explosion that damages three destroyers and the light cruiser *Birmingham*, which loses 229 men killed, 4 missing, and 426 wounded. *Princeton* is later scuttled. American pilots attack Kurita's ships, which, devoid of

air cover, suffer heavy damage. The battleship *Musashi*, hit by 19 torpedoes and 17 bombs, sinks and two other battleships, two heavy cruisers, and three destroyers are damaged, prompting Kurita to reverse course. In the meantime, carrier aircraft of Task Force 38 attack another Japanese surface force as it approaches Leyte through the Sulu Sea, damaging two battleships and sinking a destroyer. The day's actions mark the first attacks by Japanese kamikazes, which hit two freighters.

During the aerial action over Leyte Gulf, Commander David McCampbell, air group commander aboard the carrier *Essex*, along with one wingman, attacks a formation of 60 Japanese aircraft heading for the Third Fleet. The pair breaks up the enemy formation, with McCampbell shooting down nine of the attackers. For this action and his performance in the Battle of the Philippine Sea in June, McCampbell receives the Medal of Honor. He finishes the war as the U.S. Navy's leading fighter ace with 34 kills to his credit.

U.S. submarines sink eight Japanese ships in the South China Sea. However, depth charges dropped from a Japanese destroyer sink the submarine *Shark*. In other actions involving submarines, *Darter* runs aground in the Philippine Islands, and is scuttled by the submarine *Nautilus* to prevent her capture.

During operations in the Formosa Strait, Commander Richard O'Kane leads his submarine *Tang* in a surface attack against a Japanese convoy, sinking two freighters before one of his submarine's own torpedoes makes a circular run and sinks the sub. Only nine crewmen, including O'Kane, survive the sinking and are taken prisoner. For his actions in command of the submarine, O'Kane receives the Medal of Honor.

The destroyer escort *Richard M. Rowell* sinks the Japanese submarine *I-54* east of Surigao Strait, Philippines.

25 OCTOBER
ARMY

On Leyte Island, Philippine Islands, patrols from the X Corps and XXIV Corps meet, linking up the two

bridgeheads. In the X Corps, a troop of the 8th Cavalry Regiment crosses to Samar Island and secures a site. Units of the 7th Infantry Division take enemy positions on key hills, opening the Leyte Valley.

MARINE CORPS
In the Mariana Islands, the 1st Battalion, 8th Marine Regiment assumes responsibility for mopping up Tinian Island when the rest of the 8th Marines departs for Saipan Island.

NAVY
The Battle of Leyte Gulf reaches its climax, with three distinct naval engagements occurring in the waters around the Philippine Islands. Task Group 77.2 (under Rear Admiral Jesse B. Oldendorf), augmented by Task Group 77.3 and 39 motor torpedo boats, attacks a Japanese surface force in the Battle of Suriago Strait. PT boats and destroyers open the battle by launching torpedoes against the Japanese, sinking four ships, including a battleship, and damaging three others, including the battleship *Yamashiro*. Following this, the Japanese face the guns of Oldendorf's ships, which include some repaired battleships damaged during the attack on Pearl Harbor, Hawaii, in 1941. Only one enemy destroyer survives the engagement.

In one of the most controversial decisions of World War II, Third Fleet commander Admiral William F. Halsey Jr.—with reports of Japanese carriers operating to the north of the Philippine Islands and believing his pilots have successfully turned back Vice Admiral Takeo Kurita's surface force—heads north with his fast carriers. The previous day he had issued a contingency plan for creating Task Force 34, consisting of some fast battleships, cruisers, and destroyers from his carrier screen, but he does not execute an implementing order for the force to remain behind and cover the invasion force off Leyte. Thus, while Halsey's fliers strike the enemy carriers, sinking four of them (one with the assistance of naval gunfire), the only force guarding the northern approach to Leyte Gulf consists of escort carriers, destroyers, and destroyer escorts of Task Group 77.4. They soon discover that Admiral Kurita's force has reversed course when his ships appear on the horizon heading toward them. Unleashing their heavy guns, the Japanese ships wreak havoc on the thin-skinned escort carriers and the destroyers and destroyer escorts of their screens, sinking the destroyers *Hoel*, *Johnston*, and the destroyer escort *Samuel B. Roberts*. Before they go down, *Johnston*, led by her wounded skipper Commander Ernest E. Evans, closes the enemy and damages a light cruiser and a heavy cruiser, while *Samuel B. Roberts* stages a daylight torpedo attack. Evans receives a posthumous Medal of Honor for his actions. Carrier aircraft make dummy runs when their ammunition is depleted in an attempt to ward off the attackers. Despite these efforts and the laying down of smoke screens, Japanese gunfire reaches the escort carriers, damaging *Fanshaw Bay* and *Kalinin Bay* and sinking *Gambier Bay*. Miraculously, despite being outgunned, the men of Task Group 77.4 force Admiral Kurita to retire. However, Japanese suicide planes damage the escort carriers *Suwanee*, *Santee*, *Kalinin Bay*, and *Kitkun Bay* and sink *St. Lo*. Aircraft from escort carriers and Task Force 38 descend on the retiring Japanese surface forces, damaging four heavy cruisers to such an extent that they are scuttled, and sinking a light cruiser and three destroyers. U.S. submarines claim a light cruiser and destroyer, and naval gunfire sinks a destroyer.

26 OCTOBER
AIR FORCE
Over China, Fourteenth Air Force B-24 Liberator and B-25 Mitchell bombers attack Japanese shipping off the east Luichow Peninsula. Additionally, B-25s strike rail yards at Hsuchang.

Major Horace S. Carswell Jr., Fourteenth Air Force, co-pilots a B-24 Liberator against a Japanese shipping convoy in the South China Sea. The plane is crippled and his pilot is killed by flak during the attack. Upon reaching land, with only two of his four engines working, he orders the crew to bail out. His own parachute damaged beyond use, Carswell remains at the controls in an attempt to save himself and an injured crewman. He is posthumously awarded the Medal of Honor, and Carswell Air Force Base, Texas, is named in his honor.

AIR FORCE/NAVY
In the Philippine Islands, carrier aircraft and land-based Army Air Forces bombers attack the retiring remnants of the Japanese fleet following the Battle of Leyte Gulf, sinking five ships. In addition, Task Group 34.5 sinks a destroyer off Panay Island.

Right: *Bulldozers of the Army engineers cut a trail along a mountainside in India as they work to construct the Ledo Road to Burma. The road will be nicknamed "Pick's Pike" after Army engineer Major General Lewis A. Pick, the operation's commander. (U.S. Army)*

26–27 OCTOBER
ARMY

On Leyte Island, Philippine Islands, the 24th Infantry Division sends the 34th Infantry Regiment through the Leyte Valley toward Santa Fe, while the 19th Infantry fights into Pastrana. The 96th Infantry Division shells enemy positions at Tabontabon, then attacks and takes most of the town. The 7th Infantry Division clears enemy fortifications around Buri airfield and secures it.

27 OCTOBER
AIR FORCE

Pilots from the 9th Fighter Squadron become the first to fly missions from bases in the Philippine Islands since 1942. They are based at Tacloban airfield flying P-38 Lightning fighters. Major Richard I. Bong is among the first pilots to score victories from this base in the Philippines.

28 OCTOBER
AIR FORCE

The XXI Bomber Command flies its first combat mission from the Mariana Islands when 14 B-29 Superfortress bombers hit submarine pens on Dublon Island in the Truk Islands, Caroline Islands. The mission is less than a success, and Brigadier General Hansell is forced to abort due to aircraft problems.

NAVY

In the Philippine Islands, the destroyers *Helm* and *Gridley*, assisted by a TBF Avenger torpedo-bomber from the light carrier *Belleau Wood*, sink the Japanese submarine *I-46*. The Japanese submarine *I-45* torpedoes and sinks the destroyer escort *Eversole* off Leyte and is subsequently sunk by the destroyer escort *Whitehurst*.

29 OCTOBER
ARMY

The 24th Infantry Division advances toward Jaro, Leyte Island, Philippine Islands, while the 96th Division finds little resistance as it takes several towns. The 7th Infantry Division continues its attack toward Dagami and the 24th Infantry Division moves on Carigara. On 30 October, the 24th Division runs into strong enemy positions and is halted. The next day Jaro is cleared and the advance continues. By 2 November the Leyte Valley is cleared, Carigara is taken, and units are pushing into the Ormac Valley.

29–30 OCTOBER
NAVY

Task Force 38 carriers, while launching strikes against the Philippine Islands, endure repeated kamikaze attacks that damage the carriers *Intrepid*, *Franklin*, and *Belleau Wood*.

30 OCTOBER
MARINE CORPS

The 5th Marine Regiment and the last elements of the 7th Marine Regiment depart Peleliu Island, Palau Islands, for Pavuvu Island, Solomon Islands. Marine Corps casualties for the Peleliu operation total 1,336 dead or missing and 5,450 wounded. Losses among Navy personnel serving with Marine Corps units are 61 killed and 249 wounded.

31 OCTOBER
ARMY

In Burma, Major General Albert C. Wedemeyer assumes command of U.S. Forces, China Theater. Brigadier General John P. Willey replaces an injured Brigadier General Thomas S. Arms as Mars Task Force commander. Colonel Ernest F. Easterbrook takes command of the 475th Infantry Regiment and Colonel Thomas J. Heavey heads the 124th Cavalry Regiment. The task force now includes the 612th and 613th Field Artillery Battalions (pack, mule).

1 NOVEMBER
AIR FORCE

The F-13, a photoreconnaissance version of the B-29 Superfortress bomber, makes a flight over Tokyo, Japan. It is the first flight by an American aircraft over the city since the Doolittle Raid of 18 April 1942.

NAVY

Kamikaze attacks in the waters off Leyte Island, Philippine Islands, sink the destroyer *Abner Read* and, combined with conventional bombing, damage five other destroyers.

3 NOVEMBER
ALL SERVICES

The Japanese launch the first Fu-go balloons against the United States; the Zone of the Interior receives the first report of a balloon reaching the U.S. the next day. These weaponized balloons, made of paper or rubberized silk, are designed to ascend into the jet stream and detonate after reaching the American mainland. Thousands of balloons are launched over the next five months, most from the island of Honshu, Japan. Several hundred actually reach American soil, and 285 cause explosions as far inland as Michigan.

AIR FORCE

Far East Air Force fighters, many of them Fifth Air Force P-38 Lightnings, are striking targets throughout the Philippine Islands—primarily airfields in the central Philippines, and on Celebes and Halmhera Islands, Dutch East Indies.

Right: *Low-flying American bombers drop bombs with parachutes on Japanese facilities and aircraft parked at Vunakanau Airfield at Rabaul, New Britain Island. The parachutes slow the bombs until the U.S. planes are out of danger. (Dept. of Defense)*

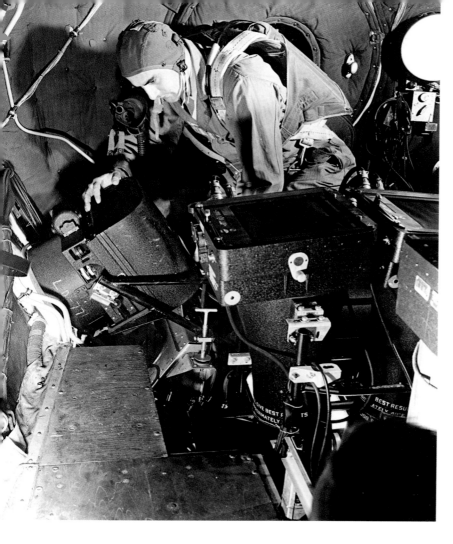

Above: *The interior of a Boeing F-13, the reconnaissance version of the B-29 Superfortress, shows the mapping cameras and operator. (NASM)*

Below: *A Japanese Fu-go balloon bomb drifts over the Pacific. Of the thousands launched from Japan, several hundred reach the U.S. homeland; one causes fatal civilian casualties. (NASM)*

Balloon in flight over the Pacific Ocean.

4–7 NOVEMBER
ARMY
The Japanese land two divisions of reinforcements on Leyte Island, Philippine Islands. The X Corps prepares defensive positions against sea attack near Carigara, while the 24th Infantry Division pushes forward to an area called Breakneck Ridge. The 96th Infantry Division continues its attack with tanks on Dagami toward Bloody Ridge. Japanese counterattacks occur nightly. On 7 November, the X Corps begins a major effort toward Ormoc. The 24th Division can take only part of Breakneck Ridge, but the 96th Division sends the entire 382d Infantry Regiment to overrun the enemy on Bloody Ridge.

5 NOVEMBER
AIR FORCE
The Twentieth Air Force sends 24 B-29 Superfortress bombers from the Mariana Islands to attack airfields on Iwo Jima Island, Japan. This attack begins tactical operations to prepare for the invasion, which will take place in February.

From Calcutta, India, 53 B-29s are sent to bomb targets in Singapore. These bombers seriously damage the King George VI Graving Dock, making it unusable for several months.

5–6 NOVEMBER
NAVY
Task Force 38 (Vice Admiral John S. McCain) strikes airfields on Luzon Island, Philippine Islands, and shipping in surrounding waters, sinking a heavy cruiser and three other vessels.

6 NOVEMBER
AIR FORCE
Seventh Air Force B-24 Liberator bombers begin flying a series of missions through 24 December, during which they will lay mines in a number of anchorages throughout the Bonin Islands.

7 NOVEMBER
MARINE CORPS
Marine Aircraft Groups 24 and 32 and Marine Scout Bombing Squadrons 133, 142, 236, 241, 243, 244, and 341 are assigned to the operational control of the Fifth Air Force for the upcoming Luzon campaign in the Philippine Islands.

NAVY
The submarine *Albacore* strikes a mine north of Honshu Island, Japan, and sinks.

8 NOVEMBER
AIR FORCE

During a strike against Iwo Jima Island, Japan, by 17 Twentieth Air Force B-29 Superfortress bombers, the XXI Bomber Command loses its first bomber during combat operations when a B-29 is forced to ditch after being attacked by Japanese aircraft that drop phosphorus bombs into the B-29 formations.

NAVY

Japanese surface ships sink the submarine *Growler* off Mindoro Island, Philippine Islands.

10 NOVEMBER
AIR FORCE

The Fifth Air Force sends 36 B-25 Mitchell medium bombers to attack a Japanese convoy near Ormoc Bay, Philippine Islands. Three ships are destroyed.

ARMY

On Leyte Island, Philippine Islands, the 1st Cavalry Division begins clearing the central mountains, while the 24th Infantry Division makes an all-out effort to take Breakneck Ridge. The 1st Battalion, 34th Infantry Regiment moves seven miles by landing craft along the coast, lands near Carigara Bay, and moves inland.

NAVY

While anchored in Seeadler Harbor, Manus Island, Admiralty Islands, the ammunition ship *Mount Hood* is blown apart and all on board are killed when the 3,000 tons of munitions she is carrying explode. Thirty-six vessels in the vicinity, ranging in size from an escort carrier to a fuel oil barge, suffer damage.

Above: *While anchored at Manus Island, Admiralty Islands, in November 1944, the ammunition ship* Mount Hood *explodes in a massive blast that kills all aboard and damages 36 other nearby vessels. (Naval Historical Center)*

Below: *Soldiers of the Mars Task Force pass a pack train of supplies as they begin a long climb up a mountainous section of the Ledo Road in Burma. (U.S. Army)*

With intelligence predicting the position of her target, the submarine *Flounder* sinks the German submarine *U-537* in the Java Sea.

11 NOVEMBER
NAVY

Carrier planes from Task Force 38 attack a Japanese convoy as it enters Ormoc Bay, Leyte Island, Philippine Islands, sinking a total of nine ships.

11–12 NOVEMBER
ARMY

On Leyte Island, Philippine Islands, the 24th Infantry Division gains the top of Breakneck Ridge and begins clearing it of resistance. The isolated 1st Battalion, 34th Infantry Regiment is resupplied by air and it moves on to its objective at Kiley Ridge, supporting a blocking position held by the 19th Infantry Regiment.

12 NOVEMBER
NAVY

The destroyer *Nicholas* sinks the Japanese submarine *I-37* south of Yap Island, Caroline Islands.

13 NOVEMBER
NAVY

The minesweeper *Ardent* and the frigate *Rockford* sink the Japanese submarine *I-12* between California and Hawaii.

13–14 NOVEMBER
NAVY

Aircraft of Task Force 38 strike targets in and around Manila, Luzon Island, Philippine Islands, sinking a total of 25 enemy vessels.

15 NOVEMBER
AIR FORCE

Flying a P-38 Lightning fighter, Major Richard I. Bong shoots down his eighth enemy aircraft since 10 October in the southwest Pacific area. Although assigned as a gunnery instructor with the Fifth Air Force, he has repeatedly volunteered to fly combat missions over Borneo Island, Dutch East Indies, as well over Leyte Island, Philippine Islands. In recognition of his actions he is awarded the Medal of Honor, which he receives from General Douglas MacArthur on 12 December.

Below: *The deep harbor of Ulithi Atoll in the western Caroline Islands becomes a staging point for the growing U.S. Pacific Fleet. (U.S. Navy)*

Opposite: *Women's Army Corps Soldiers line up to clean their mess kits by dunking them in cans of boiling water. As the war continues, more women volunteer to join the military service and do their part to defend the nation. ("Necessary Evil," Manuel Tolegian, Army Art Collection, U.S. Army Center of Military History)*

15 NOVEMBER
ARMY

After consolidation of its operational areas on New Guinea Island, New Britain Island, and the Admiralty Islands, the Eighth U.S. Army begins combat operations. The 31st Infantry Division makes amphibious landings on Mapia and Asia Islands, off the northwestern coast of New Guinea Island, meeting little resistance.

In Burma, the new Mars Task Force (the 475th Infantry Regiment under Colonel Ernest F. Easterbrook, with supporting units and 1st Chinese Separate Regiment) begins its march to help a Chinese division at Tonkwa and open the road to China. The 124th Cavalry Regiment is still in training.

17 NOVEMBER
NAVY

TBM Avenger torpedo-bombers of Composite Squadron 82 from the escort carrier *Anzio* join the destroyer escort *Lawrence C. Taylor* in sinking the Japanese submarine *I-26* in the Philippine Sea. The squadron and destroyer escort team up again the following day to sink *I-41*.

17–18 NOVEMBER
NAVY

In two days of attacks against Japanese convoy MI 27 in the East China Sea, U.S. submarines sink five enemy vessels.

19 NOVEMBER
ARMY

On Leyte Island, Philippine Islands, the advances toward Ormoc by units of both the X Corps and XXIV Corps are stalled by strong enemy resistance, rough terrain, and weather as a typhoon blows over the islands. The town of Limon is finally taken by the 32d Infantry Division on 22 November, ending the battle for Breakneck Ridge. The 77th Infantry Division arrives on 23 November and the 11th Airborne Division is diverted to reinforce Leyte. A Japanese attack hits the thinly spread 7th Infantry Division, beginning the battle for Shoestring Ridge.

NAVY

The destroyer escorts *Conklin* and *McCoy Reynolds* sink the Japanese submarine *I-37* west of the Palau Islands.

21 NOVEMBER
NAVY

The submarine *Sealion* attacks a Japanese task force off Formosa Island, sinking a battleship and a destroyer.

24 NOVEMBER
AIR FORCE

Flying their first mission against Japan from the Mariana Islands, 88 B-29 Superfortress bombers of the XXI Bomber Command hit the Mushino Aircraft Factory in Tokyo. Brigadier General Emmett O'Donnell Jr. leads the mission, and his co-pilot is Major Robert K. Morgan, the pilot of the famous B-17 Flying Fortress bomber "Memphis Belle." The mission is less than perfect; of the original 111 bombers launched, 17 abort, 50 bomb secondary targets, and a handful cannot drop their bombs due to mechanical problems. One B-29 is rammed by a Japanese fighter and becomes the first XXI Bomber Command loss to direct enemy action, and one is forced to ditch when it runs out of fuel on the way back to the base.

25 NOVEMBER
NAVY

Carrier planes from Task Force 38 strike enemy shipping off Luzon Island, Philippine Islands, sinking eight enemy vessels. Kamikazes damage the carriers *Essex*, *Intrepid*, and *Hancock*.

27 NOVEMBER
ARMY

The battle for Peleliu Island, Palau Islands, is over. The 81st Infantry Division and attached units have suffered more than 3,275 casualties.

27–29 NOVEMBER
NAVY

During operations off Leyte Island, Philippine Islands, one vessel and six ships are damaged by kamikaze aircraft.

28 NOVEMBER
NAVY

The destroyers *Saufley Waller*, *Pringle*, and *Renshaw* sink the Japanese submarine *I-46* in Leyte Gulf, Philippine Islands.

28 NOVEMBER
ARMY

The Japanese make a large night attack on Leyte Island, Philippine Islands, in an effort to overrun the 34th Infantry Regiment on Kiley Ridge. It fails, but cuts off one company of the 34th Infantry Regiment. The next day, units of the 32d Infantry Division arrive as reinforcements. Units of the 7th Infantry Division are replaced by the recently arrived 11th Airborne Division.

29 NOVEMBER
NAVY

The submarine *Archerfish* claims the biggest prize of the war, torpedoing the 64,000-ton Japanese carrier *Shinano* southwest of Tokyo Bay, Japan. The sinking marks the end of *Shinano*'s maiden voyage.

2 DECEMBER
MARINE CORPS

The first Women's Reservists report for duty in Hawaii following authorization for them to serve outside the continental limits of the United States.

2–3 DECEMBER
NAVY

The destroyers of Destroyer Division 120 enter Ormoc Bay, Leyte Island, Philippine Islands, and engage in a night action with the enemy. *Cooper* sinks after being struck by a torpedo, but not before joining other ships in sinking a Japanese escort destroyer. *Allen M. Sumner* and *Moale* are damaged in the engagement.

3 DECEMBER
MARINE CORPS/NAVY

Marine Night Fighting Squadron 541 moves from Peleliu Island, Palau Islands, to Tacloban Airfield on Leyte Island, Philippine Islands, to provide faster fighters than those of the Army Air Forces, which could not catch Japanese bombers. Marine Aircraft Group 12 and its squadrons (Fighting Squadrons 115, 211, 218, and 313) begin arriving at Tacloban from Emirau Island, Admiralty Islands, and become part of the Fifth Air Force.

In response to the threat of Japanese kamikaze attacks, the number of fighter planes on Navy carriers is increased. Since no additional Navy fighter pilots are available, Marine Corps squadrons are rushed in to fill the gap. Marine Fighting Squadron 112 goes on board the carrier *Bennington* at San Diego, California.

5–6 DECEMBER
ARMY

On Leyte Island, Philippine Islands, the Sixth Army begins an offensive to take Ormac. The 7th Division attacks north with the 184th and 17th Infantry Regiments abreast, clearing several ridges of Japanese troops. The 77th Infantry Division loads onto ships for a landing to outflank the Japanese defenses. The 112th Cavalry Regiment continues its struggle to capture Limon and open the trail in that area.

6–7 DECEMBER
NAVY

Two days of attacks by U.S. submarines against the Japanese convoy TAMA 34 in the Philippine Islands area result in the sinking of four ships and the forced grounding of another.

7 DECEMBER

Marine Aircraft Group 12 aircraft participate in attacks to destroy Japanese convoys bringing more troops to Leyte Island, Philippine Islands. The effort continues through 12 December and results in 10 ships sunk or damaged and the end of enemy reinforcement efforts.

7–21 DECEMBER
ARMY/NAVY

In the Philippine Islands, Task Group 78.3 (under Rear Admiral Arthur D. Struble) puts the 77th Infantry Division ashore in an unopposed landing at Deposito, Ormac Bay, Leyte Island. The 307th and 305th Infantry Regiments move inland at once toward the 7th Infantry Division. The Japanese react to the

Opposite: *After capturing Guam Island, Mariana Islands, Soldiers of the 77th Infantry Division are sent to Leyte Island, Philippine Islands, in late November 1944. The division soon begins combat to seize the town of Ormoc. (Naitonal Archives)*

Right: *The first B-29 Superfortress raids against Tokyo, Japan, occur on 24 November 1944 with planes taking off from the expanded airfields on Saipan Island, Mariana Islands. The raids continue and grow in intensity as more bases are built. (U.S. Air Force)*

landing with 45–50 kamikaze plane attacks, damaging the destroyers *Lamson* and *Mahan* and high-speed transport *Ward*. The two destroyers must be scuttled. The enemy defenses are broken and units advance to the Talisayan River. Ormac falls to the 77th Division on 10 December. Elements of 38th Infantry Division fight alongside the 11th Airborne Division to seize the Buri Airfield area. When the 7th Infantry Division joins the 77th Division, the enemy force is divided. By 21 December U.S. forces are in control of the Ormoc Valley.

8 DECEMBER
AIR FORCE/NAVY
Navy cruisers combine with Mariana Islands-based Twentieth Air Force B-29 Superfortress bombers and Seventh Air Force P-38 Lightning fighters and B-24 Liberator bombers to attack Japanese airfields on Iwo Jima Island, Japan. The targets are home to enemy forces launching limited attacks against U.S. bases in the Mariana Islands. These attacks continue until early 1945, during which 11 B-29s are destroyed on the ground and 43 more are damaged.

9 DECEMBER
ARMY
The 2d and 3d Battalions, 475th Infantry Regiment, arrive at Mo-hlaing, Burma, as the Japanese are attacking a Chinese unit. The Americans join in the battle, helping repulse the attack. They then relieve the Chinese and begin patrolling toward Tonkwa. Japanese counterattacks on 13 and 14 December are repelled.

11 DECEMBER
MARINE CORPS
In the Philippine Islands, F4U Corsair fighters of Marine Aircraft Group 12 shoot down 19 Japanese aircraft that are either attacking U.S. ships or defending themselves against Marine Corps air attacks.

NAVY
While en route to resupply American forces at Ormoc Bay on Leyte Island, Philippine Islands, a convoy is attacked by kamikazes, which sink the destroyer *Reid*.

12 DECEMBER
AIR FORCE

General Douglas MacArthur presents the Medal of Honor to Major Richard I. Bong for having shot down eight enemy aircraft in the southwest Pacific area from 10 October through 15 November. At the time he was assigned as a gunnery instructor with the Fifth Air Force, but repeatedly volunteered to fly combat missions in a P-38 Lightning fighter over Borneo Island, Dutch East Indies, as well as over Leyte Island, Philippine Islands.

MARINE CORPS

Marine Night Fighting Squadron 541 downs 11 enemy planes and prevents an air attack on a U.S. convoy just after dawn in the Philippine Islands.

13 DECEMBER
AIR FORCE

Twentieth Air Force B-29 Superfortress bombers from the Mariana Islands strike the Mitsubishi aircraft engine factory at Nagoya, Japan. Bombing accuracy seems improved, and significant damage is done during the raid.

MARINE CORPS

A kamikaze strikes the light cruiser *Nashville* during the movement of Army forces to Mindoro Island, Philippine Islands. Among the 135 dead on the ship are 28 men of her Marine Corps detachment.

The V Amphibious Corps Artillery departs Leyte Island for Guam Island, Mariana Islands.

14 DECEMBER
ARMY

At Puerto Princesa, Palawan Island, Philippine Islands, Japanese captors force 150 U.S. prisoners of war who had been taken from Bataan Peninsula and Corregidor Island into three covered trenches. They are doused with fuel and set afire. Those who try to escape are shot, but 11 survive to tell the story.

MARINE CORPS

Marine Aircraft Group 12 aircraft attack enemy airfields on Luzon and Masbate Islands, Philippine Islands, to reduce Japanese aerial opposition to the pending Mindoro Island landing.

15 DECEMBER
ARMY/MARINE CORPS/NAVY

A Sixth Army task force (under Brigadier General William C. Dunckel) composed of the 19th and 21st Regimental Combat Teams, 24th Infantry Division, and the 503d Parachute Infantry Regiment, lands on Mindoro Island, Philippine Islands. The task force is put ashore near San Agustin by Navy Task Group 78.3. The troops drive inland up to eight miles against light opposition to seize the airfield, and reconstruction begins immediately. Planes from Marine Aircraft Group 12 and Marine Night Fighting

Right: Soldiers of an artillery gun crew protect their ears as they fire their M1A1 155mm gun against an advancing Japanese force on Leyte Island, Philippine Islands. (U.S. Army)

Squadron 541 provide air cover. Kamikazes attack Task Group 78.3, heavily damaging two tank landing ships, which have to be scuttled, as well as the escort carrier *Marcus Island*, two destroyers, and a PT boat.

MARINE CORPS

The 2d Marine Aircraft Wing headquarters moves from Peleliu Island, Palau Islands, to Hawaii. It subsequently serves as the nucleus for the Tactical Air Force, the aviation component of the Tenth Army, which will conduct the invasion of Okinawa, Japan.

16 DECEMBER
NAVY

Task Force 38 aircraft sink a Japanese freighter in Subic Bay, Philippine Islands, unaware that she is carrying more than 1,600 Allied prisoners of war en route to Japan.

16–18 DECEMBER
ARMY

The 124th Cavalry Regiment, the second regiment of the Mars Task Force, moves to the front in Burma. Many of the men are wearing cut-down cavalry boots.

17 DECEMBER
AIR FORCE

Colonel Paul W. Tibbets Jr. takes command of the newly activated 509th Composite Group at Wendover Field, Utah. Under Tibbets' command, the group trains to deliver the first nuclear weapons in combat. A principal combat element is the 393d Bombardment Squadron (Very Heavy), equipped with B-29 Superfortress bombers. The 393d is commanded by Major Charles W. Sweeney.

Major Richard I. Bong shoots down his 40th enemy aircraft in the Pacific. Bong, who had shot down his first Japanese aircraft on 27 December 1942, is grounded by General George C. Kenney after achieving his 40th victory. Bong ends the war as America's leading ace.

18 DECEMBER
AIR FORCE

Flying from Chengtu, China, 84 B-29 Superfortress bombers carry out their first firebombing raid of the war when they attack the docks at Hankow, China, along the Yangtze River. Joining the attack are 200 Fourteenth Air Force aircraft.

ARMY

General Douglas MacArthur is promoted to the five-star rank of General of the Army.

NAVY

A typhoon decimates the ships of the Third Fleet as they operate east of the Philippine Islands. The destroyers *Hull*, *Monaghan*, and *Spence* capsize with heavy loss of life, and 21 other ships suffer damage.

Left: *The radar plot room of an aircraft carrier is the heart of its air operations, tracking both friendly and enemy aircraft. ("Radar Plot Room," Lt. Mitchell Jamieson, USNR, Navy Art Collection)*

Opposite: *A flight of B-26 Marauder medium bombers fly toward their target. The plane can carry 4,000 pounds of bombs and has 11 .50 caliber machine guns at various locations to defend itself. ("Marauder Mission," Robert Taylor © The Military Gallery, Ojai, CA)*

19 DECEMBER
NAVY

The submarine *Redfish* sinks a Japanese carrier southeast of Shanghai, China, but the resulting depth charge attacks by the carrier's escorts cause such damage that the submarine terminates her war patrol.

25–26 DECEMBER
AIR FORCE

Major Thomas B. McGuire Jr., Fifth Air Force, volunteers to lead a P-38 Lightning fighter escort mission for bombers targeting a kamikaze base on Luzon Island, Philippine Islands. Outnumbered three to one by the Japanese, he continues to fight after his guns jam. He risks his own life to protect a crippled bomber while downing several enemy aircraft.

Right: *Paratroopers of the 11th Airborne Division at Manawaret on Leyte Island, Philippine Islands, carry boxes of Christmas dinners to fellow Soldiers. The rations arrive via one of the division's L-4 light observation aircraft. (U.S. Army)*

McGuire is killed in action on 7 January 1945 over Los Negros Island, Admiralty Islands, having scored 38 victories, making him America's second highest ace of the war. He is awarded the Medal of Honor.

26 DECEMBER
NAVY

A Japanese surface force consisting of a heavy cruiser, a light cruiser, and destroyers intent on disrupting the American landings at Mindoro Island, Philippine Islands, encounters determined attacks from land-based aircraft and motor torpedo boats. Though the Japanese succeed in bombarding the Mindoro beachhead, they lose one destroyer sunk and five ships damaged.

28 DECEMBER
AIR FORCE

In the Mariana Islands, Brigadier General Haywood Hansell closes his headquarters on Saipan Island and begins moving the XXI Bomber Command Forward

Echelon Staff to Guam Island to join the ground echelon already in place.

MARINE CORPS

Marine Fighting Squadrons 124 and 213 join the carrier *Essex* at Ulithi Atoll, Caroline Islands, and become the first Marine Corps aircraft to conduct combat operations from fleet carriers during World War II.

28–30 DECEMBER
NAVY

Attacks by kamikazes against a convoy steaming to support the assault on Mindoro Island, Philippine Islands, result in the sinking of two freighters and damage to five other ships, including the destroyers *Pringle* and *Gansevoort*. Another freighter sinks after being hit in a conventional bombing attack. *LST 750*, hit by a suicide plane and later by an aircraft torpedo, is scuttled.

Left: *A B-25 Mitchell bomber swoops down on a Japanese warship in Ormac Bay, Philippine Islands, on 2 November 1944. The ship lands some of the 22,000 Japanese reinforcements sent to Leyte Island. This photograph shows the last moment before the plane's bomb squarely hits the front section of the ship, sinking her. (U.S. Air Force)*

Opposite: *A battle grimy Marine carries a near-dead infant to safety after finding it during combat operations to clear caves on Saipan Island, Mariana Islands. The baby had been hidden in the dirt under a rock. (W. Eugene Smith, Time-Life)*

31 DECEMBER
ARMY
In Burma, the Mars Task Force starts a march to join a Chinese brigade in the Northern Combat Area Command. Enemy counterattacks are launched on Leyte Island, Philippine Islands, as the 77th Infantry Division starts to relieve the 1st Cavalry Division. On Saipan Island, Mariana Islands, the 24th Infantry Regiment takes over the mop-up of Japanese holdouts.

MARINE CORPS
Marine Fighting Squadron 123 joins the carrier *Bennington*.

Right: *Soldiers of the 163d Infantry Regiment, 41st Infantry Division, along with some Army engineers, pause on the ramp of their infantry landing craft on the beach at Aitape, New Guinea Island, to watch a line of Japanese prisoners being evacuated to waiting ships. Many Japanese prisoners of war are taken to camps in the U.S. (U.S. Army)*

1945
YEAR OF RECKONING

1 JANUARY
ARMY

In Burma, the units of Mars Task Force (5332d Composite Brigade) are on the move to their next missions. The 475th Infantry Regiment departs the Tonkwa area in a march to cross the Shweli River and sets up camps near Mong Wi. It is joined there on 13 January by the 124th Cavalry Regiment. High mountains, rain, and jungle often make air resupply impossible and food runs short on many days. On 15 January, the reunited task force resumes its march over the mountains.

MARINE CORPS

In the Mariana Islands, the 1st Battalion, 8th Marine Regiment departs Tinian Island to rejoin the 2d Marine Division on Saipan Island.

2 JANUARY
AIR FORCE

Tenth Air Force troop carriers launch an amazing 546 sorties to frontline areas and resupply bases in China. During this year, they will average more than 500 sorties each day that they fly. Far East Air Forces continues to attack multiple targets in the Philippine Islands; P-38 Lightning fighters and A-20 Havoc ight bombers strike San Fernando Harbor, while B-24 Liberator bombers bomb Clark Field (still occupied by the Japanese), and B-25 Mitchell bombers hit Batangas and enemy airfields in the central Philippines. Other aircraft conduct armed reconnaissance missions across the Philippines. These missions will continue for the remainder of the war.

MARINE CORPS

Marine Aircraft Group 14, Marine Fighting Squadrons 212, 222, and 223, and Marine Observation Squadron 251 begin deploying from the Solomon Islands to an airfield on the island of Samar, Philippine Islands. The movement of aerial echelons is complete by 24 January.

3 JANUARY
MARINE CORPS

Marine Corps aircraft from the carrier *Essex* participate in their first missions from the carrier, during strikes on Formosa Island, and shoot down their first Japanese plane.

NAVY

The submarine *Swordfish*, en route to Okinawa, Japan, on her 13th war patrol, issues her last radio communication and is not heard from again. She is declared lost at sea on 15 February.

Left: *A gun crew on board the battleship* New Mexico *mans a 5-inch naval gun, one of 14 on the ship. On duty in the Atlantic at the time of the December 1941 attack on Pearl Harbor, Hawaii,* New Mexico *sailed to join the Pacific fleet in August 1942. (National Archives)*

Opposite: *Soldiers of the Mars Task Force (5332d Composite Brigade) cut their way through the Burmese jungle to strike deep into Japanese lines. ("Of Their Own Accord," James Dietz)*

3–4 JANUARY
NAVY

Aircraft from the carriers of Task Force 38 (under Vice Admiral John S. McCain) strike airfields on Formosa Island and attack shipping off shore, sinking 10 ships and damaging 8 others.

3–8 JANUARY
NAVY

U.S. Navy ships bound for Lingayen Gulf, Philippine Islands, come under attack by kamikaze aircraft. The escort carrier *Ommaney Bay* takes a hit that ignites fueled aircraft on the hangar deck, and is scuttled with the loss of 95 of her crew. The most intense day of attacks occurs on 6 January, when the battleships *California* and *New Mexico* and the heavy cruiser *Louisville* and light cruiser *Columbia* suffer damage. Among the five destroyers hit, *Walke* suffers the most damage as four suicide aircraft set their sights on her. The ship's antiaircraft gunners shoot down three of the attackers, but one enemy aircraft scores a direct hit on the bridge, which ignites in flames that seriously wound and burn its occupants, including the captain, Commander George F. Davis. Despite his wounds he continues to direct the ship's defenses until assured his command is safe. He dies hours later and receives the Medal of Honor posthumously. On 6 January the fast carriers of Task Force 38 begin concentrated strikes against Japanese airfields in the Philippine Islands. On 8 January suicide aircraft damage the escort carriers

Kitkun Bay and *Kadashan Bay,* and an Australian heavy cruiser. All told, 29 ships are sunk or damaged by kamikazes.

4–5 JANUARY
ARMY

On Mindoro Island, Philippine Islands, a company of the 503d Parachute Regimental Combat Team (Separate) joins a Philippine guerrilla group for a successful attack to seize Palauan village from the Japanese.

5 JANUARY
AIR FORCE/ARMY

Operation GRUBWORM is completed. One month after its initiation, two entire Chinese divisions, Chinese Sixth Army Headquarters, a heavy mortar company, 249 American soldiers, and two portable surgical hospitals have been airlifted from Burma to China into the combat zone. More than 1,300 transport sorties were required to complete the operation; only three aircraft went down while completing the mission.

6 JANUARY
MARINE CORPS

Marine Aircraft Group 12 aircraft participate in raids to destroy key bridges on Luzon Island, Philippine Islands. The attacks continue through 9 January.

NAVY

The first contingent of Women Accepted for Volunteer Emergency Service arrives in Hawaii. Eventually 4,009 women serve there, the only post outside the continental United States to which women are permanently assigned during World War II.

7 JANUARY
AIR FORCE/NAVY

The Far East Air Force operates with the Third Fleet in attacking enemy airfields in northern Luzon Island, Philippine Islands. In the largest joint mission of the war in the southwest Pacific, more than 130 light and medium bombers are launched against five airfields.

8 JANUARY
ARMY

In Burma, the Mars Task Force marches through rugged jungle and mountain terrain for an attack on the Burma Road. On 17 January, task force troops clear the enemy from Namhkam village and move to within three miles of Burma Road. On 18 January, the task force gains a hold on Loi-kang ridge, overlooking the road.

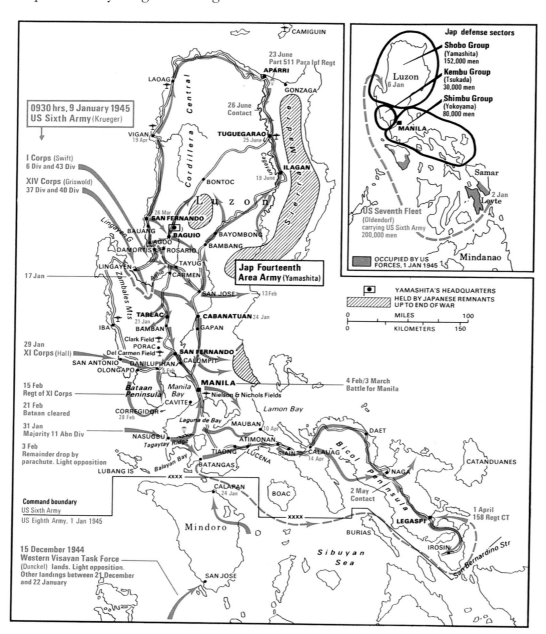

Above: *Two Soldiers of the Mars Task Force check out a Japanese foxhole on the road to Walabum, Burma, to ensure it is unoccupied. (U.S. Army)*

Left: *General of the Army Douglas MacArthur uses Lieutenant General Walter Krueger's Sixth Army divisions with Navy support to make a series of amphibious operations, bypassing Japanese defenses on Luzon Island, Philippine Islands, in the drive to liberate Manila and recapture the island. (U.S. Army)*

Opposite, top: *Both Coast Guardsmen and Navy Sailors handle the landing craft that take assault forces ashore. ("Assault Wave Cox'n," Lt. Dwight C. Shepler, Navy Art Collection)*

Opposite, bottom: *Four Army divisions assault the beaches of Leyte Island in October 1945 to start the liberation of the Philippine Islands. ("Red Beach," Paul Sample, Army Art Collection, U.S. Army Center of Military History)*

NAVY

The submarines of Task Group 17.21 (under Commander Charles E. Loughlin) attack the Japanese convoy MOTA 30 off the coast of Formosa Island, sinking three ships and damaging three others.

9 JANUARY
AIR FORCE/ARMY/NAVY

Operation MIKE 1, the invasion of Luzon Island, Philippine Islands, begins with preparatory air strikes by Army Far East Air Force and Navy planes, and a naval bombardment by Task Force 77 (under Vice Admiral Thomas C. Kinkaid). Two Army Corps are landed near the center of the island at Lingayen Gulf—the XIV Corps (under Major General Oscar W. Griswold) on the right; and I Corps (under Major General Innis P. Swift) on the left. The XIV Corps landing is virtually unopposed, and its 40th and 37th Infantry divisions quickly push four miles inland. They are to cut across the island, then turn and clear the northern part of Luzon. The I Corps' 6th and 43d Infantry Divisions are tasked to recapture the southern half of Luzon including Manila. They hit moderate resistance and make less progress. Kinkaid's fleet is attacked by Japanese assault demolition boats and kamikazes, which hit four ships, including the battleship *Mississippi*.

AIR FORCE

The Eleventh Air Force utilizes H2X radar equipment for the first time as B-24 Liberator bombers bomb Suribachi Bay Airfield, Iwo Jima Island, Japan.

10 JANUARY
AIR FORCE

The Thirteenth Air Force moves its operating base again, from New Guinea Island to Leyte Island,

Philippine Islands, as part of the Far East Air Force offensive in the Philippine area.

MARINE CORPS

Advance parties of Marine Aircraft Groups 24 and 32 go ashore at Lingayen Gulf, Luzon Island, Philippine Islands.

10–16 JANUARY
ARMY

In the Philippine Islands, the XIV and I Corps units make rapid advances against sporadic resistance on Luzon Island. In some cases, the advancing Americans find that Philippine guerrilla bands have already recaptured villages from the Japanese. The 25th Infantry Division and an armored group come ashore. On Leyte Island, the Eighth Army continues to clear pockets of Japanese defenders and sends units to secure the many small islands nearby.

Above: *The completion of the project linking the Ledo Road with the Burma Road means that supplies can be trucked from ports in India and Burma to the U.S., British, and Chinese forces fighting in north Burma and China. (U.S. Army)*

Below: *The C-46 Commando is the largest transport aircraft used by the Army Air Forces in the war. (U.S. Air Force)*

11 JANUARY
AIR FORCE

Captain William A. Shomo, Fifth Air Force, flying an F-6D (a reconnaissance version of the P-51 Mustang fighter) over Luzon Island, Philippine Islands, spots enemy aircraft and orders an attack against unknown enemy odds. Shomo destroys seven enemy aircraft and his wingman destroys three, all in one action—unparalleled success in the southwest Pacific for which he was awarded the Medal of Honor. Two other pilots, one Army and one Navy, had seven-victory days during the war, but neither received the Medal of Honor. Shomo's achievement is particularly remarkable in that reconnaissance pilots rarely engage enemy planes.

12 JANUARY
ARMY

A U.S.-Chinese convoy starts from India along the newly opened Ledo Road toward Kunming, China. On 22 January, the Ledo Road links with the Burma Road, and the long-closed supply line from India to China is reopened.

MARINE CORPS

Aircraft from the carrier *Essex* participate in major strikes along the coast of French Indochina.

NAVY

Task Force 38 (under Vice Admiral John S. McCain) strikes targets in French Indochina (a location where the admiral's grandson will fly combat missions 22 years later during another war). All told, 31 enemy vessels are sent to the bottom by the carrier planes. Task Force 38 will later hit shipping and installations at Hong Kong and shipping off the coast of China.

13 JANUARY
NAVY

The destroyer escort *Fleming* sinks the Japanese submarine *I-362* northeast of the Truk Islands, Caroline Islands.

17 JANUARY
AIR FORCE

Ninety-one B-29 Superfortress bombers take off from Chengtu, China, on a bombing mission over Shinchiku, Formosa Island. About a dozen abort before reaching the target. It is the last mission launched from Chinese bases against Japanese targets. After this mission, the XX Bomber Command B-29s will move to India where Brigadier General Roger M. Ramey will take command until they join the rest of the B-29s in the Mariana Islands in March. The 58th

Right: *On 23 January 1945, the submarine* Barb *makes a daring surface raid on a Japanese convoy in Namkwan Harbor, China. ("The Galloping Ghost of the China Coast," Ted Wilbur, U.S. Naval Institute)*

Bomb Wing, the last remaining in the XX Bomber Command, provides support for British and Indian ground forces in Burma by interdicting targets in Indochina, Thailand, and Burma. Oil refineries in distant Singapore and the East Indies are also attacked until redeployment in March.

ARMY
In Burma, the Mars Task Force clears the Japanese from the village of Namhkam, only three miles from the Burma Road. The task force digs in and begins patrols to secure the area.

On Luzon Island, Philippine Islands, the Sixth Army prepares for a fast advance on Manila and seizure of Clark Field. In the I Corps area, the 6th and 25th Infantry Divisions push their advance forward against moderate opposition.

20 JANUARY
AIR FORCE
Brigadier General Haywood S. Hansell is replaced as commander of the XXI Bomber Command by Major General Curtis E. LeMay. Hansell, an excellent administrator, has suffered from inadequate numbers of aircraft, continuing mechanical deficiencies, and extremely strong high-altitude wind conditions that have negatively impacted bombing results. Brigadier General Roger M. Ramey assumes command of the XX Bomber Command.

21–22 JANUARY
NAVY
Task Force 38 strikes targets on Formosa Island and in the Ryukyu Islands. Kamikaze attacks damage *Ticonderoga* and the destroyer *Maddox*. In addition, an aerial bomb scores a hit on the light aircraft carrier *Langley*. Carrier planes sink 23 ships in the two-day operation.

22 JANUARY
AIR FORCE
Fifth Air Force B-24 Liberator bombers with P-38 Lightning escort fighters make their first strikes on Formosa Island. Other Far East Air Force aircraft continue to support ground operations in south and central Luzon Island, Philippine Islands.

23 JANUARY
NAVY
The destroyer escorts *Conklin*, *Corbesier*, and *Raby* sink the Japanese submarine *I-48* off Yap Island, Caroline Islands.

24 JANUARY
AIR FORCE
Twentieth Air Force B-29 Superfortress bombers join Seventh Air Force B-24 Liberator bombers in bombing Iwo Jima Island, Japan. Additional B-24s act as spotters for naval bombardment.

Eleventh Air Force fighters shoot down a Japanese Fu-go balloon southeast of Attu, Aleutian Islands.

Far East Air Force B-24 bombers begin attacks on Corregidor Island, Philippine Islands. These strikes continue for three weeks in anticipation of Allied amphibious landings there.

ARMY

In the Philippine Islands, Japanese resistance strengthens on Luzon Island, as I Corps units swing north out of the beachhead. The 25th Infantry Division assaults San Manuel against firm resistance and gains a small area. XIV Corps units push south and approach closer to Manila. The 37th Infantry Division reaches the Bamban River, while the 40th Infantry Division pushes into the enemy outpost line.

MARINE CORPS

Planes of Marine Fighting Squadron 451 embark *Bunker Hill*.

25–26 JANUARY
AIR FORCE

More than 70 XX Bomber Command B-29 Superfortress bombers mine Singapore Harbor; Cam Ranh Bay and Phan Rang Bay, Vietnam; the Pakchan River, Burma; and other land approaches to the South China Sea.

25 JANUARY
ARMY

Lieutenant General Joseph Stilwell, back in the U.S. following his recall from China, is made Commanding General, Army Ground Forces.

MARINE CORPS

The first planes of Marine Scout Bombing Squadrons 133 and 241 arrive at newly built Mangalden Airfield on Luzon Island, Philippine Islands. They are the lead echelon of Marine Aircraft Groups 24 and 32, which are titled Marine Air Groups Dagupan. Within six days, seven squadrons are present.

27 JANUARY
AIR FORCE
B-29 Superfortress bombers flying from the Mariana Islands attack targets near Tokyo, Japan, and meet heavy enemy fighter attacks that shoot down 5 of the 130 B-29s. Four more Superfortresses ditch or crash-land on their return to base. B-29 gunners claim dozens of enemy fighters are shot down during the engagement.

ARMY
In the Philippine Islands, the Sixth Army receives major reinforcements as the 1st Cavalry Division and the 112th Cavalry Regimental Combat Team, along with the 32d Infantry Division, arrive at Mabilao, Lingayen Gulf, Luzon Island.

MARINE CORPS
Marine Scout Bombing Squadron 241 flies its first sorties in support of Army ground forces on Luzon Island, Philippine Islands. Marine Air Group 32 arrives at Mangalden Airfield.

28 JANUARY
AIR FORCE/ARMY
After several weeks of aerial attacks, Clark Field, Luzon Island—one of the most important air bases in the Philippines—is retaken by the 129th Infantry Regiment, 37th Infantry Division.

In Burma, the Burma Road (renamed the "Stilwell Road") is reopened, allowing supplies to flow over land from Ledo, India, to Kunming, China. Although this takes some pressure off of the airlifters who have been flying over the Himalaya Mountains since 1942, they continue to launch approximately 500 sorties during each flying day. Relocation of B-29 Superfortress bombers previously based at Chengtu, China, allows for more supplies for Tenth and Fourteenth Air Force aircraft and advancing ground troops.

29 JANUARY
ARMY/MARINE CORPS/NAVY
Navy Task Group 78.3 (Rear Admiral Arthur D. Struble) puts Army troops ashore on the west side of Luzon Island, Philippine Islands, in a series of landings to bypass Japanese defenses north of Manila. The XI Corps (under Major General Charles P. Hall)

Opposite, top: *Douglas A-20 Havoc medium bombers raid Japanese-held Clark Field, Luzon Island, Philippine Islands. ("Roarin' 20s Over Clark Field," Steve Ferguson, USAF Art Collection)*

Opposite, bottom: *Soldiers coming ashore from their landing craft wear the improved fatigue uniform, which is very different from the blue denims and cotton khakis of 1941. ("The American Soldier, 1944," H. Charles McBarron, Army Art Collection, U.S. Army Center of Military History)*

Right: *Navy PBY Catalina flying boats pass over the U.S. invasion fleet in Lingayen Gulf off of Luzon Island. (Consolidated Vultee)*

Right: *Soldiers of the 1st Cavalry Division pass an M7 Priest motorized 105mm howitzer in the Philippine Islands. (U.S. Army)*

Below: *Soldiers pass a dead enemy soldier as they move into Manila on Luzon Island, Philippine Islands, in February 1945. (U.S. Army)*

lands the 24th and 38th Infantry Divisions north of Subic Bay near San Antonio. The 34th Regimental Combat Team, 24th Infantry Division leads the assault. It quickly secures Subic, then crosses the Kalaklan River and takes Olongapo. Meanwhile the 2d Battalion, 151st Infantry Regiment, 38th Infantry Division lands on Grande Island, securing the

entrance to Subic Bay. On 31 January, with the 37th Infantry Division moving on a parallel route and attacking Fort Stotsenburg, the 1st Cavalry Division organizes its 5th and 8th Cavalry Regiments as motorized "flying columns" and launches them in a race into Manila. One of the goals is to free the civilian internees held by the Japanese. Marine Air Group 14 provides air liaison parties and continuous day sorties overhead to cover the flanks and front of the fast-moving cavalry columns. In the XI Corps area, units of the 38th Infantry Division are halted by enemy resistance at "Zigzag Pass." Task Group 78.2 (under Rear Admiral William M. Fechteler) puts the 188th Glider Infantry Regiment, 11th Airborne Division (Eighth Army) ashore on a beach near Nasugbu. The 188th moves quickly inland, seizing all objectives without opposition, and the 187th Glider Infantry follows them.

30 JANUARY
ARMY
A task force of Alamo Scouts, comprised of a company from the 6th Ranger Battalion and 200 Philippine guerrillas, penetrate 29 miles into enemy lines to raid the Japanese prison camp near Cabanatuan, Luzon Island, Philippine Islands, and free over 500 internees. The surprised Japanese guards are overrun, and the emaciated POWs are taken back to friendly lines. On 31 January, a company of the 511th Parachute Infantry, 11th Airborne Division is dropped on Tagaytay Ridge south of Manila as a diversion.

1 FEBRUARY
NAVY

The destroyers *Jenkins*, *O'Bannon*, and *Bell* join the destroyer escort *Ulvert M. Moore* in sinking the Japanese submarine *RO-115* southwest of Manila, Luzon Island, Philippine Islands.

2 FEBRUARY
ARMY

In the last major Burma combat actions for the Mars Task Force, the 1st and 2d Battalions, 475th Infantry Regiment attack and seize Japanese positions on Loi-Kang Ridge, which overlooks the Burma Road, and clear the nearby village of Loi-Kong. The 2d and 3d Squadrons, 124th Cavalry Regiment also capture key enemy held hills near Hpa-pen. There are light casualties in both regiments. First Lieutenant Jack L. Knight, commanding the F troop, 124th Cavalry Regiment, goes after a series of four enemy pillboxes on high ground. Both he and his brother, First Sergeant Curtis Knight, are wounded. Despite his wounds, Lieutenant Knight retains command and continues to attack the enemy. He is killed advancing toward Japanese lines after single-handedly destroying five enemy pillboxes. He is posthumously awarded the only Medal of Honor given to a Soldier in the China–Burma–India Theater.

3 FEBRUARY
ARMY

On Luzon Island, Philippine Islands, the 1st Cavalry Division and 37th Infantry Division link up and begin a brutal block-by-block battle into Manila against fanatical Japanese defenders. Tanks of the 1st Cavalry Division burst through the gates of the Santo Tomas University, freeing 69 Army nurses and 3,700 civilians imprisoned by the Japanese since 1942. Near Tagaytay Ridge, the 511th Parachute Infantry jumps in and links up with the 188th Glider Infantry Regiment. On 4 February, the 2d Battalion, 148th Infantry Regiment, 37th Infantry Division, "liberates" a brewery filled with cold beer as they wait for engineers to install a bridge over the nearby Tulihan River. On 5 February the 148th Infantry Regiment crosses the Pasig River, finds Bilibid prison, and evacuates 1,200 military prisoners and civilian internees. The 161st Infantry Regiment reaches San Isidro, splitting Japanese forces on Luzon. Elements of the 11th Airborne Division arrive on the outskirts of Manila. In north Luzon, the 34th Regimental Combat Team makes slow progress clearing Zigzag Pass as two more regiments from the 38th Infantry Division are directed to assist. On 6 February, most of north Manila is secured and the 11th Airborne Division (under Major General Joseph Swing) joins in the fight southeast of the city and pushes toward Nichols Field.

Right: *Alamo Scouts ford a stream on their way to raid the Japanese prison camp at Cabanatuan on Luzon Island in January 1945. The surprise attack liberates more than 500 starving Allied prisoners. (National Archives)*

MARINE CORPS

Marine Fighting Squadrons 216 and 217 begin embarking the carrier *Wasp* at Ulithi Atoll, Caroline Islands, to add fighter planes to fleet carriers to counter the Japanese kamikaze threat. Marine Fighting Squadron 511 goes aboard the escort carrier *Block Island*, the first results of the program to provide Marine Corps air support for amphibious assaults.

3–8 FEBRUARY
ARMY

In Burma, the 475th Infantry Regiment finishes clearing the Loi-kang ridge and enters the town of Loi-kang, the first significant penetration east of the Burma Road. U.S. and Chinese forces are now in control.

4 FEBRUARY
AIR FORCE

The Twentieth Air Force launches two B-29 Superfortress bomber wings against the Japanese mainland for the first time. Nearly 100 bombers attack Kobe and Natsusaka. Japanese fighter defenses are strong; one B-29 is shot down, and 35 others are damaged.

ARMY

In Burma, the 2d Squadron, 124th Cavalry Regiment (Mars Task Force) fights the regiment's last action when a platoon is caught in a Japanese ambush. The small but vicious skirmish costs 6 cavalrymen killed and 24 wounded. The task force continues patrolling and ambushing the withdrawing Japanese units, but the heavy combat action is over. Since its activation in

August 1944, the 5332d Composite Brigade, or Mars Task Force, has suffered 123 Americans killed, 938 wounded, and one missing in action. In the future, the brigade's experienced combat Soldiers will be used as advisers to the Chinese units, which will carry the fight into China.

Led by Brigadier General Lewis A. Pick, the first convoy from Ledo, India, makes a triumphal entry into Kunming, China. The convoy left Ledo on 12 January and crossed into Chinese territory on 28 January.

NAVY

Japanese aircraft sink the submarine *Barbel* in the South China Sea. There are no survivors.

5 FEBRUARY
AIR FORCE

In the heaviest bombardment of Corregidor Island, Philippine Islands, to date, 60 Far East Air Force B-24 Liberator bombers pound the island. B-25 Mitchell bombers and additional B-24s continue support missions for Allied ground troops.

7 FEBRUARY
ARMY

On Luzon Island, Philippine Islands, two battalions of the 148th Infantry Regiment, 37th Infantry Division make an assault crossing of the Pasig River in Manila. The 20th Infantry Regiment, 6th Infantry Division captures the town of Munoz and destroys several Japanese troop columns trying to escape.

NAVY

The destroyer escort *Thomason* sinks the Japanese submarine *RO-55* off Luzon Island, Philippine Islands.

10 FEBRUARY
AIR FORCE

Twentieth Air Force B-29 Superfortress bombers strike the Nakajima aircraft plant at Ota, Japan. Of the 84 XXI Bomber Command airplanes that reach the target, 12 are lost to fighters. Fighter escort for the B-29s is not yet available.

MARINE CORPS

Task Force 58 sails from Ulithi Atoll, Caroline Islands. Four of the task force fast carriers host 144 Marine F4U Corsair fighters, which account for 16 percent of the fighter planes in the task force.

12–14 FEBRUARY
AIR FORCE

B-29 Superfortress bombers based in the Mariana Islands fly reconnaissance missions for U.S. naval forces approaching Iwo Jima Island, Japan. Two dozen B-29s bomb targets there to suppress antiaircraft batteries. The Seventh Air Force relentlessly attacks defensive targets on Iwo Jima, anticipating the arrival of landing forces that will take the island.

13 FEBRUARY
ARMY

On Luzon Island, Philippine Islands, the 38th Infantry Division finishes clearing the Zigzag Pass defenses, except for a final stronghold. I Corps elements are clearing the way to the Bataan Peninsula as 6th Infantry Division elements help clear the

coastal area of Manila Bay. The 37th Infantry Division and 1st Cavalry Division continue clearing Manila while the 11th Airborne Division mops up resistance at Nichols Field.

NAVY

The submarine *Batfish* sinks the Japanese submarine *RO-113* off the Babuyan Islands, Philippine Islands.

14 FEBRUARY
ARMY

After a long imprisonment in Santo Tomas University in Manila, Luzon Island, Philippine Islands, Army nurses liberated by the 1st Cavalry Division are welcomed as heroes at Hickam Field, Oahu, Hawaii. They arrive in two Air Transport Command C-54 Skymaster transports.

Above: *These Soldiers, in the first assault wave on Leyte Island, Philippine Islands, advance toward the town of San Fabian. (U.S. Army)*

Right: *The parachutes of the Soldiers of the 503d Airborne Infantry Regiment, 11th Airborne Division, dot the landscape of "topside," the upper plateau of the fortress island of Corregidor, Philippine Islands. The paratroopers are part of a combined air-sea attack to retake the island from the Japanese. (U.S. Army)*

NAVY

During minesweeping operations off Corregidor Island, Philippine Islands, gunfire from Japanese shore batteries sinks the motor minesweeper *YMS-48* and damages escorting destroyers *Hopewell* and *Fletcher*. Shell fragments enter one of the gun magazines on board *Fletcher* and ignite some of the powder charges. Watertender First Class Elmer C. Bigelow enters the space and extinguishes the flame before it can detonate the entire magazine. He succumbs to smoke inhalation the following day and is posthumously awarded the Medal of Honor.

15 FEBRUARY
ARMY/NAVY

Task Group 78.3 lands Army troops near Mariveles Harbor, Bataan, Luzon Island, Philippine Islands.

16 FEBRUARY
AIR FORCE/MARINE CORPS

Hundreds of Far East Air Force aircraft bomb a complex target set around Corregidor Island, Philippine Islands, for most of the day in support of ground troops. At one point, Marine Corps F4U Corsair fighters are placed under the tactical control of the Far East Air Force commander to carry out napalm strikes against airfields and other tactical targets in the central Philippine Islands.

AIR FORCE/ARMY/NAVY

In the Philippine Islands, as part of the Sixth Army offensive to secure Manila Bay, Luzon Island, Task Force Rock is formed to recapture Corregidor Island. The task force is composed of the 503d Parachute

Right: *Prior to the air and sea assault on Corregidor Island, Philippine Islands, a major air bombing campaign is carried out. ("B-24s Bombing Corregidor— February 1945," Robert Laessig, USAF Art Collection)*

Regimental Combat Team (Separate) (under Colonel George M. Jones) with its airborne engineer and pack artillery units, and the 3d Battalion, 34th Infantry Regiment, 24th Infantry Division, reinforced with five tanks. The airborne assault element parachutes into two tiny drop zones—an old parade ground and a golf course to the north of Corregidor, while the amphibious assault element lands at San Jose Bay to the south. Close cooperation with the 317th Troop Carrier Group puts most of the 2,000-plus paratroopers and equipment near the drop zones. Navy PT boats are standing by to rescue the few paratroopers who are blown over the water. The 3d Battalion, 34th Infantry lands at South Dock against light resistance and seizes Malinta Hill. Naval gunfire from six destroyers provides support. Initial resistance is light, but there are 6,000 Japanese defenders hidden in caves and tunnels, not the 800 expected, and a fierce 12-day battle begins. Japanese counterattacks start after dark.

AIR FORCE
In India, Tenth Air Force transports fly more than 600 resupply sorties over the Himalaya Mountains. This pace continues though the end of the war, weather permitting. By war's end, the Air Transport Command will deliver more than 700,000 tons of material to China at a loss of 910 aircrew.

16–17 FEBRUARY
MARINE CORPS/NAVY
Task Force 58 (under Vice Admiral Marc A. Mitscher) strikes Tokyo, Japan, marking the first time that carrier aircraft attack the home islands. Marine Corps planes of Task Force 58 claim 21 Japanese aircraft shot

down and another 60 destroyed on the ground. The strikes destroy numerous shore installations and port facilities.

17 FEBRUARY
NAVY
Underwater demolition teams reconnoiter the landing beaches at Iwo Jima Island, Japan, under enemy fire. One supporting landing craft infantry (gunboat) is sunk by shore battery fire and 11 are damaged, including *LCI(G)-449* under the command of Lieutenant Rufus G. Herring. Although he is badly wounded, Herring personally maintains the position of his craft close to shore in support of the operation. For his heroism, he receives the Medal of Honor.

19 FEBRUARY
AIR FORCE
The Twentieth Air Force launches more than 150 B-29 Superfortress bombers in an effort to draw Japanese aerial reinforcements away from Iwo Jima Island, Japan. More than 110 B-29s bomb targets in Tokyo, Japan, and 6 are lost to enemy fighters.

MARINE CORPS/NAVY
Supported by naval gunfire and aircraft from Task Group 56.1, and under the overall command of Lieutenant General Holland M. Smith's Expeditionary Troops headquarters, the V Amphibious Corps' 4th and 5th Marine Divisions storm ashore on the southeast coast of Iwo Jima Island, Japan. The 28th Marine Regiment reaches the western shore at the narrow neck of the island and seals off Mount Suribachi before the end of the day, while the 27th and 23d Marine Regiments make it to

the edge of Airfield No. 1. Heavy Japanese artillery, mortar, and rocket fire, aided by mines and machine-guns, inflict over 2,400 casualties on the assault divisions. Marine Corps aircraft from Task Force 58 make air strikes in support of the landing. Japanese shore batteries and mortar fire damage a destroyer and four medium landing ships.

20 FEBRUARY
MARINE CORPS
The 28th Marine Regiment begins the assault to take Mount Suribachi on Iwo Jima Island, Japan. The 4th Marine Division and the remainder of the 5th Marine Division capture Airfield No. 1 as they begin the drive north.

21 FEBRUARY
ARMY
In the Philippine Islands, Task Force Rock on Corregidor Island continues to fight through the old buildings and fortifications to clear out Japanese defenders who stage a steady series of counterattacks. The XI Corps wraps up operations on the Bataan Peninsula as the X Corps begins a series of landings on Samar and Capul Islands looking for isolated enemy groups. The American Division is eliminating the last enemy pockets on Leyte Island.

MARINE CORPS
The V Amphibious Corps commits the 21st Marine Regiment, 3d Marine Division from corps reserve to reinforce the 4th Marine Division on Iwo Jima, Island, Japan.

NAVY
Kamikazes attack the invasion fleet assembled off Iwo Jima Island, Japan. Two suicide planes hit the escort carrier *Bismarck Sea*, starting uncontrollable fires and triggering the explosion of ammunition. She sinks in 90 minutes with the loss of 318 members of her crew. The aircraft carrier *Saratoga* is hit by five kamikazes and an aerial bomb, wrecking the forward part of her flight deck and starting fires in the hangar deck. She is forced to return to the United States for repairs, ending her combat service. Suicide planes also damage the escort carrier *Lunga Point*, the net cargo ship *Keokuk*, and the tank landing ships *LST-477* and *LST-809*. An aerial bomb damages the light aircraft carrier *Langley*.

22 FEBRUARY
MARINE CORPS
Elements of the 8th Field Depot begin going ashore on Iwo Jima Island, Japan, to manage the flow of supplies onto the island.

On northern Luzon Island, Philippine Islands, Marine Corps air liaison parties join up with Philippine guerrillas operating behind Japanese lines.

23 FEBRUARY
ARMY

On Luzon Island, Philippine Islands, the 37th Infantry Division assaults the Intramuros area of Manila, the last enemy stronghold in the city. In a joint airborne and amphibious operation, the 1st Battalion, 511th Airborne Infantry, 11th Airborne Division, strikes behind Japanese lines to liberate the 2,147 internees held at Los Banos prison camp. Among those released are 12 Navy nurses.

MARINE CORPS/NAVY

On Iwo Jima Island, Japan, elements of the 28th Marine Regiment seize the crest of Mount Suribachi and hoist an American flag obtained from the transport *Missoula* on the summit. Soon after, five Marines and a Navy corpsman replace it with a larger national ensign from the tank landing ship *LST-779*. Associated Press photographer Joe Rosenthal's photograph of this flag raising electrifies the United States and becomes the symbol for the Seventh War Bond drive.

Opposite: *Different colored parachutes indicating men, equipment, ammunition, or medical supplies open over Corregidor Island, Philippine Islands, as the 503d Airborne Infantry jumps onto the island. PT boats wait to rescue any paratroopers who may land in the water. ("PTs and Paratroopers—Corregidor," Lt. Dwight C. Shepler, USN, Navy Art Collection)*

Above: *With Corregidor Island secure, General of the Army Douglas MacArthur orders the Stars and Stripes raised once again on the island after four years of Japanese occupation. (National Archives)*

Below: *Marines of the 4th and 5th Marine Divisions storm ashore on the black sandy beaches of Iwo Jima Island, Japan, on 19 February 1945. ("Iwo Jima—19 February 1945," Donna Neary, Art Collection, National Museum of the Marine Corps, VA)*

In the Philippine Islands, Marine Fighting Squadron 115 F4U Corsair fighters sink a midget submarine off Cebu Island. Marine Aircraft Group 32 headquarters and its squadron ground echelons (Marine Scout Bombing Squadrons 142, 236, 243, and 341) begin to move from Mangaldan, Luzon Island, for sea transport toward Zamboanga, Mindanao Island, in the southern Philippine Islands.

24 FEBRUARY
AIR FORCE
Using only incendiary bombs, 105 XX Bomber Command B-29 bombers set fire to the Empire Dock area in Singapore. More than 40 percent of the warehouse space is destroyed. This is the last time that the India-based XX Bomber Command launches more than 100 bombers on any one raid.

MARINE CORPS
The 3d Marine Division, less the 21st Marine Regiment already ashore and the 3d Marine Regiment still held as Expeditionary Troops reserve, begins to go ashore on Iwo Jima Island, Japan.

25 FEBRUARY
AIR FORCE
Twentieth Air Force B-29 Superfortress bombers attack urban Tokyo, Japan, using incendiary bombs from high altitude. This is the largest XXI Bomber

Previous Spread: During the Battle of the Bismarck Sea, Japanese kamikaze planes and bombs hit the carrier Saratoga, causing extensive damage, but the ship makes it back to the U.S. for repairs. ("Kamikaze Attack on the Saratoga," by Mort Künstler, © 1963 Mort Künstler, Inc.)

Above: *B-29 Superfortress bombing raids on Japan increase in intensity as more island bases are completed for both the bombers and fighter escorts. ("Valor in the Pacific," Robert Taylor © The Military Gallery, Ojai, CA)*

Opposite: *Two Marines take cover on an Iwo Jima Island beach, a destroyed DUKW amphibious truck behind them. The men may be members of the 8th Ammunition Company. Two Army amphibious transportation companies also support the Marine Corps invasion. (USMC)*

Command raid, and the first time that three wings of B-29s have attacked the same target.

In China, the Tenth Air Force engages in combined operations with British and Chinese ground forces as they push forward. B-25 Mitchell bombers cut roads and bridges, while fighter-bombers attack enemy troop concentrations at the front line of the battle.

MARINE CORPS
The 3d Marine Division assumes responsibility for the center of the corps front on Iwo Jima Island, Japan,

with the 4th Marine Division on the right and the 5th Marine Division on the left. The V Amphibious Corps slugs its way slowly forward through the heaviest belt of Japanese defenses.

MARINE CORPS/NAVY

Task Force 58 returns to the waters around the Japanese home islands, launching strikes against factories and airfields before the onset of bad weather in the afternoon forces the cancellation of the operation. Marine Corps aircraft participate in strikes around Tokyo, Japan.

26 FEBRUARY
AIR FORCE

Lieutenant General Millard F. Harmon, the commander of the Army Air Forces, Pacific Ocean Areas, is lost when his B-24 Liberator bomber disappears during a flight between Kwajalein Atoll, Marshall Islands, and Hawaii. No wreckage or survivors are ever found.

MARINE CORPS

Two planes from Marine Observation Squadron 4 land on Airfield No. 1 on Iwo Jima Island, Japan, to begin spotting for artillery and naval gunfire.

NAVY

Off Iwo Jima Island, Japan, TBM Avenger torpedo-bombers of Composite Squadron 82 from the escort carrier *Anzio*, in concert with the carrier's escorts, sink the Japanese submarines *I-368* and *RO-43*. The destroyer escort *Finnegan* sinks the Japanese submarine *I-370* south of Iwo Jima.

27 FEBRUARY
AIR FORCE

The last B-29 Superfortress bomber wing remaining in Calcutta, India, begins deployment to the Mariana Islands. The move is completed by 6 June.

ARMY

Organized Japanese resistance on Corregidor Island, Philippine Islands, ends, but mopping up of small pockets in caves and tunnels continues for weeks.

Left: *Marines from the 3d Battalion, 28th Marine Regiment scramble up a rocky hill and move forward on Iwo Jima Island, Japan. (Marine Corps Research Center)*

Opposite: *Dozens of landing craft offload supplies for the Marines fighting on Iwo Jima Island, Japan. Moving supplies and equipment from the beach to the front lines to avoid congestion is a major effort. (Andrew Small, Naval War College)*

In the 12-day battle, the Task Force Rock has suffered 210 killed, 790 wounded, and 5 men missing. In a ceremony at 10:00 a.m. on 2 March, General of the Army Douglas MacArthur accepts the recaptured island and orders the American flag re-raised, saying to Task Force Commander Colonel George M. Jones, "I see the old flagpole still stands. Have your troops hoist the colors to the peak, and let no enemy ever haul them down." The last group of 20 Japanese soldiers give up on 1 January 1946.

MARINE CORPS

On Iwo Jima Island, Japan, the 9th Marine Regiment completes the seizure of Airfield No. 2 and also takes

Hill Peter and Hill 199 Oboe, key terrain dominating the exposed airstrip. Army forces of the Island Command begin to come ashore. Planes of Composite Squadron 5 begin arriving to bolster the spotting effort of artillery and naval gunfire.

28 FEBRUARY
ARMY/NAVY

In the Philippine Islands, Task Group 78.2 (under Rear Admiral William M. Fechteler) with gunfire support from Task Group 74.2 (under Rear Admiral Ralph S. Riggs) lands the 186th Regimental Combat Team (RCT), 41st Infantry Division on Puerto Princesa, Palawan Island. The 186th RCT seizes the island and

Right: *Soldiers in a machine gun position and on an M7 Priest motorized 105mm howitzer watch as the crew of an M18 motorized 76mm gun engages a Japanese defensive position on the road to Baguio on Luzon Island, Philippine Islands. (U.S. Army)*

establishes radar sites. On Samar Island, an America! Division battalion and 1st Filipino Infantry make progress. The attack force leaves Mindoro Island.

MARINE CORPS

The 21st Marine Regiment captures Motoyama Village and the high ground overlooking Airfield No. 3 on the northern plateau of Iwo Jima Island, Japan.

NAVY

During the fighting on Iwo Jima Island, Japan, Pharmacist's Mate First Class John H. Willis, having sneaked back to the front lines after being wounded earlier, rushes to treat a wounded Marine in a shell hole while his platoon fights off a Japanese counterattack. While Willis administers aid, nine Japanese hand grenades are lobbed into the shell hole. The corpsman throws eight of them out, but the ninth one explodes in his hand, killing him. His actions inspire the men of his platoon to press forward. Willis is awarded the Medal of Honor posthumously.

1 MARCH
ARMY

In Manila, Luzon Island, Philippine Islands, the 5th Cavalry Regiment, 1st Cavalry Division finishes clearing a large building fortified by the Japanese,

leaving only one major enemy strongpoint in the city. The 6th Infantry Division continues its assault against the Japanese "Shimbu" defensive line, while in the I Corps area, the 33d Infantry Division pushes toward Baguio in coordination with an American-led Filipino guerrilla group. The southern Philippine Island group is being cleared by a series of Eighth Army landings on suspect islands. The 21st Infantry Regiment lands on Lunag Island, and then Verde Island together with the 186th Regimental Combat Team, 41st Infantry Division.

MARINE CORPS

Transport planes of Marine Transport Squadron (VMR) 952 make the first Marine Corps air drops of supplies on Iwo Jima Island, Japan. VMR-253 and 353 join in over the next few days.

MARINE CORPS/NAVY

Task Force 58, under Vice Admiral Marc A. Mitscher, strikes Japanese airfields and installations on Okinawa Island, Japan, and sinks 15 vessels in surrounding waters. Marine Corps aircraft also participate.

2 MARCH
MARINE CORPS

On Iwo Jima Island, Japan, the 28th Marine Regiment captures Hill 362-A, the heavily fortified western

anchor of the Japanese main cross-island defensive belt. Elements of the 24th Marine Regiment seize Hill 382, the highest elevation in northern Iwo Jima.

3 MARCH
AIR FORCE/NAVY

A B-29 Superfortress bomber returning from a raid on Tokyo, Japan, makes an emergency landing on Iwo Jima Island, Japan, to repair a damaged fuel line. The huge bomber lands at Motoyama airstrip No. 1 as Seabees scurry to remove grading and construction equipment. After the aircraft is repaired, the pilot hurriedly takes off for home base. Through the end of the war, more than 2,400 such landings will be made on the small but important island.

ARMY

The 37th Infantry Division, after house-to-house urban warfare that results in heavy military and civilian casualties, declares the city of Manila, Luzon Island, Philippine Islands, to be secure. It has cost more than 1,000 Army casualties. The 11th Airborne Division puts an end to resistance in its Manila Bay sector.

MARINE CORPS

On Iwo Jima Island, Japan, the 3d Marine Division clears Airfield No. 3 and captures Hills 357 and 362B. Although Marine Corps gains on Iwo Jima have been measured in yards, at this point in the battle the V Amphibious Corps has blasted and bled its way through most of the main Japanese defensive line.

NAVY

On Iwo Jima Island, Japan, Pharmacist's Mate Third Class Jack Williams, despite being wounded and in a partial state of shock, rushes to the side of a wounded Marine, shielding the fallen leatherneck with his own body as he administers aid. He then treats another wounded Marine. While making his way to the rear to have his own wounds treated, Williams is shot and killed. He is posthumously awarded the Medal of Honor.

5 MARCH
MARINE CORPS

Lieutenant General Holland M. Smith orders his Expeditionary Troops reserve, the 3d Marine Regiment, to sail for Guam Island, Mariana Islands, despite the pleas of the V Amphibious Corps commander for use of the fresh regiment on Iwo Jima Island, Japan.

Above: *A Marine Navajo "code talker" radios information on the enemy from a destroyed Japanese bunker. ("Navajo Radio Code Talkers," Col. Charles H. Waterhouse, USMCR Ret., Art Collection, National Museum of the Marine Corps, Triangle, Virginia)*

Opposite, top: *A Sailor posted as an aircraft lookout keeps a sharp eye for attacking Japanese aircraft, especially the growing menace of kamikaze planes. The dial in front of him gives the bearing at which he is looking. (U.S. Naval Institute)*

Opposite, bottom: *The capture of Iwo Jima Island, Japan, gives U.S. bombers stationed on Saipan and Tinian Islands in the Mariana Islands an emergency airfield midway to mainland Japan, as well as a forward base for escort fighters. ("Sweating it Out," Lt. Mitchell Jamieson, USNR, Navy Art Collection)*

6 MARCH
AIR FORCE
The Seventh Air Force deploys 28 P-51 Mustang fighters and 12 P-61 Black Widow night fighters to Iwo Jima Island, Japan. The bases on Iwo Jima allow fighter escort to accompany B-29 Superfortress bombers to their targets over Japan.

MARINE CORPS
Following a day to consolidate and incorporate replacements, all three divisions of the V Amphibious Corps renew the offensive on Iwo Jima Island, Japan, behind a massive artillery, air, and naval bombardment. Gains remain small and hard-won in the extremely broken terrain falling away from Iwo Jima's northern plateau.

Marine Fighting Squadron 512 joins the escort carrier *Gilbert Islands* in San Diego, California.

NAVY
Navy nurse Ensign Jane Kendeigh arrives on Iwo Jima Island, Japan. The plane on which she is flying comes under mortar fire as it lands. She is the first Navy nurse to serve in a combat zone.

7 MARCH
MARINE CORPS
Hill 362C on Iwo Jima Island, Japan, falls to the 9th Marine Regiment.

8 MARCH
AIR FORCE/MARINE CORPS
On Iwo Jima Island, Japan, Army Air Forces fighter planes begin to assume combat air patrol over the

island and to fly some close air support missions. Elements of Marine Torpedo Bomber Squadron 242 also arrive from Tinian Island, Mariana Islands, to assist. Aircraft from Marine Transport Squadrons 253, 353, and 952 begin landing on the island to deliver supplies and evacuate wounded. Patrols from the 3d Marine Division reach the island's northeast coast. In the evening, the 4th Marine Division repulses a large-scale enemy counterattack, the first since the battle began.

NAVY

Phyllis Daley becomes the first African American woman commissioned as an ensign in the Navy Nurse Corps.

9 MARCH
AIR FORCE

Departing from three bases in the Mariana Islands, 325 B-29 Superfortress bombers from the XXI Bomber Command (under Major General Curtis LeMay) launch to strike Tokyo, Japan, on an overnight, low-level firebombing raid. Although many abort after takeoff, 279 B-29s reach the target. The attack uses 2,000 tons of incendiary bombs, creating a fire storm that burns approximately 16 square miles of the city. It is estimated that between 80,000 and 100,000 are killed and more than 250,000 buildings are destroyed in the raid. Fourteen bombers, each carrying a crew of

10 men, are lost to antiaircraft fire during the raid. This raid signals the shift from high-altitude precision bombardment to low-level night area bombing. Bombing altitudes for this raid vary between 4,900 feet and 9,200 feet. This aerial attack is the most devastating single air raid in history. In the following days the B-29s hit Nagoya, Osaka, and Kobe, Japan.

10 MARCH
ARMY/MARINE CORPS/NAVY

Task Group 78.1 (under Rear Admiral Forrest B. Royal) lands the 41st Infantry Division (under Major General Jens A. Doe) on Zamboanga Peninsula, Mindanao Island, Philippine Islands. Though four landing craft are sunk by Japanese shore batteries, the troops meet little resistance on shore. They take Wolfe Airfield and quickly drive to Mindanao City.

ARMY/MARINE CORPS/NAVY

On Iwo Jima Island, Japan, the 4th Marine Division eliminates the Amphitheater–Turkey Knob salient that has been holding it up in the center of its zone since 25 February and makes substantial gains. The 3d Marine Division largely clears the remainder of its zone. Navy escort carriers depart Iwo Jima, leaving aerial support in the hands of Army squadrons on the island.

MARINE CORPS

Marine Fighting Squadrons 124 and 213 are detached from the carrier *Essex* and depart for the United States. A portion of the maintenance crews remain on board to service replacement Navy squadrons in subsequent operations.

NAVY

The submarine *Kete* sinks a Japanese transport and two army cargo ships off Okinawa Island, Japan. Following this action no word is received from the sub, and she is declared lost at sea.

In a most unlikely long-range attack, land-based bombers fly from Japan to attack the U.S. Navy fleet anchorage at Ulithi Atoll, Caroline Islands. One Japanese aircraft crashes into the anchored aircraft carrier *Randolph*, killing 25 members of the crew and wounding 106.

11 MARCH
AIR FORCE

The Twentieth Air Force launches 285 B-29 Superfortress bombers on an overnight, low-level firebombing raid on Nagoya, Japan, with devastating results.

MARINE CORPS

On Iwo Jima Island, Japan, the 3d and 4th Marine Divisions drive to the coasts in their respective zones, leaving only a few pockets of organized resistance.

MARINE CORPS

The 9th Marine Regiment surrounds and compresses Cushman's Pocket, one of the last major Japanese strongholds on Iwo Jima Island, Japan. Operations continue against this zone for the next several days.

13 MARCH
AIR FORCE

Tenth Air Force P-47 Thunderbolt fighters provide support for the Chinese 50th Division by striking Japanese forces along the Namtu River. P-38 Lightning fighters continue to hit targets in central Burma.

The Twentieth Air Force launches its third overnight firebombing raid. This time, 274 bombers strike Osaka, Japan, destroying eight square miles of the city center.

MARINE CORPS

At Ulithi Atoll, Caroline Islands, Marine Fighting Squadrons 216 and 217 are detached from the carrier *Wasp*, although some maintenance personnel remain on board.

14 MARCH
ARMY/MARINE CORPS

As the official flag raising on Iwo Jima Island, Japan, is held at the V Amphibious Corps command post, the flag raised on 23 February over Mount Suribachi is

12 MARCH
ARMY

The 6th Infantry Division breaks through the Japanese Shimbu line defenses on Luzon Island, Philippine Islands, when the 20th Infantry Regiment seizes its objectives on the division's left flank and repels several Japanese counterattacks. In the I Corps area, the 32d Infantry Division continues its battle to clear the Villa Verda Trail. Fighting also continues on Mindanao Island.

Above: *Three Navy WAVES (Women Accepted for Volunteer Emergency Services) work on an F4U Corsair fighter at a Pacific island airbase. ("Grooming a War Dog," Howard Baer, Navy Art Collection)*

Right: *A Marine on Iwo Jima Island, Japan, dashes forward past a fallen comrade. (Marine Corps Research Center)*

Right: *A frame from 16mm movie footage shows the famous rising of the second flag on Mount Suribachi, Iwo Jima Island, by Marines of the 28th Marine Regiment on 23 February 1945. (National Archives)*

Below: *An M1 Garand rifle stuck in the ground by its bayonet and topped with a helmet marks the temporary grave of a fallen Marine on Iwo Jima Island. (National Archives)*

lowered. Army aircraft fly the last close air support mission on the island since the remaining areas under Japanese control are too small to permit further attacks.

ARMY

Major General Edwin D. Patrick, Commander, 6th Infantry Division, is mortally wounded on Luzon Island, Philippine Islands, and dies the following day. He is the first of two Army division commanders to die in World War II as a result of enemy action.

MARINE CORPS

Task Force 58 sails from Ulithi Atoll, Caroline Islands. With the addition of *Franklin* and her two Marine Corps F4U Corsair fighter squadrons (Marine Fighting Squadrons 214 and 452), there are six Marine Corps squadrons in the task force.

15 MARCH
ARMY/MARINE CORPS

In the Philippine Islands, the 24th Infantry Division troops have Romblon Province and Simara Island under control. Marine Aircraft Group 12 furnishes air support for the operation, while forward elements of its ground echelons go ashore to begin manning an existing airfield.

MARINE CORPS

Marine Fighting Squadron 115 aircraft of Marine Aircraft Group 12 lands on San Roque airfield on Zamboanga Peninsula, Mindanao Island, Philippine Islands, and begins operations the next day.

NAVY

In the last days of fighting on Iwo Jima Island, Japan, Pharmacist's Mate Second Class Francis J. Pierce is leading a stretcher party to an aid station when it comes under fire, wounding members of the party. After treating the wounded, Pierce draws his pistol and covers his comrades as they dash to safety, killing one enemy soldier. He then twice carries wounded Marines 200 yards to safety under enemy fire. The following day, Pierce is wounded while directing the treatment of a wounded Marine from a platoon patrolling the forward lines. Refusing treatment, he draws his pistol and fires it so that enemy guns concentrate on his position while the wounded man is carried to safety. Pierce survives, and receives the Medal of Honor for his actions.

Below: For weeks, Marines search the rocky ridges and hills of Iwo Jima Island looking for Japanese troops hiding in caves. (National Archives)

16 MARCH
AIR FORCE

The Twentieth Air Force launches its largest raid to date when more than 300 XXI Bomber Command B-29 Superfortresses firebomb Kobe, Japan. One-fifth of the city is destroyed by the 2,300 tons of incendiary bombs dropped. Kobe is home to a large aeronautical research facility, including a wind tunnel designed in the late 1920s for the Japanese by Professor Theodore von Kármán, then a young fluid dynamics teacher at the University of Aachen, Germany.

MARINE CORPS

On Iwo Jima Island, Japan, the 9th Marine Regiment completes the reduction of the Japanese stronghold at Cushman's Pocket, while the 21st Marine Regiment cleans out the approaches to Kitano Point. The 4th Marine Division overruns the last area of resistance in its zone along the eastern coast. Iwo Jima is declared secure, though combat operations are not yet entirely complete.

Opposite, top: *The crew of a PBY Catalina flying boat rescues a pilot shot down over Rabaul, New Britain Island. (Corbis)*

Right: *P-47 Thunderbolt fighter-bombers drop a napalm bomb on Japanese positions in the mountains east of Manila on Luzon Island, Philippine Islands. (U.S. Army)*

17 MARCH
ARMY

In the Philippine Islands, the I Corps' 25th Infantry Division attacks toward Mount Myoko, Luzon Island. In the XI Corps area, the 6th Infantry Division continues its assault on the Japanese Shimbu defensive line with the 20th and 1st Infantry Regiments, while the 43d Infantry Division struggles without success to capture Sugar Loaf Hill. On Mindanao Island, the 41st Infantry Division's advance is stopped by strong Japanese defenses near Masilay. On 18 March, Task Group 78.3 (under Rear Admiral Arthur D. Struble) lands the 185th Infantry Regiment, 40th Infantry Division unopposed on South Panay Island. The 185th Infantry Regiment moves inland to secure the villages, followed by a battalion of the 160th Infantry Regiment.

ARMY/MARINE CORPS

The 147th Infantry Regiment, including many veterans from the campaign on Guadalcanal Island, Solomon Islands, lands on Iwo Jima Island, Japan, to relieve Marines fighting cave-to-cave at the northern end of the island.

MARINE CORPS

On Iwo Jima Island, Japan, the 26th Marine Regiment reaches the coast near Kitano Point, closing the ring on Death Valley, the gorge where the Japanese commander is holding out with the last of his forces. V Amphibious Corps Artillery units complete embarkation and depart Iwo Jima.

18 MARCH
AIR FORCE

Nearly 300 XXI Bomber Command B-29 Superfortress bombers launch on low-altitude, night firebombing flights against Nagoya, Japan.

18–19 MARCH
MARINE CORPS/NAVY

Task Force 58 (under Vice Admiral Marc A. Mitscher) begins striking targets on the Japanese home islands of Kyushu and Honshu, devastating airfields and inflicting great damage on shipping, including hits on the battleships *Haruna*, *Hyuga*, and *Yamato* and carriers *Amagi*, *Hosho*, *Ikoma*, *Kaiyo*, *Katsuragi*, and *Ryuho*. Kamikazes exact revenge, scoring a hit on the aircraft carrier *Intrepid*. Conventional bombing attacks damage the carriers *Enterprise*, *Yorktown*, and *Wasp*. However, the worst damage is inflicted on the carrier *Franklin* on 19 March. Two bombs trigger a series of explosions that turn her flight and hangar decks into a blazing inferno. In the bowels of the ship, Lieutenant (junior grade) Donald A. Gary leads a group of shipmates trapped below through dark passageways to safety, and later takes charge of firefighting parties in combating the flames on the hangar deck. He also helps raise steam in one of the boilers in an effort to get the crippled ship underway. Meanwhile, on the flight deck the Roman Catholic chaplain, Commander Joseph T. O'Callaghan, brings an air of calm to the wounded and dying; he also mans hoses to fight fires and lends a hand throwing ammunition over the side. Both Gary and O'Callaghan receive the Medal of Honor. Among the 772 dead in *Franklin*'s crew, 65 are Marines from the two embarked F4U Corsair fighter squadrons. Marine Corps aircraft participate in Task

Left: *Navy Chaplain Commander Joseph T. O'Callahan ministers to an injured Sailor after Japanese bombs hit the carrier* Franklin *in March 1945. O'Callahan receives the Medal of Honor for his bravery. (Naval Historical Center)*

Opposite, top: *Only 50 miles off the coast of Japan, the carrier* Franklin *is hit by two Japanese bombs that set off a massive explosion and trigger fires in the hangar deck on 19 March 1945. Courageous actions by the crewmen save the ship, which limps back to the Pearl Harbor, Hawaii. (National Archives)*

Force 58 strikes against Kyushu Island, Japan. Marine Corps pilots claim 14 of the 102 Japanese planes shot down, plus a share of 275 destroyed on the ground.

19 March
MARINE CORPS
Marine Torpedo Bomber Squadron 233 (formerly Marine Scout Bombing Squadron 233) goes aboard the carrier *Block Island*, which sails from San Diego, California.

20 March
ARMY/MARINE CORPS
The 147th Infantry Regiment arrives on Iwo Jima Island, Japan, as the garrison force and is temporarily attached to the 3d Marine Division.

21 MARCH
AIR FORCE
A P-63 Kingcobra fighter from Walla Walla Airfield, Washington, intercepts a Japanese Fu-go balloon. The pilot must refuel twice along the way, but eventually shoots the balloon down over a desolate area near Reno, Nevada.

ARMY
In the Philippine Islands, the 33d Infantry Division links up with the guerrillas of the U.S. Army Forces near San Fernando, Luzon Island. The town and airstrip are taken without opposition. In the Mount Myoko area, the 25th Infantry Division beats back a determined Japanese counterattack. The 6th Infantry Division finds better going and pushes Japanese defenders off of Sugar Loaf Hill and two nearby ridges.

MARINE CORPS
Commandant Alexander A. Vandegrift is promoted to general, the first Marine to hold four-star rank on active duty.

23 MARCH
MARINE CORPS
Marine Corps aircraft of Task Force 58 participate in air strikes against Okinawa Island, Japan.

The four squadrons of Marine Aircraft Group 32 begin flying to Zamboanga, Mindanao Island, to join with their ground echelons and support the Eighth Army campaign in the southern Philippine Islands. The movement is complete two days later.

NAVY
Task Force 58 begins launching air strikes against Okinawa Island, Japan, in preparation for the 1 April assault on the island, while Task Force 54 (under Rear Admiral Morton L. Deyo) begins bombarding Okinawa from the sea on 25 March.

The destroyer *Haggard* spots the Japanese submarine *I-371* on the surface in the Philippine Sea and rams her, sinking the sub.

25 MARCH
MARINE CORPS

The 5th Marine Division wipes out the last resistance in Death Valley. This marks the end of organized Japanese control of any terrain on Iwo Jima Island, Japan.

26 MARCH
ARMY/MARINE CORPS/NAVY

Prior to dawn, over 200 Japanese launch a surprise attack on Marine Corps, Navy, and Army rear-area elements on Iwo Jima Island, Japan. Marine Corps units involved are the 5th Pioneer Battalion and the 8th Field Depot. The Pioneers, including many African American Marines, provide the first organized resistance and lead the effort to destroy the infiltrators after first light. Forty-four Soldiers are killed and 89 wounded. The V Amphibious Corps turns over control of Iwo Jima to Army Air Forces Major General James E. Chaney and begins departing.

In the Philippine Islands, Task Group 78.2 (under Captain Albert T. Sprague) lands three battalions of the Americal Division (Eighth Army) on Cebu Island near Talisay Point, with support from Marine Aircraft Group 14 planes. Enemy fire is light, but a beach minefield disables eight landing vehicles and initially delays inland movement. The 182d Infantry Regiment breaches the minefield and, against scattered Japanese opposition, it and the 132d Infantry Regiment push almost three miles inland by dark. Cebu City is taken on 28 March as the Japanese withdraw into the surrounding hills. Cavit Island in Cebu Bay is secured by a company of the 132d Infantry.

The invasion of the Ryukyu Islands begins as Task Force 51.1 (under Rear Admiral Ingolf N. Kiland) lands four battalion landing teams of the reinforced 77th Infantry Division on four different islands of the Kerama Retto Islands. The simultaneous landings go smoothly and on only one island is there Japanese resistance. Patrols of the Fleet Marine Force Amphibious Reconnaissance Battalion, attached to the 77th Division, land on four islets of Keise Shima Island and find it unoccupied. The 5th Fleet supports the landings with naval gunfire and air support. The islands are secured on 30 March with the 77th Infantry Division destroying more than 350 Japanese suicide boats. Artillery and planes are brought in to support the landings planned for Okinawa Island, Japan.

Left: Bands of Philippine guerrillas, often led by Americans, join U.S. forces as the liberation of the Philippine Islands spreads. This group in Batangas Province is armed with a mixture of Japanese and American weapons. (U.S. Army)

NAVY

Off Okinawa Island, Japan, kamikazes damage the battleship *Nevada*, the light cruiser *Biloxi*, three destroyers, two auxiliaries, and two transports.

27 MARCH
MARINE CORPS

The 3d and 5th Marine Divisions begin departing Iwo Jima Island, Japan. Total Marine Corps casualties

during the battle are 5,931 dead and 17,272 wounded. Losses among attached Navy personnel are 209 dead and 641 wounded.

27–28 MARCH
AIR FORCE

In the first minelaying mission by B-29 Superfortress bombers flying from the Mariana Islands, about 100 bombers drop mines in the Shimonoseki Strait between Honshu and Kyushu Islands, Japan. Many other minelaying operations are flown during the rest of the war. More than 150 other B-29s begin to strike targets in support of the upcoming invasion of Okinawa Island, Japan.

29 MARCH
ARMY/MARINE CORPS/NAVY

In the Philippine Islands, the Eighth Army makes unopposed landings on Negros Island. A reinforced platoon of the 185th Infantry Regiment, 40th Infantry Division lands at Patik to seize a key bridge while the main body of the 185th Infantry goes ashore near Pulupandan. Marine Aircraft Group 14 provides air support to the landings.

NAVY

Two carrier task groups of Task Force 58 strike targets in the Kagoshima Bay area off Kyushu, Japan, sinking 12 enemy vessels.

30 MARCH
AIR FORCE

The XX Bomber Command launches its final B-29 Superfortress bomber mission from bases in India when 26 bombers attack Japanese targets on Bukum Island near Singapore.

MARINE CORPS

Marine Bomber Squadron 611 arrives on Mindanao Island, Philippine Islands.

31 MARCH
AIR FORCE

As a diversion for the invasion of Okinawa Island, Japan, scheduled for the following day, 137 B-29 Superfortress bombers hit the airfield at Omura, Japan, and the Tachiahari machine plant.

NAVY

The destroyers *Morrison* and *Stockton* combine to sink the Japanese submarine *I-8* off Okinawa Island, Japan.

The heavy cruiser *Indianapolis*, flagship of 5th Fleet commander Admiral Raymond A. Spruance, is damaged by a kamikaze, necessitating her return to the United States for repairs. The admiral shifts his flag to the battleship *New Mexico*.

1 APRIL
ARMY/MARINE CORPS/ NAVY

Operation ICEBERG—the main invasion of Okinawa Island, Japan—begins. After intensive air and naval bombardment, Task Force 51 (under Vice Admiral Richmond Kelly Turner) lands Tenth Army forces (under Lieutenant General Simon B. Buckner Jr.) and attached Marine Corps units on the west coast of Okinawa. Marine Fighting Squadrons 221 and 451 provide air support. The 7th and 96th Infantry Division of the XXIV Corps (under Major General John R. Hodge) are put ashore on the south, while the III Amphibious Corps lands the 1st and 6th Marine Divisions to the north. The 2d Marine Division makes an amphibious feint off the southeast coast of the

Opposite, top: T45 launchers mounted on one-ton trucks of the 3d Provisional Rocket Detachment send their 4.5-inch rockets flying toward Japanese positions on Iwo Jima Island, Japan. The launchers use an automatic gravity feed system to fire all the rockets. (USMC)

Opposite, bottom: An M7 Priest self-propelled howitzer crosses a muddy stream in the Philippine Islands as Sixth Army units continue to clear Japanese troops from the islands. (U.S. Army)

Right: The joint Army–Marine Corps operation under Lieutenant General Simon B. Buckner Jr.'s Tenth Army to capture Okinawa Island, Japan, is the largest amphibious campaign of the Pacific war. More than half a million men and 1,200 ships take part. Buckner is killed in action during the fighting. (Meridian Mapping)

Map © 2008 Philip Schwartzberg, Meridian Mapping, Minneapolis, MN

Left: *Two regiments of the Americal Division wade ashore on Cebu Island, Philippine Islands, on 26 March 1945. The Soldiers meet only light resistance, and move quickly toward Cebu City. (U.S. Army)*

Below: *Operation ICEBERG, the 1 April 1945 invasion of Okinawa Island, Japan, by the Tenth Army (with two Army and two Marine Corps divisions), meets light initial opposition. The Soldiers of the 96th Infantry Division must climb a seawall to get off the beach. (National Archives)*

island. The initial landings are only lightly opposed and two airfields are quickly secured. Kamikazes damage the battleship *West Virginia* and two attack transports. By nightfall, 65,000 Soldiers, Marines, and Sailors are ashore.

ARMY/NAVY
Task Group 78.4 (Captain Homer F. McGee) puts the 158th Regimental Combat Team (RCT) ashore near Legaspi in southern Luzon Island, Philippine Islands. The landing is unopposed and the 158th RCT secures the town, port, and airstrip.

NAVY
The submarine *Queenfish* mistakenly sinks *Awa Maru*, a Japanese ship carrying Red Cross supplies to Allied prisoners of war in Singapore. The Japanese ship is marked and illuminated in a manner identifying her as a vessel on a humanitarian mission, but foggy weather prevents the sub's skipper from discerning the markings. The sub's captain is eventually court-martialed and relieved of his command.

2 APRIL
AIR FORCE
In the early morning hours, Twentieth Air Force B-29 Superfortress bombers mine the harbors around Hiroshima and Kure, Japan, and also bomb the Nakajima aircraft factory in Tokyo.

ARMY/MARINE CORPS
XXIV Corps elements reach the eastern coast of Okinawa Island, Japan, cutting the island in two. One airstrip is made ready and a light plane from a Marine Corps observation squadron is able to land. The Tactical Air Force headquarters begins setting up ashore, and the 2d Marine Division repeats its amphibious feint off the southeast beaches.

MARINE CORPS
Marine Aircraft Group 43 (formerly Marine Base Defense Aircraft Group 43) headquarters arrives on Okinawa Island, Japan, to provide the administrative echelon of its Air Defense Command.

Right: *The battleship* Idaho *fires her 14-inch main guns in support of the landings on Okinawa Island, Japan, in April 1945. (National Archives)*

3 APRIL
ALL SERVICES
The Joint Chiefs of Staff tell General of the Army Douglas MacArthur and Fleet Admiral Chester W. Nimitz to initiate planning for the invasion of Japan. MacArthur's forces are now at 1,500,000; Nimitz has 6,000 ships. Army and naval aviation assets include more than 35,000 aircraft in theater.

ARMY/MARINE CORPS
On Okinawa Island, Japan, the 1st Marine Division reaches the east coast and seals off the base of the Katchin Peninsula. Marine F4U Corsair fighters down 11 Japanese aircraft attempting to raid the Okinawa beachhead. Spotter planes from Marine Observation Squadrons 2, 3, and 6 are operational at Yontan airfield. The 7th Infantry Division moves south along the coast to Kuba.

4 APRIL
AIR FORCE
A Tenth Air Force YR-4 helicopter assigned to the Air Jungle Rescue Detachment rescues a downed PT-19 trainer aircraft pilot in enemy territory in Burma.

ARMY/MARINE CORPS
On Okinawa Island, Japan, the advance of the XXIV Corps' 7th, 27th, 77th, and 96th Infantry Regiments slows after meeting heavy Japanese defenses. The 1st Marine Regiment clears out the Katchin Peninsula while the 6th Marine Division completes its wheel to the left and begins its drive north.

ARMY
In the Philippine Islands, progress is slow in the 158th Infantry Regiment's area as it cleans out numerous Japanese positions around Busay, Luzon Island. On Negros Island, the 160th Infantry Regiment takes Concepcion without a fight, while the 185th Infantry destroys a major Japanese supply base at Guimbalon. Fighting continues on Cebu Island with the 182d Infantry capturing Horseshoe Ridge.

5 APRIL
ARMY/MARINE CORPS
On Okinawa Island, Japan, the XXIV Corps' 96th Infantry Division meets serious resistance in the south as it hits the outposts of the main Japanese defenses, known as the Shuri Line. The 7th Infantry Division moves abreast of the 96th Division. The 1st Marine Division begins mopping up rear areas while the 6th Marine Division exploits light opposition and moves rapidly northward. The Fleet Marine Force Amphibious Reconnaissance Battalion lands on Tsugen Shima Island off the east coast of Okinawa and uncovers significant enemy defenses, then withdraws.

NAVY
The destroyer *Hudson* sinks the Japanese submarine *RO-41* off Okinawa Island, Japan.

6 APRIL
ARMY
United States Army Forces in the Pacific is created to conclude the campaign in the Philippine Islands and make preparations for the invasion of Japan. General of the Army Douglas MacArthur is named commander.

6 APRIL
MARINE CORPS/NAVY

The first large-scale assault by Japanese aircraft against Allied ships operating off Okinawa Island, Japan, begins. About half of the 699 aircraft targeting the ships of the invasion force are kamikazes. Marine Corps planes of Task Force 58 shoot down 22 of the enemy. Kamikaze attacks cause extensive damage to the destroyer *Colhoun*, which is later scuttled, and sink the tank landing ship *LST-347*. Two freighters carrying ammunition for the men fighting ashore are sunk, and 26 other vessels ranging from the light carrier *San Jacinto* to a motor minesweeper are damaged during the air attack.

7 APRIL
AIR FORCE

The Twentieth Air Force launches its first escort fighters from the newly captured island of Iwo Jima, Japan, when 280 B-29 Superfortress bombers, accompanied by 91 P-51 Mustang fighters, attack three separate targets in Japan.

ARMY

On Okinawa Island, Japan, the 383d Infantry Regiment, 96th Infantry Division captures Cactus Ridge, while the 184th Infantry Regiment, 7th Infantry Division (under Major General Archibald V. Arnold) finally succeeds, after several attempts, to seize the fortified Japanese positions on a hill west of Minami village. Japanese resistance is becoming progressively stronger.

Above: *Called a "Brodie device," this hook and arm rig is put on tank landing ships to permit light aircraft like this L-4 to be launched and recovered. (Col. Gordon J. Wolf, USA, Ret.)*

Below: *("LVTs Pass USS* North Carolina *(BB-55) Bombarding Okinawa Beaches," John Hamilton, Navy Art Collection)*

MARINE CORPS

The Fleet Marine Force Amphibious Reconnaissance Battalion scouts the remaining islands off the east coast of Okinawa Island, Japan, and finds them free of the enemy. III Amphibious Corps artillery begins providing support to the XXIV Corps along the southern front. The first aircraft of Marine Aircraft Group 31's Marine Fighting Squadrons 224, 311, and 441 and Marine Night Fighting Squadron 542 begin operating ashore on Okinawa.

MARINE CORPS/NAVY

Carrier aircraft of Task Force 58 attack the Japanese battleship *Yamato*, which steams for Okinawa Island, Japan, with a light cruiser and eight destroyers. A total of 386 carrier planes score repeated hits on the Japanese ships, sinking *Yamato*, the light cruiser *Yahagi*, and four destoyers in the East China Sea. Japanese suicide planes damage six ships, including the carrier *Hancock* and battleship *Maryland*.

8 APRIL
ARMY/MARINE CORPS

On Okinawa Island, Japan, the 6th Marine Division seals off the base of the Motobu Peninsula on the island's northwest coast. The 96th Infantry Division tries unsuccessfully to advance to Kakazu Ridge. The 7th Infantry Division captures the strong point on Triangulation Hill, but is unable to take Tomb Hill.

NAVY

Following a rendezvous with the submarine *Tigrone*, the submarine *Snook* is not heard from again. She is later presumed lost with all hands in the Western Pacific.

9 APRIL
ARMY/MARINE CORPS

On Okinawa Island, Japan, battalions of the 383d Infantry Regiment, 96th Division make a pre-dawn attack on Kakazu Ridge, a major Japanese strongpoint, but withdraw after heavy losses. For its stubborn defense of its position before being forced to withdraw, Company L, 383d Infantry is awarded the first Presidential Unit Citation of the campaign. The 184th Infantry Regiment is successful in taking Tomb Hill. The 22d and 29th Marine Regiments launch patrols to determine the disposition of the strong Japanese force defending the Motobu Peninsula. The 11th Marine Regiment begins moving south to support the XXIV Corps. Kadena Airfield is opened for operational use by Marine Aircraft Group 33 (Marine Fighting Squadrons 312, 322, and 323 and Marine Night Fighting Squadron 543).

In the Philippine Islands, the 163d Regimental Combat Team, 41st Infantry Division makes an unopposed landing on Jolo Island and begins clearing it of Japanese. Marine Corps aircraft support the landing.

NAVY

The destroyers *Mertz* and *Monssen* sink the Japanese submarine *RO-56* off Okinawa Island, Japan.

Above: *Soldiers of the 158th Regimental Combat Team meet a Japanese "banzai" counterattack head-on during extensive fighting near Bicol, Luzon. ("Cuidado—Take Care, Bushmaster With Bolo!" H. Charles McBarron, National Guard Bureau)*

10 APRIL
MARINE CORPS
Marine Bomber Squadron 612 arrives on Iwo Jima Island, Japan, and begins making night anti-shipping attacks as far away as mainland Japan.

NAVY
Kamikaze attacks off Okinawa Island, Japan, damage six ships, including the battleship *Missouri* and the aircraft carrier *Enterprise*. Conventional bombing and strafing attacks by Japanese aircraft damage the carrier *Essex*, three destroyers, a tank landing ship, and a large support landing craft.

11 APRIL
ARMY
The advance on Okinawa Island, Japan, is stalled. The 96th Infantry Division makes several futile attempts to capture the ridge that comprises Kakazu and Kakazu West from the stubborn Japanese defenders. Elements of the 7th Infantry Division push into the town of Ouki, but are forced to withdraw when tanks are unable to come forward.

12 APRIL
ALL SERVICES
President Franklin Delano Roosevelt dies in Warm Springs, Georgia. Harry S. Truman is sworn in as the new President and Commander-in-Chief.

AIR FORCE
Staff Sergeant Henry E. Erwin, Twentieth Air Force, drops phosphorus smoke markers out of the mission lead B-29 Superfortress bomber over Koriyama, Japan. One of the phosphorus markers explodes in the ejector chute and shoots back into the aircraft, blinding him. Erwin realizes that if the burning bomb remains in the plane, the entire crew will be lost. Now blind and aflame, Erwin takes the smoke marker between his forearm and his body, struggles to the cockpit, and throws it out of the co-pilot's window, saving the aircraft and the crew. Remarkably, Erwin survives his extensive third-degree burns and other injuries, and is awarded the Medal of Honor on 6 June.

MARINE CORPS

Marine F4U Corsair fighters of Task Force 58 shoot down 51 kamikazes, while squadrons based on Okinawa Island, Japan, get 16 more. Major Herman A. Hansen Jr., the 25-year-old commanding officer of Marine Fighting Squadron 112, destroys three, making him an ace. Major Archie Donahue scores 5 kills, giving him a total of 14 and the status of "ace in a day." Over the remainder of the month, Marine Corps planes on the carriers rack up 30 additional kills.

Marine Torpedo Bomber Squadron 143 goes on board the escort carrier *Gilbert Islands*.

NAVY

Some 380 Japanese aircraft, in addition to piloted bombs known as "Bakas," attack U.S. ships off Okinawa Island, Japan. The Baka scores its first sinking by sending the destroyer *Mannert L. Abele* to the bottom. In addition, the large support landing craft *LCS(L)-33* is sunk by a kamikaze, while suicide planes and bombing attacks inflict damage on 18 vessels.

13 APRIL
MARINE CORPS

Patrols from the 6th Marine Division reach the northern tip of Okinawa Island, Japan, while the Fleet

Above: *Alert antiaircraft gun crews keep watch as their aircraft carrier sails into dangerous waters. ("General Quarters," Lt. William F. Draper, USNR, Navy Art Collection)*

Below: *A Japanese attack turns the night into a blaze of antiaircraft tracers and exploding aircraft. (Lt. Edward Grigware, USNR, Navy Art Collection)*

Marine Force Amphibious Reconnaissance Battalion occupies Minna Shima, an island off the northwest coast. The Amphibious Task Force flies its first close air support missions for the Tenth Army.

13–14 APRIL
AIR FORCE
More than 330 Twentieth Air Force B-29 Superfortress bombers hit the Tokyo, Japan, arsenal area.

Eleventh Air Force P-38 Lightning and P-40 Warhawk fighters scramble to intercept unknown radar returns, which turn out to be 11 Fu-go balloons. The pilots shoot down nine of the balloons over the Aleutian Islands.

14 APRIL
MARINE CORPS
On Okinawa Island, Japan, the 4th and 29th Marine Regiments launch an attack to destroy enemy forces concentrated around Mount Yae Take on the Motobu Peninsula.

NAVY
While operating in the approaches to the Yellow Sea, the submarine *Tirante*, commanded by Lieutenant Commander George L. Street III, boldly attacks the Japanese convoy MOSI 02 on the surface despite the presence of mines and numerous shoals in the water. *Tirante* sinks three ships. Street receives the Medal of Honor for his actions.

The destroyer *Laffey* is the target of 22 separate kamikaze attacks while she operates on radar picket duty off Okinawa Island, Japan. For over an hour her crew braves the onslaught, shooting down six of the attackers, while the ship is struck by suicide planes six times and holed by bombs twice. Amazingly, *Laffey* survives the attack and is towed to safety.

Right: *As the fighting draws closer to Japan and Japanese manpower and resources are strained, the Japanese turn to suicide weapons. The Kugisho MXY7-K1 Ohka is a manned, rocket-propelled flying bomb. With only about 10 seconds of fuel, it must be carried aloft by a larger bomber and released near the target. It carries more than 2,600 pounds of explosives. (U.S. Army)*

14–15 APRIL
ARMY
On Okinawa Island, Japan, the 27th Infantry Division has landed and moves forward to take its place on the XXIV Corps front line.

15 APRIL
Hard fighting continues on all fronts in the Philippine Islands. On Luzon Island, the 25th, 33d, and 37th Infantry Divisions push forward against stubborn Japanese defenses, making slow gains. In the XIV Corps area, the 11th Airborne Division opens a drive to clear Mount Malepunyo. The Americal Division is battling to clear the hills around Cebu City while the 40th Infantry Division softens up Japanese positions on Negros Island. On 16 April, the 11th Airborne Division secures Mount Malepunyo, while the 1st Cavalry Division surrounds a pocket of Japanese near Mount Mataasna Bundoc.

16 APRIL
AIR FORCE
Nearly 300 B-29 bombers strike the cities of Kawasaki and Tokyo, Japan, during the night. That day, P-51 Mustang fighters from Iwo Jima Island, Japan, attack targets in Japan for the first time. A B-29 Superfortress bomber provides navigational aid for the fighters to and from their targets at Kanoya. B-25 Mitchell bombers will pick up the navigational duties on all subsequent P-51 missions, which will continue until 14 August.

ARMY
Troops of the 77th Infantry Division land on the south and southwest coasts of Ie Shima Island, Ryuku

Islands. The enemy puts up stiff resistance. The 77th Division troops hold off a heavy counterattack to end the battle on 21 April.

MARINE CORPS
The 4th Marine Regiment seizes Mount Yae Take on Okinawa Island, Japan. Pilots of the Amphibious Task Force score 38 kills, and carrier-based Marines get another 10. Marine Fighting Squadron 441 claims 17 of the enemy.

NAVY
Kamikaze attacks off Okinawa Island, Japan, sink the destroyer *Pringle* and damage nine other vessels, including the battleship *Missouri* and the aircraft carrier *Intrepid*. *Pringle* breaks in two and sinks in five minutes with the loss of 62 of her crew.

17 APRIL
AIR FORCE
From this date until 11 May, priorities for the Twentieth Air Force shift from strategic bombardment of Japan to direct support and interdiction in the campaign to take Okinawa Island, Japan. The XXI Bomber Command will assign three-quarters of its missions to destroying aircraft and enemy operations on 17 airfields on Kyushu and Shikoku Islands. The Japanese use these airfields to launch attacks upon the invasion forces at sea and on the ground at Okinawa.

ARMY/NAVY
Task Group 78.2 (under Rear Admiral Albert G. Noble) lands the assault units of the X Corps' 24th Infantry Division near Parang, Mindanao Island,

MARINE CORPS

Transport planes of Marine Transport Squadron (VMR) 252 make their first flight to Okinawa Island, Japan, with vital supplies. VMR-253, 353, and 952 join in over the next four days. Among the pilots in VMR-253 is movie actor Tyrone Power.

NAVY

Four destroyers, assisted by a TBM Avenger torpedo-bomber of Torpedo Squadron 47 from the light carrier *Bataan*, sink the Japanese submarine *I-56* off Okinawa Island, Japan.

The submarine *Sea Owl* sinks the Japanese submarine *RO-46* just 500 yards off the beach at Wake Island.

19 APRIL
ARMY/NAVY

On Okinawa Island, Japan, the XXIV Corps launches a major assault on the outer belt of the Shuri Line, assisted by naval gunfire and the largest number of air strikes of the campaign. Deeply dug in to caves and tunnels, the Japanese withstand the bombardment and hold the attacking 7th, 27th, and 96th Infantry Divisions to minor gains at a heavy cost. The 27th Division loses 22 tanks. The ground slugging match continues the next day with no progress.

20 APRIL
MARINE CORPS

The 6th Marine Division completes the reduction of enemy defenses on the Motobu Peninsula on Okinawa Island, Japan.

Philippine Islands. No opposition is met and the initial objectives are quickly secured. On 18 April, a patrol from the 38th Infantry Division lands at Fort Drum, an island in Manila Bay, and finds it abandoned.

18 APRIL
ARMY

War correspondent Ernie Pyle is killed by a Japanese sniper while accompanying the 77th Infantry Division on Ie Shima Island, Ryukyu Islands. The division continues its assault against Bloody Ridge.

Above: *Soldiers of the 25th Infantry Division move down a ridge through the mountains of northern Luzon Island, Philippine Islands, as they approach the town of Santa Fe; they take the town on 27 May 1945. (U.S. Army)*

Left: *A Navy Landing Craft, Infantry (Rocket Ship) fires a barrage of 600 4.5-inch rockets at enemy positions on the island of Mindanao, Philippine Islands, in April 1945. Easily modified, the versatile LCI performs many missions. (National Archives)*

Right: *The largest land battle in the Pacific war takes place on Okinawa Island, Japan. ("D-Day Plus One, Green Beach, Okinawa," Lt. Mitchell Jamieson, USNR, Navy Art Collection)*

21 APRIL
ARMY

The 77th Infantry Division holds out against a final counterattack on Ie Shima Island, Ryuku Islands, and overcomes the last Japanese resistance. The island is declared secure.

22 APRIL
ARMY

In the Philippine Islands, fierce fighting continues on Luzon Island. The 37th Infantry Division attacks toward Baguio while to the west the 33d Infantry Division battles to clear the Asin tunnel positions. The 25th Infantry Division is fighting near the base of Lone Tree Hill trying to push through Balete Pass. On Jolo Island, the 163d Regimental Combat Team, 41st Infantry Division overruns the last enemy position on Mount Daho, securing the island. The clearing of Japanese on Cebu Island by the 182d Infantry Regiment makes headway as the enemy withdraws to new positions.

ARMY/MARINE CORPS

On Okinawa Island, Japan, Army and Marine regiments are rotated into the front line by the XXIV Corps, and a task force is formed to clear the last Japanese positions in the Kakazu hills. During the night of 23–24 April, the Japanese withdraw most of their troops to the main Shuri defensive line positions.

MARINE CORPS

Marine Torpedo Bomber Squadron 232 arrives on Okinawa Island, Japan. Marine Corps pilots down 33 enemy planes during a kamikaze attack. Major Jefferson D. Dorroh gets six, while Major George C. Axtell, Jr. and Lieutenant Jeremiah J. O'Keefe score five each to all become aces in a day.

In the Philippine Islands, Marine Aircraft Group (MAG) 32 aircraft conduct a major close air support mission for the Army 41st Infantry Division on Jolo Island. MAG-24 launches its first missions from the Malabang Airfield, Mindanao Island.

23 APRIL
NAVY

The submarine *Besugo* sinks the German submarine *U-183* in the Java Sea.

PB4Y-2 Privateers of Patrol Bombing Squadron 109 attack Japanese ships off Balikpapan, Borneo, Dutch East Indies, using "Bat" missiles, the first employment of the only automatic homing missiles used during World War II.

24–25 APRIL
ARMY/MARINE CORPS

On Okinawa Island, Japan, the XXIV Corps advances easily except in two areas of Japanese resistance. The 1st Marine Division becomes the Tenth Army

Reserve. Prior to dawn, the Japanese withdraw to the second layer of their Shuri defensive line.

26 APRIL
ARMY

Before dawn, the XXIV Corps begins a heavy artillery bombardment of the Shuri defensive line on Okinawa Island, Japan, then launches an assault with the 27th

Infantry Division on the right, 96th Infantry Division in the center, and 7th Infantry Division on the left. A major obstacle is the Maeda Escarpment, which runs almost halfway across the island and must be seized. Elements of the 96th Infantry Division reach the crest to discover the rear slope honeycombed with Japanese fortifications, which stops the advance. The next day, assisted by tanks and flamethrowers, the

96th Infantry Division makes slow progress, but the 7th and 27th Infantry Divisions on the flanks are held up by enemy strongpoints.

28 APRIL
MARINE CORPS/NAVY

During another large kamikaze attack at Okinawa Island, Japan, Amphibious Task Force Marines shoot down 35 planes, while carrier-based Marine Corps squadrons claim another 14. Over the next three days, kamikazes and conventional air attacks damage 15 ships off Okinawa.

29 APRIL
ARMY/MARINE CORPS

The 77th Infantry Division moves forward on Okinawa Island, Japan, and replaces the exhausted and bloodied 96th Infantry Division in the XXIV Corps center. The 77th Division takes over the battle to clear the critical Maeda Escarpment. The next day the 1st Marine Division begins replacing the battered 27th Infantry Division on the Corps' west flank.

NAVY

A TBM Avenger torpedo-bomber of Composite Squadron 92, operating from the escort carrier *Tulagi*, sinks the Japanese submarine *I-44* off Okinawa Island.

1 MAY
AIR FORCE

As the Japanese begin to withdraw from southern China, the Fourteenth Air Force concentrates on attacking transportation targets to impede the enemy's mobility in retreat. Lieutenant General George E. Stratemeyer assumes command of the Army Air Forces in the China Theater with his headquarters at Chunking. Both the Tenth and Fourteenth Air Forces fall under his control.

NAVY

Task Group 78.1 (under Rear Admiral Forrest B. Royal) puts Australian troops ashore on Tarakan Island, Borneo, Dutch East Indies, with support of the guns of Task Group 74.3 (under Rear Admiral Russell S. Berkey).

2 MAY
ARMY/MARINE CORPS

As part of the XXIV Corps offensive, the 1st Marine Division launches its first attacks against the Japanese Shuri defensive line on Okinawa Island, Japan. The 1st Marine Regiment continues a costly effort to reach the Asa River in their sector. A night counterattack pushes the 77th Infantry Division off of hard-won positions on the escarpment.

Left: *A Japanese Zeke used as a kamikaze plane barely misses hitting the deck of the battleship* Missouri *and falls into the sea. (National Archives)*

Below: *In American factories, wartime production of planes, weapons, and other equipment hits an all-time peak in 1945. (U.S. Air Force)*

NAVY

During the bitter ground fighting on Okinawa Island, Japan, Hospital Apprentice Second Class Robert E. Bush is administering plasma to a wounded Marine when Japanese soldiers attack his position. Using his pistol and a carbine he finds nearby, the corpsman beats back the enemy, killing six attackers despite losing an eye in the engagement. He refuses treatment for his own wounds until sure the injured Marine is evacuated. For his actions, Bush is awarded the Medal of Honor.

3 MAY
AIR FORCE

Rangoon, Burma, falls to the Allies, and Indian army forces occupy the city. For the rest of the month, air operations are drastically reduced, and the Tenth Air Force is relieved from combat duty and redeployed to Piardoba, India. A single squadron of P-38 Lightning fighters remains in Burma to patrol roads into China.

ARMY/MARINE CORPS

On Okinawa Island, Japan, the XXIV Corps advance almost stops. The 1st Marine Division makes little progress in the face of heavy enemy fire on the west, while the 77th Infantry Division reaches the top of the Maeda Escarpment, but is unable to go farther. In the east, the 7th Infantry Division fails to take Kochi Ridge. During the night, the Japanese counterattack and try to land troops behind American lines. The attempt is a disaster with hundreds of Japanese killed and the landing craft destroyed. On 4 May, another Japanese attack is broken up with more heavy losses by units of 7th and 77th Infantry Divisions. The 6th Marine Division relocates south, closer to the front lines, and their area is taken over by the 27th Infantry Division. Renewed Japanese attacks on 5 May hit the 7th and 77th Infantry Divisions, but are unsuccessful. The 307th Infantry Regiment, 77th Division penetrates the rear slope defenses of the escarpment and holds on to its position despite counterattacks during the night.

MARINE CORPS/NAVY

Kamikazes sink the destroyer *Little* and the medium landing ship *LSM-195* off Okinawa Island, Japan. Four other vessels suffer damage at the hands of suicide planes. Amphibious Task Force Marines shoot down 60 enemy planes.

NAVY

The Japanese minelayer *Hatsutaka* sinks the submarine *Lagarto* in the Gulf of Siam. In 2005, British divers discover the wreck, with a large rupture visible on the sub's port bow.

Above: *Marines don't pause as they pass a dead enemy on Okinawa Island, Japan, and move on to continue the months-long battle for the island. (National Archives)*

Right: *An M4 Sherman tank moves up a hill on the outskirts of the town of Baguio on Luzon Island, Philippine Islands. (U.S. Army)*

Above: *Two Marines toss hand grenades at a Japanese bunker on Okinawa Island, Japan. ("Grenade Throwers," John R. McDermott, Art Collection, National Museum of the Marine Corps, Triangle, Virginia)*

Below: *A Marine shares his rations with a refugee child on Okinawa Island, Japan. (National Archives)*

4 MAY
MARINE CORPS
The 52d Defense Battalion arrives on Guam Island, Mariana Islands.

NAVY
An intense attack by kamikaze aircraft off Okinawa Island, Japan, sinks 4 ships and damages 12 others. The ships sunk include the destroyers *Luce*, which goes down in four minutes with the loss of 149 members of her crew, and *Morrison*, which is hit four times and sinks with the loss of 153 officers and men.

4–10 MAY
NAVY
Patrol planes of Fleet Air Wing 1 fly missions off the coast of Korea and in the Tsushima Strait, sinking 21 ships.

5 MAY
CIVIL DEFENSE
Suffering the only U.S. casualties on American soil inflicted by enemy action during World War II, a woman and five children are killed when a Japanese submarine-launched Fu-go balloon bomb explodes near Lake View, Oregon.

MARINE CORPS
The 1st Marine Division reaches its initial objective on Okinawa Island, Japan, the northern banks of the Asa River. The Tenth Army orders the III Amphibious Corps to assume responsibility for the right half of the Shuri front lines by 7 May.

6 MAY
ARMY
In the Philippine Islands, the 25th Infantry Division pushes toward Balete Pass on Luzon Island. After dark, the 43d Infantry Division advances on Ipo as U.S. air and artillery disrupt a Japanese attack. The 24th Infantry Division attacks an enemy pocket on Mindanao Island, while on Negros Island the 40th Infantry Division seizes Virgne Ridge and advances along it onto the Patog Plain. The struggle on Okinawa Island, Japan, intensifies as the 77th Infantry Division in the center of XXIV Corps pushes over the escarpment and beyond to Hill 187.

MARINE CORPS
The 1st Marine Division makes little progress attacking the Awacha Pocket on Okinawa Island, Japan. The next day, the division returns to III Amphibious Corps control. Marine Observation Squadron 7 begins to arrive on Okinawa.

Right: *A flight of P-38 Lightning fighters supports the advance of the 25th Infantry Division to clear the enemy from Highway 5 by dropping firebombs on Japanese positions in the mountains north of Balete Pass on Luzon Island, Philippine Islands. (U.S. Army)*

7 MAY
MARINE CORPS
Fleet Admiral Ernest J. King approves "Base Post-War Plan No. 1," which calls for a Fleet Marine Force in the Pacific Theater consisting of a Marine Corps division and aircraft wing in California and a brigade and aircraft group in the western Pacific.

8 MAY
MARINE CORPS
On Okinawa Island, Japan, the 1st Marine Division shifts to the left of its previous frontage. The 6th Marine Division moves into position on the Asa River between the 1st Marine Division and the western coast. After darkness on 9 May, the 6th Engineer Battalion builds a foot bridge over the Asa River, which four companies of the 22d Marine Regiment cross before the Japanese blow up the bridge early the next morning.

10 MAY
AIR FORCE
A high-priority missile program is initiated to defend against Japanese suicide Baka bombs. Using jet assisted takeoff units developed at Caltech, the Naval Aircraft Modification Unit develops the "Little Joe" ship-to-air weapon. The missile is tested in July for the first time.

The Eleventh Air Force and Fleet Air Wing Four complete their most successful and largest operation against Japan to date. A dozen B-24 Liberator bombers bomb enemy ships at Kataoka naval base and follow up with photo reconnaissance of Paramushiru. Later, 16 B-25 Mitchell bombers based on Attu Island, Aleutian Islands, hit shipping targets as well.

ARMY
The 108th Infantry Regiment lands unopposed at Macajalar Bay, Mindanao Island, Philippine Islands, and moves inland to link up with other units of the 31st Infantry Division moving north along the Sayre Highway.

On Okinawa Island, Japan, the 77th Infantry Division continues to clear Japanese bunkers and trenches north of Shuri. The 383d Infantry, 96th Infantry Division secures Zebra Hill and holds it against enemy counterattacks into the night. On 11 May, a heavy artillery barrage precedes a major Tenth Army attack, with the XXIV Corps on the left and III Amphibious Corps on the right. The 306th Infantry Regiment, 77th Division makes little gain, but in the 96th Division area, the 382d Infantry Regiment secures Zebra Hill, and the 383d Infantry gains ground on Conical Hill.

Right: *Army nurses arrive on Okinawa Island, Japan, in May 1945 to tend to the wounded. Four of them wash up in front of their tents using their steel helmets as wash bowls. (U.S. Army)*

MARINE CORPS

On Okinawa Island, Japan, the 5th Marine Regiment seizes control of Awacha Draw. In a determined attack against a Japanese reconnaissance plane flying at high altitude, Marine Fighting Squadron 312's 1st Lieutenant Robert R. Klingman's guns freeze, but he uses his propeller to cut away the enemy's tail and send it into the sea. Marine Night Fighting Squadron 533 arrives on Okinawa following a long flight from Eniwetok Atoll, Marshall Islands. On 11 May, the 5th Marines wipes out the final enemy resistance in the Awacha Pocket.

MARINE CORPS/NAVY

The carrier *Block Island* and its embarked Marine Corps squadrons join the fleet off Okinawa Island, Japan. Marine Torpedo Bomber Squadron 234 joins the escort carrier *Vella Gulf.*

11 MAY
MARINE CORPS/NAVY

Kamikazes attacking the ships operating off Okinawa Island, Japan, reach the carriers, with two planes crashing into *Bunker Hill*, forcing Task Force 58 commander Vice Admiral Marc A. Mitscher to transfer his flag to the carrier *Enterprise.* Three days later the admiral must shift his flag again when the "Big E" is damaged by a suicide plane off Honshu

Island, Japan. *Bunker Hill*'s two Marine Fighting Squadrons (221 and 451) suffer 29 dead. Marine Corps pilots of the Amphibious Task Force shoot down 19 enemy.

12 MAY
MARINE CORPS

On Okinawa Island, Japan, the attack of the 22d Marine Regiment runs up against a fortified ridge, quickly dubbed Sugar Loaf Hill, that forms the western anchor of the Japanese Shuri defensive line.

Fleet Admiral Chester W. Nimitz removes the 2d Marine Division (less the 8th Marine Regiment) on Saipan Island, Mariana Islands, from Tenth Army reserve and makes it the theater reserve. That part of the division finally debarks from transports and goes ashore on Saipan. The 8th Marines remains under control of the Tenth Army.

13–14 MAY
ARMY

In the Philippine Islands, I Corps units complete clearing Balete Pass and move into the Cagayan Valley on Luzon Island. The X Corps' advance along the Sayre Highway on Mindanao Island is halted by strong enemy positions that take several days to eliminate, while on the island of Samal, the 19th

Infantry Regiment is having difficulty with Japanese defenses, but secures the island on 15 May.

On Okinawa Island, Japan, the 77th Infantry Division continues its attacks on Chocolate Drop Hill with heavy losses, but the 96th Infantry Division pushes forward, its 383d Infantry Regiment piercing the eastern end of the Shuri Line defenses to take Conical Hill and hold it against Japanese counterattacks.

NAVY
In an effort to blunt kamikaze attacks against the fleet off Okinawa Island, Japan, the carriers of Task Force 58 strike Japanese airfields on Kyushu, Japan.

14 MAY
AIR FORCE
The Twentieth Air Force launches a raid in which four B-29 Superfortress bomber wings attack northern Nagoya, Japan. During the raid, 11 of the 472 bombers are lost. The XXI Bomber Command now consists of the 58th, 73d, 313th, and 314th Bomb Wings.

15 MAY
MARINE CORPS
Marine Aircraft Group 14 ends combat operations on Samar Island, Philippine Islands, in preparation for its shift to Okinawa Island, Japan.

16 MAY
AIR FORCE
Far East Air Force P-38 Lightning fighters attack the Ipo Dam area of Luzon Island, Philippine Islands. Nearly 100 aircraft drop napalm canisters in the largest single use of that weapon in the war.

17 MAY
AIR FORCE
During early morning darkness, 457 B-29 Superfortress bombers strike Nagoya, Japan, once again, this time in the southern part of the city.

Above: *While steaming near Okinawa Island, Japan, on 11 May 1945, the carrier* Bunker Hill *is hit by two Japanese kamikaze planes and is severely damaged. The ship remains afloat and makes her way to the Hawaiian Islands. (National Archives)*

Right: *A group of Marines hitches a ride on an M4 Sherman tank during a shift of Marine Corps forces on Okinawa Island, Japan, during the last phase of the fighting in May 1945. (National Archives)*

ARMY/MARINE CORPS
Lieutenant General Simon B. Buckner Jr. takes control of all forces ashore on Okinawa Island, Japan. In the III Amphibious Corps area, the 29th Marine Regiment continues attacks on Sugar Loaf Hill with heavy air, artillery, and naval gunfire support. The 7th Marine Regiment fails in its efforts to secure Wana Ridge. A company of the 307th Infantry Regiment, 77th Infantry Division in the XXIV Corps makes a successful predawn attack to take Ishimmi Ridge, but finds itself isolated and under heavy enemy fire.

18 MAY
AIR FORCE
The Advanced Air Echelon of the 509th Composite Group arrives on Tinian Island, Mariana Islands, and sets up shop on North Field. The group is equipped with specially modified B-29 Superfortress bombers, and promptly starts to fly training missions that are shrouded in mystery. It is tasked to drop the atomic bomb on Japanese targets if needed.

MARINE CORPS
On Okinawa Island, Japan, the 29th Marine Regiment captures Sugar Loaf Hill after four days of bitter, see-saw fighting.

NAVY
Japanese shore batteries on Naha, Okinawa Island, Japan, zero in on the destroyer *Longshaw* after she runs aground, hitting her repeatedly and exploding her forward ammunition magazine. Eighty-six of her crew are lost.

19 MAY
AIR FORCE
The Twentieth Air Force sends 272 B-29 Superfortress bombers to attack the city of Hamamatsu, Japan.

ARMY
The lone company of the 307th Infantry Regiment on Ishimmi Ridge, Okinawa Island, Japan, holds out despite heavy losses until relieved during night. The 382d Infantry Regiment slowly expands its hold on the rear slope of Dick Hill, but elements of the 383d Infantry Regiment are driven back from positions gained on King Hill.

MARINE CORPS

The 4th and 22d Marine Regiments seize the Horse Shoe, another formidable position just beyond Sugar Loaf Hill on Okinawa Island, Japan.

20–21 MAY
ARMY

The XXIV Corps makes progress on Okinawa Island, Japan. The 77th Infantry Division finishes clearing the enemy from Chocolate Drop Hill and presses ahead to seize Flattop Hill. More of the fortifications on Dick Hill fall to the 382d Infantry Regiment, and the 381st Infantry moves toward Sugar Loaf Hill. On 21 May the 381st Infantry consolidates its lines on Sugar Loaf Hill and repulses a strong enemy counterattack. These actions clear the way for the 7th Infantry Division to proceed toward Buckner Bay, and force the enemy to begin to withdraw from some parts of the Shuri defensive line.

21 MAY
MARINE CORPS

The aircraft of Marine Aircraft Group 22 (Marine Fighting Squadrons 113, 314, and 422) arrive on Ie Shima Island, Ryuku Islands, from Engebi Island, Marshall Islands, and begin supporting the Tenth Army.

Marine Torpedo Bomber Squadron 132 goes on board the carrier *Cape Gloucester* at San Diego, California.

23 MAY
AIR FORCE

Of the 562 B-29 Superfortress bombers launched at night against Japan, 520 reach the designated industrial area target on the west side of Tokyo Harbor, Japan. This is the largest number of B-29s to fly during a single mission during World War II. Seventeen B-29s go down during the operation.

24 MAY
ARMY/MARINE CORPS

As part of a larger kamikaze raid, six Japanese transport planes loaded with commandos attempt to land at Yontan Airfield on northern Okinawa Island, Japan. Five planes are shot down by antiaircraft fire, but one makes a landing and the enemy soldiers destroy eight planes and cause other damage before being killed.

MARINE CORPS

The 8th Marine Regiment sails from Saipan Island, Mariana Islands, for Okinawa.

25 MAY
ALL SERVICES

The U.S. Joint Chiefs of Staff receive plans for Operation OLYMPIC—the invasion of Kyushu Island, Japan, set for 1 November, and Operation CORONET—the follow-up invasion of Honshu Island around 1 March 1946.

AIR FORCE
The Twentieth Air Force sends 464 B-29 Superfortress bombers to strike targets in Tokyo, Japan, with the loss of 26 bombers. This is the greatest loss of B-29s in one day during World War II.

The VII Fighter Command based on Iwo Jima Island,

Japan, is assigned to the Twentieth Air Force both operationally and administratively.

MARINE CORPS
In Okinawa, Japan, Marine Corps fighters from the Amphibious Task Force claim 39 of 75 Japanese planes downed in aerial combat during a mass kamikaze

Above: *A Marine covers the advance of his buddy with his Thompson submachine gun as the two move up Wana Ridge near the town of Shuri on Okinawa Island, Japan. (National Archives)*

Right: *On 29 May 1945, B-29 Superfortresses of the 500th Bomb Group drop firebombs on Yokohama, Japan, igniting a fire that consumes much of the city. (NASM)*

Opposite: *A medic helps a Soldier wounded in the fighting on Okinawa Island, Japan, to the aid station. (National Archives)*

attack. Captain Herbert J. Valentine is credited with five kills to become an "ace in a day."

NAVY
The high-speed transport *Bates* and the medium landing ship *LSM-135* are sunk by kamikazes off Okinawa Island, Japan.

26 MAY
ARMY
Lieutenant General Courtney H. Hodges and members of his First Army staff arrive in Manila, Luzon Island, Philippine Islands, to start development of plans for Operation CORONET, the invasion of Kyushu Island, Japan.

ARMY/MARINE CORPS/NAVY
Frontline observers on Okinawa Island, Japan, report the rearward movement of Japanese forces and call in massive air, artillery, and naval firepower. Over the next four days most of the Japanese withdraw to the final defensive line in the escarpments along the Kiyamu Peninsula. Second-echelon forces fight a delaying action in the Shuri line defenses.

27 MAY
MARINE CORPS
The 6th Marine Division captures Naha, the capital city of Okinawa Island, Japan.

27–28 MAY
ARMY
In the Philippine Islands, I Corps units on Luzon Island complete clearing Japanese troops from the Villa Verde Trail, move out of the mountains, and occupy Santa Fe. On Mindanao Island the 24th Infantry Division completes securing the Talomo River valley.

On Okinawa Island, Japan, the 7th Infantry Division continues to batter at enemy positions around Shuri.

28 MAY
ARMY
In the Philippine Islands, the 164th Infantry Regiment destroys the last organized Japanese resistance on Negros Island and begins mopping up operations, which continue through 31 May.

MARINE CORPS
During a massive kamikaze raid against the fleet off Okinawa Island, Japan, Marine Corps pilots claim 32 of the 49 enemy downed.

NAVY
The destroyer *Drexler* comes under attack off Okinawa Island, Japan. Hit by one suicide plane, she continues firing her guns until hit in her superstructure by another kamikaze. Following a tremendous explosion, she rolls over and sinks in less than a minute with the loss of 168 dead and 52 wounded.

29 MAY
AIR FORCE
Firebombing raids on Japan begin again as 454 B-29 Superfortress bombers, escorted by 101 P-51 Mustang fighters from Iwo Jima Island, Japan, attack Yokohama and destroy the main business district. About nine square miles of the city are in ruins. The Japanese offer stiff fighter defense and shoot down seven bombers and three fighters.

MARINE CORPS
On Okinawa Island, Japan, the 5th Marine Regiment seizes the crest of Shuri Ridge and against light opposition takes Shuri Castle, the heart of the Shuri line defenses. Marine Torpedo Bomber Squadron 131 lands on Ie Shima Island, Ryuku Islands, and begins supporting the Tenth Army.

President Harry S. Truman increases the authorized strength of the Marine Corps to 503,000.

30 MAY
ARMY

Enemy resistance weakens in the XXIV Corps area on Okinawa Island, Japan, as the Japanese withdraw to their main defensive line. The 77th Infantry Division secures three hills that were strong points of the Shuri line. Elements of the division cross into the III Amphibious Corps area to attack 100 Meter Hill. The 96th Infantry Division makes advances along its front, also taking a series of fortified hills that had been part of the enemy's defensive line. On 31 May, the 77th Division occupies the village of Shuri while the 96th Division clears its zone of action and links up with the 1st Marine Division. The 7th Infantry Division secures the hills near Chan against light opposition. Pursuit

Above: *Marine Corps F4U Corsairs take on Japanese fighters in an aerial dog-fight over Rabaul, New Britain Island. ("Rabaul—Fly For Your Life," Robert Taylor © Military Gallery, Ojai, CA)*

Left: *Navy medical corpsmen and several Marines care for the wounded in a front line aid station. ("A Gift of Life From Home," Kerr Eby, Navy Art Collection)*

Opposite, top: *A sentry and his war dog stand guard as night falls on the Okinawa Island, Japan, battlefield. The 40th, 41st, and 45th Army and the 4th and 6th Marine Corps War Dog Platoons serve in the battle for Okinawa. (National Archives)*

begins of the enemy who is retreating to its final defensive line and continues through 6 June.

NAVY
A TBM Avenger torpedo-bomber of Composite Squadron 82 operating from the escort carrier *Anzio* sinks the Japanese submarine *I-361* off Okinawa Island, Japan.

31 MAY
MARINE CORPS
The 1st Marine Division cleans out final enemy resistance in Wana Draw on Okinawa Island, Japan.

1 JUNE
AIR FORCE
During a raid on Japan flown in marginal weather, 458 B-29 Superfortress bombers attack the city of Osaka. Of the 148 fighters assigned to meet the formation, 27 collide when severe turbulence ruins their formation, and only a few dozen fighters meet the bombers as escorts. Ten B-29s do not return from the raid.

MARINE CORPS
The carrier *Gilbert Islands* and its embarked Marine Corps squadrons join the fleet off Okinawa Island, Japan.

The Fleet Marine Force Pacific Supply Service is redesignated Service Command.

2–3 JUNE
MARINE CORPS
Elements of the 8th Marine Regiment occupy the islands of Iheya Shima and Aguni Shima north and

west of Okinawa Island, Japan, respectively, to provide bases for early warning radar.

Below: *A B-24 Liberator bomber takes off from the airstrip at Yontanzan, Okinawa Island, for a mission over mainland Japan. The conquest of Okinawa by July and refurbishment of the airfields there brings American forces to the doorstep of Japan and provides a major staging base for the expected invasion of the main Japanese islands. (U.S. Army)*

Left: *A somber parade of ambulances waits at a dock on Guam Island on 4 June 1945 for the arrival of the Navy hospital ship* Solace, *which is carrying wounded men from Okinawa Island, Japan. Okinawa is one of the bloodiest battles in the Pacific. (National Archives)*

3 JUNE
MARINE CORPS

The Japanese launch a mass kamikaze attack against ships near Okinawa Island, Japan. During the four-day aerial battle, Marine Corps pilots of the Amphibious Task Force claim 35 of the 118 enemy aircraft shot down.

4 JUNE
MARINE CORPS

The 6th Marine Division launches a shore-to-shore amphibious assault against the Oroku Peninsula in southwest Okinawa Island, Japan.

5 JUNE
AIR FORCE

A firebombing attack by 473 B-29 Superfortress bombers burns four square miles of the town of Kobe, Japan. Eleven B-29s are lost on the raid.

NAVY

A typhoon batters the Third Fleet off Okinawa Island, Japan, causing damage to 4 battleships, 8 carriers, 7 cruisers, 11 destroyers, 3 destroyer escorts, and 3 fleet auxiliary ships. Heavy seas collapse the bow section of the flight decks of the carriers *Hornet* and *Bennington*, necessitating the launching of aircraft over the stern until the carriers can be detached for repairs. In addition, the heavy cruiser *Pittsburgh* loses her bow, which is later recovered. Third Fleet commander Admiral William F. Halsey Jr. and Task Force 38 commander Vice Admiral John S. McCain are found negligent in not taking the proper actions to avoid the typhoon.

6 JUNE
MARINE CORPS

The 4th Marine Regiment completes the capture of Naha Airfield on Oroku Peninsula, Okinawa Island, Japan.

7 JUNE
AIR FORCE

The Twentieth Air Force strikes Osaka, Japan, with high explosive bombs and incendiary weapons. The mission is accomplished by radar bombing techniques and destroys approximately 55,000 buildings in the city. Another small group of B-29 Superfortress bombers mine the Shimonoseki Strait between Honshu and Kyushu islands.

Opposite, bottom: *An Army engineer with his bulldozer continues to clear space for more B-29 Super-fortresses in the Mariana Islands. Hundreds of the huge bombers are sent to new bases there for the continuing air offensive against Japan.* (U.S. Air Force)

Right: *The limestone ridges of southern Okinawa Island, Japan, are honeycombed with hundreds of caves and bunkers, which form a main defensive line that the Japanese troops fight desperately to hold.* (U.S. Army)

7–8 JUNE
MARINE CORPS
Marine Aircraft Group 14 moves from Samar Island, Philippine Islands, to Okinawa Island, Japan.

8 JUNE
ARMY/MARINE CORPS/NAVY
As the Tenth Army continues the offensive on Okinawa Island, Japan, Hospital Apprentice First Class Fred F. Lester rushes beyond the front lines to render aid to a wounded Marine. Wounded by enemy fire, which paralyzes him on his right side, Lester nevertheless manages to drag the Marine to safety and refuses aid himself, instead directing the treatment of the wounded man until his own death. Lester receives the Medal of Honor posthumously.

MARINE CORPS
The carrier *Bennington* departs the operational theater around Okinawa Island, Japan, the last fast carrier with embarked Marine Corps squadrons. Marine Fighting Squadrons 112 and 123 had been in action almost continuously with the ship since 16 February.

9 JUNE
AIR FORCE
A force of 110 B-29 Superfortress bombers attack aircraft factories in Akashi, Nagoya, and Narao, Japan. During a mission flown by Eleventh Air Force B-25 Mitchell bombers, one is shot down over the Kamchatka Peninsula, USSR, by Soviet antiaircraft gunners. Another is damaged and crash-lands in Petropavlovsk, USSR. This is the first instance of Soviet shootdown of an American aircraft.

ARMY
On Okinawa Island, Japan, the XXIV Corps begins preparatory attacks for its offensive the next day. The 7th Infantry Division pushes up to the Yuza-Dake Escarpment, a key feature in the Japanese defenses. The main two-division assault begins with tank support the next morning. The 96th Infantry Division drives toward the town of Yuza and is able to get two companies onto the escarpment ridge. The 32d Infantry Regiment, 7th Division uses artillery and flame-throwing tanks to capture a key ridge near Hill 95.

NAVY
Task Group 17.21, a submarine attack group consisting of nine subs and commanded by Commander Earl T. Hydeman, begins operating against Japanese shipping in the Sea of Japan. Through 23 June, U.S. submarines sink 33 Japanese vessels, losing one sub when *Bonefish* goes down after being attacked by a Japanese destroyer and coast defense vessels.

10 JUNE
NAVY
Following bombardment by cruisers and destroyers of Task Group 74.3 (under Rear Admiral Russell S. Berkey) the ships of Rear Admiral Forrest P. Royal's Task Group 78.1 land Australian troops at Brunei Bay, Borneo, Dutch East Indies.

Off Okinawa Island, Japan, a kamikaze narrowly misses the destroyer *William D. Porter,* causing her to burn fiercely. In command of the nearby large support landing craft *LCS(L)-122*, Lieutenant Richard M.

Left: *An M4A3R3 Sherman flame tank directs its deadly stream of liquid fire into the mouth of a Japanese-occupied cave on Okinawa Island, Japan. (U.S. Army)*

Opposite: ("*Japs Feel the Sting of Our AA,*" *Lt. William F. Draper, USNR, Navy Art Collection*)

McCool Jr. places his vessel alongside the stricken destroyer to take off her crew before the destroyer sinks. The following day, when a suicide plane crashes into his ship, McCool is wounded, but musters the strength to personally free men trapped in a compartment. For his actions on these two days, McCool is awarded the Medal of Honor.

11 JUNE
AIR FORCE
Combat aircrews of the 509th Composite Group begin to arrive on Tinian Island, Mariana Islands, with specially modified Silverplate B-29 Superfortress bombers. The modified aircraft—with all gun turrets removed, extra fuel tanks installed, new propellers, and special radar and radio monitoring equipment—are designed for the secret mission of dropping an atomic bomb on Japan, if needed.

MARINE CORPS
As fighting continues on Okinawa Island, Japan, the 1st Marine Division comes up against Kunishi Ridge, the western anchor of the final Japanese defensive line on Kiyamu Peninsula. In a night attack, the 7th Marine Regiment seizes the crest of part of the ridge, though the Japanese retain control of the area all around it for several more days.

Right: *Marines of the 5th Marine Division battle for control of a ridge on Okinawa Island, Japan, in May 1945. (National Archives)*

12 JUNE
ARMY

A night attack on Okinawa Island, Japan, by the 17th Infantry Regiment, 7th Infantry Division takes the Japanese by surprise and breaks through the southeast end of their defenses. The 383d Infantry Regiment, 96th Infantry Division pushes past Yuza, while the 381st Infantry Regiment assaults with three battalions, penetrates enemy fortifications on the escarpment, and occupies positions on it.

13 JUNE
ARMY

On Luzon Island, Philippine Islands, the 37th Infantry Division's commander, Major General Robert S. Beightler, forms an armored column with tanks and a motorized infantry company plus the 145th Infantry Regiment, and sends the task force out of the recently secured Orioung Pass to capture Cordon and Santiago.

MARINE CORPS

On Okinawa Island, Japan, the 6th Marine Division completes the reduction of enemy positions on Oroku Peninsula. In another night attack, elements of the 1st Marine Regiment take additional parts of Kunishi Ridge.

15 JUNE
AIR FORCE

Forty-four B-29 Superfortress bombers attack Osaka, Japan, in the last firebombing raid against a large Japanese city.

MARINE CORPS

The 8th Marine Regiment comes ashore on Okinawa Island, Japan, and is attached to the 1st Marine Division.

16–20 JUNE
ARMY

On Okinawa Island, Japan, the Shuri defensive line is broken. Continuing its assault on the Yuza-Dake hills on Okinawa, the 96th Infantry Division captures the highest peak and begins clearing the caves and tunnels on its slopes. On 17 June, the 7th Infantry Division seizes Hills 153 and 115. The final pockets of stubborn resistance are eliminated as they are encountered, and the advance of the 96th and 7th Infantry Divisions continues toward the end of the island. The 7th Infantry Division captures the Japanese headquarters on 20 June.

Above: *A Navy band and friends wait for a submarine returning from a long combat patrol. ("Patrol's End," Paul Sample, Army Art Collection, U.S. Army Center of Military History)*

16 JUNE
MARINE CORPS
The 1st Marine Division captures most of the rest of Kunishi Ridge on Okinawa.

17–18 JUNE
AIR FORCE
Incendiary attacks against a series of small Japanese cities begin when more than 450 B-29 Superfortress bombers target Omuta, Hamamatsu, Yokkaichi, and Kagoshima. Additional B-29s mine the waters around Kobe and the Shimonoseki Strait. Night and day intruder missions begin, flown by Seventh Air Force P-47 Thunderbolt fighters and P-61 Black Widow night fighters over Kyushu Island and the Ryukyu Islands. A dozen such missions are accomplished during June.

17 JUNE
MARINE CORPS
On Okinawa Island, Japan, the 6th Marine Division moves up to assume responsibility for the right half of the 1st Marine Division zone of action. The XXIV Corps captures the commanding ground along the Yuza Dake Escarpment on the eastern side of the Kiyamu Peninsula.

Marine Fighting Squadron 513 joins the carrier *Vella Gulf* at San Diego, California.

18 JUNE
ARMY/MARINE CORPS

Prior to dawn, the 8th Marine Regiment moves into position and assumes responsibility for the right half of the 1st Marine Division front line on Okinawa Island, Japan. While observing the regiment in action that morning, Army Lieutenant General Simon B. Buckner Jr., commander of the Tenth Army, is killed by Japanese fire. He is the most senior U.S. Army officer to die in action in the Pacific. Major General Roy Geiger assumes command of the Tenth Army, becoming the first Marine Corps officer to command a field army in combat. Geiger is promoted to Lieutenant General the next day. With the aid of tanks, the 2d Battalion, 5th Marine Regiment wipes out the last enemy resistance on Kunishi Ridge.

19–20 JUNE
AIR FORCE

Twentieth Air Force targets Toyohashi, Fukuoka, and Shizuoka, Japan, with 480 B-29 Superfortress bombers. Mining operations also continue throughout Japanese waters.

21 JUNE
ALL SERVICES

Organized resistance in the III Amphibious Corps' zone ends when the 1st Marine Division takes Hill 81 and the 6th Marine Division reaches the southernmost point of Okinawa Island, Japan. Kamikaze attacks sink one vessel and damage four others. All told, in 89 days at sea off Okinawa, the U.S. Navy loses 36 vessels sunk and 243 damaged. Over 4,900 sailors give their lives and 4,824 are wounded.

The Tenth Army commander, Lieutenant General Geiger, declares Okinawa Island, Japan, secured. The American flag is officially raised over the island. The next day, the Japanese commander and his chief of staff commit suicide. American losses in this campaign of the war have been great—49,151 battle casualties, with 12,520 killed or missing and 36,361 wounded.

22 JUNE
AIR FORCE

Far East Air Force bombers continue to pound Balikpapan, Borneo, Dutch East Indies, in preparation for Allied landings scheduled for early July.

Nearly 300 Twentieth Air Force B-29 Superfortress bombers target several aircraft plants and the naval arsenal at Kure, Japan.

23 JUNE
ARMY

In the Philippine Islands, the reinforced 1st Battalion, 511th Airborne Infantry (Task Force Gypsy) parachutes behind enemy lines to link up with Philippine guerrilla units near Aparri, Luzon Island, and push toward the 37th Infantry Division.

Opposite, bottom: *Army Lieutenant General Simon B. Buckner, Tenth Army commander, walks with Marine Corps Major General Roy S. Geiger, III Amphibious Corps commander, along a path on Okinawa Island, Japan. On 18 June 1945, Buckner is killed by a Japanese shell and Geiger takes command of the Tenth Army. (National Archives)*

Right: *Marine Corps stretcher bearers use a smokescreen to cover their retrieval of a wounded comrade under Japanese fire. (National Archives)*

ARMY/MARINE CORPS

Lieutenant General Joseph W. Stilwell arrives on Okinawa Island, Japan, and assumes command of the Tenth Army from Lieutenant General Roy S. Geiger who becomes commander, Fleet Marine Force, Pacific. The 1st and 6th Marine Divisions participate in a mop up of southern Okinawa, in which the five assault divisions turn about and slowly begin to sweep over the ground they have taken in preceding weeks. In the evening, the Japanese launch another wave of banzai attacks.

26 JUNE
AIR FORCE

More than 450 Twentieth Air Force B-29 Superfortress bombers attack aircraft plants, light metal works, weapons arsenals, oil refineries, and the city of Tsu, Japan.

ARMY

In Burma, the Mars Task Force is officially disbanded with the inactivation of the 475th Infantry Regiment and the 124th Cavalry Regiment. The veterans of the task force have already been scattered to the Office of Strategic Services, the Service of Supply, or to the Chinese Combat Command Chinese (under Lieutenant General Albert C. Wedemeyer) to provide training, supply, and tactical advice to Chinese Army units.

27 JUNE
ARMY

On Luzon Island, Philippine Islands, the 129th Infantry Regiment, 37th Infantry Division captures the last major towns still in the hands of the Japanese, including Aparri.

NAVY

A PV-1 Ventura patrol-bomber of Patrol Bombing Squadron 142 sinks the Japanese submarine *I-16* east of Saipan Island, Mariana Islands.

28–29 JUNE
AIR FORCE

Incendiary bombardment by 487 B-29 Superfortress bombers damages the Japanese towns of Okayama, Sasebo, Moji, and Nobeoka.

30 JUNE
AIR FORCE

The 509th Composite Group begins training missions operating out of Tinian Island, Mariana Islands. Each crew is expected to fly five or six practice flights to familiarize themselves with the Pacific Theater. Many will drop large practice bombs, called "pumpkins," to simulate the effect of a 10,000-pound bomb dropped from their modified B-29 Superfortresses.

ARMY

The 24th Infantry Division captures Mindanao Island, Philippine Islands. The X Corps will continue mopping up there until the end of the war, but all major tasks in the main islands of the Philippine Islands are completed.

MARINE CORPS/NAVY

The mop-up of southern Okinawa Island, Japan, is completed. Marine Corps casualties during the campaign are 3,443 dead and 16,017 wounded. Losses among Navy personnel serving with Marine Corps units are 118 killed and 442 wounded. The strength of the Marine Corps on active duty is 37,067 officers and 437,613 enlisted.

1 JULY
AIR FORCE

Far East Air Force B-24 Liberator bombers continue to attack Balikpapan, Borneo, Dutch East Indies, as the Australians carry out amphibious landings there. B-25 Mitchell and B-24 bombers support the landings by hitting nearby enemy airfields. These attacks continue into the next day as Australian forces capture the island and its oil facilities.

The Twentieth Air Force launches more than 530 B-29 Superfortress bombers with incendiary bombs against the Japanese cities of Ube, Kure, Shimonoseki, and Kumamoto. Mines are also dropped in Japanese waters.

Above: *In June, the monsoon rains drench Okinawa Island, Japan, making life on the front lines even more miserable. ("Messing in the Open in Okinawa," John A. Rudge, Army Art Collection, U.S. Army Center of Military History)*

Below: *Even four-wheel-drive trucks have difficulty moving on the muddy and flooded roads on Okinawa Island, Japan. (U.S. Army)*

Above: *An M1 155mm howitzer fires on Japanese troops blocking the Balete Pass and delaying the U.S. advance on northern Luzon Island in the Philippine Islands. (U.S. Army)*

Below: *A Soldier cautiously searches a surrendering Japanese soldier outside the cave where the enemy has been hiding. (National Archives)*

ARMY

The campaign in Luzon Island, Philippine Islands, officially ends at midnight. The Eighth Army takes control of the XXIV Corps for the final mop-up, with the 6th, 32d, 37th, and 38th Infantry Divisions. The Sixth Army starts to regroup for Operation OLYMPIC, the invasion of Kyushu Island, Japan.

MARINE CORPS

Marine F4U Corsair fighters escort the first Army Air Forces medium bomber attack on the Japanese home islands since the carrier-launched Doolittle Raid of April 1942. The 8th Marine Regiment departs Okinawa Island, Japan, to rejoin the 2d Marine Division on Saipan Island, Mariana Islands.

MARINE CORPS/NAVY

In the final amphibious assault on Borneo, Dutch East Indies, Rear Admiral Albert G. Noble's Task Group 78.2 lands the Australian 7th Division at Balikpapan. Marine Corps pilots and Marine Air Support Group 48 headquarters on the carriers *Block Island* and *Gilbert Islands* support the landing.

2 JULY
ARMY

The U.S. Tenth Army (under Lieutenant General Joseph W. Stilwell) mops up remaining Japanese defenders and brings the costly campaign in the

Right: *A flight of B-29 Superfortresses passes Mount Fuji during a mission to attack Japan. The bombers use the mountain as a landmark to guide them. (U.S. Air Force)*

Ryukyu Islands to a close. On 1 August, Stilwell is promoted to four-star rank, the last of 17 Army officers promoted to full general in World War II.

MARINE CORPS
The III Amphibious Corps is released from mop-up operations on Okinawa Island, Japan.

NAVY
In the first employment of bombardment rockets by a submarine, *Barb* attacks shore installations at Kaiyho Island in the Kurile Islands.

3 JULY
AIR FORCE
Fighters from the Fifth Air Force fly their first missions over Japan. The Twentieth Air Force launches incendiary attacks with 560 B-29 Superfortress bombers against the cities of Kochi, Himeji, Takamatsu, and Tokushima, Japan.

4 JULY
MARINE CORPS
The 6th Marine Division begins moving from Okinawa Island, Japan, to Guam Island, Mariana Islands. The carrier *Cape Gloucester* and her two embarked Marine squadrons arrive off Okinawa.

6 JULY
AIR FORCE
Lieutenant General George E. Stratemeyer officially assumes command of the Army Air Forces, China Theater.

The Twentieth Air Force launches 517 B-29 Superfortress bombers to firebomb the Japanese cities of Chiba, Akashi, Shimizu, and Kofu.

9 JULY
AIR FORCE
The Twentieth Air Force launches B-29 Superfortress bombers to attack Sendai, Sakai, Gifu, and Wakayama, Japan. An additional 60 bombers strike the oil refinery at Yokkaichi.

10 JULY
NAVY
The carriers of Task Force 38 (under Vice Admiral John S. McCain) launch air strikes against Japanese airfields around Tokyo, Japan.

12 JULY
AIR FORCE
The Twentieth Air Force sends 453 B-29 Superfortress bombers to firebomb the Japanese cities of Utsonomiya, Ichinomiya, Tsuruga, and Uwajima. Another 53 bombers attack the petroleum center at Kawasaki.

Above: *Navy carrier planes attack Japanese cruisers in Kure Harbor at Honshu Island, Japan. (U.S. Navy)*

Below: *A Navy gunner on a PT boat stays ready behind his twin .50 caliber machine guns and keeps a lookout for Japanese planes. (National Archives)*

ARMY
The 1st Battalion, 21st Infantry Regiment makes an amphibious landing on Mindanao Island, Philippine Islands, in the Sarangani Bay area as part of an operation to clear Japanese holdouts in that area. There is no opposition.

13 JULY
MARINE CORPS
Many III Amphibious Corps units begin re-deployment from Okinawa Island, Japan, to Guam Island, Mariana Islands. The 1st Marine Division, III Amphibious Corps Artillery, and the 1st Armored Amphibian Battalion remain on Okinawa and go into rehabilitation camps on the Motobu Peninsula.

14 JULY
AIR FORCE
The Seventh Air Force is officially assigned to the Far East Air Forces. The aircraft will be completely moved to Okinawa Island, Japan, by 28 July.

MARINE CORPS
The Amphibious Task Force is dissolved and all Marine Corps aircraft in the Okinawa, Japan, area revert to control of the 2d Marine Aircraft Wing.

14–15 JULY
NAVY
In attacks against enemy shipping in northern Honshu and Hokkaido Islands, Japan, aircraft from

Task Force 38 sink 46 enemy vessels. At the same time battleships, cruisers, and destroyers of Task Units 34.8.1 and 34.8.2 (Rear Admiral John F. Shafroth and Rear Admiral Oscar P. Badger, respectively) bombard of Kamaishi, on Honshu Island, and Muroran on Hokkaido Island. Attacks on the Japanese home islands continue into August.

15 JULY
MARINE CORPS
The III Amphibious Corps is detached from the Tenth Army and comes under control of Fleet Marine Force Pacific. The corps headquarters begins displacing to Guam Island, Mariana Islands.

16 JULY
ALL SERVICES
At the Trinity site in near Alamogordo, New Mexico, the first atomic bomb, sometimes called "the gadget," is successfully tested. The weapon produces a yield of 19 kilotons of TNT. The success is reported to President Harry S. Truman, who is attending the Potsdam Conference in Germany with British Prime Minister Winston S. Churchill and Soviet Premier Joseph Stalin.

AIR FORCE
General Carl A. Spaatz takes command of the U.S. Army Strategic Air Force in the Pacific, while Major General Curtis E. LeMay assumes command of the Twentieth Air Force (in actuality the XXI Bomber Command since the inactivation of the XX Bomber Command). Until this date the Twentieth Air Force has been under the direct control of the Joint Chiefs of Staff through General of the Army Henry H. Arnold.

NAVY
A TBM Avenger torpedo-bomber of Composite Squadron 13 from the escort carrier *Anzio*, operating with the destroyer escort *Lawrence C. Taylor*, sinks the Japanese submarine *I-13* off Yokohama, Japan.

16 JULY
AIR FORCE
The Twentieth Air Force launches 466 B-29 Superfortress bombers to firebomb Numazu, Oita, Kuwana, and Hiratsuka, Japan.

19 JULY
AIR FORCE
Along with minelaying operations and attacks on Japanese oil facilities at Amagasaki, 470 B-29 Superfortress bombers firebomb the cities of Fukui, Hitachi, Chosi, and Okazaki, Japan.

20 JULY
AIR FORCE
The 509th Composite Group begins precision bombing practice over previously bombed Japanese cities. The practice missions, also flown on 24, 26, and 29 July, are intended to familiarize the crews with

Right: *An SB2C Helldiver comes home to the carrier* Hornet *after a mission to attack Japanese ships in the China Sea. (National Archives)*

Left: The battleships Missouri *and* Iowa *steam side-by-side off the coast of Japan. (Naval Historical Center)*

Opposite: *The secret Manhattan Project achieves success with the explosion of an atomic device in the desert at Alamagordo, New Mexico, on 16 July 1945. A coded message is sent to President Harry S. Truman, who is meeting with other Allied leaders in Potsdam, Germany. (National Archives)*

tactics that will be used during actual atomic missions. An additional reason for these practice missions is to allow the Japanese to see small formations of B-29 Superfortress bombers overhead during daylight hours, as if they were reconnaissance missions.

ARMY
In the last combat amphibious operation of the war, Company F, 34th Infantry Regiment, 24th Infantry Division lands on Balut Island in Sarangani Bay,

Philippine Islands. Its mission is to locate and eliminate holdout Japanese defenders; only a few are found.

24 JULY
AIR FORCE
Using high-explosive weapons, 570 B-29 Superfortress bombers strike Japan, hitting aircraft factories at Hando, Nagoya, and Takarazuka. Metal works at Osaka and the cities of Tsu and Kawana are also attacked.

Right: Crewmen of a Navy seaplane tender signal four PBM-3 Mars seaplanes to taxi into mooring positions. ("Making the Buoy," Joseph Hirsch, Navy Art Collection)

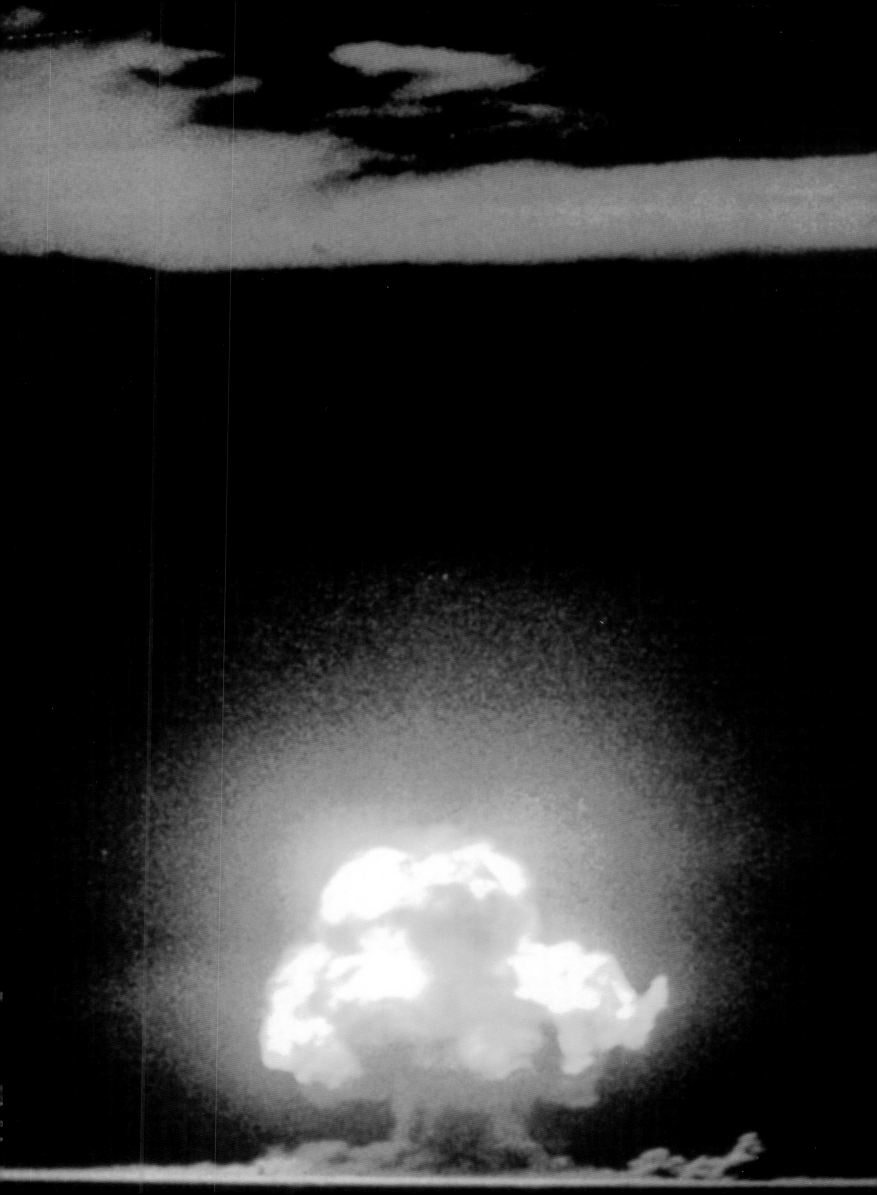

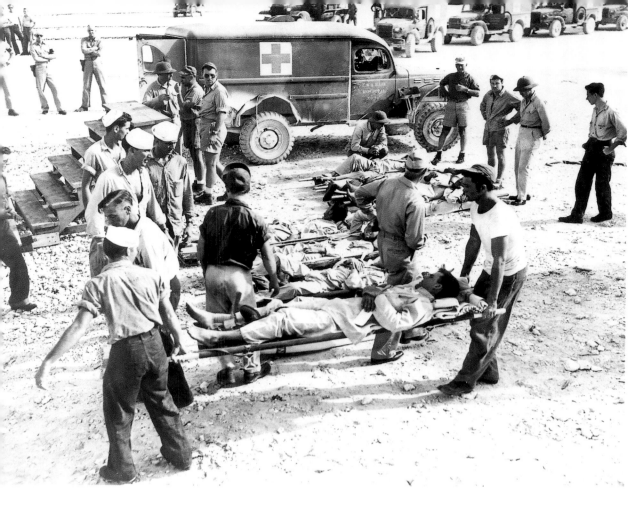

Left: Survivors of the heavy cruiser Indianapolis, *sunk by Japanese torpedoes on 30 July 1945, are carried to waiting ambulances on Guam Island. (Naval Historical Center)*

Below: A landing signal officer uses his glowing paddles to give landing instructions to pilots approaching the carrier's deck. ("Night Landing Signals," Lt. Dwight C. Shepler, USNR, Navy Art Collection)

NAVY

In strikes against Japanese airfields and the Kure naval base, pilots from Task Force 38 sink the battleship-carrier *Hyuga*, heavy cruiser *Tone*, and two other vessels. Sixteen Japanese ships are damaged in the strikes.

Off Luzon Island, Philippine Islands, the destroyer escort *Underhill* is scuttled after being damaged by "Kaitens"—manned torpedoes—from the Japanese submarine *I-53*.

24–26 JULY
MARINE CORPS

Embarked Marine Corps squadrons on board the carrier *Vella Gulf* fly sorties against Pagan and Rota Islands north of Guam Island, Mariana Islands.

26 JULY
ALL SERVICES

The Potsdam Conference in Germany results in an ultimatum for Japan. The "Big Three"—President Harry S. Truman, British Prime Minister Winston Churchill, and Soviet Premier Joseph Stalin—direct Japan to surrender or face "utter destruction."

AIR FORCE

The components of the first atomic weapon—"Little Boy"—arrive and are unloaded at Tinian Island. This small island in the Mariana Islands is the home base for the 509th Composite Group, which will drop the new weapons. Firebombing of Japan continues when 350 B-29 Superfortress bombers launch attacks on the cities of Matsuyama, Tokuyama, and Omuta.

28 JULY
NAVY

In strikes against the Kure naval base in Japan and shipping in the Inland Sea, carrier aircraft from Task Force 38 sink the battleship *Haruna*, battleship-carrier *Ise*, and 19 other ships and craft. Off Okinawa Island, Japan, the destroyer *Callaghan* is hit by a kamikaze. She becomes the last ship sunk by the "divine wind" during World War II.

Right: *Modified to carry atomic bombs called Silverplates, the special detachment of Boeing B-29 Superfortresses from the 509th Bomb Group flies over Tinian Island, Mariana Islands. (NASM)*

28–29 JULY
AIR FORCE

With no word of surrender from the Japanese, 471 B-29 Superfortress bombers launch to firebomb the cities of Tsu, Aomori, Ichinomiya, Ujiyamada, Ogaki, and Uwajima. Seventy-six additional B-29s hit the oil refinery at Shimotsu.

29 JULY
AIR FORCE

Far East Air Force B-24 Liberator and B-25 Mitchell bombers from Okinawa, Japan, and P-47 Thunderbolt fighters from Ie Shima Island, Ryuku Islands, strike a multitude of targets on the Japanese home islands. A-26 invader bombers target the naval base and engine works at Nagasaki, Japan.

MARINE CORPS

The medium bombers of Marine Bomber Squadron 612 arrive on Okinawa Island, Japan, and begin flying anti-shipping missions off Kyushu Island, Japan.

30 JULY
NAVY

After delivering top-secret components for the atomic bomb to Tinian Island, Mariana Islands, the heavy cruiser *Indianapolis* steams for Leyte Island, Philippine Islands. That evening a torpedo fired from the Japanese submarine *I-58* sinks the ship in just 12 minutes. Over 800 members of the crew are able to abandon ship, but the cruiser's last distress signals are not heard. Aircraft do not spot the survivors until 2 August, and by that time sharks and the elements have reduced their number to 316 emaciated men. Captain Charles B. McVay III is convicted by court-martial for "suffering a vessel to be hazarded through negligence" by failing to zigzag. He is the only ship captain to receive such punishment during World War II.

1 AUGUST
AIR FORCE

In the single largest operational day for Twentieth Air Force B-29 bombers during World War II, 836 B-29 Superfortresses are launched against Japan to firebomb the cities of Hachioji, Toyama, Nagaoka, and Mito; bomb the Kawasaki oil plant; and drop mines in the Shimonoseki Strait.

MARINE CORPS

Most of the 2d Marine Aircraft Wing passes to the control of the Army's Far East Air Forces.

The carrier *Cape Gloucester* and her embarked Marine Corps squadrons sail from Okinawa Island, Japan, for the East China Sea to cover minesweeping operations and launch strikes near Shanghai, China.

Marine Aircraft Group 32's four dive-bomber squadrons cease tactical operations in the Philippine Islands and prepare for return to the United States.

3 AUGUST
AIR FORCE
Fighter aircraft of the VII Fighter Command stationed on Iwo Jima, Japan, fly 100 sorties over Tokyo, Japan, striking airfields and rail equipment.

5 AUGUST
AIR FORCE
Far East Air Force aircraft strike targets from Luzon Island, Philippine Islands, to Kyushu Island, Japan, with impunity. More than 330 aircraft participate in this far-reaching aerial offensive. Sortie numbers will increase each day for the next 10 days.

Incendiary raids continue against Japan as 470 B-29 Superfortress bombers launch to attack the cities of Saga, Mae Bashi, Imabari, and Nishinomiya-Mikage. Another 100 B-29s bomb the coal processing plant at Ube.

The VII Fighter Command is officially assigned to Twentieth Air Force for the remainder of the war.

2 AUGUST
AIR FORCE
Major General Nathan F. Twining assumes command of the Twentieth Air Force. Major General Curtis E. LeMay moves to be Chief of Staff for U.S. Army Strategic Air Forces in the Pacific. Twining will rise to the rank of full general and become Chief of Staff of the U.S. Air Force in 1953. In 1957, he becomes the first Air Force officer to be the Chairman of the Joint Chiefs of Staff.

6 AUGUST
AIR FORCE/NAVY
Colonel Paul W. Tibbets Jr., Commander of the 509th Composite Group, pilots the B-29 Superfortress bomber "Enola Gay" (named after his mother) from Tinian Island, Mariana Islands, to Hiroshima, Japan. Two additional B-29s, the "Great Artiste" and aircraft number 91, accompany Enola Gay to observe the

Left: *The crew and other members of the 509th Bomb Group gather under the nose of the "Enola Gay" at their base on Tinian Island, Mariana Islands. (NASM)*

Opposite, top: *"Little Boy," the first operational atomic bomb, is prepared for loading into the bomb bay of the B-29 "Enola Gay." (NASM)*

Right: *The center of the city of Hiroshima, Japan, after the detonation of the atomic bomb on 6 August 1945. (National Archives)*

operation, drop measuring equipment, and take photographs. Enola Gay's weapons officer, Navy Captain William S. Parsons, arms the "Little Boy" atomic bomb. The gun-type, uranium weapon detonates approximately 2,000 feet above the ground in the center of the city, almost precisely over the aiming point. Within moments, the bomb destroys much of Hiroshima, immediately killing between 70,000 and 80,000 of its inhabitants. Among those killed in the atomic blast at Hiroshima are two Navy prisoners of war being held in the city, Lieutenant (junior grade) Raymond Porter and Aviation Radioman Third Class Normand Brissette, a Bombing Squadron 87 crew shot down in late July. Meanwhile, about 100 Twentieth Air Force P-51 Mustang fighters attack Tokyo from their bases on Iwo Jima. In the U.S. America's "Ace of Aces," Major Richard I. Bong, dies when the F-80 Shooting Star jet he is flying stalls on takeoff. He ejects but is too low for his parachute to fully deploy.

NAVY
The submarine *Bullhead* sinks in the Java Sea, apparently after being struck by Japanese aircraft.

7 AUGUST
AIR FORCE
B-29 Superfortress bombers begin targeting Kyushu Island, Japan, accompanied by Far East Air Force P-47 Thunderbolt fighters.

8 AUGUST
AIR FORCE
Far East Air Force and Twentieth Air Force aircraft relentlessly pound Japanese targets on Kyushu Island,

while additional B-29 Superfortress bombers attack Yawata with incendiary bombs. Later that day, 60 B-29s attack targets in Tokyo, while during the night another incendiary raid is accomplished over Fukuyama.

9 AUGUST
AIR FORCE/NAVY
Major Charles W. Sweeney pilots the B-29 Superfortress bomber "Bockscar" from Tinian Island, Mariana Islands, to Kokura, Japan, the intended target for the second atomic bomb, but poor weather prevents visual bombing. Sweeney proceeds to the secondary target, Nagasaki, where weather is also poor, but a cloud break allows a visual attack. Commander Frederick W. Ainsworth is the air crew weapons officer and he arms the bomb. The "Fat Man," an implosion-type, plutonium weapon, is dropped over the city and detonates approximately 2,000 feet above the target area, creating nearly double the energy of the "Little Boy" bomb. Approximately 35,000 occupants of Nagasaki are killed instantly, which is fewer than might have been the case had Sweeney's bomb fallen more accurately on the aiming point.

MARINE CORPS
PBJ patrol-bombers of Marine Bombing Squadrons 413, 423, and 443 conduct the last Marine Corps air strikes on Rabaul, New Britain Island.

10 AUGUST
ALL SERVICES
The Japanese government offers to surrender with the condition that the emperor would remain in power.

Above: *The "Fat Man" atomic bomb is dropped on Nagasaki, Japan, on 9 August 1945. Unlike the first bomb, which used uranium, the more powerful "Fat Man" is plutonium-based. (National Archives)*

Below: *The cloud over Nagasaki, Japan, following the explosion of "Fat Man" over the city. (National Archives)*

Opposite*: The gunners of a B-32 Dominator score the last air kill of the war when Japanese fighters attack their plane on 18 August 1945. ("Last Aerial Combat of World War II," William Reynolds, USAF Art Collection)*

On 12 August, the Allies reply to the Japanese offer stating the emperor could remain in a ceremonial capacity only. The Japanese do not reply, and air raids against Japan resume on 13 August.

AIR FORCE
During a 95-plane B-29 Superfortress bomber strike on Amagasaki, Japan, a record average bomb load per plane of 20,648 pounds is delivered to the target.

MARINE CORPS
Fleet Marine Force Pacific directs the 6th Marine Division to provide a regimental combat team to the Third Fleet for possible occupation duty in Japan. On 11 August, a Fleet Landing Force headquarters is formed with a Marine Corps staff for future occupation duty. The III Amphibious Corps makes preliminary plans for Task Force Able, to consist of an infantry regiment, an amphibian tractor company, and a medical company.

12 AUGUST
MARINE CORPS
Marine Torpedo Bomber Squadron 144 goes on board *Salerno Bay* in San Diego, California.

13 AUGUST
AIR FORCE
The Eleventh Air Force flies its final combat mission of the war. Six B-24 Liberator bombers attack the staging area at Kashiwabara, Japan, by radar bombing.

MARINE CORPS
Marine Corps aircraft make their last raid on the Japanese garrison on Wake Island.

14 AUGUST
AIR FORCE
The final B-29 Superfortress bomber missions are flown against targets throughout Japan. Some 400 bombers accompanied by P-51 Mustang fighters drop mines and strike six cities with conventional bombs. A record total number of effective aircraft sorties—754 bombers and 169 fighters—are in the air. As the P-51s return to Iwo Jima Island, Japan, they strike airfields near Nagoya. These are the last U.S. fighter attacks flown against Japan. The final night incendiary raid is flown by more than 160 B-29 bombers, which attack Kumagaya and Isezaki. A mission launched from the Mariana Islands to attack the Nippon Oil Company in Tsuchizakiminato is the longest round-trip, unstaged mission flown during the war, covering 3,650 miles.

Left: *An American B-25 Mitchell bombers escort a specially marked G4M Betty bomber carrying a Japanese surrender delegation on the first leg of their journey to meet the Allied staff of General of the Army Douglas MacArthur in Manila, Luzon Island, Philippine Islands. (Jeffery Ethell Collection)*

Below: *A released prisoner of war recovers on board the hospital ship* Benevolence *after months of captivity. (Naval Historical Center)*

Opposite: *Soldiers at a Red Cross club in Paris celebrate the surrender of Japan. (National Archives)*

NAVY

The submarine *Spikefish* sinks the Japanese submarine *I-373* southeast of Shanghai, China.

15 AUGUST
ALL SERVICES

In a radio broadcast to the people of Japan, Emperor Hirohito announces the unconditional surrender of the Japanese Empire. President Harry S. Truman

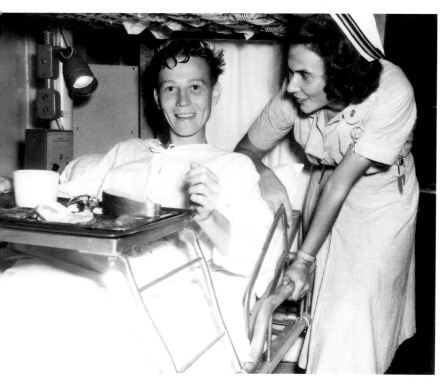

announces that a cease fire is in effect with Japan. He also appoints General of the Army Douglas MacArthur as Supreme Commander Allied Powers, with authority to accept the surrender of Japan on behalf of the United States, the Soviet Union, Great Britain, and the Republic of China. The formal surrender ceremony is set for 2 September. The 11th Airborne Division (under Major General Joseph M. Swing) moves by air from the Philippine Islands to Okinawa Island, Japan, to be ready for rapid transfer to Japan.

18 AUGUST
AIR FORCE

Two B-32 Dominator bombers fly a reconnaissance mission over Tokyo, Japan, and are attacked by more than a dozen Japanese fighters. During the attack, one U.S. crewman is killed and two more wounded by the fighters' guns. The Dominator crews shoot down two of the attackers and damage others. The aircraft are able to land at a base in Okinawa Island, Japan. This is the final air combat action against Japan by American forces.

19 AUGUST
AIR FORCE

The Japanese surrender delegation lands on Ie Shima Island, Ryuku Islands, and is flown by an Army Air Forces C-54 Skymaster transport to Manila, Luzon Island, Philippine Islands, to meet with General of the

Army Douglas MacArthur, to receive surrender instructions.

ARMY
In the Philippine Islands, the 27th Infantry Division continues the collection and processing of Japanese prisoners until November, when it leaves for the U.S. to demobilize after 41 months of overseas service. The 31st Infantry Division (under Major General Clarence A. Martin) takes the surrender of all Japanese forces remaining on Mindanao Island.

MARINE CORPS
Task Force 31 is formed on Guam Island, Mariana Islands, for the mission of occupying Japan. The headquarters of 1st Marine Aircraft Wing and Marine Aircraft Group 61 complete their movement to the Philippine Islands.

20 AUGUST
AIR FORCE/ARMY
American Office of Strategic Services agents parachute into northeast Manchuria to rescue prisoners from a Japanese camp about 100 miles from Mukden. Among those rescued are Lieutenant General Jonathan M. Wainwright, the last

commander of American forces in the Philippine Islands, as well as four participants in the April 1942 Doolittle Raid who had been held prisoner since then.

MARINE CORPS
The reinforced 4th Marine Regiment joins Task Force 31 on Guam Island, Mariana Islands.

21 AUGUST
NAVY
In the last surface action of World War II, two Chinese junks—commanded by U.S. Navy Lieutenant Livingston Swentzel Jr. and manned by Americans and Chinese guerrillas—are attacked by a Japanese junk between Hainan and Shanghai, China. The Chinese vessels, their crews firing bazookas and machine guns and lobbing grenades, soundly defeat the Japanese junk. Swentzel receives the Navy Cross for his actions during the engagement.

23 AUGUST
MARINE CORPS
Aircraft Fleet Marine Force assigns Marine Aircraft Group 31 on Okinawa Island, Japan, as the air component of the Marine Corps occupation force for Japan.

Above: *Having brought Japanese harbor pilots from shore, the destroyer* Nicholas *goes alongside the battleship* Missouri *to transfer the Japanese so the battleship can safely move into Tokyo Bay for the surrender ceremony. ("Triumph and Peace," Tom Freeman)*

Below: *Japanese negotiators meet on 19–20 August with Allied staff in Manila, Luzon Island, Philippine Islands, where General of the Army Douglas MacArthur, Supreme Commander for the Allied Powers in the Pacific, has his headquarters. Terms for the surrender of all Japanese forces and occupation of Japan are presented. (Carl Mydans, Time-Life)*

27 AUGUST
AIR FORCE
Twentieth Air Force B-29 Superfortress bombers drop supplies to Allied prisoners of war held in Japan, Korea, and China. The first drop is made into Weihsien Camp near Peking, China. Over the next month, more than 900 sorties are flown and 4,470 tons of supplies are dropped to more than 150 camps. About 63,000 prisoners are still alive throughout the theater.

MARINE CORPS
The forward echelon of Marine Bomber Squadron 611 departs the Philippine Islands for Peleliu Island, Palau Islands, to join 4th Marine Aircraft Wing there.

NAVY
Ships of the Third Fleet (under Admiral William F. Halsey Jr.) enter Sagomi Wan outside the entrance to Tokyo Bay, Japan.

28 AUGUST
AIR FORCE/ARMY
After a two-delay delay due to a typhoon in the Ryukyu Islands, the 11th Airborne Division is airlifted into Atsugi airfield near Yokohama, Japan. It is quickly followed by the 27th Infantry Division

(under Major General George W. Griner Jr.) as the Army Air Force assembles C-54 Skymaster transport planes.

MARINE CORPS/NAVY
The ships of Task Force 31 enter Tokyo Bay, Japan, and anchor off the naval base at Yokosuka.

29 AUGUST
AIR FORCE
While a B-29 Superfortress drops supplies to allied former prisoners in Korea, a Soviet fighter shoots it down.

MARINE CORPS
Plans are issued for the III Amphibious Corps to move to northern China, with a tentative departure date of 15 September.

29 AUGUST
NAVY
Landing craft arrive at Omori, the first prisoner of war camp in Japan liberated by the Allies.

30 AUGUST
ARMY
Lieutenant General Robert L. Eichelberger arrives at Atsugi airfield near Yokohama, Japan, with advance elements of his U.S. Eighth Army.

MARINE CORPS
The 4th Marines, Fleet Marine Landing Force (a three-battalion regiment composed of the 2,000 men in the fleet's Marine Corps detachments), U.S. and British sailors, and Royal Marines go ashore at Yokosuka, Japan.

31 AUGUST
MARINE CORPS
The Marine Corps is at its peak strength of the war (and all time) with a total of 485,833 officers and men. The Headquarters and Service Battalion of Fleet Marine Force Pacific is disbanded. In Japan, a company of the 3d Battalion, 4th Marine Regiment lands at Tateyama Naval Air Station at the mouth of Tokyo Bay.

1 SEPTEMBER
ARMY
General Douglas MacArthur arrives in Japan and is escorted to quarters at the New Grand Hotel in Yokohama.

2 SEPTEMBER
ALL SERVICES
The war in the Pacific ends. Allied and Japanese delegations sign the official surrender documents on the deck of the battleship *Missouri*, which is anchored in Tokyo Bay, Japan. General of the Army Douglas MacArthur is the senior Allied representative. Among the dozens of American and Allied servicemen and other officers present are Fleet Admiral Chester W. Nimitz and recently released prisoners of war, including Lieutenant General Jonathan M. Wainwright, who is also informed that he has been awarded the Medal of Honor. Massive formations of Navy, Marine Corps,

Right: *Following acceptance of the terms, the formal surrender documents are signed on 2 September 1945 on the deck of the battleship* Missouri, *while it is anchored in Tokyo Bay.* (National Archives)

Left: *A mixed crowd of American and Japanese reporters interviews General of the Army Douglas MacArthur following his landing at Atsugi Airport, Japan, on 1 September 1945. (National Archives)*

Opposite, top: *Soldiers of the 81st Infantry Division make a peaceful landing at Aomori, Japan, to begin their role as occupation troops. (National Archives)*

and Army Air Forces planes over-fly the Allied fleet in the bay. After the ceremony, films of the event are transferred to a waiting C-54 Skymaster, which then makes a record flight from Tokyo to Washington, D.C. The flight takes 31 hours and 25 minutes, but because of crossing the international dateline, the plane lands on the same calendar day it departed Japan.

3 SEPTEMBER
ARMY
Fresh from the surrender ceremonies in Tokyo Bay, Japan, Lieutenant General Jonathan M. Wainwright takes the surrender of General Tomoyuki Yamashita, commander of the Japanese Fourteenth Area Army, at Baguio, Philippine Islands. Yamashita is later tried by an American Military Court in Manila, Luzon Island.

He is found guilty of permitting atrocities and other high crimes, including the Palawan Massacre, and is executed by hanging on 23 February 1946.

4 SEPTEMBER
AIR FORCE
Two Eleventh Air Force B-24 Liberator bombers are intercepted by Soviet fighter planes during a high-altitude reconnaissance mission, foreshadowing similar events which will take place during the Cold War over the next five decades. All Eleventh Air Force missions are cancelled two days later.

MARINE CORPS/NAVY
A force of Marines and Seabees moves onto Rota Island, Mariana Islands, and begins repairing its

airstrip. The Japanese garrison on Wake Island formally surrenders to Brigadier General Lawson H. M. Sanderson, commander of 4th Marine Aircraft Wing. Marine Fighting Squadron 511 and Marine Torpedo Bomber Squadron 233 on the carrier *Block Island* assist in rescuing Allied prisoners of war from Formosa Island.

6 SEPTEMBER
MARINE CORPS

Nearly all elements of the Fleet Marine Landing Force are relieved of occupation duties in Japan and return to their ships. The 4th Marine Regiment parades for 120 former members of the regiment who survived Japanese imprisonment after the fall of Corregidor Island, Philippine Islands.

7 SEPTEMBER
MARINE CORPS

The headquarters of Marine Aircraft Group 31 and the planes of Marine Fighting Squadron 441 fly onto the Yokosuka airfield and become the first U.S. aviation unit to operate from Japan. They are followed in the next few days by Marine Fighting Squadrons 224 and 311, Marine Night Fighting Squadron 542, and Marine Torpedo Bomber Squadron 131.

8 SEPTEMBER
ARMY/NAVY

Flanked by Admiral William F. Halsey Jr. and Lieutenant General Robert L. Eichelberger, General of the Army Douglas MacArthur makes the 22-mile journey from Yokohama to Tokyo, Japan. In the former enemy capital MacArthur is saluted by an honor guard from the 1st Cavalry Division on the grounds of the former U.S. Embassy. At hand is the flag which flew over the U.S. Capitol in Washington, D.C., during the attack on Pearl Harbor, Hawaii, on 7 December 1941. General MacArthur turns to the Eighth Army commander and states, "General Eichelberger, have our country's flag unfurled, and in Tokyo's sun let it wave in its full glory as a symbol of hope for the oppressed and as a harbinger of victory for the right."

ARMY

The 1st Cavalry Division (under Major General William C. Chase) formally occupies Tokyo, Japan, becoming the first U.S. division to enter the Japanese capital. In Korea, the XXIV Corps (6th, 7th, and 40th Infantry Divisions), under Lieutenant General John R. Hodge, arrives to begin occupation duty. First to arrive is the 7th Infantry Division (under Major General Archibald V. Arnold). Hodge designates Arnold to head the U.S. Army Military Government in Korea. The 40th Infantry Division (under Brigadier General Donald J. Myers) returns home from Korea in March 1946; the 6th and 7th Infantry Divisions continue to train Korean troops until they are withdrawn in 1948.

Right: *A cheering crowd of South Koreans welcomes Soldiers of the 7th Infantry Division as liberators into their capitol of Seoul. The division is one of three arriving in Korea in September 1945 to disarm the Japanese troops who have been occupying the country for more than 30 years. (National Archives)*

SEPTEMBER–OCTOBER
ARMY

The Eighth Army assumes the occupation of Japan. Lieutenant General Robert L. Eichelberger deploys and disperses Eighth Army elements in Japan throughout IX Corps (under Major General Charles W. Ryder), XI Corps (under Lieutenant General Charles P. Hall), and XIV Corps (under Major General Joseph M. Swing). In addition to the units already in Japan, he soon has the Americal Division, the 43d, 77th, and 81st Infantry Divisions, and the 112th Cavalry and 158th Infantry Regimental Combat Teams.

10 SEPTEMBER
ARMY

Army search and rescue teams fan out in Japan to locate known prison camps and to find many former Allied and U.S. prisoners of war who are on their own after leaving detention centers following news of the Japanese surrender. Before the end of the month more than 35,000 former prisoners are repatriated.

11 SEPTEMBER
NAVY

Operation MAGIC CARPET, in which U.S. Navy warships serve as makeshift transports returning U.S. servicemen to the United States, commences.

19 SEPTEMBER
ARMY

Thirty-one months after its arrival in Australia, Lieutenant General Walter Krueger's Sixth Army headquarters lands in Japan to start its tour of occupation duty. The Sixth Army controls the I Corps (under Major General Innis P. Swift), X Corps (under Major Gerneral Franklin C. Sibert), and the V Amphibious Corps (under Major General Harry Schmidt).

20 SEPTEMBER
MARINE CORPS

The advance echelons of Marine Aircraft Group 22 fly onto Omura Airfield on Kyushu Island, Japan.

22 SEPTEMBER
MARINE CORPS

The V Amphibious Corps headquarters and the 5th Marine Division arrive at the Sasebo naval base on Kyushu Island, Japan. The 5th Marine Division assumes responsibility for occupying the northern half of the island. The 1st Marine Aircraft Wing begins to move from Mindanao Island, Philippine Islands, to China via Okinawa Island, Japan.

23 SEPTEMBER
ARMY

The veteran 97th Infantry Division (under Major General Herman F. Kramer) arrives at Yokohama, Japan, from Europe to join Eighth Army occupation forces in Japan. The 97th Infantry, with 41 combat days in the European Theater, is ordered to relieve the 43d Infantry Division.

Left: *Curious South Koreans eye the strange looking American Soldiers who now occupy their country. ("Seoul Street Scene," Steven P. Kidd, Army Art Collection, U.S. Army Center of Military History)*

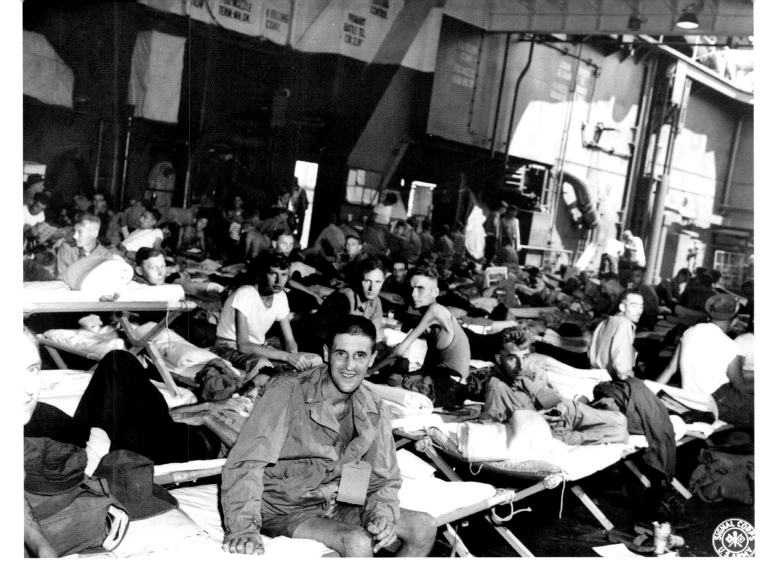

MARINE CORPS

Marine Fighting Squadron 113—the lead squadron of Marine Aircraft Group 22—lands on Omura Airfield on Kyushu Island, Japan. It is followed in the next few days by Marine Fighting Squadrons 314 and 422 and Marine Night Fighting Squadron 543. The 2d and 6th Marine Regiments land at Nagasaki and relieve the Marine detachments of the cruisers *Biloxi* and *Wichita*. The 2d Marine Division assumes responsibility for occupying the southern half of Kyushu Island. The V Amphibious Corps assumes command of the 2d and 5th Marine Divisions.

24 SEPTEMBER
ARMY/MARINE CORPS

The 8th and 10th Marine Regiments and Marine Observation Squadron 2 come ashore at Nagasaki, Japan. The U.S. Sixth Army assumes control of all ground forces in Japan.

25 SEPTEMBER
ARMY

The I Corps' 6th, 25th, and 33d Infantry Divisions take control of the area south of Osaka, Japan. Its 98th Infantry Division lands in Japan on 27 September.

Above: *Repatriated American prisoners relax on their cots in temporary quarters on the hangar deck of an aircraft carrier. The men start the process of medical check-ups, care, and recovery before heading home. (U.S. Army)*

Below: *The Americal Division discovers bars of silver hidden by the former Japanese government in the village of Atomi, Japan. (U.S. Army)*

Left: *A selection of unit insignia worn by American Army, Army Air Forces, Navy, and Marine Corps units who served in Asia–Pacific Theater. (National Archives)*

Below: *Left to right—The American Defense Service Medal and Asia-Pacific Campaign Medal are awarded to all who serve in those theaters of war. (U.S. Army Institute of Heraldry)*

Opposite: *A list of 78 amphibious operations by Army and Marine Corps units during the Pacific war. (Library of Congress)*

30 SEPTEMBER
MARINE CORPS
The III Amphibious Corps (under Major General Keller E. Rockey) arrives at Tangku, China. The 2d Battalion, 7th Marines lands and secures the city. The 3d Battalion goes ashore and boards a train for Tientsin.

3 OCTOBER
ARMY
With its elements arriving in Japan from Mindanao Island, Philippine Islands, the X Corps deploys its major units in the Kure–Hiroshima sector of western Honshu Island, where it also occupies the Okama area with the 24th and 41st Infantry Divisions.

5 OCTOBER
ARMY
The 43d Infantry Division is the first of the veteran divisions in the Asia–Pacific area to be inactivated.

12 OCTOBER
ARMY
The Americal Division in the area of Yokohama–Kawasaki–Yokosuka, Japan, reports a startling discovery. A division patrol searching the Atomi city hall finds clues that lead to a stash of 2,660 silver ingots, weighing about 103.4 tons, with an estimated value of $1.3 million.

13 OCTOBER
AIR FORCE
The Army Air Forces holds a large open house at Wright Field near Dayton, Ohio. On display for public viewing are many pieces of captured enemy aeronautical technology. The Army Air Forces uses the opportunity to tell the public, more than one

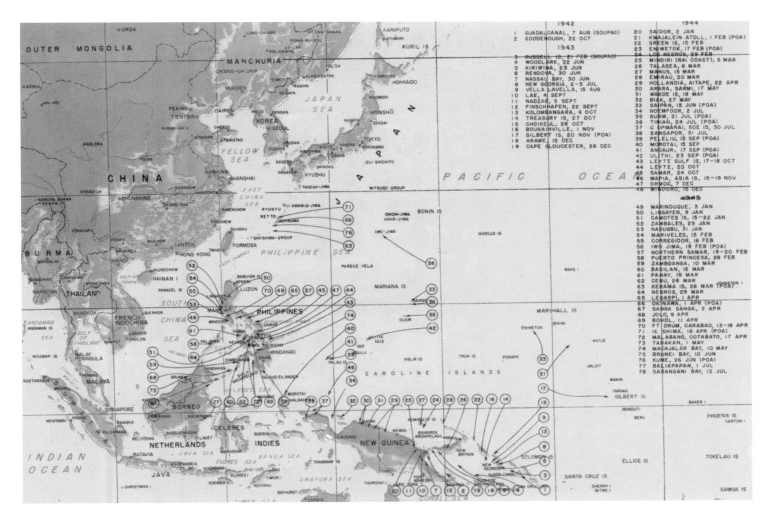

million during one week, about its contribution to victory in World War II.

15 NOVEMBER
NAVY
While monitoring shipping activity off the coast of Manchuria near Port Arthur, a PBM Mariner patrol-bomber is fired upon by a Soviet fighter plane, an event symbolic of the beginning of the Cold War.

1 DECEMBER
ARMY
The Americal Division moves to its final assembly point at Fort Lawton, Washington. The successor to Task Force 6814, the division was born on foreign soil (on New Caledonia Island in the South Pacific), and is mustered out of the service on 12 December, after an existence of 43 months.

24 DECEMBER
ARMY
The XIV Corps (under Major General Joseph M. Swing) returns to the United States after wartime service which began on Guadalcanal Island, Solomon Islands. It is inactivated on 31 December.

31 DECEMBER
ARMY
By 31 December seven of the Asia–Pacific divisions (27th, 31st, 37th, 39th, 41st, and American Infantry Divisions) are off the Army's rolls. As the Pacific Ocean region welcomes its first peacetime, postwar New Year, the costs of war are counted in more than 300,000 Americans killed in action or wounded in the campaigns of the Asia–Pacific Theater.

1946
A RETURN TO PEACE

31 DECEMBER
ALL SERVICES
World War II is over for the United States when President Harry S. Truman declares hostilities are terminated.

THE WAR IN EUROPE
1942-1945

THE WAR IN EUROPE

1942-1945

"We've got to go to Europe and fight."
—Brigadier General Dwight D. Eisenhower, entry in personal diary, January 1942

"You are hereby designated as Supreme Allied Commander of the forces placed under your orders for operations for liberation of Europe from the Germans. . . . Task: You will enter the continent of Europe and, in conjunction with the other United Nations, undertake operations aimed at the heart of Germany and the destruction of her armed forces."
—Extract of Combined Chiefs of Staff directive to General Dwight D. Eisenhower, 12 February 1944

PLANS AND PREPARATIONS

As the United States officially entered the war, Germany had occupied most of Europe, and Great Britain—America's lone remaining potential ally—was being hammered day and night from the air, starved by a submarine blockade, and in danger of losing its foothold in the Middle East to German advances in North Africa.

Close cooperation between the U.S. and Britain would become the key to defeating the enemy in Europe. What had begun as informal military discussions between the two nations in early 1940 evolved into formalized staff meetings which continued throughout the war and matured into a close combined strategic relationship. The staff meetings were complemented by periodic conferences between President Franklin D. Roosevelt and British Prime Minister Winston S. Churchill, who became the ultimate deciders of Allied strategy.

While planners struggled with strategic issues, Americans were already getting directly involved in the war. In the opening months of 1942, the first Soldiers of the 34th Infantry Division arrived in Northern Ireland to relieve British troops. In July, six Army Air Forces crews struck back by flying British bombers in a low level attack against German targets, and in August, 50 Army Rangers participated in a British raid on Dieppe, France.

By mid-1942, American planners concluded that support to the Pacific had to be restricted, and instead began focusing on an intense debate with their British colleagues as to how best to defeat Germany. Despite repeated proposals, even demands, for increased support to China, the Middle East, the Pacific, and the Soviet Union, President Roosevelt stressed that operations in Europe needed to have priority. American planners proposed a direct approach with a cross-channel invasion of Europe as early as 1942. The British disagreed. Concerned about losing the Middle East, as well as the defense of their own home islands, the British favored a more indirect strategy to "close the ring" around Germany, then attack Germany itself from several fronts. After weeks of analyzing various options, a decision was made to land a combined American–British force in North Africa in November 1942. The operation, code-named TORCH, drew so heavily on

Left: *Italian dictator Benito Mussolini (front left) walks alongside German Chancellor Adolf Hitler (center front) at a meeting in Munich in September 1938. (Hugo Jaeger/Timepix/Rex Features)*

ships, men, and equipment that a cross-channel invasion had to be delayed at least a year.

INTO ACTION AT LAST

The TORCH assault forces came ashore at three general locations on the North African coast in Algeria and Morocco on 9 November 1942. The Allies overcame Vichy French resistance by 11 November, then reorganized and turned east to challenge the German–Italian forces of Field Marshall Erwin Rommel in Tunisia. The Allied engineers placed captured airfields into operation as soon as possible, and Army Air Forces planes were brought from the carrier *Ranger*. Operation TORCH was the source of many lessons in amphibious and airborne operations for both the Army and Navy, and laid the groundwork for joint Army–Navy cooperation that was invaluable for future operations.

In February 1943, the advancing American and British forces were hit hard by a German counterattack near Kasserine Pass, Tunisia. The inexperienced American units were thrown back, but the Germans could not sustain their gains and had to withdraw. Caught between the advancing U.S. II Corps from the west and British troops pushing out of Egypt from the east, the German and Italian forces in North Africa surrendered in May 1943. Allied bombers and fighters stationed at North African airfields struck Italy and into middle Europe as Allied preparations for an invasion of Sicily and Italy, favored

by the British as a "back door" into Europe, were made. Another combined American–British amphibious-airborne operation in July gave the Allies a foothold on Sicily. When initial enemy resistance faltered, the Allied advance turned into a race between American and British units to secure the northern port of Messina, Sicily. It fell on 17 August 1943 to Lieutenant General George S. Patton's Seventh Army, but too late to prevent the bulk of the German army from escaping to Italy.

Allied naval forces crossed the straits from Sicily to Italy in September, and landed American and British troops on beaches in the Salerno area. Allied air and naval support sustained the beachheads against strong German counterattacks until reinforced ground forces could gradually push inland. Mountainous terrain and terrible winter weather favored the defending Germans, giving them time to prepare a successive series of strong defensive lines that slowed the Allied advance to a crawl. An amphibious landing just south of Rome at Anzio in January 1944 was an attempted end-run around the German lines, but it was contained by the Germans, and almost ended in disaster for the assault force. It was four long months before a link-up between the struggling units in the beachhead and the Allied units advancing from Salerno was made. The Allied push up the Italian boot remained a bitter and bloody struggle. Rome was finally liberated in June 1944, but fighting in northern Italy continued for another 11 months.

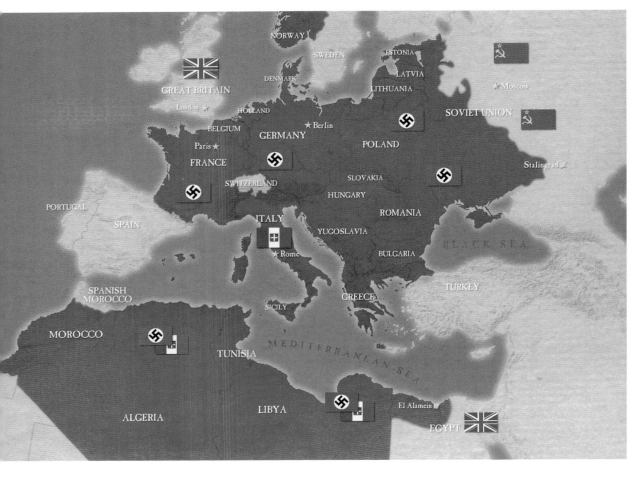

Left: *By the time the U.S. enters the war, Germany controls all of western Europe and is pushing the Soviet forces back to Moscow, USSR. (National Archives)*

Opposite: *The Coast Guard cutter* Campbell *performs convoy escort duty despite heavy seas in the stormy North Atlantic. (Lt. Cdr. Anton O. Fischer, USCGR, U.S. Coast Guard Collection)*

TURNING THE TIDE

By mid-1943, the nature of the U.S. Navy's battle against German submarines, and to a lesser extent German surface ships and aircraft, had begun to shift from primarily defensive convoy escort duty to actively hunting and killing German targets. While enemy submarines continued to attack convoys with deadly results, the number of German U-boats lost to Allied attacks steadily increased. New improved warships, and more of them, as well as use of PBY flying boat patrol aircraft from newly built bases in the Azores Islands, Iceland, and Africa gave the Navy what it needed to break the German stranglehold on Great Britain. The Atlantic was gradually becoming an American ocean. Convoys of dozens of new *Liberty* ships made increasingly safer voyages as the build-up of air and ground forces in Great Britain continued in anticipation of a cross-channel invasion.

During this same time, dominance in the air also shifted from the Germans to the Allied, mainly American, air forces. Hundreds of airmen never returned from their missions, but their places were filled by better trained pilots and crews from the mobilized training bases in America; planes that were shot down were replaced by new, better aircraft. Thousands of fighters, bombers, and transports were ferried from the full-time industrial production lines

in the U.S. over the Atlantic to the airfields that dotted Great Britain and North Africa. By the early months of 1944, Germany and its occupied territories were being struck by Allied air attacks around the clock from two directions—North Africa/Italy and England. Desperate German efforts to regain air superiority were unable to effectively counter Allied strength. Under this umbrella of air protection, the Allied expeditionary ground and naval force gathered like a coiled spring, and waited for release against occupied Europe.

CRUSHING THE REICH

During the late night and early morning hours of 5–6 June 1944, the massive Allied invasion of occupied France began—Operation OVERLORD. Long planned and painstakingly prepared, the D-day invasion began with an assault by airborne forces to seal off the routes to the beachheads and disrupt German defenders. This was followed at dawn with amphibious landings by American, British, and Canadian divisions on five Normandy beaches. Hard fighting through tangled French hedgerow countryside lasted until July when Allied forces broke out, and fighter-bombers and fast-moving armored columns pursued the retreating German army. A second landing in southern France, Operation

ANVIL, crumpled German efforts to hold back the advancing Allies. When the U.S. VIII Corps moved in September to seize Cologne, Germany, and control the Roer River dams, it became involved in a long, bloody fight in the dense Hurtgen Forest. Before the fighting ended, five American divisions had suffered heavy losses. That same month, a combined British-American operation—Operation MARKET-GARDEN—used airborne and armored units to try to seize four Dutch bridges and cross the Rhine River. The operation fell short of its goal, but by November, ground advances covered by the Allied dominance of the air, drove the Germans back to their homeland.

The Germans made a desperate last effort in mid-December 1944 to retake the critical Allied supply port of Antwerp, Belgium, and split the American and British forces. This surprise attack, the largest battle ever fought by the U.S. Army, was contained by heroic stands of Army units in the wooded and rolling Ardennes region around Bastogne, Belgium. The crisis ended in January, and American units began breaking through the concrete bunkers and tank traps of the Siegfried Line along the German border while overhead thousands of Army Air Forces bombers and fighters battered the heart of Germany.

Early 1945 found American divisions advancing on all fronts. In a stroke of luck in March, a bridge over the Rhine River was found still standing, and units were rushed across under German fire. Navy landing craft were brought forward to ferry more troops across the river while planes of the Eighth and Ninth Air Forces gave support. Another airborne assault, Operation VARSITY, secured additional bridgeheads over the Rhine, and the push into Germany continued toward the Elbe River. That river was the agreed limit of American advance and the planned meeting point with the approaching Soviet army. In April, the first concentration camps were discovered and the stunned inmates liberated. In northern Italy, the Fifth Army continued to batter through the last German defensive lines.

In May, the European war ended. American and Soviet troops met on the Elbe River, and a link-up was made between Fifth Army units from Italy and Seventh Army units from France and Austria. On 2 May 1945, the German forces in Italy surrendered after more than 600 days of combat. Five days later, in a small schoolhouse in Rheims, France, the surviving German High Command officially surrendered all German forces effective 9 May 1945. The war against Germany was over, and the occupation began.

1942
MEETING THE ENEMY

1 JANUARY
ARMY
The Army has 36 divisions under arms—29 infantry, 5 armored, and 2 cavalry. Production and procurement for 1941 included 600 howitzers and 1,461 medium tanks.

NAVY
Admiral Royal E. Ingersoll assumes the duties of Commander in Chief, U.S. Atlantic Fleet.

6 JANUARY
AIR FORCE
President Franklin D. Roosevelt calls for a greatly expanded air force. He challenges America and the aircraft industry to produce 100,000 combat planes during the coming year.

10 JANUARY
MARINE CORPS
The Glider Detachment is formed at Parris Island, South Carolina.

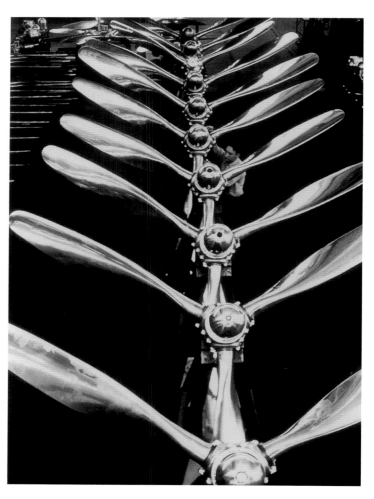

11 JANUARY
NAVY
Five German U-boats commence Operation DRUMBEAT off the East Coast of the United States, sinking 26 Allied ships over the next month.

14 JANUARY
AIR FORCE
The Army Air Forces awards the first contract to build a helicopter designed to meet military requirements.

20 JANUARY
MARINE CORPS
Legislation authorizes the promotion of Commandant Thomas Holcomb to lieutenant general, the first Marine to ever hold that rank.

26 JANUARY
ARMY
Company B, 133d Infantry Regiment, 34th (Red Bull) Infantry Division is the first American unit to arrive in Europe. The unit lands at Belfast, Northern Ireland. The men wear World War I–style helmets, olive drab blouses with ties, full field packs, gas masks, and canvas leggings.

28 JANUARY
AIR FORCE
The Eighth Air Force is activated under Brigadier General Asa Duncan, an old-time Army Air Corps flier, at Savannah Army Air Base, Georgia. During the war, the "Mighty Eighth" will become America's strategic bombardment powerhouse and participate with the Royal Air Force during the Combined Bomber Offensive.

NAVY
While flying convoy escort off the coast of Newfoundland, Canada, a PBO Hudson patrol bomber of Patrol Squadron 82 piloted by Aviation Machinist's Mate First Class Donald F. Mason attacks a surfaced U-boat. Mason transmits, "Sighted sub, sank same," a memorable radio message that unfortunately turns out to be incorrect, for no U-boat is lost on this date.

7 FEBRUARY
NAVY
President Franklin D. Roosevelt establishes the War Shipping Administration to consolidate operational control of all American merchant vessels. The first director of the new agency is Rear Admiral Emory S. Land.

Right: *The members of the Joint Chiefs of Staff are key in determining U.S. strategy during the war. Clockwise from lower left are: Admiral Ernest J. King, Lieutenant General Henry H. Arnold, Admiral William D. Leahy, and General George C. Marshall. (National Archives)*

9 FEBRUARY
AIR FORCE/ARMY/NAVY

The U.S. Joint Chiefs of Staff evolves to provide U.S. Army and Navy input for the newly established Combined Chiefs of Staff. The Army is represented by General George C. Marshall; the Army Air Corps by Lieutenant General Henry H. Arnold; and the Navy by Admiral William D. Leahy and Admiral Ernest J. King. The wartime JCS becomes the principal agency for coordination between the Army and Navy.

19 FEBRUARY
MARINE CORPS

The 9th Defense Battalion arrives at Guantanamo Bay, Cuba, to assume responsibility for protecting that base.

20 FEBRUARY
AIR FORCE

The War Production Board announces that aircraft production has been elevated to the same priority as that of tanks and ships. Government allocations of materials for wartime production are modified accordingly.

Major General Ira C. Eaker and six staff officers arrive in the United Kingdom. Three days later,

Eaker takes charge of VIII Bomber Command. Eaker's staff continues to arrive in England to establish his headquarters.

28 FEBRUARY–1 MARCH
NAVY

A PBO Hudson patrol bomber of Patrol Squadron 82 spots *U-656* on the surface off Newfoundland, Canada. The subsequent bombing run sinks the German submarine, the first U.S. Navy U-boat kill scored during World War II.

6 MARCH
AIR FORCE

The first class of African American pilots graduates from the aviation school established at the Tuskegee Institute, Alabama.

8 MARCH
ARMY/MARINE CORPS

The 1st Marine Brigade (Provisional) is relieved by the U.S. Army Indigo Force (under Major General Charles H. Bonesteel) and departs Iceland.

9 MARCH
AIR FORCE/ARMY

The Army reorganizes into three principal divisions— Army Air Forces, Services of Supply, and Army

Left: *Unit insignia, top, left to right: Army Ground Forces; Army Service Forces; Army Air Forces. Bottom, left to right: Anti-Aircraft Command; USMC detachment in Iceland; Army Iceland Command. (U.S. Army)*

Below: *Admiral Ernest J. King, left, newly appointed Commander in Chief, U.S. Fleet, welcomes his chief of staff, Rear Admiral Russell Wilson. (Naval Historical Center)*

Ground Forces. Respective commanders are Lieutenant General Henry H. Arnold, Lieutenant General Brehon B. Somervell, and Lieutenant General Lesley J. McNair. The Air Corps operates as the combatant arm of the Army Air Forces.

ARMY

Under Major General Joseph Green, the Antiaircraft Command is activated as an element of the Army Ground Forces. The Antiaircraft Artillery School is established at Camp Davis, North Carolina.

13 MARCH
ARMY

The first war dogs join the Army at Front Royal, Virginia. This Army branch quickly becomes known as the "K-9 Corps." In months to come, 20,000 dogs are "recruited," of which 10,526 are accepted for service; most serve overseas and 2,290 are killed in action.

15 MARCH
NAVY

While flying escort over convoy ON 74, a PBO Hudson patrol bomber of Patrol Squadron 82 sinks the German submarine *U-503* off Argentia, Newfoundland, Canada.

17 MARCH
NAVY

Vice Admiral Robert L. Ghormley assumes the newly established post of Commander Naval Forces Europe.

19 MARCH
AIR FORCE/ARMY/NAVY

A group of five scientists from Caltech form the Aerojet Engineering Company. Dr. Theodore von Kármán is the president. Aerojet will produce both liquid- and solid-fuel rockets for the Army and the Navy. The company becomes one of the largest rocket engine producers in the world.

NAVY

The destroyer *Dickerson* is accidently fired upon by the U.S. freighter *Liberator* while operating off the coast of Virginia. The destroyer's captain is one of three men killed; six are wounded.

21 MARCH
MARINE CORPS

The 3d Marine Brigade is established at New River, North Carolina. Its major elements are the 7th Marine Regiment and 1st Battalion, 11th Marine Regiment. Its mission will be garrisoning Western Samoa.

25 MARCH
AIR FORCE

Flying a British Spitfire fighter with the Royal Air Force, Major Cecil P. Lessing becomes the first Eighth Air Force pilot to fly a combat mission over France. His 36-plane formation is recalled when it is determined that they are facing a force of 50 German planes.

26 MARCH
NAVY

Under the provisions of an executive order combining the duties of Commander in Chief, U.S. Fleet and Chief of Naval Operations, Admiral Ernest J. King relieves Admiral Harold R. Stark and becomes the ninth Chief of Naval Operations.

In an effort to reinforce the British Home Fleet, Task Force 39—consisting of the battleship *Washington*, aircraft carrier *Wasp*, heavy cruisers *Tuscaloosa* and *Wichita*, and eight destroyers—depart Portland, Maine, for Scapa Flow in the Orkney Islands. The next day, task force commander Rear Admiral John W. Wilcox Jr. is washed overboard while walking on the deck of the flagship *Washington* and is lost at sea. Rear Admiral Robert C. Giffen assumes command of the task force.

In a spirited gun battle 300 miles east of Norfolk, Virginia, the antisubmarine vessel *Atik* damages the German submarine *U-123*, but in turn is sunk with the loss of all 139 on board. *Atik* is the only U.S. "Q-ship," an armed ship disguised as a merchantman, lost in action during World War II. Commissioned on 5 March 1942, her operational career lasts just three weeks.

27 MARCH
AIR FORCE/NAVY

The War Department and the Department of the Navy jointly announce that the U.S. Navy will take command of antisubmarine operations, with jurisdiction over both American coastlines. The Navy will hold authority over Army Air Forces aircraft in accomplishing this mission.

Right: *Army war dogs and their handlers receive extensive training in patrolling, sentry duties, and message delivery at the Army's training center in western Virginia. (U.S. Army)*

Left: *Brightly colored hand-held paddles help pilots preparing to land on an aircraft carrier see the signals for a correct approach. This landing signal officer is Lieutenant David S. McCampbell, who later becomes the Navy's top fighter ace. (Naval Historical Center)*

Below: *The Hat-in-the-Ring insignia identifies the fighter planes of the famous 94th Pursuit Squadron in World War I. (U.S. Army)*

8 APRIL
ARMY
The 5th Air Support Command at Bowman Field, Kentucky, is redesignated the Ninth Air Force.

12 APRIL
AIR FORCE
At the request of the pilots of the 94th Pursuit Squadron, famed World War I ace Eddie Rickenbacker asks Lieutenant General Henry H.

Arnold to reinstate the "Hat in the Ring" emblem for the 94th. In 1924, the emblem had been changed to the Indian Head of the 103d Aero Squadron.

14 APRIL
NAVY
After spotting the German submarine *U-85* on the surface off North Carolina, the destroyer *Roper* gives pursuit and scores repeated hits on the sub. The destroyer subsequently drops depth charges that help send *U-85* to the bottom; she is the first German submarine sunk off the coast of the United States during Operation DRUMBEAT.

16 APRIL
MARINE CORPS
The 3d Barrage Balloon Squadron is formed at Parris Island, South Carolina.

20 APRIL
NAVY
The aircraft carrier *Wasp*, having ferried 47 British Royal Air Force Spitfire fighters to the Mediterranean, flies the aircraft off to bolster the defenses of the besieged island of Malta.

25 APRIL
ARMY/MARINE CORPS/NAVY
In tests conducted at Norfolk, Virginia, Andrew Higgins' 50-foot tank lighter (a larger version of his bow-ramp landing craft) proves superior to a Navy-

designed craft. It goes into production and is designated the Landing Craft Mechanized. The craft provides the first practical means to get medium tanks from ship to shore during an amphibious assault.

ARMY
The Sixth Army at San Francisco, California, begins implementing orders to gather and confine Japanese-Americans into relocation camps in the western U.S.

26 APRIL
NAVY
The destroyer *Sturtevant* strikes a mine off Marquesas Key, Florida, and sinks with the loss of 15 members of her crew.

28 APRIL
NAVY
A joint Anglo–American force that includes the battleship *Washington*, heavy cruisers *Wichita* and *Tuscaloosa*, and four destroyers sails from Scapa Flow in the Orkney Islands to the waters northeast of Iceland to cover convoy PQ 15, bound for the Soviet Union.

30 APRIL
NAVY
Admiral Harold R. Stark assumes command of U.S. Naval Forces Europe.

Above: *The destroyer* Roper *is the first U.S. Navy ship to sink a German submarine in the war. (Naval Historical Center)*

Below: *The mechanized landing craft, developed by Andrew Higgins and used for moving troops, vehicles, and equipment between ship and shore, becomes known as the "mike boat." (USMC)*

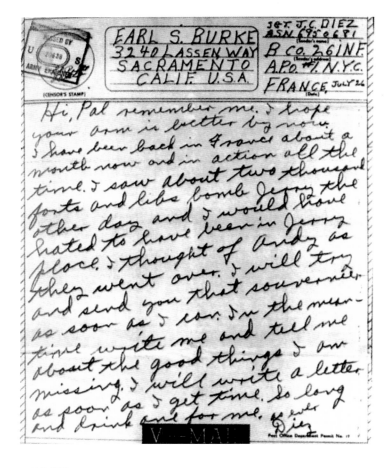

10 MAY
AIR FORCE/NAVY
The aircraft carrier *Ranger*, off the Gold Coast of Africa, launches 68 Army Air Forces P-40 Warhawk fighters for a flight to Accra. She repeats the operation on 19 July, sending 72 P-40s off her deck.

11 MAY
MARINE CORPS
Marine Barracks, Fleet Air Base Iceland is established.

12 MAY
AIR FORCE
The Eighth Air Force advance echelon arrives at High Wycombe, England. A group numbering 39 officers and 348 enlisted troops begins preparations for the arrival of the flying units soon to follow. One of the first arrivals (14 May) is the 15th Bombardment Squadron (Light), equipped with A-20 Havoc attack bombers.

13 MAY
NAVY
The Bureau of Navigation is renamed the Bureau of Naval Personnel.

14 MAY
ARMY
The president signs "An Act to establish a Women's Army Auxiliary Corps for service with the Army of the United States." This is soon known as the WAAC.

9 MAY
NAVY
The aircraft carrier *Wasp* once again launches British Royal Air Force Spitfire fighters to help strengthen the defense of Malta, prompting British Prime Minister Winston S. Churchill to comment, "Who said a Wasp couldn't sting twice!"

Above: *To save weight and space, a V-Mail letter is written on a special form and photographed on microfilm, which is then shipped, reprinted, and given to the recipient. More than 18,000 letters fit on a single roll of film. (Earl Burke)*

Left: *The Army is tasked with the management of internment camps for Japanese–American civilians, like this one in Amache, Colorado. (Library of Congress)*

15 MAY
ARMY
The Army Postal Service, working with the Army Signal Corps, hits upon a photographic concept to improve mail delivery time to overseas troops. Senders are encouraged to write letters on V-Mail forms, which are photographed and flown to V-Mail stations. At the receiving end the film is developed, enlarged, and printed as 4 1/2 x 5-inch reproductions for distribution to recipients. Peak volume will be 63 million letters processed in April 1944.

ARMY
The Army's Parachute School is activated at Fort Benning, Georgia, as a separate entity apart from the Infantry School activities.

16 MAY
ARMY
Mrs. Oveta Culp Hobby takes the oath of office as director, WAAC, and is awarded silver eagles symbolic of her "equivalent grade" as an Army colonel.

17 MAY
AIR FORCE
Igor Sikorsky and C. L. "Les" Morris deliver the Army Air Forces' first helicopter, the Sikorsky XR-4 Hoverfly, to Wright Field, Ohio. It is accepted by the AAF on 30 May. The XR-4 will be the only U.S. helicopter to see action during World War II.

18 MAY
ALL SERVICES
U.S. and Panamanian officials sign base loan agreements that provide for the use of a number of bases to defend the Panama Canal.

20 MAY
MARINE CORPS
Cunningham Field is commissioned at Marine Corps Air Station Cherry Point, North Carolina. It is capable of supporting a Marine Air Wing.

23 MAY
MARINE CORPS
The Training Center, Fleet Marine Force, is established at New River, North Carolina. During the course of the war, the base becomes the home of numerous schools and training programs.

Above: *Major General George A. Lynch, Chief of Infantry (in civilian clothes), and Brigadier General Frank M. Andrews, Army G–3 (on left), observe the Army's parachute test platoon during training. (National Archives)*

Left: *With General George C. Marshall on her right and Secretary of War Henry Stimson on her left, Mrs. Ovetta C. Hobby is sworn in as Director of the Women's Army Auxiliary Corps (WAAC). (U.S. Army)*

Left: *A young man ponders his choices for a military future. (Smithsonian Institution)*

25 MAY
NAVY

While operating off Martinique in the French West Indies, the destroyer *Blakeley* is torpedoed by the German submarine *U-156*. The blast takes away 60 feet of the destroyer's bow, kills 6 crewmen, and wounds 21 others. However, she survives to fight again.

26 MAY
AIR FORCE

The Northrop P-61 Black Widow night fighter, piloted by Vance Breese, flies for the first time near Hawthorne, California. The P-61 is designed specifically to fight at night using radar.

1 JUNE
MARINE CORPS

In accordance with the orders of President Franklin D. Roosevelt and Secretary of the Navy Frank Knox, the Marine Corps begins recruiting African Americans. Initial enlistees Alfred Masters and George O. Thompson are the first African Americans to join the Marine Corps since the Revolutionary War.

12 JUNE
AIR FORCE

A secretly trained detachment of Army Air Forces crews commanded by Lieutenant Colonel Harry Halverson carries out the first strategic air raid in the European–African–Middle Eastern Theater. Halverson leads 13 B-24 Liberator bombers from Fayid, a base in the Egyptian desert, against oil fields near Ploesti, Romania, with little effect.

15 JUNE
MARINE CORPS

The 11th Defense Battalion is formed at Parris Island, South Carolina.

16 JUNE
ARMY

Originally codenamed the "Plough Project," the 1st Special Service Force comes into being at Camp Hale, Colorado. U.S. and Canadian soldiers are united to form a unique and deadly light infantry combat team ostensibly destined for cold weather operations. Their collar insignia takes the form of crossed arrows in place of crossed rifles.

MARINE CORPS

The 3d Marine Regiment is reactivated at New River, North Carolina.

18 JUNE
AIR FORCE

Major General Carl A. Spaatz assumes command of the Eighth Air Force in London, England, where approximately 85 airfields are prepared and handed over for operations to the Army Air Forces.

19 JUNE
ARMY

The U.S. V Corps organizes the 1st Ranger Battalion at Carrickfergus, Northern Ireland, with Major William O. Darby as commander; 520 volunteer officers and men head for training at the British Commando School in Scotland.

21 JUNE
AIR FORCE

The Arnold–Portal–Towers Agreement is signed in London. It addresses U.S. air commitments in Europe and provides support for Operation BOLERO, the buildup of Army Air Forces in Europe. The first aircraft deployed in support of the operation leave Presque Isle, Maine, for bases in Great Britain on 23 June. The agreement is approved by the Joint Chiefs of Staff on 25 June, and by the Combined Chiefs of Staff on 2 July.

24 JUNE
AIR FORCE/ARMY

Major General Dwight D. Eisenhower becomes commanding general of the European Theater of Operations, U.S. Army.

ARMY

The United States Military Iranian Mission in Basra, Iraq, is redesignated the Iran–Iraq Service Command, with the mission to expedite the flow of war materials to the Soviet Union from Persian Gulf ports. This is soon redesignated the Persian Gulf Service Command.

25 JUNE
ARMY

Major General Mark W. Clark becomes the chief of staff for U.S. ground forces in Europe and commander of the II Corps.

Above: *Volunteers of the newly formed 1st Ranger Battalion undergo rigorous training at the British Commando school in northern Scotland. (U.S. Army Military History Institute)*

Below: *The uniform insignia of the American–Canadian 1st Special Service Force is a red arrowhead. Members wear the crossed-arrows insignia of the old Indian Scouts on their lapels, like this enlisted man's insignia. The unit is a forerunner of the modern Army Special Forces. (U.S. Army)*

Above: *A Navy PBM Mariner patrol bomber drops a depth charge on a German submarine during the battle to control the sea lanes of the Atlantic. ("P-Boat One, U-Boat Nothing," Don Feight)*

Below: *The damaged destroyer* Blakely *makes her way slowly to port in May 1942 after having her bow blown off by a German torpedo. (Naval Historical Center)*

LATE JUNE
MARINE CORPS
Marine Barracks, Londonderry is established in Northern Ireland to protect naval facilities.

30 JUNE
NAVY
A PBM Mariner of Patrol Squadron 74 sinks the German submarine *U-158* with depth charges off Bermuda.

1 JULY
AIR FORCE
The first B-17 Flying Fortress bomber of the 97th Bombardment Group arrives at Polebrook, England.

4 JULY
AIR FORCE
Members of the 15th Bomb Squadron accomplish the first Army Air Forces bomber mission over western Europe. Flying six Royal Air Force Boston III bombers (RAF versions of the Douglas A-20 Havoc built in the U.S.), these airmen are part of a 12-plane British low-level attack against enemy airfields in the Netherlands. Results are not encouraging. One lost pilot is the first U.S. airman taken prisoner in Europe. The plane of American commander of the 15th Bomb Squadron, Captain Charles C. Kegelman, suffers severe damage from flak but he manages to coax his aircraft back to Swanton Morley. A week later, Kegelman is decorated with the Distinguished Service Cross for extraordinary gallantry and heroism during the raid. He is the first in the Eighth Air Force to receive this award.

Right: *Soldiers sit with their jeep and towed howitzer in a C-47 Skytrain transport early in the war. In addition to parachutes and gliders, the Army sought every possible way to use aircraft to increase mobility of the ground forces. (U.S. Air Force)*

7 JULY
AIR FORCE

An A-29 Hudson of the 396th Bombardment Squadron, assigned to the Zone of the Interior off the coast of North Carolina, sinks the submarine *U-701*. This is the first time an Army Air Forces aircraft sinks a German submarine during World War II.

10 JULY
AIR FORCE

The Douglas XA-26 Invader medium bomber prototype flies for the first time when company pilot Ben O. Howard takes it into the air near El Segundo, California. Initially plagued by problems with control during conditions of asymmetric thrust, the aircraft is eventually made safe and is used with great effect during the war.

Left: *Igor Sikorsky (left) stands by the nose of one of his XR-4 Hoverfly helicopters after delivering it in May 1942 to the Army Air Forces for testing. The "X" indicates it is still an experimental aircraft. (NASM)*

15 JULY
NAVY

The U.S. merchantman *Unicoi* rams the German submarine *U-576*, and an OS2U Kingfisher observation plane from Scouting Squadron 9 joins in to sink the sub off the coast of North Carolina.

20 JULY
ARMY

The first Women's Auxiliary Army Corps Officer Candidate School program starts with 440 members at Fort Des Moines, Iowa. The goal is to have 1,300 trained WAAC officers before the enlistment of "enrolled personnel."

NAVY

Recalled to active duty, Admiral William D. Leahy becomes Chief of Staff to President Franklin D. Roosevelt.

21 JULY
AIR FORCE

Lieutenant General Dwight D. Eisenhower assigns the Eighth Air Force the mission, with the Royal Air Force, of achieving air dominance over western France by 1 April 1943.

22 JULY
ARMY

A Japanese submarine shells Fort Stevens, Washington (a coastal Army post). This is the first foreign sea attack against U.S. continental soil since the War of 1812.

The Army's old Corps Areas are renamed Corps Service Commands as the Army's corps are now tactical commands.

30 JULY
NAVY

The Women Accepted for Volunteer Emergency Service (WAVES) is established. Lieutenant Commander Mildred H. McAfee becomes

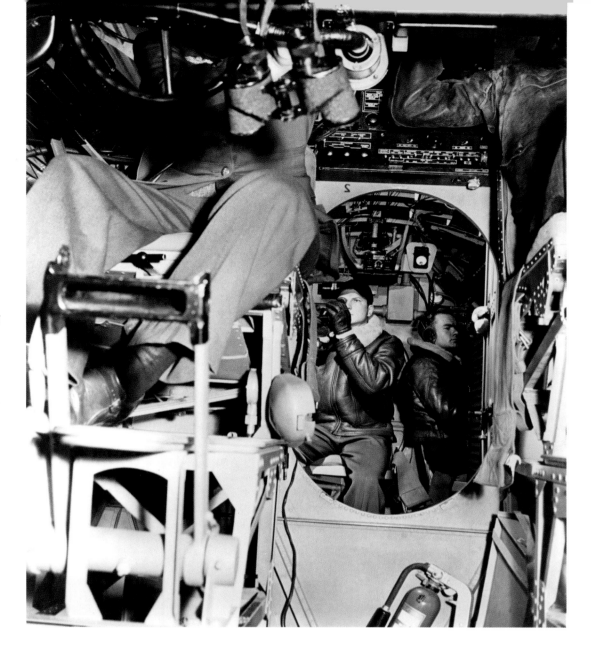

commanding officer on 2 August. By the end of 1942 total WAVES strength is 3,879 officers and enlisted personnel. By 31 July 1945, that number will grow to 86,291.

31 JULY
ARMY
The Transportation Corps is officially formed, taking on many of the missions formerly handled by the Quartermaster Corps. Major General Charles P. Gross, as the head of the Transportation Corps, is the chief transportation officer of the Army.

7 AUGUST
ARMY
The 1st Infantry Division (Big Red One) is the first U.S. division to reach England. Its newly assigned commander is the colorful ex-cavalryman Major General Terry de la Mesa Allen. Its assistant commander is Brigadier General Theodore Roosevelt Jr., a Reserve officer, the son of former president Theodore Roosevelt.

12 AUGUST
ALL SERVICES
British Prime Minister Winston S. Churchill and American ambassador to Moscow W. Averell Harriman meet with Soviet Premier Joseph Stalin in Moscow. The discussions last for three days. Stalin is informed about Operation TORCH—the planned Allied invasion of northern Africa—and a possible second front in the European War.

NAVY
In the first operational testing of antiaircraft projectiles incorporating proximity fuses, gunners on board the light cruiser *Cleveland* shoot down three target drones in the skies over the Chesapeake Bay. The proximity fuse greatly enhances the air defense capability of U.S. Navy ships during World War II.

13 AUGUST
MARINE CORPS
Marine Corps Air Station Santa Barbara, California, is established.

14 AUGUST
AIR FORCE

2d Lieutenant Joseph D. Shaffer and 2d Lieutenant Elza E. Shahan, flying a P-40 Warhawk and P-38 Lightning fighter, respectively, team up to shoot down a German FW 200 Condor off the coast of Iceland. This is the first aerial victory for the Army Air Forces in the European Theater.

15 AUGUST
ARMY

The 82d Division, under Major General B. Matthew Ridgway, activated in March, is redesignated the 82d Airborne Division, making it the first such division in the Army.

MARINE CORPS

Marine Aircraft Wings (MAW), Pacific, is organized at San Diego, California, to provide administrative and logistic oversight for all MAWs.

16 AUGUST
ARMY

A second airborne division, the 101st, is activated at Camp Claiborne, Louisiana. First commander, Major

General William C. Lee, notes that "it has a rendezvous with destiny." The division becomes the famed "Screaming Eagles."

NAVY

While flying a patrol off the California coast, the airship *L-8* of Blimp Squadron 32 is damaged. She makes it back to the coast and lands at Dale City, but her control car is empty, the two-man crew having disappeared without a trace.

17 AUGUST
AIR FORCE

Colonel Frank A. Armstrong leads 12 B-17 Flying Fortress bombers of the 97th Bomb Group in an attack against Rouen–Sotteville rail yards in occupied France. This is the Eighth Air Force's first bombing raid conducted over Europe. During the raid, Sergeant Kent R. West shoots down a German fighter, becoming the first Eighth Air Force gunner to receive credit for a combat kill.

MARINE CORPS

The 51st Defense Battalion is activated at Montford Point, New River, North Carolina. It trains the

Marine Corps' first African American recruits and becomes the service's first African American operational unit.

19 AUGUST
AIR FORCE/ARMY

Fifty Army Rangers participate in a British–Canadian raid on the German-held port of Dieppe, France. They are the first U.S. troops to fight in France in World War II. British and Canadian losses are heavy. The Rangers lose 3 killed, 5 wounded, and 3 captured. An observer from Army Air Forces is also wounded. In an effort to decoy German fighters away from the location of the raid, 22 Eighth Air Force B-17 Flying Fortress bombers drop more than 30 tons of bombs on airfields near Abbeville and Drucat. Not only is it successful at deceiving enemy fighters, the bombers cause extensive damage to the airfield targets.

20 AUGUST
AIR FORCE

The Twelfth Air Force is activated at Bolling Field, Washington, D.C. Three months later, the Twelfth moves to the Mediterranean Theater, providing airpower support for the invasion campaigns in North Africa and Italy.

21 AUGUST
AIR FORCE

Lieutenant General Dwight D. Eisenhower assigns Major General Carl A. Spaatz additional responsibilities as Air Officer, European Theater of Operations, U.S. Army and head of the air section of its staff. This assignment ensures that the theater air arm is fully represented in operations planning meetings.

22 AUGUST
AIR FORCE

Sixth Air Force aircraft from the 45th Bomb Squadron sink the German submarine *U-654* off Panama.

23 AUGUST
NAVY

A force consisting of the heavy cruiser *Tuscaloosa* escorted by the destroyers *Rodman* and *Emmons* and the British destroyer *Onslaught* delivers men and equipment of two British Royal Air Force squadrons to Murmansk, Russia.

Right: *A German photo shows the bodies of some of the Rangers killed in action while accompanying the British–Canadian commando raid on Dieppe, France, in August 1942. (Library and Archives Canada)*

Above: *The trip to bring supplies to the Soviet Union port of Murmansk is one of the most dangerous for Allied convoys. In addition to the constant submarine threat, the ships must pass within range of German land-based planes and ships. Heavy escort by Allied ships and planes brings most of the more than 1,500 ships in safely. ("Arctic Convoy," James Dietz)*

Below: *New African American Marine Corps recruits prepare for their first inspection at Montford Barracks (later Camp Lejune) at New River, North Carolina. (National Archives)*

24 AUGUST
ARMY/MARINE CORPS

Major General Holland M. Smith turns over command of the Amphibious Force Atlantic Fleet to the Army. Smith and his staff then form the Amphibious Training Staff, Fleet Marine Force.

26 AUGUST
MARINE CORPS

The first African American recruits arrive at Montford Point, New River, North Carolina, to begin training.

28 AUGUST
NAVY

A PBY Catalina of Patrol Squadron 92 joins the Canadian corvette HMCS *Oakville* in sinking the German submarine *U-94* in the Caribbean.

5 SEPTEMBER
AIR FORCE

Major General Carl A. Spaatz convinces Lieutenant General Dwight D. Eisenhower to rescind his previous order suspending the Eighth Air Force's bomber operations from Britain in order to support the Twelfth Air Force's preparations for Operation TORCH.

6 SEPTEMBER
AIR FORCE

Two B-17s Flying Fortresses from the 8th Bomber Command fail to return from a combat mission over Meaulte, France, becoming that unit's first aircraft lost in combat.

Right: *In September 1942, the Army Air Forces' new experimental bomber built by Boeing, the XB-29, makes its first test flight. Initially conceived to make long range attacks on Germany, the B-29 Superfortress finds the most use in the Pacific, where it will be the plane that ends the war. (National Archives)*

9 SEPTEMBER
AIR FORCE

Lieutenant General Henry H. Arnold submits Air War Plans Division-42, the Army Air Forces plan to achieve air ascendancy over the enemy, to General George C. Marshall. The plan, approved through the president's office by November, contains the basic tenets of both American bombing doctrine and the Combined Bomber Offensive, which will be placed into action during the following year.

12 SEPTEMBER
AIR FORCE

The 4th Fighter Group is activated at Bushey Hall, England. Anchored by former Eagle Squadron pilots, the 4th takes up the task of providing fighter escort for heavy bombers during raids over Europe. The official transfer of personnel from the Royal Air Force to the VIII Fighter Command begins on 29 September.

16 SEPTEMBER
MARINE CORPS

The 3d Marine Division is activated at Camp Elliott, California. It is initially composed of five regiments—9th Marines, 21st Marines, 23d Marines, 12th Marines (artillery), and 19th Marines (engineer). The 3d Parachute Battalion is organized in southern California.

17 SEPTEMBER
ARMY

Army engineer Brigadier General Leslie R. Groves takes command of the super-secret Manhattan Project, the objective of which is to build an atomic bomb for wartime use.

21 SEPTEMBER
AIR FORCE

The Boeing XB-29 Superfortress flies for the first time, with test pilot Eddie Allen at the controls at the Boeing factory near Seattle, Washington. The future superbomber is 99 feet long and has a 140-foot wing span. By the end of August 1945 Army Air Forces inventories show 2,132 B-29s on hand.

23 SEPTEMBER
AIR FORCE

Brigadier General James H. Doolittle assumes command of the Twelfth Air Force in Great Britain—known during its build-up as Eighth Air Force "Junior."

27 SEPTEMBER
NAVY

In an engagement between the U.S. freighter *Stephen Hopkins* and the German auxiliary cruiser *Stier* and supply ship *Tannenfels* in the South Atlantic, gunners of the freighter's Armed Guard and civilian volunteers score hits on *Stier*, sinking her. Unfortunately, *Stephen Hopkins* is also sunk in the engagement. For his actions, Lieutenant (junior grade) Kenneth M. Willett, a naval reservist and commander of the Armed Guard detachment, receives a posthumous Navy Cross.

1 OCTOBER
AIR FORCE

The Bell XP-59 Airacomet, America's first turbojet-powered fighter (powered by two GE Type 1-A engines modeled after the Whittle engine prototype) accidentally makes its first flight at Muroc Field,

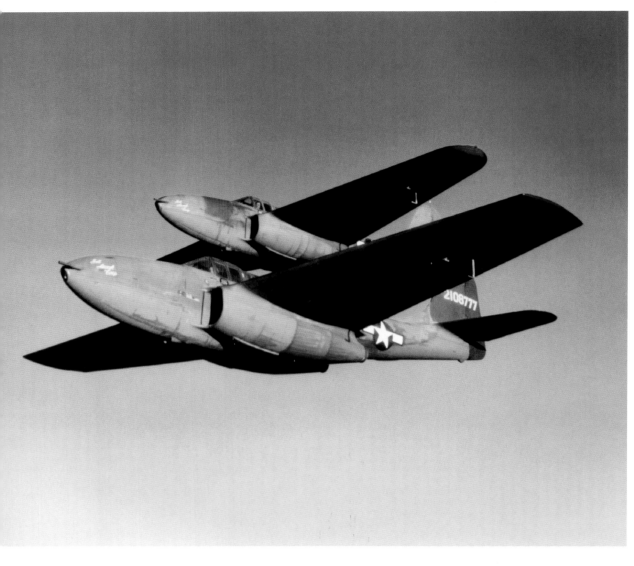

California. During high-speed taxi tests, the plane becomes airborne, but test pilot Robert Stanley lands immediately. The aircraft is officially flown for the Army Air Forces brass the next day. Stanley flies two sorties and then the Army project officer, Colonel Lawrence C. Cragie, becomes the first military pilot to fly a jet when he takes the plane on its third mission of the day.

2 OCTOBER
AIR FORCE/ARMY
At the Aeromedical Laboratory located at Wright Field, Ohio, Major J. G. Kearby ascends to a simulated altitude of 60,200 feet in the altitude chamber as part of a series of full-pressure–suit tests.

5 OCTOBER
NAVY
A PBY Catalina of Patrol Squadron Patrol Squadron 73 sinks the German submarine *U-582* with all hands off Iceland.

22 OCTOBER
AIR FORCE
The Twelfth Air Force begins moving its headquarters from England to North Africa.

ARMY
Major General Mark W. Clark leads a small party ashore in Algeria, North Africa, at night from a submarine with the hope of negotiating with pro-Allied French officials to ensure an unopposed landing in the upcoming Operation TORCH. Clark is assured that the French will cooperate, and he returns to the sub.

23 OCTOBER
AIR FORCE/ARMY
British General Bernard Montgomery leads his Eighth Army in a massive ground offensive at El Alamein, Egypt. Heavy fighting continues into the next day. American B-25 Mitchell bombers provide close support operations west of El Alamein to assist the British advance.

ARMY/NAVY

The first detachment of the Western Naval Task Force under Rear Admiral H. Kent Hewitt departs from Hampton Roads, Virginia, for Operation TORCH, the invasion of North Africa. The remainder of the task force sails the next day.

4 NOVEMBER
NAVY

Members of the Armed Guard detachment on board the U.S. freighter *John H. B. Latrobe* defend the ship against an attack by German He.115 seaplanes east of Iceland. Their efforts, and the captain's skillful shiphandling, cause all seven enemy torpedoes to miss the mark. Strafing wounds three men of the Armed Guard and damages the freighter to such an extent that she returns to Iceland for repairs.

5 NOVEMBER
NAVY

Captain Jerauld Wright temporarily commands the British submarine *Seraph* as she evacuates French General Henri-Honoré Giraud and his staff from occupied France.

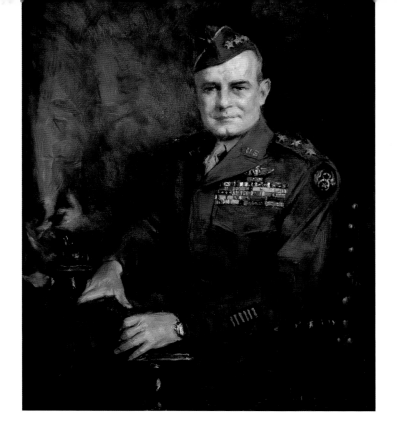

Above: *("Lieutenant General James H. Doolittle," Howard C. Christie, NASM Art Collection)*

Below: *Soldiers of the 34th Infantry Division train on the wet moors of northern Scotland. Months pass before new equipment under development in the U.S. reaches them. (Hulton Getty)*

A PBY Catalina of Patrol Squadron 84 sinks the German submarine *U-408* off Iceland.

7 NOVEMBER
MARINE CORPS
The Commandant authorizes the Marine Corps Women's Reserve, although actual enlistments are not taken until February 1943.

8 NOVEMBER
ALL SERVICES
With Lieutenant General Dwight D. Eisenhower in overall command, Operation TORCH, the landings in North Africa, begins. The three Allied invasion task forces—American Army and Navy elements operating in conjunction with British forces—arrive off the coasts of Algeria and Morocco.

The Eastern Naval Task Force under British command lands the Eastern Assault Force (Major General Charles W. Ryder) on beaches east and west of Algiers, Algeria, at 1:00 a.m. There is only light resistance. Two British destroyers with troops of the 135th Regimental Combat Team make a successful direct assault into the harbor, and Algiers surrenders by evening.

The Central Naval Task Force, also under British command, begins landing the Center Assault Force units of the U.S. II Corps (under Major General Lloyd R. Fredendall) east and west of Oran, Algeria, at 1:30 a.m. Among the units landing is the 48th Surgical Hospital with 60 Army nurses, the first nurses to take part in an invasion. As troops move toward the city, French resistance stalls the attack in several locations. The 2d Battalion, 509th Parachute Infantry makes the first U.S. parachute combat assault

Above: *Lieutenant General Mark W. Clark, deputy commander of Allied Forces in North Africa (center right) stands with Major General Lloyd R. Fredendall, commander of the II Corps (right) and Major General James H. Doolittle, commander of the 12th Air Force (center), along with other officers. (Dept. of Defense)*

Below: *A map showing the Operation TORCH landings in November 1942. (U.S. Army)*

Opposite: *SBD Dauntless dive-bombers and F4F Wildcat fighters wait on the deck of* Ranger *as the Operation TORCH invasion fleet steams for North Africa. (U.S. Navy)*

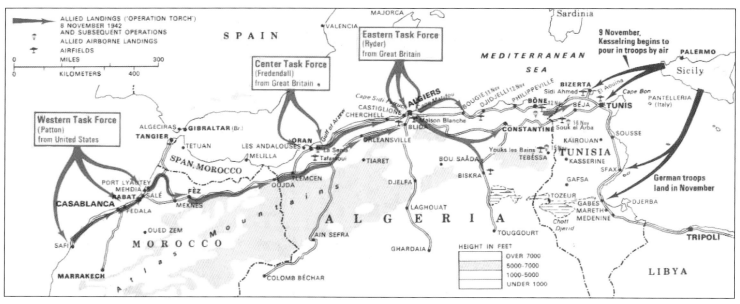

to help seize an airport at Tafaraoui, but the C-47 Skytrain air transport drops are scattered and the assault is ineffective. An attempt to capture the Oran harbor by direct assault ends in disaster. Two British destroyers are sunk with heavy losses to the 3d Battalion, 6th Armored Infantry and a group of U.S. Sailors and Marines. French resistance continues.

Landings by the three Attack Groups of the Western Naval Task Force (under Rear Admiral H. Kent Hewitt) on beaches in Morocco are delayed. The Southern and Central Attack Groups meet light resistance, and by evening the towns of Safi and Fedala are taken. However, the landings of the Western Attack Group are confused and the units scattered. French resistance is heavy. A daring attempt is made to secure a truce with the French when a small team led by Army Air Forces Major Pierpont M. Hamilton passes through the lines under a flag of truce to talk with the French commander at Port Lyautey. Team member Colonel Demas T. Craw is killed by French fire and the team is placed in custody in the town. Craw is later awarded the Medal of Honor. Landing plans are modified as two destroyers put troops ashore while the battleship *New York* and light cruiser *Philadelphia* silence the guns of shore batteries. Once ashore, the Attack Groups reorganize and secure their beachheads. Stiff French defenses halt the advance toward Port Lyautey and its key airfield.

The Twelfth Air Force supports the operation with airlift and fighter support. C-47 Skytrain transports attempting to land troops are attacked by hostile French fighter planes, which shoot down several transports. Spitfire fighters of the 31st Fighter Group respond by downing three of the French fighters.

U.S. Navy forces are active against Vichy French ships and shore installations contesting the landings in North Africa. Off Morocco, the heavy cruiser *Augusta* and destroyers *Ludlow* and *Wilkes* silence shore batteries in the Casablanca/Fedala areas. *Augusta* also joins the light cruiser *Brooklyn*, heavy cruisers *Wichita* and *Tuscaloosa*, and battleship *Massachusetts* in turning back two attempts by the French to disrupt the landings. The Vichy ships are driven back into the harbor where they are bombed repeatedly by aircraft from U.S. escort carriers. *Massachusetts* is hit by shore batteries as she shells the defenses and the French battleship *Jean Bart*.

9 NOVEMBER
ARMY
The 1st Infantry Division and 1st Armored Division push against French defenses to close on Oran, Algeria. In Morocco, Rear Admiral H. Kent Hewitt passes command of the ground troops of the Western Task Force to Major General George S. Patton Jr. at Fedala. Despite high surf, reinforcements land and three French counterattacks with tanks are beaten off. Night operations by the 60th Infantry Regiment to seize the Port Lyautey Airfield are only partially successful.

AIR FORCE/ARMY/NAVY

The Piper L-4 flies into combat for the first time when three of these Army observation aircraft are launched from a Navy carrier to assist ground forces. The planes are piloted by Lieutenant William Butler, with observer Captain Brenton Deval; Lieutenant John R. Shell; and Captain Ford Allcorn.

10 NOVEMBER
ARMY

French troops holding Oran, Algeria, surrender.

AIR FORCE/ARMY/NAVY

In Morocco, a nighttime raid by a demolition engineer party under Navy Lieutenant M. K. Starkweather partially cuts the barrier boom blocking the Sebou River, which flows past Port Lyautey airfield. At daylight, the destroyer *Dallas* rams through the boom and fights its way upriver with Army Rangers to seize the field. The Rangers storm ashore from rubber boats with coordinated infantry attacks from the land side. The airfield is under control in 30 minutes. More than 100 P-40 Warhawk fighters from the 33d Fighter Group arrive from the carriers *Chenango* and *Archer* over three days. One by one, French defenses around Port Lyautey are eliminated. In the evening the senior French area commander contacts Major Pierpont M. Hamilton, who had been in custody in Port Lyautey since 8 November, to arrange a truce. Hamilton relays this to

the Attack Group commander, Major General Lucian K. Truscott Jr., and a meeting is set for the morning.

As Army units move on Casablanca, aircraft from the carrier *Ranger* bomb the French battleship *Jean Bart*, causing heavy damage as the French ship attempts a second sortie from the city's harbor. The 2d Armored Division heads for Marrakech.

11 NOVEMBER
AIR FORCE/ARMY/NAVY

In Morocco, French commanders agree to the terms of an armistice, and Admiral François Darlan broadcasts orders to French forces to cease resistance. Casablanca surrenders, and the 3d Infantry Division enters the city. In Algeria, fighting continues. Members of the 31st Fighter Group launch from Gibraltar in British spitfire fighters to start operations ashore at an airfield 15 miles south of Oran.

12 NOVEMBER
AIR FORCE/ARMY

The U.S. Middle East Air Force is dissolved and the Ninth Air Force is established in Cairo, Egypt, commanded by Lieutenant General H. Lewis Brereton. His new command is to include the IX Bomber Command and the Ninth Air Service Command, which will provide tactical air support to the British Army as it presses its attacks to the west against the enemy.

Opposite: *Soldiers of the 39th Infantry, 9th Infantry Division, land at Surcouf, east of Algiers, Algeria. There is almost no resistance and pro-Allied French help seize the city of Algiers. (Imperial War Museum)*

Right: *Paratroopers of the 2d Battalion, 509th Airborne Infantry Regiment make the first combat parachute assault in U.S. Army history as they leap into the sky over Algeria on 8 November. ("You Have Your Orders," James Dietz)*

15 NOVEMBER
AIR FORCE

Lieutenant Harold Comstock and Lieutenant Roger Dyer set a speed record for airplanes when they dive their P-47 Thunderbolt fighter from 35,000 feet and accelerate to a remarkable 725 miles per hour.

16 NOVEMBER
AIR FORCE

Supporting the British First Army's march into Tunisia, Twelfth Air Force C-47 Skytrain transports drop British paratroopers near Souk el Arba. Additionally, six B-17 Flying Fortresses of the 97th Bomb Group in Algiers fly a raid on Sidi Ahmed

Left: *Rangers from the 1st Ranger Battalion hold a neutralized French bunker at Arzew, Algeria. As part of the invasion of North Africa, the Rangers have surprised French defenders and seized fortifications and coastal gun batteries around the town. (U.S. Army)*

airfield at Bizerte. The 97th had flown the first heavy bomber mission against enemy targets from the United Kingdom on 17 August; now, having been transferred to the Twelfth, they fly their first combat mission in Africa as well.

MARINE CORPS

The first night fighter squadron, Marine Night Fighting Squadron 531, is organized at Cherry Point, North Carolina.

NAVY

The destroyers *Woolsey*, *Swanson*, and *Quick* team up in a coordinated depth charge attack to sink the German submarine *U-173* off Casablanca, Morocco.

17 NOVEMBER
ARMY

Lieutenant General Dwight D. Eisenhower flies to Algiers to finalize the French–American truce agreement with Admiral François Darlan. The 2d Battalion, 509th Parachute Infantry occupies Gafas airfield, as the first U.S. troops in Tunisia.

20 NOVEMBER
ARMY
The 1,422-mile Alaska Military Highway, built mostly by seven Army Corps of Engineer regiments, many of them having African American soldiers, opens nine months after the project began. The strategic road connects Alaska with Dawson Creek, Canada.

24–25 NOVEMBER
ARMY
Combat Command B, 1st Armored Division enters Tunisia and raids Djedeida airfield, destroying 30 German planes.

27 NOVEMBER
ARMY
The famous K-ration is put into the distribution system. Named after its developer, Mr. A. Keyes, the meals include three packages designated breakfast, dinner, and supper.

1 DECEMBER
AIR FORCE
Eighth Air Force commander Major General Carl A. Spaatz is transferred to the Mediterranean Theater. He flies to Algeria to act as Lieutenant General Dwight D. Eisenhower's air advisor. Major General Ira C. Eaker is named as his replacement to command the Mighty Eighth.

2 DECEMBER
ALL SERVICES
Scientists at the University of Chicago successfully accomplish the first nuclear chain reaction in history.

4 DECEMBER
AIR FORCE
B-24 Liberator bombers of the Ninth Air Force flying from bases in Egypt attack targets in Italy for the first time. The targets include harbor installations, a rail yard, and several ships, including a battleship, located near Naples.

5 DECEMBER
ALL SERVICES
President Franklin D. Roosevelt orders the end of voluntary enlistments for those 18–37 years old for all services effective in January. Those 17, or older than 37, are still allowed to enlist.

AIR FORCE
It is announced that Major General Carl A. Spaatz will become the Deputy Commander in Chief for Air, Allied Forces in Northwest Africa.

ARMY
A German counterattack penetrates Combat Command B 1st Armored Division positions at El Guessa, Tunisia.

8 DECEMBER
AIR FORCE

A VIII Bomber Command study of attacks on German submarine pens reveals that current weaponry is not capable of penetrating the facilities' structure from any safe bombing altitude. The resulting programs to develop weapons capable of penetrating such defenses include Project Aphrodite, which focuses on designing unmanned aerial bombs.

10–11 DECEMBER
ARMY

During the night, Combat Command B 1st Armored Division withdraws to the Bedja, Tunisia, area with heavy loss of equipment.

20 DECEMBER
MARINE CORPS

Marine Barracks New River, North Carolina, is renamed Camp Lejeune.

24 DECEMBER
AIR FORCE/ARMY/NAVY

The Allied command decides to halt the advance toward Tunis until the end of the rainy season in Tunisia.

1943

ON LAND, SEA, AND AIR

JANUARY
ARMY
The Army calls for volunteers to make up an all Japanese-American combat unit. In Hawaii, thousands clamor to join the 100th Infantry Battalion, soon to be followed by the 442d Infantry Regiment.

1 JANUARY
ARMY
Major General Lloyd R. Fredendall takes command of the II Corps, and he begins planning Operation SATIN, the capture of Sfax, Tunisia.

3 JANUARY
AIR FORCE/ARMY
In the first attack against German submarine pens at Saint-Nazaire, France, 68 VIII Bomber Command aircraft use precision formation bombing techniques. Although considerable damage to the target is achieved, opposition over the target is stiff. Seven aircraft are lost, 47 are damaged, and 70 aircrew are missing and another 5 are reported killed in the raid. This attack is the first in which formation precision bombing is attempted.

5 JANUARY
AIR FORCE
Lieutenant General Dwight D. Eisenhower activates the Allied Air Force in the North African Theater. Major General Carl A. Spaatz assumes command as the Air Commander in Chief. The aviation element includes the Twelfth Air Force plus Royal Air Force and potentially some French units.

ARMY
Lieutenant General Mark W. Clark, first commander of the U.S. Fifth Army, opens his headquarters at Oujda, Morocco. It becomes responsible for planning the U.S. portion of the invasion of Italy.

6 JANUARY
NAVY
During a patrol off Brazil, a PBY Catalina of Patrol Squadron 83 sinks the German submarine *U-164*.

13 JANUARY
NAVY
PBY Catalinas of Patrol Squadron 83 send the German submarine *U-507* to the bottom off Brazil.

14–24 JANUARY
ALL SERVICES
The Casablanca Conference opens in Morocco. President Franklin D. Roosevelt and Prime Minister Winston S. Churchill agree to defeat Germany first while accepting only unconditional surrender of Axis forces. Churchill and Roosevelt decide to invade Sicily; outline a Pacific strategy with offensives through the central and southwest Pacific; and agree to send more troops to the China–Burma–India Theater. Brigadier General Ira C. Eaker, at the insistence of Lieutenant General Henry H. Arnold, presents the Army Air Forces' daylight bombing strategy to Churchill, which eventually leads to the Allies' around-the-clock bombing strategy known as the Combined Bomber Offensive.

15 JANUARY
ALL SERVICES
The Pentagon, built in 16 months under the direction of the Army Corps of Engineers, opens ahead of schedule in Arlington, Virginia.

MARINE CORPS
Anne A. Lentz becomes the first female Marine Corps officer reservist when she is commissioned a captain following her civilian work in designing the uniforms for the Women's Reserve program.

20 JANUARY
NAVY

Brennan becomes the first destroyer escort commissioned. Though her activity is confined to duty as a training ship, her successors see action with Atlantic convoys and hunter-killer groups, and will fight with distinction at the Battle of Leyte Gulf in October 1944.

27 JANUARY
AIR FORCE

Heavy bombers from the Eighth Air Force attack U-boat construction pens, power-generating facilities, and docks at Wilhelmshaven and Emden. Conducted by 1st Bombardment Wing, these raids are the first American bombing raids of the war against enemy targets in Germany.

ARMY

The 149th Post Headquarters Company, the first Women's Army Auxiliary Corps unit deployed overseas, arrives in Algiers, North Africa. It is an African American unit.

29 JANUARY
MARINE CORPS

Ruth Cheney Streeter is commissioned a major and named as director of the Marine Corps Women's Reserve.

Opposite: *Lieutenant General Mark W. Clark is named the commander of the Fifth Army in January 1943 and tasked with planning the invasion of Italy. (National Archives)*

Above: *In Casablanca, Morocco, President Franklin D. Roosevelt, second from left, and Prime Minister Winston S. Churchill, far right, meet with two leaders of the Free French forces—General Henri Giraud, far left, and Brigadier General Charles DeGaulle. (Imperial War Museum)*

Below: *Major Ruth C. Streeter, USMC, is sworn in as the second female Marine Corps officer in January. She becomes the first director of the Marine Corps Women's Reserve. (Marine Corps Historical Center)*

3 FEBRUARY
ARMY/NAVY

While crossing the Atlantic, SS *Dorchester* is torpedoed by a German submarine. The ship is carrying 902 troops headed for the U.S. base on Greenland. Four Army chaplains—Lieutenants George L. Fox, Alexander D. Goode, John P. Washington, and Clark V. Poling—remove their own lifebelts and give them to others. The four chaplains go down with the ship.

4 FEBRUARY
AIR FORCE/ARMY

Lieutenant General Frank M. Andrews assumes command of the European Theater of Operations, U.S. Army. Lieutenant General Dwight D. Eisenhower assumes command of the North African Theater of Operations, U.S. Army.

13 FEBRUARY
MARINE CORPS
The first women are enlisted into the Marine Corps for World War II.

14 FEBRUARY
ARMY
In Tunisia, advancing Allied units including the 1st Infantry and 1st Armored Division are forced back by a major German attack. Some U.S. elements are cut off on Djebel Lessouda ridge and suffer heavy casualties.

15 FEBRUARY
AIR FORCE
Major General Ira C. Eaker replaces Major General Carl A. Spaatz as commander of the Eighth Air Force. Spaatz moves to the Mediterranean to command the air operations in North Africa.

ARMY
Counterattacks to relieve surrounded U.S. units in Tunisia fail with heavy tank losses, but some of the trapped force escape during the night. Major General Lloyd R. Fredendall's II Corps is ordered to withdraw to new positions.

16–17 FEBRUARY
ARMY
Reinforcement by its Combat Command B allows the 1st Armored Division to halt the German advance in Tunisia for the night as the II Corps falls back to defend passes at Sbiba, Kasserine, and Dernaia. Reinforcements from the 1st and 9th Infantry Divisions move forward and isolated forces caught behind German lines are wiped out.

17 FEBRUARY
AIR FORCE
The Mediterranean Air Command is activated. Air Chief Marshal Sir Arthur Tedder assumes overall command of three subordinate operational commands. One of these, the Northwest African Air Forces, is commanded by Lieutenant General Carl A. Spaatz.

18 FEBRUARY
AIR FORCE
During a test flight of the Boeing XB-29 bomber, all aboard are lost when it crashes—including Edmund T. Allen, "the greatest test pilot of them all."

Above: *An Army Air Forces ground crew prepares a plane for an upcoming mission in North Africa. ("In Good Weather," Carlos Lopez, Army Art Collection, U.S. Army Center of Military History)*

Below: *The crew of an M3 half-track (T28E1), armed as an antiaircraft vehicle with a 37mm gun and two .50 caliber machine guns, watches for German planes in North Africa. (Dept. of Defense)*

19 FEBRUARY
ARMY
Units from the 1st and 34th Infantry Divisions together with British and French troops hold against a German armored attack on Sbiba Pass, Tunisia.

20–22 FEBRUARY
AIR FORCE/ARMY
A strong German attack breaks through II Corps defenses at Kasserine Pass, Tunisia, and moves north as corps units withdraw to new positions. U.S. reinforcements help to barely contain the German thrusts after hard fighting. Stiffening Allied defenses finally force the Germans to give up their offensive and withdraw. The 1st Armored Division with air support attacks and pushes the Germans out of the Ousseltia Valley.

21 FEBRUARY
AIR FORCE/ARMY
The 93d Bombardment Group is relieved from duty in the Middle East and is reassigned to the Eighth Air Force in England. The 93d will jump back and forth between England and North Africa, and by war's end will log the highest total number of combat missions

of any Eighth Air Force bomb group, flying 396 missions as a group, including 43 from north Africa.

22 FEBRUARY
NAVY
The battleship *Iowa* is commissioned.

26 FEBRUARY
AIR FORCE
Major General James H. Doolittle assumes command of the XII Bomber Command.

1 MARCH
AIR FORCE
In Algeria, Lieutenant General Carl A. Spaatz assumes command of the Twelfth Air Force.

MARINE CORPS
Marine Bombing Squadron 413, the first of 12 Marine Corps bombing squadrons established during World War II, is organized at Cherry Point, North Carolina.

1–5 MARCH
ARMY
Patrols from the II Corps follow the German units retreating from Ousseltia Valley, Tunisia, while British forces continue to be attacked.

6 MARCH
ARMY
Major General George S. Patton Jr. takes command of the U.S. II Corps, relieving Major General Lloyd R. Fredendall. Major General Omar N. Bradley becomes deputy corps commander.

NAVY
The auxiliary escort carrier *Bogue*, forming the centerpiece of a pioneer hunter-killer group, begins operations in the Atlantic, marking the first time that a ship of her type operates strictly in the antisubmarine role protecting convoys. All told, *Bogue*'s embarked aircraft and escorts send 13 German U-boats to the bottom during World War II.

8 MARCH
MARINE CORPS
The 1st Marine Depot Company is formed, manned primarily by African American enlisted Marines. It is the first of 51 such units, which have the mission of unloading supplies at the beach and moving them inland during an amphibious assault.

NAVY
A PBY Catalina of Patrol Squadron 53 sinks the German submarine *U-156* off Trinidad.

Right: *All of the U.S. military services are segregated during the war. African American men who join the Marine Corps are placed in the 51st or 52d Defense Battalion or in service units of some kind. (USMC)*

Left: *American Soldiers examine an abandoned German Mark VI Tiger tank and the large 88mm main gun. (Dept. of Defense)*

Below: *General Henry H. Arnold, commanding general of the Army Air Forces, pauses in front of his official sedan to observe planes passing overhead. (Robert and Kathleen Arnold Collection)*

10 MARCH
NAVY

The light cruiser *Savannah* and destroyer *Eberle* encounter the German blockade runner *Karin* in the South Atlantic. After crewmen from the destroyer board her in hopes of obtaining intelligence documents, scuttling charges set by *Karin*'s crew explode, killing seven and wounding two members of the boarding party. The surviving members of the boarding party continue their intelligence gathering until forced to abandon ship.

12 MARCH
NAVY

The destroyer *Champlin*, while escorting convoy UGS 6 west of the Azores Islands, obtains a radar contact ahead of the convoy. Racing to the contact point, she observes the surfaced German submarine *U-130*. The destroyer attempts to ram the sub, which makes a crash dive. *Champlin* drops depth charges on the submerging submarine, sinking it.

13 MARCH
ARMY

The first Women's Army Auxiliary Corps officer candidates report for training at Mount Holyoke College in Massachusetts.

15 MARCH
NAVY

A system of numbering the Navy's fleets is instituted, assigning those in the Pacific odd numbers and those in the Atlantic even numbers.

17 MARCH
ARMY

The II Corps, with the 1st Infantry Division leading, attacks and seizes El Guettar, Tunisia; hard fighting continues.

18 MARCH
AIR FORCE

First Lieutenant Jack W. Mathis, Eighth Air Force, is assigned as the lead bombardier for the 359th Bomb Squadron of 22 B-17F Flying Fortress bombers attacking submarine yards at Vegesack, Germany. His aircraft is hit with antiaircraft fire and he is mortally wounded, knocked from the bombsight to the rear of the bombardier compartment. Mathis drags himself back to the sight, releases his bombs, and then dies at his post. Mathis becomes the first Eighth Air Force Medal of Honor recipient. His brother, Mark, replaces

him as a bombardier in the 359th and is lost over the North Sea during a bombing mission on 14 May 1943.

19 MARCH
AIR FORCE

Lieutenant General Henry H. Arnold is promoted to general. His four stars are the first for an Army Air Forces commander.

21–23 MARCH
ARMY

The 1st Infantry Division moves east from El Guettar, Tunisia, to push Germans from Djebel Naemia. The 1st Ranger Battalion and 26th Infantry Regiment trap a German force and take 700 prisoners of war. German counterattacks to retake El Guettar are contained after fierce fighting with heavy losses.

24 MARCH
MARINE CORPS

The first female recruits report for boot camp at Hunter College in New York City, New York. The Marine Corps' Women's Reserve training facility is co-located with the Navy's Women Accepted for Volunteer Emergency Service training program at this prestigious university.

26 MARCH
MARINE CORPS

The 24th Marines, an infantry regiment, is organized at Camp Pendleton, California.

28–29 MARCH
ARMY

The II Corps renews attacks toward Gabes, Tunisia, with the 1st and 9th Infantry Divisions abreast. The 1st Division makes only limited advances, while the 9th, in action for the first time, suffers costly failures due to confusion and heavy enemy fire. For the next two weeks futile efforts are made to break the German positions.

1 APRIL
MARINE CORPS

Marine Aircraft Group 51, the first Marine night fighter group, is established at Cherry Point, North Carolina.

Below: *A column of advancing American Soldiers uses a hasty bridge and ford to cross over a river in North Africa. ("River Crossing," Fletcher Martin, Army Art Collection, U.S. Army Center of Military History)*

Above: *An Army Air Forces bombardier sets the calibrations on the super-secret Norden bombsight that gives Allied planes the capability to do very high-level daylight bombing with improved accuracy. (U.S. Air Force)*

Below: *The blue and white insignia of the U.S. II Corps includes a rising eagle and a rampant lion, both symbolizing the corps' service in World War I. (U.S. Army)*

Opposite: *Officers confer over a map in front of an M3 command half-track while another M3 with a 75mm gun is positioned in a small ravine near El Guettar, Tunisia. (Dept. of Defense)*

NAVY

Naval Air Station Patuxent River, Maryland, is established. The base will eventually replace Naval Air Station Anacostia, Washington, D.C., as the site of the Navy's flight testing, and will become home to the Naval Test Pilot School.

2 APRIL
AIR FORCE/ARMY

The research building of the Army Air Forces School of Aviation Medicine, which houses four altitude decompression chambers, opens at Randolph Field, near Austin, Texas. Twenty-seven officers and 35 civilians man the facility.

MARINE CORPS

The 4th Parachute Battalion begins organizing in southern California.

4 APRIL
AIR FORCE

Eighth Air Force heavy bombers strike industrial targets near Paris, France. These 85 bombers inflict heavy damage on the Renault armaments factory and motor works. Four U.S. bombers are lost when enemy fighters attack the formation.

5 APRIL
AIR FORCE/ARMY

Operation FLAX begins. This campaign is designed to destroy the enemy's system of ferrying personnel and supplies to Tunisia by attacking air transports and their escorts. North African Air Force aircraft destroy more than 60 enemy planes during the operation, which continues through 22 April.

8 APRIL
AIR FORCE

The Eighth Fighter Command bolsters its capability by adding the 56th and 78th Fighter Groups to the already operational 4th Fighter Group. Increased activity is now possible that will eventually allow deep fighter penetration with long-range heavy bombers.

9 APRIL
NAVY

The Navy reestablishes the rank of commodore.

12 APRIL
AIR FORCE/ARMY

Details of the highly secret Norden bombsight are released by the War Department. The sight is said to remain locked to a target regardless of aircraft speed or other movement.

15 APRIL
ARMY
Lieutenant General George S. Patton Jr. turns command of the II Corps over to Major General Omar N. Bradley and begins planning for the invasion of Sicily.

NAVY
A PBY Catalina of Patrol Squadron 83 sinks the Italian submarine *Archimede* off the coast of Brazil.

16 APRIL
NAVY
In a major change to uniform regulations, the color of the Navy's working uniform is changed to slate gray. "Grays" prove unpopular among the officer corps, and on 15 October 1946 khakis are reinstated as the working uniform for the Navy.

17 APRIL
AIR FORCE
The Eighth Air Force launches its first 100-plane raid against one single target—the Focke-Wulf factory in Bremen, Germany. Fifteen bombers are shot down and another is brought down by antiaircraft fire. German fighter opposition is so strong that fighter commanders call for 20 additional fighter groups to balance the odds over Europe.

23 APRIL
ARMY
The U.S. II Corps under Major General Omar N. Bradley moves 100,000 men an average distance of

Above: Promoted to lieutenant general in June 1943, Omar N. Bradley travels from North Africa to England, and is made commander of First U.S. Army in August. He becomes deeply involved in the planning for the invasion of France. (National Archives)

Below: The crew of an M4 Sherman tank prepares the large flail device on the front of the tank, called a "scorpion," which whirls chains ahead of the vehicle to detonate enemy mines. (Dept. of Defense)

Right: *Soldiers from the 47th Infantry Regiment, 9th Infantry Division move cautiously into the outskirts of the town of Bizerte, Tunisia, in May 1943. (Dept. of Defense)*

Below: *Lieutenant General Frank M. Andrews, commander of U.S. Forces in Europe, dies in a plane crash in Iceland in May 1943. (U.S. Air Force)*

150 miles in deployment from southern to northern Tunisia to launch the final phase of the campaign—Operation VULCAN. Bradley orders four U.S. divisions into action—the 1st Infantry, 9th Infantry, 34th Infantry, and 1st Armored Divisions. He has the 3d Infantry Division ready to assist as needed.

27 APRIL
NAVY
A PV-1 Ventura patrol-bomber of Bombing Squadron 125 sinks the German submarine *U-174* while covering convoy SC 128 off Halifax, Nova Scotia.

1 MAY
MARINE CORPS
The 25th Marines, an infantry regiment, is organized at Camp Lejeune, North Carolina.

3 MAY
AIR FORCE/ARMY
Lieutenant General Frank M. Andrews is killed when his aircraft crashes into the side of a mountain in Iceland during an approach to land. Andrews, the Commanding General, European Theater of Operations, U.S. Army, had been instrumental in educating Army senior staff officers in the use of American airpower.

ARMY
In Tunisia, II Corps elements force the enemy to retreat to the last hills protecting the roads to Bizerte and Tunis. The second phase of the campaign begins on 4 May as the II Corps breaks through to seize Bizerte and Chouigui.

4 MAY
AIR FORCE
Sixty-five Eighth Air Force heavy bombers strike the former Ford and General Motors factories at Antwerp, Belgium. As part of the mission, a group of 30 B-17 Flying Fortress and B-24 Liberator bombers launch a diversion toward the French coast. More than 100 German fighter planes sent to intercept the feint are distracted long enough to allow the main strike force to attack with limited interruption. P-47 Thunderbolt fighters escort the bombers for 175 miles.

Above: *Lieutenant General Jacob L. Devers, commander of the European Theater of Operations, congratulates Captain Robert K. Morgan, commander of the B-17 Flying Fortress "Memphis Belle," on completion of 25 combat missions over Europe. (Getty Images)*

Below: *Soldiers of the 319th Parachute Field Artillery Battalion, 82d Airborne Division, load a 75mm pack howitzer into a CG-4A glider during a training exercise in Morocco. (82d Airborne Division War Memorial Museum)*

6 MAY
AIR FORCE/NAVY
Captain H. Franklin Gregory makes the first helicopter landing on a ship when he lands a Sikorsky XR-4 Hoverfly on the deck of the carrier *Bunker Hill*, at anchor in Long Island Sound, New York.

8 MAY
AIR FORCE
Aircraft of the North African Air Force and the Ninth Air Force—B-26 Marauder and B-25 Mitchell bombers, and P-40 Warhawk fighters—begin bombardment of the Pantelleria landing ground. Additionally, P-40s strafe and attack other targets in the Gulf of Tunis. The aerial attacks at Pantelleria, an island located between Italy and Tunisia, will continue through June.

12 MAY
ARMY
The end of the battle for North Africa is marked by the surrender of the Fifth Panzer Army at Ferryville, Tunisia.

14 MAY
AIR FORCE
A "maximum force" bombing effort—just over 200 VIII Bomber Command bombers—is launched simultaneously on four separate objectives. Primary targets are submarine yards and naval facilities at Kiel, Germany, and factories near Antwerp, Belgium. This is the first time that more than 200 Army Air Forces bombers have been dispatched on a single mission.

15 MAY
NAVY
OS2U/OS2N Kingfisher aircraft of Scouting Squadron 62 join the Cuban submarine chaser *SC 13* in sinking the German submarine *U-176* in the waters off Cuba.

15–25 MAY
ALL SERVICES
The Trident Conference between British Prime Minister Winston S. Churchill, President Franklin D. Roosevelt, and the Combined Chiefs of Staff in Washington, D.C., results in a reaffirmation of the "Germany first" strategy; decisions to invade Italy and plan for a cross-channel invasion of Europe; and approval for an offensive across the Central Pacific.

Above: *Soldiers carry duffle bags with their personal gear up the gangway into a troopship as their unit prepares to depart. ("Blue Duffle Bags," Barse Miller, Army Art Collection, U.S. Army Center of Military History)*

16 MAY
NAVY
The destroyer *MacKenzie* executes two depth charge attacks against the German submarine *U-182* near the Madeira Islands west of Morocco, sinking the sub.

17 MAY
AIR FORCE
The crew of the B-17F Flying Fortress "Memphis Belle" completes 25 combat missions in the European Theater. Led by Captain Robert Morgan, the crew returns to the U.S. with their bomber and fly it on a nationwide tour selling war bonds.

After 10 of 11 322d Bomb Group B-26 Marauders are lost on a single low-level bombardment mission, the Eighth Air Force suspends such operations for medium bombers indefinitely.

NAVY
After being damaged in an attack by a PBM Mariner of Patrol Squadron 74, the German submarine *U-128* is sunk in the South Atlantic by 5-inch gunfire from the destroyers *Moffett* and *Jouett*. Forty-seven of the sub's crew survive the sinking.

18 MAY
AIR FORCE
The Combined Chiefs of Staff approves the plan for the Combined Bomber Offensive. The offensive is aimed at the destruction of the German military military, industrial, and economic system with around-the-clock bombing of selected targets. Destruction of the German aircraft industry is the first priority; other targets include German submarine bases, oil refineries, and factories.

20 MAY
NAVY
The 10th Fleet is established with headquarters in Washington, D.C., to direct the antisubmarine warfare effort in the Atlantic.

22 MAY
NAVY
While protecting convoy ON 184 in the Atlantic, TBF Avenger torpedo-bombers of Composite Squadron 9 from the escort carrier *Bogue* sink the German submarine *U-569* and damage *U-305*.

Above: *Crewmen of the subchaser* PC-565 *man the 3-inch deck gun as the little ship patrols the Atlantic looking for German submarines. She already has one kill,* U-521, *posted on her bridge. (U.S. Naval Institute)*

Below: *Subchasers such as the* PC-472, *shown here off the east coast of Virginia, are used extensively to guard American coastal waters. (Naval Historical Center)*

25 MAY
NAVY
A PBY Catalina of Patrol Squadron 84 sinks the German submarine *U-467* in the waters off Iceland.

1 JUNE
MARINE CORPS
The 14th Marines, an artillery regiment, is activated at Camp Lejeune, North Carolina.

2 JUNE
AIR FORCE
Lieutenant William B. Campbell and Lieutenant Charles B. Hall fly the first combat mission of the 99th Fighter Squadron out of Fardjouna, Tunisia.

NAVY
While operating off the Virginia Capes, the submarine chaser *PC-565* obtains an underwater sound contact on the German submarine *U-521*. A depth charge attack brings the sub to the surface, and gunners on board the submarine chaser batter the sub with 20mm fire, forcing her to submerge again. A second depth charge sinks *U-521*; only one member of her crew survives.

5 JUNE
NAVY

Having damaged three U-boats the previous day, TBF Avenger torpedo-bombers of Composite Squadron 9 sink the German submarine *U-217* off the Canary Islands.

10 JUNE
AIR FORCE

The Combined Bomber Offensive against Germany begins. The Royal Air Force attacks German targets by night while the Eighth Air Force attacks industrial targets during the day. The around-the-clock bombardment is intended to destroy Germany's wartime capability and morale. The Combined Operational Planning Committee is established as the agency for coordinating efforts between Allied air forces.

NAVY

The German submarine *U-66* attacks the tanker *Esso Gettysburg* as she carries crude oil to Philadelphia, Pennsylvania. The attack triggers fires that feed on the ship's cargo. Despite the flames, Ensign John S. Arnold II of the ship's Armed Guard detachment orders the forward gun manned and opens fire on the submarine.

10–11 JUNE
AIR FORCE/ARMY

North African Air Force Wellington bombers, naval aircraft, and Ninth Air Force B-25 Mitchells bomb the island of Pantelleria while escorted by P-40 Warhawk fighters. This concludes more than one month of aerial bombardment of the small island between Italy and Tunisia. The British 1st Division lands on Pantelleria unopposed, and the enemy forces surrender unconditionally without a shot being fired. This marks the first time that a major military objective surrenders solely because of the impact of airpower.

12 JUNE
NAVY

A TBF Avenger of Composite Squadron 9 from the escort carrier *Bogue* sinks the German submarine *U-118* near the Canary Islands.

The U.S. submarine *R-12* (SS 89) sinks while conducting training operations off Key West, Florida. All 42 members of her crew perish in the accident.

15 JUNE
AIR FORCE/ARMY

The 58th Bombardment Wing is formed at Marietta, Georgia. It is the first Army Air Forces unit to fly the B-29 Superfortress bomber operationally.

Right: German submarines often take the risk to surface in the dark to better conduct their attacks on Allied convoys. ("Sea Wolves," James Dietz)

Left: *A German submarine is attacked by TBF Avenger torpedo-bombers from the escort carrier* Bogue *in the Atlantic. (National Museum of Naval Aviation)*

Below: *A Soldier examines his cans of C-rations with some skepticism. (U.S. Army)*

Opposite: *Women's Army Corps officers are sworn in after completing their training at Fort Des Moines, Iowa. Almost 500,000 women volunteer to serve in the military during the war. (U.S. Army)*

MARINE CORPS

The 20th Marines, a regiment of engineers and pioneers, is established at Camp Lejeune, North Carolina.

20 JUNE
NAVY

A PBY Catalina of Patrol Squadron 84 sinks the German submarine *U-388* and damages *U-420* in the

waters off Iceland. A landmark event in antisubmarine warfare, this action marks the first employment of the Mark 24 homing torpedo, nicknamed "Fido."

21 JUNE
ARMY

Nurse 2d Lieutenant Edith Greenwood receives the first Soldier's Medal awarded to a woman for heroism in saving patients during a hospital fire at Yuma, Arizona.

22 JUNE
AIR FORCE

Conducting the first large-scale daytime raid on targets in the Ruhr area of Germany, 182 Eighth Air Force bombers strike chemical works and synthetic rubber plants. Another formation bombs the former Ford and General Motors plants at Antwerp, Belgium.

24 JUNE
AIR FORCE

Lieutenant Colonel William R. Lovelace of the Army Air Forces Aeromedical Laboratory makes a record-setting parachute jump near Ephrata, Washington. He leaps from an altitude of 40,200 feet.

25 JUNE
ARMY

The Army quartermaster corps announces the "Ten-in-One" ration, a package that contains complete food supplies for 10 men for one day, or for one man for 10 days.

30 JUNE
MARINE CORPS
The strength of the Marine Corps on active duty is 21,384 officers and 287,139 enlisted.

NAVY
Unaware that he is an African American, the Navy designates Ensign Oscar Holmes a naval aviator, making him the first man of color to receive the coveted wings of gold. Holmes' experience as a civilian pilot means that he is winged following completion of an instructor's course, rather than the entire Navy flight syllabus.

JULY
AIR FORCE
A Romanian pilot flies a German Ju 88D-1/Trop long-range photographic reconnaissance plane to Cyprus to defect to British forces there. The Royal Air Force turns it over to the U.S. Army Air Forces. Test pilots later fly the aircraft extensively at Wright Field, Ohio.

MARINE CORPS
The Women's Reserve officer candidate school and recruit training programs are transferred from civilian institutions to Camp Lejeune, North Carolina.

1 JULY
ARMY
President Franklin D. Roosevelt signs a bill establishing the Women's Army Corps (WAC) as a component of the Army of the United States. The Army has 90 days to dissolve the Women's Army Auxiliary Corps and to determine how many of the enrolled women and commissioned officers will join the new WAC.

MARINE CORPS/NAVY
The Navy Department establishes the V-12 program at various universities to train enlisted Sailors and Marines for commissioning.

4 JULY
AIR FORCE
After a staged flight totaling 28 hours, the first C-47 Skytrain to fly across the Atlantic lands in Great Britain. This is also the first time a Skytrain tows a glider across the ocean. The CG-4A glider carries medical supplies for Russia and a variety of other mechanical parts.

Above: *The American-built CG-4 glider can carry up to 13 troops and is used in all major U.S. airborne assaults in Europe. (U.S. Air Force)*

Below: *Uniform insignia for an Army Air Forces flight instructor. (U.S. Army)*

In the Zone of the Interior, the Army Air Forces Training Command is established and takes up the responsibility formerly assigned to the Technical Training Command and Flying Training Command.

8 JULY
AIR FORCE
Colonel Malcolm G. Grow, a surgeon in the Eighth Air Force, develops the flak vest and steel pot helmet for use by aircrew in aerial combat.

9 JULY
AIR FORCE/ARMY/NAVY
Under overall command of British General Sir Harold Alexander, Operation HUSKY, the Allied invasion of Sicily, begins. The air offensive since mid-June by the Northwest African Air Forces with air bombardment and fighter sweeps has been successful in gaining air superiority over the island. After dark, while convoys of the two naval task forces with the assault units steam toward the beaches, 226 C-47 Skytrains of the

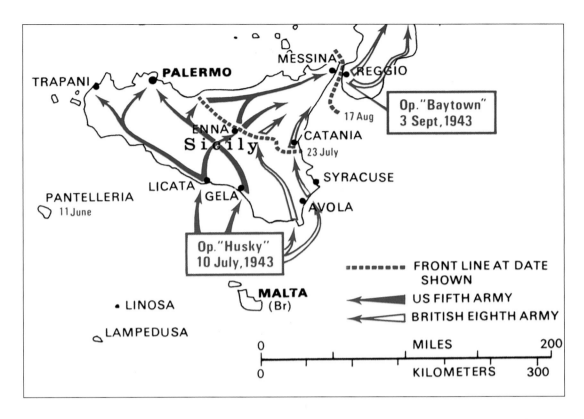

Right: *In Operation HUSKY, the invasion of Sicily, a joint American–British assault force lands on the south coast and proceeds up both sides of the island. (U.S. Army)*

Troop Carrier Command drop paratroopers of the 82d Airborne Division to capture the high ground near the Ponte Olivo airfield. The landings are widely scattered, yet the men take the objective. British landings are also successful. It is the first major Allied airborne assault of the war. On one of the landing ships, Ensign John J. Parle suffers fatal injuries when he prevents alerting the enemy to the amphibious landings by tossing overboard a prematurely ignited smoke pot. He is awarded the Medal of Honor.

NAVY
A PBY Catalina of Patrol Squadron 94 sinks the German submarine *U-590* at the mouth of the Amazon River in Brazil.

10 JULY
AIR FORCE/ARMY/NAVY
On board the attack transport *Monrovia*—of the Western Naval Task Force under Vice Admiral H. Kent Hewitt—the U.S. Seventh Army (formerly the I Armored Corps) is created with Lieutenant General George S. Patton Jr. as commander. It is the first U.S. field army in action. Landing craft, including the new Army DUKW ("duck") amphibious trucks, puts three U.S. assault forces ashore before dawn near Licata and Gela, Sicily. Despite some confusion with the landing craft on the beaches, the two assault task forces— composed of units from the 1st, 3d, and 45th Infantry Divisions, the 2d Armored Division, and three battalions of Rangers—land without serious delay or casualties. U.S. Navy ships provide gunfire support.

Linkup is made with the 82d Airborne units, and towns are seized as the U.S. forces move along the southwestern coast. The British Eighth Army landings to the east are also successful. Axis aircraft attack the Allied ships, sinking the destroyer *Maddox*, *LST 313*, and the minesweeper *Sentinel*, which endures five attacks. Fire from shore batteries also damages *LCT 242*.

11 JULY
AIR FORCE/ARMY/NAVY
Allied forces expand their bridgeheads in Sicily. The II Corps under Lieutenant General Omar N. Bradley turns back several Axis counterattacks with the support of gunfire from Navy cruisers and destroyers. After dark, a reinforcing airdrop by the 504th Regimental Combat Team, 82d Airborne Division suffers heavy losses when the C-47 Skytrains are mistakenly fired on by Allied ships and shore gunners as the planes pass overhead. Surviving planes scatter, dropping men across the island. Of 144 C-47s, 23 never return.

12 JULY
ARMY
Moving inland from the Sicilian coast, U.S. forces meet sporadic resistance and counterattacks from German and Italian units. Comiso and its airstrip are taken as are other towns, and linkup is made with units of the British Eighth Army. Late in the day Lieutenant General George S. Patton Jr. moves his Seventh Army headquarters ashore.

13 JULY
AIR FORCE/ARMY/MARINE CORPS

With Brigadier General William J. Donovan designated to take charge, President Franklin D. Roosevelt orders creation of the Office of Strategic Services for special operations behind enemy lines. This is the forerunner of the Central Intelligence Agency.

ARMY/NAVY

The 45th Infantry Division assists British forces in taking Vizzini, and Rangers with naval gunfire support the capture of Butera, Sicily. Despite continued American success, an order from Allied commander British General Sir Harold Alexander limits the U.S. Seventh Army's ability to advance, placing it in a supporting role covering the British left flank and rear. Lieutenant General George S. Patton Jr., however, approves a "reconnaissance in force" by the 3d Division (under Major General Lucian K. Truscott Jr.) north along the coast toward Agrigento using the 7th Infantry Regiment and 3d Ranger Battalion.

NAVY

A TBF Avenger of Composite Squadron 13 operating from the auxiliary aircraft carrier *Core* sinks the German submarine *U-487* in the Atlantic.

14 JULY
NAVY

TBF Avenger and F4F Wildcat aircraft of Composite Squadron 29 from the auxiliary aircraft carrier *Santee* sink the German submarine *U-160* south of the Azores Islands.

14–15 JULY
ARMY/NAVY

Navy cruisers provide naval gunfire support as the 7th Infantry Regiment and Rangers secure their objectives on Sicily against sporadic resistance. Lieutenant David C. Waybur, 3d Infantry Division, later receives the Medal of Honor for stopping a column of Italian tanks with a submachine gun. Lieutenant General George S. Patton Jr. reorients his units to the north, creates a Provisional Corps under Major General Geoffrey Keyes, and with it on the west of the II Corps prepares to continue the "reconnaissance."

15 JULY
NAVY

A PBY Catalina of Patrol Squadron 92 assists three British warships in sinking the German submarine *U-135* west of the Canary Islands.

A TBF Avenger of Composite Squadron 29 operating from the escort carrier *Santee* sinks the German submarine *U-509* south of the Azores Islands.

A PBM Mariner of Patrol Squadron 32 sinks the German submarine *U-159* in the Caribbean south of Haiti.

16 JULY
NAVY

TBF Avengers from Composite Squadron 13 operating from the escort carrier *Core* sink the German submarine *U-67* in the Atlantic.

17 JULY
ARMY

Lieutenant General George S. Patton Jr., angry over a new British order that places Seventh Army in an even more passive role in Sicily, flies to British General Sir Harold Alexander's headquarters in Tunisia. Patton gains approval of a new plan to let U.S. forces advance against Palermo on the north coast. He returns to Seventh Army and orders his two corps to advance. A later British "clarification" of the agreement again imposes limits on U.S. forces, but Patton ignores it.

18 JULY
NAVY

The blimp *K-74* is shot down by deck gunners on the surfaced German submarine *U-134* in the Florida Straits. This is the only loss of an airship to enemy action during World War II.

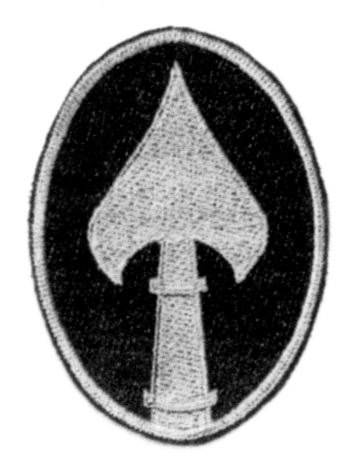

19 JULY
AIR FORCE

Flying from bases in Benghazi, Libya, Northwest African Strategic Air Force B-17 Flying Fortresses carry out the first Army Air Forces bombing raids on

Opposite: *High winds and antiaircraft fire force paratroopers of the 82d Airborne Division to drop in widely scattered locations during the invasion of Sicily. Forming small bands, the determined Soldiers attack and delay Germans whenever they can, spreading confusion in the German lines. ("In The Beginning," James Dietz)*

Above: *Uniform insignia for the members of the Office of Strategic Services.*
(U.S. Army)

Right: *A destroyer fires one of her 5-inch guns. ("Number 2 Gun," Lt. Mitchell Jamieson, USN, Navy Art Collection)*

Previous spread: *Anxious ground and air crews on one of the many bases in England count the returning planes, hoping for a glimpse of their comrades. ("The Return of the Raid Over Rouen," Peter Hurd, Army Art Collection, U.S. Army Center of Military History)*

Above: *Navy dirigibles on convoy escort duty keep watch for lurking German submarines. ("The Convoy Brood," Adolph Dehn, Navy Art Collection)*

Rome, Italy, attacking the rail yards there. B-25 Mitchell and B-26 Marauder medium bombers strike nearby airfields.

19 JULY
NAVY
A PBM Mariner of Patrol Squadron 74 sinks German submarine *U-513* off Brazil.

21 JULY
AIR FORCE
While flying his eighth mission, 99th Fighter Squadron pilot Lieutenant Charles B. Hall shoots down a German FW-190 fighter over Sicily. Hall is the first African American Army Air Forces pilot to shoot down an enemy aircraft.

NAVY
A PBY Catalina of Patrol Squadron 94 sinks the German submarine *U-662* off the mouth of the Amazon River in Brazil.

23–31 JULY
AIR FORCE/ARMY/NAVY
Units of Major General Geoffrey Keyes' Provisional Corps capture Palermo, Sicily, and then begin mopping up operations of bypassed Axis elements in its sector. Against occasional fierce resistance, the II Corps closes on the north coast road. On 31 July, Lieutenant General George S. Patton Jr. issues orders for the II Corps to turn east toward Messina in pursuit of the fleeing Germans and Italians. Army Air Forces and Navy units support the advance.

23 JULY
NAVY

TBF Avengers of Composite Squadron 9 operating from the escort carrier *Bogue* sink the German submarine *U-527* south of the Azores Islands.

The destroyer *George E. Badger* sinks the German submarine *U-613* south of the Azores Islands.

PB4Y-1 Liberator patrol bombers of Bombing Squadron 107 sink the German submarine *U-598* off Brazil.

24 JULY
ALL SERVICES

Italy's Fascist Grand Council removes Head of Government Benito Mussolini and places him under arrest.

AIR FORCE

In its first attack in Norway, Eighth Air Force heavy bombers attack nitrate works at Horoya. Aluminum and magnesium plants are also attacked and subsequently abandoned by the Germans. On this raid, new techniques are used by the bombers to join above overcast weather conditions using "splasher beacons." Future poor weather missions are made possible by such rejoin methods.

24 JULY–3 AUGUST
AIR FORCE/ARMY

The Royal Air Force and Army Air Forces begin Combined Bomber Offensive raids against the German port city of Hamburg. On the first night, 750 RAF heavy bombers do considerable damage to the city. The following day, more than 200 Eighth Air Force heavy bombers attack the Hamburg shipyard and the U-boat base at Kiel. Effective German fighter tactics bring down 19 American planes. These attacks are costly, as escort fighters are unable to accompany the bombers all the way from England to targets in Germany.

26 JULY
AIR FORCE/ARMY/NAVY

As part of a psychological campaign to induce surrender, the bombing of Italy is suspended. The Combined Chiefs of Staff authorize General Dwight D. Eisenhower to implement plans for Operation AVALANCHE—the invasion of Italy—as soon as possible.

NAVY

A PBM Mariner of Patrol Squadron 32 sinks the German submarine *U-359* off Haiti.

Opposite: *Lieutenant Charles B. Hall, one of the "Tuskegee Airmen" of the 99th Fighter Squadron, celebrates his first aerial kill on 21 July with a Coke. He is the first African American pilot to down a German plane. (NASM)*

Right: *The Combined Bomber Offensive against Germany begins on 24 July with a massive night raid on Hamburg by the Royal Air Force, followed the next day by 200 heavy U.S. bombers. ("Hamburg Raid, July 1943," Floyd Davis, Army Art Collection, U.S. Army Center of Military History)*

28 JULY
AIR FORCE

More than 300 Eighth Air Force heavy bombers attack Germany. Because of horrible weather, only about 80 reach their targets, the aircraft factory at Kassel and the major Focke-Wulf factory at Oschersleben. These raids mark the deepest penetration into Germany yet by American bombers from England. Although the targets suffer significant damage, 22 of the bombers are lost when the Luftwaffe fighters attack their formations with rockets. P-47 Thunderbolt fighters, flying their first mission equipped with jettisonable auxiliary fuel tanks,

escort the bombers into Germany, but not all the way to their targets. Another formation of P-47s meets them after the attack and engages about 60 enemy fighters. One P-47 is shot down but the Germans lose nine aircraft.

2nd Lieutenant John C. Morgan, Eighth Air Force, serving as co-pilot on a 326th Bomb Squadron mission, earns a Medal of Honor for his bravery. Prior to reaching the German coast his B-17 Flying Fortress is attacked by a large force of enemy fighters, and the pilot's skull is split open by enemy fire, leaving him in a crazed condition. Fighting off the pilot, Morgan

flies the aircraft over the target and back to a friendly base wholly unassisted. Morgan is later shot down over Germany and spends more than one year as a prisoner of war.

29 JULY
AIR FORCE

More than 200 Ninth Air Force P-40 Warhawk fighters attack a number of targets around Messina, Sicily.

30 JULY
NAVY

A PV-1 Ventura patrol bomber of Bombing Squadron 127 sinks the German submarine U-591 while flying cover for convoy TJ 2 off Brazil.

TBF Avengers and F4F Wildcats of Composite Squadron 29 from the escort carrier *Santee* sink the German submarine U-43 in the Atlantic.

The submarine chaser PC-624 sinks the German submarine U-375 off Tunisia.

31 JULY
ARMY

Lieutenant General George S. Patton Jr. issues orders for the Seventh Army to prepare for a major attack eastward toward Messina, Sicily. The II Corps under Lieutenant General Omar N. Bradley with the 1st, 3d, and 9th Infantry Divisions is to make the main effort. Patton's goal is to beat the British to Messina.

NAVY

A PBM Mariner of Patrol Squadron 74 joins Brazilian aircraft to sink the German submarine U-199 off Rio de Janeiro, Brazil.

1 AUGUST
AIR FORCE

Consolidated B-24 Liberator bombers from the Ninth and Eighth Air Forces conduct a treetop raid on the oil refineries at Ploesti, Romania. Although 40 percent of the refineries' capacity is destroyed, 54 planes of the 177 launched are lost along with 532 aircrew. Operation TIDALWAVE demonstrates without doubt the dire need for long-range fighter escorts for heavy bombers. Five Medals of Honor are awarded for this single mission.

In Sicily, more than 230 Ninth Air Force P-40 Warhawk fighters attack multiple targets around Messina. This is the Ninth Air Force's single largest attack to date.

2 AUGUST
AIR FORCE/ARMY

The campaign that is to culminate in the invasion of Italy gets underway with a heavy bombing raid on Naples. The II Corps' advance in Sicily is slowed by its determined enemy-delaying actions.

3 AUGUST
NAVY

A PBM Mariner of Patrol Squadron 205 sinks the German submarine U-572 north of Dutch Guiana.

Above: *This crew of Women's Airforce Service Pilots (WASP) walks with justifiable pride away from the B-17 Flying Fortress bomber "Pistol Packin' Mama" that they have just delivered. The WASPs are the first women in U.S. history trained to fly military planes. They fly every type of aircraft and perform every type of mission except combat. Thirty-nine die in the line of duty. (NASM)*

The destroyer *Buck* sinks the Italian submarine *Argento* off Tunisia.

5 AUGUST
AIR FORCE/ARMY
Merging the Women's Flying Training Detachment with the Women's Auxiliary Ferrying Squadron, the Army Air Forces forms the Women's Airforce Service Pilots (WASP). Famed aviatrix Jacqueline Cochran assumes duties as the director, while Nancy Harkness Love becomes the WASP executive with the Ferrying Division of Air Transport Command.

NAVY
The German submarine *U-566* sinks the gunboat *Plymouth* off Cape Henry, Virginia.

7 AUGUST
NAVY
A PB4Y-1 Liberator of Bombing Squadron 105 sinks the German submarine *U-84* in the North Atlantic.

F4F Wildcat fighters and TBF Avenger torpedo-bombers of Composite Squadron 1 operating from the escort carrier *Card* sink the German submarine *U-117* while operating west of the Azores Islands. Two days later an Avenger from the squadron sinks *U-664.*

7–8 AUGUST
ARMY/NAVY
A night amphibious operation by a reinforced 2d Battalion, 30th Infantry (Task Force Benard) bypasses enemy positions on Mount San Fratello, Sicily, and opens the way for the 3d Division to advance along the coast road.

10–11 AUGUST
ARMY/NAVY
Task Force Benard makes another night amphibious landing behind German lines near Brolo, Sicily, to cut off German units. The 7th and 15th Infantry Regiments must break through German positions to link up with the task force. The landing progresses smoothly until the Americans are discovered shortly before dawn. The cruiser *Philadelphia* and two destroyers provide support, but the German reaction is fierce. After heavy fighting all day, the surviving Germans break out and withdraw. The race to Messina continues.

11 AUGUST
ALL SERVICES
The Quebec Conference begins. President Franklin D. Roosevelt and Prime Minister Winston S. Churchill hold discussions covering all phases of military operations around the globe and decide upon future actions for the Allies. May 1944 is set as the target for

Operation OVERLORD—the invasion of France—and Operation POINT BLANK, the preceeding bomber campaign. Plans to invade Italy are approved.

11 AUGUST
NAVY
Previously damaged by U.S. air and surface attacks, the German submarine *U-604* is scuttled in the South Atlantic by her crew.

A TBF Avenger torpedo-bomber and F4F Wildcat fighter of Composite Squadron 1 operating from the escort carrier *Card* sink the German submarine *U-525* in the Azores Islands.

13 AUGUST
AIR FORCE
Bombers of the Northwest African Strategic Air Force, flying from bases in Italy, attack targets in Germany for the first time.

16 AUGUST
MARINE CORPS
The 4th Marine Division is activated at Camp Pendleton, California. It primarily consists of five regiments: 23d, 24th, and 25th (infantry), 14th (artillery), and 20th (engineers and pioneers).

Above: *Lieutenant General George S. Patton Jr., commander of the II Corps, visits the 1st Infantry Division in Sicily and talks with Brigadier General Theodore Roosevelt Jr., assistant division commander, on the street of a liberated town. (U.S. Army)*

Below: *("B-17s Over Europe," David Ray, USAF Art Collection)*

Right: *Paratroopers of the 82d Airborne Division use some old-fashioned means of transportation as they move through the town of Vittoria, Sicily, several days after the invasion of the island. (National Archives)*

17 AUGUST
AIR FORCE

The Eighth Air Force launches 315 B-17 Flying Fortress bombers on a mission farther into Germany than any raid to date. The primary targets are the Messerschmitt aircraft factory at Regensburg and the anti-friction-bearing plant at Schweinfurt. During the unescorted, two-pronged attack, B-17s unload 724 tons of bombs over their targets with mixed results.

German fighters attack the bomber formations at will. By the end of the day 60 of the original 315 B-17s have been lost.

ARMY

The Sicily Campaign officially ends at 10 a.m. when the Seventh Army's 3d Division enters Messina. Lieutenant General George S. Patton Jr. is there to greet the British when they arrive.

Left: *A high-flying flight of B-17 Flying Fortresses leaves a pattern of contrails as the planes head for targets in Germany. (U.S. Air Force)*

Opposite: *Operation AVALANCHE begins the long campaign to free Italy from Italian Fascist and German control. (U.S. Army)*

17–24 AUGUST
ALL SERVICES

The Quadrant Conference between Prime Minister Winston S. Churchill, President Franklin D. Roosevelt, and the Combined Chiefs of Staff at Quebec, Canada, results in the decisions to devote more effort to the Pacific Theater, increase emphasis on defeating Italy, and work more closely with the Soviet Union.

25 AUGUST
AIR FORCE

Operation STARKEY begins when Eighth Air Force heavy bombers are assigned to attack the German Air Force to entice the Germans to keep their forces contained in Western Europe rather than transferring them to the Eastern Front. The Allies hope to prod the Luftwaffe into an air battle of attrition before the actual invasion of France in 1944.

27 AUGUST
AIR FORCE

In the first Eighth Air Force attacks on German missile-launching sites, more than 180 heavy bombers are used to attack construction sites at Watten. V-weapon sites are later given the code name NOBALL.

NAVY

F4F Wildcat fighters and TBF Avenger torpedo bombers of Composite Squadron 1 from the escort carrier *Card* sink the German submarine *U-847* in the Atlantic.

1 SEPTEMBER
ARMY

All eligible Women's Army Auxiliary Corps officers are sworn into the Army. The conversion for the 50,000 (more than 75 percent of the force) who volunteered for Army status is underway. Director Oveta Culp Hobby is now a colonel.

NAVY

The Navy is given full responsibility for airborne antisubmarine warfare in the Atlantic Ocean.

2 SEPTEMBER
MARINE CORPS

Marine Corps Air Base Kearney Mesa, California, is renamed Marine Corps Air Depot Miramar.

3 SEPTEMBER
ALL SERVICES

The first units of the British Eighth Army land on the heel of Italy, and the Italian government signs an armistice to be made public on 8 September.

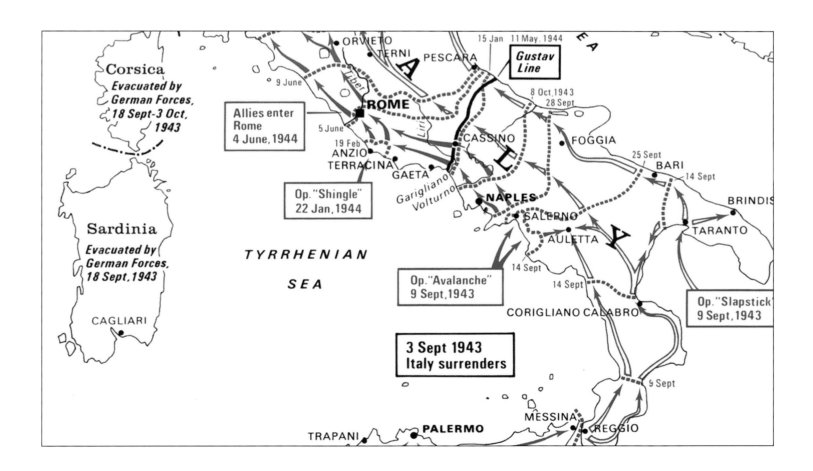

4 SEPTEMBER
ARMY

The 100th Infantry Battalion, composed of Hawaii-born Japanese-American (Nisei) volunteers, joins the 34th (Red Bull) Infantry Division, near Oran, North Africa.

6 SEPTEMBER
AIR FORCE

In the first raid of more than 400 bombers, the Eighth Air Force launches a multipronged attack on targets near Stuttgart, Germany. Poor weather wrecks the primary plan but secondary strikes are accomplished under heavy enemy fighter attacks. Forty-five American bombers are lost.

ARMY

Lieutenant General Omar N. Bradley departs the II Corps for England where he will form the First Army in preparation for Operation OVERLORD—the invasion of France.

9 SEPTEMBER
AIR FORCE/ARMY/NAVY

Operation AVALANCHE, the U.S.–British invasion of Italy, begins at 3:30 a.m. with the Fifth Army's VI Corps (Southern Assault Force) under Major General Ernest J. Dawley landing south of Salerno while a British force (Northern Assault Force) lands on its left. Strong air and Navy support (Task Force 80) is provided and the shallow beachheads are held against several German counterattacks in the 36th Infantry Division's area. By the end of the day most initial objectives are taken. A U.S.–British task force of 1st, 3d, and 4th Ranger Battalions and British commandos land unopposed near Sorrento. German air attacks and shore batteries sink one vessel and damage eight others.

AIR FORCE

Operation STARKEY, intended to lure the Luftwaffe into the sky to fight, is a relative failure. More than 300 heavy bombers hit targets around Paris and on the French coast, but enemy fighters stay away for much of the raid.

10–13 SEPTEMBER
AIR FORCE/ARMY

Increasingly stronger German attacks continue against the slowly expanding Italian beachheads of both U.S. and British forces, pushing some units back. On 13 September, the 36th and 45th Divisions barely stop major German attacks in their areas. The 52d Troop Carrier Wing drops 1,200 men of the 504th Parachute Infantry, 82d Airborne Division into the beachhead as reinforcement. No men or planes are lost.

11 SEPTEMBER
NAVY

In continuing action off the beachhead at Salerno, Italy, the destroyer *Rowan* sinks in just one minute after an engagement with German motor torpedo boats, taking 202 of her 273-man crew with her. Rocket bombs dropped by German Do. 217 bombers score a direct hit on a gun turret on the deck of the light cruiser *Savannah*.

14 SEPTEMBER
AIR FORCE

Eighth Air Force heavy bombers conduct an important strike against roller and ball bearing factories at Schweinfurt, Germany.

One of America's leading glider experts, Richard DuPont, is killed in a glider accident at March Field, California. DuPont is working as an advisor to the Army Air Forces glider program.

14–15 SEPTEMBER
AIR FORCE/ARMY/NAVY

The situation in Salerno, Italy, remains serious. Reserves and service troops of the Fifth Army are committed to hold the beachhead. Heavy air and Navy fire support are critical. The 52d Troop Carrier Wing drops the 505th Regimental Combat Team into the VI Corps area and drops the 2d Battalion, 509th Parachute Infantry behind German lines near Avellino.

15–18 SEPTEMBER
ARMY

German attacks slacken as Fifth Army and British units link up and begin pushing out of the beachhead at Salerno, Italy. German units withdraw north to new positions.

18 SEPTEMBER
ALL SERVICES

Italy surrenders to the Allies; Italian forces not under German command and control reenter the war on the Allied side. The Fifth Army secures the Salerno area and pushes north.

Opposite: *Landing craft from the U.S. invasion fleet in Naples Bay make their way onto the beachhead at Salerno, Italy. An umbrella of moored antiaircraft balloons hovers overhead to defend against German or Italian aircraft that may try to attack the ships. ("Castellamarre, Bay of Naples, August 13, 1944," Lt. Albert K. Murray, USN, Navy Art Collection)*

Right: *On very short notice, paratroopers of the 504th Infantry Regiment, 82d Parachute Division, prepare to make a combat jump to reinforce the threatened beachhead at Salerno, Italy, on 13 September 1943. (National Archives)*

20 SEPTEMBER
ARMY
Major General John P. Lucas takes command of the VI Corps from Major General Ernest J. Dawley.

22–23 SEPTEMBER
AIR FORCE
For the first time, American B-17 Flying Fortress bombers fly a night bombing mission with the Royal Air Force. The few aircraft that participate are experimenting with possible alternatives to daylight raids, which had resulted in tremendous losses the month before.

The Ninth Air Force flies its last bombing mission from Africa when its B-24 Liberators hit two enemy airfields. The bomb groups of the IX Bomber Command are transferred to the Twelfth Air Force.

23 SEPTEMBER
ARMY
In the VI Corps sector of the Salerno, Italy, beachhead, the 3d and 45th Infantry Divisions are slowed by demolitions. Engineers are called upon to keep routes of advance open.

27 SEPTEMBER
AIR FORCE
For the first time in Europe, American bombers fly daylight bombing raids led by pathfinder aircraft equipped with H2S direction-finding equipment. More than 1,000 tons of bombs are dropped from above complete overcast. For the 244 bombers that attack the port of Emden, Germany, P-47 Thunderbolt fighters equipped with belly tanks escort the formation all the way to the target in Germany and

Above: *Two Army combat engineers use a mine detector to locate enemy mines containing metal so they can be deactivated and removed. Small wooden mines used by the Germans are not detectable and present a particular danger. (National Archives)*

Left: *The 305th Bomb Group sends 15 B-17 Flying Fortresses to participate in the daylight raid against Schweinfurt, Germany, on 14 October 1943; only two planes return. The entire bomber group suffers 20 percent losses that day, and most of the planes that do return arrive damaged. ("Incredible 305th at Schweinfurt," James Dietz)*

Right: *In October 1943, dive-bombers, torpedo planes, and fighters from the carrier* Ranger *make the only U.S. carrier-launched attack on enemy ships in northern Europe. (Naval Historical Center)*

return with the bombers to their home bases, setting a new distance record of more than 600 miles. This marks the beginning of long-range fighter escort for American bombers.

NAVY

While flying patrol off Brazil, a PBM Mariner of Patrol Squadron 74 attacks and sinks the German submarine *U-161*.

29 SEPTEMBER
ALL SERVICES

General Dwight D. Eisenhower and Marshal Pietro Badoglio sign Italian surrender documents on board the battleship HMS *Nelson* off the coast of Malta.

1 OCTOBER
ARMY

The 82nd Airborne Division enters Naples, Italy. By 7 October VI Corps troops are at the Volturno River preparing for further offensive operations.

MARINE CORPS

The 1st Marine Ammunition Company is formed at Montford Point, North Carolina. It is the first of 12 such units, with the mission of moving and storing ammunition during an amphibious assault.

4 OCTOBER
NAVY

The aircraft carrier *Ranger* launches attacks against German shipping in Norway in the only operation conducted by U.S. carriers in northern European waters. F4F Wildcat fighters of Fighter Squadron 4

splash two German aircraft that approach the carrier, while other squadron Wildcats join SBD Dauntless and TBF Avenger aircraft in sinking four steamers and a transport and damaging five other vessels.

TBF Avengers and F4F Wildcats of Composite Squadron 9 operating from the escort carrier *Card* spot four German U-boats engaged in a resupply operation north of the Azores Islands. The aircraft sink two of the boats, *U-460* and *U-422*.

A PV-1 Ventura of Bombing Squadron 128 sinks the German submarine *U-279* southwest of Iceland.

6 OCTOBER
NAVY

The submarine *Dorado* departs New London, Connecticut, bound for Panama. She is never heard from again and is declared lost at sea.

7 OCTOBER
AIR FORCE

Aircraft of the Eighth Air Force conduct a night proganda leaflet drop, the first in a series of such missions.

8 OCTOBER
AIR FORCE

In Germany, more than 350 heavy bombers attack industrial areas and the city of Bremen as well as the U-boat facilities at Vegesack. At Bremen, about 30 U.S. aircraft are lost. This is the first bombing mission to use airborne jammers against German radar.

9 OCTOBER
NAVY

The destroyer *Buck* sinks after being torpedoed by the German submarine *U-616* in the Gulf of Salerno, Italy. She sinks in just four minutes with only 97 survivors.

10 OCTOBER
AIR FORCE

The Army Air Forces demonstrates control of a drone aircraft using television to provide visual feedback.

12–15 OCTOBER
ARMY

In Italy, Fifth Army units begin assault crossings over the Volturno River on a 40-mile front, slogging into the upper valley against stiff resistance. The VI Corps makes a third crossing of the twisting Volturno as the 34th and 45th Infantry Divisions maneuver to help the 3d Infantry Division take the Mignano Gap.

13 OCTOBER
NAVY

A TBF Avenger of Composite Squadron 9 operating from the escort carrier *Card* sinks the German submarine *U-402* north-northeast of the Azores Islands.

The German submarine *U-371* sinks the destroyer *Bristol* off Algeria.

14 OCTOBER
AIR FORCE

American heavy bombers return to attack the plants at Schweinfurt, Germany. Of the 230 bombers launched on the raid, 60 are shot down, many by German fighters firing long-range rockets, and 138 more are so badly damaged that the Eighth Air Force is forced to cancel operations deep into Germany without escort fighters.

15 OCTOBER
AIR FORCE

Eighth Air Force commander Lieutenant General Ira C. Eaker assumes additional responsibility when Headquarters U.S. Army Air Forces, United Kingdom, is activated to coordinate operations between the Eighth and Ninth Air Forces in Britain, with Major General Lewis H. Brereton in command. The establishment of the new command is essential as the Ninth Air Force forces arrive in England from the Mediterranean Theater, filling the role of the tactical air arm for the Army Air Forces in Europe.

16 OCTOBER
AIR FORCE

General Henry H. Arnold proposes that the Fifteenth Air Force be established in Italy. The new command would supplement Combined Bomber Offensive operations against Germany. Experienced weather forecasters believe that better weather in Italy will allow a greater number of effective combat missions to be flown during the winter months.

20 OCTOBER
NAVY

TBF Avengers of Composite Squadron 13 operating from the escort carrier *Core* sink the German submarine *U-378* north of the Azores Islands.

21 OCTOBER
NAVY

The destroyer *Murphy*, serving as an escort for convoy UT 4, is accidentally rammed and cut in two by the American tanker *Bulkoil* in the Atlantic. Her bow section sinks; her after portion remains afloat and is towed to New York. Fitted with a new forepart, *Murphy* returns to the fleet in time to support the landings in Normandy, France, in June 1944.

27 OCTOBER
ARMY

A War Department decision establishes two special badges to provide special recognition for the Infantry: the Combat Infantryman badge and the Expert Infantryman badge.

Right: *A selection of the Army Air Forces insignia of units active during the war: Top, left to right: First Air Force; Third Air Force; Sixth Air Force; Eighth Air Force; Ninth Air Force. Second row, left to right: Twelfth Air Force; Fifteenth Air Force; U.S. Strategic Air Forces in Europe; Desert Air Force; Mediterranean Allied Air Force. Bottom, left to right: Air Ferry Command; 12th Tactical Air Force; Airborne Troop Carrier Command. (U.S. Army)*

Above: *Winter in Italy brings unusually heavy rain, flooding from swollen rivers, and deep mud. Even four-wheel-drive vehicles like this jeep need help. (National Archives)*

Below: *A patrol of the 133rd Infantry Regiment, 34th Division, moves through the first snow high in the mountains before Bologna, Italy. ("A Patrol," Edward A. Reep, Army Art Collection, U.S. Army Center of Military History)*

Opposite: *A Navy PB4Y-1 Liberator, having completed its patrol, flies along the cliff shores of England as it heads for its home base. (National Archives)*

31 OCTOBER
NAVY
A TBF Avenger of Composite Squadron 9 operating from the carrier *Card* sinks the German submarine *U-584* north of the Azores Islands. *U-584* is on her tenth patrol, an earlier one in June 1942 involved the landing of saboteurs at Jacksonville, Florida.

NOVEMBER
AIR FORCE
General Henry H. Arnold, Commanding General, Army Air Forces, directs an expanded guided missile program based upon German advances in the field. His scientific advisor, Dr. Theodore von Kármán, submits a proposal to develop long-range surface-to-surface missiles.

1 NOVEMBER
AIR FORCE
The Fifteenth Air Force is activated at Tunis, Tunisia. Major General James H. Doolittle assumes command. His forces will move to Italy to accomplish bombing missions in preparation for the invasion of France.

2 NOVEMBER
AIR FORCE

The Fifteenth Air Force flies its first combat missions of the war. Seventy-four B-17 Flying Fortresses and 38 B-24 Liberators bomb an aircraft factory and industrial complex at Wiener-Neustadt, Germany. B-25 Mitchells and B-26 Marauders bomb targets near Amelia.

3 NOVEMBER
AIR FORCE

A new blind bombing tool, the H2X, is used in combat for the first time. More than 530 Eighth Air Force B-17 Flying Fortress and B-24 Liberator bombers, nine of them using the new device, attack the German port of Wilhelmshaven. P-38 Lightning fighters escort the bombers nearly the entire trip in their first European Theater operation.

5 NOVEMBER
AIR FORCE/NAVY

PB4Y-1 Liberators of Bombing Squadron 107 join Army Air Forces B-25 Mitchell bombers of the First Composite Squadron in sinking the German submarine *U-848* southwest of Ascension Island.

5–15 NOVEMBER
ARMY

With terrible weather conditions enveloping Italy, the decision is made to make an all-out effort to get into the Liri Valley. The Fifth Army begins its efforts to breach the German defenses known as the "Winter Line." The 3d Infantry Division meets stiff enemy defenses at Mount la Difensa. To the right, the 45th Division is having better luck taking the high ground flanking the Mignano Gap. Its efforts are reinforced

by the 1st Ranger Battalion and the 509th Parachute Infantry. In the U.S. II Corps sector, the 36th Infantry Division is bolstered with attachment of the First Special Service Force under Colonel Robert T. Frederick.

6 NOVEMBER
NAVY

While escorting convoy KMF 25A bound for Naples, Italy, the destroyer *Beatty* is sunk by a torpedo dropped by a German aircraft, which also torpedoes the troop transport *Santa Elena*. The following day, *Santa Elena* collides with another transport and sinks.

10 NOVEMBER
NAVY

PB4Y-1 Liberators of three Navy squadrons join British Royal Air Force aircraft in sinking the German submarine *U-966* in the Bay of Biscay.

12 NOVEMBER
NAVY

President Franklin D. Roosevelt boards the battleship *Iowa* for his journey to conferences at Cairo, Egypt, and Tehran, Iran, the latter the first meeting of the so-called Big Three—President Franklin D. Roosevelt, Prime Minister Winston S. Churchill, and Soviet Premier Joseph Stalin. A close call occurs two days later when, during battle practice at sea, the destroyer *William D. Porter* accidentally launches a live torpedo at the battleship. *Iowa* receives a warning in time to avoid being hit.

A PB4Y-1 Liberator of Bombing Squadron 103 sinks the German submarine *U-508* in the Bay of Biscay.

Above: *P-38 Lightning fighters from the 20th Fighter Group sweep low over an English village as they fly on a mission to France. ("Dawn Chorus," Nicholas Trudgian, USAF Art Collection)*

13 NOVEMBER
AIR FORCE

In the longest escort mission by American fighters to date, 115 Eighth Air Force heavy bombers attack the port of Bremen, Germany. Another 100 bombers abort due to poor weather. Of the 47 P-38 Lightning fighters escorting the bombers, 7 do not return after facing an overwhelming number of German fighters over the target.

14 NOVEMBER
AIR FORCE

In the first Army Air Forces raids on Bulgaria, 90 Twelfth Air Force B-25 Mitchell medium bombers drop 135 tons of bombs on targets in Sofia.

16 NOVEMBER
ARMY

Responding to suggestions from troops in the field, the Army approves a standard combat boot to replace the field shoe worn with canvas leggings for field wear.

18 NOVEMBER
ARMY

The II Corps (under Major General Geoffrey Keyes), recently arrived from Sicily, assumes control of the 3d and 36th Infantry Divisions and takes its place in the center of the Fifth Army's battle line.

20 NOVEMBER
AIR FORCE
The Army Air Forces–sponsored play *Winged Victory* opens on Broadway. Telling the story of the struggles made by flying cadets to earn their wings, the play's cast of 300 actors are nearly all military service members. It will later be made into a movie.

25 NOVEMBER
NAVY
A PB4Y-1 Liberator of Bombing Squadron 107 sinks the German submarine *U-849* in the South Atlantic.

26 NOVEMBER
AIR FORCE
The Eighth Air Force launches 440 bombers against Bremen, Germany. Weather is poor and 29 U.S. aircraft are shot down.

28 NOVEMBER
ALL SERVICES
At the Tehran Conference, President Franklin D. Roosevelt, Prime Minister Winston S. Churchill and Soviet Premier Joseph Stalin give Operation OVERLORD, the invasion of northern France, and Operation ANVIL, the invasion of southern France, priority over all other operations. Stalin agrees to enter the war against Japan after Germany is defeated.

29 NOVEMBER
AIR FORCE
The Army Air Forces accomplishes its first raid against targets in Sarajevo, Yugoslavia, when the Twelfth Air Force sends 25 B-25 Mitchell medium bombers to attack rail yards and military bases.

DECEMBER
MARINE CORPS
The first Reserve Officer Class is formed for newly commissioned female lieutenants.

1 DECEMBER
MARINE CORPS
Making use of lightweight search radars, the Marine Corps creates the first air-transportable air warning squadron, AWS(AT)-5, at Cherry Point, North Carolina.

2 DECEMBER
ARMY
Hundreds of burn casualties follow destruction of the transport *John Harvey* in an enemy air raid in the harbor of Bari, Italy. The transport was carrying mustard gas to be used only if the enemy used chemical agents first.

Opposite, below:
Paratroopers from the 82d Airborne Division demonstrate the operation of a 2.36-inch "Bazooka" rocket launcher. They are using mortar shell vests to carry extra rockets. (U.S. Army)

Right: *Soldiers of the 168th Infantry Regiment, 34th Infantry Division, surprise German defenders to seize and hold Mount Pantano, Italy, a key position of the German Winter Line. ("The Red Bull in the Winter Line," Donna Neary, National Guard Heritage Series)*

Left: *Soldiers of the 16th Engineer Battalion carry a wounded officer out of the flooding Volturno River in Italy. The officer was directing work to restore the pontoon bridge in the background when he was hit by enemy fire. (National Archives)*

After two weeks of bitter fighting, the German Winter Line in Italy is finally broken. The 36th Infantry Division with the 1st Special Service Force attached, carries out an attack on the Difensa-Maggiore complex in rain and cold. By 8 December this complex, a key obstacle on the road to Rome, is in U.S. hands.

5 DECEMBER
ALL SERVICES

The Second Cairo Conference begins. During the three-day talks, President Franklin D. Roosevelt and Prime Minister Winston S. Churchill discuss global operations, set a timetable for offensive operations in the Pacific Theater, and establish a unified command for the Mediterranean Theater effective on 10 December. Roosevelt decides that General Dwight D. Eisenhower will hold Supreme Allied Command for the invasion of France.

AIR FORCE

Of 250 B-26 Marauder bombers launched to attack enemy targets in France, 200 turn back due to poor weather. Ninth Air Force P-51 mustang fighters of the 354th Fighter Group, equipped with long-range fuel tanks, escort Eighth Air Force heavy bombers nearly 500 miles to targets in northern Germany. This is the first escort mission flown by American P-51 Mustangs.

7 DECEMBER
AIR FORCE/ARMY

Supported by heavy air strikes, II Corps units begin a 10-day battle to seize and clear the area around San Pietro, Italy, as part of the final push through the Winter Line. Losses are high.

7–15 DECEMBER
MARINE CORPS

The 1st, 3rd, 5th, and 6th Barrage Balloon Squadrons are deactivated and most of their personnel are assigned to defense battalions.

8 DECEMBER
AIR FORCE

General Henry H. Arnold notifies Lieutenant General Carl A. Spaatz that he will become the overall air commander in Europe for the invasion scheduled for summer 1944.

ARMY

After several probes by the Rangers, 36th Infantry Division troops move up the slope of Mount Sammucro toward San Pietro, Italy. After three days of bitter fighting the attack is called off. A second attack is launched on 15 December. The division is reinforced with the 504th Parachute Infantry and a battalion of tanks. By 17 December San Pietro is in U.S. hands.

10 DECEMBER
ARMY

The Persian Gulf Service Command in Tehran, Iran, is redesignated the Persian Gulf Command and placed directly under the War Department.

13 DECEMBER
AIR FORCE

In Germany a massive air attack is launched against port areas in Bremen and Hamburg as well as the U-boat yards at Kiel by 649 B-17 Flying Fortress and B-24 Liberator bombers. This is the first Eighth Air Force raid in which more than 600 bombers attack targets.

NAVY

The destroyer *Osmond Ingram* suffers damage in a gun battle with the German submarine *U-172* west of the Canary Islands. *Osmond Ingram*, along with sister destroyers *George E. Badger* and *Clemson*, and F4F Wildcats of Composite Squadron 19 from the escort carrier *Bogue* cooperate to sink the enemy sub.

Following a 32-hour chase, the destroyer *Wainwright*, operating with the British frigate, sinks the German submarine *U-593* off Algiers.

Above: *Insignia for the U.S. Army Persian Gulf Command. (U.S. Army)*

Below: *Paratroopers of the 82d Airborne Division trudge up an Italian mountain trail toward their positions near San Pietro, Italy. A string of mules carries additional supplies and ammunition. (National Archives)*

Left: *A U.S. Navy destroyer (top left) makes full speed toward the German submarine U-172, which has been forced to the surface by depth charges near the Canary Islands on 13 December 1943. (Naval Historical Center)*

Opposite: *A damaged and smoking B-17 Flying Fortress bomber signals its base that it needs assistance by shooting off two flares as it limps in for landing. ("B-17 in Distress," Floyd Davis, Army Art Collection, U.S. Army Center of Military History)*

20 DECEMBER
AIR FORCE

The Eighth Air Force launches a massive attack against the port of Bremen, Germany. Enemy fighters knock down 27 bombers, while P-51 Mustang and P-38 Lightning fighters engage the Luftwaffe in a fierce air battle. The Germans use twin-engine, rocket-firing fighters that are protected by single-engine fighters. The Eighth Air Force uses anti-radar strips of metal foil, called window, in combat for the first time.

The Mediterranean Allied Air Forces is established under the overall command of Air Chief Marshal Sir Arthur Tedder. Lieutenant General Carl A. Spaatz commands the U.S. element, U.S. Army Air Forces North African Theater of Operations.

NAVY

TBF Avengers and FM Wildcats of Composite Squadron 19 from the escort carrier *Bogue* attack the German submarine *U-850* southwest of the Azores Islands. The sub engages in a gun battle with the aircraft but is sunk.

24 DECEMBER
ALL SERVICES

President Franklin D. Roosevelt announces General Dwight D. Eisenhower as Supreme Commander of the Allied Expeditionary Force for the future invasion/liberation of France.

AIR FORCE

In the largest single raid against enemy targets in Europe to this date, the Eighth Air Force sends 670 B-17 Flying Fortress and B-24 Liberator bombers on their first Operation CROSSBOW mission to destroy German V-1 and V-2 missile sites in the Pas de Calais area of northern France. No American aircraft are lost during the attacks.

NAVY

Attacked unsuccessfully the previous day, the antisubmarine task group led by the carrier *Card* suffers losses by German U-boats in the North Atlantic. Torpedoes sink the destroyer *Leary*, with the loss of 97 crewmen, but the destroyer *Schenk* counters by sinking *U-645*.

28 DECEMBER
NAVY

A PB4Y-1 Liberator of Bombing Squadron 105 sights German destroyers and torpedo boats in the Bay of Biscay. Later in the day, Navy PB4Y-1s join two British light cruisers in attacking the force and sinking one destroyer and two torpedo boats.

30 DECEMBER
ARMY

The Army activates the 555th Parachute Infantry Company, the first African American airborne unit, at Fort Benning, Georgia. This becomes the core of the future 555th ("Triple Nickel") Parachute Infantry Battalion. The unit remains in the U.S. during the war, fighting forest fires.

MARINE CORPS

Commandant Lieutenant General Thomas Holcomb issues an order abolishing the Marine Corps parachute and raider programs.

31 DECEMBER
AIR FORCE

The Eighth Air Force launches a 500-plane raid against targets near the coast of France. Twenty-five planes do not return. After this raid, the total tonnage of bombs dropped by the Eighth exceeds that dropped by Royal Air Force Bomber Command for the first time.

Opposite: *A 155mm howitzer answers back with counter-battery fire, as German artillery shells rain down on the beachhead at Anzio, Italy. (U.S. Army)*

Left: *Paratroopers of the all African American 555th Parachute Infantry Company prepare for a training jump. The unit eventually expands to a battalion and deploys in the U.S. Pacific northwest as "smoke jumpers" to help fight forest fires caused by Japanese Fu-go balloons. (National Archives)*

Below: *When it is necessary to transfer crews between ships, a dangerous and difficult trip by lifeboat is the only way. ("Ship-to-Ship," Lt. Cdr. Anton Fischer, U.S. Coast Guard Collection)*

1944
PIERCING THE WALL

1 JANUARY
ARMY

Caltech's rocket laboratory begins research and development of a long-range missile at the request of the Army. Project Ordcit eventually results in the development of the Private "A" and Corporal missiles.

2 JANUARY
NAVY

While on patrol south-southwest of Ascension Island, PB4Y-1 Liberators of Bombing Squadron 107 spot the German blockade runner *Weserland*. The destroyer *Somers* intercepts the ship and fires one salvo, forcing the enemy crew to abandon ship. *Weserland* subsequently explodes and sinks.

4 JANUARY
NAVY

The light cruiser *Omaha* and destroyer *Jouett* intercept the German blockade runner *Rio Grande* off the coast of Brazil, damaging her with gunfire to such an extent that she is scuttled by her crew. The pair of ships

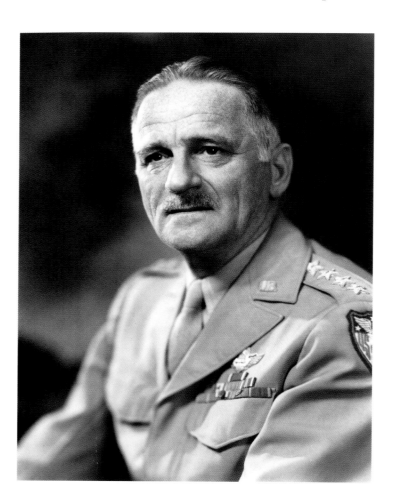

repeats the scenario the following day, sinking the German blockade runner *Burgenland*.

4–5 JANUARY
AIR FORCE

During the day, more than 500 Eighth Air Force heavy bombers attack German ports. That evening, U.S. aircraft begin flying supplies supporting the underground resistance in western Europe. Lieutenant Colonel Clifford Heflin flies the first of these nighttime Operation CARPETBAGGER missions from Tempsford, England, to locations in France.

6 JANUARY
AIR FORCE

Lieutenant General Carl A. Spaatz assumes command of the U.S. Strategic Air Forces in Europe (USSAFE). The acronym is changed to USSTAF on 4 February. Lieutenant General James H. Doolittle takes over the Eighth Air Force, and Lieutenant General Ira C. Eaker moves to Italy as commander of the Mediterranean Allied Air Forces. Additionally, to better coordinate the Combined Bomber Offensive attacks across Europe, control of the Fifteenth Air Force is placed under Spaatz as Commanding General, USSAFE.

MARINE CORPS

Captain Peter J. Ortiz, a former member of the French Foreign Legion, parachutes into southeastern France with two Allied officers to assist the French in establishing additional guerrilla units. His team from the Office of Strategic Services remains on the ground until early May, then returns to England.

8 JANUARY
AIR FORCE

The Lockheed XP-80 experimental jet fighter flies for the first time at the Muroc test center in California. Piloted by Milo Burcham, the "Lulu Belle," named after a popular cartoon character, blazes the trail for future production jet aircraft that will exceed 500 miles per hour in level flight. Development of the prototype took only 143 days.

ARMY

In Italy, Task Force B, 36th Infantry Division outflanks and captures Hill 1109. The enemy withdraws back to Monte Trocchio to defend approaches to Rome.

10 JANUARY
MARINE CORPS

The 26th and 27th Marine Regiments (infantry) and 13th Marine Regiment (artillery) are organized at Camp Pendleton, California, for duty with the soon-to-be-created 5th Marine Division.

11 JANUARY
AIR FORCE/ARMY

Some 600 Eighth Air Force B-17 Flying Fortress and B-24 Liberator bombers strike enemy industrial targets in Germany. Enemy fighter opposition is fierce, with an estimated 500 enemy fighters in the fight. A total of 60 bombers are lost during the raid. For the first time, B-24 Liberators are used as Pathfinder aircraft to accomplish bombing through overcast skies.

Major James H. Howard, Ninth Air Force, leads a group of P-51 Mustang fighters over Halberstadt, Germany, to provide support for a heavy bomber formation. Fighting off a formation of more than 30 enemy airplanes, Howard single-handedly destroys three German fighters—a FW-190 and two Bf-110s along with another probable Me-109 fighter. Howard is the only P-51 pilot to receive the Medal of Honor during the war.

Fifteenth Air Force B-17 Flying Fortress bombers, escorted by P-38 Lightning fighters, attack the harbor near Piraeus, Italy. Although the attackers claim eight enemy kills, flying in extremely poor weather results in midair collisions that claim six B-17s.

Opposite: *General Carl A. Spaatz commands the U.S. Strategic Air Forces in Europe. (U.S. Air Force)*

Above: *The P-80 Shooting Star is a follow-on to the earlier XP-59A Airacomet that the Army Air Forces tested in 1942. The first P-80 is designed and built in 143 days. The plane has a speed of 600 mph and a ceiling of 50,000 feet. A few P-80s are sent to Italy before the end of the war, but they never see combat. (U.S. Air Force)*

Below: *The P-51 Mustang is a long-range fighter that when equipped with external fuel tanks can escort bombers all the way into Germany and back. ("P-51 Mustang and Me 109," J. D. Deneen, NASM Art Collection)*

13 JANUARY
AIR FORCE

During a raid against German missile-launching sites in France by nearly 200 Ninth Air Force B-26 Marauders, several aircrews report being fired upon by antiaircraft rockets.

14 JANUARY
AIR FORCE

While more than 500 Eighth Air Force heavy bombers attack 20 V-weapon sites in Pas de Calais, France, Twelfth Air Force aircraft blast targets throughout Italy in support of the Fifth Army's efforts in the Monte Trocchio area. B-25 Mitchell bombers, A-20 Havoc bombers, A-36 Apache dive-bombers, and P-40 Warhawk fighters participate in the coordinated close support missions.

15 JANUARY
AIR FORCE

Lieutenant General Ira C. Eaker assumes overall command of Mediterranean Allied Air Forces and also takes responsibility for the Army Air Forces units serving in that combined command.

16 JANUARY
AIR FORCE/ARMY/NAVY

General Dwight D. Eisenhower assumes his post as the Supreme Allied Commander, Allied Expeditionary Force. In this position, he holds overall command of Operation OVERLORD, the invasion of France.

NAVY

A TBF Avenger of Composite Squadron 13 flying from the escort carrier *Guadalcanal* sinks the German submarine *U-544* in the Atlantic.

20–22 JANUARY
ARMY

The 36th Infantry Division crosses the Rapido River near the Italian town of San Angelo, establishing a fragile hold on the far bank. German counterattacks hit the bridgehead, resulting in heavy U.S. casualties.

21 JANUARY
AIR FORCE

More than 500 Eighth and Ninth Air Force bombers strike V-weapon sites across northern France. Low clouds force an additional 400 bombers turn back to England without attacking 19 other targets.

MARINE CORPS

The 5th Marine Division is officially activated at Camp Pendleton, California.

22 JANUARY
AIR FORCE/ARMY/NAVY

Operation SHINGLE, the U.S.–British invasion at Anzio, Italy, begins at 2:00 a.m. The operation is an effort to bypass German defenses that have kept Allied forces bogged down in southern Italy. Aircraft from the Twelfth and Fifteenth Air Forces launch more than 1,200 sorties in support of the Fifth Army's VI Corps, to isolate the battlefield and maintain air superiority during the landings at the Anzio beachhead. U.S. Naval Task Force X-Ray (under Rear Admiral Frank K. Lowry) lands VI Corps troops (under Major General John P. Lucas) south of town at 2:30 a.m. The 3d Infantry Division (under Major General Lucian K. Truscott Jr.) and a reinforced Provisional Ranger Force (under Colonel William O. Darby) conduct these landings, while the British land a division north of town. The Germans are surprised and by noon the initial beachhead is secured. The U.S. Navy suffers a minesweeper sunk and damage to a large infantry landing craft; ground force losses are small.

24 JANUARY–1 FEBRUARY
ARMY/NAVY

The 1st (Old Ironsides) Armored Division (under Major General Ernest N. Harmon) and the 45th (Thunderbird) Infantry Division (under Major General William W. Eagles) come ashore at Anzio, Italy, to reinforce the beachhead, which is starting to receive ground attacks. German aircraft and mines damage three Navy ships.

Above: *General Dwight D. Eisenhower, shown in a later portrait with the insignia of a General of the Army, is selected to be the Supreme Allied Commander of the Allied forces invading France in 1944. (Nicodemus Hufford, Army Art Collection, U.S. Army Center of Military History)*

Below: *Soldiers of the Fifth Army unload and move supplies and equipment over the beach at Anzio, Italy. Two DUKWs lead a stream of vehicles from a tank landing ship over the sand dunes while other landing craft, large and small, move through the bay. (U.S. Army)*

24 JANUARY–11 FEBRUARY
ARMY/NAVY

In Italy, elements of the 34th Infantry Division cross the Rapido River upstream of the 36th Division as the first battle for Monte Cassino starts.

27 JANUARY
AIR FORCE

In a very active day, Twelfth Air Force P-40 Warhawk and Fifteenth Air Force P-38 Lightning and P-47 Thunderbolt fighters provide close air support and air cover to the Fifth Army while shooting down dozens of enemy fighters over Rome and Florence, Italy.

28 JANUARY
AIR FORCE

Eighth Air Force B-24 Liberator bombers equipped with the Gee-H blind-bombing device strike V-weapon sites near Bonnieres, France. This is the first time Gee-H is used in combat. It is more accurate than previous devices, but is range-limited, only effective up to 200 miles.

NAVY

A PB4Y-1 Liberator of Bombing Squadron 103 sinks the German submarine *U-271* off the river Shannon estuary, Eire, Ireland.

29 JANUARY
AIR FORCE

Eighth Air Force Pathfinder aircraft lead a force of 763 B-17 Flying Fortress and B-24 Liberator bombers to strike targets near Frankfurt, Germany. The aircraft drop almost 1,900 tons of bombs on the city; nearly 30 bombers are lost to enemy fighters. This is the first Eighth Air Force mission with more than 700 bombers.

29–30 JANUARY
ARMY

As part of an effort to break out of the small Anzio beachhead in Italy, the 3d Infantry Division begins a night attack to seize Cisterna. Lead elements are the 1st and 3d Ranger Battalions, which find themselves in a German trap that destroys the two units during a desperate, daylong man-against-tank battle. Of the 767 Rangers, only 6 escape death or capture. The division's following units also hit strong German resistance and are halted.

30 JANUARY
AIR FORCE

During the Eighth Air Force's second 700-plane raid, blind-bombing devices allow the formation to attack industrial targets near Brunswick, Germany. A smaller force of airplanes bombs targets near Hanover. During the raid, 20 bombers are lost to enemy fighter attacks. Meanwhile, Twelfth Air Force fighters find no enemy air opposition over Anzio, Italy, during their daily fighter sweeps over the beachhead. The 451st Bomb Group, flying B-24 Liberators, is activated in the Fifteenth Air Force, bringing the total number of heavy bomb groups in that command to nine.

FEBRUARY
AIR FORCE/ARMY

The Army Ordnance Division and the Army Air Forces initiate the development of a surface launched, supersonic, guided, high-altitude missile designed to intercept aircraft. This project develops the Nike I surface-to-air missile.

The first VB-1/2 Azon controllable, vertical glide bombs are sent to Europe. These weapons are controllable in azimuth only (from side to side) and are guided through a bombsight by means of radio remote control. A total of 15,000 Azons are produced through November 1944.

Above: *Ground crews make last preparations before the P-51 Mustangs of the 4th Fighter Group depart on their first escort mission into Germany in March 1944. ("Blakeslee Before Berlin," James Dietz)*

Below: *Two of the Army nurses caring for the wounded in the field hospitals on the Anzio, Italy, beachhead take a break outside their tents. They keep their steel helmets on in case of German artillery bombardment. Six nurses and almost 100 other medical personnel are killed on the beachhead. (George Silk, Getty Images)*

1 FEBRUARY
AIR FORCE

Major General Elwood Quesada takes charge of the IX Air Support Command, which controls all of the fighter and reconnaissance units of the IX Fighter Command.

2 FEBRUARY
ARMY

The 1st Special Service Force (under Brigadier General Robert T. Frederick) arrives at Anzio, Italy, and takes a position on the right flank. Anticipating a major German offensive against the beachhead, Lieutenant General Mark W. Clark, Fifth Army commander, orders the VI Corps to shift to a defensive posture, tighten its lines, and dig in. He is correct—the German attack begins the next day.

3 FEBRUARY
AIR FORCE

The 358th Fighter Group joins the 354th Fighter Group already flying missions for the Ninth Air Force. By 1 May, 16 more fighter groups will be added to the Ninth for duty during Operation OVERLORD.

3–10 FEBRUARY
ARMY

The Germans launch the first of three major efforts to break through the beachead at Anzio, Italy, and destroy the VI Corps and British units. U.S. units receive probing attacks while the British are forced to fall back with heavy losses. Enemy artillery reaches all areas of the beachhead and hampers naval support operations. German units penetrate British defensive positions and U.S. units are shifted to block and reinforce. Major Walter Kerwin, the 3d Division's artillery officer, introduces a new technique to coordinate artillery fire from many locations and concentrate it on a critical spot. Adopted by the whole VI Corps, the technique plays a critical role in stopping the German attacks. On 7 Februrary, the 95th Evacuation Hospital on the beach is hit, causing numerous casualties. The hospital gains the name "Hell's Half Acre."

6 FEBRUARY
NAVY
A PB4Y-1 Liberator of Bombing Squadron 107 sinks the German submarine *U-177* west of Ascension Island.

8 FEBRUARY
AIR FORCE
The Fifteenth Air Force activates the 454th Bomb Group flying B-24 Liberator bombers. This brings the total of heavy bomb groups in the Fifteenth to 10.

B-17 Flying Fortresses continue to bomb targets near Orvieto, Piombino, and Prato, Italy, under escort by P-47 Thunderbolt and P-38 Lightning fighters.

MARINE CORPS
The 28th Marine Regiment is organized at Camp Pendleton, California, to round out the 5th Marine Division.

9 FEBRUARY
ALL SERVICES
President Franklin D. Roosevelt authorizes the new Bronze Star Medal to be awarded "for heroic or meritorious service against the enemy not involving aerial flight."

AIR FORCE
Twelfth Air Force aircraft strike hard in support of Fifth Army operations around Cassino, Italy.

11 FEBRUARY
ARMY
Over one million U.S. troops have been transported across the Atlantic. Divisions are now training in England, Northern Ireland, and Scotland.

Right: *Soldiers cram into a jeep with their belongings and some furniture. ("We Move Again," Edward A. Reep, Army Art Collection, U.S. Army Center of Military History)*

13 FEBRUARY
AIR FORCE

The Combined Chiefs of Staff alter the Combined Bomber Offensive plan to refine and reduce the number of targets essential to the campaign prior to planned landings at Normandy, France. The modifications reflect adaptations based upon Germany's industrial revitalization and dispersal plans.

15 FEBRUARY
AIR FORCE

In an effort to soften up the enemy for the U.S. Fifth Army and the British Eighth Army as they push toward Rome, Italy, Lieutenant General Mark W. Clark, Fifth Army commander, approves the use of air and artillery to destroy the Benedictine Abbey of Monte Cassino, which is erroneously suspected of sheltering enemy forces. A bomber force of 254 American B-17 Flying Fortresses, B-25 Mitchells, and B-26 Marauders attack in two waves and destroy the abbey. Another 60 B-24 Liberator bombers strike other targets surrounding Cassino. Follow-on attacks occur over the following three days.

ARMY

The VI Corps prepares defenses in Italy in anticipation of a counterattack by German forces, while the II Corps continues efforts to cross the Rapido River south of Cassino.

16–19 FEBRUARY
ARMY

The second major German attack using six divisions hits the VI Corps at Anzio, Italy, this time in the area of the 45th Infantry Division's 157th and 179th Infantry Regiments. Some units are surrounded while others are able to make fighting withdrawals to new positions that cost the Germans heavy losses. By 19 February, the German attack is halted by a desperate defense supported by exceptionally heavy U.S. air and artillery support, but the Germans have a salient into the beachhead a mile deep and two miles wide.

18 FEBRUARY
AIR FORCE

Headquarters Eighth Air Force establishes the 8th Reconnaissance Wing (Provisional) in Cheddington, England, to provide independent capability as the invasion of Normandy, France, approaches. Colonel Elliot Roosevelt, President Franklin D. Roosevelt's son, is given command of the unit.

AIR FORCE/ARMY

In Italy, Twelfth Air Force A-20 Havoc light attack bombers, A-36 Apache dive-bombers, and P-40 Warhawk fighters struggle to hold off the advancing Germans around the Anzio beachhead. The German troops make their deepest advance, but are pushed back the next day by more than 200 close support sorties and a determined VI Corps counterattack.

ARMY

To address a shortage of infantrymen, the Army issues orders to move 110,000 students from the Army Specialized Training Program (ASTP) to the ground forces by 1 April. Remaining in ASTP status are 30,000 soldiers enrolled in advanced medicine, dentistry, and engineering programs.

20 FEBRUARY
AIR FORCE/ARMY

The Eighth Air Force launches more than 1,000 heavy bombers for the first time, initiating Big Week.

Nearly 900 reach their targets in Germany. During the week they attack aircraft factories and airfields, and attempt to draw German fighters into the skies where massive numbers of escort fighters are waiting. Losses are heavy but less than expected. From this week forward, the German air forces continue to lose effectiveness. Although the Luftwaffe is still formidable at times, this campaign marks the turn in the tide of the air war over Europe.

Left: *An artillery gun crew prepares their M1 240mm howitzer for its next fire mission against the German defensives of the Gothic Line near Mignano, Italy. This is the largest field piece used by the Army in the war. (National Archives)*

Above: *Enemy artillery shells are not the only hazard for Army drivers in the combat zone. A Military Police motorcyclist observes while on traffic duty near an ammunition supply point. (National Archives)*

20 FEBRUARY–3 MARCH
ARMY

The VI Corps counterattacks against the German penetration at Anzio, Italy, with limited success. A third, and final, German offensive to try to expand their penetration hits the 3d Infantry Division. A bitter fight called "Battle of the Caves" takes place in the 2d Battalion, 157th Infantry area as it fights against German infantry and tank forces. By holding its positions and inflicting heavy casualties, the 3d Infantry Division begins the slow and bloody reversal of German forces that restores the beachhead line.

21 FEBRUARY
AIR FORCE

A force of 764 B-17 Flying Fortress and B-24 Liberator bombers attack aircraft factories and storage facilities near Brunswick and Diepholz, Germany. Weather prevents further attack by other forces.

22 FEBRUARY
AIR FORCE

In a coordinated attack between Eighth and Fifteenth Air Force heavy bombers, 101 B-17 Flying Fortresses strike aircraft factories around Halberstadt, Germany. Another 154 bombers attack a variety of aircraft production and airfield targets across Germany, including the aircraft works around Regensburg. During the attacks, more than 50 heavy bombers are lost to enemy fighters.

23 FEBRUARY
AIR FORCE

Poor weather grounds the majority of Eighth Air Force air operations over Europe, while Fifteenth Air Force B-24 Liberator bombers attack the industrial complex at Steyr, Austria. Escort fighters claim 30 victories during the raid.

ARMY

Major General John P. Lucas is relieved and Major General Lucian K. Truscott Jr. is put at the helm of the faltering VI Corps effort in Anzio, Italy.

Left: *A flight of Boeing B-17 Flying Fortresses takes off over an English farmer's hay wagon for another bombing mission. (Peter Hurd, Army Art Collection, U.S. Army Center of Military History)*

Opposite: *There is little shelter from the winter weather in the Italian mountains for the Soldiers of this 105mm artillery battery. ("Artillery Position Above Loilano," Savo Radulovic, Army Art Collection, U.S. Army Center of Military History)*

24 FEBRUARY
AIR FORCE/ARMY

When the weather breaks, the Eighth Air Force launches three bombardment missions against Germany. First, 231 B-17 Flying Fortresses strike ball bearing works at Schweinfurt; second, 238 B-24 Liberators hit the aircraft factory and airfield at Gotha, losing 33 bombers; third, 236 bombers attack targets near Rostow after poor weather forces a shift to their secondary target. Overnight, Royal Air Force Bomber Command aircraft target Schweinfurt again. Fifteenth Air Force B-17s attack the factories in Steyr, Austria, and also the oil refinery at Fiume, Yugoslavia, where they lose 19 bombers to enemy defenses.

NAVY

In the first employment of magnetic anomaly detection gear for tracking a submerged submarine, PBY-5A Catalinas of Patrol Squadron 63 join a PV-1 Ventura of Bombing Squadron 127 and British aircraft in attacking the German submarine *U-761* as she attempts to enter the Atlantic through the Straits of Gibraltar. The submariners abandon their heavily damaged boat and scuttle her. In reference to this new technology, VP-63 is known throughout the remainder of the war as the "MAD Cats."

25 FEBRUARY
AIR FORCE/ARMY

In a major combined effort, Allied heavy bombers strike German targets at Regensburg, Augsburg, Furth, Stuttgart, as well as Zara Harbor and Fiume, Yugoslavia. The strikes are flown both day and night, and German fighters take punishing losses against Allied fighter escort and B-17 Flying Fortress and B-24 Liberator gunners.

26 FEBRUARY
AIR FORCE

Big Week comes to an end when poor weather grounds most Eighth Air Force aircraft during the day. Big Week succeeds in halting the momentum of German airpower. From this point forward, Germany becomes more and more defensive in the air.

29 FEBRUARY
MARINE CORPS

The 1st Parachute Regiment and its subordinate battalions officially disband. Their personnel are transferred to form the core of the infantry regiments of the 5th Marine Division.

MARCH
AIR FORCE/ARMY

The U.S. Office of War Information reports that as of the end of 1943, more than 7,800 aircraft—mostly combat planes—have been shipped to the Soviet Union through the Lend-Lease program.

Above: *B-17 Flying Fortresses of the 95th Bombardment Group, escorted by P-51 Mustang fighters, make the first American attack on Berlin. ("First American Bombing of Berlin, 4th March 1944," John Rayson, USAF Art Collection)*

1 MARCH
NAVY
The destroyer escort *Bronstein* sinks the German submarine *U-603* in the North Atlantic and later in the day joins the destroyer escorts *Thomas* and *Bostwick* in sinking *U-709.*

2 MARCH
AIR FORCE
The Fifteenth Air Force gains another group of B-24 Liberators, the 459th Bomb Group, and employs 300 B-17 Flying Fortress and B-24 bombers, escorted by 150 P-47 Thunderbolt and P-38 Lightning fighters, to provide support for the Fifth Army's operations at Anzio, Italy.

ARMY
Lieutenant General Alexander M. Patch is advised that he will command Operation ANVIL—the invasion of Southern France. The operation is later renamed DRAGOON.

3 MARCH
ARMY
At Ponte Rotto, Italy, the 3d Infantry Division successfully holds off the last major enemy effort to break the Anzio beachhead.

4 MARCH
AIR FORCE
Thirty-one Eighth Air Force B-17 Flying Fortresses bomb Kleinmachnow in southwest Berlin. Originally, more than 200 B-17s are launched, but many abort the mission when German radio transmissions "recall" the bombers, citing bad weather. The 95th Bombardment Group presses ahead anyway and bombs the target from 28,000 feet. This is the first time that U.S. bombers have attacked the German capital city.

6 MARCH
AIR FORCE
The Eighth Air Force launches a major offensive strike against Berlin, Germany; 658 heavy bombers attack the city and surrounding areas, dropping more than 1,600 tons of bombs on the capital. More than 10 percent of the attacking bombers (69 aircraft) are lost on the raid, the highest number of bombers lost on any single day of the war. Meanwhile, medium bombers of the Ninth Air Force continue to strike

German V-missile sites in France while Twelfth Air Force aircraft hammer targets around the Anzio beachhead in Italy.

8 MARCH
AIR FORCE

The Eighth Air Force sends 460 bombers to strike the ball bearing factory at Erkner, Germany. Seventy-five additional aircraft strike Wildau and Berlin. Resistance is stiff, and 36 bombers are shot down.

9 MARCH
AIR FORCE

More than 450 Eighth Air Force bombers continue to attack deep into Germany, including strikes on Berlin, Brunswick, Hannover, and Nienburg.

NAVY

The German submarine *U-255* torpedoes the destroyer escort *Leopold* in the North Atlantic, damaging the ship to such an extent that she sinks the following day. Only 28 of her 199 crewmen survive.

13 MARCH
NAVY

A TBF Avenger torpedo-bomber of Composite

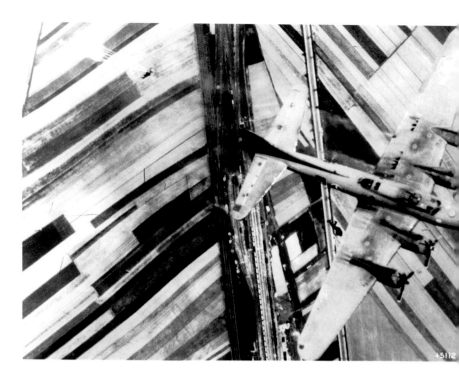

Above: *Two crewmen parachute away from their crippled B-17 Flying Fortress. (NASM)*

Below: *Infantrymen watch from their foxholes along an Italian road as German prisoners are taken to the rear. For these Germans, the war is over. (Dept. of Defense)*

Squadron 95 from the escort carrier *Bogue* joins U.S. and Canadian ships and a British patrol bomber in sinking the German submarine *U-575* in the North Atlantic.

15 MARCH
AIR FORCE/ARMY

In an all-out effort, Allied aircraft destroy the abbey at Monte Cassino, Italy, with 1,200 tons of bombs followed by an intense artillery barrage. Cassino defies Allied efforts for nearly four months. The battle-weary 36th Infantry Division is withdrawn for rest and refitting.

16 MARCH
NAVY

A PBY Catalina of Patrol Squadron 63 employs magnetic anomaly detection gear to detect the

submerged German submarine *U-392* in the Straits of Gibraltar. The Catalina and British ships attack the boat, with the British frigate *Affleck* delivering the blows that sink the sub.

17 MARCH
NAVY

TBF Avengers of Composite Squadron 6 from the escort carrier *Block Island* join the destroyer *Corry* and destroyer escort *Bronstein* in sinking the German submarine *U-801* west of the Cape Verde Islands.

18 MARCH
AIR FORCE

The Eighth Air Force sends 679 bombers against aircraft factories across Germany. The Luftwaffe comes out in force. Forty-three American bombers and 13 escort fighters are lost, but the enemy suffers heavy losses. The loss of German pilots begins to impact the effectiveness of defensive responses over Germany. The Fifteenth Air Force continues to pound targets in Italy, destroying a sizeable number of enemy planes during their raids.

19 MARCH
AIR FORCE

Lieutenant General Ira C. Eaker's Mediterranean Allied Air Force launches Operation STRANGLE in support of Allied ground forces in Italy. The objective of the seven-week campaign is to interdict enemy supplies across Italy by disrupting rail service, and damaging marshalling yards and ports. By mid-May, the Allies will have dropped more than 26,000 tons of bombs while flying more than 50,000 sorties during this operation.

NAVY

A TBF Avenger and F4F Wildcat of Composite Squadron 6 from the escort carrier *Block Island* sink the German submarine *U-1059* in the Atlantic west-southwest of Dakar, Africa.

20 MARCH
AIR FORCE

The 67th Tactical Reconnaissance Group completes a series of 83 missions to map the French coast in preparation for the invasion of Normandy. More than 9,500 photographic prints are made of the beaches, and no aircraft are lost during this one-month project.

21 MARCH
ARMY

The 34th Infantry Division arrives at Anzio, Italy, in preparation for the planned VI Corps breakout from the beachhead. Meanwhile, other corps units continue to press against stubborn German resistance in an effort to expand the beachhead.

22 MARCH
AIR FORCE

Mount Vesuvius, near Naples, Italy, erupts during combat operations. B-25 Mitchell bombers from the Twelfth Air Force fly through the ash, which burns through control surfaces made of fabric, and pits and chips the windshields.

25 MARCH
AIR FORCE

Fifteenth Air Force bombers successfully close the Brenner Pass between Italy and Austria, disrupting enemy transportation of supplies and communications.

26 MARCH
AIR FORCE

The Eighth Air Force sends more than 500 B-17 Flying Fortress and B-24 Liberator bombers to attack V-weapon sites in the Pas de Calais and Cherbourg areas of France. The Ninth Air Force sends 338 B-26 Marauder bombers and A-20 Havoc light attack bombers to strike torpedo-boat pens near Ijmuiden, while 140 P-47 Thunderbolt and P-51 Mustang fighters attack marshalling yards at Creil and other military installations in France.

27 MARCH
AIR FORCE

In a massive effort against airfields and aircraft works, the Eighth Air Force launches 700 heavy bombers to strike targets across France.

28 MARCH
AIR FORCE

The Fifteenth Air Force launches the first of a series of massive strikes in support of Operation STRANGLE to interdict movement of enemy supplies in Italy. Nearly 400 B-17 Flying Fortress and B-24 Liberator bombers strike marshalling yards and railroads around Verona and Cesano in their first "thousand-ton raid." P-38 Lightning and P-40 Warhawk fighters cover the bombers; no bombers are lost, but three of the fighters are shot down. The next day, more than 400 heavy bombers are launched, topping the record number for attacks over Turin, Milan, and Bolzano. Six aircraft are lost during these raids.

APRIL
AIR FORCE

During this month, the 100,000th Rolls-Royce Merlin engine is produced. Used on American P-51 Mustang fighters, the Merlin also powers 13 other operational aircraft, from Royal Air Force Halifax bombers to the Spitfire.

1 APRIL
MARINE CORPS

The 9th Marine Aircraft Wing is established at Cherry Point, North Carolina. Its mission is to train and equip aviation units for deployment to combat theaters.

2 APRIL
AIR FORCE

The Fifteenth Air Force, now with 16 heavy bomber groups at the ready, launches more than 530 bombers against the ball bearing factory at Steyr, Austria, and other targets near Mostar, Yugoslavia. Escort fighters claim more than 100 enemy fighters are destroyed, while 19 bombers are lost.

3 APRIL
AIR FORCE

The IX Bomber Command establishes a new operational leave policy as aircrew shortages develop. Bomber crews are allowed a maximum of one week of leave between their 25th and 30th missions. They are allowed a maximum of two weeks between their 40th and 50th missions.

The Fifteenth Air Force launches two days of strong attacks against aircraft industrial targets around Budapest, Hungary. More than 450 bombers conduct the first strike, and escorts and bombers claim two

Opposite: *Despite the efforts of its P-51 Mustang fighter escort, (foreground), the B-24 Liberator "E-Z Duzit" (upper right) is shot down on this mission over Germany and the crew is put in a prison camp. ("Brunswick, 8 April 1944," Paul Jones, USAF Art Collection)*

Above: *Soldiers bound for fighting in Europe board a transport with their weapons and duffle bags. ("Embarkation," Barse Miller, Army Art Collection, U.S. Army Center of Military History)*

Below: *A battery of M7 self-propelled 105mm howitzers provides artillery support to the 45th Infantry Division. (Dept. of Defense)*

Left: *A deck crewman gives the signal for takeoff to the pilot of an F4F Wildcat. ("To the Attack," Lawrence Beal Smith, Navy Art Collection)*

dozen kills during the raid. More than 300 heavy bombers strike the next day, and an intense fighter-to-fighter battle ensues. Ten bombers and dozens of enemy aircraft are shot down.

5 APRIL
AIR FORCE
Fifteenth Air Force bombers return to Ploesti, Romania, and target the refineries and marshalling yards near the town. Enemy fighters and antiaircraft fire claim 13 bombers.

ARMY
The 90th Infantry Division (Texas–Oklahoma) arrives at Liverpool, England. It is the first of the "draftee" infantry divisions deployed to the United Kingdom.

7 APRIL
NAVY
The destroyer *Champlin* intentionally rams the German submarine *U-856* in the Atlantic. Although damaged, she joins with the destroyer escort *Huse* in sinking the sub. *Champlin*'s commanding officer, Commander John J. Shaffer III, is wounded by shrapnel during the attack and dies the following day.

8 APRIL
AIR FORCE
In a major assault upon German airfields and aircraft factories, 13 combat wings from the Eighth Air Force launch in three separate forces. The largest single force of 192 B-17 Flying Fortress bombers attacks factories in Brunswick, with the loss of 34 aircraft. More than 200 B-26 Marauder bombers and P-47 Thunderbolt fighters of the Ninth Air Force attack targets near Hasselt, Belgium, in one of the largest tactical raids of the war.

9 APRIL
AIR FORCE
Eighth Air Force B-24 Liberator and B-17 Flying Fortress bombers continue to pound away at airfields and aircraft factories in Germany and Poland. Of 399 bombers launched, 32 are shot down. No diversionary raids are flown, allowing the enemy to concentrate on the attacking formations.

NAVY
TBM Avengers and F4F Wildcats of Composite Squadron 58 from the escort carrier *Guadalcanal* join the destroyer escorts *Pillsbury*, *Pope*, *Flaherty*, and *Chatelain* in sinking the German submarine *U-515* in the Atlantic off Madeira Island. The following day the Avengers also sink *U-68*.

11 APRIL
AIR FORCE

More than 800 Eighth Air Force B-17 Flying Fortress and B-24 Liberator bombers attack fighter production factories and airfields across Germany. Enemy fighters shoot down 64 bombers in what becomes the Eighth Air Force's second bloodiest day of the war. The Ninth Air Force launches more than 300 aircraft against a variety of targets in France. B-26 Marauder bombers, A-20 Havoc light attack bombers, and P-47 Thunderbolt fighters participate in these attacks.

13 APRIL
AIR FORCE

General Dwight D. Eisenhower, the Supreme Allied Commander, Allied Expeditionary Force, assumes direction of most air operations from his headquarters in the United Kingdom. He also assumes command of the majority of ground and naval forces that will participate in the invasion of France. The Eighth and Ninth Air Forces will make more frequent attacks in northern France as D-day approaches. Continued attention is given to attacking V-weapon sites and lines of communication. The Twelfth Air Force continues to hit hard in Italy, supporting ground forces engaged there.

The Fifteenth Air Force launches its largest raid of the war to date. More than 530 heavy bombers attack multiple aircraft factories and airfields across Germany and Hungary. More than 200 fighter sorties support the raids, the Fifteenth's largest number to date. More than 120 enemy aircraft are destroyed on the ground while fighters claim an additional 40 victories in the air.

16 APRIL
NAVY

The battleship *Wisconsin* is placed in commission.

17 APRIL
NAVY

While operating in the North Atlantic, the minesweeper *Swift* joins the submarine chaser *PC-619* in sinking the German submarine *U-986*.

Above: *Wounded Soldiers of the 15th Infantry Regiment, 3d Infantry Division, make their way to an aid station behind the battle lines in Italy. (Corbis)*

Right: *Supreme Allied Commander General Dwight D. Eisenhower, center, meets with senior members of his combined American–British staff in London to plan the invasion of France. (U.S. Army)*

Left: *An M7 self-propelled 105mm howitzer makes a careful crossing on a pontoon tread-way bridge over the swollen Volturno River in Italy. (Dept. of Defense)*

20 APRIL
NAVY

An attack by German torpedo planes against convoy UGS 38 off Algeria sinks the destroyer *Lansdale*, killing 47 members of her crew.

26 APRIL
ARMY

General Dwight D. Eisenhower watches helplessly as nine German torpedo E-boats attack landing ships of Army troops, mostly from the 1st Engineer Special Brigade, practicing for the landings at Normandy, France. Almost 750 Soldiers and Sailors die in the night tragedy off Slapton Sands, England.

NAVY

In the Atlantic north of the Canary Islands, four destroyer escorts—*Frost*, *Huse*, *Barber*, and *Snowden*—sink the German submarine *U-488* with naval gunfire.

28 APRIL
NAVY

Secretary of the Navy Frank Knox dies in Washington, D.C. He is replaced by undersecretary James V. Forrestal, who becomes the 48th Secretary of the Navy on 19 May.

MAY
MARINE CORPS

The 29th Marine Regiment (infantry) is organized at Camp Lejeune, North Carolina.

5 MAY
AIR FORCE

The Fifteenth Air Force reaches 20 heavy bombardment groups in strength, allowing it to launch more than 640 bombers against targets near Ploesti, Romania. Fighters fly 240 support sorties for the largest bomber force ever dispatched by the Fifteenth.

MARINE CORPS

The Marine Corps promulgates the new F-series tables of organization for its divisions. The main changes include enlargement of the rifle squad from 12 to 13 and the adoption of the four-man fire team; removal of the amphibian tractor battalion; deletion of the infantry battalion weapons company (with its machine guns and mortars dispersed to other companies); and abolition of the engineer regiments (though not its component engineer and pioneer battalions). The divisions implement the changes over the coming months.

6 MAY
NAVY

Pursuing the German submarine *U-66* west of the Cape Verde Islands, the destroyer escort *Buckley* evades enemy torpedoes and gunfire and rams the U-boat. After the destroyer escort backs off, the sub slams into her starboard side, opening a hole. The ensuing pitched battle at close quarters ends when *U-66* sinks.

7 MAY
AIR FORCE

The Eighth Air Force sends more than 900 heavy bombers to attack industrial centers near Munster and Osnabruck, Germany. Additional sorties are flown later that day against marshalling yards near Liege. This marks the first time that the Eighth Air Force launches an attack of that size.

8 MAY
ALL SERVICES

General Dwight D. Eisenhower sets 5 June as the date for the invasion of France.

9 MAY
AIR FORCE

An Allied offensive against airfields in France begins. The Eighth Air Force sends a total of 797 heavy bombers to attack more than a dozen airfields in France and other targets in Luxembourg, Germany. The objective is to keep Germany from rebuilding these fields for use prior to the planned 5 June invasion of France. The Ninth Air Force joins in the pre-invasion airfield offensive two days later.

Operation STRANGLE, the air offensive in Italy which began on 19 March, comes to a close. The Mediterranean Allied Air Force drops a total of 26,000 tons of bombs during 50,000 sorties flown in the campaign.

11–19 MAY
ARMY

Under cover of artillery fire, the Fifth Army breaks through the German Gustav Line, a stronghold south of Rome, Italy. The II Corps attacks with the 85th Infantry Division on the left and the 88th on the right. Both divisions make good progress and force the Germans to withdraw to a new defensive position.

Above: *An "old Army" horse cavalryman prepares to put his modern "steed" out of its misery. (Sergeant William Mauldin, Army Art Collection, U.S. Army Center of Military History)*

Right: *Infantrymen and tankers of the 1st Armored Division enter a war-ravaged Italian town. ("Into the Shadow," James Dietz)*

Left: *In the face of heavy antiaircraft fire, B-17 Flying Fortresses bomb Frankfurt, Germany, in January 1944. ("Shatzi Over Frankfurt," Michael Resmussen, USAF Art Collection)*

Below: *To cross some of the German anti-personnel minefields that block advances into Italy, the 3d Infantry Division tries a new armored vehicle that pulls a number of steel containers carrying infantrymen through the minefield. The vehicle sets off the mines while the containers protect the Soldiers behind. The device is declared a failure. (Dept. of Defense)*

12 MAY
AIR FORCE

The Eighth Air Force sends 800 bombers to attack oil production targets at Merseburg and Chemnitz, Germany, as well as Brux, France. Facing massive enemy fighter concentrations, 46 heavy bombers are shot down. The Ninth Air Force executes a dress rehearsal for the airborne element of the invasion of Normandy, France. Operation EAGLE tests the tactics and techniques of all specific missions related to the predawn plan to land paratroopers and supplies inland to help establish the beachhead. Weather is a mitigating factor, but the exercise goes on as planned. The Fifteenth Air Force, now expanded to its full

combat strength of 21 heavy bombardment groups, launches its largest raid against German headquarters at Massa d'Albe and Monte Soratte, Italy. The 730 bombers launched also strike airfields and transportation targets north of Rome. More than 250 fighters escort the bomber formations during the day.

13–14 MAY
AIR FORCE/ARMY

Twelfth Air Force aircraft put pressure on enemy forces in Italy as the Fifth Army and the French Expeditionary Force make a hard-fought breakthrough against the Germans' Gustav Line south of Rome. Country-wide attacks north of Rome continue throughout the day. The Fifteenth Air Force sends approximately 700 heavy bombers on interdiction strikes supporting the ground forces engaged at the Gustav Line.

13 MAY
NAVY

The destroyer escort *Francis M. Robinson* sinks the Japanese submarine *R-501* en route from Germany to Japan, south-southwest of the Azores Islands.

15 MAY
NAVY

PBY Catalinas of Patrol Squadron 63 join British ships in sinking the German submarine *U-731* off Tangiers.

17 MAY
NAVY

Eight U.S. Navy destroyers join a British bomber in damaging the German submarine *U-616* off the coast of Algeria, forcing her crew to scuttle the U-boat.

18 MAY
ARMY

The 36th Infantry Division begins an amphibious move to the beachhead at Anzio, Italy, where the 3d and 45th Infantry Divisions are preparing for an attack toward Cisterna.

19 MAY
AIR FORCE

As the Fifteenth Air Force pushes its attack to the north of Rome, enemy fighter opposition disappears.

NAVY

The destroyers *Niblack* and *Ludlow* join British aircraft in sinking the German submarine *U-960* off Algeria.

22 MAY
AIR FORCE

The Eighth Air Force occupies its last station in Britain, bringing the total to 77, including 66 airfields, which are home to 82 operational or headquarters units.

ARMY

Ten days after its arrival in Italy, the Eighth Army is redesignated the Ninth Army to forestall any possible confusion with the British Eighth Army. The new Ninth Army is under the command of Lieutenant General William H. Simpson. At Anzio, Italy, the 36th Infantry Division comes ashore, bringing the number of divisions in the beachhead to six plus other combat and support units. While keeping pressure on the Germans, the VI Corps is resupplying and refitting for the coming offensive toward Rome.

23 MAY
ARMY

After more than four months, the reinforced VI Corps breaks out of the beachhead at Anzio, Italy, and resumes the attack north toward Rome. Two days later, the II Corps and VI Corps link up, making a unified Fifth Army front for the first time.

25 MAY
AIR FORCE/ARMY

In one of its busiest days of the war, the Twelfth Air Force strikes targets throughout Italy while the German army retreats from Anzio, Italy. Support operations for the Fifth Army are critical as all ground forces from Anzio and from the west coast finally meet, forming a solid Allied front in the move to the north.

27 MAY
AIR FORCE

More than 2,000 aircraft attack targets across France, Germany, and Italy. Losses are heaviest over Germany as 24 Eighth Air Force bombers are shot down. Raids by the Mighty Eighth routinely number more than 800 bombers plus escort aircraft. Ninth Air Force missions number between 300 and 600 escorts. The Fifteenth Air Force is capable of launching more than 800 bombers on one mission.

29 MAY
AIR FORCE

In a daring experiment, Captain Charles T. Everett flies a test A-20 Havoc light attack bomber nicknamed "Alclad Nag," which is fired upon by the top turret gunner of a YB-40 (a modified B-17 bomber). They are testing the "frangible" bullet. This ceramic bullet is made to disintegrate on contact with the target plane for aerial gunnery training.

NAVY

The German submarine *U-549* slips through a screen of escorts and torpedoes the escort carrier *Block Island*, and sinks her, the only U.S. Navy aircraft carrier lost in the Atlantic. The destroyer escorts *Ahrens* and *Eugene E. Elmore* subsequently attack *U-549* and sink her.

30 MAY
ALL SERVICES

In England, assault forces for Operation OVERLORD begin loading equipment and supplies for the upcoming invasion of France. Theater-wide aerial assaults continue to ensure that the Luftwaffe has no operational capability near the landing zones.

31 MAY
AIR FORCE

The VB-7 vertical bomb is tested for the first time. It is one of the earliest attempts to guide a weapon using remote radio signals, to move control fins for steering.

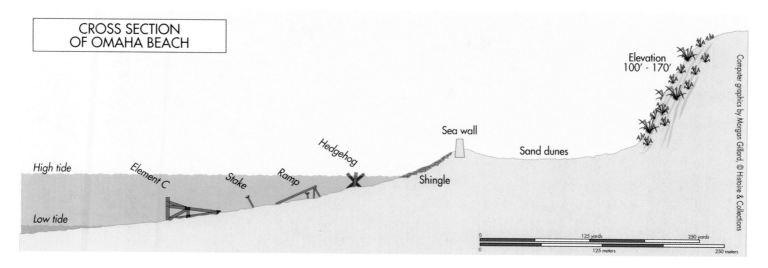

Elevation
100' - 170'

Sea wall

Sand dunes

Hedgehog

High tide

Element C

Stake

Ramp

Shingle

Low tide

125 yards   250 yards

125 meters   250 meters

Computer graphics by Morgan Gillard. © Histoire & Collections

ARMY

North of Anzio, Italy, the 36th Infantry Division seizes the heights of Mount Laziali, outflanking German defenses and forcing them to withdraw north beyond Rome.

2 JUNE
AIR FORCE

In preparation for Operation OVERLORD, heavy bombers continue to attack transportation and airfield targets in northern France. Heavy attacks upon the coastal defenses at Pas de Calais are made as part of Operation COVER—the deception campaign designed to disguise the actual landing zones for the invasion—that continues until 4 June. Two waves of bombers totaling more than 1,000 aircraft accomplish these strikes with minimal enemy fighter contact. Only eight bombers are lost to antiaircraft fire. American tactical forces meet with ground liaison officers to finalize targets to be struck before and during the landing. V-weapon sites, fuel depots, bridges, and railroads are high on the list.

Lieutenant General Ira C. Eaker commands the first raids flown during Operation FRANTIC, the shuttle-bombing strikes on Axis-controlled Europe from bases in the UK, Italy, and the USSR. Eaker leads 130 B-17 bombers escorted by 70 P-51 Mustang fighters of the Fifteenth Air Force from bases in Italy to bomb marshalling yards at Debreczen, Hungary, then go on to land at an airfield in Poltava, Soviet Union. Later, more than 400 heavy bombers taking off from airfields in both Italy and the United Kingdom attack deep targets and then land in the Soviet Union.

In Italy, the Twelfth Air Force continues to fly sorties in support of the Allied push north of Rome.

Above: *A cross-section of the Normandy beach designated "Omaha" shows the under-water obstacles placed by the Germans to stop landing craft. (© Histoire & Collections)*

Left: *Navy underwater demolition teams and Army engineers are tasked to create clear lanes through the German obstacles to permit landing craft to reach the invasion beaches in Normandy, France, in June 1944. ("Naval Demolition Men Blowing Up Obstacles," Lt. Mitchell Jamieson, USNR, Navy Art Collection)*

Above: *Marked with their D-Day stripes, hundreds of C-47 Skytrain transports tow CG-4A gliders full of Soldiers. Escorted by P-51 Mustangs, they pass over the invasion fleet en route to the drop zones behind the beaches in Normandy, France. ("D-Day—The Airborne Assault," Robert Taylor, NASM Art Collection)*

Below: *Thousands of parachutes carrying Soldiers from two airborne divisions descend in the night sky behind the American landing beaches in Normandy, France. ("Hours of Liberation," Larry Selman)*

4 JUNE
ALL SERVICES
General Dwight D. Eisenhower postpones Operation OVERLORD for 24 hours due to poor weather for the amphibious landings. Aerial preparation of the landings continues as more than 500 tactical strikes are made against bridges and coastal gun batteries. Convoys full of the ground landing forces are already at sea, and turn back.

AIR FORCE
The Twelfth and Fifteenth Air Forces continue to support advancing ground forces and hit targets in the northwest of Italy near the French border in preparation for Operation DRAGOON, the invasion of southern France.

ARMY
Rome, Italy, falls to Allied forces. The first unit to enter the city is the 88th Reconnaissance Troop, 88th Infantry Division. The Fifth Army converges on the city, and the 3d Infantry Division is tasked to garrison the area. The VI and II Corps pursue the Germans.

NAVY
In the first capture of an enemy vessel on the high seas by a U.S. Navy warship since 1815, Task Group 22.3, a hunter-killer group that includes the escort carrier *Guadalcanal* and five destroyer escorts under the command of Captain Daniel V. Gallery, drive the German submarine *U-505* to the surface off Africa. Subsequently, the destroyer escort *Pillsbury* puts a boarding party aboard the captured submarine.

Lieutenant (junior grade) Albert L. David receives the Medal of Honor for leading the men to enter the sub despite the danger of scuttling charges exploding. *U-505* is kept afloat and eventually towed to Trinidad.

5 JUNE
ALL SERVICES

After dark, Operation OVERLORD begins as the naval invasion fleet moves toward the coast of Normandy, France, and more than 1,400 C-47 Skytrain transports and gliders of the Ninth Air Force take to the air with the first airborne assault units of the U.S. 101st and 82d Airborne Divisions and the British 6th Airborne Division.

6 JUNE
ALL SERVICES

The invasion of Normandy, France, begins with pre-dawn airborne landings. More than 1,400 Ninth Air Force transport planes and gliders drop Allied airborne troops and land in the rear of German-occupied France. These three full airborne divisions are to secure the inland approaches to the Normandy beachhead. The pre-dawn airborne landings are scattered, but surprise the Germans. American and British paratroopers begin seizing their objectives and severing the roads to the beaches to block German reinforcements.

Above: *Senior American commanders anxiously watch Normandy landing beaches from the cruiser* Augusta. *Standing at the rail from left to right are Rear Admiral Alan G. Kirk, Lieutenant General Omar N. Bradley, Rear Admiral Arthur D. Struble, and Major Hugh Keen. (Naval Historical Center)*

Below: *A map showing the D-Day invasion beaches and landing zones. (U.S. Army)*

Following spread: *("The Battle for Fox Green Beach," Lt. Dwight C. Shepler, Navy Art Collection)*

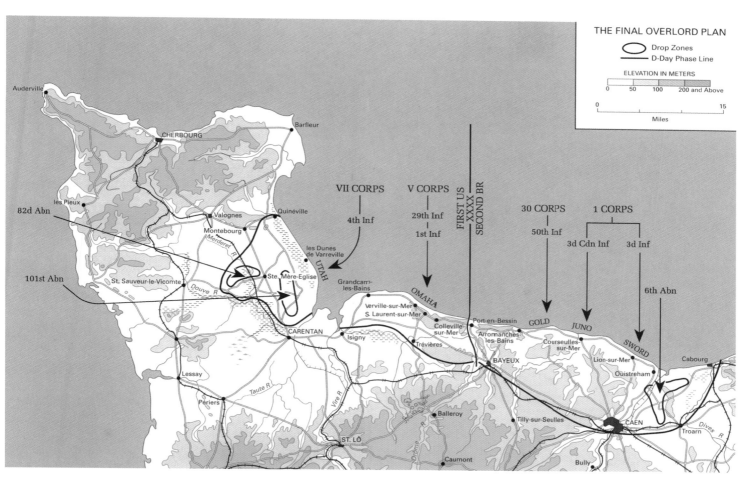

Above: *Soldiers heading for one of the D-Day invasion beaches in Normandy, France, on 6 June 1944, peer over the side of their landing craft as it approaches the shore. (U.S. Army)*

Below: *B-24 Liberator bombers fly through a dense barrage of German antiaircraft fire. (U.S. Air Force)*

At dawn, in the largest amphibious attack in history, Allied forces staging from England land on the beaches of Normandy. The naval aspect of the landings, Operation NEPTUNE, includes the American Western Task Force (under Rear Admiral Alan G. Kirk), which provides gunfire support and lands Army troops ashore. The main U.S. amphibious landings are by Lieutenant General Omar N. Bradley's First Army at two beaches code-named "Omaha," on the left (the V Corps, under Major General Leonard T. Gerow) and "Utah," on the right (the VII Corps, under Major General J. Lawton Collins). Between the two, the 2d Ranger Battalion scales the cliffs at Pointe du Hoc to destroy German coastal guns.

German resistance is heaviest at Omaha Beach, where the 1st and 29th Infantry Divisions land. The 4th Infantry Division battles its way ashore on Utah Beach under the leadership of its Assistant Division commander, Brigadier General Theodore Roosevelt Jr., the only Army general to accompany the initial assault waves.

Off Omaha Beach, destroyers risk grounding to move in close to fire at point blank range in support of the troops ashore. At Utah Beach, mines sink the destroyer *Corry* and 18 landing craft; 3 others are sunk by German shore batteries. On the beaches 114 landing craft are wrecked. Navy demolition teams, Seabees, and naval beach battalions suffer heavy casualties working alongside Army units to clear obstacles, direct unloading, and move the landing forces over the beaches. Doctors and corpsmen provide critical medical care to the casualties evacuated from the beaches. Marine Corps detachments also participate in the landings, and a number of Marine Corps officers are assigned as observers with Army and Navy units.

During the first 24 hours of the mission, American and British air forces fly more than 15,000 sorties in support of the invasion force. The Eighth Air Force (under Lieutenant General James Doolittle) sends more than 1,000 bombers to attack enemy positions near the landings and attack targets inland. They drop about 3,000 tons of bombs, with the loss of three aircraft. More than 1,800 fighters participate in escort and ground attack missions, with 25 lost at low level to antiaircraft fire. The Ninth Air Force (under Major General Lewis H. Brereton) supports the invasion with 800 medium bombers along with 2,000 fighter sweeps over the beaches and inland. Total losses are 30 aircraft. The Ninth Air Force continues to support ground operations as the Allies prepare to break out of the beachheads.

AIR FORCE
The Fifteenth Air Force continues shuttle-bombing missions, flying nearly 700 sorties against targets in

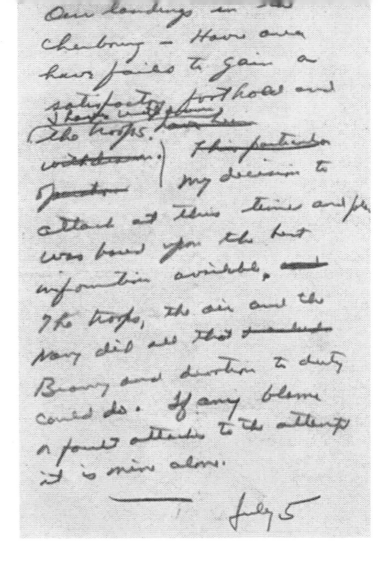

Above: *Anticipating a possible failure of the landings in Normandy, France, General Dwight D. Eisenhower prepares this handwritten statement taking responsibility for the operation. With the landings a success, he discards the note, but a staff member saves it. (Dwight D. Eisenhower Presidential Center)*

Below: *The 4th Infantry Division lands on Utah Beach. ("Overlord, Utah Beach," James Dietz)*

Ploesti and Brasov, Romania, and Turin, Italy. Primary targets are oil facilities in Hungary and Yugoslavia. The Twelfth Air Force continues to strike tactical and strategic targets throughout Italy.

7 JUNE
AIR FORCE

Following the landings at Normandy, France, the Eighth and Ninth Air Forces continue to interdict incoming German reinforcements while also resupplying airborne troops dropped into the enemy rear the night before. More than 2,000 sorties are flown in support of the invasion forces now established on five beaches in northern France. The Fifteenth Air Force reaches its peak strength of 21 heavy bomber groups and 7 fighter groups and continues strikes against targets in northwestern Italy. As long as weather cooperates, thousands of aircraft are airborne across Europe, accomplishing close support, interdiction, and strategic bombardment missions.

ARMY/NAVY

Headed for Utah Beach in Normandy, France, the transport *Susan B. Anthony* hits a mine near Reuville, France, and sinks in less than two hours. The ship is carrying an advance party of the 90th Infantry Division and 2d Battalion, 359th Infantry. There is no loss of life, but the bulk of equipment and weapons is lost.

NAVY

The construction of artificial harbors called "mulberries," necessary because of the lack of port facilities on the coast of Normandy, France, begins with the sinking of blockships and concrete caissons.

The United States Naval Academy Class of 1945 is graduated a year early due to the national emergency. Sixteen members of the class are killed during the remaining months of World War II.

8 JUNE
AIR FORCE

General Carl A. Spaatz places oil targets as the highest priority target for aircraft of the U.S. Strategic Air Forces.

ARMY

In the First Army area, the U.S. VII Corps begins an all-out drive to gain Cherbourg, France, with elements from the 82d Airborne Division and 4th Infantry

Division. On the VII Corps' south flank the 101st Airborne Division battles for control of the Carentan area, the key to a linkup with the V Corps. Elements of the 29th Infantry Division (under Major General Charles Gerhardt) relieve the hard-pressed 2d Ranger Battalion at Pointe du Hoc. The 2d Infantry Division (under Major General Walter M. Robertson) is in action in the V Corps zone.

NAVY

A mine damages the destroyer *Glennon* off Normandy, France. As the destroyer escort *Rich* maneuvers close by to assist her, three mines detonate nearby in quick succession, one blowing off 50 feet of the destroyer escort's stern. *Rich* sinks with the loss of 27 killed, 73 wounded, and 62 missing.

9 JUNE
AIR FORCE

Allied Air Forces units begin operating from bases in northern France.

NAVY

The destroyer *Meredith* sinks off Normandy, France, from damage incurred after striking an enemy mine off Utah Beach on 7 June.

10 JUNE
ARMY

Near Civitavechchia, Italy, the newly arrived 442d Regimental Combat Team, mostly Hawaiian Japanese-Americans, is attached to the 34th Infantry Division and is joined by the 100th Infantry Battalion, which becomes a battalion of the 442d. The VI Corps headquarters pulls out of the frontline to start planning for the forthcoming invasion of southern France. The II Corps and IV Corps remain to command the 34th, 85th, 88th, 91st, and 92d Infantry Divisions, 10th Mountain Division, and 1st Armored Division.

NAVY

Off Normandy, France, the destroyer *Glennon*, having already been damaged by a mine, sinks after being hit by German artillery fire.

11 JUNE
AIR FORCE

Fifteenth Air Force B-17 Flying Fortress bombers and P-51 Mustang fighters take off on a shuttle-bombing mission from bases in the Soviet Union, bomb several oil distribution and refinery targets, and return to bases in Italy.

Right: *The crew of the Coast Guard cutter* Campbell *fires depth charges from deck launchers at a suspected German submarine. (Lt. Cdr. Anton Fischer, USCG, U.S. Coast Guard Collection)*

NAVY

The battleship *Missouri* is commissioned, becoming the last American battleship to enter active service.

11–12 JUNE
ARMY/NAVY

Gunfire from U.S. Navy battleships operating off Normandy, France, provide much-needed support to paratroopers of the 101st Airborne Division in their capture of Carentan.

12 JUNE
AIR FORCE/ARMY/NAVY

The Joint Chiefs of Staff cross the English Channel in a landing craft and inspect the six-day-old beachhead at Normandy, France.

13 JUNE
AIR FORCE

The Germans launch V-1 weapons against England for the first time. The first one explodes at Swanscombe, Kent, at 4:18 a.m. Eleven are detected, and four of these strike random locations in London. General Henry H. Arnold, in England to monitor the air war, insists on being driven to one of the V-1 impact locations to inspect the damage.

15 JUNE
ARMY

As the Army celebrates "Infantry Day," the Replacement Training Center at Fort McClellan, Alabama, welcomes the 200,000th man to arrive for infantry basic training—Private Norman W. Crew of Brookline, Massachusetts.

NAVY

TBF Avengers and F4F Wildcats of Composite Squadron 9 operating from the escort carrier *Solomons* sink the German submarine *U-860* in the South Atlantic.

17–18 JUNE
ARMY

The 9th Infantry Division (under Major General Manton S. Eddy) breaks through at Barneville-sur-mer, France, to seal off the Cotentin Peninsula, trapping German defenders. Other units continue to press north and east out of the beachhead. In the XIX Corps (under Major General Charles H. Corlett), the 29th Infantry Division advances are contained.

21–22 JUNE
AIR FORCE

The Eighth Air Force continues Operation FRANTIC shuttle-bombing missions, sending 144 heavy bombers to strike oil targets en route to two landing fields in the Soviet Union. This raid is flown in conjunction with a massive 900-plane attack against targets in and around Berlin, Germany. More than 900 fighters are involved in escorting these bombers to and from the targets. Additional B-24 Liberator bombers strike German missile launching and rocket sites at Siracourt. During the night, German bombers damage or destroy almost all of the

Fortress bombers parked on the airfield at Poltava, Soviet Union. The Ninth Air Force provides 700 escort fighters for the Eighth Air Force bombers over Berlin.

22 JUNE
ALL SERVICES
President Franklin D. Roosevelt signs the "GI Bill," giving broad benefits to veterans. The Servicemen's Readjustment Act of 1944 makes higher education attainable for millions of returning veterans of World War II and all future conflicts.

23 JUNE
AIR FORCE
Across northern France, Allied efforts are made to strike at German V-1 missile sites in an effort to curtail continued attacks against southern England. Weather keeps many aircraft on the ground, but the Fifteenth Air Force launches a raid against oil targets near Ploesti, Romania. More than 400 bombers and 300 escort fighters are tasked for this mission; more than 100 of them are shot down.

ARMY
The 9th Infantry Division breaks into the defenses of the port city of Cherbourg, France. It will take another three days of fighting to clear the city and start to exploit its harbor facilities.

24 JUNE
NAVY
A TBM Avenger of Composite Squadron 69 off the escort carrier *Bogue* sinks the Japanese submarine *I-52* southwest of the Azores Islands.

25 JUNE
NAVY
Ships of Task Force 129 engage in a gun battle with German shore batteries at Cherbourg, France, with three destroyers and the battleship *Texas* suffering damage during the action. Straddled 65 times by enemy fire, the battleship is hit twice, including one that strikes the fire control tower. German defenders at Cherbourg surrender the following day.

30 JUNE
MARINE CORPS
The strength of the Marine Corps on active duty is 32,788 officers and 442,816 enlisted.

Above: *The German V-1 "buzz bomb" is the first surface-to-surface long distance unmanned weapon used in warfare. The weapons are often launched at British towns from sites in France. (NASM)*

Right: *A surprised German submarine crew discovers their intended prey is an armed Coast Guard cutter. ("Brief Encounter," Lt. Cdr. Anton Fischer, USCG, U.S. Coast Guard Collection)*

Above: *Soldiers of the 35th Infantry Division fight to break through the German positions dug into the hedgerows in Normandy, France. ("From Cornrow to Hedgerow," Keith Rocco, National Guard Heritage Series)*

Below: *The four-engine Douglas C-54 Skymaster can carry 50 troops and has a range of 4,000 miles, making it the main long-distance transport. (NASM)*

2 JULY
NAVY
A TBM Avenger of Composite Squadron 58 off the escort carrier *Wake Island* sinks the German submarine *U-543* southeast of the Azores Islands.

3 JULY
AIR FORCE
The P-61 Black Widow, America's only aircraft built specifically as a night fighter, flies its first operational mission in Europe.

ARMY
The First Army launches a general offensive into what is soon described as "the Battle of the Hedgerows." The VIII Corps, in a driving rain that prevents air support and hampers movement, attacks down the west coast of the Cotentin Peninsula, France.

NAVY
The destroyer escorts *Frost* and *Inch* sink the German submarine *U-154* in the Atlantic Ocean off Madeira.

5 JULY
NAVY
Off Nova Scotia, Canada, the destroyer escorts *Thomas* and *Baker* attack the German minelaying

submarine *U-233*. A depth charge attack by *Baker* forces the submarine to the surface, after which *Thomas* sets a collision course and bears down on the submarine with all guns firing. She slices through *U-233*'s pressure hull, causing the U-boat to sink in less than a minute.

7 JULY
AIR FORCE

The Eighth, Twelfth, and Fifteenth Air Forces hit petroleum, oil, and lubricant targets throughout the European Theater. In the approximately 3,000 sorties flown during the day, around 60 planes are shot down.

8 JULY
AIR FORCE

Lieutenant Colonel Clifford Heflin flies a C-47 Skytrain transport into France to rescue Allied airmen forced to parachute from damaged aircraft behind enemy lines. This is the first time such a mission has been attempted.

NAVY

While moored at the Naval Advance Amphibious Base at Deptford, England, the tank landing ships *LST-312* and *LST-384* become the first naval vessels damaged by German V-1 missiles.

9 JULY
AIR FORCE

The Fifteenth Air Force launches its first Pathfinder-led mission against oil targets at Ploesti, Romania. The escorting P-38 Lightning and P-51 Mustang fighters meet more than 40 enemy fighters, shooting down 14 of them.

Pieces of a wrecked V-1 "buzz bomb" (Fiesler Fi 103) are delivered to Wright Field, Ohio, for evaluation. In 17 days, the Ford Motor Company builds a copy of the pulse-jet motor. By October, the Republic Aircraft Company has been able to copy the weapon's airframe design. U.S.-built duplicates are called the JB-2.

11 JULY
AIR FORCE

The Eighth Air Force launches a multi-day raid against targets in Munich, Germany. Nearly 800 fighters fly escort support for the strike. The next day, more than 1,000 bombers and 750 fighters attack Munich, again striking marshalling yards and aircraft engine factories. On the 13th, 888 bombers strike again with 548 fighters as escort. The Fifteenth Air Force begins to strike targets in southeast France while continuing raids against oil production in Romania, as ground forces continue to press north through Italy.

13–14 JULY
ARMY

At the 2d Infantry Division command post in Normandy, France, Lieutenant General Omar N. Bradley and Major General Leonard T. Gerow observe a hedgerow-cutting device improvised by the

102d Cavalry Reconnaissance Squadron, 102d (Essex Troop) Cavalry Group (Mechanized). The V Corps Ordnance officer soon has production lines cranking them out for attachment to light and medium tanks. In the meantime the 4th Armored Division (under Major General John S. Wood) comes ashore to join the fight.

15 JULY
ARMY

The 29th and 35th Infantry Divisions engage in the battle for Saint-Lô, France. The capture of Saint-Lô on 18 July concludes the Battle of the Hedgerows.

17 JULY
AIR FORCE

A P-38 Lightning fighter drops napalm, a jellied form of gasoline, during a close support mission against a fuel depot at Coutances, France. This is the first use of napalm in combat by U.S. forces.

NAVY

During the loading of ammunition into the holds of the merchant vessels *Quinault Victory* and *E. A. Bryan* at the Port Chicago Naval Magazine in California, a series of explosions ignites nearly 5,000 tons of munitions. *E. A. Bryan* is blown to pieces and the adjacent pier disintegrates. The force of the explosions causes damage in San Francisco 48 miles away. A total of 320 men working on the loading parties are killed instantly, 202 of them African Americans. In the wake of the disaster, surviving African American munitions loaders refuse to obey orders directing them to perform the hazardous duty, and 258 of them face courts-martial. In January 1946 all of the men are given clemency and the opportunity to receive honorable discharges.

18 JULY
AIR FORCE

Lieutenant C. D. Lester, flying a 100th Fighter Squadron P-51 Mustang fighter out of Ramitelli, Italy, is part of an escort mission for a group of B-17 Flying Fortresses bombing targets over southern Germany. His flight engages a formation of German Bf-109 fighters, and in the ensuing six minutes of combat, he shoots down three enemy aircraft. Through his many aerial engagements, he never received as much as a bullet hole in his aircraft. The 100th was one of four African American fighter squadrons that made up the 332d Fighter Group. African American military pilots flew more than 15,000 missions while destroying 261 enemy aircraft during the war.

ARMY

The 34th Infantry Division begins its final assault on Leghorn, Italy, with Task Force Williamson (under Brigadier General Raymond Williamson) attached from the 91st Infantry Division. Other 91st Infantry Division elements reach the Arno River at Pontadera. On 19 July Leghorn falls and the 88th Infantry Division joins the 91st Infantry Division in patrolling to the Arno. By 20 July the 34th Infantry Division nears Pisa.

19 JULY
AIR FORCE

The Eighth Air Force launches 1,100 bombers against targets in Germany, including Munich, followed one hour later by the Fifteenth Air Force, which launches 400 bombers against targets in the same area. During the raids, fighters fly more than 1,000 sorties in support of the bombers. For the rest of the month, Munich will be targeted regularly by near-1,000-plane raids.

22 JULY
AIR FORCE

The first shuttle-bombing mission flown exclusively by fighter aircraft occurs when P-38 Lightning and P-51 Mustang fighters based in Italy attack an airfield near Ploesti, Romania, and then go on to land at Russian bases.

ARMY

The U.S. 12th Army Group (originally formed in England as the First United States Army Group) moves to France and Lieutenant General Omar N. Bradley opens the Group Command Post in a Normandy, France, apple orchard. He exercises command and control of the First Army (under Lieutenant General Courtney H. Hodges) and the Third Army (under Lieutenant General George S. Patton Jr.).

25 JULY
AIR FORCE/ARMY

After being postponed for 24 hours due to poor weather, Operation COBRA—the breakout from Normandy, France—begins. In preparation for the breakout attempt in the VII Corps area, 1,495 Eighth Air Force heavy bombers use saturation bombardment on targets in front of Allied-held lines. Unfortunately, 35 aircraft drop their bombs on the American side of the forward line of troops, resulting in the deaths of 102 soldiers, including Lieutenant General Lesley J.

Above: *An Army patrol, including a medic, enters the old city gate of Pisa, Italy. (Dept. of Defense)*

Right: *("Sherman Tanks Passing Streams of German Prisoners," Ogden Pleissner, Army Art Collection, U.S. Army Center of Military History)*

Right: *As part of the deception to conceal the real plans for the invasion of Normandy, France, the non-existent First U.S. Army Group, with a "ghost army" of 20 divisions, is created in England. Unit insignia are created, radio traffic is sent, and some Soldiers representing the units are seen in public. These are some of the ghost unit insignia. (American Society of Military Insignia Collectors)*

14th Army   XXXI Corps   XXXIII Corps   6th Airborne Division   9th Airborne Division   11th Division

14th Division   17th Division   18th Airborne Division   21st Airborne Division   22nd Division   46th Division

46th Division (variation)   48th Division   50th Division   55th Division   59th Division   108th Division

119th Division   119th Division (variation)   130th Division   135th Airborne Division   141st Division   157th Division

McNair, commander of the U.S. Army Ground Forces. Additionally, 380 troops are wounded. Ninth Air Force medium bombers also drop some of their bombs short, killing and wounding more American soldiers.

1 AUGUST
ARMY

Lieutenant General Courtney H. Hodges is announced as First Army commander. Hodges remains in command throughout the war.

After a secret existence for many months, the Third Army is identified as being in the field. Lieutenant General George S. Patton Jr., whose role was under wraps to mislead the Germans, is now openly named as its commander, with the VIII, XII, XV, and XX Corps under his wing.

The headquarters of the Sixth Army Group is organized at Bastia, Corsica, under the command of Lieutenant General Jacob L. Devers. Its mission is to provide overall operational control for the Seventh Army (under Lieutenant General Alexander M. Patch) and the future French First Army, which are the major command elements of Operation ANVIL—the planned invasion of southern France. The southern France landing is delayed due to an acute shortage of landing craft.

MARINE CORPS

Major Peter J. Ortiz and Sergeants John P. Bodnar, Jack R. Risler, and Frederick J. Brunner parachute into German-occupied southeastern France. They are part of a seven-man team from the Office of Strategic Services inserted to assist French guerrilla units. All but Brunner are captured by German forces on 16 August.

2 AUGUST
NAVY

The German submarine *U-804* sinks the destroyer escort *Fiske* east of Newfoundland, Canada. The ship breaks in two after being hit amid ships by a torpedo.

Right: *Soldiers of the 30th Infantry Division prepare to meet a German counterattack near Mortain, France. ("Battle of Mortain," Keith Rocco, National Guard Heritage Series)*

Below: *Prolonged street fighting by the 2d Infantry Division becomes necessary before the German defenders of Brest, France, surrender. (National Archives)*

4 AUGUST
AIR FORCE

In response to the first direct Soviet request for U.S. air strikes, more than 70 P-38 Lightning and P-51 Mustang fighters of the Fifteenth Air Force take off from Italy, attack targets in Romania, and land at bases in the USSR.

The Eighth Air Force launches 1,250 heavy bombers against industrial targets, airfields, and the Peenemünde rocket research facility in Germany, as well as two coastal batteries in the Pas de Calais area, two V-weapon sites, airfields, and other installations in France. Additional strikes against industrial targets in Germany and France, including V-weapon sites, take place over the next two days. On 8 August 359 B-24 Liberator bombers hit 10 V-weapon sites in northeastern France.

The first Project Aphrodite launches occur against V-weapon sites in Pas de Calais, France. In these missions, a pilot and weaponeer fly war-torn B-17 Flying Fortress and B-24 Liberator bombers, modified with an open cockpit, near the coast of England. The crew arms the 20,000 pounds of nitrostarch packed into the airframe, and then parachute to safety. A control ship then directs the bombers from a safe distance behind. A dozen such attempts are made before the heavy bomber part of Project Aphrodite is cancelled. Glide bombs fitted with radio and television guidance devices are still used during the project.

ARMY

The plan to attack the Gothic Line in Italy is revised with the Fifth Army strengthened by the attachment of the British 13th Corps, to make a subsidiary attack from Florence to Bologna. The offensive is delayed to 19 August. The main effort is to be led by the II Corps.

6 AUGUST
AIR FORCE

The Eighth Air Force conducts its second shuttle-bombing mission, launching 78 B-17 Flying Fortress bombers from the UK, which are joined later by P-51 Mustang fighters, to strike targets in Germany en route to the USSR. The Fifteenth Air Force also launches 60 fighters from bases in the USSR, which attack targets in Romania and land in Italy. Operation FRANTIC shuttle-bombing missions continue through 12 August.

Major George E. Preddy Jr., a P-51 Mustang pilot with the Eighth Air Force, shoots down six enemy

fighters in only five minutes, while escorting a formation of B-17 Flying Fortress bombers en route to bomb factories near Brandenburg, Germany. Preddy becomes the highest scoring P-51 pilot of the war, with 24 kills, but he is killed by antiaircraft fire on Christmas Day 1944.

8 AUGUST
AIR FORCE
Lieutenant General Hoyt S. Vandenberg assumes command of the Ninth Air Force.

ARMY
The VIII Corps demand for the German surrender of

Above: Lieutenant Colonel Benjamin O. Davis, commander of the 332d Fighter Group, begins the war as commander of the 99th Pursuit Squadron in North Africa. The 332d Fighter Group—African American pilots who became known as the "Tuskegee Airmen"—earns a distinguished combat record. (U.S. Air Force)

Right: VI Corps Soldiers pour ashore from their landing craft during the landing in southern France on 16 August 1944. ("Hitting the Beach, Lt. Albert K. Murray, Navy Art Collection)

Brest, France, is ignored. The 6th Armored Division prepares to assault until an approaching enemy division is intercepted. Bitter fighting continues near Saint-Malo where elements of the 83d Infantry Division meet heavy opposition. The XV Corps overruns Le Mans. General Dwight D. Eisenhower moves his headquarters to France.

10–14 AUGUST
AIR FORCE
Despite being hampered by poor weather, Twelfth Air Force B-25 Mitchell and B-26 Marauder bombers and P-47 Thunderbolt fighters strike targets on the French and Italian coast west of Genoa. On 12 August, Fifteenth Air Force heavy bombers join in the strikes in preparation for the invasion of southern France. The Eighth and Ninth Air Forces continue to cover operations around Paris.

13 AUGUST
AIR FORCE
As part of Project Aphrodite, two GB-4 television-guided, radio-controlled glide bombs are launched against E-boat pens in Le Havre, France. Additional strikes are launched through 13 September.

14 AUGUST
AIR FORCE
Captain Robin Olds, son of famed aviator General Robert Olds, shoots down his first enemy fighter. By 4 July 1945, Olds accumulates 11 more victories. Almost 22 years later, on 2 January 1967, Olds shoots

down an enemy MiG fighter in Southeast Asia. This victory makes Olds the only American ace ever to shoot down enemy aircraft in nonconsecutive wars.

15 AUGUST
AIR FORCE/ARMY/NAVY

Operation DRAGOON, the invasion of southern France, begins. Before dawn, the 1st Airborne Task Force (under Major General Robert T. Frederick), a combined U.S.–British unit of division size, makes a parachute assault into the Le May area to isolate the beachhead. Meanwhile a naval task force (under Vice Admiral H. Kent Hewitt) lands the 1st Special Service Force on the island of Levante. At the same time, a VI Corps (under Major General Lucian K. Truscott Jr.) amphibious assault force of three divisions (3d, 45th, and 36th Infantry Divisions) comes ashore on the French Riviera coast. Nineteen landing craft are damaged by German mines, underwater obstructions, and artillery. Hewitt's ships provide naval gunfire support while planes from the Twelfth and Fifteenth Air Forces use hundreds of light and medium bombers escorted by about 200 fighters to bomb enemy defenses. The 3d Infantry Division has three landing ships modified into mini-aircraft carriers to fly light observation aircraft for artillery target spotting. Only moderate resistance is met in all areas on shore and the beachhead is quickly expanded.

Above: *DUKWs of an Army amphibious transportation unit bring supplies onto the beach at Cavalaire Bay, France, during Operation DRAGOON in August 1944. The six-wheeled dual-drive trucks are invaluable to Allied landings. (U.S. Naval Institute)*

Below: *Infantrymen of the 550th Glider Infantry Battalion, 1st Airborne Task Force, find portions of their landing zone studded with German anti-glider poles linked to mines. ("Glider Landing in Southern France," Tom Craig, Army Art Collection, U.S. Army Center of Military History)*

16 AUGUST
AIR FORCE

Five German Me-163 Komet rocket planes attack a formation of B-17 Flying Fortress bombers near Merseburg, Germany. The rocket-plane attack, the first of its kind, is ineffective. Only 279 Komets, which can sustain flight for 8–10 minutes and obtain speeds in excess of 590 miles per hour, are built by the end of the war.

Right: The breakout from the Normandy beachhead in July sends the Allied armies racing after the retreating Germans. To keep the supplies flowing as the battle front moves farther from the coastal ports, a special system of dedicated one-way roads is set up with military police to ensure the high-priority, 24-hour-a-day flow of supply trucks is not delayed. ("Keep 'Em Rolling," Don Stivers)

17 AUGUST
AIR FORCE

The Fifteenth Air Force returns to hammering away at petroleum and oil industrial targets while the Twelfth Air Force continues to provide tactical air support to the DRAGOON invasion forces.

18 AUGUST
AIR FORCE

Ninth Air Force B-26 Marauder bombers and A-20 Havoc light attack bombers, having begun their forward deployment to continental Europe from England, strike fuel and ammunition dumps, and road and rail chokepoints in France, Belgium, Holland, and Germany in an effort to disrupt retreating German ground troops. More than 1,000 fighters fly cover during these operations and provide close support and interdiction for the ground armies as they return to their bases.

MARINE CORPS

Marine Barracks Londonderry in Northern Ireland is disbanded and most of the Marines sail for the States. An 80-man detachment remains behind to guard the naval radio station.

20 AUGUST
NAVY

TBF Avenger torpedo-bombers and F4F Wildcat fighters of Composite Squadron 42 from the escort carrier *Bogue* sink the German submarine *U-1229* in the North Atlantic.

Opposite, top: *A military policeman stands at a checkpoint along one of the "Red Ball Express" routes, taking a tally of the tons of cargo passing by his post and encouraging the drivers to "keep 'em rolling." (National Archives)*

Above: *The 28th Infantry Division parades through the center of Paris as a symbolic gesture of Allied unity and success in reclaiming Europe from German domination. Hard fighting is still ahead. (National Archives)*

21 AUGUST
ARMY

The closure of the Falaise Gap results in the capture of 50,000 German soldiers. This brings the Battle of Normandy to a conclusion. The French 2d Armored Division is alerted to liberate the French capital. The 4th Infantry Division is instructed to support the French as needed.

The Army Transportation Corps announces its "Red Ball Express," a unique fast-delivery system using over 6,000 Quartermaster and Transportation Corps trucks and one-way road traffic to speed supplies to the advancing U.S. forces. The original Red Ball route is from Saint-Lô, France, to Paris and back. Other "express" routes are soon in operation. Red Ball convoys operate through 13 November 1944, traveling 1,504,616 ton-miles. Nearly 75 percent of the truck companies in the Motor Transport Service in Europe are manned by African American troops.

MARINE CORPS

2nd Lieutenant Walter W. Taylor, working with an Office of Strategic Services team in front of Allied lines in southern France, is captured by German forces.

25 AUGUST
ARMY

The honor of leading the way into Paris, France, is given to the U.S.-equipped French 2d Armored Division supported closely by the U.S. 4th Infantry Division (under Major General Raymond O. Barton). The advance is screened by the 102d Cavalry Group (Mechanized).

27 AUGUST
ARMY

In response to French request, an impromptu parade is arranged in Paris. The 28th (Keystone) Infantry Division is diverted for a march down the Champs-Elysées. The men continue through streets of Paris toward the front lines.

28 AUGUST
AIR FORCE

Two Eighth Air Force P-47 Thunderbolt fighter pilots, Major Joseph Myers and 2nd Lieutenant Manford Croy Jr., shoot down a German Me-262 jet fighter in the first Allied aerial victory over a jet aircraft.

Above: *Soldiers of an antiaircraft battery man their 40mm Bofors gun during a practice drill in front of the recently liberated Trocadéro area museums in Paris. The gun is positioned to protect a nearby bridge over the Seine River. (National Archives)*

Below: *Soldiers of a quartermaster laundry platoon perform the unglamorous but necessary duty of providing clean uniforms to the troops on the front line. (National Archives)*

29 AUGUST
MARINE CORPS
As part of the Allied invasion of southern France, the Marine Corps detachments on board the cruisers *Augusta* and *Philadelphia* land on islands in Marseilles Harbor and oversee the surrender and disarmament of the German garrisons there.

30 AUGUST
ARMY
The 1st Airborne Task Force pushes to Beaulieu, France. Meanwhile the main body of the Seventh Army moves up the Rhone Valley (via Avignon), while the VI Corps, after action at Montelimar, races on toward Lyon.

1–5 SEPTEMBER
ARMY
In Italy, the IV Corps patrols across the Arno River in pursuit of withdrawing enemy forces. Task Force 45 crosses the Serchio River and clears the northern part of Pisa while the 1st Armored Division clears Mount Pisano. In the II Corps area, the 88th Infantry Division patrols contact the British at Sesto. On 5 September, the 1st Armored Division takes the walled town of Lucca.

2 SEPTEMBER
ARMY

The XIX Corps advances from France into Belgium and pushes toward Tournai. VII Corps units also cross the border. Also in Belgium, the 3d Armored Division advances to Mons; the 9th Infantry Division swings northeast near Charleroi.

Major General Lucian K. Truscott Jr., VI Corps commander, is promoted to lieutenant general. He soon learns he is to return to Italy to take command of the Fifth Army. Major General Edward H. Brooks takes Truscott's place at the head of VI Corps.

5 SEPTEMBER
ARMY

The Ninth Army (under Lieutenant General William H. Simpson) is officially operational, taking over the siege of Brest, France, and the port cities of Lorient and Saint-Nazaire.

The Army newspaper *Stars & Stripes* reappears in Paris, France, 25 years after it was suspended with the end of World War I. The Paris edition will use the equipment and offices of the *New York Herald Tribune*. *YANK*, the Army weekly, is already in business using captured German paper and ink.

8 SEPTEMBER
ALL SERVICES

The world's first ballistic missile—the German V-2—

is launched in combat. The first explodes in a suburb of Paris, France, and the second in a suburb of London, England, a few hours later. Scientist Wernher von Braun developed the missile at the secret research facility at Peenemünde, Germany. After the war von Braun comes to America, where he will continue his work developing rockets for the U.S.

9 SEPTEMBER
AIR FORCE

While Ninth Air Force bombers fly leaflet-dropping missions over coastal France and Belgium, more than 700 transport planes deliver supplies, evacuate

Above: *Many French villages along roads used by the Germans suffer from Allied bombs. (National Archives)*

Left: *Eight senior American leaders meet with General Dwight D. Eisenhower. Left to right, front row: Lieutenant Generals George S. Patton Jr. (Third Army) and Omar N. Bradley (12th Army Group); Eisenhower; Lieutenant Generals Courtney H. Hodges (First Army) and William H. Simpson (Ninth Army). Second row, 2nd to 4th right: Charles E. Corlett (XIX Corps); J. Lawton Collins (VII Corps); Leonard P. Gerow (V Corps); and Elwood R. Quesada (IX Tactical Air Command). (Dept. of Defense)*

wounded, and pick up interned Allied personnel across the rapidly expanding theater of operations.

10 SEPTEMBER
AIR FORCE
While more than 1,000 Eighth Air Force heavy bombers attack aircraft, tank, and jet propulsion plants in south central Germany, the Ninth Air Force assigns railroad targets in an effort to cut them both west and east of the Rhine River. More than 800 transports complete supply and evacuation missions across France as the Normandy invasion force meets the Operation DRAGOON force. Luxembourg is liberated as the advance toward Berlin continues.

The Fairchild C-82, the first World War II aircraft exclusively designed to carry cargo, flies for the first time near Hagerstown, Maryland.

ARMY
The II Corps opens the drive toward the Gothic Line in Italy with the 34th and 91st Infantry Divisions abreast. In the IV Corps sector, Task Force 45 and the 1st Armored Division also advance.

11 SEPTEMBER
ARMY
In the V Corps sector of France, a dismounted patrol of the 85th Reconnaissance Squadron, 5th Armored

Above: *As a part of Operation MARKET-GARDEN in September 1944, paratroopers of the 502d Parachute Infantry Regiment, 82d Airborne Division assault and seize a German-held bridge over the Maas River near Grave, Netherlands. ("Making It Happen," James Dietz)*

Division is the first Allied unit to cross the border into Germany. In the Third Army area the 90th Infantry Division clears the heights of Thionville, France, and reaches the Moselle River.

11–16 SEPTEMBER
ALL SERVICES

President Franklin D. Roosevelt and British Prime Minister Winston S. Churchill, along with the Combined Chiefs of Staff, meet at the Second Quebec Conference, with the discussions centering mainly on the British Royal Navy's role in the campaign against Japan. They approve Admiral William F. Halsey Jr.'s suggestion to push ahead with the invasion of Leyte Island, Philippine Islands, which is based in part on intelligence gathered from Philippine rescuers by a fighter pilot shot down off Leyte.

12 SEPTEMBER
AIR FORCE

In a rare demonstration of defensive airpower, the Luftwaffe launches approximately 400 fighters against an Eighth Air Force bomber package of more than 800 bombers and hundreds of fighters. The bombers suffer 45 losses and about 12 P-51 Mustangs are shot down.

ARMY

The V Corps launches a reconnaissance in force toward the Siegfried Line—enemy defenses consisting of tank traps and concrete bunkers along the German border. The 5th Armored Division and the 4th and 28th Infantry Divisions, with the 102d Cavalry Group, attack on 14 September. The terrain discourages employment of armor and the enemy reinforces defenses. The effort ends short of its objective on 16 September.

12 SEPTEMBER–27 OCTOBER
ARMY

The Fifth Army hits the Gothic Line in the west and penetrates toward Bologna, Italy, taking heavy losses. Gothic Line defenders resist until the spring of 1945.

Right: *German Me 109 fighters make a head-on attack against a formation of B-17 Flying Fortresses over Germany. ("Fortress Engaged in Commemoration of the B-17," Keith Farris, USAF Art Collection)*

Below: *While his assistant waits behind him, a gunner uses the shoulder stock of his M1919A .30 caliber light machine gun to aim through a hole in a wall in Italy. (National Archives)*

13 SEPTEMBER
ARMY

The 3d Armored ("Spearhead") Division (under Major General Maurice Rose) is committed to advance through the heavily wooded terrain on the border of Germany near Roetgen. On 14 September, the 9th Infantry Division (under Major General Louis A. Craig) enters the battle for the Huertgen Forest. The 9th Division advances against stubborn resistance.

14 SEPTEMBER
AIR FORCE

An A-20 Havoc light attack bomber intentionally penetrates a hurricane to collect scientific data. The first "Hurricane Hunters" are Colonel Floyd B. Wood, Major Harry Wexler, and Lieutenant Frank Reckord.

17 SEPTEMBER
AIR FORCE/ARMY

Operation MARKET-GARDEN begins. More than 1,500 Allied air transports and nearly 500 gliders carry 20,000 troops of the First Allied Airborne Army to the Netherlands. The U.S. 82d and 101st Airborne Divisions conduct a daylight parachute assault at Eindhoven and Arnhem, Netherlands. Their initial objective is to secure a road to the Rhine River bridges at Arnhem for the advance of the British Second Army. A second wave drops the next day, and the air battle is intense around Arnhem as 16 B-24 Liberator bombers and 21 fighters go down during operations. For the next two weeks, Allied airpower provides support to the First Allied Airborne Army by bombing targets throughout the Netherlands.

20 SEPTEMBER
AIR FORCE

Republic Aircraft Company rolls out the 10,000th P-47 Thunderbolt at Farmingdale, New York. It will take another 10 months to build the next 5,000 of these durable, multipurpose fighter aircraft.

21 SEPTEMBER
AIR FORCE

Eighth Air Force B-24 Liberator bombers fly more than 80 sorties to deliver fuel to ground and air forces in France. More than 100 such missions are flown the next day. By the 28th, nearly 200 B-24s will be delivering fuel to advancing forces in France while B-17 Flying Fortress and other B-24 bombers continue to attack German fuel resources.

25 SEPTEMBER
NAVY

While operating off Le Havre, France, the minelayer *Miantonomah* strikes an enemy mine and sinks in 20 minutes with the loss of 58 crewmen.

29 SEPTEMBER
NAVY

PB4Y-1 Liberators of Bombing Squadron 107 sink the German submarine *U-863* in the South Atlantic.

30 SEPTEMBER
NAVY

The destroyer escort *Fessenden* sinks the German submarine *U-1062* west of the Cape Verde Islands.

1 OCTOBER
AIR FORCE

With the assignment of the 5th Photo Group, Reconnaissance, the Fifteenth Air Force reaches its full wartime authorization of 21 heavy bomber groups, seven fighter groups, and one reconnaissance group.

NAVY

Vice Admiral Richard S. Edwards is named to the new posts of Deputy Commander in Chief, U.S. Fleet as well as Deputy Chief of Naval Operations.

2 OCTOBER
AIR FORCE

Over the next 30 days, when not stopped by poor weather, the Eighth Air Force launches 12 raids of more than 1,000 bombers and another 6 raids of more than 450 bombers. Between 5 and 17 groups of fighter escorts accompany each mission. Priority targets remain airfields, oil production and refineries, motor works, and munitions plants. Targets surrounding the city of Cologne, Germany, are hit particularly hard and often during the month. German defenses are inconsistent, but are still formidable when launched en mass. On 7 October, 52 bombers and 15 fighters are shot down. Some of the bombers fall victim to new Me 262 jet fighters. Four of the enemy Me 262 jets are shot down on that same day.

4 OCTOBER
ARMY

The Ninth Army assumes responsibility for the sector between Bollendorf and Saint-Vith in the Luxembourg-southern Belgium region to enable the First and Third Armies to concentrate in narrow fronts for offensive action. Initially, only the VIII Corps is available.

Left: *Dedicated medics and stretcher bearers work in the dark to bring a wounded Soldier down from his mountain position. ("Night Shift," Joseph Hirsch, Army Art Collection, U.S. Army Center of Military History)*

Above: *In Italy, Soldiers wearing the "Buffalo" shoulder insignia of the 92d Infantry Division stand for inspection by Lieutenant General Lucian K. Truscott Jr., Fifth Army commander. (U.S. Army)*

Below: *Soldiers of the 110th Infantry Regiment, 28th Infantry Division advance cautiously through the dense Huertgen Forest of Germany in November 1944. Strong German resistance causes heavy losses to the five U.S. divisions and other units that fight in the forest for three months. (National Archives)*

Opposite: *Crewman manage to bail out of their burning B-17 Flying Fortress, one of 56 B-17s lost during a 1,000-plane raid on a German oil refinery in Merseburg, Germany. ("Leuna Oil Refinery, Merseburg, November 30, 1944," Alfred Vetromile, USAF Art Collection)*

5 OCTOBER
ARMY
Major General Raymond S. McLain is named to command the XIX Corps in Lieutenant General George S. Patton Jr.'s Third Army. The former Oklahoma banker is the first National Guard officer in modern times to command a corps in combat.

Adverse weather conditions hamper the 9th Infantry Division in its attack at Schmidt, Germany, which commands the Roer River's Schwammenauel Dam. On 6 October, the division launches two regiments into the Huertgen Forest against tenacious opposition. Advance elements make gains but the main body fails to catch up. On 8 October tanks and tank destroyers arrive to assist. On 9 October troops break out of Huertgen in two places.

12 OCTOBER
AIR FORCE
In support of the Fifth Army offensive near Bologna, Italy, the Twelfth Air Force sends 700 B-17 Flying Fortress and B-24 Liberator bombers to strike ammunition and fuel dumps, barracks, vehicle repair facilities, and munitions factories. Another 160 P-51 Mustang fighters strafe rail, airfield, and river targets.

19–20 OCTOBER
ARMY
German efforts to break out of encirclement by U.S. forces are abandoned as the Aachen garrison is told to fight to the end. Troops of the 1st Infantry Division, assisted by the 28th Infantry Division, force the enemy toward the suburbs of the city. Task Force Hogan, 3d Armored Division gains Lousberg Heights.

1 NOVEMBER
AIR FORCE
At Caltech, the nation's first rocket research and development center is reorganized and renamed the Jet Propulsion Laboratory. The laboratory will become the center of American rocket development during the early years of the Cold War.

1–3 NOVEMBER
ARMY
In Germany, the V Corps launches an attack to clear the Vossenack–Schmidt–Lammersdorf triangle to the headwaters of the Roer River. A regiment of the 28th Infantry Division crosses the Kall River and takes Kommerscheidt and Schmidt despite the lack of progress on its flanks.

Right: *Army Air Forces ground crews at a base in England prepare P-47 Thunderbolts for their next mission. (Ogden Pleissner, Army Art Collection, U.S. Army Center of Military History)*

Below: *Two M10 tank destroyers of the 893d Tank Destroyer Battalion drive up the muddy Kall Trail in the Huertgen Forest, Germany. (National Archives)*

2 NOVEMBER
AIR FORCE

During a 1,100-plane raid at the synthetic oil plant at Merseburg/Leuna, Germany, approximately 500 enemy fighters attack wave after wave of American bombers. Although 17 fighter groups provide escort for the mission, 40 bombers and 28 fighters are lost. American fighter pilots claim more than 150 victories during the massive air battle.

3 NOVEMBER
ARMY

The 92d Infantry Division (under Major General Edward M. Almond) starts operations in the Serchio River Valley, Italy. The 92d Infantry Division is composed predominantly of African American troops, but many of its officers are white.

4 NOVEMBER
AIR FORCE

In Italy, the Twelfth Air Force sends more than 300 medium bombers to bomb rail lines and roads in Brenner Pass and west of the Po River Valley. Four P-47 Thunderbolt fighters attack a Milan hotel, where it is believed that German ruler Adolf Hitler is staying.

MARINE CORPS

In California, Marine Base Defense Air Group 48 at Santa Barbara and Marine Aircraft Group 51 at Mojave are redesignated as Marine Air Support Groups (MASG). Each will be composed of four Marine Corps carrier air groups, each slated to operate from a single escort carrier with a fighter squadron and a torpedo bomber squadron. The mission of the MASGs is to provide close air support to ground troops during an amphibious assault and subsequent fighting ashore.

5 NOVEMBER
AIR FORCE

In their largest operation against one single target during the war, the Fifteenth Air Force sends 500

B-24 Liberator and B-17 Flying Fortress bombers to bomb the oil refinery at Vienna/Florisdorf, Austria. Nearly 140 P-38 Lightning and 200 P-51 Mustang fighters provide escort and support for the mission.

7 NOVEMBER
AIR FORCE

General Henry H. Arnold tasks Dr. Theodore von Kármán to investigate the potential of airpower for the future. The report and recommendations of Kármán's report, "Toward New Horizons," will form the basis of the scientific foundation of the future U.S. Air Force.

9 NOVEMBER
AIR FORCE

As the Third Army launches a full-scale ground attack on Metz, Germany, the Eighth Air Force sends more than 1,100 heavy bombers to attack targets near Metz, Thionville, and Saarbrucken. Eleven fighter groups escort, but still 40 bombers and fighters are lost during the operation.

10 NOVEMBER
MARINE CORPS

The 4th Marine Base Defense Aircraft Wing is redesignated 4th Marine Aircraft Wing and its groups are redesignated as Marine Aircraft Groups 41, 42, 44, 45, and 46.

12 NOVEMBER
AIR FORCE

Fighter pilot combat tour length is set at 270 flight hours.

15 NOVEMBER
AIR FORCE/ARMY

Army Ordnance initiates a program of research and development of ballistic missiles. Project Hermes begins with a prime contract issued to the General Electric Company, and includes plans to study captured German V-2 rockets.

16 NOVEMBER
AIR FORCE

More than 4,000 Allied aircraft drop over 10,000 tons of bombs in front of the First and Ninth Armies in preparation for a major ground offensive in Germany.

ARMY

At Schevenhuette, the farthest point of penetration yet made into Germany, the First Army's VII Corps launches the main effort toward Cologne and the Roer River.

21 NOVEMBER
AIR FORCE

During another 1,000-plus plane raid over oil targets at Merseburg/Leuna, Germany, Eighth Air Force bombers are hit hard despite having 16 groups of

Right: *In October 1944, Soldiers of the 18th Infantry, 1st Infantry Division assault German positions on Hill 239 (Crucifix Hill), a critical German position in the defenses around Aachen, Germany. ("Battle of Crucifix Hill," Don Stivers)*

many had diverted to emergency landing fields in Allied-occupied territory.

21–27 NOVEMBER
ARMY

The V Corps joins the offensive to take Huertgen and Kleinhau, Germany. The 8th Infantry Division (under Major General Donald A. Stroh) attacks through rain, fog, and mud. The 121st Infantry Regimental Combat Team registers only modest gains. Tanks sever the Huertgen–Kleinhau highway. On 27 November the 121st RCT reports the fall of Huertgen village.

27 NOVEMBER
AIR FORCE

During an Eighth Air Force raid against German targets in the Magdeburg–Munster–Hannover area, American aircrews observe approximately 750 German fighters. This is the single largest aerial defense mounted by the Luftwaffe during the war, demonstrating its ability to concentrate forces when needed.

fighters as escort. Approximately 35 bombers and fighters go down during the fighting. In a similar raid four days later, Pathfinder bombers will lead a force of 900 bombers over these same targets. Weather is extremely poor and more than 65 aircraft fail to return to their home airfields. It is later determined that

29 NOVEMBER
ARMY

The Combat Command Reserve (CCR), 5th Armored Division, under 8th Division command, seizes Kleinhau, Germany. The nine-day fight costs the 121st Infantry Regiment, CCR 5th Armored Division, and

Above: *Brigadier General Anthony C. McAuliffe, 101st Airborne Division artillery commander, is the acting division commander on 22 December 1944 when the Germans demand that the American forces defending the town of Bastogne, Belgium, surrender. McAuliffe replies, "Nuts!" (National Archives)*

Right: *This map shows the German attacks during the Battle of the Bulge in December 1944. (U.S. Army)*

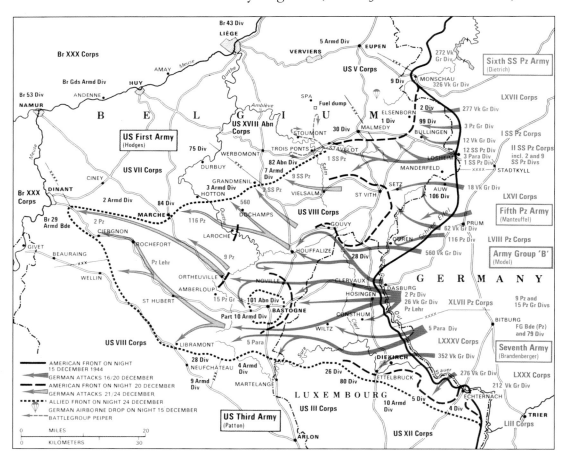

the 1st Battalion, 13th Infantry Regiment more than 1,200 casualties. The 8th Infantry Division is ordered to continue the attack. The 8th Infantry Division is soon on the west bank of the Roer River, recovering from the brutal fight in the Huertgen Forest.

30 NOVEMBER
AIR FORCE
The Eighth Air Force sends 1,200 heavy bombers against German synthetic oil plants at Bohlen, Zeitz, Merseburg/Leuna, and Lutzkendorf. A total of 19 fighter groups (16 from the Eighth and 3 from the Ninth) escort the package. Flak is intense and brings down 29 bombers. Another dozen are shot down by enemy fighters.

1–16 DECEMBER
ARMY
Only 11 months after the establishment of Project Ordcit, the Jet Propulsion Laboratory launches two dozen Private A rockets at Camp Irwin, California.

5 DECEMBER
AIR FORCE
Launching more than 500 bombers against targets over Berlin and Munster, Germany, the Eighth Air Force escort fighters meet 300 Luftwaffe fighters in heated aerial combat and claim dozens are destroyed.

Above: *Paratroopers of the 82d Airborne Division help stop and turn back the advancing German armor columns in the northern sector of the "bulge." ("Stopped Dead in Their Tracks," James Dietz)*

Below: *The personal flag for a five-star General of the Army. (NASA)*

6 DECEMBER
ARMY

In Germany, the 83d Infantry Division relieves the battered 4th Infantry Division as the Huertgen Forest campaign comes to a close. Since 14 September, when elements of the 9th Infantry Division enter the fringes of the forest near Roetgen, five U.S. infantry divisions—the 1st, 4th, 8th, 9th, and 28th, along with the 2d Rangers and elements of the 5th Armored Division—suffer 5,000 casualties per division.

7 DECEMBER
ARMY

The 2d Ranger Battalion attacks and captures the critical Castle Hill (Hill 400) in Bergstein, Germany. The Rangers hold the hill for two days against German artillery and counterattacks, suffering over 25 percent casualties.

15 DECEMBER
ALL SERVICES

President Franklin D. Roosevelt signs legislation authorizing new five-star ranks, with seven promotions taking place over the next six days. Promoted to General of the Army are Generals George C. Marshall (16 December); Douglas MacArthur (18 December); Dwight D. Eisenhower (20 December); and Henry H. Arnold (21 December). Promoted to Fleet Admiral are Admiral William D. Leahy (15 December); Ernest J. King (17 December); and Chester W. Nimitz (19 December). Two others, Admiral William F. Halsey Jr. and General Omar N. Bradley, are promoted after the war.

AIR FORCE

Army Major Glenn Miller, famous band leader, departs from France bound for England as a passenger aboard a Noorduyn C-64 Norseman aircraft. His aircraft disappears and no wreckage is ever found.

ARMY

Lieutenant General Mark W. Clark departs the Fifth Army for command of the new 15th Army Group. Lieutenant General Lucian K. Truscott Jr. takes over the Fifth Army.

16 DECEMBER

In Belgium, the Battle of the Bulge begins. Striking under cover of darkness, two German Panzer armies launch a surprise attack on First Army frontline units in the Ardennes Forest, battering the 28th Division and the 14th Cavalry Group, surrounding—and virtually destroying—the green 106th Infantry Division, and forcing back the 4th Infantry and 9th Armored Divisions.

17–18 DECEMBER
AIR FORCE/ARMY

Although no Ninth Air Force bombers fly, more than 1,000 fighters launch against the German counteroffensive in the Ardennes Forest in Belgium. The 9th Tactical Air Force attacks the leading edge of the enemy troops by strafing and bombing German Panzer tanks. After 18 December, poor weather grounds most planes until 23 December.

18–19 DECEMBER
ARMY

The 101st Airborne Division, with elements of the 9th and 10th Armored Divisions and other units, establishes a defensive perimeter around Bastogne, Belgium. Efforts to reach the 28th and 106th Infantry Divisions are abandoned as the German Panzer tank columns advance swiftly into Belgium.

20 DECEMBER
ARMY

In Belgium, Army engineers frustrate advancing Germans by destroying bridges and creating roadblocks, while U.S. reinforcements attempt to stem the German tide. General George S. Patton Jr. rapidly moves his Third Army from Metz, Germany, to Arlon, Belgium, and assembles the 4th Armored Division and 26th and 80th Infantry Divisions for rapid movement to the Bastogne area.

22 DECEMBER
ARMY

The attacking Germans surround Bastogne, Belgium; the 101st Airborne Division and the other U.S. units man the perimeter in freezing weather. Brigadier General Anthony C. McAuliffe, acting commander of the 101st Airborne Division, replies to a German demand to surrender with "Nuts!" Although their supplies are scarce, the defenders are determined to hold out.

23 DECEMBER
AIR FORCE

In Belgium, weather finally allows the Ninth Air Force to launch some 500 B-26 Marauder and A-20 Havoc bomber sorties in support of the engaged Allied forces at the Bulge. Although 31 bombers are

Opposite: *("Berlin, December 5, 1944," Alfred Vetromile, USAF Art Collection)*

Right: *Soldiers on the front line in Italy take a break and use a haystack as a table to enjoy their Christmas dinner in December 1944. (Dept. of Defense)*

shot down, many more German fighters are destroyed by the escort forces.

24 DECEMBER
AIR FORCE/ARMY
In Belgium, the Ninth Air Force continues to fly support sorties for the III, VIII, and XII Corps along the south flank at the Bulge. These missions continue as weather permits for the remainder of the month, including direct support for the U.S. 4th Armored Division as it breaks through to the besieged 101st Airborne Division, which has been surrounded at Bastogne since 22 December.

AIR FORCE
In the largest Eighth Air Force operation to date, more than 2,000 heavy bombers are dispatched to targets across Europe. Eleven airfields, 14 communications centers, five cities, and dozens of targets of opportunity are bombed by more than 1,900 of the original force. Thirteen Allied fighter groups in an escort role—more than 1,000 fighters—meet 200 enemy fighters, shooting down about 25 percent of the enemy planes.

Brigadier General Frederick W. Castle, Commander, 4th Bomb Wing, Eighth Air Force dies in the skies over Belgium after his crippled B-17 Flying Fortress is shot down by enemy fighters. Brigadier General Castle initially loses an engine, but loses maneuverability while attempting to keep from endangering friendly ground troops. He remains at the controls of his aircraft to allow four of his crewmembers to escape. He receives the Medal of

Below: *When casualties cause an acute infantry manpower shortage in December 1944, African American Soldiers serving in rear area support units are offered the opportunity to volunteer for front line duty. Several thousand do, and form platoons that are sent to augment understrength infantry companies. (Waymond Ransom)*

Honor; in addition, Castle Air Force Base in Merced, California, is later named in his memory.

ARMY

En route to Cherbourg, France, the troopship SS *Leopoldville* is torpedoed by a German submarine. The ship carries troops of the 262d and 264th Infantry regiments, 66th (Panther) Infantry Division, plus other units. The crew panics and the soldiers are never given the command to abandon ship. More that 500 men die in the frigid water or trying to reach rescue ships that finally come to help. It is the Army's worst ship disaster during the war.

26 DECEMBER
ARMY

Lieutenant General John C. H. Lee announces to troops in his rear area Communications Zone units that they may request assignment to units "where assistance is most needed" without regard to color or race. This opens the door for African American soldiers serving in service and support units in England and France to serve alongside white soldiers in undermanned combat units.

In Belgium, Lieutenant Colonel Creighton Abrams' 37th Tank Battalion, 4th Armored Division breaks

Above: *Lieutenant Colonel Creighton W. Abrams waves the men of his 37th Armor Battalion, 4th Armor Division forward to break through the German line and link up with the surrounded 101st Airborne Division in Bastogne, Belgium, on 26 December 1944. ("To Relieve Bastogne," Don Stivers)*

through from the south to relieve the Bastogne defenders. At 6:45 a.m. the first M4 Sherman tank enters the U.S. positions and the siege is over.

28 DECEMBER
ARMY

Lieutenant General Alexander M. Patch's Seventh Army is attacked as a secondary German counteroffensive is launched in the Saar region of Germany. The Seventh Army initially yields west of the Rhine River.

29 DECEMBER
ARMY

In Italy, reversals in the Serchio River valley delay the Fifth Army's offensive toward Bologna. By the end of the year U.S. positions are about the same as they were at the end of October.

1945
THE FINAL ACT

I JANUARY
AIR FORCE

The Eighth Air Force's three Bomb Divisions are redesignated as Air Divisions. During the month, weather permitting, hundreds of bombers and fighters are sent to attack targets throughout Europe. Transportation targets (bridges over the Rhine River, rail junctions, and tank and troop concentrations in the western sections of Germany) are added to the target list with increased priority. Hundreds of escort fighters accompany the bombers on every mission, striking lines of communications as they return to base. Weather throughout the continent limits bombing operations throughout the winter months. The German air force attacks Allied airfields in Brussels, Belgium; Eindhoven, Netherlands; and Metz, Germany. More than 120 Allied aircraft are destroyed on the ground. Allied fighters shoot down an estimated 460 of the 700–800 attacking aircraft.

NAVY

During the last year of World War II, Navy personnel strength reaches a wartime high of 3,405,525.

4 JANUARY
ARMY

As the weather turns bad in Europe, the bombing campaign in the area of the Brenner Pass linking Italy and Austria shifts to hitting open stretches of railroad tracks and hitting bridges to disrupt enemy traffic between Austria and northern Italy.

Above: *The bodies of American Soldiers lie in the snow near Malmedy, Belgium, where they were executed by advancing Germans during the Battle of the Bulge in December 1944. (U.S. Army)*

Below: *M4 Sherman tanks of the 10th Tank Battalion sit covered by snow near Saint-Vith, Belgium, where they will battle advancing German tanks to a standstill in late January 1945. (National Archives)*

Opposite: *This map shows the Allies' advance into Germany. (U.S. Army)*

8 JANUARY
ARMY

The U.S. Fifteenth Army becomes operational at Ferme de Suippes, France.

13 JANUARY
ARMY

The 87th Infantry Division reaches the Ourthe river in Belgium and makes contact with the British. In the XVIII Airborne Corps area the reconstituted 106th Infantry Division attacks alongside the 30th Infantry Division near the Salm River. During the bitter campaign the U.S. casualties are 19,000 killed in action and 15,000 taken prisoner.

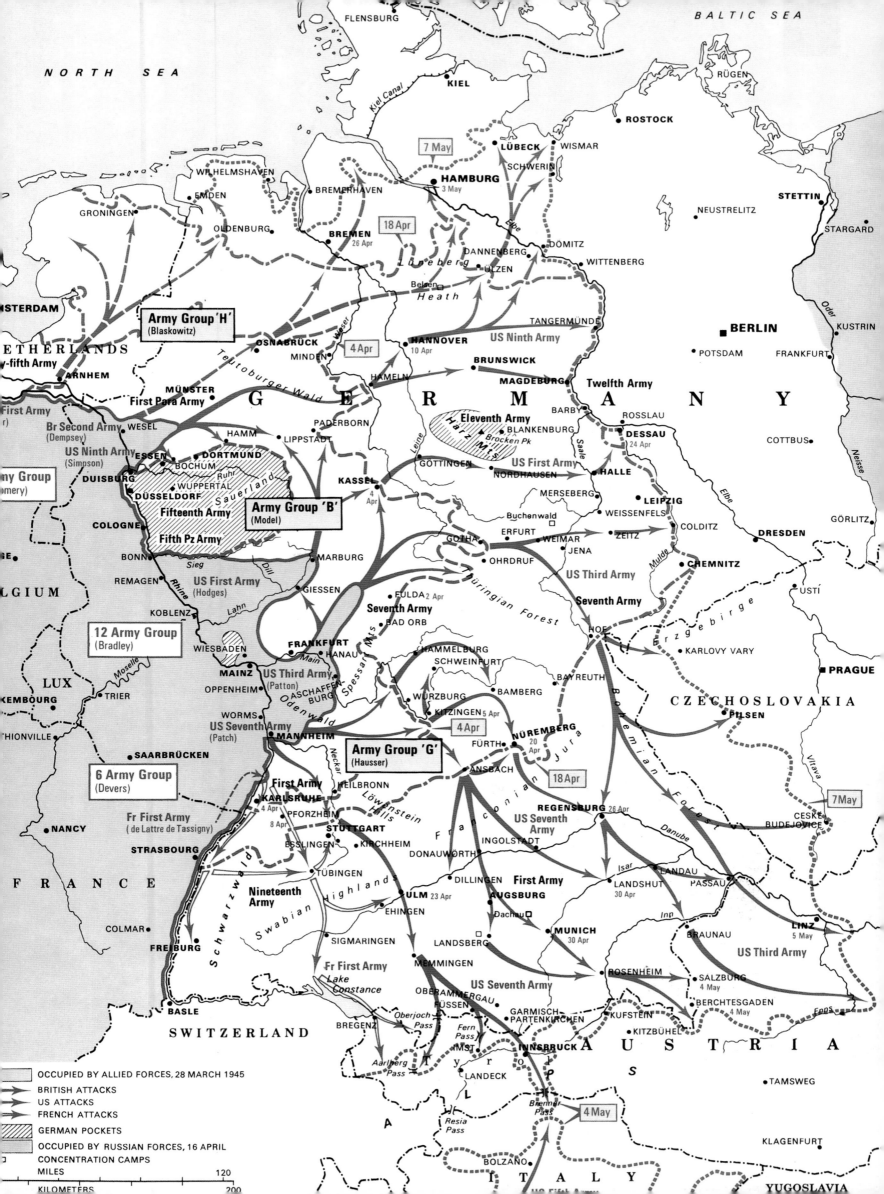

15 JANUARY
ARMY

The first of 4,562 African American volunteers for combat duty report to the 16th Reinforcement Depot at Compiegne, France. The goal is to have the first detachment ready for assignment to units by 1 March. Lieutenant General Leonard T. Gerow leaves the V Corps to take command of the Fifteenth Army, with the immediate mission of rehabilitating and refitting the losses from the Battle of the Bulge.

16 JANUARY
NAVY

The destroyer escorts *Otter*, *Hubbard*, *Hayter*, and *Varian* sink the German submarine *U-248* off the Azores Islands.

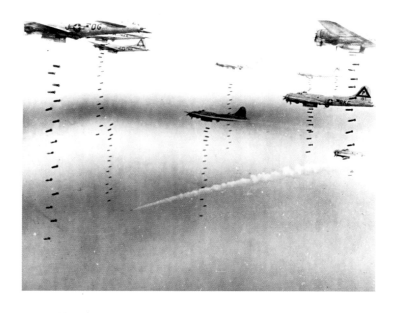

17 JANUARY
ARMY

At midnight control of the First Army (under Lieutenant General Courtney Hodges), which has been under British Field Marshal Bernard Montgomery's command, reverts back to the 12th Army Group (under Lieutenant General Omar N. Bradley).

20 JANUARY
ARMY

The 45th Infantry Division Regiment is unable to reach an encircled battalion of the 157th Infantry near Drusenheim, France. Elements of the 314th Infantry Regiment, 79th Infantry Division, escape the enemy trap, but many members of the 2d Battalion are missing in action.

21 JANUARY
ARMY

The 65th Infantry Division (under Major General Stanley E. Reinhart) starts its precombat training at Camp Lucky Strike near Le Havre, France. Since September 1944, 22 new U.S. divisions, including six armored divisions, have reached France.

22 JANUARY
ARMY

The 3d Infantry and 5th Armored Divisions start a southward drive on Colmar, Germany. To the west the 28th Infantry Division begins two days of raids.

23 JANUARY
NAVY

President Franklin D. Roosevelt boards the heavy cruiser *Quincy*, which will carry him to Malta on the first leg of his trip to Yalta in the Crimea for conferences with British Prime Minister Winston S. Churchill and Soviet Premier Joseph Stalin.

28 JANUARY
ARMY

The 1st Infantry Division and 82d Airborne Division lead the XVIII Airborne Corps advance toward the German Siegfried Line—a defensive line of bunkers and tank traps along Germany's western border. The 7th Armored Division seizes stubbornly held positions in Saint-Vith, Belgium. The Third Army deploys the VIII, III, XII, and XX Corps as it attacks German forces.

31 JANUARY
AIR FORCE

After nine days grounded by winter weather, the Fifteenth Air Force resumes bombing targets in Germany. More than 670 B-17 Flying Fortress and B-24 Liberator bombers, escorted by P-51 Mustang and P-38 Lightning fighters, attack oil refineries at Moosbierbaum and marshalling yards at Graz and Maribor. More B-24 bombers drop supplies to ground forces in northern Italy. Another 300 bombers attack the Moosbierbaum refinery again the next day.

31 JANUARY
ARMY

Found guilty by court martial of desertion, Private Eddie Slovik of the 28th Division is shot by firing squad near the village of Ste.-Marie aux Mines, France. He is the only U.S. Soldier executed for desertion during the war, and the first Soldier to be so punished since the Civil War.

3 FEBRUARY
AIR FORCE

In a typical good-weather, daylight raid for the Eighth Air Force, more than 1,200 B-17 Flying Fortress and B-24 Liberator bombers launch to attack Germany—marshalling yards in Berlin as well as a synthetic oil plant and transportation targets in Magdeburg. More than 900 escort fighters provide top cover. The mission against Berlin, which includes 959 bombers, is the largest of the war thus far. The Mighty Eighth will deliver a similar blow to the same target area three days later.

4 FEBRUARY
ALL SERVICES

The Yalta Conference begins, with the Big Three—President Franklin D. Roosevelt, British Prime Minister Winston S. Churchill, and Soviet Premier Joseph Stalin—discussing the timing of the Soviet Union's entry into the war against Japan. The conference concludes on 11 February, having also

Right: *Paratroopers of the 82d Airborne Division move through the snow toward Herresbach, Belgium, accompanied by an M4 Sherman tank of the 740th Tank Battalion. The men wear white sheets and hoods as camouflage. (National Archives)*

examined postwar issues that will impact East–West relations, such as the division of Germany, the future of Poland, and the Soviet influence in Europe.

5 FEBRUARY
AIR FORCE
The Twelfth Air Force strikes a variety of tactical targets in the Po River Valley in northern Italy with more than 270 medium bombers.

In Germany, the Fifteenth Air Force sends more than 730 heavy bombers to take out petroleum storage tanks at Regensburg, as well as communications targets. Huge numbers of P-38 Lightning and P-51 Mustang fighters escort the bombers and also cover B-24 Liberator bombers delivering supplies to Yugoslavia. Two days later, the Fifteenth will use a similar number of bombers and fighters to attack eight different oil production facilities.

ARMY
In Germany the Colmar Pocket is cut in two as the XXI Corps (under Major General Frank W. Milburn) and French 1st Corps make contact.

9 FEBRUARY
ARMY
In Germany, German army engineers deliberately open the discharge valves to unleash 111 million cubic

Above: *American P-51 Mustang fighters dogfight with German FW-190 fighters. ("Aces Meet," Loren Blackburn, USAF Art Collection)*

meters of Roer River water contained in two reservoirs. This stalls the proposed Allied offensive for two weeks and complicates plans for crossing the Roer.

In eastern France, operations on the Alsatian plain come to a close as U.S. forces operating with the French 1st Army virtually destroy the German 19th Army. The XXI Corps, with significant support from the XII Tactical Air Command, has contributed significantly to the success.

13 FEBRUARY
AIR FORCE
Allied bombers begin raiding targets in Dresden, Germany. Late in the evening, Royal Air Force aircraft carefully mark the target for the attacking bombers, which strike just after 1:00 a.m. on the morning of the 14th. American B-17 Flying Fortress bombers continue the bombardment during the day after launching more than 1,300 aircraft to attack several marshalling yards and oil depots. Sixteen groups of escort fighters fill the skies over Germany during these raids, which continue again that night and the following day. The bombing starts a firestorm in the city, killing 25,000.
15 FEBRUARY

ARMY

The Army reports 172,879 enemy prisoners of war under Army control in the U.S. By the end of the war there are almost 400,000 German prisoners detained in the U.S.

18 FEBRUARY
ARMY

In Italy, Soldiers of the 86th Infantry Regiment, 10th Mountain Division move in darkness to scale the steep 2,000-foot cliff of Mount Manicenello in the Pizzo di Campiano Ridge and defeat the surprised German defenders. The regiment holds for three days against German counterattacks.

22 FEBRUARY
AIR FORCE

Operation CLARION—an Allied attempt to systematically destroy all forms of transportation available to Germany throughout occupied territory in Europe in 24 hours—begins. Approximately 9,000 aircraft launch strikes from bases in England, France, Holland, Belgium, and Italy over an area covering 250,000 square miles. The Eighth Air Force launches

more than 1,350 bombers against more than 40 different targets; the Ninth Air Force launches some 1,500 medium bombers and more than 800 fighter/bomber sorties; the Twelfth Air Force sends aircraft although still committed to supporting the Fifth Army; the Fifteenth Air Force sends more than

Above: An M10 tank destroyer crosses the Our River in Belgium. The tank and its companion vehicle have the "rhino" plow attachment on the front from fighting in the hedgerows of Normandy, France. (Dept. of Defense)

Right: Soldiers from the 10th Mountain Division in northern Italy stay hidden as they observe activity in the valley below. ("Patrol in Mt. Belvedere Area," Savo Radulovic, Army Art Collection, U.S. Army Center of Military History)

350 bombers and more than 300 fighters to more than 50 specific targets in southern Germany and Italy. Additional missions against similar targets are flown on the 23rd in anticipation of Allied ground forces crossing the Rhine River into Germany.

22 FEBRUARY
ARMY

The 10th Mountain Division reports all of its objectives are secure and division elements are moving to seize Mount Torraccia, near La Serra, Italy, which is taken two days later.

23 FEBRUARY
ARMY

In Germany, Operation GRENADE (the drive from the Roer River to the Rhine River) is underway. In the Ninth Army sector, the combat-experienced 29th, 30th, 35th, 79th, 83d, 84th, and 102d Infantry Divisions successfully cross the Roer. On 2 March advance elements of the Ninth Army reach the Rhine River south of Neuss.

25 FEBRUARY
AIR FORCE/ARMY

The Bell XP-83 flies for the first time. This pressurized turbojet aircraft evolves from Bell's earlier P-59 Airacomet—America's first jet aircraft.

27 FEBRUARY
NAVY

A PB4Y-1 Liberator patrol-bomber of Patrol Bombing Squadron 112 teams with British ships in sinking the German submarine U-327 in the English Channel.

28 FEBRUARY
AIR FORCE

The Army Air Forces announces the successful arrival of the new P-80, the Army's first jet-propelled combat aircraft. It is nicknamed "Shooting Star."

MARCH
AIR FORCE/ARMY

Plans for Project Paperclip, the recruitment of German missile scientists, begin in the Pentagon, Washington, D.C.

1 MARCH
ARMY

The first graduates of the African American combat volunteer program at Compiegne, France, are deemed ready for assignment. Twenty-five platoons go to Twelfth Army Group divisions; 12 to the Sixth Army Group. In most cases they serve as members of all-African American platoons integrated into line companies.

Above: *Paratroopers of the 101st Airborne Division march on a forest road into Germany. (U.S. Army)*

Left: *This map depicts the Allies' northern advances in Italy in the last months of the war. (U.S. Army)*

Above: *Soldiers of the 27th Armored Infantry Regiment, 9th Armored Division, race through German fire to seize control of the railroad bridge at Remagen, Germany, before enemy engineers destroy it. It is the only remaining bridge over the Rhine River. ("Bridge at Remagen," H. Charles McBarron, Army Art Collection, U.S. Army Center of Military History)*

In Germany, the VII Corps attacks toward Cologne and expands its bridgeheads over the Erft River as the 3d Armored Division and the 99th Infantry Division make gains. In the XX Corps sector, the 10th Armored Division enters Trier and clears it.

The Detachment d'Armée des Alpes is established under the 6th Army Group (under Lieutenant General Jacob L. Devers) with responsibility for the Alpine sector along the French–Italian border. A French general commands the new force, which includes French and American soldiers.

7 MARCH
ARMY
In a lightning move the 9th Armored Division captures the damaged, but usable, Ludendorff railroad bridge over the Rhine River at Remagen, Germany.

First to fight their way across are the infantrymen of the 27th Armored Infantry Battalion, with other units close behind. By nightfall five infantry and tank battalions are on the east bank.

8 MARCH
ARMY
The Sixth Army Group commander, Lieutenant General Jacob L. Devers, is promoted to full general. His command includes the Seventh Army and the First French Army.

8–12 MARCH
ARMY
In the northern part of the Third Army's XII Corps zone in Germany, the 80th Infantry Division is pinched out of line by spearhead elements of the 11th Armored Division and the 90th Infantry Division striking east toward the Rhine River. The 10th Armored Division and 4th Armored Division clear the north bank of the Moselle River with assistance of the 5th Infantry Division (under Major General Stafford L. Irwin). The 90th Infantry Division passes from VIII Corps to XII Corps control.

11 MARCH
AIR FORCE
In a raid on Essen, Germany, Allied aircraft drop the greatest tonnage on one raid during the war as more than 1,000 bombers release 4,738 tons of bombs on the town.

ARMY/NAVY
Though normally used in the surf of an ocean shore, U.S. Navy landing craft are hauled on trucks from the Atlantic to the Rhine River, where sailors ferry Army troops across the river and assist in building a pontoon bridge at Remagen, Germany. On 17 March the landing craft ferry 2,500 soldiers across the Rhine.

NAVY
A PB4Y-1 Liberator patrol-bomber of Patrol Bombing Squadron 103 sinks the German submarine *U-681* off Great Britain's Isles of Scilly.

12 MARCH
ARMY
Lieutenant General Omar N. Bradley, commander of the Twelfth Army Group, is promoted to general.

14 MARCH
AIR FORCE
In Italy, Allied bombers in cooperation with Russian war planners strike targets in Austria, Hungary, and Yugoslavia in support of the Red Army.

15 MARCH
NAVY
An accident involving improper operation of the torpedo tube doors on the submarine *Lancetfish* results in the sinking of the boat at the Boston Navy Yard in Massachusetts.

17 MARCH
ARMY
The Army announces the presentation of the Presidential Unit Citation to the 101st Airborne Division for "extraordinary heroism and gallantry" in the defense of Bastogne, Belgium, during the Battle of the Bulge. It is the first time this award, the highest Army unit decoration, has been given to an entire division. Previously, the Army restricted the award to regimental level and below.

Opposite: *A Navy Landing Craft Vehicles/Personnel motors on the Rhine River toward the fallen bridge at Remagen, Germany. Landing craft ferry advancing troops over the river when the bridge collapses. (U.S. Naval Institute)*

Right: *A radioman helps control the one-way traffic over a treadway bridge put in place by Army engineers near the remains of the Remagen bridge. It is one of the longest pontoon bridges ever constructed and is in place in record time. (The Robert Hunt Library)*

In Germany, Army engineers have pontoon bridges in place as the railroad bridge at Remagen collapses. Engineers accelerate work on a 1,752-foot single-track bridge to span the Rhine River near Wesel. In Belgium, Major General James A. Van Fleet takes command of the III Corps as it advances under the Third Army. He relieves Major General John Millikin.

18 MARCH
NAVY
The destroyer escorts *Menges*, *Mosley*, *Pride*, and *Lowe* sink the German submarine *U-866* off Nova Scotia, Canada.

18–21 MARCH
ARMY
A powerful XII Corps effort with four infantry and two armored divisions rocks the enemy back and seals the fate of enemy forces defending Germany's Saar-Palatinate. The 4th Armored Division and 90th Infantry Divisions head for Mainz and Worms, Germany. Seventh Army frontline divisions smash through the Siegfried Line defenses.

Left: *The round-the-clock air attack on Germany continues. ("B-17s of the 91st Bomb Group Over Germany," George Guzzi, USAF Art Collection)*

Above: *Soldiers of the 6th Cavalry Group lead the attack against German troops holding positions near Harlange, Luxembourg. ("Breaking the Harlange Pocket," Don Stivers)*

Below: *Wounded Americans board a hospital ship headed back to the U.S. ("All Aboard for Home," Joseph Hirsch, Army Art Collection, U.S. Army Center of Military History)*

22–23 MARCH
ARMY

The XII Corps caps its drive with an assault crossing of the Rhine River near Mainz, Germany. The 5th Infantry Division bolts across in a bold night move using rafts and small boats. In the XXI Corps, the 71st and 100th Infantry Divisions cover the XV Corps' right flank, which has the 3d and 45th Infantry Divisions at the Rhine looking for crossing sites. The First Army attacks east toward Kassel.

23 MARCH
ARMY/NAVY

In Germany, Navy landing craft of Task Unit 122.5.1 ferry over 4,000 men of General George S. Patton's Third Army across the Rhine River, continuing the operation on 24 and 26–27 March, the latter crossings occurring under heavy enemy fire.

24 MARCH
AIR FORCE

In support of Allied ground forces crossing the Rhine River into Germany (Operation VARSITY), the Eighth and Ninth Air Forces conduct Operation PLUNDER, flying approximately 7,000 sorties, and striking rail yards and bridges, flak positions, communications centers, and many other targets. The Ninth Air Force continues support missions for the Allied ground forces as they push forward into Germany. Meanwhile the Fifteenth Air Force strikes Berlin for the first time, sending 150 B-17 Flying Fortress bombers to drop more than 350 tons of bombs on industrial targets in the city.

ARMY

The U.S. 17th Airborne Division and 6th British Airborne Division launch Operation VARSITY, a daylight parachute and glider assault east of the Rhine River near Wesel, Germany. The mission is to secure bridgeheads for other units to cross. Although one of the most successful airborne drops in history, some 50 aircraft and 11 gliders are shot down during the offensive. Of 1,305 gliders employed, only 172 are salvageable, leading to the cancellation of the proposed drop of the U.S. 13th Airborne Division.

25 MARCH
ARMY

In Germany, the Third and Seventh Armies complete the reduction of the Saar-Palatinate triangle, having decimated two German armies in the 10-day campaign. The banks of the Rhine River as far south as Speyer are cleared of enemy troops. The VI Corps completes the clearing of northern Alsace, France, and enters Germany.

26 MARCH
ARMY

Under orders from General George S. Patton Jr., the 4th Armored Division sends a task force commanded by Captain Abraham Baum (assigned to Combat Command B, under Lieutenant Colonel Creighton Abrams) to attempt the rescue of allied prisoners in the vicinity of Schweinfurt, Germany. Task Force Baum is severely mauled. Nearly all survivors are missing in action and the prisoners they liberated are returned to confinement. Patton is widely criticized when it is learned that his son-in-law is among U.S. prisoners held in the camp.

28 MARCH
ARMY

The Fifteenth Army has the two-fold mission of containing bypassed enemy troops in coastal areas of France and of governing the Rhineland sector of Germany. The 4th Armored Division spearheads the Third Army moving north to join forces with the 9th Armored Division (First Army). Both armies advance steadily to the east. Meanwhile General of the Army Dwight D. Eisenhower redirects the final advance of

Above: *A lieutenant colonel and aid man from the Fifth Infantry Division walk past a column of Sherman tanks from one of the armored divisions. The men wear the latest field uniforms, which are very different from those Soldiers wore less than four years earlier. ("The American Soldier, 1944," H. Charles McBarron, Army Art Collection, U.S. Army Center of Military History)*

Below: *Enemy fighter planes and antiaircraft fire are not the only threats in the air over Germany. Formation flying with hundreds of other aircraft introduces other dangers. Here a B-17 Flying Fortress loses part of its tail to a bomb dropped by a companion bomber. (U.S. Air Force)*

Left: *Soldiers exhibit some of the priceless art found hidden throughout Germany in tunnels, old mines, and castle basements. The Nazi hierarchy pilfers and hides hundreds of millions of dollars worth of Europe's finest art, as well as precious metals. Special Army teams search it out. (National Archives)*

Opposite: *The Army artillery caisson carrying the body of President Franklin D. Roosevelt rolls in a solemn funeral procession down Pennsylvania Avenue in Washington, D.C., on 14 April 1945. (National Archives)*

the Allied forces and reorients toward Leipzig rather than Berlin as a terminal objective. His decision leaves the Russians to take the Nazi capital.

30 MARCH
ARMY
Major General Maurice Rose, commander of the 3d Armored Division, becomes the second U.S. Army division commander to be killed in action. He and his command group are surprised by German

tanks along a wooded trail in the advance on Paderborn, Germany.

APRIL
AIR FORCE/ARMY
Supersonic wind tunnel tests of sweptback wing sections are accomplished at the Aberdeen Proving Ground, Maryland. Dr. Theodore von Kármán suggests such tests be run at Mach numbers approaching 1.75.

Right: *Infantrymen advance along a dusty Italian road near the Po River in April 1945 as the Allies continue to push the Germans north. (Dept. of Defense)*

1 APRIL
AIR FORCE/ARMY
The first Private F rocket is fired by Jet Propulsion Laboratory at the Hueco Range at Fort Bliss, Texas. Seventeen rockets will be fired through 13 April.

ARMY
The Ninth and First Armies join forces at Lippstadt, Germany, trapping two German army groups. The 5th Armored Division spearheads the drive toward the Weser River; the 17th Airborne Division prepares to assault Muenster; and the 84th Infantry Division (under Major General Alexander R. Bolling) begins to assemble east of the Rhine River.

4 APRIL
AIR FORCE
Eighth Air Force bombers begin a week-long bombardment of targets throughout Germany. More than 1,000 bomber raids are launched each day against ordnance depots, armament factories, airfields, aircraft plants, rail yards, industrial complexes, oil storage facilities, marshalling yards, headquarters buildings, and jet aircraft operating bases. Enemy jet fighters attack formations regularly but only in small numbers, which limits their effectiveness as the bombers are escorted by hundreds of P-51 Mustang escort fighters. On 10 April, 10 U.S. bombers are shot down by jet fighters, the highest total in one day, but 20 American pilots shoot down German Me-262 jet fighters. Hundreds of German aircraft are destroyed on the ground during these raids.

ARMY
Troops from the 90th Infantry Division uncover a treasure trove in an industrial salt mine near Merkers, Germany. On investigation, this proves to be the German gold bullion reserve. An inventory finds 4,500 25-pound gold bars and millions more in Reichsmarks, as well as a cache of foreign currency and art treasures looted by the Germans.

5 APRIL
ARMY
The 92d Infantry Division begins a diversionary attack toward Massa and La Spezia, Italy. The attached 442d Regimental Combat Team takes Mount Fragolito and Mount Carchio and prepares to attack heavily defended Mount Belvedere. The 92d Infantry Division continues its drive up the Serchio River valley.

Right: *Major General E. F. Reinhard, commander of the 69th Infantry Division, shakes the hand of Major General Rusakov of the 58th Guards Division, 1st Ukrainian Army, at Torgau, Germany, as the two Allied armies link up on the Elbe River. (National Archives)*

11 APRIL
ARMY

Lead elements of the 2d Armored Division are the first to reach the Elbe River 80 miles west of Berlin, the line of separation for Soviet troops advancing from the east.

12 APRIL
ALL SERVICES

President Franklin Delano Roosevelt dies. Vice President Harry S. Truman, a World War I Army veteran, takes the oath of office as the new President and Commander-in-Chief.

14 APRIL
ARMY

In Italy, the U.S. Fifth Army launches its final offensive—the Po Valley campaign. The IV Corps sends the 10th Mountain Division toward the Po River Valley as the 1st Armored Division battles for Vergato. There is heavy fighting in both the II Corps and IV Corps sectors.

15 APRIL
AIR FORCE

In its largest operational effort of the war, the Fifteenth Air Force sends 830 B-17 Flying Fortress and B-24 Liberator bombers to attack gun positions, supply dumps, troop concentrations, and headquarters areas along the highway that leads from Bologna, Italy. P-38 Lightning fighters escort the formations. An additional 300 aircraft strike bridges and ammunition dumps in northern Italy. Hundreds of fighters fill the skies, providing close support of the Fifth Army as it pushes north. During this 24-hour period, 1,142 bombers strike targets. This day marks the greatest number of fighters and bombers launched for attack and the heaviest bomb tonnage dropped by the Fifteenth during the war. Concentrated raids on transportation and petroleum production targets continue during the next six days.

In Germany, Eighth Air Force bombers drop napalm weapons on German ground forces in pillboxes, tank trenches, and artillery batteries. Even though more than 850 bombers drop these weapons, they are considered ineffective. This is the sole operational employment of napalm by Eighth Air Force bombers during the war.

NAVY

The destroyer escorts *Frost* and *Stanton* sink the German submarine *U-1235* west of the Azores Islands. The pair scores another kill there the following day, sending *U-880* to the bottom.

MID-APRIL
ARMY

The Third Army overruns a Nazi concentration camp in Ohrdruf, Germany. In the Seventh Army sector, elements of the XX ("Ghost") Corps cross the Saale River and soon liberate concentration camps at

Above: *A reconnaissance patrol from the Third Army's 43d Cavalry checks its location as it moves ahead of the main body of advancing units into the heart of Germany. ("Brave Rifles," Don Stivers)*

Below: *Paratroopers of the 17th Airborne Division raise the American flag over Duisburg, Germany. (National Archives)*

Buchenwald, Erla, Belsen, and Dachau. Other camps soon fall to Allied forces.

17 APRIL
ARMY
Shifting to the south, the 45th and 3d Infantry Divisions (XV Corps) converge on Nuremburg, Germany. In the XXI Corps sector the 42d Infantry Division pursues the enemy toward Fuerth, working closely with the 14th Armored Division. The 4th Infantry Division's motorized 8th Infantry task force races toward Ansbach. The 10th Armored Division (under Major General William H. H. Morris Jr.), the 63d Infantry Division (under Major General Louis E. Hibbs), and 100th Infantry Division (under Major General Withers A. Burress) speed down the Neckar Valley.

19 APRIL
ARMY
In Germany, the 2d and 69th Infantry Divisions complete the capture of Leipzig. In the VII Corps sector, the 1st Infantry Division advances in the Harz Mountains and reaches the Corps' northern boundary. The 104th Infantry Division elements capture Halle and move on.

NAVY
While operating off Halifax, Nova Scotia, Canada, the destroyer escorts *Buckley* and *Reuben James* sink the German submarine *U-548*.

Left: *Soldiers of the 88th Infantry Division drive German defenders from a northern Italian town. (Army Art Collection, U.S. Army Center of Military History)*

Opposite: *Liberated inmates from the concentration camp at Buchenwald, Germany, gather around some of the Soldiers who liberated them. (National Archives)*

21 APRIL
ALL SERVICES
Soviet forces reach Berlin, Germany.

AIR FORCE/ARMY
Twelfth Air Force A-20 Havoc and B-26 Marauder bombers press the attack upon retreating enemy forces in Italy. By 25 April, all combat operations are aimed at plugging retreat routes and disrupting transportation in the northern Po River Valley. The attacks destroy more than 1,000 vehicles, drop bridge spans, and strafe airfields.

22 APRIL
NAVY
The destroyer escorts *Carter* and *Neal A. Scott*, operating off the Azores Islands, sink the German submarine *U-518*.

24 APRIL
NAVY
The German submarine *U-546* sinks the destroyer escort *Frederick C. Davis* east of Newfoundland, Canada. Seven other destroyer escorts avenge their sister ship, sending *U-546* to the bottom.

25 APRIL
AIR FORCE
The Eighth Air Force flies its last combat mission against industrial targets in the war. Around 275 B-17 Flying Fortress bombers strike the armament works at Plzen-Skoda, Czechoslovakia, while a similar number of B-24 Liberator bombers hit a transformer near Traunstein and other nearby targets.

ARMY
The First Army is taken out of action to prepare for transfer to the Far East. This affects only the Army headquarters as troop elements are distributed to the Ninth and Third Armies.

The German Gothic Line—initially attacked by U.S. forces on 12 September 1944—ceases to exist as the 92d Infantry Division completes its capture of Aulla, Italy.

Patrols from the 69th Infantry Division make first contact along the Elbe River near Torgau, Germany, with Soviet forces advancing from the east.

NAVY
A PB4Y-1 Liberator patrol-bomber of Patrol Bombing Squadron 103 sinks the German submarine *U-326* off Brest, France.

26 APRIL
ARMY
Task Force Darby (under Colonel William O. Darby, assistant division commander, 10th Mountain Division), enters Verona, Italy, and finds elements of the 88th Infantry Division in control. The task force proceeds along the east side of Lake Garda where Darby is killed in action. He is posthumously promoted to brigadier general. The 85th Infantry Division gains a bridgehead across the Adige River in the Verona area.

27 APRIL
ALL SERVICES
Italian partisans capture and hang former Head of Government Benito Mussolini and his family.

AIR FORCE

By this date, P-51 Mustang fighters and B-17 Flying Fortress and B-24 Liberator bombers used as replacement aircraft in Europe stop flowing into combat units. Aircraft strength authorization for bomber groups is reduced from 68 planes to 48 planes, while fighter group strength is reduced from 96 planes to 75 planes. This is the first step in the massive demobilization that is about to occur in the European Theater.

28 APRIL
ARMY

The 92d Infantry Division seizes Alessandria, Italy, on Highway 10; the 10th Mountain Division clears the east shore of Lake Garda. The 34th Infantry Division rounds up enemy remnants west of Brescia as the 1st Armored Division reaches Lake Como near the Swiss border. The 88th Infantry Division clears Vicenza; the 91st Infantry Division elements cross the Brenta River, driving toward Treviso.

29 APRIL
ARMY

Troops of the 45th and 42d Infantry Divisions batter down the gates of the Dachau, Germany, concentration camp to liberate surviving prisoners.

In Italy, as the 1st Armored Division nears Milan, the 91st Infantry Division (under Major General William G. Livesay) crosses the Brenta River. Commander of the German Army Group Southwest agrees to unconditional surrender at Caserta, Italy, effective 2 May.

30 APRIL
ALL SERVICES

German dictator Adolph Hitler commits suicide in his Berlin chancellery bunker.

ARMY

Lieutenant General Courtney H. Hodges, First Army commander, greets the commanding general of the Soviet 5th Guard Army on the east bank of the Mulde River near Eilenberg, Germany. Headquarters First Army relinquishes its duties, turns over its units to adjacent U.S. Armies, and prepares for redeployment to the Pacific.

In Italy, the 92d Infantry Division reaches Turin. The 473d Infantry Regiment, containing many soldiers

Right: P-47D Thunderbolt fighters of the 56th Fighter Group, commanded by Colonel Hubert Zemke. Many pilots of "Zemke's Wolfpack" paint their planes with cartoon characters as nose art. The Wolfpack ends the war with the highest score of enemy planes shot down by any fighter group—679. ("A Wolfpack Salute," Roy Grinnell)

Left: Sailors on the frigate Moberley *watch the pattern of "hedgehog" depth charges off the bow of their ship to see if there is a response from the German submarine suspected to be hiding there. (Naval Historical Center)*

Below: Three weary infantrymen keep on the move as the war nears its last weeks. (Howard Brodie, Army Art Collection, U.S. Army Center of Military History)

from disbanded antiaircraft artillery units, links up with French troops on the Franco–Italian border. The 10th Mountain Division puts down enemy resistance in the vicinity of Lake Garda and deploys elements to take Gargnano and Riva. The IV Corps formally occupies Milan and the II Corps takes Treviso, north of Venice.

NAVY
While conducting an antisubmarine patrol off the Virginia Capes, the destroyer escorts *Thomas*, *Bostwick*, and *Coffman* along with the frigate *Natchez* sink the German submarine *U-879*.

A PBY Catalina patrol-bomber of Patrol Squadron 63 sinks the German submarine *U-1107* off Brest, France.

1 MAY
AIR FORCE
In the face of poor weather, Fifteenth Air Force B-17 Flying Fortress bombers hit the main marshalling yard at Salzburg, Austria, with P-38 Lightning and P-51 Mustang fighter escorts. This is the final Fifteenth Air Force bombing raid during World War II.

Operation CHOWHOUND begins as Allied bombers drop nearly 8,000 tons of food to starving civilians in the Netherlands. The drops are made in open areas and airfields by agreement with the Germans. Through 7 May the Eighth Air Force sends about 400 B-17 Flying Fortress bombers each day to drop food in a variety of locations.

2 MAY
ALL SERVICES
German forces surrender in Italy, marking the end of 604 days of continuous combat for Fifth Army troops. The German capital of Berlin falls to the Soviet army.

Right: *In a small brick school house in Rheims, France, Colonel General Alfred Jodl signs the document of unconditional surrender of all German armed forces to the Allies on 7 May 1945. (National Archives)*

AIR FORCE/ARMY

Wernher von Braun and the rest of his V-2 technical group surrender to American forces in Germany near the Austrian border. Many are transferred to Fort Bliss, Texas, to continue their work on V-2 technology. Later, some are relocated to Huntsville, Alabama, where they assist in the development of America's missile forces. The Redstone and the Saturn V launch vehicles are developed after the war under von Braun's guidance.

4 MAY
ARMY

The motorized column from the 411th Regimental Combat Team, 103d Infantry Division, Seventh Army advances through Brenner Pass, enters Italy, and at 1:50 a.m. near Vipiteno, Italy, makes contact with the Intelligence and Reconnaissance Platoon, 349th Infantry Regiment, 88th Infantry Division (Fifth Army).

In Germany, XIII Corps commander Major General Alvan C. Gillem Jr. meets with the Soviet commander following the juncture with Soviet forces. In the XV Corps sector, 3d Infantry Division elements advance through Salzburg to German dictator Adolph Hitler's retreat at Berchtesgaden. In the Third Army area, the 5th and 90th Infantry Divisions start to clear passes into Czechoslovakia through which the 4th Armored Division plans to toward Prague. Following Soviet protests, General George S. Patton Jr. is cautioned not to advance beyond Pilsen.

6 MAY
NAVY

While operating near Block Island off New England,

the destroyer escort *Atherton* and frigate *Moberley* sink the German submarine *U-853*.

In the last sinking of a German submarine by American forces, the destroyer escort *Farquhar* sinks *U-881* in the North Atlantic.

7 MAY
ALL SERVICES

A modest school building in Rheims, France, takes center stage as the German High Command surrenders all land, sea, and air forces unconditionally to the Allies effective 9 May. President Harry S. Truman declares 8 May as "V-E Day" for Victory in Europe.

8 MAY
AIR FORCE

All Fifteenth Air Force combat operations cease on V-E Day. All subsequent operations are related to transport, supply, and training missions. The Twelfth Air Force continues to fly evacuation and supply missions throughout the theater. Ninth Air Force aircraft are tasked to fly "demonstration missions" over a variety of once-hostile target areas and also over liberated concentration camps. By the end of the month, the redeployment of most air forces in Europe is proceeding at full speed. As the war in Europe comes to a close, General of the Army Dwight D. Eisenhower has a total of 90 divisions—60 U.S., 13 British, five Canadian, 10 French, and one Polish— as well as the 1st Allied Airborne Army, 1st Tactical Air Force, Ninth Air Force, and Second British Tactical Air Force. Some elements are quickly alerted for redeployment to the Pacific.

Above: *A German woman stares in dismay at the ruins of her town as the new conquerors walk past. (Jerry Rutberg, Black Star)*

Below: *The captured German submarine* U-858 *arrives at Cape Henlopen, Delaware, under command of a U.S. Navy prize crew. The sub surrendered at sea and is being escorted to port by a Sikorsky HNS-1 helicopter and a Navy airship. (National Archives)*

9 MAY
AIR FORCE/ARMY/NAVY
All hostilities in the European Theater of Operations are officially terminated, and the occupation phase begins. It has been 338 days since the D-day invasion of Normandy, France.

10 MAY
AIR FORCE
Lieutenant General James Doolittle is relieved of his Eighth Air Force command and reassigned to Headquarters, Army Air Forces in Washington, D.C. Major General William E. Kepner replaces him.

21 MAY
ARMY
Headquarters, First U.S. Army, embarks from Le Havre, France, under orders to proceed, via the U.S., to the Pacific area to prepare for a major role in the forthcoming invasion of Japan.

2 JUNE
ARMY
Major General Wade H. Haislip assumes command of the Seventh Army.

6 JUNE
NAVY
The U.S. Naval Academy Class of 1946 graduates one year early due to the national emergency.

14–15 JUNE
ARMY
The Ninth Army is directed to turn over its

Right: *Columns of American vehicles advancing deeper into Germany pass a long stream of German prisoners headed to prisoner-of-war camps. (National Archives)*

occupation area and all troops to the Seventh Army as it returns to the U.S. for redeployment to the Pacific.

15 JUNE
ARMY
The Third Army (under General George S. Patton Jr.) and the Seventh Army (under Major General Wade H. Haislip) are designated as the major command headquarters for U.S. forces in the occupation of the captured territory in Europe.

16 JUNE
NAVY
The Naval Air Test Center is established at Patuxent River, Maryland.

19 JUNE
AIR FORCE
Dr. Frank L. Wattendorf, an engineer at Wright Field, Ohio, and a member of the Army Air Forces' Scientific Advisory Group (later the Scientific Advisory Board), recommends to the Chief of the Engineering Division that a major Air Force Development Center be built far away from facilities in Dayton, Ohio, and located near a large, cheap source of power. This center would include facilities for the development of supersonic aircraft and missiles. The center becomes a reality, and in 1950 is dedicated as the Arnold Engineering Development Center in Tullahoma, Tennessee.

25 JUNE
AIR FORCE/ARMY
Ground is broken and construction begins at the White Sands Proving Grounds in New Mexico. Dozens of captured V-2 rockets as well as the first American large-scale, liquid-fuel rockets will be tested there in the coming years. The center officially opens on 13 July.

30 JUNE
ARMY
A summary of production for the "Arsenal of Democracy" shows that between July 1940 and July 1945 U.S. industry produced 17.4 million rifles, carbines, and pistols, 315,000 artillery weapons (including mortars), 86,338 tanks, and 297,000 aircraft.

1 JULY
ARMY
General Jacob L. Devers assumes command of the Army Ground Forces.

7 JULY
NAVY
President Harry S. Truman embarks in the heavy cruiser *Augusta* for the first leg of his trip to a conference with British Prime Minister Winston S. Churchill and Soviet Premier Joseph Stalin at Potsdam, near Berlin, Germany.

Left: *Allied political and military leaders meet in Potsdam, Germany, to discuss postwar issues in August 1945. Front row, left to right: British Prime Minister Clement Atlee, President Harry S. Truman, and Soviet Premier Joseph Stalin. Back row, left to right: Truman's Chief of Staff Fleet Admiral William D. Leahy, British Foreign Minister Ernest Bevin, U.S. Secretary of State James F. Byrnes, and Soviet Foreign Minister Vyacheslav Molotov. (National Archives)*

14 JULY
ALL SERVICES
With its mission accomplished, Supreme Headquarters Allied Expeditionary Force is discontinued. General of the Army Dwight D. Eisenhower is now commanding general, United States Forces, European Theater as well as Military Governor of the U.S. Occupied Zone in Germany.

16 JULY
ALL SERVICES
The Big Three leaders meet in Potsdam, Germany. President Harry S. Truman, Soviet Premier Joseph Stalin, and British Prime Minister Winston S. Churchill disagree about postwar Europe arrangements. The war in the Pacific is also discussed and Truman is advised of the atomic bomb test success at the New Mexico test site. The conference concludes on 2 August, and results in an Allied declaration calling for the unconditional surrender of Japan.

AIR FORCE/ARMY
A nuclear device is tested deep in the desert of New Mexico. It is a "Fat Man"–type of weapon rather than the less complicated version that is eventually dropped over Hiroshima, Japan.

28 JULY
AIR FORCE
A B-25 Mitchell bomber flying in dense fog crashes

Right: *A U.S. Army tugboat welcomes troops returning from Europe as their transport enters New York harbor. (Jeffery Ethell Collection/Eppstein)*

Opposite, bottom: *Soldiers board a transport in France for a long trip to the Pacific where they will be a part of the anticipated invasion of Japan. (National Archives)*

into the 79th floor of the Empire State Building in New York City, New York. Nineteen people are killed and 29 more are hurt.

31 JULY
ARMY
General Omar N. Bradley's 12th Army Group is dissolved as operational control of all American forces in Germany passes to United States Forces in the European Theater. Bradley returns to the U.S. to take charge of the Veterans' Administration.

12 AUGUST
MARINE CORPS/NAVY
Plans are initiated for the establishment of separation centers at Great Lakes, Illinois, and Bainbridge, Maryland, to quickly demobilize eligible personnel. Three days later, the Commandant and the Undersecretary of the Navy approve a point system to guide demobilization. Points are awarded for time in service, for time deployed overseas, for combat awards, and for minor children. Those with the most points are separated from active duty first.

25 AUGUST
ARMY
The 85th Infantry Division, a veteran of three Italian campaigns since its arrival on 23 December 1943, is inactivated—the first inactivation of the many combat divisions organized for World War II. Soldiers not eligible for return home are reassigned. As the news spreads of the Japanese surrender in the Far East, the Army responds to the public clamor "to get the boys home." By 31 December, 42 of the divisions in Europe are off the Army's rolls.

SEPTEMBER
AIR FORCE
The first U.S. jet aircraft, the Bell XP-59 Airacomet, goes on exhibit at the Smithsonian Institution. Today, the XP-59 hangs in the Milestones of Flight Gallery in the National Air and Space Museum.

1 SEPTEMBER
MARINE CORPS
Marine Barracks Guantanamo Bay, Cuba, is redesignated as a Marine Corps Base.

4 SEPTEMBER
MARINE CORPS
The Marine Corps replaces the F series tables of organization (adopted in early 1944) with the G series. The change increases the size of a full-strength division by 1,700 men, much of it due to beefed-up service and support elements in light of the planned disbandment of corps-level reinforcing units.

Above: *As the Soviet Army closes in on Austria, General George S. Patton Jr. sends Soldiers to the breeding farm for the famous Royal Lippizzaner horses, to bring the horses into American lines, saving them from possible destruction. ("Rescuing the Lippizzaners," Don Stivers)*

5 SEPTEMBER
AIR FORCE

The Douglas C-74 prototype, the Globemaster, flies for the first time at Douglas facilities in Santa Monica, California.

8 SEPTEMBER
ARMY

Lieutenant General Geoffrey Keyes takes command of the Seventh Army, which remains in Heidelberg, Germany, as an occupation army.

10 SEPTEMBER
NAVY

Midway, the first of the large aircraft carriers built reflecting wartime experience, is placed in commission. In terms of displacement, she is the largest warship built by the U.S. Navy to date.

11 SEPTEMBER
ALL SERVICES

Operation MAGIC CARPET, in which U.S. Navy warships serve as makeshift transports returning U.S. servicemen to the United States, commences.

21 SEPTEMBER
ARMY

After more than five years in office during a turbulent period in history, Henry L. Stimson retires as Secretary of War. He is replaced by his wartime deputy, Judge Robert P. Patterson, a World War I combat veteran.

23 SEPTEMBER
NAVY

A reorganization of the Navy Department results in the creation of an Office of Naval Material and billets for five Deputy Chiefs of Naval Operations for Personnel, Administration, Naval Operations, Logistics, and Aviation.

26 SEPTEMBER
ARMY

The Army WAC Corporal, with a Tiny Tim booster, is launched on its first development flight at the White Sands range in New Mexico. The missile establishes a U.S. altitude record of 43.5 miles, and is the first liquid propellant rocket developed with government funding.

29 SEPTEMBER
NAVY

An executive order eliminates the post of Commander in Chief, U.S. Fleet, leaving the position of Chief Naval Operations as the senior Navy position.

Right: *Former German Luftwaffe commander Hermann Goering undergoes initial questioning after his capture. He is brought to trial as a war criminal, found guilty, and sentenced to hang. He commits suicide the night before the sentence is to be carried out. (National Archives)*

Below: *Soldiers take souvenir snapshots at a Nazi memorial in Munich, Germany. Such symbols of Hitler's reign will soon be destroyed. (National Archives)*

1 OCTOBER
ARMY
The Persian Gulf Command is deactivated at Khorramshahr, Iran, and replaced by the Persian Gulf Service Command under control of U.S. Army Forces, Africa–Middle East Theater. Its principal task now is the liquidation of U.S. installations and activities in the region.

2 OCTOBER
ARMY
Thirty-four months after its activation in Morocco, the Fifth Army is inactivated.

3 OCTOBER
ARMY
Following a conflict with General of the Army Dwight D. Eisenhower over occupation policies, General George S. Patton Jr. is relieved as commander of the Third Army and placed in command of the Fifteenth Army, an administrative headquarters.

7 OCTOBER
ARMY
Lieutenant General Lucian Truscott Jr. is appointed commanding general of the Third Army and Eastern Military District (Bavaria) to replace General George S. Patton Jr.

11 OCTOBER
ARMY
The 1st Guided Missile Battalion is activated at Fort Bliss, Texas.

20 OCTOBER
AIR FORCE/ARMY
Lieutenant General Nathan F. Twining is commander of a flight of three B-29 Superfortress bombers which fly from Guam Island, Mariana Islands, to Washington D.C. via India and Germany—a new route to the American capital. The 13,000-mile journey takes just under 60 hours.

Above: *The ocean liner* Queen Mary, *pressed into service as a troop transport during the war, steams slowly to her pier at the New York docks. She makes many such Atlantic crossings, returning thousands of happy American servicemen and women to their homes and families. (National Archives)*

27 OCTOBER
NAVY
The aircraft carrier *Franklin D. Roosevelt* is placed in commission, with President Harry S. Truman present for the ceremony.

5 NOVEMBER
NAVY
An FR-1 Fireball jet aircraft piloted by Ensign Jake West makes the first successful landing of a jet aircraft on board a U.S. Navy carrier. The combination piston-engine/jet-powered aircraft makes an arrested landing on the flight deck of the escort carrier *Wake Island* in the Pacific Ocean.

7 NOVEMBER
AIR FORCE/ARMY
A remote controlled version of the P-59 Airacomet jet fighter is flown by the Bell Aircraft Corporation. A television affixed to the inside of the cockpit reads the flight instruments while in the air.

18 NOVEMBER
ARMY
General of the Army George C. Marshall retires from active service. General of the Army Dwight D. Eisenhower replaces him as Army Chief of Staff the next day.

20 NOVEMBER
ALL SERVICES
The Nuremberg Trials begin. An International Military Tribunal will try 24 Nazi leaders as well as a host of lesser war criminals during the second phase of the legal proceedings. The trials continue until 1949.

AIR FORCE/ARMY
A B-29 Superfortress bomber sets a world non-stop, non-refueling distance record of 8,198 miles during a flight from Guam Island, Mariana Islands, to Washington, D.C. The flight takes just over 35 hours.

26 NOVEMBER
ARMY
General Joseph T. McNarney becomes commander of United States Forces, European Theater.

29 NOVEMBER
AIR FORCE
The Army Air Forces School moves from Orlando, Florida, to Maxwell Field in Montgomery, Alabama. The school, a major command, later becomes the Air University.

Opposite, bottom:
*Campaign medals awarded
for wartime service include
the European–African–
Middle Eastern Campaign
Medal, left, and the World
War II Victory Medal, right.
(U.S. Army Institute of
Heraldry)*

Right: *The smallest veteran
on the transport* Queen
Mary, *"Spotty," a mascot of a
70th Infantry Division unit,
is held by one of two Red
Cross nurses who rescued the
dog. Spotty had been left
behind because the unit
thought he could not be
brought to the U.S. Within a
few weeks of "emigrating" to
America, Spotty reunites with
his master. (National
Archives)*

1 DECEMBER
NAVY

Fleet Admiral Chester W. Nimitz, the leader of the
U.S. Navy in the Pacific during World War II,
becomes the tenth Chief of Naval Operations.

3 DECEMBER
AIR FORCE

The 412th Fighter Group at March Field, California,
becomes the first Army Air Forces unit to be equipped
with jet fighters—the P-80 Shooting Star.

5 DECEMBER
NAVY

Flight 19, consisting of five TBM Avengers, takes
off from Naval Air Station Fort Lauderdale, Florida,
on a routine training flight. Although contact is
maintained with the aircraft for a time, the radios
eventually go silent and the aircraft are never seen
again, spawning theories about their disappearing over
the Bermuda Triangle.

17 DECEMBER
AIR FORCE

General Carl A. Spaatz accepts the Collier Trophy
from President Truman for "demonstrating the
airpower concept" in the air war over Europe.

19 DECEMBER
ALL SERVICES

President Harry S. Truman submits a plan to
Congress for the unification of the armed forces.

21 DECEMBER
ARMY

General George S. Patton Jr., former commander of
the Third Army, dies in the hospital at Bad Nauheim,
Germany, of injuries suffered in a vehicle accident 11
days earlier. He is buried in the American military
cemetery at Hamm, Luxembourg.

ACKNOWLEDGMENTS

CONTRIBUTORS

Colonel Raymond K. Bluhm Jr., USA (Ret.) graduated from the University of Illinois in 1962 with a BA in Political Science. He was commissioned from ROTC in 1963 and received a Regular Infantry commission. After 30 years as an Infantry and Foreign Area Officer, he retired in 1993. His service includes commands and staff duty with light, airmobile, and mechanized Infantry; two tours to South Korea; 18 months in South Vietnam as an ARVN Infantry advisor, then company commander with the 1st Cavalry Division (Airmobile); and two tours to Europe. Colonel Bluhm was the U.S. Defense and Army Attaché to Belgium and Luxembourg. He has an MA in International Relations, and attended the Army's Command and Staff College and War College. His last position was with the U.S. Army Center of Military History. He earned the Combat Infantryman Badge, Expert Infantryman Badge, Parachute Badge, Ranger Tab, Army General Staff, and DOD Staff Badges. His awards and decorations include the Valorous Unit Award, Silver Star, Bronze Star with V, Legion of Merit, and the Belgian Order of Leopold II. After retirement he served as Executive Director of the Army Historical Foundation. Among other works, Colonel Bluhm co-authored *The Soldiers Guidebook;* was the graphics editor/author of *The Army;* and was the Editor-in-Chief/author of *U.S. Army: A Complete History* and *U.S. Army Infantry*. He is currently a freelance editor/author/historian and assistant gardener to his wife. They live in Fairfax, Virginia.

Major General Bruce Jacobs, USA (Ret.) was commissioned in the Army Reserve following enlisted service in World War II. He was detailed as a combat historian in the Marianas, Iwo Jima, and Okinawa. He transferred to the Army National Guard in 1957. He served with the U.S. Army in Vietnam, 1968–1969, and after a detail to the White House in 1970, was appointed Chief of Public Affairs, National Guard Bureau, 1971–1974. He was Secretary of the Army Reserve Forces Policy Committee, 1975–1979. He joined the staff of the National Guard Association of the U.S. in 1979 and was Chief Historian when he retired in 1995. He is the author of books and articles on military topics and served as an editor and author of *The Army* and *U.S. Army: A Complete History*. He earned an M.A. in diplomatic history at Georgetown University. He became an adviser to the Army Historical Foundation in 1983, joined the Board of Governors in 1995, and has served two terms as its secretary.

M. Hill Goodspeed received his undergraduate degree from Washington and Lee University, where he was a George C. Marshall Undergraduate Scholar, and his master's degree in history from the University of West Florida. Currently, he serves as Historian and Head of Artifact Collections at the National Museum of Naval Aviation and lectures in strategy and policy for the Naval War College in the College of Distance Education. He served as Editor-in-Chief of the books *U.S. Naval Aviation* and *U.S. Navy: A Complete History,* and is the author of articles and book reviews that have appeared in *U.S. Naval Institute Proceedings, The Journal of Military History, Naval History, Naval Aviation News, Wings of Fame, International Air Power Review, Foundation,* and *The Public Historian*.

Colonel Jon T. Hoffman, USMCR (Ret.) has spent his entire career as an infantry officer and military historian. During his 17 years of active duty, he commanded two companies in an infantry battalion, taught history at the U.S. Naval Academy, and served as the deputy director of the History and Museums Division. He has published dozens of articles and two books, including *USMC: A Complete History*. His first book, *Once a Legend: "Red Mike" Edson of the Marine Raiders,* received the Marine Corps Heritage Foundation's 1994 Greene Award. His most recent volume, *Chesty: The Story of Lieutenant General Lewis B. Puller, USMC,* earned the 2002 Greene Award and was on the *New York Times* bestseller list. In 1998 he was honored as a *Marine Corps Gazette* Distinguished Author.

Lieutenant Colonel Dik Alan Daso, USAF (Ret.) is curator of Modern Military Aircraft at the Smithsonian Institution, National Air and Space Museum, Washington, D.C. As an Air Force pilot, he logged more than 2,700 flying hours in RF-4C Phantom II and F-15A Eagle fighters and T-38 Talon supersonic training aircraft. During his Air Force career, he also served as a history instructor at the USAF Academy, an executive officer on the Air Force Scientific Advisory Board, and chief of Air Force doctrine in the Pentagon. He earned a PhD in military history from the University of South Carolina. Dr. Daso is the curator for *Military Unmanned Aerial Vehicles*, an exhibition at the Smithsonian National Air and Space Museum on the National Mall; the Modern Military Aircraft Collection on display at the Smithsonian National Air and Space Museum, Steven F. Udvar-Hazy Center; and is co-curator for a permanent exhibition at the National Museum of American History—*The Price of Freedom: Americans at War*. He compiled and edited the exhibition books for The Udvar-Hazy Center and for *The Price of Freedom: Americans at War*. As a contributor, he has written chapters that were included in *Winged Crusade: The Quest for American Air and Space Power*, *West Point: Two Centuries and Beyond*, and *The Air Force*. As book author, he has written *U.S. Air Force: A Complete History*; *Hap Arnold and the Evolution of American Airpower*, which won the American Institute of Aeronautics and Astronautics History Manuscript Award, and *Doolittle: Aerospace Visionary*.

SPECIAL THANKS

The publisher would like to thank the following individuals for their enthusiasm and dedication in bringing this project to fruition:

Brigadier General Creighton Abrams, Executive Director, USA (Ret.), Army Historical Foundation; Captain Charles T. Creekman, USN (Ret.), Executive Director, Naval Historical Foundation; Colonel Walt Davis, USMC (Ret.), former Chief Operating Officer, Marine Corps Association; Colonel Tom Bradley, USAF (Ret.), Executive Director of The Air Force Historical Foundation; Matt Seelinger, Senior Historian, Army Historical Foundation; John Reilly, Naval Historical Foundation; Jack Neufeld, Air Force Historical Foundation; Renée Klish, Army Art Curator, U.S. Army Center of Military History; Gale Munro, Navy Art Collection; Laura Waayers, Naval Historical Foundation; Joan Thomas, Assistant Curator of the Art Collection, National Museum of

the Marine Corps, Triangle, Virginia; U.S. Marine Corps Research Library at Quantico, Virginia; Russell Kirk, Air Force Art Collection; Colonel Roger Barnard, USMC (Ret.); indexer Beth Crumley; and copyeditor Wendy Leland.

The following images are used with permission from the National Air and Space Museum archives. (NASM images used with Boeing special permission are in BOLD type).

p. 18; 87-6048
p. 26; 82-1729
p. 28; 98-20680
p. 43; A19960595000
p. 59; 89-4708
p. 71; 98-20529
p. 138; 82-14280
p. 202; 75-5394
p. 222; 90-2374
p. 236; 2006-6753
p. 252; 98-15681
p. 256; 87-13689, 86-12160
p. 262; 89-22018
p. 294; A19840466000
p. 324; 2004-41000
p. 343; 76-17743
p. 344; 87-9675, 99-42697
p. 442; 2000-1601
p. 453; unnumbered
p. 475; 76-3443
p. 476; 87-9655

Please reference the following web site for Mort Künstler paintings: www.mortkunstler.com